Public Administration

Challenges,
Choices,
Consequences

Public Administration

Challenges, Choices, Consequences

Charles H. Levine

B. Guy Peters
University of Pittsburgh

Frank J. Thompson
State University of New York, Albany

SCOTT, FORESMAN/LITTLE, BROWN HIGHER EDUCATION
A Division of Scott, Foresman and Company
Glenview, Illinois   London, England

For those committed to public service

Library of Congress Cataloging-in-Publication Data

Levine, Charles H.
    Public administration : challenges, choices, consequences /
Charles Levine, B. Guy Peters, Frank J. Thompson.
      p. cm.
    Includes bibliographical references.
    ISBN 0-673-39997-4
    1. Public administration. I. Peters, B. Guy. II. Thompson,
Frank J. III. Title.
JF1351.L47   1990
350—dc20   90-8034
                                               CIP

1 2 3 4 5 6—RRN—95 94 93 92 91 90

Preface

Attempting to capture a field as broad and diverse as public administration within the covers of a single book may appear to be an exercise in hubris. Whatever else, it is a humbling experience. In *Public Administration: Challenges, Choices, Consequences,* we have attempted to cover the major literature and perspectives within the field, and at the same time to add our own thoughts and observations. We have also tried to strike a balance between the intellectual basis of public administration and the actual practice of management in the contemporary public sector. This is a difficult but necessary balance to achieve. If the balance leans toward the intellectual side, it is the result of our attempt to place the conduct of government and public program administration in a broad social, economic, and, above all, political context.

With this broad context in mind, we have chosen to concentrate on the administration of federal programs. While most public employees in the United States work for state and local governments, and many of Washington's programs are administered by subnational governments, federal policy and management practices tend to dominate American public life. No other single government matters so much to so many people. Hence, we believe it is important to understand the operations of the federal government first, and then to plumb the complexities of state and local government. Furthermore, many of the concepts and propositions embedded in this book apply to all public agencies. We use federal examples to illustrate these principles but could draw as easily on state and local case material for that purpose.

In this attempt to be comprehensive, we have examined and analyzed public administration at three levels. We begin with a broad "macro" analysis of American public administration in the context of its socioeconomic environment. We examine the demands placed on government by that environment, and the ways that the constitutional and legal foundations of government shape its responses to these demands. These matters of *haut politique* may appear far removed from the local Social Security office, but actually they are closely intertwined. Without a solid understanding of the framework of government, there is little hope of understanding any level of American public administration as anything other than a sterile exercise in management.

The second level—a "meso" level—is concerned with the intersection of those broad socioeconomic and political forces and the service delivery demands of a large and complex government. Fundamental questions include: How should government be organized? How can programs be administered in ways that respect economy, efficiency, effectiveness, responsiveness, and accountability? Responding to these questions requires an understanding of organizational theory and a comprehension of relationships between administration and politics. The President's efforts to provide direction and enforce the responsibility of the remainder of the executive branch are examined, as are the relationships between administrative agencies and such entities as Congress, the courts and interest groups.

Finally, on the "micro" level, we deal with the questions of management and service delivery within agencies. Political leaders and senior civil servants pride themselves on holding decision-making positions in government, but most of the decisions in government are made at the lower operating level. These decisions include choices about which potential clients should receive benefits, which malefactors should be arrested, and which farmers should receive permits to graze their cattle on public lands. These decisions also include numerous judgments about personnel, the budget, the use and dissemination of information, and the management of space in public buildings. These matters may appear very mundane when viewed from the heights of Capitol Hill, but they comprise the guts of government, they are crucial for clients, for employees, and ultimately for the success of federal programs. There is little reason that government in many spheres cannot be as efficient and effective as the private sector; much of the effort, though, must occur at these lower echelons of public service.

Finally, we examine the future of public administration and its pursuit of excellence. While there are no easy predictions, the previous discussion of all three levels of public administration—macro, meso, and micro—lays the foundation for the comprehensive understanding of the possible future of public service. We also give close attention to the legacy of the Reagan administration.

A number of people should be thanked for their contributions in making this book a reality. First, we need to thank each other. This has been a team effort, with each author contributing equally to the final intellectual product. Editors at Little, Brown and Company and later Scott, Foresman and Company were patient and persistent. We believe that their patience has allowed us to produce a much better book. Along the way, various individuals generously took the time to read the manuscript and offer perceptive advice on all or portions of it. In this regard, we wish to thank Richard Campbell, David Cingranelli, Phil Cooper, Dennis Dresang, Robert Durant, Richard Elling, Rebecca Hendrick, Fred Lane, Naomi Lynn, Bob Nakamura, John Nalbandian, James Perry, Dave Schmitt, Dave Smith, Lana Stein, Paul Thompson, and Marcia Whicker. As much as they influenced us, we still absolve them from any responsibility for flaws in this edition. Finally, we acknowledge a special debt to our families, who have endured the disruption associated with a project of this magnitude.

There is one final thing which must be written. As we write this preface, only two of the three authors are present. Charles Levine died suddenly in September 1988 just after we completed the manuscript. Charlie was instrumental in assembling this team, and in the beginning he was the glue that held us together.

He will be sorely missed, by us and by countless others in universities and in government. We only hope that his commitment to public service and to public administration will be demonstrated in *Public Administration: Challenges, Choices, Consequences*, and that this text will encourage another generation to consider what they can achieve, for themselves and for society, through public service.

BGP
FJT

Contents

List of Tables, Figures, and Exhibits

Public Administration

Challenges,
Choices,
Consequences

Chapter One

A Framework for Studying Public Administration

Introduction

In the United States, government is involved in almost every facet of our lives. The food we eat, for example, is produced by farmers supported by crop subsidies, government loans for equipment and land, and technical assistance from civil servants. It is likely to be graded by government inspectors, subjected to regulation, delivered to market on public roads or publicly supported railroads, and refrigerated with electricity provided by government-funded or regulated utilities. Every other part of our society, from the houses we live in to the entertainment that amuses us, lies within the reach of government.

Such a government must be not only big but also complex. In addition to the federal government, which alone has close to three million civilian workers and two million military employees, there are fifty state governments and more than 80,000 units of local government. The overlapping functions of these units of government and their interactions with one another, with citizens, and with private-sector firms are sometimes unclear to even the most knowledgeable people.

Because of government's size and complexity, people who try to make sense of it often limit themselves to one of three main avenues: (1) Some specialize. They choose a specific policy area such as agriculture, labor, or foreign affairs; an institution or agency such as the presidency, Congress, or the Office of Personnel Management; or a function, for instance, budgeting, regulation, or personnel management. (2) Some focus on the impacts of government on other units of society such as businesses, the family, or the poor. (3) Some damn the whole thing as hopelessly complicated, intrusive and inefficient.

No one of these three ways of thinking can provide a comprehensive understanding of the role of government in society. For example, studying only a part of government precludes a larger understanding of government's place in society. Likewise, focusing on the effects of government on society fails to clarify how the public sector works or how it grew so powerful. Finally, concentrating on government's "waste, fraud, and abuse" and wishing it would "get off the backs of the American people" fails to acknowledge the positive contributions of government to society. Consequently, this book strives for a broader perspective in order to sort out the parts without losing sight of the whole and to understand the positive contributions of government as well as its failures.

A Conceptual Lens

A conceptual lens focuses the attention on a specific aspect of a subject and blurs out the irrelevant. Take a car for example. The potential car buyer may use a lens that focuses on the car's reliability, its road handling, the comfort of its ride, its gas mileage, its cost of upkeep, and its styling. A loan officer at a bank chooses a lens that focuses on the car's cost, its projected depreciation, and the ability of the buyer to pay back the loan on it. An auto mechanic's lens focuses on the car's engine, ignition system, and electrical system; a designer's, on its lines, color, and interior decoration. Clearly, each of these people has special needs in choosing a conceptual lens for studying a car, and each chooses a different lens for sorting out relevant parts and making judgments about them.

The study and evaluation of government generally and public administration in particular also requires a conceptual lens. The choice of lens depends on who is doing the studying and for what purpose. Several possibilities exist. The student of government may be a public official eager to become a more effective administrator or a taxpayer interested in learning where the taxes are going, or a client of government programs, curious about how to get benefits from government.

The conceptual lens used in this volume relies on certain assumptions about its readers: (1) that most readers are advanced undergraduate or graduate students taking their first course in public administration; (2) that they know something about American government and politics but not much about the details of its policies, programs, organizations, and operations; (3) that they want to understand the whole of public administration rather than specializing in specific functions of government or policy issues. Although it is intended primarily for prospective specialists in public administration, this volume also strives to provide a perspective and propositions that will interest seasoned students of the subject.

This book concentrates on the federal government, which directly employs fewer personnel than its state and local counterparts but whose programs are at least as important to the average citizen. Expenditures of the national government from its own revenues surpass those of all state and local governments combined. In the mid-1980s federal expenditures amounted to about 25 percent of the gross national product (GNP), and state and local outlays approximated 10 percent. The federal government has in several respects come to dominate the public sector. This focus on the federal government provides a depth of analysis that is impossible when discussing all of public administration. Much of this volume, however, will be quite germane to public administration at subnational levels. In many policy spheres, state and local governments essentially serve as implementing agents of Washington. Hence, this volume will of necessity consider certain aspects of public administration in states and localities. Of even greater importance, there are substantial commonalities in the theory and practice of public administration between the federal and other levels of government, so that an understanding of one system will advance understanding of the others.

This is not a how-to-do-it book. It seeks to cast light on government and its basic problems, policies, programs, operations, and products. Its philosophy is that before one seeks to master the body of tools and techniques used by people who work in public administration, one needs to understand the context and the logic behind the use of these tools. To the extent that this book improves the reader's understanding of this context and the appropriate use of these tools, it will have contributed significantly to better public management. Finally, readers may be especially interested in the problems and controversies that surround government. These issues will be clearer if readers first study why they arise rather than immediately seeking solutions. In other words, this book is more concerned with description and explanation than with how to "fix" government.

In focusing the conceptual lens that orients this study, a critical question remains: What is public administration? People who study the subject differ in their definitions and their notions of the proper scope of the field.[1] For instance, one author succinctly asserts that "the field of public administration is the study of the activities and impact of governmental bureaucracies."[2] While this definition certainly captures much of what one means by the term, a broader conceptualization may well be more appropriate—one that more explicitly recognizes the substantial role played by private organizations (for example defense contractors) in implementing government policy.

Thus, public administration is centrally concerned with the organization of government policies and programs as well as the behavior of officials (usually nonelected) formally responsible for their conduct. This definition implies a focus on what administrators do to shape the laws as well as to implement them. "Officials" refers to government executives with responsibility for whole programs, offices, or departments. It refers to middle managers who supervise the work force. Finally, it refers to government workers who have no supervisory authority at all. Scientists in the National Institutes of Health, program analysts in the Office of Personnel Management, secretaries in the Department of Housing and Urban Development, agents of the Internal Revenue Service are all officials—all public administrators.

Public administration does not include such mainly nongovernmental entities as business firms, families, and civic organizations unless the nongovernmental entity is formally designated (and usually paid) to implement government policies, in which case their behavior assumes center stage in public administration. One cannot come to grips with the dynamics of public programs without considering such entities. It would be ludicrous, for instance, to study the administration of government health policy without addressing roles played by private insurance companies, physicians, and hospitals. The field of public administration runs grave risks of irrelevance if it fails to probe the behavior of private agents in their capacity as implementing agents of government. Given this conceptual underpinning, the remainder of this chapter sets the table for the meal to follow (a banquet, it is hoped).

From Macro to Micro

Issues of public administration can be arrayed on a continuum that runs from *macro* to *micro*. At the macro end of the continuum, one grapples with fundamental questions of how large government should be relative to the private sector. One focuses on whether government should get involved at all in dealing with a particular social problem or should instead leave it to private institutions, groups, and dynamics (for example, religious bodies, the family, market forces). In deciding this issue, considerations do not include only whether government can better ameliorate a particular problem than can the private sector. They also center on the effects of government intervention on social stability, economic growth, and the legitimacy of public authority.

Fundamental questions of governmental structure also come into play at this level. How, for instance, do such constitutional matters as federalism and the separation of powers shape the desirability and feasibility of government intervention? The highest-level problems often receive scant attention in public administration books because it is assumed that program administrators can do so little to influence them. Nevertheless, these macro concerns profoundly shape the behavior of public employees and other implementing agents in their day-to-day activities.

Formal policymaking is the next step on the continuum. How does government make policy? What difference do policies make? What tools are available to policymakers? What criteria should be used to judge programs, and how can one evaluate programs? These and related questions prompt a focus on the major lawmaking institutions of government in the United States—the Congress, the courts, and the presidency. Public administrators also play a major role in shaping this process.

Specific issues of policy implementation and government organization form yet another level on the macro-to-micro continuum. At this level the spotlight is on administrators, administrative structure, what happens after a bill becomes law. How should government shape its formal structure (for instance, lines of authority) to carry out policy? What do implementing agents do as they carry out (or fail to carry out) government programs? What outputs and outcomes result from their activities?

At the micro end of the continuum, the focus is on government operations and management. What constraints and opportunities do public managers face as they attempt to use certain resources—legal authority, personnel, information, money, equipment, and facilities—in the day-to-day conduct of agency operations? What basic technologies do they employ? Do they succeed in fostering efficiency and effectiveness?

A central question is how the various levels of concern—from macro to micro—become integrated through processes of political decisionmaking and public administration. Decisions at one level are interwoven with those at other levels; events at one level help explain choices and activities at another. Existing theory and evidence do not permit a precise specification of the complex relationships among levels, but this volume will cast at least some light on the matter.

In considering the various levels of concern, certain factors that influence them deserve note. First, on each level politics affects who gets what from a government activity. For example, what may at first glance seem to be a straightforward administrative problem of organizing a service, such as providing information to farmers on how best to raise corn, turns out at closer examination to be a hotly contested political issue. Should the service be provided by the government at all? If so, who should provide it (the federal government or the state university)? Who should receive the service (large or small farms), and what kind of corn should be covered by the program (corn for feeding cattle or for feeding people)? At each level there are political issues embedded in democratic theory. It is necessary to consider the relationships among efficiency, effectiveness, accountability, and responsiveness. Second, at each level there are empirical questions. How do people and institutions behave, and why? If public administration is to mature as a field, it must develop better theories to describe and explain behavior at all levels. Third, at each level there are normative issues. Questions of whether government should get involved in an issue or problem and how the activities of government ought to be conducted remain central to the field.

The Macroeconomic Division of Labor

Citizens' values strongly influence the demand for and supply of public policies. In large part, these values are received; that is, they are part of a society's cultural heritage.[3] In the United States we hold a set of expectations for our lives that rest on some central tenets of social and economic order. Above all, Americans cherish personal economic progress, security, and political autonomy, that is, the opportunity to share in the nation's prosperity, to lead safe and secure lives, and to have a broad range of political, economic, and social choices.[4]

Public policies are often best understood as governmental responses to crises that threaten to stand in the way of citizens' attaining or approaching these values. For example, the first ten amendments to the Constitution—the Bill of Rights—and many of the other amendments provide guarantees for personal freedom. Economic policies—fiscal, monetary, regulatory, and labor—are designed to promote the growth of national wealth and a stable economic environment, that is, a rising gross national product (GNP) and politically acceptable levels of inflation and unemployment.

Much economic policy has been formulated in response to the catastrophic breakdown of the economy during the Great Depression of the 1930s. Similarly, national defense and foreign policy have striven to maintain secure national borders and a favorable balance of trade in a world characterized by growing interdependence, high technology, and recurring military and economic warfare. Likewise, much domestic policy, especially social welfare programs, reflects deep-seated values of security and opportunity. Many of these programs, like Social Security, started during the Depression to provide a floor of support for the economically hard-pressed. Other such programs commenced in the 1960s to provide better living conditions and upward mobility to the poor. Similar patterns unfold at the state and local levels of government; services like police and fire departments, schools, libraries, roads, licensing, and regulation sought to improve conditions that segments of the citizenry found unacceptable.

The nation's value system also shapes the way government handles problems. Society places a high value on rationality and efficiency, that is, solving problems with the least expenditure of resources and with the best information attainable. This leads to respect for professionalism, or the application of education and expertise to solving specific problems. At the same time, citizens cherish the right to be involved, to participate in decisions that affect their lives. Americans are not content to delegate policymaking and implementation to experts. They want administrators to be held accountable to their wishes—to their personal definitions of the problem and the best way to solve it. In this way citizens make administrators responsible to their particular needs. Above all else, the principle of equal opportunity has a firm place in the nation's culture. Although the country has frequently failed to live up to this ideal in practice, the standard does much to shape government design. Hence, political and administrative systems have rules and regulations to promote equal rights to participate in politics and equal access to public programs and benefits.

Thus, the system for defining and resolving problems in the United States reflects the multiplicity of values held by the American people. The system is imperfect; its solutions almost always seem imperfect, partly because these solutions involve trade-offs among values, and policymakers cannot forge consensus on the relative importance of the different values. If government relies on a military draft to obtain the human resources it needs to protect its international position, it must also infringe on individual freedom. If government seeks to provide education economically, people who are culturally deprived, handicapped, or otherwise expensive to serve will face barriers. In short, the value system laced into the fabric of the culture often leads to a complex and contradictory method of identifying and evaluating problems and solutions. Public agencies must try to reconcile the irreconcilable, deal with problems that defy solution, and design solutions that only approximate the ideal. Nevertheless, citizens and legislators expect progress toward solving problems, and these expectations do much to drive the behavior of public administrators and their organizations.

Whatever the multiplicity of American values, the fact remains that there is considerable public support for government activism. Table 1.1 reveals the attitudes of the populace toward government spending in fourteen areas. In only one area did as much as a quarter of the populace favor decreases in federal expenditures (military armaments and defense at 37 percent); in nine areas, fewer than 10 percent of the respondents wanted less spending. In contrast, at least half the public expressed support for spending increases in six areas. In many areas there is substantial support for spending hikes, even if such action requires new taxes (see source cited in Table 1.1).

The climate of support for government activism in turn raises critical issues for mixed economies, in which the government and the private sector exist side by side. Many in the United States accept the view that when private-sector markets produce a reliable and appropriate quantity of goods and services at a reasonable price, they should be let alone. Some sectors of the private economy do work well and meet these criteria, but others do not. Consequently, government often seeks to regulate the reliability of products, foster competition and fair pricing, protect the unwary, and compensate the harmed through regulatory programs, inspection services, grant programs, income maintenance initiatives, and other vehicles.

Chapter 2 of this volume plumbs the empirical and normative issues typically raised in discussions of the balance between the public and private sectors in mixed economies. For present purposes, certain general observations seem pertinent. Different nations use different divisions between the public and private sectors, depending largely on their economic development, national culture, ruling elite, and dominant ideology. In the 1980s government spending at all levels in the United States typically hovered around 35 percent of GNP. This percentage ranks relatively low among industrialized nations. Japan and Spain had lower percentages, but most advanced nations had larger public sectors. (See Chapter 2.)

TABLE 1.1   Attitudes Toward Federal Spending, 1989

"If you had a say in making up the federal budget this year, for which of the following programs should spending be increased, for which should spending be decreased, or for which should spending be kept the same?"

Program	Increased	Same	Decreased	Don't Know
Combatting the drug problem	65%	28%	4%	3%
Health care	57	36	4	3
Programs for the homeless	53	40	4	3
AIDS research	52	38	6	4
Programs for the elderly	50	45	3	2
Public school system	50	43	5	2
Social security	46	47	3	4
Environmental protection	39	49	7	5
Aid for farmers	33	47	16	4
Scientific research	32	55	9	4
Financial aid for college students	31	49	15	5
Government assistance to the unemployed	26	57	14	3
Programs for blacks and other minorities	20	55	21	4
Military armaments/defense	11	49	37	3

Source: Gallup Organization in "Opinion Roundup." *Public Opinion* 11 (March-April, 1989): 25. Reprinted with the permission of the American Enterprise Institute for Public Policy Research.

Figure 1.1 casts further light on cross-national variation, depicting the extent of state ownership in various industrialized societies. Again, the commitment of the United States to private ownership stands out. Unlike those of many other nations, such critical industries as telecommunications, electricity, gas, coal, and airlines remain substantially in private hands in the United States. Over the last ten to fifteen years, there had been some movement toward greater state ownership in other countries.[5] However, some countries whose public sector has loomed particularly large as a proportion of economic activity (Sweden and Great Britain, for example) have begun to move in the opposite direction.

The debate over public versus private dominance continues to ferment. Markets, for example, frequently produce unacceptable inequalities between the haves and the have-nots; governmental arrangements tend to produce disincentives that augur against the efficient allocation of scarce resources. Proponents of the private sector frequently emphasize that reliance on it will stimulate economic growth by allowing entrepreneurs to flourish; presumably, benefits also trickle down to the poor. Others express doubts about the potency of these dyamics. They point to the paucity of firm evidence of a clear relationship between the extent of state-owned enterprise and national economic growth. Some economies that grew rapidly from 1960 to 1980 (for example, Germany and Brazil) had substantial public ownership, whereas others

	Posts	Tele-commun-ications	Elec-tricity	Gas	Oil Produc-tion	Coal	Rail-ways	Airlines	Motor Industry	Steel	Ship-building
Australia	●	●	●	●	○	○	●	◕	○	○	NA
Austria	●	●	●	●	●	●	●	●	●	●	NA
Belgium	●	●	◕	◕	NA	○	●	●	○	◔	○
Brazil	●	●	●	●	●	●	◕	○	●	◕	○
Britain	●	◕	●	◕	◕	●	●	◕	◑	◕	●
Canada	●	◕	●	○	○	○	◔	◕	○	○	○
France	●	●	●	●	NA	●	●	◕	◑	◕	○
West Germany	●	●	◕	◔	◕	◔	◑	●	●	◕	◕
Holland	●	●	◕	◕	NA	NA	●	◕	◑	◕	○
India	●	●	●	●	●	●	●	●	○	◕	●
Italy	●	●	◕	●	NA	NA	●	●	◕	◑	◑
Japan	●	●	○	○	NA	○	◔	◕	○	○	○
Mexico	●	●	●	●	●	●	●	◑	◕	◕	●
South Korea	●	●	◕	○	NA	◕	◕	○	○	◕	◔
Spain	●	◑	○	◔	NA	◑	◑	●	○	◑	◑
Sweden	●	●	◑	●	NA	NA	●	◑	○	◕	◑
Switzerland	●	●	●	●	NA	NA	●	◕	○	○	NA
United States	●	○	◔	○	○	○	◔ *	○	○	○	○

Privately owned all or nearly all ○   Publicly owned all or nearly all ●   75% ◕   50% ◑   25% ◔

NA–not applicable or negligible production
* Including Conrail

Adapted from a chart in *The Economist* (London) December 30, 1978 and reprinted with special permission

FIGURE 1.1.
Extent of State Ownership

Adapted from: Thomas K. McCraw, "Business & Government: The Origins of the Adversary Relationship," *California Management Review* 26 (Winter 1984): 34.

(Japan) had relatively little. Some countries that achieved only limited growth had relatively few state enterprises (Canada, the United States) while others (Great Britain) had many. Economic theory simply has not progressed far enough to predict the exact consequences of different private and public sector arrangements. This uncertainty helps to fuel the debate and the persistent effort to seek a better balance.

Claims that private-sector enterprises inevitably achieve greater efficiency than their public-sector counterparts are to be taken with a grain of salt. Many economists believe that business organizations are more attuned to profit and loss and that their management enjoys greater freedom of action and incentives to perform. Thus, they are alleged to be more efficient and better contributors to national economic growth.

In contrast, these theories see public administrators as accountable to elected officials as well as constrained by rules and regulations. Such factors, along with the absence of competition, presumably push these administrators toward less efficiency and effectiveness.[6] As will become clearer later in this volume, differences between the public and private sectors are much less clear-cut. For example, many public managers have substantial incentives to pursue efficiency, and their counterparts in the private sector often face considerable pressure to be accountable to government regulations.

The Policy Process

Broad discussions of the mix of public and private activities lend a limited understanding of who gets what from government. The dynamics of policy processes also require careful scrutiny. These processes deserve attention whether an analyst focuses on macro policies that involve large-scale efforts to shape society over an extended period (for example, major tax policies) or micro decisions that have a relatively small impact over a short time (for example, decisions about eligibility by workers for the Social Security Administration). Chapter 3 provides a backdrop for policy processes and subsequent chapters in the book. It examines the major actors in the policy process and notes how the nation's political culture helps shape their behavior. Chapter 3 pays particular attention to the kinds of administrative agencies involved in the process and the tools they use. Chapter 4 presents an overview of the key phases of the policy process—agenda setting, policy formulation, legitimation, resource attachment, implementation, evaluation, and response. The role of administrative agencies in each phase receives particular consideration.

In attempting to understand policymaking, students of public administration have chosen several different paths. Some have sought to describe how government makes policy, that is, how a public problem and a policy idea come together to become a law.[7] Others have sought to analyze the effects of institutions and rules on the way government addresses policy issues and the choices it makes, often with the aim of improving the way problems are handled.[8] Still others have sought to develop, describe, or explain decision-making tools used by government in formulating public policy.[9] Finally, some people have sought to explain foreign and domestic policy failures in terms of breakdowns in decision-making processes.[10]

This volume views public policies as *formally specified responses to public problems*. They generally find expression in such documents as public laws and court opinions. In terms of content, policies tend to articulate (with varying degrees of clarity) goals for a program and the means to accomplish them. Of course, the statement of objectives is one thing and their realization is another. Policies often yield outputs and outcomes that the drafters did not intend or anticipate.

Public policymaking is a complex process for several reasons. First, policymaking usually involves changing a state of affairs when not everyone agrees that the present state is unsatisfactory or that the proposed state will be better. To illustrate, although many believe that acid rain constitutes a major environmental hazard, states with many sulfur-producing industries regard it much differently than do those without such industries, especially those downwind from the source of the sulphur. Second, participants in the policy process often disagree about the means for achieving a better state of affairs. In the case of acid rain, affected industries may oppose federal legislation to minimize or prohibit sulphur coming from their smokestacks. State governments and congressional delegations may join the resistance as well. Proposals to develop hardier strains of timber and vegetation for downwind states may be seen by their officials as too long-term and halfhearted. Third, the Constitution ensures that in the United States, policymaking will be a complicated process. Suspicious of a strong, unified executive, the framers of the Constitution chose a structure of government that provided for the separation of powers with several types of checks and balances, because they "were more concerned about *preventing tyranny* than they were about *facilitating policy development.*"[11]

These three features of the American political system stand in contrast to problem solving in simpler systems. Effective decision making tends to be more feasible when these circumstances prevail:

1. There are few goals, little conflict over goals, and few ambiguities about them.
2. Goal-attainment measures are readily available and indicators are precise and tangible.
3. Cause-and-effect relationships are well understood; that is, social technologies are highly predictable and efficiencies are well understood.
4. The environment provides quick and accurate feedback on organizational performance.
5. All necessary resources are under the control of a single manager and organization.

Some tasks in the public sector, such as bridge construction by the Army Corps of Engineers and claims processing by the Social Security Administration, meet these conditions. Unfortunately, few of these conditions prevail in the management of public organizations at more politically sensitive levels of authority. Instead, the reality of the policy system—fragmented political authority, institutionalized competition for scarce resources, and multiple checks and veto points at different levels of government and at different stages in the policy process—confronts public-sector managers with problems both complex and politically infused. The misperception of problems or the inappropriate choice of means to solve them can lead to unintended consequences and dysfunctional outcomes. In micro problem solving, this development can threaten the survival of an agency or program. Faulty problem solving at the macro level—especially of those problems involving economic, defense, and foreign policy—can produce negative effects that threaten the stability and even the survival of a government.

Administrative Questions, Political Answers

The involvement of administrative agencies in the policy process highlights the political role of these agencies. Students of public administration have attempted to come to grips with the appropriate relationship between politics and administration for over a century.[12] For much of that time, experts believed that a workable arrangement could be based on the premise that the politics of policymaking and the implementation of programs could be kept separate, so that political officials would be responsible for policy and career civil servants would be responsible for implementation. Since World War II, this doctrine, known as the politics/administration dichotomy, has faced severe challenge. Career civil servants tend to be inexorably drawn into policy matters while implementing programs and serving as major sources of expertise during policy formulation.

Chapters 5 through 8 cast some light on the issues involved in understanding the relationship between politics and administration. Chapter 5 sorts out various definitions of *politics* and *political* as they pertain to public administration. It suggests that given certain definitions, administration can be seen as more or less politicized. Chapter 6 focuses on another arena that can claim great political importance—budgetary processes. Money is the mother's milk of administration. The processes that shape the appropriations to agencies, as well as the amounts they actually spend on particular items, loom large in any effort to understand public administration. Chapter 7 examines issues of administrative law. Somewhat paradoxically, the forces that shape administrative law simultaneously constrain civil servants and energize them. Clearly, interaction in this arena profoundly influences the role of civil servants in shaping who gets what from government. Finally, Chapter 8 probes the issues raised by public administration for a democratic society. The realization of the artificiality of any attempt to separate politics from administration casts public adminstration doctrine into a state of confusion. If civil servants are not simply neutral instruments of elected public officials, what should be their proper role in a democracy? How should they be held accountable? As these questions suggest, one cannot judge the merits of public administration purely in terms of efficiency and effectiveness. Political criteria rooted in democratic theory also apply.

Theories of Public Organization

As a factor influencing the relationship between politics and administration, structure makes a difference. The framers of the Constitution were quite conscious of the importance of structural arrangements. Indeed, one can view the Constitution as an organizational design intended to promote limited government.[13] Later, as government grew, concern with the way it delivered services took root, and a doctrine of administrative management for government agencies evolved. This doctrine, articulated in the late 1930s by the Brownlow Committee and by the two Hoover commissions a decade and a half later, implicitly accepted the notion that government programs could best be administered by large-scale bureaucracies directly accountable to the president. Explicitly, this meant strengthening the president's control of the bureaucracies through structural arrangements.[14]

As the government grew, however, it became increasingly clear that the large-scale bureaucracy reporting directly to the president was only one kind of tool. Such alternatives as government corporations (for example, the post office and Synfuels Corporation), grants-in-aid to state and local governments, and tax incentives emerged and were used to implement federal policy. In many of these cases, the involvement of the president was less direct. Clearly, in choosing alternatives to bureaucracy, policymakers believed that structure made a difference in the effectiveness of programs and the distribution of benefits. However, no overarching theory of public organizations evolved to demonstrate what structures work best for specific kinds of policies. Instead, the government has made choices on an ad hoc basis with little concern for the desirability of one structure over the others.[15]

This suggests that public administration in the United States is in a period of great uncertainty. The efficiency, effectiveness, and accountability of the executive branch affect how citizens judge their government. For students of public administration, the urge to study and then improve or "reform" (often reorganize) the executive branch has been a major concern during the past century. Chapters 9 and 10 of this book review the major theories and perspectives that have shaped thinking about public organizations, especially at the federal level.

Government Operations and Public Management

Students of public administration must also be attentive to the day-to-day concerns and strategies of public managers. These activities in the aggregate do much to spell the success or failure of government programs.

Public managers face many constraints that limit their discretion and flexibility. The control of public organizations and employees has always been a central issue in public administration. Layer after layer of laws, rules, regulations, procedures, and related mechanisms serve the ostensible purpose of holding civil servants accountable to elected officials. Procurement, budgetary, and personnel processes require periodic reporting and careful documentation to guard against malfeasance, nonfeasance, and favoritism. Indeed, a principal distinction between public and private management is the degree to which these procedural controls apply.[16] While undoubtedly fostering lawful and accountable administration in many instances, the plethora of rules often makes managerial work in the public sector more difficult. To achieve goals, managers must generally make choices with these constraints in mind.

The rule-bound environment that many public managers face is not clear, neat, and orderly. To the contrary, managing governmental intervention in human affairs usually implies work filled with ambiguity, complexity, conflict, confusion, and scarce resources. Furthermore, the higher a public manager goes in the hierarchy, the likelier it is that he or she will face problems for which no clear-cut solution can be found, no obvious strategy is politically feasible, or no choice can be made without someone or everyone becoming the worse for it.[17]

Public management is a continuing struggle against instability caused by social and technical change and the tendency of political and organizational arrangements to break down and come apart.[18] Instability, combined with the complexity of most modern administrative arrangements, forces public managers to make decisions and operate under varying conditions and degrees of uncertainty or ignorance. Similarly, the dispersal of political power and authority among agencies, interest groups, and levels of government requires that public managers contribute to the building and maintenance of a consensus among interested parties. Finally, limits to the revenue-raising power of government, combined with the imbalance between almost unlimited demands for programs and limited funds, mean that public managers will usually have to manage with scarce resources. These factors present public managers with some continuing problems: the necessity to generate useful information; the necessity to build broad consensus in support of policies; the necessity to coordinate and integrate complex administrative arrangements; and the necessity to ration resources.

From the beginning, students of public administration have sought to improve the performance of public agencies. This volume focuses on the challenges top executives face as they seek to manage certain critical resources, or factors of production. Thus, Chapter 11, showing the nature of managerial work and the way in which culture, technology, and certain imperatives shape it, focuses on formal legal authority as a resource. To achieve their ends, managers at times call on the authority granted to them by legislation, court opinions, administrative regulation, and other documents.

Chapter 12 zeroes in on personnel as a critical resource. Success in government programs depends partly on the ability of managers to obtain, deploy, remove, train, and motivate employees. The opportunities and barriers to personnel management deserve careful attention. Chapter 13 targets three other resources that managers must use to achieve effectiveness: information, facilities and equipment, and money. Managers often have limited ability to control the deployment of these resources. Executives, however, are far from impotent in shaping their use, and these resources often figure prominently in the strategic and procedural calculations of public managers.

Conclusion

This volume takes the reader from the macro to the micro concerns of public administration. Exhibit 1.1 presents an overview of its landscape. The reader should not assume that the cells embedded in the matrix are conceptually airtight. Government processes and activities flow and merge into one another in complex, interactive ways. The left-hand column of the matrix specifies four levels along the macro-to-micro continuum. The second column fleshes out the basic processes that occur at each level, and the third points out the particular institutional foci that tend to capture attention. For instance, students of policymaking frequently examine issue networks as they study processes leading to the passage of legislation by Congress. The fourth column suggests some critical questions embedded in choice processes at each level. The final column uses the issue of gaps in health insurance coverage to illustrate the kinds of matters likely to arise at the various levels.

The matrix suggests how a macro problem can have implications for micro processes and vice versa. For example, an issue such as poor economic growth may stem from problems with the fundamental division of labor between the public and private sectors. This problem influences policymaking, implementation, and organizational strategies and comes home to roost in such problems as reductions in force and poor employee morale. Poor management practices in government may yield to better organization and implementation. Officials may reconsider how best to design policies or even whether, given the problems of performance, government ought to be involved in the policy arena at all. Similar linkages could pertain in the case of medical insurance coverage—the illustration used in Exhibit 1.1.

In probing the problems encountered at various points on the macro-to-micro continuum, certain propositions deserve emphasis. Because government intervenes

EXHIBIT 1.1   The Landscape of Public Administration

Levels of Analysis	Basic Processes	Some Institutional Foci	Some Critical Questions	Illustration
Macroeconomic division of labor (What government does)	From social issues to government intervention	The structure and functions of American government and the elements of the private sector	Can government effectively intervene to ameliorate a problem, or will the public interest be better served by leaving the problem to private-sector groups and dynamics? Will intervention facilitate social stability, spur (or at least not impede) economic growth, and foster government legitimacy?	Should the federal government intervene to provide medical insurance to 37 million Americans who lack any coverage? Or, given the deficit and the persistent problem of inflation in the medical sector, would it be best to live with the inequity created by the current patchwork of private sector as well as state and local programs?
Policymaking (How government decides what to do)	From policy agendas to public policies	Issue networks, policy arenas, and the sub-governments of policy formulation	Which public-policy alternative seems most likely to be effective? Which will be more affordable or efficient? Which alternative is the most politically feasible? Who should reap the benefits? Who should pay the costs?	Assuming the desirability of federal intervention, would it be better to attack the problem by (a) requiring all employers to provide adequate health plans for their employees, (b) extending coverge under the Medicaid program, or (c) launching a national health insurance plan for all citizens modeled on the Canadian system?

EXHIBIT 1.1 *Continued*

Levels of Analysis	Basic Processes	Some Institutional Foci	Some Critical Questions	Illustration
Policy implementation and government organization (How government carries out its decisions)	From public policies to public programs	The structure and culture of executive branch organization, administration by proxy, program structure	What organizational and program arrangements should be used to implement the program? Should the federal government rely on states, localities, or private entities for implementation? How can a balance be struck between effectiveness, responsiveness, and accountability?	Should a new agency be set up to administer the program? Or should it be assigned to the Health Care Financing Administration, the federal agency that is responsible for Medicaid and Medicare? How, exactly, should the program be structured to guarantee that those currently without insurance coverage receive program benefits efficiently and without sacrificing accountability?
Government operations and management (How the day-to-day operations of government are managed)	From public programs to operational efficiency and effectiveness	The roles and responsibilities of public managers and employees	How can managers set priorities, create and use resources, sustain and improve technologies, and generally pursue strategies that will foster the efficiency and effectiveness of agency operations?	How can managers balance their obligations to this new program with other programmatic responsibilities? How can they be sure to receive sufficient information about the conduct of the program without suffering from information overload? How can personnel with adequate skills to operate the program be recruited and retained?

in almost every facet of life, often in critically important ways, public administration is a *very* special field of study. Its successes and failures generally have great implications for the quality of life and at the extreme bear on the very survival of society itself. As those involved in public administration grapple with this responsibility, they must discard the stereotypical notion of administration as centralized, hierarchical decision making. The policymaking core of government is pluralistic, multilevel, and multistage. The policy process tends to produce compromises and piecemeal solutions against a backdrop of individual and group needs, ambitions, power, ideology, and coalitional loyalties. Actions taken at both macro and micro levels often have unintended and dysfunctional consequences.

If public administration ranks high in importance and complexity, it also has come under considerable criticism during the 1970s and 1980s. A performance gap exists; people see a discrepancy between what they want from government and what they receive.[19] Perceiving many of the social policy initiatives of the 1960s as failures and preferring lower taxation, many people questioned the sense of government involvement in many areas of social and economic life. The debate over purposes and the role of government in a mixed economy has resurfaced with a vengeance. Where critics of government acknowledge the need for some government programs, they often advocate greater application of business techniques or privatization strategies so that private contractors perform much of the work of the public sector.

Public discontent, whether or not based on accurate perceptions of government performance, requires that the search for excellence in public administration intensify. In this regard, Chapter 14 reviews some of the enduring issues—from macro to micro—that intersect with efforts to foster excellence in public administration. This volume holds that there are often basic differences between the problems of business and those of governmental organizations. While business methods can on occasion be fruitfully imported by the public sector, efforts to do so often prove counterproductive. Finally, Chapter 15 reviews the legacy of the Reagan years, highlighting some of the challenges to public administration in the year 2000.

In sum, the approach to public administration in this volume is both political and managerial. It strives to link political issues and processes with managerial challenges so that the special role played by public organizations in the administrative state can be better understood.

Notes

1. For discussions of the paradigm crisis in American public administration, see Dwight Waldo, ed., *Public Administration in a Time of Turbulence* (Scranton, PA: Chandler, 1971); Frank Marini, ed., *Toward a New Public Administration: The Minnowbrook Perspective* (Scranton, PA: Chandler, 1971); and Vincent Ostrom, *The Intellectual Crisis in American Public Administration* (University, AL: The University of Alabama Press, 1973). For a discussion of the difficulty of defining the scope of public administration, see Dwight Waldo, *The Enterprise of Public Administration: A Summary View* (Navato, CA: Chandler and Sharp, 1980), 58–60; and "Scope of the Theory of Public Administration," in James C. Charlesworth, ed., *Theory and Practice of Public Administration: Scope, Objectives, and Methods* (Philadelphia: The American Academy of Political and Social Science, 1968), 1–26.

2. Frederick S. Lane, ed., *Current Issues in Public Administration*, 3d ed. (New York: St. Martin's, 1986), xv.

3. This idea is developed in the context of public administration in Eugene Lewis, *American Politics in a Bureaucratic Age: Citizens, Constituents, Clients and Victims* (Cambridge, Mass.: Winthrop, 1977).

4. For an extensive discussion of these core values and how they shape public policy, see Robert A. Dahl and Charles E. Lindblom, *Politics, Economics, and Welfare* (New York: Harper, 1953).

5. See Thomas K. McCraw, "Business & Government: The Origins of the Adversary Relationship," *California Management Review* 26:2 (Winter 1984): 35.

6. For a review of these distinctions, see Hal G. Rainey, Robert W. Backoff, and Charles H. Levine, "Comparing Public and Private Organizations," *Public Administration Review* 36:2 (March-April 1976): 233–244.

7. See, for example, John W. Kingdon, *Agendas, Alternatives and Public Policies* (Boston, Mass.: Little, Brown, 1984).

8. See, for examples, Vincent Ostrom and Elinor Ostrom, "Public Choice: A Different Approach to the Study of Public Administration," *Public Administration Review*, 31:2 (March-April 1971): 203–216; and Richard R. Nelson, *The Moon and the Ghetto* (New York: Norton, 1977).

9. In the budgeting area, for example, see Aaron Wildavsky, *The Politics of the Budgetary Process*, 4th ed. (Boston: Little, Brown, 1984).

10. See, for example, Irving L. Janis, *Group Think,* 2d ed. (Boston: Houghton Mifflin, 1982).

11. Charles O. Jones, *An Introduction to the Study of Public Policy,* 3d ed. (Monterey, CA: Brooks/Cole, 1984), 6.

12. This juxtaposition of ideas comes from Claude E. Hawley and Ruth G. Weintraub, eds., *Administrative Questions and Political Answers* (Princeton, N.J.: Van Nostrand, 1966), a compilation of representational articles from the first twenty-five years of the *Public Administration Review.*

13. See Charles E. Lindblom, *The Intelligence of Democracy* (New York: The Free Press, 1965).

14. See Harold Seidman, *Politics, Position and Power,* 3d ed. (New York: Oxford University Press, 1980).

15. See Frederick C. Mosher, "The Changing Responsibilities and Tactics of the Federal Government," *Public Administration Review* 40:6 (November-December 1980): 541–548; and Lester M. Salamon, "Rethinking Public Management: Third-Party Government and the Changing Forms of Government Action," *Public Policy* 29:3 (Summer 1981): 255–275.

16. See Rainey, Backoff, and Levine, "Comparing Public and Private Organizations"; and Graham T. Allison, Jr., "Public and Private Management: Are They Fundamentally Alike in All Unimportant Respects?" in Lane (ed.), *Current Issues in Public Administration,* 184–199.

17. See Guido Calabresi and Philip Bobbitt, *Tragic Choices* (New York: Norton, 1978).

18. See Victor A. Thompson, *Bureaucracy and the Modern World* (Morristown, N.J.: General Learning Press, 1976), especially Chapter 1.

19. For a discussion of performance gaps see Anthony Downs, *Inside Bureaucracy* (Boston, Mass.: Little, Brown, 1967).

Part One

The Superstructure of Public Administration

Public administrators need some understanding of how broad socioeconomic and political forces shape government programs in order to do their job honestly and well. The three chapters in this section focus on aspects of this macro context. Although many of these environmental factors appear remote from the everyday concerns of federal employees, they set off ripples (at times, waves—even tidal waves) that affect the efficiency, effectiveness, responsiveness, and accountability of public workers.

Chapter 2 focuses on the nature and degree of government's general involvement in the society and economy. In comparison with other industrialized democracies, government in the United States tends to play a small role in the economy. Nonetheless, government takes a noticeable tax bite out of each paycheck (federal witholding, Social Security) and impinges on the lives of virtually all citizens through its programs. The decisions by government on how much to tax and to spend, what to spend on and what to tax, as well as how large a public deficit to accept, significantly influence the performance of the entire economy. The federal government has increasingly found itself in the role of economic manager and guarantor of the quality of life for the nation. In this capacity government must respond to demands generated by social and economic trends.

Political and morphological factors also significantly affect public program administration. Certain basic features of the governmental structure ordained by the Constitution—especially federalism and the separation of powers—come home to roost in administration. So too does an idea anchored in the intellectual legacy of the Founding Fathers—suspicion of centralized governmental power. Morphological factors include broad administrative structures and program tools. As will become evident in Chapter 3, these structures and tools come in myriad forms. In addition to the regular line agencies of government, administrative structures include "independent" commissions, public corporations, and institutes. Tools may be direct, for example health care in Veterans Administration hospitals, or indirect, for example guaranteeing loans made by private parties in order to encourage conservation.

Socioeconomic, political, and morphological elements ultimately become intertwined with the policy process—the focus of Chapter 4. They shape and are shaped by processes involved in agenda setting, policy formulation, legitimation, resource attachment, implementation, evaluation, and response. Public administrators play a role in all of these phases of the policy process. In this and other respects they are inescapably actors in a political drama. Astute public administrators must remain sensitive to their roles in this drama, the forces that shape it, and its implications for the proper conduct of their day-to-day duties.

Chapter Two

What Governments Do: Problems and Prospects

Introduction

Traditionally Americans are suspicious of government and have developed an implicit ideology that stresses the role of the free market and individual freedom as the best way to maximize human happiness. Despite that ideology, and politicians such as Ronald Reagan who espouse it freely and frequently, government in the United States has developed into a very big business. This holds true whether one considers the gross division of labor between the public and private sectors, the range of activities carried on by government, the amount of money collected and spent, or the number of people employed. This chapter discusses the division of labor in the economy as well as the size and shape of government. It then addresses some possible justifications for the increasing role of government, considers the case for limiting government involvement in the economy and society, and addresses implications of these issues for public administration.

"Big Government" in the United States

American government is not so large as many people think. Compared with other industrialized democracies, federal, state, and local governments in the United States are hardly gargantuan. This is especially evident if one considers the proportion of GNP accounted for by the public sector. Table 2.1 indicates that government in the United States spends more than 36 percent of GNP. Public expenditures in many other industrialized democracies account for an appreciably larger share of GNP. As of the mid-1980s, for example, the public sector accounted for more than 60 percent of GNP in Sweden and the Netherlands. Further, government employs less than one-fifth of the work force in the United States, whereas in several European countries government employs more than two-fifths. The relative size of American government does not prevent the growth of government from begin an important political issue, however.

While American government is not large in comparison with those of other industrialized democracies, it is much larger than for most of American history. Table 2.2 reveals appreciable increases in the public-sector portion of GNP from 1950, when it accounted for just over 20 percent. The federal share of GNP grew from

TABLE 2.1 Public Expenditure as a Percentage of Gross National Product:
The United States Compared, 1985

United States	36.7
Switzerland	30.9
Japan	32.7
Canada	47.0
West Germany	47.2
United Kingdom[1]	47.9
France	52.4
Italy	58.4
Netherlands	60.2
Sweden	64.5

[1] Estimated

Source: Organization for Economic Cooperation and Development, *Economic Outlook* (June 1987), p. 170.
Reprinted by permission of the Organization for Economic Cooperation and Development.

roughly 14 percent in 1950 to nearly 25 percent by the mid-1980s. State and local expenditures from their own revenues climbed from about 7 percent of GNP in 1950 to roughly 10 percent in the mid-1980s.[1]

A broader historical perspective provides additional vivid testimony to the growth of government. When George Washington became President, the American federal government consisted of a "Foreign Office with John Jay and a couple of clerks . . . there was a Secretary of War with an authorized Army of 840 men; there

TABLE 2.2 The Public Sector in Relation to Gross National Product in the
United States (in percentage)

	Total Expenditures	Federal Expenditures
1950	21.3	14.3
1955	24.5	17.0
1960	26.9	18.3
1965	27.2	17.9
1970	31.6	20.6
1975	34.5	23.0
1978	31.5	21.1
1980	33.1	22.9
1982	35.5	25.0
1984	35.6	24.7
1986	35.0	24.6

Source: U.S. Office of Management and Budget, *Budget of the United States Government, 1987, Historical Tables* (Washington, DC: Government Printing Office, 1986).

were a dozen clerks whose pay was in arrears."[2] With these humble beginnings American government began performing the core functions of government such as defending its territories, engaging in foreign relations, collecting taxes, and administering justice.[3] Until 1849 the Cabinet consisted of the Secretaries of State, Treasury, War, and Navy and the Attorney General.

Even before the Department of the Interior was formed in 1849, however, American government began to promote economic development. The least controversial creation was the Patent Office in 1802, followed closely by the General Land Office, which regulated the sales of vast amounts of land as pioneers opened the West. With great spaces to be developed, the federal government became involved in a number of transportation and communication enterprises, most notably the railways. For example, in 1850 the federal government granted 3.7 million acres of land to the Illinois Central Railroad. During this time and even before, state and local governments invested in canals, railroads, and highways.[4] What government gives it can also take away, and toward the end of the nineteenth century, the federal government increasingly regulated business, beginning with the Interstate Commerce Commission in 1887.

The latest functions to be undertaken by American government—especially the federal government—are social services.[5] The Public Health Service was initiated in 1789, but the first major involvement of the federal government in a social policy was the Morrill Act of 1862. This act provided each state a grant of land for higher education in "agriculture and mechanics" and was the source of the system of land grant universities. The great burst of social intervention did not occur until the New Deal of President Franklin Roosevelt, which began Social Security and programs that have evolved into Aid to Families with Dependent Children (AFDC) and Supplemental Security Income (SSI).[6] The second great social policy initiative was the Johnson administration's Great Society programs such as Medicaid, Medicare, Head Start, and the Job Corps. Thus government grew by adding new functions and rarely abandoning old ones. Government in the late 1980s did most of what government in the late eighteenth and nineteenth centuries did and a great deal more.

It is important to remember that this volume discusses only the federal part of big government. The Constitution and the Tenth Amendment assign each level of government a set of functions as its exclusive domain: The federal government holds explicit constitutional authority to print money, manage international relations, and conduct war. The states and localities are responsible for social functions such as education, public assistance, and health regulation.[7] However, by the 1980s there was no neat division of labor in these areas. In particular, the federal government has become involved in a number of functions that fifty or even ten years ago would have been considered the proper preserve of state and local governments. These include elementary and secondary education, fire protection, and consumer protection. Most of the exclusively federal functions, for instance, international affairs and minting currency, have remained the federal government's sole concern, although even here some blending of functions occurs. For example, many state and local governments send trade missions to foreign countries, actions which are sometimes seen as intervening in the authority of the federal government to control international commerce.

TABLE 2.3   Federal Expenditures by Function (in percentage)

	1952	1960	1970	1980	1984	1986	1988
Defense	64.8	49.8	40.0	23.4	28.9	27.1	27.3
Income Maintenance	7.7	19.5	21.9	33.3	33.3	34.0	32.8
Health	0.5	0.8	6.6	10.0	10.7	11.7	11.6
Education	0.5	1.4	4.4	5.3	3.0	3.1	3.0
Housing	0.9	1.1	1.2	1.7	1.5	1.7	1.3
Debt Interest	9.1	9.0	9.3	11.1	12.2	14.6	15.1
Other	16.5	18.4	16.6	15.2	11.0	7.8	8.9
Total	100.0	100.0	100.0	100.0	100.0	100.0	100.0

Source: U.S. Office of Management and Budget, *Historical Tables, Budget of the U.S. Government, 1990.*

What Government Buys

To list the activities of the federal government would require several entire books. The appendix to the fiscal 1990 federal budget, with detailed information, exceeded 1,000 pages; the budget for even a small department (Justice, which spends $5.4 billion out of a federal budget of more than a trillion dollars) had over 200 expenditure lines. Federal government funding impacts virtually all policies and programs in the United States. Much of the work of the federal government does not involve direct provision of services to citizens. Rather, state and local governments, or private individuals and organizations, carry on much of its work.[8] For example, although the federal government in fiscal 1989 spent approximately $11 billion for AFDC, it hired very few social workers or others to administer the program; instead it used state and local governments to make the decisions about eligibility and to disperse the money. Likewise, Medicare cost more than $70 billion in 1988, but the federal government hired very few physicians for the program; instead it paid nonfederal physicians and hospitals to care for Medicare patients. Thus, many of the activities of the federal government are indirect—only the dispersal of money and the eventual monitoring of its expenditure. For some such dispersals, for instance general revenue sharing, the federal government allows the governments receiving the money to impose their own priorities for expenditures.[9]

Whatever the vehicle for expenditure, by the end of the 1980s the federal government spent more than a trillion dollars each year. The mixture of public expenditures at the federal level had changed markedly during the postwar period. As Table 2.3 suggests, expenditures reflect a welfare shift as the federal government shifts spending from defense to social services. In 1952 almost two-thirds of federal public expenditures were for defense; by 1980 this proportion had decreased to 23 percent. During the Reagan years defense spending began to rise again, but by the mid-1980s it still remained much less than in 1970. In contrast, social expenditures were less than 10 percent of federal spending in 1952 and almost half in 1984. During the Reagan years discretionary domestic expenditures dropped significantly. However, the Reagan administration was able to do very little about social entitlement

TABLE 2.4 State and Local Expenditures by Function (in percentage)

	1952	1960	1970	1975	1980	1985
Education	25.7	30.7	35.6	32.6	30.7	29.3
Welfare	19.0	13.8	14.8	18.4	17.5	17.6
Health	6.3	6.2	6.5	7.0	7.4	7.6
Highways	13.6	15.5	11.1	8.4	7.7	6.8
Public Safety	4.5	4.7	4.4	4.5	4.4	4.5
Other	30.9	29.1	27.6	29.1	32.3	34.2
Total	100.0	100.0	100.0	100.0	100.0	100.0

Source: Tax Foundation, *Facts and Figures on Government Finances, 1988–89* (Baltimore, MD: Johns Hopkins University Press, 1988).

programs such as Social Security and Medicare. These programs guarantee certain income or services to citizens. Entitlement programs are not necessarily inviolate, but it generally requires a great deal of political effort to cut them. Moreover, elected officials often pay substantial political costs for such attempts. For instance, Social Security has achieved so high a level of popularity as to become virtually immune from attack, despite its rapid growth in expenditures.

As of the mid-1980s state and local expenditures, excluding federal grants, amounted to roughly $380 billion. The states' outlays from their own sources comprised almost 60 percent of this sum.[10] State and local governments spend money for a plethora of functions (see Table 2.4).[11] Education is by far the largest single item, but public welfare and health also loom large, followed by highways and public safety. State and local government expenditures make the United States much more a welfare state than do federal outlays alone.

So far this chapter has assumed that one can be absolutely sure of what a public expenditure is. This is not the case; many items not directly counted as expenditures represent outlays of public money. Further, some types of commitments *may* involve expenditures in the future but are not counted until they generate costs. For example, in 1984 the federal government provided $135 billion in new loans to farmers for crops, to businesses via the Small Business Administration (SBA) and the Export-Import Bank, to individuals for college, and to others. When analysts calculate that 35 percent of GNP is devoted to public expenditures, these loans are not counted because of the assumption that they will be repaid and net expenditures will be zero.

Governments also guarantee loans and insure economic activities. By so doing, they incur potential obligations but again do not count these obligations as a part of expenditures or potential expenditures. This accounting practice may seem reasonable. After all, the Chrysler Corporation repaid its federally guaranteed loan on time. However, in order to understand the full effect of government on the economy, one must consider the amount of money moved about by government actions in so many areas. Washington insures not only loans but also farm crops and citizens' deposits in banks and savings and loan institutions. In short, the real and possible obligations of the United States make a total substantially larger than 35 percent of GNP.

Moreover, government is committed to certain *tax expenditures*. These are tax preferences for certain types of income and spending. For instance, the federal government generally does not provide grants or otherwise send checks so that people can buy their own homes. Instead it allows people to deduct mortgage interest from taxable income. Thus, government improves the living conditions of many citizens, capital accumulation in the economy, and the health of the construction industry. Some of the incentives that government manipulates do not seem so benign as those for buying homes. Critics frequently charge that such loopholes allow wealthy individuals and corporations to escape paying their fair share of taxes.

Picking Up the Tab: Public Revenue

The concept of tax expenditures leads to another critical macro issue—obtaining money to pay for government. Government sells some services. For instance, the citizens of Athens, Georgia, a college community, pay a monthly fee to the city for water and sewer service, and they pay the recreation department when they enroll their children in a summer program. Like other Americans, they buy postage stamps so that the U.S. Postal Service will deliver their letters. Many children are born in a local public hospital that charges fees for deliveries. When those children reach college age, many of them pay tuition to the University of Georgia, a state institution. Often, the amounts charged by such public agencies do not recoup the full cost of providing services, but the sums paid go a long way. In principle government could market services such as highways, education, and fire protection. Despite some pressure to make government services pay for themselves, however, the bulk of the costs of government are met through taxation.[12]

The personal income tax is the largest single source of federal tax revenue, amounting to more than 45 percent as of the mid-1980s (see Table 2.5). It has sustained this position as the major source of revenue throughout the entire postwar period. During this period, however, a major shift has occurred in the relative role of corporate income tax and social insurance taxes. In 1952 the corporation tax provided almost one-third of total federal taxes; by 1984 this share was less than 9 percent. Moreover, tax loopholes allowed many large and profitable corporations, such as General Electric, Boeing, DuPont, and General Dynamics, to pay no income tax in one or more of the years 1981 to 1984.[13] In contrast, social insurance, for example Social Security and Medicare taxes, increased from less than 10 percent of total taxes to more than one-third. This means that almost two-thirds of federal tax revenue comes directly from the income of workers. Federal excise taxes on such commodities as alcohol, tobacco, and gasoline have also declined appreciably as a percentage of total revenue.

On October 22, 1986, President Reagan signed the Tax Reform Act of 1986, claiming it was "the best anti-poverty bill, the best pro-family measure and the best job-creation program ever to come out of the Congress of the United States."[14] However inflated these claims, it may be altering the composition of federal taxes to some degree. Among other goals, the law seeks to stem the decline in the relative share of taxes coming from corporations. Analysts estimate that the corporate income tax will rise from about 8 percent of all taxes in the mid-1980s to nearly 14 percent by the early 1990s.[15]

TABLE 2.5   Federal Taxes by Source (in percentage)

	1952	1960	1970	1980	1984	1986	1988
Personal Income Tax	41.1	45.0	47.8	48.7	46.4	45.5	45.1
Corporation Tax	31.2	23.7	20.1	12.9	8.6	9.1	10.6
Social Insurance[1]	9.6	15.3	20.6	30.8	37.0	36.1	37.6
Excise Taxes	13.1	12.9	8.3	4.9	3.8	4.4	4.0
Other[2]	5.0	3.1	3.2	2.7	4.2	4.9	2.7
Total	100.0	100.0	100.0	100.0	100.0	100.0	100.0

[1]Approximately half of social insurance contribution comes from employers.
[2]Customs, estate and gift taxes, miscellaneous
Source: U.S. Office of Management and Budget, *Historical Tables, Budget of the United States, 1990.*

When state and local as well as federal taxes are considered, the personal income tax becomes less central, although it still amounts to about 35 percent of total taxation (see Table 2.6). In 1984 state and local sources of revenue were about 20 percent income tax; 30 percent property tax, mostly local; and 36 percent sales tax. Subnational governments also levy excise taxes, frequently on the same commodities as the federal government, but the general sales tax brings in the biggest share of their revenue. The administration of the general sales tax differs from place to place, such items as food, medicine, and clothing being exempted from taxation in some states but not in others.

Discussion of sales tax brings up the question of progressivity. A tax is progressive if the affluent pay a higher share of their income than those in lower income brackets. It is proportional if all citizens pay the same percentage of their income to it. It is regressive when those with lower incomes pay at a higher rate than those who are richer. The sales tax is regressive; it takes more from the less affluent because the less affluent spend a higher proportion of their income than the affluent. The federal income tax is progressive. Assessment of the progressivity of tax structures at different levels of government depends in part on basic assumptions about the incidence of the property tax and corporation taxes, but whatever the

TABLE 2.6   Total Taxes by Source (in percentage)

	1952	1960	1970	1980	1982	1984	1986
Personal Income Tax	32.1	34.1	36.8	39.3	40.0	36.9	35.7
Corporation Taxes	24.5	17.9	13.3	10.7	9.9	7.6	7.1
Social Insurance	8.8	10.8	15.3	21.2	23.7	24.7	28.2
Property	9.6	12.9	12.4	9.3	9.1	9.9	9.6
General Sales	3.6	4.2	5.8	7.0	7.3	7.7	7.7
Excises	13.3	14.4	11.0	7.3	6.9	7.9	7.3
Other	8.1	5.7	5.4	5.2	3.1	5.3	4.4
Total	100.0	100.0	100.0	100.0	100.0	100.0	100.0

Source: Bureau of the Census, *Government Finances,* Series GF, no. 5, annual.

assumptions, state and local tax structures generally are less progressive than their federal counterpart.

However, since 1966 the progressivity of the tax structure in general has declined. Changes in the federal tax system appear to account for this diminution. The increase in payroll taxes such as for Social Security, as well as revenue policy modifications in 1981, contributed to this trend. It remains to be seen whether the Tax Reform Act of 1986, which reduced the top federal income tax rate from 50 percent to 28 percent, will reinforce movement toward less progressivity. As of the early 1980s it appeared that the large majority of Americans paid about the same proportion of their income in taxes of all sorts (federal, state, local), but the very rich and the very poor on average paid a higher proportion. [16]

Note that the public appears to prefer taxes notorious for their regressivity. Asked to choose between a sales tax hike and an income tax boost, 57 percent chose the sales tax; 23 percent endorsed the income tax. Furthermore, if pushed to endorse some form of federal tax increase, most of the public prefers a national sales tax to a hike in the federal income tax. [17] A value-added tax might be considered if the federal government decides to respond to these sentiments. This tax, common in Europe, is levied on goods and services at each stage of production, and the amount of the tax is included in the final price of the product. The value-added tax tends to be invisible, which may make it less politically controversial than taxes that take a noticeable bite out of one's paycheck. [18]

In addition to being less progressive, state and local taxation is less buoyant; it tends to respond less to changes in either economic growth or inflation. Local governments have improved their assessment systems but may still fall behind in the real value of property. In addition, the ownership of property is not always a good indicator of the ability to pay taxes. Elderly homeowners on fixed incomes may not be able to keep up with property tax payments when assessments increase. Likewise, unemployed people or struggling businesses may not be able to pay during hard economic times. Therefore, local governments might be better served if they taxed liquid (accessible) capital rather than property. In part because of these problems, local governments often turn to Washington for additional funding. In fiscal 1986 state and local governments received approximately 20 percent of revenue from the federal government. [19]

Tax revenues and charges for service are major means for funding government. Another increasingly prevalent method, especially at the federal level, is borrowing. By the end of fiscal 1988 (September 30, 1988), gross federal debt was an estimated $2.6 trillion (see Table 2.7). Since 1980 the deficit has more than doubled, even controlling for inflation and the decline in the value of the dollar. In fiscal 1986 alone, the federal deficit amounted to roughly $221 billion, which meant that Washington was borrowing $1 of every $5 it spent. This represents borrowing at a rate not previously seen except during times of war. Table 2.7 also indicates that the gross federal deficit as a percentage of GNP has risen since 1970. However, the percentage in 1950 and in 1960 stood at higher levels than in the 1980s.

State and local governments do not have such capacity to borrow. As of the mid-1980s the per capita debt of subnational governments was approximately $2,139, whereas the per capita figure for the federal government was $6,677. [20] Nearly all states and localities are forbidden by their own laws and constitutions to

TABLE 2.7   Federal Debt, 1950–1987

Year	Gross Federal Debt in Millions of Dollars	As Percentage of GNP
1950	256,853	96
1960	290,862	57
1970	382,603	39
1980	914,317	34
1986	2,132,913	51
1987	2,345,578	53
1988	2,600,753	54
1989 (est.)	2,868,792	56

Source: U.S. Office of Management and Budget, *Historical Tables, Budget of the United States Government, Fiscal Year 1990* (Washington, DC: Government Printing Office, 1989).

incur deficits in their operating budgets. They can issue bonds for capital projects, but the amounts are frequently limited by a linkage to the tax base or other economic variable. Further, state and local governments cannot print money; if the federal government does not want to borrow money directly from citizens and organizations, it can seek authorization to print more money. Borrowing for revenue eases political problems in one time period, but it imposes long-range restrictions on government. Interest payments have been increasing as a proportion of total public expenditures, especially for federal expenditures. Debt interest is a contractual obligation on which no government is inclined to default. To pay greater amounts of interest, however, limits government's ability to spend for other policy goals.

Public Employment

Government employed more than 16 million part- and full-time civilian employees as of the mid-1980s (see Table 2.8). Although the federal government spends the most money, it employs fewer than 20 percent of government workers. The majority of public employees, close to 10 million, serve local governments. School districts employ nearly half of these workers.

While public expenditures and revenues have increased as a proportion of the GNP, public employment has been relatively stable. State and local employment (full- and part-time combined) increased by roughly 35 percent from 1970 to 1985 although the population of the United States grew by only about 16 percent over the same period. However, from 1970 to the mid-1980s, the number of federal employees declined as a percentage of the total labor force and of the population in the United States.[21] This fact plus the large increases in the federal budget illustrates the degree to which the federal sector is money-intensive rather than labor-intensive. Except for the armed forces, the post office, and some direct services such as those provided by the Veterans Administration, the federal government mainly sends out checks to individuals, organizations, and other governments and arranges for third

TABLE 2.8   Governmental Employment 1985

Government	Full-time and Part-time Employees (in thousands)
Federal Civilian	2,964[1]
State	3,984
Local	(9,685)
County	1,891
Municipalities	2,467
School Districts	4,416
Townships	392
Special Districts	519
Total	16,633

[1]This figure excludes some 55,000 federal employees who work for the legislative and judicial branches as well as the White House staff. Full-time equivalent employment in the executive branch approximated 2,854,000 in the mid-1980s. See U.S. Office of Management and Budget, *Special Analyses, Budget of the United States Government, Fiscal Year 1988.* (Washington, D.C.: Government Printing Office, 1987), I-2.
Source: U.S. Department of Commerce, *Statistical Abstract of the United States, 1987* (Washington, DC: Government Printing Office, 1986), 280, 311.

parties to provide services. This requires some people to program computers and some to monitor contracts and expenditures, but requires fewer people than do state and local government services such as police and fire protection, maintenance of streets and highways, and the delivery of social welfare.

Some labor-intensive services have found ways to function with fewer personnel. Modern military forces rely on fewer people to deliver massive destructive power. The post office now delivers 65 billion more pieces of mail than in 1950 and does it with fewer people, in part because of automation. Computers and telecommunications technologies allow fewer federal workers to provide the same services. Finally, the federal government has been under pressure to appear as small as possible as recent Presidents have tried to trim the federal bureaucracy. This has provided potent incentives to use subnational governments, quasi-governmental organizations, and private parties as implementing agents.

Just as the composition of public expenditures has changed, so too has the composition of public employment (Table 2.9). In particular, the same trend has shifted personnel away from defense and the other defining functions of government and toward the social functions.[22] The shift of employment has not been so pronounced as the shift in expenditures. Moreover, the types of social functions absorbing the greatest amount of expenditure have not necessarily had the greatest increases in employment.

These variations to some degree reflect the differences in the economics of different public services. For example, educational services require large numbers of public employees. Most governments hire teachers, administrators, bus drivers, cafeteria workers, and all others needed to make a school function. On the other hand, health services are frequently contracted out, and large public expenditures for health may not be reflected in the number of government employees. Finally, services such as public pensions require little direct public employment even though the service is

TABLE 2.9 Total Public Employment by Function (in percentage)

	1952	1962	1972	1984	1986
Defense	45.7	32.2	20.4	16.9	17.3
Education	17.2	26.4	34.0	36.4	37.8
Post Office	4.8	4.8	4.1	3.6	4.0
Health	5.0	7.4	8.0	9.0	8.8
Police & Fire	3.8	4.7	5.2	5.6	5.7
Other	23.5	24.5	28.3	28.5	26.4
Total	100.0	100.0	100.0	100.0	100.0

Source: Bureau of the Census, *Public Employment*, Series GE, 1, annual.

direct. The Social Security Administration is mostly an efficient check-writing machine, especially since the development of the computer. Large-scale increases in income maintenance expenditures may be carried out with the same or fewer staff.

Several other changes in the composition of total public employment deserve note. One is the increasing public employment for police and fire protection. The real and perceived increase in crime in the United States over the postwar period has resulted in large increases in the number of public safety employees—and there are even larger increases in private-sector employment in protection and security agencies.[23] All of the myriad functions of government other than the five large employing functions detailed in Table 2.9—including such large-expenditure programs as Social Security—can be delivered by approximately one-quarter of total public employment.

The Justification for Government Intervention

Society has long questioned the role of government and sought minimal government interference in the lives of citizens, so it is only natural to wonder at the large-scale expansion of the public sector. Is this trend indicative of a failure of the democratic process to translate the wishes of citizens into policy? Is government out of control? Some have argued that the increases in the size of the public budget result from the abilities of aggressive "bureaucratic enterpreneurs" to hide the true costs of producing services and to gain excessively large appropriations from Congress.[24] Another argument is that in times of crisis—wars, depressions—the public is willing to see the amount of government revenue expand to meet the crisis. However, after the crisis politicians manage not to return the "surplus" revenues, but spend them instead.[25] Others have argued that governments cannot readily reduce costs through new technologies (despite the post office example above). Many jobs performed by government are labor-intensive, and new technologies can help little. In addition, for services such as social work, personal time and contact are as important as financial benefits, so that introducing labor-saving technologies might be counterproductive.[26]

A number of other more fully developed theories, with both normative and empirical aspects, have roots in the dynamics of democracy, economics, and moral philosophy.

Democracy Propels Growth

Rather than a failure of democracy, the expansion of government may represent democracy run wild. The birth of new programs and the expansion of existing ones in part occurs because the public, or some segment of it, demands such action. The population of the United States has a schizophrenic attitude toward government and public programs. On one hand, people want government services—especially those benefiting them directly. On the other hand, they are reluctant to pay the taxes that support those programs. At times this schizophrenia is quite pronounced. A majority of those in favor of Proposition 13, which severely cut local taxes, supported cuts in only a single program—public welfare—and that was a bare majority. More voters wanted programs expanded than wanted them cut.[27] As Free and Cantril argue, Americans tend to be ideological conservatives and operational liberals.[28] Citizens oppose "big government" with great vigor but are quite willing to spend money for particular programs, especially the ones that benefit them directly. In his discussion of what he calls interest group liberalism, Theodore Lowi argues that the nature of American government is to appropriate the power of the public sector for private advantage.[29]

Even if the majority of the public were in favor of the elimination of public programs, the nature of the political process makes it easier to spend. James Q. Wilson refers to this phenomenon as the politics of concentrated benefits and dispersed costs.[30] Most public programs benefit segments of the population differentially. Farmers benefit from agricultural programs, businessmen from subsidies, the poor from welfare and food stamps, the elderly from Social Security, and so forth. Because any individual taxpayer pays only a small portion of the costs of any program, citizens have a much greater incentive to organize to protect and expand benefits than they do to reduce programs. There have been some notable taxpayer efforts to reduce public expenditures—Proposition 13 in California and the federal War on Waste associated with the Grace Commission on cost control.[31] However, these are exceptions rather than the general rule in policy making, and spending generally has more political appeal than saving.

The structure of federal policymaking contributes to the ability of interest groups to generate benefits. Interest groups, congressional committees, and public agencies work together to protect and expand government programs. Congressional oversight committees and subcommittees tend to be composed of congressmen from districts directly affected by the programs in question. As shown in Exhibit 2.1, the composition of some committees places the foxes in charge of the henhouse. That is, the officials who oversee the expenditures have most to gain from increased spending.

Some citizen demands need not be expressed so overtly and politically to fuel growth in outlays. Most social expenditures in the United States are made through entitlement programs, so that if a citizen meets certain criteria, for instance, age and previous contributions to Social Security, he or she is entitled to benefit. Government

EXHIBIT 2.1   Subcommittees of the House Agriculture Committee, 1987

Cotton, Rice, and Sugar

Democrats	*Republicans*
Huckaby (Louisiana)	Stangeland (Minnesota)
Jones (Tennessee)	Emerson (Missouri)
Stallings (Idaho)	Lewis (Florida)
English (Oklahoma)	Combest (Texas)
Harris (Alabama)	Herger (California)
Coelho (California)	Holloway (Louisiana)
Stenholm (Texas)	
Tallon (South Carolina)	
Rose (North Carolina)	

Tobacco and Peanuts

Jones (North Carolina)	Hopkins (Kentucky)
Hatcher (Georgia)	Roberts (Kansas)
Tallon (South Carolina)	Combest (Texas)
Thomas (Georgia)	Holloway (Louisiana)
English (Oklahoma)	
Stenholm (Texas)	

Wheat, Soybeans, and Feed Grains

Johnson (South Dakota)	Marlenee (Montana)
English (Oklahoma)	Stangeland (Minnesota)
Huckaby (Louisiana)	Roberts (Kansas)
Evans (Illinois)	Emerson (Missouri)
Penny (Minnesota)	Smith (Oregon)
Nagle (Iowa)	Schuette (Michigan)
Jontz (Indiana)	Grandy (Iowa)
Volkmer (Missouri)	
Espy (Mississippi)	
Jones (North Carolina)	

Source: *Congressional Quarterly*, 45:18, *Supplement*, 2 May 1987.

has little control over how much it will spend for programs of that type; expenditures depend largely on demographic and economic changes.

If people who benefit from public programs are anxious to have them continued, so too are the public employees who administer those programs. Government is a large employer, and its employees are also voters. They have strong incentives to fight any cuts in their programs or changes in the nature of programs that would reduce their job opportunities. Some argue that one of the major sources of resistance to change in existing welfare programs, especially AFDC, toward less labor-intensive programs has been organized social workers. Opposition to budget cuts and program modifications is rarely expressed in terms of job protection but rather in such terms as "the quality of service" and "protection of the client." Nevertheless, the interests of public and private providers as well as clients must be taken into account, especially since they exert influence as voters as well as policy advisers or members of interest groups. Furthermore, it is natural for administrators to value the programs they serve and to believe quite sincerely that they are providing important services.

Several dynamics affect the role of public agencies as sources of pressure for expansion. For instance, agencies often have the most information about the field when a program is being implemented. These street-level bureaucrats gain a great deal of information from their clients. That information may be about specifics of the program, for example inadequate benefits or contradictory regulations, or it may be about other aspects of the client's life that impinge upon the success of the program in question. The role of lower-level administrators is usually discussed within the context of social programs, but much the same would be true of programs designed to aid arms merchants or other businesses. Administrators regularly in touch with beneficiaries are likely to have the most information about how the program functions and what the clients need, and they often use that information to suggest improvements in existing programs or supplements to them.

An increasing number of public employees are professionals or para-professionals.[32] Because of their professional training and continued association with professional organizations, such employees look beyond the bureaucracy and its rules to discover what is good practice in their field. Doctors will look for guidance to the American Medical Association or specialist boards rather than to the rule books of a government agency, and teachers look to educational groups. Further, public management itself is becoming defined as a profession with its own standards. Professional associations for public employees may encourage their members not to remain quiet if an agency is implementing a substandard program; they will be more likely to demand improvements.

At times public employees do rally in defense of their jobs as employees rather than as professionals or service providers. This was notable during the Reagan administration, which mounted large-scale attacks on the size of the civil service, its pay and perquisites, and its political independence.[33] Such direct defense of civil service employment is relatively rare, in part because the civil service—the bureau-cracy—has not been a positive symbol for most Americans.

This discussion of the size of the public sector in the United States has em-phasized the government's responsiveness to the demands of clients and service providers. It has also suggested that government itself is not simply reactive and that many within the public sector are developing proposals for new programs. One study argued that the principal cause of expansion was that "entrepreneurial" members of Congress seek to make a name for themselves by sponsoring new programs.[34]

The executive branch may push strongly for new programs, especially the President and appointed political executives who come to Washington with ideas about what needs to be done to make the country better.[35] Career civil servants, because of expertise, experience, and concern for policy—as well, perhaps, as concern for an increased budget—push for expansion. Thus, the institutions of government may be a good deal more autonomous than they are sometimes thought to be, and pressure groups may actually be pressured groups.

Thus, democratic politics is a powerful explanation of why our governments grow and grow. Taken as a whole, the array of public programs may appear huge and almost extravagant, but each program benefits some, who are likely to prize it highly. Those programs employ individuals who want to keep their jobs. They represent the political efforts of elected and appointed officials who are determined to see their pet programs prosper. In such a political environment it is easy to see why government has become a big business.

Economic Impetus

The political justifications for government intervention stress demands from citizens, especially from organized citizens, for benefits. The justifications for government action in the economics literature stress the characteristics of the goods and services provided. Even economists enamored of the free market as an optimal means of allocating most goods and services recognize that some types of goods and some problems require authoritative action by government.

The concept of the public good provides one of the classic economic justifications for the role of the public sector. A public good has one major defining characteristic—namely, that it is difficult or impossible to exclude anyone from consuming it once it is created. Moreover, consumption by one person does not prevent consumption by another.[36] The classic example of a public good is defense. Once government chooses to maintain defense, all citizens are defended. Police and fire protection are also close to pure public goods, although fire services at least can be marketed, and at least one fire department has refused to answer a call from nonpaying citizens.[37] Commodities such as clean air and water can also be thought of as public goods.

The economic problem with public goods is that a person cannot be excluded from receiving the benefit of the good once it is produced, so no one has an incentive to pay for the good. They instead have an incentive to be a "free rider" and let everyone else pay. Therefore governments, having the power to tax and coerce citizens to pay for their benefits, are the logical institutions to supply public goods. Even here, however, individuals may have an incentive not to make their desire for public goods known to government. That way they can minimize their taxes while still receiving some of the benefit of the public goods created. Hence, public goods may be produced in less than desirable amounts.[38]

The concept of externalities is another justification for government. An externality is a social cost or benefit of production that is not reflected in the market price of a product. The most obvious example of a negative externality is pollution. Leaving aside the aesthetic costs of pollution, it produces real economic and social costs. Owners of houses downwind from a polluting plant have to repaint them more often; people living near the source frequently fall ill and lose time at work; plants and animals may be killed. The polluting industry does not include those social costs in the price of its products; they are borne by society at large, or at least by that part of society affected by the pollution. Of course, firms that create positive externalities, for example new recreation opportunities in a reservoir behind a dam, do not charge for them.

Again, government is the logical institution to deal with externalities. It often regulates the producers of negative externalities, for example requiring discharge permits for various types of pollution. A mechanism proposed by the Reagan administration is to impose effluent charges on firms that generate pollution. Presumably this would be an efficient means of controlling pollution because it would allow the more profitable and cleaner firms to produce at a high level, and less-clean firms might be driven out of business. Of course, environmentalists argue that this merely makes increased pollution more likely and that it sets a price on life. Fundamentally the market is incapable of dealing effectively with externalities, and some form of governmental intervention often becomes necessary.

Some other types of goods and services cannot be produced efficiently in the free market. Such goods have declining marginal costs of production; that is, the larger they are, the more efficient they become. Public utilities such as electricity are the classic example of goods of this type. In addition to the efficiency of larger generating plants, the jumble of wires and cables that would be associated with competitive electrical suppliers argues in favor of granting a monopoly for a single firm in a geographical area and then using the power of the public sector to ensure that the firm does not extract unfair payments from its customers because of its position as a monopoly. Interestingly, analysts once thought that telephone service had the same characteristics as electric service, but the development of satellite technologies made competition in long distance phone service a booming industry after the deregulation of communications systems.

The economist's model of the free market rests on a number of assumptions. One is that consumers have adequate (or even perfect) information about the goods and services they purchase. This condition fails to apply in many instances, and government intervenes in any number of ways to correct the inadequate supply of information. For instance, government has long required the licensing of professions. A patient visiting a physician may not know just how competent he or she is, but will at least know that the physician had to meet certain standards before the state would grant a license.[39] The same is true for a large number of other professions and occupations. Similarly, governments require restaurants to post their sanitary ratings and meat-packers to stamp the quality grade on the carcasses. More recently, governments have required manufacturers to provide complete information on the content of packaged foods, to post the estimated gas mileage of automobiles, and to warn smokers about threats to their health. None of these actions prevent the consumer from buying a gas-guzzling automobile or from smoking three packs of cigarettes a day; consumers can, however, have information about the products they consume.

Governments have also become managers of economies. The Keynesian revolution during and after the 1930s led many politicians and economists to believe that appropriate interventions by the public sector could produce full employment, economic growth, and low inflation.[40] The historical cycles of boom and bust in industrial economies would be a thing of the past. No one—politician, economist, or citizen—is now so optimistic about government's ability to control macroeconomic movements as in the 1950s and 1960s. However, having accepted the task of economic management, governments appear to be stuck with it. Further, if any institution is capable of steering the economy, it is the federal government. Governments can influence their economies directly, as by regulating wages and prices, or indirectly, by manipulating revenue and expenditure (fiscal policy) or the money supply (monetary policy). While the ability of governments to manage the economy effectively is increasingly in doubt, the responsibility for trying is not likely to be removed.

Governments are a source of investment and subsidy for the private sector, if only to preserve employment. In an economy with a few large firms rather than a large number of small firms, allowing any one firm to go out of business can have serious consequences for employment and economic growth. Therefore government has accepted the role of lending money or guaranteeing loans to a number of large firms in danger of bankruptcy. Many of the risks usually associated with capitalism have been shifted to government and the population at large. The federal government bailed out Lockheed and Chrysler, and state and local governments have attempted to prop up declining industries. Some scholars and politicians have argued for an even greater concern with industrial policy.[41] Governments also indirectly subsidize firms by educating future workers (an increasingly important function in a technological age) and providing the infrastructure—roads, water, weather bureaus—necessary for economic success.

Finally, the market does not always produce the most desirable distribution of goods and services. Even free market economists see some justification for redressing severe inequalities produced by the marketplace. Thus, programs such as Social Security, which aids workers after they can no longer work, win the approval of some conservatives. Liberal economists see the market producing a number of distortions and more readily favor government intervention. For example, they support measures to ameliorate the undervaluing of jobs that have traditionally been considered women's work.

Just as war is too important to be left to the generals, the economy is too important to be left to the private sector. The neoclassical free market model may work well in the classroom, but the complexity of the world requires the use of public policy and exchange to manage the economy and its consequences.

Social Ethics as Impetus

Government intervention in the economy and society also derives from philosophy and social ethics. The economist or the businessman may compare government outcomes on a measuring rod of money; the philosopher may apply different and more ambiguous criteria to assess the proper role of government. Both sets of criteria are important in understanding the role of government. For example, the businessman may find it profitable to invest in South Africa, whereas the philosopher may find a number of moral objections to such actions and argue for government intervention to enforce those moral judgments.

One ethical question concerns the degree to which the state is justified in acting to protect citizens from external threats or from themselves. *State paternalism* (government as parent) may be contrasted with a position arguing for the freedom of citizens to make their own choices. This question is resolved in a number of ways. First, certain types of citizens—children and the mentally handicapped, for example—who are incapable of making fully informed and rational choices can be treated differently from competent adults. Thus, citizens under twenty-one may be deemed incapable of dealing with the effects of alcohol and are prohibited from purchasing liquor; those under sixteen or eighteen may be deemed incapable of making competent choices about smoking and are prohibited from purchasing cigarettes.

This chapter pointed to steps government has taken to rectify the information deficit of citizens yet allow citizens to make their own decisions. In some cases, however, government will not allow citizens to buy products even if they understand the risks. Each year the Consumer Products Safety Commission requires a number of products to be removed from the market, just as the Food and Drug Administration prevents other products from being put on the market. Governments may also require citizens to perform certain actions, for example to wear a motorcycle helmet, even if the rider understands the risks of not wearing a helmet. Governments may remove individual choice even for adults and substitute the judgment of lawmakers. The principal justification for such action is that no reasonable person would be willing to accept the risk of an untried drug or of riding a motorcycle without a helmet; anyone willing to do so is prima facie incapable of a rational decision.[42] A more utilitarian view is that the cost to society of permitting such risk taking (for example, higher health insurance premiums and taxes for services to crippled motorcyclists) provides justification for restricting choice.

In other instances government intervenes in order to preserve the freedom of the individual in the marketplace. For example, some argue that wage and hour laws are necessary to allow the individual an equal bargaining position against large firms. Similarly, the guarantee of collective bargaining by government—for instance by the National Labor Relations Board—also strives to promote greater equality between labor and management. Proponents of legislation against prostitution have justified it on the basis of preserving the dignity of the individual.

Reasonable individuals may disagree on the extent to which individual choice should reign over collective choice and the regulations imposed by government.[43] Some argue that individuals should have the right to take all the informed risks they wish and that government has no right to impose its will on individuals, no matter how well-intentioned the government may be. Others argue that family members, friends, society, and other groups can be affected by the actions of the risk taker. They believe that government has the positive obligation to use its powers and its information to preserve the life and health of its citizens.

The desire for greater equality is another important philosophical and political justification for government intervention. We know that the marketplace does not generate equal shares for people, but reasonable people disagree on the extent to which equality should be generated by public action. The important ends of that dimension have been staked out by John Rawls and Robert Nozick.[44] Rawls asks people to consider what sort of society they would choose were they ignorant of their own position in society. If one is affluent, one can easily argue in favor of inequality, but such a choice is risky if it is made from behind a "veil of ignorance."[45] Rawls therefore argues that an egalitarian society is more justifiable than a society of inequality. Further, government is justified in intervening in any manner that improves the lot of those worse off in society.[46] Interestingly, such a stance would justify large-scale expenditures associated with social welfare programs but not for business, agricultural, and other middle-class subsidies.

Robert Nozick takes a position based upon property rights. He argues that any income legally received is the property of the individual and that government must have extraordinary claims to deprive the individual of that rightfully earned income. Nozick considers inherited income or other income received without work as legal and defensible as income earned through the labor and the talents of the individual. Such a stance justifies the perpetuation of economic inequalities across generations.

Historically the ideology of the American people has been more in tune with Nozick than with Rawls. American public policy has tended to be *distributive,* giving a portion of the benefits of public expenditure to all groups in society, rather than *redistributive,* aiding the most needy. The proper role of government in society remains a source of political and ideological controversy.

The concept of equality relates closely to that of *equity,* the access of citizens to certain benefits of society. Thus, governments may intervene in favor of equal access to education or employment or public service. Similarly, governments may have to consider the rights of future generations of citizens when short-term economic or social logic dictates the exhaustive use of some resources. The concept of equity is difficult to define, but it is one value that governments may have to pursue as they formulate public policies. They may be the only institutions capable of coping with problems of equity.

Efforts to Sustain the Mix

The forces contributing to the growth of government have spawned concern among those who wish to maintain an economy in which the private sector furnishes the lion's share of goods and services. The concerns of this segment find only limited expression in sporadic initiatives to cut taxes or balance the budget. Efforts to slash particular kinds of taxes need not constrain government growth as a proportion of the GNP if public policymakers substitute one tax for another or resort to deficit financing to boost government outlays. So, too, one can have a perfectly balanced budget by raising revenues to cover greater public expenditure. Thus, those who seek to sustain the broad division of labor between public and private sectors often focus on the percentage of GNP accounted for by government.

The National Tax Limitation Committee, an interest group that claimed to have six hundred thousand members as of the early 1980s, stood as a major advocate of this perspective.[47] This group supported an amendment to the Constitution to require that total federal budget outlays in a given fiscal year could not increase by a greater percentage than the proportion of increase in GNP in the prior calendar year. Hence, if GNP rose by 4 percent, federal spending could rise by 4 percent. In this fashion the ratio of public to private sector in the economy could be stabilized. (Note that the amendment applied to federal but not to state or local outlays.) The amendment also provided certain safety valves. For instance, federal outlays could surpass the limit if the President declared an emergency and each house of Congress voted by a two-thirds majority to exceed the ceiling.

Why do its proponents believe in the necessity of this amendment? At least two central themes undergird the proposal. First, supporters believe that a relatively large private sector ultimately promotes certain desirable values. Some believe that over the long term a robust private sector replete with markets will enhance economic growth, help ensure efficient production of goods and services, and give consumers what they want. One leading proponent of the amendment notes that if the government sector grew too large, "there would be less innovation; new ideas would languish. . . . There would be less variety because government guarantees collectivity not individuality." Carrying the point still further, he asserts: "Why don't I like big government? It breeds dependency, which is bad for the moral fiber of the citizenry. It breaks down, which breeds disrespect."[48]

Belief in the positive effects of private markets mingles with the second concern—that democratic forces deny government the will to resist constant expansion of the tax base and expenditures. Government allocates benefits to many groups, each of which vigorously fights to defend its program from cuts. Political institutions come under relentless pressure from countless special interests to sustain and enlarge benefits to them. A constitutional amendment linking expenditures to GNP would presumably force government to set priorities and make choices rather than practice something-for-everyone politics.

On April 5, 1979, Senators John Heinz (Republican of Pennsylvania) and Richard Stone (Democrat of Florida) formally introduced a constitutional amendment patterned after the proposal of the National Tax Limitation Committee. Colleagues in the House of Representatives introduced a similar measure. The proposal languished. The election of President Reagan in 1980 unleashed new initiatives to limit government expenditures. Almost all of them, however, marched under the banner of a "balanced budget amendment"—a phrase that tended to trigger broader public support than the more complex notion of limiting federal expenditures as a proportion of GNP. Balanced budget requirements do not necessarily address issues of the appropriate size of government relative to the private sector. A version endorsed by President Reagan early in his administration would, however, have done much to address issues of public and private proportions of a mixed economy. This legislation required a balanced budget and limited any increase in federal receipts to a figure no greater than the percentage growth in the national income of Americans in the previous year.[49] Again, however, Congress turned its back. Supporters of limits on spending increasingly turned their attention to the states. Article V of the Constitution requires Congress to call a convention to consider proposed constitutional amendments if two-thirds of the states (thirty-four) request such action. By the mid-1980s thirty-two states had passed resolutions calling for a convention to consider a balanced budget amendment. The National Tax Limitation Committee as well as another major group, the National Taxpayers Union, lobbied other state legislatures in an effort to rally the necessary thirty-four states. But some states, including Connecticut and Michigan, refused to join the call, and the movement lost momentum in the latter 1980s. Even if a constitutional convention did materialize, delegates might not adopt a proposal that would tie the growth in government expenditures to increases in the GNP or national income.

In sum, the experience of the 1980s points to the political difficulties of using the Constitution to keep the lid on the public proportion of the economy. More fundamentally, the desirability of these efforts remains open to question. As proponents of the limitation readily admit, the current federal share of GNP is hardly sacrosanct. Societies in which government claims a much larger share often enjoy as much economic growth as those in which it is smaller. Moreover, many important social problems cry out for government attention and possibly growth (for example the AIDS epidemic). For these and many other reasons, critics challenge the normative and empirical underpinnings of efforts to limit federal expenditures as a

percentage of GNP. Whatever the limitations of the proposal, however, its proponents deserve credit for directly addressing the question of the "right mix" in a mixed
economy. What proportion of GNP should government provide? Is the political
system so lacking in discipline as to make the establishment of priorities nearly
impossible and the something-for-everyone growth of big government inevitable?
Even those sympathetic to public programs can benefit from wrestling with these
questions.

Public Administration and the Macro Level

Students of public administration cannot safely ignore the macro issues discussed
to this point. Broad economic, social, and political trends ultimately come home to
roost in government policy, organization, and day-to-day management of public
activities. The ways political factors intertwine with public administration receive
persistent attention in the remainder of this volume. For present purposes, some
salient implications of economic, social, and technological trends for public administration deserve note.

Reverberations from the Economy

Implementing agents of the federal government often feel the aftershocks of
broad economic trends and government efforts to steer and manage the economy. In
never-never land, agencies get more or fewer resources depending on how efficiently
and effectively they operate, and increases in gross government expenditures depend
on whether most agencies perform well. In the United States, public bureaucracies'
resources often depend heavily on economic trends and governmental decisions made
in the name of the economy. Government has accepted the major responsibility for
steering the economy and therefore for assuring orderly economic growth, a
favorable balance of payments, a sound dollar vis-à-vis foreign currencies, low
inflation, and low unemployment. This is very difficult, and presidential popularity
depends heavily on at least the appearance of success in this realm.

In considering the economy and public administration, annual growth in the GNP
looms as critical. During the years following World War II, the high rate of economic
growth strongly influenced policymaking. From 1948 to 1984 GNP in the United
States more than tripled in real terms (after allowing for inflation). This enabled the
government to provide increasing public services while allowing for increased private
consumption.[50] Policymakers could provide new social programs and more defense
spending without making difficult choices about how large they wanted the public
sector to be.

The several oil crises of the 1970s and the subsequent economic difficulties
changed that. Growth in GNP fell to an average of 1.8 percent in the years
immediately after 1973 from more than 4 percent per annum for the years 1948–1973.
Not only were there shocks to the American economy from abroad, but the
productivity of American workers did not keep pace with that of workers in other
countries. Moreover, American goods were priced high in an increasingly interdependent world economy. The United States remained a very wealthy nation, but its

economic growth was no longer certain. Without economic growth, increases in the consumption of publicly provided goods were paid for out of private consumption; if the public wanted more schoolteachers, it would risk having fewer refrigerators. Yet substantial opposition to higher taxes to finance these ventures remained.

By the mid-1980s economic growth had begun to rebound. Earlier scenarios about limits to growth became less compelling, but the sense of scarcity and pressure to curtail federal spending programs grew. Soaring federal deficits were the primary engine of this pressure. These huge deficits (see Table 2.7) largely resulted from the supply-side economic strategy of the Reagan administration. This strategy for sustained economic growth called for reduced taxes—especially for the more affluent. This in turn would provide greater incentives for work and investment. Proponents argued that the economic growth resulting from this strategy would provide sufficient government revenues to cover expenditures even at lower tax rates. In fact, however, economic growth was not high enough to compensate for tax cuts. Pressure to balance the budget arose, including provisions for across-the-board cuts in expenditures so that a balanced budget might be reached by 1991. The huge increase in the public debt and the associated interest payments will present a continuing problem.

This era of perceived scarcity presents real difficulties for public administration. First, it has changed much of the ethos of working in the public sector. Instead of expecting to improve the world, most employees can hope for no more than that their portion of the world will not get much worse.[51] Even programs with long-established commitments to clients may be threatened by scarcity.

Second, public employees are one of the most vulnerable groups during scarcity. Politicians often gain a good deal of political mileage by cutting civil service pay, perquisites, and numbers of employees. In the United States, federal civil service pay has not kept pace with salaries in the rest of the economy, and total compensation for civil servants is now approximately 79 percent of that for comparable jobs in the private sector.[52] The especially pronounced pay differential at the upper levels has contributed to a loss of experienced career executives just when talented executives may be most necessary.

International matters affect public administration in relation to broader economic issues. As a superpower, the United States plays an important global role. The size of the defense budget and the extensive commitment of American armed forces bear vivid testimony to this fact. So do involvement in foreign aid and various international organizations such as the United Nations, the International Monetary Fund, and the World Bank. Superpower status entails large responsibilities to other nations and consequent financial and administrative strains on the federal government.

Of at least equal importance, the United States increasingly must compete in an international economy. American markets are open to many imported goods; one estimate holds that 75 percent of American manufacturers face strong foreign competition, whereas only a few years ago the figure approximated 25 percent.[53] Certain industries—steel, automobiles, and microelectronics—have been particularly vulnerable to international competition, and some of the movement away from the Rustbelt, the Northeast and Midwest industrial states, may be attributable to the loss of jobs to imported steel and automobiles. The United States consistently runs a large deficit in its *balance of trade*, the difference between the value of imports and the value of exports. By the mid-1980s, for the first time in more than a century, the United States owed more overseas than foreign countries owed to it. Greater involvement in world economics has placed even greater strains on an economy in transition and has generated calls for increased use of trade barriers such as tariffs and import quotas to protect American industry.

This international development has triggered demands that the United States adopt a comprehensive industrial policy as a means of promoting new industries and propping up old ones. Such a national policy would be a substitute for the large number of state and local programs designed to attract new industry to their locales through tax incentives, direct loans, and a variety of other inducements. These piecemeal programs do little to foster overall economic development. However, an integrated national industrial policy would require more centralized decisions than the federal government is usually capable of making and would require large public organizations for assessing the growth potential of certain industries and making decisions about how to allocate industrial aid.[54] Organizations of that nature have not existed in the United States since the end of World War II, and it is not clear that in the absence of a military threat they would be acceptable to large segments of the population.

Social Reverberations

Trends in the structure and culture of society interact with economic forces to shape the environment of public administration. One major social trend is the shift toward multiple wage earners in a single household, some or all of whom work less than full-time. This development has substantial implications for the patterns of child rearing and may increasingly impel governments to foster and subsidize child care programs. Likewise, a good deal of social and labor policy is premised upon the full-time worker who is the sole breadwinner for a family. It appears that such premises must be reconsidered and more appropriate policies developed. In fact, changes are apparent in the structure of the family unit in general; for example, more than one-fourth of all children in 1984 were reared in single-parent households.

Second, large population shifts from the Rustbelt toward the Sunbelt, the South and West, present declining cities and industries in one section of the country and the need for massive investment in infrastructure such as roads, sewers, and waterworks in another.[55] It is unclear to what extent these movements are accentuating regionalism, which may become especially heated over the control of natural resources such as oil and gas.[56]

Finally, the changing age structure of the population presents great challenges for public policy and administration. America, along with other industrial countries, is getting older day by day. The population over age sixty-five represented 11.9 percent of the population in 1984 and is projected to represent almost 14 percent by the year 2000. Thus, the squeeze will be on the working-age population, who will have to pay the taxes to support public pensions, health care, and other services to the elderly. Of course, policymakers may begin to explore options for reducing the pressure on those at work. Given greater longevity and the decline of physical labor in the economy, they may increase the retirement age or make it more feasible for those over sixty-five to work part-time. These changes would require modifications in Social Security. At the opposite end of the age structure, the school-age population has declined, in some areas sharply. This has forced many state and local officials to close schools and consider ways to deal with a surplus of teachers. Whatever the specifics, these cases illustrate the role of demographic trends in shaping demands on public policy and administration.

Forces of Technology

Technological change has always influenced social and economic life, and the pace appears to have quickened. Government, no different from other institutions, is significantly influenced by technology, although some influences are quite subtle.

One effect is in the composition of the work force. Many functions once performed by public employees can now be performed by machines, and one individual may now do a job that used to require several. The image of rows and rows of green-eyeshade civil servants shuffling piles of paper has given way to that of government by computer; one study identified 17,000 computers in the federal government with a quarter of a million employees minding them. It is likely that the public work force will drop in numbers relative to total employment in the economy and will have a higher proportion of technical and professional personnel. Further, such employees as secretarial and clerical personnel may need higher skill levels to use sophisticated office equipment.

As well as making public employees more productive, technological change will alter the tasks of government. Governments must now regulate activities that were nonexistent just a few years ago, such as recombinant DNA research. The regulation of these new technologies may be especially important given their destructive potential and the uncertainty about their possible effects, as at Three Mile Island and Times Beach. However, in some instances the development of new technologies has enabled the deregulation of some industries. For instance, the emergence of satellite communications has enabled government to eliminate the monopoly on telephone services and to foster competition in that area.

Conclusion

American government has grown large, expensive, and complex. Nonetheless, the private sector of the economy continues to be larger than the public sector. Proxy administration by private organizations stands as one of the most salient consequences of implementing programs in this context. Spurred in part by the presence of a large private sector and a concern that massive government bureaucracies not accompany major boosts in public spending, government contracts out an increasing amount of work to private entities. Procurement for military weapons, for example, has long depended on private contractors. Government has created a range of organizations at the margins of the state to perform tasks that government does not perform with its own employees and its own authority. As one commentator has expressed it:

> Pervasive sharing of governmental authority with a host of "third parties" (hospitals, universities, states, cities, industrial corporations, etc.) has significantly altered the practice of public management and rendered the traditional preoccupations of public administration, if not obsolete, then at least far from adequate.[57]

Contracting out government functions, or using other intermediary organizations, permits government to appear smaller to many citizens than its proportion of GNP would suggest. As will become evident later in this volume, administration by proxy also poses significant problems.

The presence of a large private sector and proxy administration should not mask the fact that the public bureaucracy is a major political actor in both the formulation and implementation of policy. In some ways it mirrors broad social and economic trends; in other respects it does much to shape programs with major implications for macro issues. Thus, the examination of public administration in this book involves more than the mere execution of laws; it involves a central political process in American government.

Notes

1. U.S. Advisory Commission on Intergovernmental Relations, *Significant Features of Fiscal Federalism,* 1984 edition. (Washington, DC: Government Printing Office, 1985), 8.
2. Leonard White, *The Federalists: A Study in Administrative History* (New York: Macmillan, 1948), 3.
3. Richard Rose, "On the Priorities of Government," *European Journal of Political Research* 4 (1976):247–89.
4. Jonathan T. R. Hughes, *The Governmental Habit* (New York: Basic Books, 1977), 67–71.
5. From the beginning of the United States, local governments have to some degree been involved with social policies, such as relief for the poor and elementary education.
6. The original Social Security Act established programs of categorical relief for the blind, aged, and disabled. These programs were combined into the Supplemental Security Income program during the Nixon administration.
7. For an extremely useful review of the development of federalism in the United States, see Deil S. Wright, *Understanding Intergovernmental Relations,* 2d ed. (Monterey, CA: Brooks/Cole, 1982).
8. Frederick C. Mosher, "The Changing Responsibilities and Tactics of the Federal Government," *Public Administration Review* 40 (1980): 541–53; Lester M. Salamon, "Rethinking Public Management: Third Party Government and the Changing Forms of Government Action," *Public Policy* 29 (1981): 255–75; Ira Sharkansky, *Wither the State?* (Chatham, NJ: Chatham House, 1979).
9. See George F. Break, *Financing Government in a Federal System* (Washington, DC: The Brookings Institution, 1980).
10. U.S. Advisory Commission on Intergovernmental Relations, *Significant Features of Fiscal Federalism,* 8–9.
11. U.S. Department of Commerce, *Statistical Abstract of the United States, 1987* (Washington, DC: Government Printing Office, 1986), 251.
12. One of the best explications of the logic of user charges is Arthur Seldon, *Charge* (London: Temple Smith, 1977).
13. "Biggest Profits, Zero Taxes," *National Journal* (6 April 1985): 767.
14. *Congressional Quarterly Weekly Report* 44, (25 October 1986): 2668.
15. U.S. Office of Management and Budget, *Historical Tables, Budget of the United States Government, Fiscal Year 1988* (Washington, DC: Government Printing Office, 1987), Table 2.2.
16. Using a number of different models of tax effects, Joseph Pechman estimated the

effects of taxes on income groups in the United States. The most progressive assumptions showed that those in the $500,000-to-$1 million group paid only a 6.7 percent higher rate of tax than someone earnng $5000 to $10,000. All of his nine models showed those in the $0-to-$5000 group paying the highest real rate. Joseph A. Pechman, *Who Paid the Taxes, 1966–1985?* (Washington, DC: The Brookings Institution, 1986).

17. U.S. Advisory Commission on Intergovernmental Relations, *Changing Public Attitudes on Government and Taxes* (Washington, DC: Government Printing Office, 1983), 9–11.

18. On the visibility of taxes, see Harold L. Wilensky, *The "New Corporatism": Centralization and the Welfare State* (Beverly Hills, CA: Sage, 1976).

19. U.S. Department of Commerce, *Statistical Abstract of the United States, 1989*, 258.

20. Ibid., 249.

21. See B. Guy Peters, "Public Employment in the United States," in Richard Rose, Richard Parry, Andrea C. Pigniatelli, Edward Page, and B. Guy Peters, *Public Employment in Western Democracies* (Cambridge: Cambridge University Press, 1985); U.S. Department of Commerce, *Statistical Abstract of the United States, 1987*, 230, 309.

22. Rose, "On the Priorities of Government," and Peters, "Public Employment in the United States."

23. B. Guy Peters, "Providing Public Services: The Public and Private Employment Mix," in Dennis L. Thompson, ed., *The Private Exercise of Public Functions* (Lexington, MA: Lexington Books, 1989).

24. William Niskanen, *Bureaucracy and Representative Government* (Chicago: Aldine/ Atherton, 1971).

25. Alan T. Peacock and Jack Wiseman, *The Growth of Public Expenditure in the United Kingdom*, 2d. ed. (London: George Allen and Unwin, 1967).

26. William J. Baumol, "The Macroeconomics of Unbalanced Growth," *American Economic Review* 57 (1967): 415–26.

27. David O. Sears and Jack Citrin, *Tax Revolt: Something for Nothing in California* (Cambridge, MA: Harvard University Press, 1982).

28. Lloyd Free and Hadley Cantril, *The Political Beliefs of Americans* (New York: Simon and Schuster, 1968).

29. Theodore J. Lowi, *The End of Liberalism* (New York: Norton, 1969).

30. James Q. Wilson, *The Politics of Regulation* (New York: Basic Books, 1980).

31. Jonathan Rauch, "Grace Commission Still Wooing Converts," *National Journal* (6 April 1985): 727, 748–9.

32. Frederick C. Mosher, "Professions in the Public Service," *Public Administration Review* 38 (1978): 144–50.

33. See Charles H. Levine, *The Unfinished Agenda of Civil Service Reform* (Washington, DC: The Brookings Institution, 1985).

34. Advisory Commission on Intergovernmental Relations, *The Growth of Government in the United States* (Washington, DC: Government Printing Office, 1980).

35. See Colin Campbell, *Governments Under Stress* (Toronto: University of Toronto Press, 1983).

36. Vincent Ostrom and Elinor Ostrom, "Public Goods and Public Choice," in E. E. Savas, ed., *Alternatives for Delivering Public Services* (Boulder, CO: Westview Press, 1977), 12ff.

37. Robert M. Spann, "Public versus Private Provision of Governmental Services," in Thomas E. Borcherding, *Budgets and Bureaucrats* (Durham, NC: Duke University Press, 1977), 71–89.

38. Anthony Downs, "Why the Government Budget Is Too Small in a Democracy," *World Politics,* 12 (1960): 541–63.

39. See Simon Rottenberg, ed., *Occupational Licensure and Regulation* (Washington, DC: American Enterprise Institute, 1980).

40. See, for example, the first three essays in Peter Jay, *The Crisis for Western Political Economy* (London: Andre Deutsch, 1984).

41. See Chalmers Johnson, ed., *The Industrial Policy Debate* (San Francisco: ICS Press, 1984).

42. D.F. Thompson, "Paternalism in Medicine, Law and Public Policy," in D. Callahan and Sisela Bok, eds., *Ethics Teaching in Higher Education* (New York: Plenum, 1980).

43. Donald VanDeVeer, "Paternalism and Restrictions on Liberty," in Tom Regan and Donald VanDeVeer, eds., *And Justice for All* (Totowa, NJ: Rowman and Littlefield, 1982), 17–41.

44. John Rawls, *A Theory of Justice* (Cambridge, MA: Harvard University Press, 1971); Robert Nozick, *Anarchy, State and Utopia* (Oxford: Basil Blackwell, 1974).

45. Rawls, *A Theory of Justice.*

46. Rawls referred to this as the "difference principle."

47. *Congressional Quarterly Weekly Report* (27 March 1982): 659; Aaron Wildavsky, *How to Limit Government Spending* (Berkeley, CA: University of California Press, 1979), 127–36.

48. Wildavsky, *How to Limit Government Spending,* 7.

49. *Congressional Quarterly Weekly Report,* 40 (27 March 1982): 659.

50. See Richard Rose and B. Guy Peters, *Can Government Go Bankrupt?* (New York: Basic Books, 1978).

51. See, for instance, *Washington Post,* 24 April 1984.

52. Advisory Commission on Federal Pay, *Report on the Fiscal 1985 Pay Increase Under the Federal Statutory Pay Systems* (Washington, DC: Advisory Commission on Federal Pay, 1984).

53. U.S. House of Representatives Committee on Banking, Finance and Urban Affairs, *Industrial Competitiveness Act* (Washington, DC: Government Printing Office, 1984).

54. On the debate over industrial policy, see Barry Bluestone and B. Harrison, *The Deindustrialization of America* (New York: Basic Books, 1982); Robert Z. Lawrence, *Can America Compete?* (Washington, DC: The Brookings Institution, 1984).

55. Pat Choate and Susan Walter, *A Nation in Ruins* (Washington, DC: Council of State Planning Agencies, 1981).

56. Ann Markusen, *The Politics of Regions* (Totowa, NJ: Rowman and Littlefield, 1985).

57. Salamon, "Rethinking Public Management."

Chapter Three

Political Context and the Morphology of the Public Sector

Introduction

A citizen who consults the United States Constitution to determine the proper role of the career civil service in government receives little guidance. In fact, the Constitution provides few clues about the organization of the executive branch. The Constitution merely gives the President the right to request written opinions from the heads of departments and if Congress approves, to appoint such inferior officers in government as are necessary. On this slim constitutional peg hangs the employment of millions of public employees, as well as the powers of the modern presidency in dealing with matters of personnel.[1] Undoubtedly the Founding Fathers knew that we would need public employees, although they probably thought in terms of only hundreds or a few thousand. Until the Civil War the federal work force consisted of thirty thousand civilian employees, most of them in the Post Office.[2] The American civil service developed largely without explicit constitutional or even legal status for most of the nation's history; it simply grew.

This volume occasionally calls public administration in American government the *bureaucracy*. To some this term implies rigid adherence to rules and an overabundance of regulations, red tape, and buck-passing.[3] More analytically, the German sociologist Max Weber defined *bureaucracy* as a hierarchical organization relying upon formal authority and rules to govern the activities of the members of the organization. He used *bureaucracy* to mean management based on written documents or files.

By contrast, as used here, *bureaucracy* will refer simply to the executive branch of government. The authors do not intend this term (or its close kin, *bureaucrats*) to have a negative connotation.

Public bureaucracy in the United States functions within a complex political system. Any set of institutions employing more than 16 million people and spending more than $1.5 trillion is almost certain to be complex, but in this regard American government is quite special. To some extent this complexity results from conscious choice throughout American history. Some complexity sprang from the desire to restrain public officials. Complexity has also evolved with government institutions, society, and the economy.

This chapter discusses critical factors affecting public administration in the United States. It looks at the structures of public administration—much as a biologist looks at the structure of an organism—because formal structure may not reveal exactly how government will function, but it provides clues and points to some critical parameters. Finally, this chapter examines the tools with which government influences the economy and society.

The Political Context

Politics in the United States features a host of variables that shape public administration. Four in particular stand out: federalism, the separation of powers, political culture, and interest groups. Of course, public administration in turn shapes the four critical contextual factors.

Federalism

The Constitution established federalism in American government. In particular it recognized and reserved substantial powers for state governments. Before the drafting of the Constitution in 1787, the central government occupied a precarious position. Under the Articles of Confederation it possessed almost no powers outside foreign affairs; it could not even raise an army, but had to request troops from the states. As originally interpreted, the Constitution limited the central government to narrow enumerated powers; the Tenth Amendment reserved the remaining powers to the states and to the people. The concept of federalism has evolved, but the division of powers among the levels of government is still an important issue.[4]

Many complexities arise from the concurrent powers of the state and federal governments. In many policy areas both levels of government legislate; at times federal and state ideas conflict. For example, state and federal governments disagree over the proper scope of environmental regulation, especially of toxic wastes. In addition, state governments have discretionary control over federal funds for a number of grant programs. For only one example, not only do levels of payment for AFDC, a form of welfare, vary among the states (the average monthly payment is $89 in Mississippi and $515 in Alaska), but the eligibility criteria differ as well. The variations in what is presumably a national program introduce a great deal of complexity and inequality into the federal system of government.

So far this chapter has focused on the fifty states and the District of Columbia out of more than 83,000 units of government in the United States. The remaining governments are local (see Table 3.1). Some local governments are as old as or older than the United States itself, but for most of the nation's history they were viewed as creatures of state government. Dillon's Rule limited local governments to powers specifically granted to them by the states; the states could create or dissolve local governments at will.[5] By the mid-twentieth century, however, many local governments—especially city governments—had home rule charters and broader grants of power from the states. In addition, local governments began to enter directly into arrangements with the federal government, usually for direct federal grants. Thus, federalism became more complex and "intergovernmental," involving public-sector units not covered in the Constitution.[6] In addition, relationships among governments

TABLE 3.1   Number of Governments in the United States, 1987

Federal	1
State	50
County	3,042
Municipal	19,205
Township and Town	16,691
School District	14,741
Special District	29,487
Total	83,217

Source: U.S. Bureau of the Census, *Statistical Abstract of the United States, 1988* (Washington, DC: Government Printing Office, 1987), 256.

increasingly turned to bargaining and negotiation, which accentuated problems of coordination.

Federalism has ramifications for another factor—interest groups. Since the mid-1960s the intergovernmental lobby has risen to be a major factor in American politics. This lobby in large measure works through such groups as the National Governors Conference, the Council of State Governments, the National Association of Counties, and the International City Managers Association. Even so, the most important lobbying probably occurs day-to-day as individual state and local office-holders press advice and requests upon federal officials.

The Separation of Powers

The Constitution divides government into three branches. The legislative, executive, and judicial branches possess substantial powers. The sharing (rather than separation) of powers among the three branches enables any branch to slow or thwart the activities of the others. To accomplish anything, political leaders must often be able to "win" in all three branches. The complex interactions among the several institutions and even within single institutions, for example the two houses of Congress, prompt the depiction of American governments as "all anchor and no sail." Numerous means can prevent action or force modifications of proposals, but very few produce prompt action.

The constitutional division of powers did not include the public bureaucracy. Constitutionally, the bureaucracy is merely a part of the executive branch, formally under the control of the President. In practice, however, a President may have difficulty controlling the bureaucracy. In addition, the bureaucracy, as a whole or in parts, may join forces with Congress to fight the President. For example, public employees asked Congress to restore some of the Reagan administration's pay and perquisite cuts.[7] Moreover, groups of career employees in organizations such as the Environmental Protection Agency and the Department of the Interior cooperated with Congress in opposing Reagan administration plans for the environment.[8]

A Skeptical Political Culture

In the early 1980s Electronic Arts, a company in San Mateo, California, produced a video game whose hero, a blip called Mack, attempts to construct a high-rise building; he can be killed by an inspector blip representing the Occupational Safety and Health Administration, a federal agency. The game package refers to the inspector blip "as living proof of the banality of evil."[9] While this is an extreme example, it bears testimony to a political culture that disparages the federal government and its bureaucracy. Survey after survey suggests the sorry state of Washington's reputation. According to a Gallup poll, a substantial majority of people in the United States believes that the federal government hires too many people and that these employees do not have to work as hard as those in the private sector.[10] Another survey reports that most people think the federal government wastes a lot of money. Some 57 percent feel that those running the government do not know what they are doing.[11]

To be sure, the public often expresses more positive sentiments about particular agencies or programs. People often acknowledge satisfaction with the services they receive.[12] However, individuals can sustain contradictory values and views. The particular context activates one or another set of views. Election campaigns often draw on and reinforce the blame-the-bureaucrat component of the political culture. In this regard, the faceless career executive in Washington (as opposed to the friendly postmaster down the block) becomes a particularly inviting target. On balance, there is much to support Dwight Waldo's view that the belief in "the ineffectiveness and inefficiency" of the public sector is "so widely and firmly held that one . . . can regard it as a unifying theme of our national creed: something that might be inserted after 'We hold these truths to be self-evident. . .' "[13]

This negative political culture holds many implications for the practice of public administration. For instance, it encourages perennial and often futile reform initiatives to adopt practices used in the private sector—to make government run like a business. It also galvanizes support for administration by private proxy. If one lacks faith in the efficacy of public agencies, contracting with private firms to deliver programs naturally becomes more appealing. A skeptical political culture also heightens the risk that public managers will become less bold and innovative than their counterparts in the private sector (an argument to be developed at greater length in Chapter 11).

A Plethora of Organized Interests

Organized interests are another critical element in public administration. Literally thousands of interests, ranging from foreign governments to the Boy Scouts, have representatives in Washington. In *The Federalist Papers,* James Madison warned about the dangers of factions imposing their narrow, parochial interests on government at the expense of the broader public interest. If he were to return to Washington today, Madison would find factions involved in virtually all aspects of policymaking.

Partly in response to court activism and new federal programs, interest groups have multiplied over the last quarter of a century. Robert H. Salisbury goes so far as to proclaim "an explosive growth in the number of groups and institutions seeking Washington representation as well as in the number of individuals providing it." As of the 1980s, an estimated seven thousand organizations of this kind had more or less permanent residence in Washington. Individuals representing these organizations numbered more than forty thousand, many of whom were lawyers.[14] As these figures suggest, groups have multiple representatives, each of whom specializes in particular policy areas. This specialization helps to make politics highly technical—a brand of politics played by experts representing diverse points of view.

The organizations seeking representation in Washington vary greatly. Besides groups speaking for private-sector economic interests such as the AFL-CIO and the Chamber of Commerce, those speaking for state and local governments abound. There are also so-called public interest groups such as Common Cause, and those representing particular ideological positions in specific policy areas such as the Sierra Club and the National Abortion Rights Action League. Furthermore, there is a pertinent distinction between conventional interest groups and institutions. The term *interest group* typically conjures up an image of a voluntary association of individuals or institutions who pay membership fees to the organization. In turn the organization represents them and provides other benefits. While these voluntary associations continue to play an important role, such individual institutions as corporations, local governments, and universities have also hired individuals to advance their interests.[15] The University of Georgia, for example, keeps a lawyer on retainer to represent its point of view in Washington.

Americans tend to regard interest groups, pressure groups, and lobbyists quite unfavorably, as protecting "special interests." Since virtually any interest imaginable is now represented, government is increasingly an aggregation of special interests. In addition, interest groups have been made a legitimate part of the policymaking process. Interest groups staff thousands of bodies that advise the federal government on their own behalf. Some such advisory bodies are empowered by law, while others act unofficially. Organized interests may also implement government policy, as when state medical and legal associations implement professional licensure laws. Similar medical interests helped to write and implement federal health planning laws.

State and society do not exist in separate compartments in the United States. The blending of public and private roles is evident in a number of ways.

Unlike the majority of industrialized democracies, the United States gets much of its executive talent from the private sector, and many of those individuals remain in Washington only a few years. There has been a revolving door for political executives, several thousands coming into office when there is a change of administration. For each policy area there is a network of persons in office, in think tanks (research organizations such as the Brookings Institution and the American Enterprise Institute), in consulting firms, in universities, in law firms, and so on.[16] These people move in and out of public office depending upon administrations, opportunities, and policy issues. Beyond the overlap, the federal government extensively relies on third parties to implement its programs. These third parties in turn become a kind of organized interest seeking to influence public administration.

The Bottom Line: Potent Centrifugal Forces

Federalism, the separation of powers, a skeptical political culture, and organized interests combine with the economic, social, and demographic factors described in Chapter 2 to provide a complex, fluid environment for public administration in the

United States. The fundamental political institutions of the country frequently make it difficult for officials to design and implement coherent public policies. The forces for power dispersal already present in a mixed economy gain reinforcement from fragmented political institutions.

The fragmentation of power in public administration is reflected in the bureaucracy. There is no single federal bureaucracy, but rather many competitive organizations loosely bound by a few central organizations such as the president's personal staff, the Office of Management and Budget, and the Office of Personnel Management. Even within the executive branch, there is a great deal of fragmentation, and it is sometimes difficult to find much coordination and control.

The divisions within the executive branch are mirrored in the legislature, which is divided into many committees and subcommittees. It is characteristic of American government to make a number of separate decisions about individual policy areas rather than to consider more comprehensive decisions, taking from one policy area and giving to another. Similarly, a parochial imperative tends to produce distributive decisions, allocating resources relatively equally among geographical areas (states and congressional districts) rather than making bolder decisions (called *targeting*) to concentrate resources. For example, the Model Cities program, intended to be a redistributive program for a few inner cities, evolved into a pork barrel program that had to aid at least one city in each state.

On balance, the American system operates to divide public organizations into subsystems and to insulate policy areas. A public organization may exist within an executive department or be formally independent. It may be an agency, a bureau, an office, or a service. In any case it provides services to clients and may have established a relatively stable relationship with Congress. Further, public employees tend to give their principal allegiance to this level of organization rather than to the executive department or to the federal government in general.

One may think of the agency in the federal government as one side of an iron triangle composed of the agency, the relevant congressional committees and one or more pressure groups. All the sides in this triangle need each other. In the first place, the agency needs the political support of the interest group. When agencies go to Congress for their annual budgets or for new legislative authority they need political support, and who can provide that better than the client group being served by the agency's programs? Organized client support is sufficiently important that if an interest group does not exist the agency will usually attempt to develop one.

The agency also needs the support of at least four subcommittees: the functional subcommittees (for example, the Tobacco and Peanuts subcommittees of the two agriculture committees) and the relevant appropriations subcommittees in the two houses of Congress. Winning approval of all these bodies may appear to be a formidable task. The burden is eased somewhat, however, by the tendency of members of Congress with a particular interest in the policy area, often based on their constituencies, to be assigned to the pertinent committees. Thus, members of these committees are more likely to empathize and sympathize with the agencies they supervise than would randomly selected House or Senate members. The burdens of political mobilization are further eased by the stability of the career staffs in the agency and of the members of Congress on the subcommittees. The process of mobilizing support does not begin anew each year but goes on for years or even decades.

Members of Congress in their subcommittees have a great deal to gain by the preservation of this system. Within it they are in a position to protect the agencies that serve their constituents. In addition, the subcommittees' ties with interest groups are in many ways ties with their own constituents. Hence they can represent certain constituents via the iron triangle. In addition, the interest groups are a source of political support for members of Congress in elections, especially for raising funds to finance electoral campaigns. Interest groups also provide information, even if biased, for policymaking.

Finally, interest groups have a great deal to gain by their cozy relationships with Congress and the agencies. Through these relationships they acquire access and influence, which may be less easy to gain than is sometimes assumed. Even though the iron triangles are showing some rust around their edges (see below), agencies and subcommittees still tend to limit the number of interest groups to whom they grant access and to make one interest group the semiofficial representative of clients. For example, the Department of Agriculture has tended to accept the national Farm Bureau Federation, fostered by the Department of Agriculture, as the legitimate representative of agricultural interests; other groups, for instance, the more militant National Farmers Union, have had substantially less influence on policy. An interest group has a great deal to gain by being the accepted representative in a policy area and may for that privilege be willing to take a less militant line in opposing policy initiatives.

A system of policymaking based on iron triangles has little to unify it. Rather than *a* government in Washington, there are many governments.[17] Without coordination of individual policymaking triangles, the federal government sometimes adopts quite contradictory policies; for example, the Department of Agriculture subsidizes tobacco while the Surgeon General warns against smoking it.[18] Top leaders in a department frequently find it difficult to coordinate and control their own agencies. The Secretary and his or her staff are short-term political appointees, but career civil servants in the agencies often have well-developed links to congressional committees and individual members of Congress.

For similar reasons, iron triangles undermine presidential control. To be sure, the budget process and a relatively unified personnel system provide the President with some mechanisms for leverage, but at a minimum iron triangles substantially increase the amount of time and effort needed to achieve centralized coordination.

The iron triangle remains a useful metaphor for policymaking in the federal government, but changes in the policy process and its environment have made it less valid. Access to agencies has become less exclusive as more and more organizations try to influence government; norms of openness have become accepted. A transition from iron triangles to *issue networks* has occurred.[19] An issue network is a much looser aggregation of interest groups and political and technical elites, all concerned with a certain policy area. The growing importance of federal policies and the use of so many subsidiary government and private organizations to implement those policies has increased the openness of policymaking and converted triangles into more complex forms. In the words of Hugh Heclo:

> Preoccupied with trying to find the few truly powerful actors, observers tend to overlook the power and influence that arise out of the configurations through which

the leading policymakers move and do business with each other. Looking for the closed triangles of control, we tend to miss the fairly open networks of people which increasingly impinge upon government.[20]

Types of Agencies in the Federal Government

The agencies of the federal government come in many forms. One could attempt to classify them using a number of major dimensions: size, organizational culture, hierarchical levels, technology, and many more. For present purposes, however, it may be useful to employ the formal nomenclature generally common to students and practitioners of public administration at the federal level. In doing so, however, one needs to keep in mind that a given category can encompass agencies that differ in a great many respects.

The Executive Office of the President

The President's staff assists him in managing the executive branch and providing policy leadership for government as a whole. The Executive Office of the President (EOP) employs some 1,700 people. Those closest to the President, including the President's personal advisers, press aides, and the like, are in the White House Office. The largest number of people in the EOP are in the Office of Management and Budget, which prepares the annual budget and monitors public expenditures and government management. Other groups in the EOP develop and prepare policy advice for the President. They are often members of such bodies as the National Security Council, the Office of Policy Development, and the Council on Environmental Quality.

A large personal staff indicates several things about the presidency and the executive branch. (The authors use *large* advisedly, as the personal staffs of the political leaders of other industrialized democracies number in the dozens rather than the thousands. For example, the Prime Minister's Office in the United Kingdom employs approximately seventy people.) The substantial size of the staff emphasizes the active role of the President in policymaking and the apparent distrust of Presidents for the advice from established executive branch organizations. The various policy bodies in the EOP to some degree shadow other executive branch organizations performing rather similar tasks; if postwar Presidents were willing to accept the advice of the Department of State and the Department of Defense, there might be little or no need for the National Security Council. Most have felt, however, that they needed advice not colored by departmental views but from personally loyal employees. In addition to benefiting from his relationship to these policy bodies, the President gains great policymaking power because of his control of the Office of Management and Budget and the related ability to set the agenda for debate on budgetary issues.

Second, the structure of the Executive Office of the President highlights the personalism of the office. With a staff of several hundred people just to serve the President and to enhance the image of the office, the presidency is indeed a position of great personal power and some isolation. The employees of such a "republican officer," George Washington's term for the office, are not bureaucrats in the traditional sense of being devoted to the organization and its functions. They are more like the household of a monarch. This further indicates the degree to which government in Washington is "government against subgovernment" and that the principal actor with an ability to be the government is the President.[21] Staff is one resource he can use to unify what is otherwise a very decentralized and differentiated governing system.

Executive Departments

The organizational form most familiar to Americans is the executive department headed by a Secretary with a seat in the Cabinet. The thirteen executive departments have more than 1.7 million civilian employees, or approximately 60 percent of all civilian employees in the federal government, and roughly 85 percent of all civilian workers outside the post office. When one adds uniformed military employees in the Department of Defense, these thirteen organizations employ more than 3.8 million people, or about 75 percent of federal employees.

Executive departments are heterogeneous. They vary greatly in size, whether measured by budget or by employment (see Table 3.2). Their internal structures also differ. Some of these organizations, such as the Department of Agriculture (see Figure 3.1), encompass a large number of bureaus providing services to clients and use the secretary's staff (undersecretaries, assistant secretaries, and so on) to supervise the operations of those bureaus. Other departments, such as the Department of Housing and Urban Development (Figure 3.1), have fewer bureaus and place more of the operating burden on field personnel. The former type of departmental structure may well approximate the iron triangle model, and any Secretary may have difficulty in getting such a department to march to his or her orders. However, even in a department apparently under control of the Secretary, staff are not necessarily loyal to the Secretary. They may have very different conceptions of how the department should function.[22] Thus, Cabinet departments often resemble large holding companies with a number of individual firms. For example, the Department of Defense encompasses the several armed forces, which compete for funds and power among themselves and with the Office of the Secretary of Defense.

"Independent" Agencies

The organization manual of the United States government lists dozens of agencies as independent establishments. *Independent* in this context refers primarily to the fact that they are formally outside the thirteen main executive departments. Some independent agencies are larger than many cabinet departments. Consider, for instance, the old Veterans Administration (238,000 employees), the National Aeronautics and Space Administration (23,000 civil servants), and the General Services Administration (30,000 employees). Other independent establishments are much smaller. For example, the Farm Credit Administration employed about 300 people, and the Merit System Protection Board, about 500 as of the mid-1980s.

Independent agencies also vary in their leadership structure. Some of them, such as the Environmental Protection Agency and the Central Intelligence Agency, are single-headed. That is, the President, with the advice and consent of the Senate, appoints a single individual to lead and manage a particular agency. Others, such as

TABLE 3.2   Civilian Employment in Selected Federal Government Organizations, 1983

Executive Departments	
Defense	1,026,461
Education	5,268
Independent Executive Agencies	
Veterans Administration	238,739
Farm Credit Administration	308
Independent Regulatory Agencies	
Nuclear Regulatory Commission	3,534
International Trade Commission	420
Public Corporations	
Tennessee Valley Authority	37,181
Pennsylvania Avenue Development Corp.	36
Foundations, etc.	
National Science Foundation	1,257
Harry S. Truman Scholarship Foundation	4
Quasi-Public Organizations	
Federal Home Loan Mortgage Corporation	730[1]
Advisory Bodies, etc.	
Federal Mine Safety and Health Review Committee	62
Advisory Committee on Federal Pay	3
Executive Office of the President	
Office of Management and Budget	564
Office of the U.S. Trade Representative	3

[1] Not direct federal employees.

Source: U.S. Bureau of the Census, *Statistical Abstract of the United States, 1987* (Washington, DC: Government Printing Office, 1986), 311–312.

the Appalachian Regional Commission and the Merit System Protection Board, are multiheaded. Subject to certain legal requirements, the President appoints a board that is responsible for major decisions affecting the agency. Agencies headed by commissions at times gain an additional measure of independence from the President, who may have limited authority to intervene directly in agency matters and to appoint all of the commissioners.

Why make an executive agency independent rather than put it under the control of a Cabinet department? Four factors, among others, account for such action. First, independent status often enhances the political clout of the agency. Veterans organizations are among the most powerful lobbies in the United States. They successfully fought to gain independent status for the Veterans Administration. They were able to maintain the agency's status despite sporadic threats to its position. For example, President Carter attempted to split up the functions of the VA, giving some to the Department of Health and Human Services and some to the Department of Education; the veterans lobbies resisted and Carter's initiative failed.[23] It was finally made a Cabinet department in 1989.

FIGURE 3.1

DEPARTMENT OF HOUSING AND URBAN DEVELOPMENT

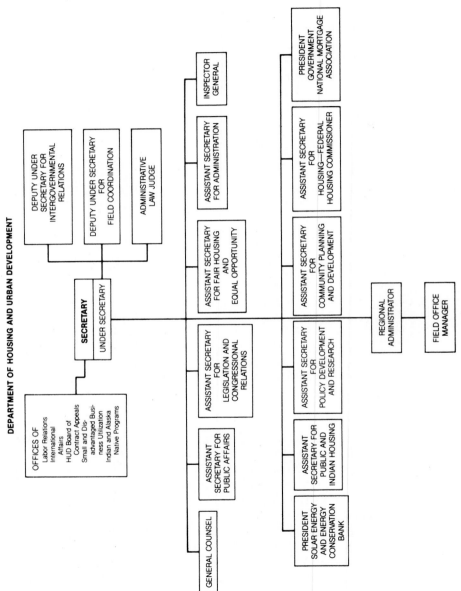

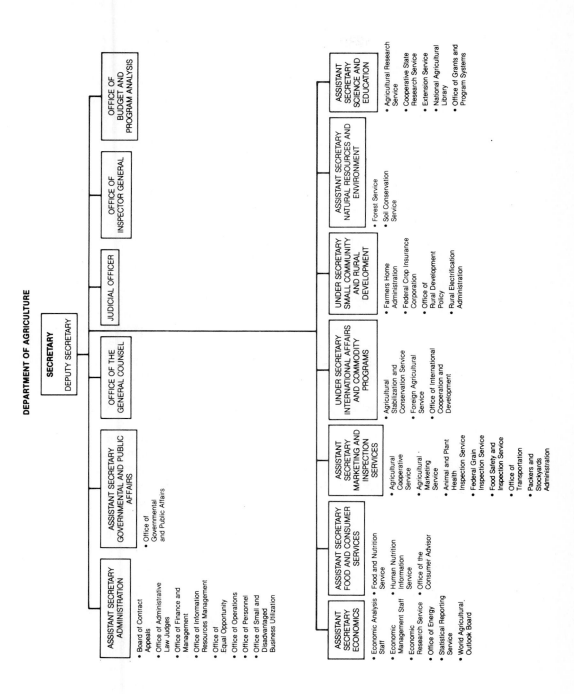

DEPARTMENT OF AGRICULTURE

A second reason for independent status is so that new approaches can be tried. For example, when President Lyndon Johnson initiated the War on Poverty, he placed the Office of Economic Opportunity outside the Department of Health, Education, and Welfare, then the major federal organization responsible for human services. He feared that that department's prevailing ideas about social insurance and welfare would prevent the Office of Economic Opportunity from trying new and inventive programs to alter the climate and culture of poverty. Likewise, the Small Business Administration was originally organized outside the Department of Commerce because top officials saw the department as biased toward big business.

Third, some organizations serve most other government organizations, and it is better to have them independent and able to serve all equally. For example, the General Services Administration provides office space, pens, paper, and other material to government agencies. The Office of Personnel Management is responsible for standards of recruitment and retention for most federal civilian employees, and its status as an independent organization allows it to establish systemwide standards and operate with greater prospects for fairness for all organizations.

Finally, independent executive agencies have an advantage over agencies within cabinet departments in that their heads report directly to the President. This can help them in recruiting their managers. The federal government often has a hard time competing with the private sector for top executives. Executive pay is much lower than pay for equally responsible jobs in the private sector. Moreover, managing a public organization with complex civil service rules, freedom of information requirements, and Congress looking over one's shoulder is probably more difficult than managing a private firm. The ability to deal directly with the President of the United States, rather than through an intermediary, is one small inducement that can be offered to recruit top quality executives to government service.

Independent Regulatory Commissions

A number of regulatory agencies operate as independent commissions in order to "take politics out of administration" by weakening the direct authority of the President over agency activities. The first of these organizations was the Interstate Commerce Commission, organized in 1886 to regulate interstate freight rates on the railways. Other commissions regulate trade, employment, communications, nuclear power, and a variety of other activities. As of the late 1980s, the roster of such organizations included the Federal Trade Commission, the Equal Employment Opportunity Commission, the Nuclear Regulatory Commission, and the Federal Communications Commission.

The concept of independent regulatory bodies came from the Progressive, or "good government," movement, which held that if regulatory decisions could be depoliticized, they would be fairer, more objective, and generally better. However, reformers overestimated the independence of these commissions from political forces. To be sure, members of various regulatory commissions serve for a long time, typically four- to seven-year overlapping terms, so that a President cannot always alter the complexion of a commission in a single term of office. Moreover, commissions typically possess substantial rule-making authority under the laws governing them. Nonetheless, they must appeal to the President and Congress for staff and budget. In this regard, one empirical analysis of the performance of regulatory commissions across several presidential administrations concludes that Presidents achieve a substantial measure of direction and control over them.[24] Further, Congress may intervene with legislation limiting an agency's scope of authority or may specifically overturn certain regulations. Therefore, regulatory bodies need political allies, just as do other agencies. In their quest for support they may turn to the very groups they are supposed to be regulating.

The close ties between the regulated industries and the regulatory bodies have led to claims that the commissions have been captured by the industries. A classic example of a captured commission is the Interstate Commerce Commission, which transformed over time from a regulator of railroads to an advocate of railroads.[25] Likewise, the principal opponent of deregulating interstate trucking (also under ICC jurisdiction) was the trucking industry itself. Even if unintentionally, a regulatory agency often reduces competition in rates and types of service and can shelter industry from the entry of new competitors.

Several factors appear to be lessening the extent of regulatory capture. One is consumer lobbies and public interest groups. These groups have actively monitored regulatory bodies and advocated changes in regulations to aid consumers. In addition, a series of Presidents have pressed for greater deregulation of industries, such as trucking and the airlines, and have raised questions about the effects of economic regulation. A specialist press with a readership limited to those interested in a specific policy area or industry prevents decisions from being hidden from those who might be affected. Finally, several new regulatory bodies, for example, the Consumer Product Safety Commission, cut across industry lines, and as a rule they are more difficult for an industry to capture. Still, the problem of regulatory capture and the operations of independent regulatory bodies are important considerations in policymaking. The idea of independent rulemaking bodies appears deeply ingrained in reformist thinking in the United States. If these bodies are to persist and perhaps expand, then one needs to focus on mechanisms to help them function in the more broadly defined public interest.

Public Corporations

Despite the prevailing free enterprise doctrines in the United States, the federal government does engage in a number of economic activities, some of which actually make a profit. Most of these are public corporations with an issue of stock owned either by the Department of the Treasury or by some other department principally concerned with their operations. Some public corporations, such as the Tennessee Valley Authority, are independent entities; others are not. For example, the St. Lawrence Seaway Development Corporation is in the Department of Transportation. These corporations operate under federal charters granting them specific powers, much as a statute details the powers of another federal organization, and under the Government Corporation Control Act.

Government corporations typically do not enjoy the latitude of their counterparts in the private sector.[26] However, corporate organization does give administrators more discretion than their colleagues elsewhere in government. Moreover, the corporate form may protect government from certain difficulties. As a separate legal entity, a government corporation can borrow money without pledging the credit of the United States, with the additional advantage that its borrowing is not counted in the public debt. Government corporations are also free of some of the financial and expenditure regulations imposed on other government organizations; for example, the General Accounting Office cannot disallow the expenditures of a government corporation as it can other federal organizations. Most funds used by a government corporation do not come from annual appropriations, so these bodies have greater latitude in the timing of expenditures. Finally, although the employees of public corporations are usually employees of the United States government, several corporations have been allowed to develop their own personnel systems and have escaped some strictures of the civil service system. This may permit corporations to pay competitive salaries. In sum, the public corporation allows its leadership greater flexibility than is found in other public organizations, although that flexibility is limited by the corporate charter.

A broad range of agencies are government corporations. Some organizations one might think of as corporations are not. The *Government Manual* describes the National Railroad Passenger Corporation (Amtrak) as a quasi-official agency and does not list it with other government corporations. Amtrak has characteristics of both public and private sector organizations. Policymakers developed this partnership between the federal government and the railways as a means of retaining passenger rail service in the face of declining demand, rising costs, and deteriorating equipment. The nine-member board of directors of Amtrak consists of the Secretary of Transportation ex officio, the president of the corporation, three members appointed by the President of the United States and confirmed by the Senate, two members representing commuter authorities, and two members selected by the preferred stockholders. Unlike corporations wholly owned by government, Amtrak is formally responsible to federal policymakers and private shareholders. Although policymakers amended Amtrak's original charter as a for-profit corporation, it still attempts to operate in some ways like a private-sector organization. The Reagan administration persistently sought to minimize government support and return it to market accountability.[27]

Even more than the conventional corporate form, quasi-official corporations give government the flexibility to intervene in a policy arena while retaining some distance from the problems and political failures in that area. No President would like to be directly responsible for trains running on time, but demands from citizens—especially those in the Northeast and in remote areas of the West—now have government deeply involved in the railroad business. Amtrak, however, buffers elected officials from some responsibility and holds out hope (perhaps fanciful) that at some point policymakers will not have to provide tax subsidies to keep the corporation afloat. Similarly, the Legal Services Corporation (another quasi-official entity) permits the federal government to subsidize the access of indigents to the court system without making it seem that Washington itself has declared legal war on some individual or group. Since the corporation often subsidizes legal action against state and local governments, federal policymakers can escape politically embarrassing confrontations.

Corporations do not abolish politics from administration. One systematic analysis concludes that "the experience with government corporations is replete with cases of organizations whose presumed autonomy and insulation from external intervention have been breached by elected officials protecting their own political interests."[28] Officials at Amtrak, for instance, remain sensitive to the importance of serving districts represented by certain members of their congressional oversight committees. However, the corporate form of organization does raise issues of accountability. The independence granted to such corporations often means that they pay more attention to the market than to political signals. Moreover, they may be less accountable in financial terms. Systems of accounting in the public sector tend to ignore many of the problems of corporations, and loans to them made within government itself do not necessarily appear in the public budget as an outflow of funds. These practices may disguise both the true nature of these corporate activities and the real magnitude of public sector intervention.

Foundations and Institutes

The federal government engages in a number of activities influencing education, science, and the arts in the United States. Government is a major source of support for both the sciences and the humanities through organizations such as the National Science Foundation, the National Institutes of Health, and the National Foundation for the Arts and Humanities. Government funds these organizations through a foundation or endowment. Just as the corporate form mimics the organization of business, the foundation or endowment form mimics the organization of private philanthropy and research support. Government foundations have developed an elaborate system of advisory committees and peer review in order to ensure that the awards reflect the criteria used within the respective disciplines rather than the criteria of politicians or civil servants. The federal government in this way seeks to avoid fostering "official" science or art, as has happened in more authoritarian governments.[29]

Despite efforts to establish political buffers, elected officials intrude on the decisions of these institutes and foundations. Congress and the President decide how much money to give them each year. At times, members of Congress question the agencies' decisions. Senator Proxmire of Wisconsin, for instance, has ridiculed several research projects funded by these agencies. Such criticism can weaken an agency's will to rely on professional judgments in allocating funds. Aside from these manifestations of penetration by politicians, policymakers at times move toward establishing institutes or foundations that have ideological purposes. For example, conservatives have proposed that a government Freedom Foundation be established to fund projects consistent with their views.

Legislative Organizations

The legislative branch of government now employs almost forty thousand people. The majority of these work for individual members of Congress or for a committee or subcommittee. However, three legislative organizations—the Library of Congress, the Government Printing Office, and the General Accounting Office (GAO)—each employ more than five thousand people. Besides being the national library, the Library of Congress houses the Congressional Research Service. As its name suggests, the Government Printing Office publishes many (not all) of the documents and hearings associated with federal activities. Its publications are indispensable if the citizenry is to keep abreast of such activities. The GAO retains the auditing in the federal government as one more check on the executive branch. However, the GAO has adopted a much larger analytic role as well; it reports to Congress not only on whether money was spent legally, but also on whether it was spent on efficient and effective programs.[30] While the GAO focuses largely on what occurs after agencies spend money, the Congressional Budget Office (CBO) targets decisions made in the budgetary process. It therefore is a legislative analogue to the Office of Management and Budget. The CBO provides expert analysis to Congress, not only on specific expenditures but also on the macroeconomic effects of the federal budget.

Overview

In a sense the federal government is a large zoo; it houses many species of organizations—executive departments, independent agencies, regulatory commissions, corporations, legislative agencies, and many more. Furthermore, each type of organization includes a great many variations on the theme. Agencies vary as much within categories as across them. In this regard one can make a strong case that those who label the species in the federal zoo need to work much harder on developing a refined typology. Those who operate zoos with animals in them have achieved a higher level of sophistication in classifying the beasts they house.

In broad terms, however, this description of the various types of federal agencies demonstrates the importance of selecting the proper form for the achievement of policy. Organizational type has implications for the degree to which public administration ultimately proves to be accountable, efficient, and effective. Accountability refers to whether implementing agents remain deferential to the law and the preferences of top elected officials. Accountability also advances when citizens can more readily comprehend government activities. In this regard, conventional executive departments often seem to offer more advantages than do complex corporate structures. Efficiency focuses on achieving a high ratio of benefits to costs, and effectiveness, on the degree to which programs achieve stated goals. The degree to which various organizational types promote these values remains unclear. Conceivably, however, the corporate form may perform well in terms of efficiency and effectiveness, thus raising the classic tension between the attainment of these values and the norms of accountability. However, social science has yet to develop a theory that precisely predicts the implications of relying on one organizational type vis-à-vis another.

Tools

Besides broad organizational types, governments can choose different tools to achieve policy.[31] Like organizational types, the tools of government vary considerably, and a single generic tool may have several manifestations. Underlying all the tools described below, however, are certain basic vehicles that governments use to achieve their ends. Typically, the administration of government policies depends upon some combination of *authority, exchange,* and *persuasion.*[32] Governments use their legitimate authority to pass laws and issue formal interpretations of them. Governments also carry on exchanges with society, in a sense trading certain benefits for certain behavior. For example, government may trade a tax break on mortgage interest to citizens in the hope that citizens' demand for housing will increase to absorb construction of new homes. So, too, government officials use the media and other devices to persuade citizens of the wisdom of the means they use and ends they pursue. Authority, exchange, and persuasion are the key materials of the more specific instruments described below.

Direct Provision of Services or Goods

Governments at times use their own employees to deliver a service or good. The Veterans Administration hires its own medical personnel, builds its own hospitals, and directly delivers health care to many veterans. By contrast, Medicaid and Medicare provide medical insurance for clients to permit them to shop in nongovernmental markets for service. As of the 1980s, the federal government provided relatively few services directly; one major exception is the Postal Service. In contrast, state and local governments directly provide services for health, education, recreation, and welfare. Governments directly perform relatively few services. In principle even defense could be contracted out to mercenaries, and there is a history of franchising tax collection to private individuals in a number of countries. However, strong traditions in the United States and elsewhere dictate that government should directly provide certain services, such as defense.

There are often good reasons for direct service. Primarily, it ensures—as far as possible—that a service will be delivered as intended by laws. The Department of Health and Human Services has less control over services to clients than has the Veterans Administration. Similarly, governments seldom contract out police services because they want a function so closely linked to the authority of government, and with such complex and difficult interactions with citizens, to be provided by their own employees.

Interestingly, although it may involve building and hiring, direct provision can be cheaper for government than indirect service. A Veterans Administration physician has little or no incentive to provide extra services and cannot escalate charges; a doctor in private medicine makes money by providing additional (and sometimes unnecessary) services and has the power to raise fees. Direct provision implies direct control over the quality and cost of service.

Direct provision of services can work well. However, it has the disadvantage of being relatively inflexible. Occasionally an ill-conceived hospital or school is built, and then it must be used or be recognized as a white elephant—another of the failures of government. Such sunk costs sometimes can increase waste because governments sometimes keep redundant facilities operating.

Finally, direct service has the disadvantage of the state's operating in loco parentis, removing substantial degrees of personal choice. This is generally considered acceptable in dealing with children or others who do not have full capacity to make decisions but is less desirable when dealing with competent adults. For instance, government could deal with the financial needs of the elderly by directly providing them housing, food, and other necessary services. Instead, the elderly get Social Security pension checks and discretionary power over them.

Transfer Payments

A major alternative to direct provision of services is to make transfer payments to citizens. Most transfer payments (Social Security pensions, welfare benefits) go directly to citizens and can be used for any purpose. Such payments rest on the assumption that the citizens receiving the money spend it wisely. This is not always true. Some Social Security recipients may spend all their money on their pets or cigarettes or alcohol rather than wholesome food. Transfers lack the certainty of direct service but are much more flexible. Furthermore, economists argue that transfers do not supplant the market the way direct services do. That is, when money is handed over to citizens, they can buy what they want, and if the market works at all as it is supposed to, a more efficient allocation of resources will emerge.[33]

Transfer payments may be a very efficient means of reaching certain policy goals. It costs little administratively to provide a Social Security recipient with a check each month; with computers the Social Security Administration is quite an efficient check-writing machine.[34] The success of Social Security officials in holding down administrative overhead reflects the ease and permanence of their decisions about eligibility. The agency has access to good records on those entitled to receive pension payments; moreover, once Mrs. Citizen receives eligibility based largely on age, she will in all probability sustain that eligibility for the rest of her life. Thus, Social Security does not have to invest heavily in monitoring pensioners as to continued eligibility. Other transfer programs, such as Aid to Families with Dependent Children, face more perplexing issues in determining eligibility. In AFDC eligibility is largely based on income. If the incomes of clients increase, they must be removed from the eligibility rolls. Eligibility error rates (especially those whereby citizens receive excess benefits) remain a constant concern to welfare administrators. Such errors can drive up costs and produce great political embarrassment. Thus, administrative overhead costs in welfare programs for the poor tend to be high.

The effectiveness of transfer payments depends upon citizens voluntarily signing up for program benefits. Not all eligible persons apply. They may lack information, and often those most in need of program benefits (the very poor and uneducated) have the least knowledge of how to obtain them. Some programs, in order to reduce costs, fuel this problem by disseminating little or no information about their services. Abrasive, uncooperative intake workers as well as arduous application processes may deter candidates for service. Welfare programs require applicants to prove they are poor, which involves considerable probing into their personal lives. Rather than put up with this screening process and the stigma of being "on welfare," many people scratch for the necessities of life.[35]

Not all transfer payments are fungible. Government may limit transfers to the purchase of particular services and goods. Government sometimes pays providers for services to eligible citizens. Medicare and Medicaid are health care programs for the elderly and the poor respectively. Physicians and hospitals usually bill government for services provided to patients in these programs.

Vouchers are another form of noncash transfer. Recipients of food stamps, for instance, can use them only to buy certain kinds of edibles. Some people advocate voucher systems to introduce competition in services that government has dominated. For example, some endorse education vouchers as a means of making elementary and secondary education more competitive and hypothetically better.[36] The idea is to give parents a voucher good for a certain amount of money usable at any accredited school good for the entire cost of the student's education. This is presumed to allow middle- and lower-class parents the same choices in education that the more affluent enjoy.

This form of transfer is intended to create a market where none existed, an efficient way of reaching an expensive policy goal. However, success depends very much on parents' accepting the vouchers and using them wisely, and on education providers' willingness to risk opening new schools, knowing that their existence depends upon government's continuing the voucher program. Further, if the goal of such a program is to improve the quality of education, it also assumes that competition will work in that type of service as well as it does in dry-cleaning. An indirect method such as the voucher places a number of steps between the adoption of a program and the achievement of its goal. Given what we have learned about these chains of events from the implementation literature, there is reason to question the effectiveness of such indirect instruments.[37]

Intergovernmental Grants

One particular type of transfer that deserves more extensive discussion is the intergovernment grant, by which one level of government, usually Washington, delivers money to another level. Grants given for specific purposes are called *categorical grants*. Grants offered for limited general purposes are *block grants*. General revenue sharing is entirely *unrestricted*. Each of these forms of transfer has different effects.[38]

State and local governments usually prefer unrestricted grants. This money is used either to increase services to citizens or to reduce their tax costs for providing the same level of services. In either case, it makes local governments look better to citizens, as the apparent benefit-to-cost ratio rises. This is especially valuable for local governments heavily dependent upon the visible and unpopular property tax. On the other hand, critics of federal expenditure programs have argued that if the states and localities want to spend money, they should bear the political costs of raising the revenues.

The categorical grant provides the federal government a great deal of control over the actions of local governments. Some grants are awarded competitively to execute policy. For example, Urban Development Action Grants from the Department of Housing and Urban Development awarded cities funds for projects to improve the economic viability of inner cities. Other categorical grants allocate awards according to a formula, so that the amount depends upon certain characteristics, such as the number of families living in poverty. Still other categorical grants have matching and maintenance-of-effort provisions: a city may have to put up a percentage of the costs of a program or promise to keep paying for the program.

Categorical grants tend to produce *priority inversions,* in which the city government does what federal funds encourage rather than what it might otherwise do.[39] Some cities spend a good portion of the budget simply trying to match federal funds. More generally this form of grant tends to centralize control of policymaking in Washington.

Block grants fall somewhere between revenue sharing and categorical grants. Although they are given for a particular purpose, the degree of specificity is much less than for categorical grants, and the money is discretionary within the designated policy area. The Community Development Block Grant is an example. The Reagan administration converted a number of categorical grants to local governments into block grants to the states. This has had the advantage of returning some decision making to a lower level of government. However, passing the money through state hands combined with overall reductions in funding, has produced substantial hardships for some cities.[40]

Long-term problems may arise for local governments that become dependent upon block grants for basic services. For example, block grant manpower funds, through the Comprehensive Employment and Training Act (CETA), have been used by cities to subsidize the personnel costs of basic city services such as sanitation and even the police and fire departments. This enabled city taxes to be lower than they otherwise would have been but presented severe difficulties once CETA funds began to dry up and CETA-funded employees had to be laid off or paid out of local taxes.

Federal grants can encourage state and local governments to engage in new activities, and the subnational governments may continue the programs even if Washington withdraws financial support. This possibility has ramifications for more general fiscal policy. It means that while the federal government can often stimulate spending at the state and local levels during a recession, it may find it difficult to reduce expenditures during inflationary times if politicians in these governments want to tax and spend.

Of course, an unattractive federal matching rate can deter participation, and state and local governments can reject federal grants in the first place. Although the Occupational Safety and Health Act of 1970 (OSHA) provides grants to the states for the program, as of the late 1980s, fewer than half the states had accepted these grants. States had to come up with about a dollar from their own revenues for every dollar Washington supplied under the Occupational Safety and Health Act. Other programs may show little benefit to subnational units. As regards the federal occupational safety and health program, for example, state officials know that Washington will use its own employees to implement the program within the area they represent if they decline to participate. Subnational governments may also resent reporting requirements, overstrict specifications, and other restrictions.[41]

The Tax System

In the classic Supreme Court case *McCulloch* v. *Maryland*, Chief Justice Marshall argued that the "power to tax involves the power to destroy."[42] The tax system certainly establishes disincentives for particular activities, but it also creates incentives for other activities. The tax system can be used to do many things other than simply raise revenue for government.

Governments may use taxes to reduce demand for some items or to establish a clear case of tax evasion if the prohibitive tax is not paid. For example, one way to control especially dangerous firearms, such as automatic weapons and sawed-off shotguns, is to tax them at $10,000 per weapon. Given that those who want such weapons have little interest in the federal government knowing that they own them, owners have an incentive to evade the tax. This in turn gives government a way of prosecuting them for possessing the weapon in a climate that does not favor gun control. In addition to absolute prohibitions, taxes can be used to deter or slow consumption of certain types of goods. Tariffs (taxes on imports) have traditionally been used to deter the consumption of foreign-produced goods. Likewise, high taxes on alcoholic beverages—as well as being a sure revenue source—are also used to slow consumption of that product.

The United States government now "spends" huge amounts through tax expenditures, which allow citizens not to pay taxes on money spent in certain ways.[43] For example, Americans can deduct interest on home mortgages along with the property taxes they pay state and local government. These two tax expenditures amounted to a middle-class housing subsidy of some $31.8 billion in 1984, as compared with the direct subsidy of $3.8 billion for housing for the poor. Tax expenditures are not always for purposes as noble as housing for underpaid college professors, and there have been a number of campaigns to reduce or eliminate loopholes—for example, for the purchase of race horses or three-martini lunches.

Tax expenditures are popular with those who receive them and unpopular with those who don't. Perhaps their most appealing feature for politicians is their relative invisibility. Until it became a political issue in the 1980s, tax expenditure was known about but poorly understood. The complexity of tax law and the relative invisibility of the writing of that law made concessions a fact of life, not something that generated much citizen concern.[44]

As a means of implementing public policies, tax expenditures are efficient. Because Americans prepare their own federal income tax forms rather than paying a tax bill, citizens shoulder the major burden of record keeping and decision making. Of course, some citizens take advantage of the system of self-assessment, and government must hire auditors to protect itself against fraud and abuse. In general, however, tax expenditures have lower direct administrative costs than transfer programs.

Still, tax expenditures are an extremely indirect way to accomplish a public purpose. They depend entirely upon taxpayers' response to incentives, but the predicted response may not materialize. Provisions seeking to encourage investments in risky industries may become loopholes allowing planned losses in motion pictures, cattle and the like. Movies may be a worthwhile form of entertainment but are not the type of growth industry Congress intended the writeoffs for. During the 1970s a large industry promoting tax shelters surfaced. In turn, the Internal Revenue Service focused increased attention on these shelters until the Tax Reform Act of 1986 closed most of them.

Finally, tax expenditures may be inequitable. For tax expenditures to be of much use to a citizen, he or she must face an otherwise substantial tax bill. Further, in a progressive tax structure a credit or deduction has most value to the person in the highest bracket. Evidence shows that the middle class uses these tax provisions, but they are often not available to the poor. Thus, when the goal is income maintenance, direct methods may be more efficient and effective.

Law and Regulation

Law is a unique resource of government. Other organizations have money and some use force, but governments have a monopoly on formal political authority—the law. In the United States these instruments have the advantage of requiring relatively little enforcement. People obey most laws every day without government intervention. Thus, by simply enacting a law or regulation government can exercise great authority over the population. Nonetheless, government maintains mechanisms for monitoring compliance with the law. For example, inspectors from OSHA and other federal bodies monitor industry's compliance with a host of regulations. The FBI and other federal law enforcement organizations monitor compliance with federal criminal laws. The costs of these employees is trivial, however, compared to the expenditure that would be required if the population did not consider government authority to be legitimate, or if the government sought to ensure compliance with all its decrees, as some totalitarian regimes might.

While the costs of enforcing regulations may be low, some laws and regulations impose substantial costs on individuals and firms. By one estimate, in 1980 the government's costs of economic regulation in data collection, inspections, hearings, and so forth amounted to "only" $6 billion, while the costs imposed on firms and ultimately on consumers was $120 billion.[45]

The choice of the regulatory instrument to achieve the goals of a policy is by no means a given. For example, instead of requiring automobile manufacturers to install seat belts in new cars and consumers to pay for them, government could buy the seat belts and give them to the manufacturer or even have federal employees install them. This is not as farfetched as it may appear, for some states purchase automobile safety seats for infants whose parents cannot afford them. Direct provision appears more difficult to administer than regulation. It incurs greater government costs and may provoke a greater outcry than the current regulatory program.

Because of the burdens that regulations are assumed to place on the economy, some policy analysts—including many in the Reagan administration—argued that the same objectives could be reached by imposing fees for pollution and other incentives for compliance rather than direct regulations.[46] Incentives for firms to reduce emissions and save money would presumably allow the market to take care of the problem. Despite their appeal in a political system that values such ideals, market approaches have run into a number of practical and ethical problems. One is the difficulty of accurately monitoring and measuring a firm's pollution; another is the question of rate setting. The ethical question is the desirability of opening a government-run market in pollution.[47]

Loans and Loan Guarantees

Government at times turns to banks to accomplish policy objectives; it lends money or guarantees private loans for certain projects. This strategy can remove pressure for transfer payments to a group and may save public funds, since those receiving the loans presumably will repay them. However, if borrowers can repay their debts, why not allow private financial institutions to make the loans? One answer is that interest on government-backed loans is often below market rates. Such loans may send students to college or let financially strapped farmers borrow against future crops at rates no bank would offer.

The great financial resources of government allow it to *socialize risk*—to distribute any cost over a much broader base than banks can. This phenomenon is especially evident in loan guarantees. Only the federal government could afford the risk of the loans to the Lockheed Corporation and the Chrysler Corporation. Government guaranteed the loans and private banks made them. This excursion into the money market did not cost the government one penny other than the quite modest administrative costs, because both companies did repay their loans. Further, no money left the public coffers, but only a written guarantee that if the company did default, the United States would repay the banks.

Not only large companies benefit from loan guarantees. A number of very large programs, such as Federal Housing Administration (FHA) and Veterans Administration loans for house purchases, have benefited millions, some of whom would not otherwise have been homeowners. Loan guarantees are a means of intervening in the market at very low costs, albeit with the risk that costs will mushroom.

The limited probability of loss leads to one anomaly of accounting: loans and loan guarantees are typically not counted as public expenditure.[48] This practice, like tax expenditures and shifting costs to the private sector via regulatory policy, makes the public sector appear smaller than it is and hides a good deal of real cash movement. The federal government has begun to publish a credit budget, but the media do not report much about it, especially compared with public expenditure in the budget. Thus, in a society that is dubious about public interventions into markets, loans and loan guarantees provide a politically and economically handy means for intervening.

Loans, like transfers, require the target of a program to seek out the benefit and apply for it. Information about loan programs may not be distributed widely, and few loans may be made. It is also difficult to hold the administration of such a program accountable. Administrators cannot necessarily tell whether recipients of loans will default. Also, lenders may try to ensure a high rate of repayment, to demonstrate the effectiveness of the program. They may therefore lend to those most likely to repay, in effect targeting borrowers who could have obtained the money commercially. If the purpose of the program is to benefit those who cannot raise a commercial loan, the program may fail and a good deal of public money may be misused.

Insurance

Another indirect means for government to achieve its policy goals is insurance. In some ways guaranteeing a loan is like issuing an insurance policy; government also directly insures a variety of activities. The government insurance program most Americans know about is federal insurance for bank deposits through the Federal Deposit Insurance Corporation (FDIC). This program grew out of the Depression, when depositors fueled economic decline by rushing to withdraw their money from the banks. The Federal Crop Insurance Corporation covers against crop loss caused by storms, droughts, plagues of locusts, and other natural disasters. The Overseas Private Investment Corporation insures American investors in overseas projects against expropriation, damage caused by wars and revolutions, and other dangers.

In most years insurance programs let government influence the economy at relatively little direct cost. If government offers insurance at a price approaching an actuarially sound one, on average it should lose very little across the years. Even subsidized insurance tends to cost less than direct assistance.

Insurance does, however, present some problems similar to those of other indirect policy instruments. Failures of insured savings and loan institutions cost the federal govenment billions of dollars in 1989. Most insurance programs depend upon consumers to apply for coverage, although some programs have required certain classes of individuals, for instance, new homeowners in flood-prone areas, to buy private insurance. In addition, insurance coverage may encourage citizens to engage in activities they might otherwise find too risky. The federal flood insurance program that protects homeowners in flood plains has protected developers of many coastal areas, sometimes with serious environmental consequences.

Contracting Out

Government uses contracts as a policy tool. "Old" contracting is associated with procurement of goods ranging from missiles to paper clips. Government procurement, especially by the Department of Defense, sporadically erupts as a political issue. Such procurement is a well-established means of acquiring the material to operate the government; very early in the nation's history the Navy contracted for the building of the frigates *Constitution* and *Constellation*. Government could build its own weapons, but many believe that competition produces better and less costly weapons systems. They further argue that it would be inefficient for government to build all its own equipment when the private sector can shift between public- and private-sector contracts depending upon demands, keep its work force more efficiently employed, and therefore reduce overall costs.

In practice much of the justification for procurement contracting is suspect. There is limited competition for most weapons contracts. The economic barriers to new firms limit bidding. Some contracts, especially for spare parts and maintenance, are not bid out at all but offered to a sole source, usually the firm that produced the system. Finally, many defense contractors do almost nothing else. General Dynamics, for instance, receives almost all of its revenues from defense contracts and therefore depends as much on the government as direct public employees. In addition, the close linkage between the large defense contractors and the Pentagon has raised a number of concerns about the honesty and effectiveness of the procurement process and its effects on American democracy. Concern with this problem goes back at least as far as President Eisenhower, who pointed to the rise of the "military industrial complex."[49] Firms outside the defense industry also rely heavily on government contracts. Consulting firms providing services to the domestic side of the federal government as well as to state and local governments are often as dependent upon government work as are defense contractors.

"New" contracting follows from ideological and practical pressures to privatize government functions. Since the private sector "invaded" the territory once reserved for the public sector, many governmental tasks are being performed by private sector firms. Since the mid-1970s, the federal government has been encouraging contracting through the Office of Management and Budget Circular A-76 by requiring federal managers to consider which of their functions could better be performed by private-sector firms and to make such contractual arrangements where appropriate.[50]

Proponents believe that the new form of contracting will reduce the costs of government. They assume that market competition can lower the costs of many public functions. Their proposal bears some resemblance to arguments for vouchers, although in this case government rather than the citizen would control the consumption of the benefit. Contracting has been assumed to be especially effective in reducing costs of relatively routine activities such as janitorial service. The assumption is that large private firms can provide service to a large number of office buildings more cheaply than can public employees. This is especially true when a small facility provides less than full-time work for a janitor.

Although there is conflicting evidence about the cost savings associated with contracting, it does provide a flexible means of performing public-sector functions. Direct employment by government presents some cost and managerial difficulties because of the rigidity of some civil service rules and the possibility of personnel acquiring permanent employment rights. Contracting lets government adjust personnel and costs to a changing environment. Thus, contracting may be especially suitable for functions whose workloads vary across time. Contracting is especially useful when the tasks are not directly associated with public functions such as law enforcement and public safety.

Contracting can be used to reach other goals. Government can impose noneconomic policies through the specifications and regulations for awarding contracts. For example, Lyndon Johnson threatened to refuse government contracts to steel companies that did not honor his price guidelines. Further, the federal government enforces some of its equal employment opportunity programs through its contracting powers. Since the 1960s it has reserved some contracts for minority-owned firms. The huge volume of purchases that government must make in the private sector gives it substantial power over private firms.

Some Criteria of Assessment

Which of the sundry tools presented above serve the policy ends of government? Certain of the strengths and weaknesses of each tool have received attention. A more systematic assessment requires consideration of somewhat overlapping criteria:

- Certainty
- Timeliness
- Cost
- Efficiency
- Effectiveness
- Flexibility
- Visibility
- Accountability
- Citizen choice

Policy tools vary in the degree to which they score well on these criteria. However, considerable uncertainty characterizes any effort to appraise them in these terms. Social scientists simply do not have enough empirical understanding of government programs to state definitively that one tool will score better than another in a certain case. Nonetheless, these criteria assist preliminary assessments of tools.

Certainty.   Policy tools vary in predictability of the administrative processes, outputs, and outcomes they engender. Direct delivery of services, goods, or transfers often achieves a greater level of certainty than allowing the individual to identify and accept an incentive, for example a tax expenditure. Of course, direct services are far from foolproof. Children forced to attend public schools do not necessarily learn.

Timeliness.   The question of when a program will work often is as important as whether it will work. Some programs take years to become effective, and others take off rapidly. The desire for quick results at times encourages government to contract with private organizations or provide grants to other governments rather than develop a federal bureaucracy. In addition to the commonsense reasons for wanting a policy to be effective promptly, there are political reasons. Federal politicians have a maximum of six years before they have to run for election again, and they want to be able to show the folks back home what good they have done. If a program is very slow to produce desired effects, the politician can only promise that great things are on the way. Career civil servants may be attracted to programs that yield superior results at a lower cost even if they take longer to produce. Thus conflicts between politicians and career officials may arise over whether a certain type of policy is desirable and over the timetable for results.

Cost.   In these budget-conscious days, the relative cost of providing services in different ways is important. Cost is not entirely a function of the instrument selected to deliver a program, since way direct services or transfers can be made more or less generous. However, there are often significant differences in the direct costs of various instruments. Direct costs show up explicitly in the government budget, but indirect costs do not. Advocates of varying ideological stripes often emphasize the indirect costs of a particular tool. For instance, conservatives point to costs imposed on business and consumers by government regulation, which as a tool has small direct costs. On the other hand, liberals have argued that low funding for social programs may cost more in the future than they save in the present by perpetuating the social conditions that create poverty.

Efficiency.   Efficiency raises questions about the ratio of outputs to costs. This in turn spawns one of the ultimate and perhaps unanswerable questions of public policymaking: how to measure and evaluate the output of the public sector.[51] Assuming that direct measurement of efficiency is impossible, one may be forced to employ surrogate measures. These are based primarily on the amount of administrative overhead required for a program. Therefore, programs that require large staffs to make determinations about benefits or obligations may be less efficient than those that use indirect methods; for the federal government to make out all income tax bills would require a huge bureaucracy. However, self-assessment allows a moderate-size bureaucracy to monitor compliance and enforce the tax laws. Although the comparison is far from perfect, the Inland Revenue in the United Kingdom (which assesses taxes on individuals) is not a great deal smaller than the Internal Revenue Service in the United States, although the United States has approximately four times as many taxpayers.

Of course, some of the means by which costs can be lowered for one level of government impose equal or greater costs on other levels or on nongovernmental organizations. The federal government uses states and localities to implement most social programs other than Social Security. Therefore, one must be extremely careful to recognize that one actor's efficiency may be another's inefficiency.

Effectiveness.   A policy tool may be inefficient yet highly effective. Effectiveness refers to whether a program achieves goals. Medicare and Medicaid have increased access to medical care for the poor and elderly. In all probability they have improved health among these groups. Thus, one can plausibly argue that these programs, especially Medicare, are highly effective. However, serious questions about their efficiency have arisen. Medical providers have often enjoyed generous, even wasteful payments from these programs. The costs of the programs have relentlessly increased, and they and private insurance plans have contributed to rapid price escalations in medicine. Some analysts argue that their major tools, heavy reliance on contracts with private insurance companies and transfer payments to nonfederal physicians and hospitals, have created effectiveness accompanied by inefficiency. The degree to which alterenative tools would sustain effectiveness while facilitating efficiency is an important question.

Flexibility.   Some tools permit government to respond readily to change and error.[52] The literature on policy implementation repeatedly proclaims that errors and unintended consequences can creep in at any number of points in a program. Hence, tools with some built-in capacity for error detection and correction have considerable appeal. Some suggest that contracting will afford greater flexibility than regulation or direct services. On balance, however, the degree to which various tools foster error detection and correction remains the subject of speculation.

However, flexibility may present problems if legislators want a firm structure for purposes of enforcing accountability (see below); flexibility may also be unwelcome to clients, who want their program to be safe and secure. Finally, a flexible or unstructured program may not be welcome to administrators, who may want clearer direction for self-protection and for making decisions about clients.

Visibility.   A low profile—in some cases, near invisibility—can make a tool attractive to policymakers and other interested groups. The political appeal of a low public profile comes in two major forms. First, in a society that does not always approve of governmental action, keeping a program invisible may be the only way of sustaining it; therefore, politicians who wish to retain programs may devise mechanisms that let them do so with minimum visibility. The second political advantage is the dark side of the first. Invisible policy mechanisms are difficult to control politically; many never appear as budget items, and only the best informed are aware of their existence. Therefore, it is easier to build in rewards for special interests that the population at large probably would not support. The perceived unfairness of the tax expenditure system is one example of a system of benefits constructed in relative secrecy and frequently denounced for failing to promote the public interest.

In essence, the pursuit of invisibility can become the reverse of truth telling. One can plausibly argue that public officials have special obligations to tell the truth and to avoid deceptive practices.[53] Thus, to the extent that indirect policy tools deceive the population or make informed political and policy choices impossible, indirect policy tools have definite ethical flaws.

Accountability.   A classic problem in public administration is how to hold implementing agents accountable for their actions, either to elected officials or to the general public. Some policy tools promote accountability better than others. In certain respects accountability tends to improve when government directly provides services, goods, transfers, or regulatory programs. Accountability problems do not vanish with the use of these tools, but such indirect tools as intergovernmental grants, contracting, and loans often are worse. For some programs, such as law enforcement, in which the authority of government is invoked and the possibility of the use of force is always present, strict attention must be paid to accountability. Functions that more closely approximate market activities may require less accountability and generate greater concern for other criteria.

Citizen Choice.   Although the United States supplies a number of goods and services to citizens, much of the ethos of the free market remains. Therefore, many people discussing policy interventions argue that maximum citizen choice in the nature of a service—or whether to receive it at all—is an important attribute of any policy tool. Some government goods and services—*merit goods*—are considered sufficiently important that citizens may be coerced to consume them. School for children up to the age of sixteen is a merit good.

Even merit goods may allow some choice. Children may have to go to school, but a voucher plan would allow their parents to send them to the school they choose rather than to the public school in their district. For public goods and services not considered vital, government may be willing to allow the citizen greater freedom of decision. Citizens spend transfer payments in almost any way they choose, while tax expenditures depend upon the citizen's making certain types of decisions. Pure privatization may be the ultimate form of consumer choice, as it simply allows a market to function, albeit at times with some government support and regulation. In all forms of policymaking there must be consideration about whether citizens are willing and capable of making good choices; where they are, it may be less costly and more humane to allow them to make those decisions.

Tools and Competing Values.   Several scholars have developed schemes for assessing policy instruments. Savas examined major characteristics of programs, noting especially the implications of various tools for the size of government and consumer choice.[54] Hatry used eight somewhat overlapping criteria in assessing a slightly different array of policy instruments.[55] Exhibit 3.1 presents an overview of the assessment criteria employed in this volume with speculation about how well a given tool serves certain criteria. A plus indicates that, other things being equal, a tool probably scores better on the particular dimension than do most alternatives; a minus indicates the opposite. In some cases neither a plus nor a minus appears because even informed speculation provides few clues about the relative merits of the tool vis-à-vis that dimension.

Exhibit 3.1 makes it even more obvious that the selection of a policy tool frequently involves trade-offs. No one instrument scores well on all criteria. In choosing tools, policymakers do not usually proceed with a systematic assessment of the advantages and disadvantages of each vehicle. Chance, past experience, practical politics, ideology, intuition, habit, custom, inertia, and related factors are often more important than careful analysis in the selection of tools.

EXHIBIT 3.1 Probable Characteristics of Policy Instruments

	Direct Service Provision	Transfers	Grants	Tax Expenditures	Regulations	Loans	Insurance	Contracts
Certainty	+	+	−	−	+	−		−
Timeliness						−	+	−
Less Cost						+	+	
Efficiency				+				−
Effectiveness								
Flexibility	−	−	−					
Visibility	+	+	+		+	−	−	+
Accountability	+	−	+	−	+	−	−	−
Choice	−	+	+	+	−	+	+	+

Conclusion

This chapter provides a broad-brush treatment of some important institutions shaping public administration in the United States. The separation of powers, federalism, a skeptical political culture, and organized interests do much to generate the particular challenge faced by top political officials and implementing agents. These features of American politics spawn potent centrifugal forces, which heighten the complexity of public administration. They fuel division within the executive branch and make it difficult for government to speak with one voice. Policymaking in the United States tends toward distribution rather than redistribution, each interest group and geographical area receiving a piece of government's pie.

Moreover, the federal bureaucracy encompasses many types of organizations and employs many tools. Even the most seasoned student of government has a hard time keeping up with all the variations. Each organizational form and tool has certain advantages and disadvantages. Perhaps the wide choice of organizational types and tools has in the aggregate contributed to greater efficiency and effectiveness. Whatever its virtues in these respects, however, this proliferation has further heightened the complexity of public administration.

Notes

1. See G. Calvin MacKenzie, "The Paradox of Presidential Personnel Management," in Hugh Heclo and Lester M. Salamon, eds., *The Illusion of Presidential Government* (Boulder, CO: Westview Press, 1981), 113–46.
2. B. Guy Peters, "Public Employment in the United States," in Richard Rose et al., eds., *Public Employment in Western Democracies* (Cambridge: Cambridge University Press, 1985).
3. James O. Freedman, *Crisis and Legitimacy* (Cambridge: Cambridge University Press, 1978).
4. Deil S. Wright, *Understanding Intergovernmental Relations*, 2d ed. (Monterey, CA: Brooks/Cole, 1983).
5. See John G. Grummand and Russell D. Murphy, "Dillon's Rule Reconsidered," *The Annals* 416 (November 1974): 120–32.
6. Wright, *Understanding Intergovernmental Relations*, 45–68.
7. See B. Guy Peters, "Administrative Change and the Grace Commission," in Charles H. Levine, ed., *The Unfinished Agenda of Civil Service Reform* (Washington, DC: The Brookings Institution, 1985).
8. Paul R. Portney, "Natural Resources and the Environment: More Controversy Than Change," in John L. Palmer and Isabel W. Sawhill, eds., *The Reagan Record* (Cambridge, MA: Ballinger, 1984).
9. *Wall Street Journal*, 17 November 1983, 33.
10. *The Gallup Opinion Index* 146 (September 1977): 20–24.
11. Institute for Social Research, University of Michigan, *1980 Election Survey* (Ann Arbor: University of Michigan, 1981).
12. See Charles T. Goodsell, *The Case for Bureaucracy* (Chatham, NJ: Chatham House, 1983).
13. Dwight Waldo, *The Enterprise of Public Administration* (Novato, CA: Chandler and Sharp, 1980), 17.

14. Robert H. Salisbury, "Interest Representation: The Dominance of Institutions," *American Political Science Review* 78 (March 1984): 72.

15. Ibid.

16. Hugh Heclo, "Issue Networks and the Executive Establishment," in Anthony King, ed., *The New American Political System* (Washington, DC: American Enterprise Institute, 1978), 87–124.

17. B. Guy Peters, "The Problem of Bureaucratic Government," *Journal of Politics* 43 (1981): 56–82.

18. A. Lee Fritschler, *Smoking and Politics,* 3d ed. (Englewood Cliffs, NJ: Prentice-Hall, 1983).

19. Heclo, "Issue Networks and the Executive Establishment."

20. Ibid., 88.

21. Richard Rose, "Government against Subgovernment," in Richard Rose and Ezra N. Suleiman, eds., *Presidents and Prime Ministers* (Washington, DC: American Enterprise Institute, 1982).

22. See James L. Sundquist, "A Comparison of the Policy-making Capacity in the United States and Five European Countries: The Case of Population Distribution," in Michael E. Kraft and Mark Schneider, eds., *Population Policy Analysis* (Lexington, MA: D.C. Heath, 1978).

23. Rufus E. Miles, Jr., "A Cabinet Department of Education: An Unwise Campaign Promise or a Sound Idea?" *Public Administration Review* 39 (1979): 103–110.

24. See Terry M. Moe, "Regulatory Performance and Presidential Administration," *American Journal of Political Science* 26 (May 1982): 197–224.

25. Samuel P. Huntington, "The Marasmus of the ICC," *Yale Law Journal* (April 1952): 467–509.

26. See Harold D. Seidman, *Politics, Position and Power* (New York: Oxford University Press, 1975), 253–263.

27. U.S. National Archives and Records Administration, *The United States Government Manual, 1986/87* (Washington, D.C.: Government Printing Office, 1986); Lloyd Musolf, *Uncle Sam's Private, Profitseeking Corporations* (Lexington, MA: D.C. Heath, 1983).

28. John T. Tierney, "Government Corporations and Managing the Public's Business," *Political Science Quarterly* 99 (Spring 1984): 83.

29. Z. A. Medvedev, *The Rise and Fall of T.D. Lysenko* (New York: Columbia University Press, 1969).

30. Frederick C. Mosher, *The GAO: The Quest for Accountability in American Government* (Boulder, CO: Westview Press, 1979).

31. See Christopher Hood, *The Tools of Government* (Chatham, NJ: Chatham House, 1985).

32. Eugene B. McGregor, Jr., "Administration's Many Instruments: Mining, Refining and Applying Charles Lindblom's Politics and Markets," *Administration and Society* 13 (1981): 347–75.

33. See, for example, David Heald, *Public Expenditure* (Oxford: Martin Robertson, 1983).

34. The actual distribution of the checks is relatively inexpensive. Administrative expenses such as record keeping and determining eligibility are higher.

35. One of the classic statements of this point is Francis Fox Piven and Richard A. Cloward, *Regulating the Poor* (New York: Pantheon, 1971).

36. Rochelle L. Stanfield, "If Vouchers Work for Food, Why Not for Housing, Schools, Health and Jobs?" *National Journal* (23 April 1983): 840–44.

37. See Jeffrey L. Pressman and Aaron Wildavsky, *Implementation,* 3rd ed. (Berkeley, CA: University of California Press, 1984).

38. Wallace F. Oates, ed., *The Political Economy of Fiscal Federalism* (Lexington, MA: D.C. Heath, 1977).

39. Charles H. Levine and Paul Posner, "The Centralizing Effects of Austerity on the Intergovernmental System," *Political Science Quarterly* 96 (1981): 67–85.

40. George F. Peterson, et al., *Block Grants* (Washington, DC: The Urban Institute, 1984).

41. David R. Beam, "Washington's Regulation of States and Localities: Origins and Issues," *Intergovernmental Perspective* 7 (Summer 1981): 8–18.

42. *McCulloch v. Maryland,* 4 Wheaton. 316 (1819).

43. Stanley S. Surrey and Paul R. McDaniel, *Tax Expenditures* (Cambridge, MA: Harvard University Press, 1985).

44. Thomas J. Reese, *The Politics of Taxation* (Westport, CT: Quorum Books, 1980).

45. Murray L. Weidenbaum, *Business, Government and the Public,* 2d ed. (Englewood Cliffs, NJ: Prentice-Hall, 1981), 344.

46. Allen V. Kneese and Charles L. Schulze, *Pollution, Prices and Public Policy* (Washington, DC: The Brookings Institution, 1975).

47. Steven Kelman, *What Price Incentives?* (Boston: Auburn House, 1981).

48. Dennis S. Ippolito, *Hidden Spending: The Politics of Federal Credit Programs* (Chapel Hill, NC: University of North Carolina Press, 1984).

49. Council on Economic Priorities, *The Iron Triangle* (New York: CEP, 1981).

50. Stephanie Smith, *Contracting Out and OMB Circular A-76: The Current Situation* (Washington, DC: Congressional Research Service, February 10, 1983).

51. See Robert H. Haveman and Burton A. Weisbrod, "Defining Benefits of Public Programs," in Robert H. Haveman and Julius Margolis, *Public Expenditure and Policy Analysis,* 3d ed. (Boston: Houghton Mifflin, 1983); I.C.R. Byatt, "Theoretical Issues in Expenditure Analysis," in Michael V. Posner, ed., *Public Expenditure: Allocation Among Competing Ends* (Cambridge, MA: Cambridge University Press, 1977).

52. Sam D. Sieber, *Fatal Remedies* (New York: Plenum, 1981).

53. Sisela Bok, *Lying: Moral Choice in Public and Private Life* (New York: Random House, 1979); Joel Fleishman et al., eds., *Public Duties* (Cambridge: MA: Harvard University Press, 1981).

54. E.S. Savas, *Privatizing the Public Sector* (Chatham, NJ: Chatham House, 1982), 78–88.

55. Harry P. Hatry, *Alternative Service Delivery Approaches Involving Increased Use of the Private Sector* (Washington, DC: Greater Washington Research Center, 1983).

Chapter Four

The Public Bureaucracy in the Policy Process

_____
_____

Introduction

Typologies of organizations and tools are important, but they convey little about the dynamics of the public agency in the policy process. Most people think of public agencies as involved in one phase of policymaking—the implementation, or execution of laws.[1] More sophisticated observers realize that by implementing policy administrators are major political actors. Many have considerable discretion to shape the conduct of programs—to determine who gets what, when, where, and how from government. Furthermore, lower-level officials, even street-level bureaucrats, make choices that in the aggregate influence profoundly the benefits and costs of a program.[2]

The political power of public agencies extends well beyond policy implementation. Administrators shape agenda setting, policy formulation, policy legitimation, resource attachment, evaluation, and program change or termination. Thus, the study of public administration goes to the core of comprehending government more generally. Bureaucrats are not bit players in the political drama; they serve as major protagonists even if their names usually do not appear on the marquee outside the theater. To describe the role of administrative agencies in the policy process, this chapter examines certain decision models. Second, this chapter sketches a model of the policy process, defining its critical phases in greater detail. A third section plumbs the role of administrative agencies in each of the phases.

Decision Models

Policymaking involves choice. Social scientists concerned with how large organizations make choices have developed a number of aids to understanding decision-making processes. These models of decisionmaking are abstractions from the complex process of choosing in government generally and in public administration in particular; they capture the central characteristics of the processes and constitute a useful standard for comparison of what actually occurs. The fact that the models are abstractions does not negate their usefulness. They contribute to empirical theory about how organizations behave and why, and they can help even the most practical participant in the policy process.

These models of decisionmaking have normative as well as empirical implications. Their proponents argue that selecting one or another model will lead to better decisions. Even if there can be no agreement about the respective quality of decisions, it does appear that different models will produce different types of outcomes. As is shown below, the incremental model tends to be conservative but is more certain, whereas the synoptic model may produce greater change—but at high risk. Whether from a normative or an empirical perspective, these models have sparked a number of important disagreements among scholars. These disagreements have colored the study of public administration and influenced efforts to understand how government functions.

The Synoptic Model

Synoptic, or rational comprehensive, decisionmaking has great appeal. This is the model most people have in mind for decisionmaking, and it is a useful standard. Conventional economic theory sees this model as how people and firms are supposed to make decisions.[3] The person making the decision is required to decide upon a goal or a hierarchy of goals, to determine the alternative paths of reaching the goal, to analyze the paths and their consequences, to assign a value to each of the consequences, and then to select the path most likely to lead to the desired goal(s) at a minumum cost. Decisionmakers are assumed to be optimizers of their own or their organization's utility.

While this rational approach is best in an ideal world, in reality it presents enormous difficulties. First, goals are not always so clear, especially in large, complex bureaucracies with many organizational and personal objectives. Even if the goals were clear, it might be difficult to rank them and to decide which to pursue first. Second, to consider all possible policies would make the process interminable; there is always one more option or one more criterion to consider. Society needs some means of shortening the process and reducing complexity, particularly given the limitations of human intelligence and time. Third, accurately projecting the outcomes, and hence the costs and benefits, of various alternatives is often impossible. Finally, it may be difficult to evaluate the effects of different choices. Outcomes that some people consider desirable, others consider extremely undesirable. How can we bring alternative means of evaluating policies into a single rational decision? There may be some means, for instance through hierarchical authority, but most of these methods would violate the norms of political democracies.

Incrementalism

Incrementalism is the prevailing mode of describing and explaining decisionmaking in government in the United States. Public decisionmaking in the United States is seen as muddling through rather than as a comprehensive search for the best policy possible.[4] Incrementalism is used as both a descriptive and a prescriptive model of decisionmaking. Chapter 6 on budgeting will discuss the descriptive use of incrementalism; here the prescriptive aspects receive attention.

Prescriptive incrementalism argues that public decisions are best made in small steps. Human intelligence and decisionmaking capacity are limited; the world and its policy problems are complex. Therefore, incrementalists contend that better policy will result if decisionmakers launch only small departures from existing policies, assess how well those small departures work, and then make any additional adjustments that are necessary or desirable. Decisionmaking is by successive limited comparisons rather than by large leaps into the unknown and perhaps unknowable.[5] This presumably helps officials avoid major expensive errors, makes decisionmaking easier, and permits erroneous decisions to be reversed.

In its own way an incremental approach is perfectly rational, despite the greater intellectual appeal of the more comprehensive approaches. Incremental decisions minimize costs rather than maximize benefits. If a policy area is difficult to understand and policymakers lack any firm knowledge about the root causes of the problems, searching for the perfect policy may be not only illogical but also impossible. In such cases, the decisionmaker is better advised to adopt a more experimental approach, try small steps, and look for solutions that are good enough rather than perfect. Administrators must search for acceptable alternatives rather than optimize.[6] These satisfactory solutions are found by bargaining and adjustment rather than through any single vision of good policy.

Incrementalism suffers from some weaknesses.[7] One weakness is that it is sometimes hard to know when to consider a step big or little.[8] A seemingly small change in a regulation may have consequences worth millions of dollars to some industries and consumers. Rarely do decisionmakers understand their policy area well enough to know just what their interventions will do. More important, this conservative approach to policymaking assumes that policymakers are using an adequate model of the problem. With incremental policymaking, change comes slowly, and some problems need radical surgery, and quickly.

One of the arguments for incrementalism is that small steps are reversible. This is not always true. Clients, once created, tend to persist, especially when many clients base important personal decisions on the program, for example not saving for retirement because of Social Security. Finally, the experimental nature of the incremental method may raise ethical questions, given that the lives and livelihoods of individuals are the subjects of the experiments. Does government not have some responsibility for trying to get policy right the first time?

The Garbage Can

Both synoptic and incremental decisionmaking assume goal-seeking behavior on the part of individuals and organizations; policies reach for certain goals. However, the connection between goals and particular policies is not always so clear. Some government organizations, especially less hierarchical ones without firmly estab-lished technologies, approach what Cohen, March, and Olsen called organized anarchies.[9] According to this model, decisionmaking results from the fortuitous confluence of four streams—participants, solutions, problems, and choice opportunities. Certain individuals with certain notions about solutions and problems happen to come together at a particular time when the opportunity for decision presents itself. Chance and luck have a lot to do with what happens.

In government there may be little time to plan and decide upon hierarchies of preferences. The agendas of government organizations may be set by unpredictable events, for instance a five-hundred-point drop in the stock market. Moreover, preferences often emerge from action rather than the reverse; while making and implementing policy, decisionmakers develop a set of goals to rationalize what they are doing. Then, too, solutions seek problems as much as problems seek solutions. Individuals and organizations often have particular technologies, such as social insurance or loan guarantees, that they want to apply or that they are used to applying to problems; they seek problems for which they can make these tools work. Finally, issues and values are rarely discussed outside the context of a particular decision. The choices resulting from the routines or events of the organization, for example, the annual budget request, become the occasions for discussion of goals, instead of goals leading to choices.

Although this anarchic vision of government decisionmaking captures much about the dynamics of many agencies, one must be careful not to assume that it is true in all instances. Tightly controlled, "rationally" planned hierarchies exist in many agencies—especially in those performing routine tasks. Many government actors are goal-directed, even if incremental, in their day-to-day activities.[10]

Bureacratic Politics

Yet another model sees decisionmaking arising from the strategic interaction of many players, each of whom brings certain values and resources to the administrative arena. These players plot strategies, build coalitions, bargain, and compromise to promote their objectives. They may strive to expand the power of the agency vis-à-vis its competitors. They may promote their agency's mission and their particular version of the public interest. The conflicts among the armed services within the Department of Defense exemplify bureaucratic struggles. The end result of strategic interaction may not be the first choice of any player, but it often reflects an acceptable short-term solution to conflicts among values.

The bureaucratic politics model conveys much about the nature of decisionmaking (a point to be developed further in Chapter 5). Like other models, however, it has its limits. It pays somewhat excessive homage to the rational model in that it sees strategically rational actors vying for power within the bureaucracy, so it often assumes too strongly that actors in the bureaucracy have clear preferences they strive to promote. The model also gives insufficient attention to the force of standard operating procedures. It can inappropriately downplay the role of inertia, custom, false reasoning, and so on.

The synoptic, incremental, anarchic, and political models by no means make up the entire list of decision models, and to some degree they overlap. They do, however, capture important perspectives on decisionmaking. In one way or another, each has considerable relevance at each phase of the policy process.

Phases of the Policy Process

Many factors fuel policy processes in the United States. The multiple branches and levels of government provide many points of access to the process and help to ensure the involvement of many actors. Given the great number of access points, it is difficult to say that issues are ever finally resolved in the United States.[11] For example, interest groups offended by presidential or congressional decisions may thwart action through the courts. If that fails, they can attempt to influence implementing agents. Since the federal government frequently relies on state and local governments to carry out its policies, affected interests can often use their political connections at these levels to get their way.

Overall, multiple points of access make it easier to block than to create action. The framers of the Constitution in some respects designed the system to accomplish this end. This propensity also stems from the growth in procedural requirements written into law from the 1960s onward. Environmental impact statements, regulatory cost-benefit analyses, and the like have made action all the harder. Barriers to action can arise at any phase of the policy process.

Policy processes can be divided into seven major phases: agenda setting, policy formulation, legitimation, resource attachment, implementation, evaluation, and response, particularly change and termination.[12] Although discussed sequentially below, these phases do not necessarily progress in so orderly a fashion. Evaluation may occur before any serious attempt to implement a program has occurred. The processes of implementation may without formal evaluation shift the items on government's agenda.

Agenda setting requires that influential elements in a society recognize a certain social condition as a public problem. Poverty, for example, existed in the United States for years before it was recognized as a problem on which government should spend time and money. Other recognized problems may be thought to lie outside the range of permissible government intervention; the problems of many families in the United States are thought to be more suitably addressed by religious organizations or private counselors than by large-scale government intervention.[13]

Governments have two types of agendas.[14] The *systemic agenda* consists of items deemed appropriate for legislation, whether actively being considered or not. The *institutional agenda* consists of the items under active consideration by any policymakers. A great deal of the activity in making public policy involves getting particular issues onto institutional agendas so that there is some hope of producing new policy.

Getting an item on an institutional agenda may be difficult. Characteristics of the issue play a role. Some problems simply cannot be put on an agenda, given the rather conservative nature of American politics. In general, problems that affect a large number of people or that are concentrated geographically so that they appear to affect large numbers of people have the best chance of getting on an agenda. Chances are improved if such problems affect victims rather severely—everyone catches colds, but dread diseases get the money from government. It is easier to legislate on behalf of certain social groups—the elderly and children—than for others. Finally, symbols such as defense and national pride can be manipulated to improve the chances of an issue's getting on an agenda. The National Defense Education Act was much more about education than defense, but the availability of that symbol helped to ensure consideration of the legislation. The clever politician—including organizational politicians—will package issues so that they appear to have some of these characteristics. "Policy windows" are times when circumstances are right to consider an issue.[15] In many instances hard political work is the key to moving an issue onto the agenda.

Policy formulation is the development of solutions for the problems on the agenda. This may be the least-understood portion of the policymaking process. Governments often are not very innovative in the way they respond to problems. A great deal of policy is formulated by analogy—often false analogy—experience, or just plain guesswork.[16] Perhaps the fundamental difficulty is that government frequently must address problems about whose underlying causes it has limited information. Policymakers have little guidance in the selection of appropriate responses.

One standard pattern is to select a solution off the shelf and do what has been done in the past. A number of well-tried mechanisms for intervention are used time and again even when they are not particularly appropriate. In the United States we tend to use social insurance even when inappropriate. For example, Medicare in its early days did little to address the problem of price inflation in the medical sector. Its emphasis on minimal regulation and on giving beneficiaries the right to select their medical providers did, however, have substantial political appeal.

After policymakers have identified a problem and selected a response, their proposal must be *legitimated,* or enacted. That is, the new policy must receive the force of law. The idea behind legitimation is that people believe they have an obligation to obey the law. In some instances, in the absence of formal law, officials can use an informal process to make a proposal appear to be government policy. For present purposes, however, laws passed by Congress and signed by the president more directly capture the meaning of the term. The legislative process is not the only way to legitimate policies. The bureaucracy makes more rules in a single day than Congress makes in a whole year. These regulations are based on powers delegated to the agencies by acts of Congress and are made according to statutes, especially the Administrative Procedures Act, that specify the process. In addition, the courts make policy and legitimate it by reference to the Constitution and other laws. Finally, at least in states and localities in the United States, the populace may be directly involved in legitimating policy through referenda and initiatives. Lawmaking is important, but legitimation is a much broader activity.

After a policy is adopted, government must generally *attach resources* to make it effective. A few policies go into effect by decree, but most require organizations, personnel, and money. This volume has already discussed the types of organizations in the federal government and will give extensive treatment to both budgeting (Chapter 6) and public personnel (Chapter 12). Government can undo a policy after a bill becomes law simply by providing inadequate resources. At times policymakers pursue this option as a conscious strategy. Even if legislators do not favor a program, they may feel compelled to pass it because of political pressures. They can convert the program into a merely symbolic response to a problem by providing few or no resources. For example, government's failure to provide funds for hiring qualified inspectors has rendered some occupational safety legislation almost meaningless.

The failure to provide adequate resources need not be a political trick. A functional committee may want a certain program although the appropriations subcommittee does not. Money may not materialize because of a genuine policy disagreement within Congress. The point is that once there is a policy on the books, the game is not over; it must be played every year, when the budget returns to the Congressional agenda.

Once there is a policy with resources, that policy must be *implemented*.[17] Although analysts have known for some time that many or perhaps even most policies do not work as intended, emphasis on implementation has highlighted the difficulties of making programs work well. In particular, the idea of clearance points has emphasized that a number of separate decisions must be made before the program can be put into effect.[18] Successful implementation often requires federal civil servants, local officials, and even individuals in the private sector to act favorably.

There are a number of barriers to effective implementation. The legislation itself may specify impossible goals or impractical means. The new policy may conflict with other established goals and programs. An increasingly important source of implementation failure is administration by proxy, which often features many clearance points involving other governments or private-sector organizations. Those organizations may have goals or procedures of their own that block implementation. One must be careful not to blame all policy failure on implementation; errors at the formulation stage may doom the program to failure even if it is implemented effectively.[19]

Evaluation is the appraisal of a policy or program, that is, a judgment of how well it works. Policymakers and others have always informally appraised programs. These judgments often amounted to superficial impressions based on episodic evidence (a constituent complaint, for example, or an article in the *Washington Post*). The increase in government programs that resulted from President Johnson's social initiatives of the 1960s spawned greater commitment to more formal and extensive evaluation of programs. Often the laws mandating a program require formal evaluations. Thus, evaluation research became a growth industry.

Just as barriers impede implementation, numerous obstacles derail evaluation. Chapter 13 will discuss in greater detail the difficulties of generating useful studies. The legislation authorizing a program may be vague or unrealistic. This poses a challenge for evaluators. Should the evaluator attempt to determine the original intent of the legislation or assess performance in light of other criteria and standards? If the latter, which ones? The practice of relying heavily on assessments of costs and benefits also presents intriguing issues. It can lead evaluators to undervalue such political factors as accountability, equity, and individual choice.[20]

Evaluations generate a range of *responses* among policymakers and others. These include doing nothing (a common complaint of evaluators), changing the program, and terminating it. For reasons to be explored in Chapter 13, policymakers often do nothing in response to formal evaluations. They may disagree with a report's conclusions; they may not read the evaluation; or they may lack the time, energy, or political support to act on recommendations.

Some evaluations, whether informal or systematic, do generate initiatives to change or terminate programs.[21] To some degree, an attempt to modify or terminate a program requires going through the policy process again.[22] There are some important differences, however, most of which arise from the fact that once a program is in place, it has clients and employees with a vested interest in perpetuating it. Attempts to change an existing program are generally not greeted with the same hostility as attempts to terminate it, but even so, change may be threatening. Although faced with the entrenched political strengths of clients and workers, a would-be terminator or modifier does not have to place the program on the systemic agenda of government. Moreover, certain repetitive items on the institutional agenda such as budgets let the issue be brought forward as a matter of routine. Finally, changing policy may not be as easy as implementing a program the first time. Organizations tend to resist change and may implement a new program very much as they did an old one. Forcing policy change may require more effort than proponents anticipate.

Administrative Agencies As Participants

The public bureaucracy is an extremely important actor in the policy process. The bureaucracy provides greater stability than the other institutions of government. Politicians may come and go; even when a president remains in office for eight years, the administration typically undergoes changes that affect the conduct of policymaking.[23] President Reagan had a relatively stable administration, but in its first six years there were changes in cabinet secretaries and thousands of other personnel. On average political appointees remain in office less than two years and rarely return to Washington. In the midst of all this change the civil service is a force for stability. To be sure, civil servants also vacate positions and leave government, but frequently those who replace them are promoted through the ranks. Often they come from within the same organization. This experience can be contrasted with that of new political appointees, many of whom come into office from outside Washington without prior experience in government. The continuity of the civil service may make change difficult at times, but it does help to prevent extremely rapid divergence from proven policy directions.

Associated with the experience and continuity of the civil service is the expertise bureaucrats bring to their tasks. This is the product not only of experience but also of formal academic and professional education. Although some political appointees have backgrounds in the policies they administer, this is by no means always the case. The civil service, on the other hand, constitutes a reservoir of physicians, lawyers, engineers, agronomists, psychologists, and others who have the training to advise about policy and to make professional judgments about the content of policy decisions.[24] This expertise gives them a great deal of influence over adopted policies, especially in a society that tends to respect technical proficiency.

Finally, the civil service offers commitment. In many instances commitment cannot be easily separated from knowledge, because professional training tends to teach the best ways of performing public functions and the proper standards of practice. Commitment to a program of a specific type may come from professional training, from experience, or simply from ideology. In any case, it is an important

EXHIBIT 4.1 The Role of the Public Bureaucracy in the Policy Process

Stage	Description	Role of Public Bureaucracy
Agenda Setting	Deciding which issues government will consider and act on	Promoting issues of special concern to an agency; filtering ideas from the public
Policy Formulation	Development of specific instruments to achieve goals	Source of ideas and experience on policy instruments and on program design
Legitimation	Invoking a legal or constitutional process to make laws or rules	Administrative rulemaking
Resource Allocation	Funding programs through the budgetary process; personnel authorization	Agency advocacy for its own budget and personnel
Implementation	Putting programs into effect through public bureaucracy or other organizations	Central concern of the bureaucracy with service delivery
Evaluation	Assessment of the effects of programs, concern with effectiveness, efficiency, other values	Self-evaluation of programs
Response: Maintenance, Change, or Termination	Deciding whether programs should be continued as they are, altered, or terminated	Defense of its own programs; proposals for changes to meet findings of evaluation

source of energy for maintenance and change. Analysts frequently think of civil servants as applying most of their energy to preserving existing programs, but in many instances they are also important in advocating new programs and producing change. Such commitment need not be self-serving. As much as politicians, civil servants are interested in improving existing programs and developing new ones. Further, the civil service is in an excellent position to produce many types of changes. Its employees are in government, not trying to get access as are pressure groups. Civil servants are permanent and have the luxury of fighting long guerilla wars to get the policies they want, but politicians have to try to achieve their goals in as little as two years. Finally, most civil servants have the requisite political and managerial abilities to make positive changes in programs.

These considerations suggest the important role of civil servants at each stage of policymaking. Those who think of civil servants as paper pushers with green eyeshades miss an important point. Although usually anonymous, civil servants play an increasingly important part in the policy process. Exhibit 4.1 shows typical contributions of the civil service at each stage of policymaking.

Public bureaucracies are usually associated with incremental decisions. Given their continuity and their commitment to existing programs, rapid policy change is rarely uppermost in the minds of most civil servants. However, public workers often do have ideas about how policy could be improved, including radical departures from the status quo. These ideas are synoptic and often have roots in the ideologies embedded in various professions, for instance visions of national health insurance among workers in public health. The garbage can model also bears on the process specified in Exhibit 4.1. Chance or luck can play a role at each stage. Moreover, the stages do not necessarily proceed in the neat sequence suggested by Exhibit 4.1. For instance, a solution such as a breakthrough in computer technology may lead a small group in the bureaucracy to formulate a policy option before they attempt to put it on the agenda. Each stage of the policy process typically features public administrators with diverse resources and preferences jousting with other players.

Agenda Setting

The role of civil servants in setting the agenda springs in part from their technical expertise. Although Congress has built its own information base through larger committee staffs and such organizations as the Congressional Budget Office, administrative agencies continue as a dominant source of information about social conditions and play a significant role in defining problems requiring government action. For instance, just by systematically collecting and reporting data on unemployment, poverty, inflation, and the number of individuals without health insurance, administrative agencies often fuel concern. Financial projections for Medicare can prompt interested parties to place its costs and funding on the public agenda. In this way public agencies anticipate major problems and may propose solutions to them. Such anticipatory proposals are often difficult to sell on Capitol Hill. Even so, if an agency has built credibility over time, it can exert significant influence on Congress.

Use of data on social indicators is only one aspect of the bureaucracy's ability to shape policy agendas. Administrators also interpret whether a problem can be solved through government action. The National Institute of Occupational Safety and Health (NIOSH) studies many threats to health in the workplace and points out some problems requiring immediate government action. By sharing this interpretation with OSHA, labor unions, and health professionals, NIOSH can create political pressure for changed standards.

Several factors other than expertise also give the bureaucracy leverage in agenda setting. The longevity of civil servants relative to elected political officials and their appointees lets them wait for the right moment to get a problem on the agenda. Moreover, civil servants can activate others to include certain issues on the policy agenda. In some cases agencies have stronger ties to pressure groups and clients than do political leaders. Civil servants may activate these groups by providing and interpreting information. In other instances the quest by politicians for new issues and ideas may help the bureaucracy set government's agenda. One study attributes the expansion of the public sector in the United States largely to the activities of "enterpreneurial congressmen" who want their names attached to new programs.[25] Although some new issues come from increasingly large congressional staffs, the bureaucracy seeks out other problems for these ambitious politicians to ameliorate.

At times the bureaucracy shapes agendas in ways administrators prefer to avoid.

Thus, the clandestine activities of the CIA in some far corner of the world may suddenly thrust a foreign policy issue onto the agenda. The explosion of a space shuttle or the malfunction of an expensive weapons system may likewise shape the congressional agenda.

Policy Formulation

Important participants in agenda setting, public agencies play an even more important role in policy formulation. A number of organizations and actors are prepared to help formulate proposals for "solving" the issues arising on the public agenda. The numerous think tanks and consulting firms in Washington stand ready to provide assistance in policy formulation, usually for a price. The staffs of individual congressmen and senators supply advice. Politicians occasionally develop ideas of their own. However, the great majority of detailed proposals come from the bureaucracy.

The proposing of solutions is facilitated simply because there are relatively few new and completely innovative ones. Organizations in government, like those in the private sector, have a stock of solutions to problems and attempt to employ them widely. To some extent this reflects the inertia of well-entrenched methodologies; civil servants act on what they know and what they can do. A stock solution may be used because it worked in the past. A particular methodology for delivering a service will at times be extended to new policy spheres. If another organization featuring a different methodology is chosen, it can signal a loss in status and power for the first agency. Agencies that have delivered services in a certain manner tend to regard that method as a natural and desirable way to provide those or similar services.

Expertise and staff time are critical resources for public agencies in shaping policy. When policymakers change tax law, they can hardly ignore the Treasury Department's estimates of tax receipts under the proposal. The departments have staffs with the time and commitment to draft legislation to promote their objectives. The presumed feasibility of a proposed solution is an important selling feature, and there are few better sources for determining feasibility than the agency that will implement the policy. If agency personnel support a proposal, it becomes much more difficult to oppose it on grounds of workability.

Agencies frequently work with interest groups in drafting legislation. These groups not only have issues to place on government's agenda, they also have pet solutions they want adopted.[26] In teaming up with interest groups, top executives in departments may provide both technical expertise and critical information on what will fly politically. In the mid-1960s, for instance, the Department of Health, Education, and Welfare played a critical role in drafting Medicare legislation. The AFL-CIO had long lobbied for increased federal intervention in health insurance and took an active interest in shaping the legislation. During the final phases of policymaking, Wilbur Cohen, Secretary of the department, and Wilbur Mills, Chairman of the House Ways and Means Committee, negotiated critical details. A member of the AFL-CIO staff lobbying for the legislation recalls:

In many ways we were in the same position with regard to Wilbur Cohen as some of the Committee members were in respect to Wilbur Mills. We were very much dependent on his judgment. . . . He had the power that comes with a tremendous amount of technical know-how. He really knew his stuff, and he had the relationship with Wilbur Mills. And that was an absolutely critical component. . . . If we had been in on all the meetings between Wilbur Mills and Wilbur Cohen, then it would be very easy to say, "But, gee, Wilbur Cohen, Mills doesn't seem to feel very strongly about this, and I think you could get him to maneuver on that." We never had that kind of information. And so when Wilbur said, "Look, this is what Mills will take," we had to believe him.[27]

Thus, top executives in the public bureaucracy may have disproportionate political as well as technical information.

Legitimation

Legitimation refers to the enactment of a policy proposal by those who have the formal authority to take such action. The passing of legislation and the promulgation of formal rules in the *Code of Federal Regulations* are key arenas, and public agencies play a major role in both. The president frequently expects top bureaucrats to push the administration's bills. In this service they appear before congressional committees, give interviews to *The New York Times,* appear on television news shows, give speeches to groups, and so on. In general, political executives at the highest levels represent public agencies in these activities. Still, they often depend heavily on career civil servants to brief them before they make public appearances.

Career civil servants influence legislative enactment in other ways as well. While politics requires them to support the president's proposals, or at least not openly oppose them, they may work behind the scenes to expedite or impede these proposals. Many career civil servants have close ties with members of Congress and their staffs, with members of interest groups, and with the news media. Career executives can fuel opposition or support for the president's program through off-the-record conversations with any of these parties. Where iron triangles exist, members of Congress may introduce legislation preferred by the agency. Civil servants may tacitly support the legislation and ultimately get their way without ever having a proposal cleared through the White House.

Public administrators play a more open and visible role in administrative rulemaking. The rules, which ultimately appear in the *Code of Federal Regulations,* do much to interpret the law. Issues of administrative law receive more extensive examination in Chapter 7. For present purposes a case involving the Department of Health, Education, and Welfare in the late 1970s illustrates some of the pulling and hauling that can go into the enactment of rules by the bureaucracy.

In 1974 Congress approved the Health Planning and Resources Development Act. One of its goals was to improve the distribution of health care.[28] In response to the law, administrators at Health, Education, and Welfare proposed guidelines for local health planning agencies. In 1977 the department published the proposed guidelines in the *Federal Register*. These guidelines attempted to set quantitative health resource standards in several areas. For example, they prescribed that, barring special circumstances, there should be fewer than four nonfederal short-term hospital beds per thousand persons in a health service area, and any hospital performing open heart surgery ought to do at least two hundred procedures a year. The former standard sought to cut down on excess resources, and the latter rested on the assumption that lack of practice reduced quality and risked the health of the patients. The standards hit most heavily at small rural hospitals that often had excess beds per capita and in the judgment of many health professionals should not be performing complex medical procedures.

Administrators expected the new guidelines to spark public comment. Nonetheless, the magnitude of the reaction caught many of them by surprise. Letters poured in, first by the hundreds and then by the thousands. All told, federal administrators received fifty-five thousand written communications on the guidelines, nearly all negative. Some congressional offices received as many as ten thousand. The postmarks on the letters bore the names of many obscure small towns. The nature of the communications left little doubt that hospital associations and related groups of medical providers had helped orchestrate the protest. Many of the communications were form letters. In some cases elementary and high school teachers organized class projects to protest. No doubt many of those who complained felt that the guidelines would reduce their access to hospital care in rural communities (no matter how suspect the quality of that care). The issue had economic and symbolic overtones as well. Like post offices, hospitals contribute to the local economy and become sources of community pride; they can put a place on the map.

The gusher of complaints prompted a congressional resolution ordering the bureaucracy to consider the needs of rural areas, and the final guidelines reflected a substantial retreat.

Although this case is unusual in the amount of public outcry, it does illustrate the importance of administrative decrees that enact policy. Processes surrounding rulemaking frequently feature a fairly aggressive posture by the bureaucracy followed by negotiation over final rules with interest groups and possibly members of Congress. The final rules usually do more to promote consensus than the initial proposals.

Of course, legitimation can proceed through the courts.[29] Public agencies often employ considerable legal talent and may use the courts to press their concerns. Courts may, in response to program clients, require that agencies undertake certain actions. Environmental groups have taken the Environmental Protection Agency to court for lax pollution control standards. Many civil servants in the agency are sympathetic to the environmentalists and may well enjoy a loss that lets them tighten the rules.

Resource Attachment

Deciding to do something is the easiest part of making public policy. Now the government must put policy into effect. This requires certain basic resources. Chapter 1 pointed to five particularly important ones—formal authority, personnel, money, information, and physical resources. Congress does much to allocate resources, and civil servants strive to influence it by inserting their preferences into the original bill and by obtaining subsequent amendments to the legislation.

Policymakers assign formal authority over programs to particular organizations. The most common practice is to assign a program to an existing agency, often the one that proposed the program. The agency attempts to integrate the programs into its formal authority structure. Some new programs require a new organization.

The scope of authority granted to implementors deserves attention. Consider regulatory authority. The statute creating the Occupational Safety and Health Administration gives that agency direct authority to impose penalties on businesses that violate health and safety standards. In contrast, the Equal Employment Opportunity Commission must pursue violators through the court system. The courts, rather than the agency, have the authority to punish lawbreakers. Policymakers must choose whether to concentrate or disperse the formal authority granted. In some cases the statute parcels out authority over the program to many different organizations (several federal agencies, state and local governments, private organizations, advisory commissions). In other instances, it grants top executives in a department more exclusive authority to make critical decisions. The degree to which policymakers disperse formal authority has profound implications for subsequent implementation dynamics.

Resource allocation also involves assigning people to programs. The sheer number of different types of positions allocated to public agencies can obviously make a considerable difference in subsequent implementation patterns. The commitment and skills of program personnel also loom large in importance. If a policy is to succeed, the people empowered to make it work must have at least a modicum of faith in the program and a willingness to try to make it work. For new and innovative programs, such as many New Deal programs in Roosevelt's administration or those of the Environmental Protection Agency in the 1970s, there has been little difficulty in finding people who are committed to program goals. They even may be willing to make personal sacrifices to accomplish agency objectives. (In fact, zealotry, or too much commitment, may be the more serious problem in these cases.) For many of the mundane functions of government, such as the housekeeping duties of the General Services Administration, high levels of commitment may be more difficult to sustain. In some instances, programs can be assigned to people who lack commitment to them. In the 1970s, for example, a health planning program designed to restrict expansion of medical facilities was assigned to an agency that inherited many employees from the Hill-Burton program—a policy initiative that sought to encourage (not discourage) the construction of hospitals.

Programs also need money. The budgetary process produces the central recurring policy decision for a public agency. This process receives considerable attention in Chapter 6, but one should note here that policymaking makes little real difference if an agency lacks the funds to carry out a program. It bears repeating that one set of committees and subcommittees in Congress authorizes programs, and another set allocates funds. This is why agencies must not only be adroit at shaping substantive policy but also shrewd at budget strategy. An agency staffed by people who are able and knowledgeable in dealing with the program per se, but who lack budgetary skills, is likely to flounder.

There may be extensive information resources for implementing agents attached to policies. A statute could, for example, authorize welfare agencies to draw on the information banks of the Internal Revenue Service or the Social Security Administration for purposes of determining client eligibility for means-tested benefits. A law could require agencies to collect certain kinds of data useful for monitoring and evaluation. A mandate may go to some lengths to generate an information source for an agency. For instance, the Occupational Safety and Health Act established NIOSH to prepare studies for OSHA to use in promulgating rules. In these and countless other ways, a policy can make it more or less difficult for agencies to acquire the information they need to accomplish their missions.

Resources include buildings, equipment, and other supplies. In the Defense Department, for instance, decisions about the number and kind of weapons for the various armed services go to the heart of their efficiency and effectiveness. Each branch of the armed service holds distinctive views on which purchases make the most sense (although they share a propensity to see more as better). Beyond these dramatic issues, computers and telephones can greatly affect a program's efficiency and effectiveness.

Implementation

After enactment and resource attachment, basic tasks of translating the law into action and program outputs (e.g., inspections, clients processed) remain. Public agencies as well as the hired hands of government in the private sector assume center stage during these processes. The president, members of Congress, and the courts occasionally appear, and interest groups and clients often play major supporting roles.

During the 1970s scholars took great pains to point out that implementation was far from automatic. An influential study of the Economic Development Administration in Oakland, California, bore the subtitle "How Great Expectations in Washington Are Dashed in Oakland: or Why It's Amazing That Federal Programs Work at All."[30] Another analyst set out to proffer recommendations for ameliorating implementation, only to become so impressed with the magnitude of these difficulties as to conclude that "government ought not to do many of the things liberal reform has traditionally asked of it."[31] This analysis chronicled numerous implementation games that divert resources, deflect program goals, and generally dissipate energies.

In retrospect the gloom and doom of some of these analyses seems quite excessive; others suggest that many federal programs work quite well.[32] Nonetheless, the highly perceptive early studies of implementation graphically illustrated the enormous importance of this phase of the policy process.

Although this chapter cannot possibly treat all major issues of implementation, three receive particular note: delay, clearance points, and control versus evolution. Students of implementation have devoted much attention to delay. Programs often seem to have enormous difficulty getting off the ground. A law is approved, but nothing seems to happen—or at least very little. Civil servants may be extremely deliberate in promulgating the rules required to energize the program. One analysis goes so far as to assert that delay "is often difficult to distinguish from program failure."[33] Delay can do much to undermine the efficiency, effectiveness, and general credibility of a program, but that fact should not obscure the difficulties produced by a rush to judgment. For instance, officials at OSHA hurried to promulgate large numbers of safety and health standards, in part to demonstrate their commitment to the program. However, many of the new rules were pointless, needless irritants to employers. It subsequently took considerable time and energy to remove these nuisance standards.

Clearance points refer to the decision sites a program must traverse to be implemented. In their seminal study of implementation in Oakland, Pressman and Wildavsky found that even if one assumes very high probabilities of participants reaching agreement at each decision site, a large number of sites presents a substantial risk that the program will break down at least for a period.[34] If the probability of agreement at each of seventy clearance points is 0.99 (an optimistic estimate), the probability of eventual success is slightly less than half. If one assumes the probability of agreement to be 0.95 (still quite high), the odds of success after 70 clearance points are less than 0.03. This kind of statistical analysis makes certain assumptions that do not always hold and so exaggerates prospects for breakdown. Clearly, however, the presence of a large number of decision sites adds to the difficulty of implementation. This has prompted some scholars to call for a reduction in the number of clearance points, but fragmentation of power and the persistent commitment to administration by proxy make the adoption of this proposal difficult.

The problems of implementation have spawned suggestions for improvement. One view is that the structuring of the statute is critical for success. This view is that precisely defined and clearly ranked goals within a law facilitate success. An alternative bottom-up approach sees considerable virtue in allowing implementing agents ample discretion to shape goals and strategies. This latter approach tends to view implementation as the evolution of policy goals and means.[35] Aside from the implications for programs' effectiveness and efficiency, these views raise interesting questions about democratic accountability, which receives more extensive treatment in Chapter 8.

From any perspective, implementation is a major responsibility of the public bureaucracy. In implementing programs, agencies must understand the law as well as the interests of their clients and themselves. Implementation typically features bureaucratic politics. Control over a program is a valuable resource the agency can use to influence other administrative units. Implementation is usually not a function of just a single, lonely organization but a number of public and private organizations.

Evaluation

After implementation has begun, the nagging question quickly arises: How well is the program performing? Another question is whether the program is worth the resources committed to it. Thus, evaluation can be a threatening stage of the policy process for government agencies. It can cast aspersions on the competence of administrators and precipitate a quest to transform or even terminate a program. Evaluation is more than a "scientific" assessment of a program's effectiveness; it is a political event that can alter who gets what from government, when, and how.

The evaluation of public programs poses several important questions. One is which criteria and standards should apply. Legality is the minimal requirement. Is the program performing its tasks as required by law, and is it spending money legally? This form of evaluation focuses on compliance and auditing. While useful, it often slights questions of efficiency and effectiveness. For many decades the federal government emphasized this type of evaluation supplemented by the oversight activities of congressional committees.

As policy analysis and the applied social sciences became more sophisticated, evaluation began to measure and explain program (a) outputs, for example the number and nature of safety inspections performed by OSHA; (b) outcomes, for example whether the inspections reduced injuries in the workplace; and (c) impact, for example the dent in the entire problem of workplace injuries made by the inspection program. No matter how sophisticated the research design, its complexities as well as data limitations almost invariably leave a residue of uncertainty concerning effectiveness. Nonetheless, these evaluations appreciably advance understanding of the costs and achievements of various programs.

Some evaluative approaches draw heavily on economics. Cost-benefit analysis requires evaluators to derive a dollar value for all benefits of a program. Hence, analysts estimate the monetary value of the injuries avoided and the lives saved by OSHA. A ratio of benefits to costs could be neatly specified and the program's ratio could readily be compared to those of other programs. The difficulties of placing a dollar value on program benefits suggest other modes of analysis that emphasize cost-effectiveness. In the case of a child health care program, for instance, one might estimate the mean cost per life saved. This ratio could facilitate comparisons of effectiveness (lives saved) with economic costs but need not set a dollar value on an infant's life.

As valuable as cost-benefit and cost-effectiveness analyses can be, they cannot tell the entire story about a program's accomplishments. Other criteria may include citizen participation, responsiveness to constituents' demands, and other factors.

Another question is which organizations will perform the assessment. In the federal government, organizations conduct evaluations in a number of ways. Congress is one of the major players. The congressional oversight committee can be an important agent of evaluation, although rarely so formal as evaluation research. Congress is also responsible for the General Accounting Office, which conducts more extensive evaluations. The GAO has been especially important since the mid-1970s, when it expanded its realm from auditing to efficiency and effectiveness.[36] The GAO now has substantial analytic capacity to determine how well money is being spent.

The executive branch also conducts evaluations of agencies. The Office of Management and Budget helps the president make decisions about expenditures. Also, each organization of any size in the bureaucracy has the capability of conducting evaluations of its own programs. Although at times ideological concerns drive out analysis, there is no major shortage of analytic capacity in the federal government.

Where such shortages exist, consulting firms sometimes sell their analytic capacity to agencies. The "Beltway bandits" eager to provide evaluations ring Washington. Many of these firms specialize in a particular policy area, and others specialize in particular forms of evaluation. The degree to which evaluation by proxy produces high-quality studies remains debatable. Contractors have some incentive to tell clients what they want to hear in order to get subsequent contracts. Of course, in-house evaluation staffs sometimes come under pressure to provide a favorable assessment.

The competition between in-house evaluation and external research firms raises intriguing questions about the politics of evaluation. An organization is not likely to determine that its own programs should be terminated except when opponents to existing programs gain control of the White House and impose new priorities. Thus, it may seem sensible to employ outside evaluators. However, these outsiders may not grasp the details and nuances of operations well enough to make meaningful evaluations, and program officials may therefore discount their conclusions. As

Wildavsky points out, the only effective evaluation may be an ongoing internal one within the organization itself, if for no other reason than it may be the only type to which the relevant decision makers pay any attention.[36]

Unofficial evaluations are frequent. The program's clients express their assessment via complaints, nonparticipation, noncompliance, and other means. Via investigative journalism, the media conduct many unofficial evaluations. Finally, think tanks produce and disseminate ongoing evaluations of government programs. In short, evaluation abounds; of course, a critical question is how the agency responds to the assessment.

Response: Change or Termination?

The public bureaucracy is central to issues of policy change and succession. Most important is that proposed changes in existing policies imply modifications in the organizations responsible for the policy. Civil servants may welcome these changes, even initiate them. In many instances, however, they see change as unwelcome and resist it. It is a human characteristic to find comfort in business as usual—to keep social systems operating as they have been. In addition, administrators may believe that any changes in the program will harm its clients. Whether for self-preservation or for the benefit of its clients, an agency often resists attempts to change policy.

Organizations are in an excellent position to resist such changes. If an agency has been operating for a long period, it tends to have good working relationships with the congressional oversight committees and appropriations subcommittees that approve major modifications in existing policies. In addition, the agency has close ties to clients and so can mobilize popular support for threatened programs. The members of the organization may also use federal personnel procedures to defend their own positions and thereby defer the transition. Finally, anticipated reactions may redound to the benefit of administrators inclined to resist change. Those who foster change may view the task of accomplishing it in large government agencies as so formidable that they prefer to invest their time and energy in other causes.

Given the nature of organizations and clients, the process of changing a policy often involves more extensive bargaining than does initiation, and the style of bargaining is different. When deciding to initiate a policy, governments tend to consider ideological questions about the desirability of the program and whether government should set a policy at all. When policy succession is the issue, however, the argument is more likely to address the relative efficacy of different approaches to the problem in question. In such an argument an existing organization has an advantageous position, in part because its employees have expertise in the technicalities of implementation and alternatives to existing practice. The agency may use its expertise as a force for the status quo, arguing that whatever the limits of a program, alternatives suffer from worse defects.

In spite of the barriers to change and the many successful attempts to preserve the status quo, much change occurs. Modern governments continually make and remake policies. In the process public agencies are charged with implementing the revised programs. For the employees of public organizations and their clients, new or modified programs to address the same problems may present several difficulties. For the clients numerous programs can create a sense of *déjà vu* and a reluctance to believe that any program really presents an answer. This skepticism can be particularly debilitating when a new program requires beneficiaries to invest their own time, energy, and resources. If clients believe that the original program will not exist or will be substantially modified in the near future, they may be less willing to participate. For their part, implementing agents may be reluctant to commit time and energy to a new program, knowing that it will soon change. If nothing else, to do so might make them look naive or deceptive to clients.

Thus encouraging constructive change while minimizing its downside is a central challenge for public administration. Those who wish for less permanence may turn to several devices. Some favor sunset laws, which require the reconsideration and the positive reaffirmation of a program after a period if it is to continue.[38] Others focus on the techniques of organization development to create an agency culture more receptive to change.[39] Also, an organization may be designed with internal incentives to foster change. Far from panaceas, these strategies may help agencies achieve greater efficiency and effectiveness.

Scholars have given less attention to the question of how to damp destructive change. Countering the rush to evaluation ranks high in importance here. Congress and other oversight agencies frequently impose unrealistic time limits on programs. Driven by election cycles and other pressures, politicians frequently expect major results sooner than anyone can reasonably expect them. Consequently, they may rush to change a program rather than allow the original policy to be tested.

The final option available after the evaluation of a program is to terminate it and possibly the organization that delivers it.[40] Given the difficulties of changing a program, one can readily anticipate the even more acute problems of termination. Many programs, such as Social Security, have so much political support as to be beyond termination, at least barring major political upheaval. As if these political pitfalls were not sufficient, the transition costs of terminating a program, then constructing a new one to deal with the problem, may seem so great that even politicians who favor termination desist from advocating it.

In spite of these difficulties some termination does occur. In some cases, the laws initiating programs or organizations require termination. Many boards, study commissions, and the like receive a limited amount of time to do a specific job. In other instances the need expires as the social and economic environment or technology changes. A number of New Deal agencies shut down as economic recovery began at the start of World War II. Finally, political leaders may make political and ideological decisions to terminate programs. The attempts (not all successful) of the Reagan administration to eliminate a number of social programs exemplify this impetus for termination. In short, while most government programs and organizations continue from year to year, more go out of business than might be expected. Termination may be difficult, but it is not impossible.

Conclusion

Public agencies are major political actors in all phases of the policy process—agenda setting, policy formulation, legitimation, resource attachment, implementation, evaluation, and response (retention, change, or termination). To say that these agencies influence all facets of the policy process is not to suggest that the public bureaucracy is omnipotent. The vast dispersal of power in the American political system means that no one actor can realize all its preferences and that actors are usually in a much better position to veto action than to realize initiatives.

Public agencies in the policy process serve as a force for both stability and change. People often think of public agencies as champions of the status quo—as working zealously to protect their programs and turf. To some extent this description hits the mark. Yet public agencies also press for change. Career civil servants have experience in their programs and know what can be improved. Further, an increasing number of public employees have professional training and use it to build their own ideas of good policy as well as to make a set of contacts outside the organization to give them new ideas. Civil servants may have to wait years before they push a new policy forward, but push they do. To be sure, civil servants frequently advocate incremental change. They usually do not call for radical restructuring of government programs all at once, but over a decade the many small steps that are the hallmark of incrementalism can lead to major changes in public policy.

Notes

1. See, for example, Jeffrey L. Pressman and Aaron Wildavsky, *Implementation* (Berkeley: University of California Press, 1973); Christopher Hood, *The Limits of Administration* (New York: John Wiley, 1976).

2. See Michael Lipsky, *Street-level Bureaucrats: Dilemmas of the Individual in Public Services* (New York: Russell Sage, 1980).

3. See chapters by Zeckhauser and Schaefer and Bower in Raymond E. Bauer and Kenneth J. Gergen, *The Study of Policy Formation*. (New York: The Free Press, 1968); Herbert A. Simon, "Rationality as a Process and a Product of Thought," *American Economic Review* 68 (1978): 1–16.

4. Charles E. Lindblom, "The Science of Muddling Through," *Public Administration Review* 19 (1959): 79–88; "Still Muddling, Not Yet Through," *Public Administration Review* 39 (1979): 517–26. Incrementalism has taken on a variety of meanings in the literature on decisionmaking. As used here, it describes a process of less than complete searches for new policy options, with only limited movement away from existing policies. Another name for this process of decisionmaking is *bounded rationality*. See Herbert A. Simon, *Administrative Behavior* (New York: The Free Press, 1947).

5. David Braybrooke and Charles E. Lindblom, *A Strategy of Decision* (New York: The Free Press, 1963).

6. Herbert A. Simon, *Administrative Behavior*.

7. Robert E. Goodin, *Political Theory and Policy Analysis* (Chicago: University of Chicago Press, 1982), 19–38; but see David Braybrooke, "Scale, Combination, Opposition: A Rethinking of Incrementalism," *Ethics* 95 (1985): 920–33.

8. M. A. H. Dempster and Aaron Wildavsky, "On Change: Or There Is No Magic Size for an Increment," *Political Studies* 28 (1980): 371–89.

9. Michael D. Cohen et al., "A Garbage Can Model of Organizational Choice," *Administrative Science Quarterly* 17 (1972): 1–25.

10. See Anthony Downs, *Inside Bureaucracy* (Boston: Little, Brown, 1967); B. Guy Peters, "The Problem of Bureaucratic Government," *Journal of Politics* 43 (1981): 56–82.

11. Lawrence B. Mohr, "The Concept of Organizational Goal," *American Political Science Review* 67 (1973): 470–81.

12. See Charles O. Jones, *An Introduction to the Study of Public Policy,* 3d ed. (Monterey, CA: Brooks/Cole, 1984); B. Guy Peters, *American Public Policy* 2d edition, (Chatham, NJ: Chatham House, 1986).

13. The discovery of the concept of poverty in the United States is usually associated with Michal Harrington, *The Other America* (New York: Macmillan, 1963); see also Gilbert Y. Steiner, *The Futility of Family Policy* (Washington, DC: The Brookings Institution, 1981).

14. Roger W. Cobb and Charles D. Elder, *Participation in American Politics: The Dynamics of Agenda-Building* (Baltimore: Johns Hopkins University Press, 1972).

15. John W. Kingdon, *Agendas, Alternatives and Public Policies* (Boston: Little, Brown, 1984), 173–204.

16. See Jones, *An Introduction to the Study of Public Policy,* 76–109.

17. See Daniel A. Mazmanian, *Implementation and Public Policy* (Glenview, Ill.: Scott, Foresman, 1983).

18. Pressman and Wildavsky, *Implementation,* 118.

19. William S. Pierce, *Bureaucratic Failure and Public Expenditure* (New York: Academic Press, 1981); Brian W. Hogwood and B. Guy Peters, *The Pathology of Public Policy* (New York: Oxford University Press, 1985); William D. Sieber, *Fatal Remedies* (New York: Plenum, 1981).

20. See Peter Self, *Econocrats and the Policy Process* (London: Macmillan, 1967).

21. The Reagan administration has been particularly prone to attempt to terminate programs because of political and ideological disagreements with their purposes. See, for example, John E. Chubb and Paul E. Peterson, *The New Direction of American Politics* (Washington, DC: The Brookings Institution, 1985).

22. Brian W. Hogwood and B. Guy Peters, *Policy Dynamics* (New York: St. Martin's Press, 1983).

23. For example, although President Reagan has been somewhat more successful than most Presidents in holding onto his officials, only four of the thirteen cabinet secretaries that began with him in 1981 were still in office in 1987. The turnover among lower-echelon personnel was even higher.

24. Frederick C. Mosher, "Professions in Public Service," *Public Administration Review* 38 (1978): 144–50.

25. Advisory Commission on Intergovernmental Relations, *The Federal Role in the Federal System* (Washington, DC: ACIR, 1980).

26. J. Leiper Freeman, *The Political Process* (New York: Random House, 1965); A. Grant Jordan, "Iron Triangles, Woolly Corporatism and Elastic Nets: Images of the Policy Process," *Journal of Public Policy* 1 (1981): 95–123.

27. Cited in Martha Derthick, *Policymaking for Social Security* (Washington, DC: The Brookings Institution, 1979), 329.

28. This example is drawn from Frank J. Thompson, *Health Policy and the Bureaucracy: Politics and Implementation.* (Cambridge, MA: MIT Press, 1981), 60–61.

29. Donald L. Horowitz, *The Courts and Public Policy* (Washington, DC: The Brookings Institution, 1977); Richard Neely, *How the Courts Govern America* (New Haven: Yale University Press, 1981).

30. Pressman and Wildavsky, *Implementation.*

31. Eugene Bardach, *The Implementation Game* (Cambridge, MA: MIT Press, 1977), 283.

32. See, for instance, Harrell B. Rodgers, Jr., and Charles S. Bullock III, *Coercion to Compliance* (Lexington, MA: D.C. Heath, 1976).

33. Pressman and Wildavsky, *Implementation,* 107.
34. Ibid.
35. Richard E. Elmore, "Backward Mapping: Implementation Research and Policy Decision," in Walter Williams, ed., *Studying Implementation* (Chatham, N.J.: Chatham House, 1982), 18–35.
36. Frederick C. Mosher, *The GAO: The Quest for Accountability in American Government* (Boulder, CO: Westview, 1979).
37. Aaron Wildavsky, "The Self-Evaluating Organization," *Public Administration Review* 32 (1972): 509–20.
38. U.S. Senate Committee on Government Operations, *Hearings on S.2925, The Government Economy and Spending Reform Act of 1976* (Washington, DC: Government Printing Office, 1976); Robert D. Behn, "The False Dawn of Sunset Laws," *Public Interest* (Fall 1977): 103–18.
39. See, for instance, Wendell L. French and Cecil H. Bell, Jr., *Organization Development* (Englewood Cliffs, NJ: Prentice-Hall, 1973).
40. Robert D. Behn, "How to Terminate a Public Policy: A Dozen Hints for the Would-be Terminator," *Policy Analysis* 4 (1978): 393–413.

Part Two

Politics and Public Administration

Introduction

Part 1 plumbed the macro issues of government's role in a mixed economy, the fundamental political framework shaping public administration, the organizational types and tools of administration, and the dynamics of the policy process. The analysis revealed the central role of government agencies in policymaking as well as the political dimensions of administrative life. Thus far, however, the political aspects of public administration are painted with a very broad brush. In Part 2 a finer brush draws administrative politics and its implications for democracy in greater detail.

For all the talk of the relationship between politics and administration, analyses frequently fail to define the term *politics*. Chapter 5 shows that public administration has several political faces. Since administrative activity invariably affects who gets what from government and cannot be value-free, all of public administration is in a sense political. But different observers see politics from different viewpoints. One perspective sees public administration as becoming more political to the degree that administrators possess greater formal authority to make discretionary decisions. Another views administration as more politicized to the extent that elected officials intervene to shape the day-to-day exercise of authoritative discretion by public workers. Yet another, whose perspective is rooted in organization theory, depicts politics as a function of the degree to which public administration features actors engaged in conflict over ends, means, or both. The implications of each of these connotations of politics for an understanding of public administration deserve attention.

In the politics of administration, no resource looms larger than money. As Chapter 6 shows, the budgetary process provides the lifeblood for the agencies of government; in turn, these agencies are major players in the budget game. Each year top adminstrators conceive strategies to mobilize support in Congress and key interest groups in order to obtain funding for their programs. In turn, the White House strives to fund its policy priorities. Elected officials and others use the budgetary process to enforce accountability on government organizations. The massive budget deficit, the growth of entitlement programs and (beginning in the 1970s) changes in the law governing budgetary processes in the 1970s and 1980s have spawned considerable modifications in budget practices and new challenges for public administrators.

Administrative discretion and politics fuel concern about accountability. Some citizens and politicians fear that if the bureaucracy can do what it wants, it will ignore the wishes of the people and their elected representatives and trample on the rights of citizens. The legal process is one means of checking any such proclivity. Hence, Chapter 7 reviews how administrative law addresses questions of accountability and control. Administrative law deals with such matters as the procedures for making rules and for applying rules to clients. Administrative law also addresses the circumstances under which judicial review occurs and public workers become legally liable for their actions.

Legal mechanisms are not the only way to pursue administrative accountability. Many mechanisms have been devised to deal with the possibility of a public bureaucracy running amok. One device is civil servants' professional and personal ethics. Another device is hierarchy within the agencies, taking accountability all the way to the top of a department. Still another device is Congress's powers to investigate and punish malfeasance. These and other forces provide ample opportunities to constrain administrative behavior—but are these opportunities seized? Is public administration safe for democracy?

Chapter Five

The Faces of Administrative Politics

―――――
―――――

Introduction

Most people tend to think of politics as the activities of Congress or the White House or as the hoopla surrounding conventions and elections. These are the most visible political activities, but a great deal goes on beneath the surface of government and is just as important to the policymaking process. Administrative agencies are major players in much backstage political activity. Some of this occurs at the highest levels of government as agency managers fight for legislation and for their budgets. At the very lowest echelons of the bureaucracy politics concerns the exercise of discretion about whom to arrest, whom to treat with what therapies in federal hospitals, and which deductions to allow in a tax audit. These actions all have political ramifications because in the end they decide who wins and who loses. Administrative struggles are not the dramatic stuff of political novels, but they are certainly politics.

Many people both inside and outside government attempt to distinguish between politics and administration. In some instances this reflects a misguided view that administrators are merely following laws and rules set down and interpreted by Congress, the President and the courts. Others find it convenient—both analytically and normatively—to distinguish between politics and administration. So long as the latter understand the fundamental sense in which all public administration is political, this distinction is sometimes useful. Consistent with this perspective, this chapter seeks to distinguish between different facets of administrative politics. First, however, the intellectual heritage of the dichotomy between politics and administration requires attention.

The Dichotomy

On November 4, 1886, the *New York Evening Post* reported that Professor Woodrow Wilson had presented a "very able paper" to a meeting of the Historical and Political Science Association the night before. Like countless academicians who followed him, Wilson published the paper, "The Study of Administration," in a scholarly journal.[1] Unlike the writings of many scholars, Wilson's essay, which was published in 1887, profoundly influenced a field of study. Of particular relevance, Wilson drove home a distinction between politics and administration. Reflecting the business culture that dominated the United States, Wilson declared that "the field of administration is a field of business. It is removed from the hurry and strife of politics." He went on to assert, "Most important to be observed is the truth already so much and so fortunately insisted upon by our civil service reformers; namely, that administration lies outside the proper sphere of politics." For Wilson, "this discrimination between administration and politics is now, happily, too obvious to need further discussion."[2]

In the years following Wilson's essay, others reasserted the principle. Writing at the turn of the century, Frank Goodnow, a professor at Columbia University, observed that a large part of administration was unconnected with politics.[3] The scientific management movement also took hold in the early 1900s. Led by Frederick W. Taylor, it emphasized the importance of time-and-motion studies of employees to find the one best way to accomplish certain tasks. Taylor's choice of the best way rested on a commitment to efficiency and research methods he touted as scientific. Hence administration was not only separate from politics, it was scientific engineering rather than art.[4]

Readers of the first chapters of this book will find a sharp distinction between politics and administration hard to swallow. Civil servants in federal agencies have substantial discretion to influence the output of government programs. The relevance of administrative discretion looms even larger when one recalls the propensity of the federal government to rely on administration by proxy.[5] The pervasive use of state and local governments, businesses, private nonprofit organizations, and other third parties to implement programs tends to enlarge administrative discretion.

Administrative discretion invites company and conflict, which further undermine the dichotomy. Sensitive to the importance of the decisions made during implementation, elected officials in the White House and Congress at times try to influence them. Elected officials and interest groups frequently have differing opinions. Conflict erupts. Participants mobilize their resources, make strategies, and create coalitions. Such imagery hardly squares with notions of administration as a pattern of neat hierarchical relationships in which administrators rely on a scientifically proven one best way to carry out precise laws.

The political quality of public administration became increasingly evident through the 1930s and 1940s. Dwight Waldo and Paul Appleby were among the leaders in pointing to the folly of rigid distinctions between politics and administration.[6] Moreover, a careful rereading of the early scholars associated with the dichotomy reveals less dogmatic commitment to it than some observers have suggested. Woodrow Wilson emphasized that the administrator "ought not to be a mere passive instrument" and "that large powers and unhampered discretion" were "the indispensable conditions of responsibility." Wilson contended that "the greater [the administrator's] power the less likely is he to abuse it, the more is he nerved and sobered and elevated by it. The less his power, the more safely obscure and unnoticed does he feel his position to be, and the more readily does he lapse into remissness." Wilson considered visibility the key ingredient making discretion palatable. Administrative power obscured became irresponsible.[7] Hence, Wilson did not envision the dichotomy between politics and administration as achievable only when the law leaves administrators with no opportunity to choose. This perspective has prompted one analyst to say that Wilson "vacillates between the two poles of thought regarding the separability and inseparability of administration from politics."[8]

If the limits to the dichotomy are apparent even in early writings, complete destruction of the distinction hardly proves gratifying. Seeing all administration as politics takes one a limited distance analytically. Does one really mean to put the computer operator, coding and punching data, into the same category as a senior executive bargaining with Congress over proposed legislation? Moreover, everyday parlance holds that some agencies and administrative activities are more political (or politicized) than others. Is it appropriate to dismiss these observations as empirically meaningless?

This chapter assumes that it remains important to consider some administration as more political, or politicized, than other forms. Efforts to understand the political aspects of administrative life must explicitly deal with the different meanings of the terms *politics* and *politicized*. No doubt linguists could develop extensive lists of definitions. This chapter discusses three: (1) politics as discretion, (2) politics as intervention by elected officials and their appointees, and (3) politics as generic conflict. The meaning of each of these and their manifestation in American public administration are the primary foci of this chapter. As will become evident, a single administrative episode can exemplify all three kinds of politics; nonetheless, each type carries different connotations. Nor is the term *politics* pejorative; at times politics serves positive ends, and on other occasions, negative ones.

Politics as Discretion

As Chapter 4 indicated, administrators influence many phases of the policy process, such as agenda setting, policy formulation, and legitimation. This section focuses more narrowly on the discretion they exercise in carrying out policy. Politicization via administrative discretion occurs to the degree that laws and written interpretations of laws leave administrators free to choose among important possible courses of action or inaction.[9] Faced with a decision, administrators typically confront some set of rules or orders, that is, a legal superstructure of statutes, court opinions, administrative regulations, and so on. To the degree that administrators cannot change the legal superstructure on short notice and are willing to obey its instructions, the superstructure helps define the scope of administrative discretion.[10] Administrators use this discretion to determine who gets what from government.

Imprecision in federal laws yields much discretion to administrators. Precision is the degree to which statutes and other documents define objectives, quantify them, specify timetables for them, indicate priorities among multiple objectives, and spell out the administrative structure to be used for a program.[11] Nebulous statutes at times spring from coalitions in Congress. Vague language may enable different factions in the House and Senate to support a bill. Each group may believe that its own interpretation of fuzzy legal provisions will prevail during the implementation process. Vague statutes may also be attractive for passing the buck to administrators. If a program produces undesirable effects that prompt public criticism, Congress can point the finger of blame at administrators for failing to implement the law effectively. Technical complexity and change have also pushed lawmakers toward ambiguity. For instance, when Congress passed the Occupational Safety and Health Act in 1970, it could not hope to prescribe allowable exposure levels for all carcinogens in the workplace. Instead it assigned administrators pivotal responsibility for discovering which substances posed threats and for proposing regulations to deal with them.

Agencies exercise discretion through a number of channels. For example, agencies have authority to fill in the ambiguities of statutes with administrative regulations, and in so doing, they choose not only which particular ambiguities should be addressed but what the substance of the rules should be. Although the law requires them to refrain from being "arbitrary or capricious" (see Chapter 7), agencies have substantial discretion in this arena. Agency personnel also make decisions about how to treat individual cases. An OSHA inspector has some latitude in deciding whether to fine an offending firm or to give it time to correct the problem. An auditor at the IRS has some discretion about what proof is sufficient for deductions. Such decisions affect one person or one firm at a time, but they add up to a pattern of interaction between government and its citizens. This pattern goes a long way in determining how citizens view government and what public policies actually mean to them. It may also determine the extent to which an agency conflicts with other bureaucracies, including central agencies such as the Office of Management and Budget.

As the number of people severely affected by a given decision grows, the importance of administrative discretion increases. A secretary working in a government typing pool determines which letters and reports to type first. A small number of government officials and citizens may notice relatively modest effects, such as delay or other inconvenience, as a result. On the other end of the scale, decisions made at the highest levels of OSHA concerning carcinogens can profoundly affect the health of many workers as well as the financial condition of firms who must reduce workers' exposure to toxic substances.

Judgments of the significance of administrative discretion are complex. A little discretion can have a cumulative impact. An OSHA inspector tends to possess less formal discretion than his or her superiors. Collectively, however, *all* inspectors may have more administrative discretion than their superiors, as they enforce regulations day after day. Aside from this issue, the effects of administrative discretion are often indirect and difficult to trace. Moreover, observers vary in their notions of significance. All may agree that discretion with life-or-death implications for many people is the most important. In other instances, however, consensus evaporates. Is administrative discretion over who has how much access to the national parks as important as discretion over comparable access to Amtrak? Opinions differ.

As this discussion suggests, measuring administrative discretion poses enormous difficulties. Whatever the measurement issues, officials in some agencies have much greater discretion than others. Agencies with wide discretion are more political in the sense that they rather than Congress make critical decisions concerning programs. This does not mean that officials with great formal discretion are ipso facto powerful. Sometimes others succeed in influencing their exercise of discretion. In this regard, the efforts of elected officials and their staffs to shape administrative decisions point to another major type of politicization.

Politicization via Elected Officials

The President and Congress at times directly intervene to influence specific administrative decisions. They also intervene indirectly through interest groups, the media, and one another; they place personnel loyal to them in key administrative positions and motivate these employees to represent their viewpoints in agency decisions. The degree of this form of politicization varies greatly among agencies. In the early 1960s career administrators in the Food Stamp Program achieved virtual autonomy in drafting major regulations governing who would be eligible for food stamps. As the program grew and became more controversial, however, the White House, members of Congress, and top political executives in the Department of Agriculture exerted much more power over the drafting of these rules.[12]

The Administrative Presidency

Presidential attempts to politicize the bureaucracy coexist easily with conventional wisdom. This "wisdom" portrays the president as ultimately accountable for the responsive and efficient operation of government programs. The buck presumably stops at the top of the ladder.

Whatever the virtues or defects of presidential leadership, many forces constrain the chief executive's ability to tilt public administration. The framers of the Constitution worked to guard against excessive centralization of power. Judges, members of Congress, interest groups, civil servants, political appointees, the media, and others compete with the President for control of administrative discretion.

Presidents are hardly helpless, however. Strategically sophisticated ones have developed and used many levers to shape administrative behavior. In fact, contemporary presidents have become increasingly sensitive to the use of public administration to accomplish what they cannot achieve through legislative action. If a president cannot change the law, he may be able to shape administrative discretion. President Nixon and his staff, for instance, came to the view that their objectives could be achieved only if the White House gained more control over domestic agencies because in many areas, operations is policy. The day-to-day management of programs decides many critical issues of who gets what from government.

A president bent on influencing administrative discretion can issue an executive order.[13] Another way is to draft specific rules for the *Code of Federal Regulations*. The Nixon White House promulgated new rules governing welfare error rates in eligibility determinations, which increased pressure on state governments to reject applications for welfare and to provide lower payments to individual recipients.[14] Reorganization is another vehicle for presidential power. President Nixon at times used to reorganize whole activities out of existence. And of course the president shapes agencies' budgets as well as when and how they spend appropriations (see Chapter 6).

In using these and other vehicles of politicization, the president may choose a centralized strategy featuring heavy reliance on the Executive Office as a kind of counterbureaucracy. Employing this approach, the president attempts to force major decisions into the White House, where he presumably can count on greater responsiveness to his particular policy agenda. The problems with this strategy loom large, however. First, the trivial often swamps the important. Richard Nathan notes that under President Nixon, "As the White House became more and more involved in routine administrative matters, the time and energy it had to devote to truly important policy issues was correspondingly reduced."[15] Second, the White House staff has limited expertise. Staff members lack the time to achieve sufficient knowledge of the issues that confront the federal departments. Third, overload seems inevitable. Discretion permeates the bureaucracy. For the White House to control it through direct intervention would require gargantuan efforts.

For these and other reasons, complete reliance on a counterbureaucracy strategy to shape administrative discretion runs an extremely high risk of failure. Instead, successful presidential politicization requires that the operations of the line agencies be penetrated. Again in the words of Richard Nathan:[16]

> An administrative presidency must emanate from the president and crucially involves his relationship with his appointees in major executive branch agencies. For this relationship to be a successful one, it cannot be encumbered by a White House bureaucracy.

Of course, no one doubts that the White House staff has a role to play. The directives and controls imposed by the Office of Management and Budget play an especially critical role in presidential efforts to shape administrative discretion. By itself, however, the Executive Office cannot do the job.

Presidential Penetration via Appointments.   Given the problems of central-izing decisions in the Executive Office, the appointment of responsive and capable personnel to key positions in the bureaucracy becomes extremely important. The president exerts substantial control over appointments to top posts—those eight hundred openings that fit into the five levels in the Executive Schedule (Level I being the highest).[17] In addition, the president can fill ten percent of the roughly seven thousand positions in the Senior Executive Service (SES). This personnel stratum falls just below the top Executive Schedule appointments in the hierarchy.

While the wisdom of using appointment powers to control administrative discretion may seem obvious, in practice it has proved difficult. Prior to the establishment of the SES, one astute observer described the struggle by the president to control the bureaucracy as a "leap into the dark."[18] While the Civil Service Reform Act of 1978 installed a few lights to show the president where he (or she) may be leaping, fine-tuned control via appointments remains elusive. The White House faces many pitfalls in recruiting competent and responsive people to translate its policy preferences into administrative action. Low salaries relative to those in the private sector are part of the problem, but the difficulties extend much further.

Political parties contribute to the problem. Spoils politics is not the major issue here, as too few jobs exist for presidents to bolster their party by rewarding large numbers of the faithful with patronage. Presidents tend to appoint people from their own political party in large part to ensure staff sympathy to their policy positions.[19] However, the weakness and ideological heterogeneity of American parties under-mine the value of this approach. The parties do not sustain recruitment networks that an incoming president can count on to furnish him with responsive, capable personnel.

Presidential dispositions to use appointments to heal election wounds also present a pitfall. After an intense campaign contest, presidents at times strike a conciliatory pose by appointing cabinets broadly representative of many groups or seek to curry favor with Congress and interest groups via appointments. However valuable for promoting good will, such appointments frequently do little to heighten presidential control over administrative discretion. In 1968, for instance, President Nixon chose a cabinet designed to represent major interests in the inner council of government. Many of these officials were minimally responsive to White House preferences on a range of issues. President Carter fell prey to similar pressures. During his 1979 midterm shake-up, he felt compelled to fire four cabinet members.

A tendency to focus excessive attention on cabinet as opposed to subcabinet appointments can come home to haunt the president. As a condition for accepting top posts, cabinet officials often demand control over other political appointments in the agency. When President Carter approached Joseph Califano to head the Department of Health, Education, and Welfare in 1976, he asked Califano whether he had any questions. "Only one," Califano responded. "Will I have the ability to pick my own people?" Expressing his commitment to "cabinet government," Carter responded affirmatively.[20] So, too, President Nixon, in one of the first cabinet meetings of his administration in 1969, delegated to cabinet officials the responsibility for filling political positions in their agencies.[21] The experience of both Carter and Nixon suggests the limits to this approach. At the subcabinet level the Carter administration had a large number of committed activists, many of whom had program agendas quite different from the President's. Nixon subsequently regretted that in his first term he "had failed to fill all key posts in the departments and agencies with people who were loyal to the president and his programs."[22]

Furthermore, political executives may go native, that is, start off committed to the White House agenda, but end up defending the programs they manage from the president. Awareness of this pitfall encouraged the Reagan administration to leave vacant many top positions. This allowed the Reagan White House to launch its assault on several government programs with less fear of encountering resistance from its own political appointees. To counter appointees' propensity to go native, some presidents have gone out of their way to inculcate loyalty through personal phone calls to underlings, by inviting them to receptions, and in other ways.

Even if the president dodges problems of unresponsiveness, issues of competence may arise. Political executives frequently lack skills needed to manage government operations. They tend to stay in government for short periods, roughly two years on the average. This means that unless they learn very rapidly, these appointees may not be ready for effective action until about the time they leave office. Many of them occupy weak and uncertain leadership positions and so become imperfect conduits for presidential power.

Skill deficiencies among political executives are often especially evident in the way they manage their relations with career civil servants. Faced with the need to make a name for themselves in a brief period, political appointees tend to push hard and to view career civil servants as a likely source of resistance. As Laurence Lynn observes, "Fearful of being coopted or outmaneuvered, political executives are tempted to go on the defensive immediately, issuing warnings that they will not be taken in and filtering or restricting their communications with bureaucrats."[23] Indiscriminate mistrust of career managers tends to undercut the effectiveness of political executives. The danger of keeping career managers in the dark is not so much in sabotage of initiatives through direct resistance, although such sabotage occurs on occasion, as in passive compliance with the wishes of political executives. Under this yes-boss approach, career officials let political executives wander into traps without warning.[24] They do not volunteer the strategic and technical information necessary for political appointees to manage effectively.

Conflictual or poorly managed relations with career civil servants can yield other negative consequences for the White House. Poor relations may precipitate a decline in the commitment, motivation, and work performance of career personnel. Turnover may increase. This deterioration may heighten the president's ability to shape administrative discretion, or it may hurt. The president may be thwarted by inadequate numbers of personnel competent to carry out his agenda. Highly conflictual relations with civil servants may also energize outside interest groups who oppose the president. Fund-raising may become easier for these groups.

Thus, political executives who trust within limits and seek help from reliable career counterparts probably perform better. One study of five political executives in the Reagan Administration concludes, "Loyalty to the president's goals . . . was not inconsistent with open, trusting, and participative approaches to agency management."[25]

Even having recruited responsive and competent political executives, the president cannot count on fine control over administrative discretion. Opportunities vary greatly from one agency to the next. White House control becomes more difficult where laws clearly specify an agency's core activities, where considerable decentralization of authority exists, where career personnel have strong professional identities, and where these personnel have close ties to outside interest groups and congressional committees.[26]

Although presidential appointments remain an uncertain instrument of power —one whose potential for error and unanticipated consequences loom large—presidents have on occasion used it effectively. In contrast to Ford and Carter, Reagan won wide respect for his sophisticated approach to selecting cabinet and subcabinet officials.[27] Well before Reagan became President, Edwin Meese and E. Pendleton James devised a plan for appointing persons to cabinet and major subcabinet posts. James continued to serve through July 1982, during which time he had an office in the White House and considerable access to the President. A staff of roughly ten professionals took great pains to screen candidates for positions, placing heavy emphasis on ideological compatibility with the President.[28] Although the quality of President Reagan's appointees varied considerably, many of them demonstrated substantial competence as well as responsiveness to the White House.

In attempting to penetrate the operations of the bureaucracy through the appointment of personnel, Reagan was the first president who from the onset stood to reap the full benefits of institutions established by the Civil Service Reform Act of 1978 (see Exhibit 5.1). In this regard the newly created Senior Executive Service offered the president a number of levers for influence.

EXHIBIT 5.1   The Civil Service Reform Act of 1978

In 1976, when President Carter was elected, the civil service system in the United States was the object of increasing scrutiny and complaint. It appeared to many people that it impeded efficiency, effectiveness, and political responsiveness. Personnel rules constrained federal executives' ability to manage. Presidents and top political officials considered that the bureaucracy often failed to respond to their policy priorities.

With strong support from President Carter, the Civil Service Reform Act of 1978 sought to address these perceived problems. The most visible reforms in the new statute are structural. The Civil Service Commission was divided into two organizations, the Office of Personnel Management (OPM) and the Merit System Protection Board (MSPB). OPM is responsible for recruitment, training, performance appraisal, and so on. OPM also advises the President on all matters of federal personnel policy. In addition, the act decentralized a number of functions, such as recruitment, to the line agencies of government.

The Merit System Protection Board assumed the appellate and quasi-judicial functions of the old Civil Service Commission. It safeguards employees' rights to due process and equitable treatment. The act created an Office of the Special Counsel in the MSPB, which in part seeks to protect whistle-blowers against unfair reprisals. To handle employee complaints of unfair labor practices and generally regulate labor relations, the act established the Federal Labor Relations Authority.

Of particular relevance here, the Civil Service Reform Act provides for the Senior Executive Service, which includes most senior civil servants and is meant to provide a high-quality, mobile, and politically responsive cadre of generalist public executives for the federal government. It gives the White House more authority to assign career civil servants to particular posts and to intersperse political executives among them. It also emphasizes merit pay to encourage excellence among top executives.

Penetration via the Senior Executive Service.   Created by the Civil Service Reform Act, the Senior Executive Service encompasses nearly seven thousand executives—approximately one for every three hundred federal employees (excluding the Postal Service). SES members are sandwiched between some eight hundred top political executives and more than a hundred thousand middle managers (General Schedule 13–15).[29] The Civil Service Reform Act did not impose the SES across the entire federal establishment. Exemptions include such agencies as the FBI and the CIA. In most federal departments, however, SES members play a major role in translating broad policy mandates into day-to-day operations.

About 10 percent of SES personnel are noncareer, or political, appointees selected outside ordinary merit system channels. The rest are career executives, whose commitments to federal service presumably extend beyond the term of a given President. These career executives have certain procedural rights concerning appointment and removal that political executives lack. The Civil Service Reform Act regulates the numerical balance between political and career officials through several provisions. It specifies that the number of noncareer appointees in all agencies cannot exceed 10 percent of total SES positions. Except in certain rare circumstances, the total number of noncareer appointees in a single agency cannot exceed 25 percent of SES positions in that unit.

Statutory provisions concerning the SES contain many elements. Among other things, the law structures the SES as a mobile force that top political executives can easily redeploy in response to changing national priorities, as a cohort of executives about whom there is excellent information on individual performance. This information is appraised and linked to rewards—pay, promotion, and retention. The SES is to sustain the appropriate balance of power between political and career executives.

Assignment As a Lever.   The Civil Service Reform Act makes it easier to transfer executives from one position to another. Such fluidity presumably facilitates greater responsiveness to shifts in presidential priorities. It may also make civil servants less beholden to various interest groups and congressional subcommittees and avoid the tunnel vision that can arise from occupying the same job for years. In this latter sense, the law might take one small step toward overcoming the balkanization of the federal government into narrow functional fiefdoms such as health, defense, and education.

To facilitate mobility, the law establishes a biennial process to allocate SES positions. Agencies request SES slots, and OPM allocates them within limits specified by Congress and the White House. Once they obtain positions, agency officials have the discretion (depending in part on funding) to *establish,* or formally create, and fill them.[30] The law also facilitates mobility through a rank-in-person system. That is, rank and salary are attached to the person rather than to the position, so that the shifts in position do not affect status or income.

In sum, the mobility of the SES not only permits the White House to appoint and strategically place political executives but also provides opportunities to transfer career executives. To be sure, these opportunities existed before the SES. During the Nixon years the White House Personnel Office drafted the "Malek Manual" (after Fred Malek, who for a time headed the office). This document prescribed various techniques for removing "uncooperative" career civil servants. According to the manual, "By carefully researching the background of the proposed employee-victim, one can always establish that geographical part of the country and/or organizational unit to which the employee would rather resign than obey and accept transfer orders." The report went on to urge that a promotion accompany the undesirable transfer to foreclose any claim of unfair action. The Malek Manual also endorsed the "traveling salesman" technique for removing career administrators. This technique, "especially useful for the family man and those who do not enjoy traveling," involved promotion and assignment to a position which required considerable travel. The individual "is given extensive travel orders criss-crossing him across the country to towns (hopefully with the worst accommodations possible) of a population twenty thousand or under." Forced to endure these hardships, the career official presumably leaves the federal service.[31]

The degree to which the Nixon White House employed such tactics remains unclear. However, it does appear that Nixon altered the composition of the top echelons of the career civil service in a manner consistent with his policy preferences.[32] While Nixon's transformation of the civil service was not massive, it does illustrate the ability of the President to make a difference. The creation of the SES further bolstered prospects for presidential impact of this kind.

Mobility in the SES appears to be considerable, reassignments averaging more than a thousand per year, at least in the initial period after passage of the Civil Service Reform Act. If reassignments are common, however, interagency transfers remain much less in evidence, amounting to approximately a hundred annually.[33] The data on interagency movement suggest that the SES system may well encounter difficulties in creating a core of generalist managers who move from one policy sphere to another.[34]

Protection of the Balance?   While the SES gave the White House new power over personnel matters, it also paid homage to the need to preserve a balance of power between political and career executives. Students of democracy generally caution against shifting excessive leverage toward either group. When too many political appointees staff the bureaucracy and influence government operations, amateurism and excessively partisan administration increase. Lack of managerial know-how makes it difficult to implement programs effectively. Carried to an extreme, loyalty to the president can breed lawlessness as officials promote the president's policy agenda or reward the party faithful through acts of dubious legality. However, career executives may acquire too much autonomy and become unresponsive to the legitimate claims and statutory interpretations of the White House. This can undercut accountability and weaken democracy.

Several provisions of the Civil Service Reform Act, especially those that eased the reassignment of SES positions and personnel, bolstered the power of political appointees and the White House. However, the law also sought to thwart excessive politicization by limiting the proportion of SES positions that political executives could fill. In addition, the Civil Service Reform Act requires that each board responsible for recruiting, evaluating, and recommending pay increases for career SES officials draw more than half its members from the career civil service. Furthermore, the reform act proclaims that individuals with five years of continuous work in the civil service prior to their initial appointment to the SES must fill at least 70 percent of SES positions. This is a modest barrier to back-door entry by political appointees into career SES jobs.

Has the appropriate balance been struck? Limited data as well as normative disagreement about how to define the "proper" balance preclude a definitive judgment. In a limited and technical sense, however, there is little evidence that widespread abuse has occurred. During the first five years of the SES system, the number of noncareer appointments did not exceed the limit established by the law (10 percent of all SES positions). To be sure, the OPM interpreted the limit as being based on allocated rather than established or filled positions. Since the number of unfilled allocated positions often surpassed a thousand, the proportion of SES personnel who were political appointees exceeded 10 percent during certain years of the Reagan administration. This overage, however, hardly amounts to a major abuse of the Civil Service Reform Act. Nor does it appear that political executives have entered the career service in large numbers through the back door. During the period from July 1979 through September 1983, only fifty individuals converted from noncareer to career appointments—twenty-seven under Carter and twenty-three under Reagan. At no time did the proportion of SES members with at least five years of continuous service in the federal government prior to joining the SES drop below 82 percent.[35]

Data such as these cannot answer the question whether the SES has placed career executives under excessive White House pressure. The statistics cannot convey whether ideological loyalty receives too much weight in evaluating and rewarding career managers. They cannot reveal whether the influence of career executives at key decision sites has fallen to inappropriate levels. Some analysts believe that this occurred during the Reagan years.[36] Furthermore, career members of the SES sensed an increase in political influence as a result of the Civil Service Reform Act. One survey found that 69 percent of SES respondents adhered to this view. Forty percent went so far as to agree with the statements, "In this organization, SES will cause politics to be more important than expertise."[37] Career SES members who work in Washington appear to be particularly conscious of growing political influence.[38]

These and related perceptions may damage the civil service. Some studies indicate that SES members have become increasingly negative toward the new executive system. One survey found that roughly twice as many senior executives believed the SES had produced a decline in motivation and job satisfaction as held the opposite view. Furthermore, 62 percent thought the SES system reduced job security, while only 2 percent disagreed.[39] Turnover data also raise questions about the new system. As of late 1983, almost thirty-five hundred career and noncareer SES members had left government service since the establishment of the SES in July 1979. Roughly twenty-seven hundred, or well over 70 percent, were career SES. The overwhelming majority of SES members who departed either resigned or retired. Only 9 SES members fell victim to termination of reduction-in-force actions—less than 1 percent. (Some executives may have resigned or taken early retirement rather than face involuntary termination.)[40] Statistics such as these have prompted some analysts to conclude that the SES is primarily a vehicle "for speeding the exit of top managers from government service."[41]

The degree to which the SES per se has precipitated disenchantment and turnover remains an open question. Given negligible pay increases as well as the austerity of the 1980s, executive dissatisfaction might have been just as evident had the SES system never been adopted. The degree to which turnover and negative attitudes about the SES persist over time and the causes of these phenomena constitute an important subject for future research.

Presidential Politicization in Perspective

Presidential politicization of the bureaucracy has its defenders. Richard Nathan argues that it is "desirable . . . for political chief executives to seek to exert greater managerial influence over the bureaucracy." The discretion wielded by the bureaucracy remains too vast and too technical to be understood by ordinary citizens. As a popularly elected official, the president must do his utmost to assure that management tasks "be performed by partisans."[42] In a similar vein, Moe points out that the beneficial effects of "politicization and centralization" have yet to be seriously entertained by students of public administration.[43] Still, politicization entails risks. Carried to an extreme, it can breed disregard for the law. It can lead to an insufficient emphasis on technical competence, thereby undermining the ability of the bureaucracy to assist the president in formulating and implementing policy.

Whatever the exact trade-off involved, the Nixon and Reagan presidencies in particular provide clear evidence of the ability of the White House to shape administrative discretion. To be sure, efforts at control often yield unanticipated consequences. Errors occur. The courts, Congress, interest groups, the bureaucracy, and others often succeed in limiting presidential clout. On balance, however, there is much to be said for the view that if Presidents fail to influence policies, "it is not usually for lack of administrative tools."[44]

Congressional Penetration

The politicization of public administration does not begin and end with efforts by the president and his immediate appointees to influence administrators. Members of Congress and their staffs also seek to shape administrative discretion. One study of federal bureau chiefs asserts that Congress stands at the center of the relationships critical to agencies and describes the chiefs as "constantly looking over their shoulders" for congressional reaction.[45] The legislative liaison offices in the federal departments formally symbolize the importance administrators attach to their relationships with Congress. But these offices comprise only the tip of the iceberg.

Like the president, members of Congress shape administrative discretion with a number of tools. For example, they understand how appointments to key positions can influence administrative discretion. Article II of the Constitution constrains presidential authority by providing for the "advice and consent of the Senate" on the appointment of ambassadors and other officers of government. The number of ambassadorships as well as appointments in cabinet departments and independent agencies subject to this approval approximated seven hundred in the early 1980s.[46]

Congressional efforts to influence executive branch appointments extend beyond advice and consent. Senators and representatives frequently lobby the president to appoint particular individuals. These attempts at influence do not invariably spring from a desire to see administrative discretion exercised in a particular way. A member of Congress may lobby for an appointment purely to reward a generous campaign contributor without much reference to the contributor's stance on pertinent issues. At other times, however, ideological compatibility matters greatly. During the 1980s Senator Jesse Helms of North Carolina sought to influence decisionmaking at the State Department by blocking the appointment of nominees who would be "too soft" in dealing with the communists. Instead, he vigorously advocated the appointment of certain hard-liners.

Members of Congress can shape administrative discretion in other ways. They can threaten to use their authority over budget processes and legislation. They can use their ties to the president, interest groups, or the media. The degree to which these tactics allow Congress to control the bureaucracy depends on many factors. Oversight looms as a particularly important one.

Oversight

The Legislative Reorganization Act of 1946 requires the standing committees of Congress "to exercise continuous watchfulness" over federal agencies. Oversight focuses on what Congress does after it has approved a law rather than what it prescribed in advance in an effort to control those charged with implementation. At its core oversight involves gathering information about agencies or programs and taking steps to correct any problems.

Congressional oversight is at times broad in scope. A Senate committee may, for instance, conduct hearings on whether Medicare payment practices provide incentives for hospitals to discharge elderly patients too rapidly. The committee may find a problem and recommend legislative changes designed to deal with it. On other occasions oversight is narrow. A member of Congress may intervene on behalf of a single constituent who has not received a Social Security check.

Oversight also varies in formality. Formal probes require explicit actions such as holding congressional hearings, requesting a report from the GAO, or sending a letter of inquiry to administrators. Informal probes tend to be less systematic and explicit. For instance, congressional staff members often know civil servants personally and frequently obtain insights at lunch or over the phone. They may also glean information from the newspaper, the evening news, interest groups, or constituents. Responses to information also vary in formality. Members of Congress may act formally, issuing a report or drafting legislation, or rely on confidential conversations with administrators to reach an informal understanding with an agency.

Observers tend to describe oversight as random, unsystematic, or haphazard.[47] In many respects it is; nevertheless, certain decision processes regularly involve programs and agencies in oversight. Agencies' need for an annual appropriation triggers oversight, as does the need to reauthorize programs that have fixed termination dates. So, too, the promulgation of formal rules by the bureaucracy (a notice and proposed rule must be published in the *Federal Register*) often serves as an occasion for congressional scrutiny. For instance, issuing rules concerning food stamps, administrators in the Department of Agriculture on one occasion received two letters, one from six Republican members of a congressional nutrition committee and the other from twenty Democratic liberals. Both letters sought to shape the interpretation of statutory intent concerning eligibility requirements for the program.[48] Given the numerous and subtle kinds of oversight, it is little wonder that precise measurement of it poses enormous methodological problems.

While important, oversight does not represent all of Congress's power or influence over the bureaucracy. Civil servants generally respect the law even in the absence of oversight. Furthermore, the possibility of adverse congressional action may well lead civil servants to defer to the preferences of key members of Congress even if there is little oversight.

Incentives for Oversight.   Congress clearly has a mandate and the resources to conduct oversight, but do its members have an incentive to ride herd on administrators? According to one view, no. From this perspective, a concern with winning reelection encourages members of Congress to spend more time campaigning or working to pass new laws than monitoring programs and shaping the exercise of administrative discretion. To the extent that oversight interests them, it is at the micro rather than the macro level. Casework, which lets members of Congress claim direct credit from individuals for concessions by the bureaucracy, appeals to them more than comprehensive inquiries into implementation.

This vision is too skeptical. Senators and representatives frequently have an incentive to oversee programs. First, some of them wish to become known as policy influentials—as having substantial power over setting a given policy. Senator Sam Nunn of Georgia, for instance, diligently built his expertise in defense policy and became a major and widely respected player in this arena. This reputation helped him in his home state at election time. Second, many legislators nurture ideological convictions about programs. They want them to work well and stand ready to encourage oversight of them. One cannot completely discount ideas and visions of the "good" program and its contribution to the "good" of society. Third, some legislators' staffs constantly search for politically promising issues. If staff members discover problems in the operation of a program, they may be able to get the boss some favorable publicity via oversight activities.[49]

Whatever the importance of these and other incentives, it appears that oversight increased during the 1970s. One analysis reports that from 1968 to 1976 hearings in the House of Representatives quadrupled, and the number in the Senate more than doubled.[50] Congressional staff numbers also more than doubled in the period 1960 to 1974.[51] Aside from these developments, agencies such as the GAO, the Congressional Budget Office, and the Office of Technology Assessment began to play larger roles in the investigation and evaluation of the bureaucracy's activities. All three of these agencies house capable staffs and report directly to Congress.

The proliferation of statutes containing legislative veto provisions also indicates growing congressional interest in shaping administrative discretion. Since 1932 more than two hundred statutes with more than three hundred separate veto provisions have won approval. Well over half of the acts containing vetoes and more than two-thirds of the individual provisions have surfaced since 1969.[52] Veto provisions take many shapes. One form provides Congress with an explicit opportunity to disapprove of a proposed administrative decision before it takes effect. Another requires Congress to approve a proposed regulation before the bureaucracy can effect it. Still another establishes a mandatory waiting period during which Congress can block proposed action through normal legislative processes.

The legislative veto has sparked considerable controversy. Critics contend that it impairs both representative and effective governmental decisionmaking. There is evidence that Congress has used the veto in behalf of interest groups that wanted special treatment under the law. The legislative veto can delay implementation.

Some, however, see considerable merit in the legislative veto. Whatever its benefits, in 1983 the Supreme Court's *Chadha* decision ruled against veto provisions that required the approval of only one house of Congress and by implication the two-house form of legislative veto as well.[53] Nevertheless, the legislative veto continues to play a role. Administrators responsible for implementing statutes containing vetoes have frequently bent over backward to be solicitous to legislators in the wake of the Supreme Court ruling. For example, one administrator from the National Aeronautics and Space Administration wrote to an appropriations committee to suggest that the veto be converted to an informal agreement between his agency and the committee.[54]

Will the impetus for oversight generated in the 1970s persist and grow? Ripley and Franklin argue that "the post-Watergate burst of interest proved to be largely a flash in the pan and did not really lead to a permanent increase in oversight or removal of any of the fundamental barriers to serious oversight. . . . In short, oversight does not come naturally or easily to Congress, and there is no reason to expect that it ever will."[55] Ripley and Franklin may prove perspicacious, but the growth of congressional staffs as well as such agencies as the Office of Technology Assessment, the Congressional Budget Office, and the GAO may institutionalize oversight more than this view allows. Clearly researchers need to trace trends in oversight in the 1980s and 1990s to tackle this question.

Committees and Subcommittees: Molecular Oversight.   To speak of congressional oversight in many respects misleads. The Senate and House of Representatives consist of diverse individuals with varying values and perceptions. Moreover, the congressional committee system substantially determines the structure of oversight. In the Ninety-ninth Congress (1985–1986), the House of Representatives had some 22 standing committees and 5 select committees, which in turn begat 139 subcommittees. The Senate had 16 standing committees and 4 select or special committees that yielded 90 subcommittees.[56] Certain committees hold jurisdiction over all federal agencies. The Senate Committee on Government Affairs and the House Committee on Government Operations have authority to review administrative procedures throughout the federal bureaucracy. Similarly, the House and Senate Appropriations Committees have responsibility for scrutinizing and recommending appropriations for agencies. Besides these committees, an agency faces specific authorization committees that draft and amend laws. Taxation committees—House Ways and Means as well as Senate Finance—have grown more powerful. These committees oversee and exert substantial leverage on the major entitlement programs such as Medicare, Medicaid, and Social Security.

Frequently several committees claim jurisdiction over a single program. In looking back on his days as Secretary of Health, Education, and Welfare under President Carter, Joseph Califano observes that he worked in a world of "molecular politics" where power over his agency was fragmented among a host of particular interests. He notes, "More than forty committees and subcommittees claimed jurisdiction over one or another part of HEW and each month demanded hundreds of hours of testimony and thousands of documents from top departmental appointees."[57]

The ability of committees to influence administrative discretion stems in large part from the deference accorded to their judgments by members of Congress in general. Although committee support cannot guarantee victory for certain measures, failure to obtain such support tends to spell their demise. Moreover, committees have nonstatutory means for influencing agency behavior. Those sympathetic to the food stamp program have often used congressional hearings to publicize regulations or agency actions that seemed likely to hurt recipients. In so doing, they have increased pressure on administrators not to take these actions. Committee reports, which rank high in importance, frequently contain detailed instructions as to what implementing agents can do, and administrators take them very seriously. Unlike statutes, however, these reports are not reviewed and revised on the floor of the Senate or House.

Various empirical analyses testify to the role of committees in shaping administrative discretion. One study of federal grant programs found that when pertinent oversight committees had more liberal members and more liberal chairs, program administrators proved significantly more vigorous in enforcing statutory provisions that required matching funds from state or local governments.[58] Hence, administrators appear to respect the dominant political ideology on oversight committees when they exercise discretion. Another analysis focused on three federal programs that allocated benefits on a geographic basis—military employment, water and sewers grants, and model cities grants. It found that as a rule administrators allocate "disproportionate shares of benefits" to districts and states whose members of Congress sit on a committee with jurisdiction over the program. The analysis goes on to point out that administrators carefully target these extra shares. Rather than reward all members of the appropriations committee, for instance, administrators tend to single out members of pertinent appropriations subcommittees for special treatment.[59]

To assert that congressional committees and subcommittees influence bureaucratic decisions does not mean that administrators invariably give away the store to them. In allocating grants to geographic areas, for instance, "between 10 and 30 percent of allocational decisions may be adjusted [by administrators] in accordance with particular congressmen's preferences."[60] A study of the Federal Trade Commission, an agency concerned with fostering competitive trade practices, found that committees had little influence over the agency unless their requests commanded wide congressional support.[61]

Agencies subject to more oversight committees do not inevitably prove more deferential to Congress. One study of federal energy policy hypothesized that agencies faced with multiple heterogeneous oversight bodies would tend to practice a pluralistic approach in dealing with interest groups. That is, agency officials would sense their vulnerability to criticism and establish numerous flexible relationships with diverse interest groups to obtain wide support. On balance, however, the study found that multiple oversight institutions were "not able to coax the bureaucracy away from its biased and exclusive private contacts," with (primarily) energy producers. Conceivably the proliferation of oversight bodies enabled agencies to play one against another and actually weakened Congress's ability to discipline the bureaucracy.[62]

This finding is consistent with what Dodd and Schott have called the oversight paradox. Their view is that while the proliferation of subcommittees has increased the number of legislators active in oversight and the number of hearings held by Congress, "it has at the same time weakened the ability of Congress to conduct serious oversight and administrative control."[63] In a sense members of Congress have become simultaneously better informed and less influential vis-à-vis the bureaucracy, because a subcommittee attempting to discipline an agency often finds another subcommittee ready to defend it.

Furthermore, when making and maintaining a coalition, administrators often include rank-and-file members of Congress. Civil servants know that the strategic allocation of projects to districts represented by these members of Congress often proves useful in the case of programs that distribute benefits on a geographic basis. Such allocations can encourage friends to continue their support and lure the disaffected to switch sides or mute their opposition.[64]

The development of more collegial processes in Congress may further fuel the tendency of administrators to think beyond immediate committees.[65] A collegial pattern lets all legislators participate in deliberations and decisions. Although Congress remains miles away from the full embodiment of this pattern, reforms in procedures in the 1970s and 1980s, as well as other factors, triggered some movement toward collegial processes. In the House of Representatives, rank-and-file members, including junior members, came to have more opportunities for participation at nearly every stage of the policy process. For instance, meetings of the Democratic Caucus became a forum for influencing policy decisions. Furthermore, the budget committees created by the Congressional Budget and Impoundment Control Act of 1974 sparked floor debates. These debates often permitted a broader cross section of Congress to influence legislative outcomes. Collegial processes tend (for better or for worse) to weaken administrators' incentives to show particular deference to committees as opposed to a broader coalition within Congress. Whether this trend will augment or detract from overall congressional influence on administrative discretion remains an open question.

The changing pattern of congressional dealings with administrative agencies and the increasing number of interest groups concerned with an agency have tended to break down the familiar iron triangles of American politics. No longer can a single committee and a single interest group determine the fate of an agency; the conflict over agencies and programs has expanded. This does not gainsay that some committees and interest groups are much more important to an agency than others. It does acknowledge that the composition of the remaining triangles tends to be of a far more flexible and elastic material than iron.

Casework: Gresham's Law of Oversight?   Like oversight via subcommittees, casework has precipitated concern. Much congressional investigation and action involve one senator or representative intervening for one individual, family, or firm. In the terms of one analyst, Congress serves as the "monopoly supplier of bureaucratic unsticking services."[66] Typically, a constituent complains to the legislator about a certain matter such as denial of eligibility for disability benefits. The legislator intervenes with the bureaucracy to aid the constituent. By one estimate, the offices of more than 90 percent of the members of the House of Representatives handled at least twenty such cases per week; 30 percent handled at least eighty per week.[67] In their capacity as processors of complaints, members of Congress serve as informal ombudsmen.

Why is casework so alluring to legislators? First, it usually does not require them to take a controversial position such as advocating cutbacks in a popular program to reduce the budget deficit. Second, a member of Congress can claim sole responsibility for solving a constituent's problem. Third, assiduous attention to casework tends to help on election day. Data indicate that challengers find the unseating of incumbent representatives to be increasingly difficult. Analysts theorize, and to some degree have demonstrated, that the willingness of representatives to do casework helps account for their growing job security. Partisan ideological issues matter less in House elections; experience and seniority in dealing with the bureaucracy matter more.[68] Of course, casework carries some risks. A representative may be unable to get the bureaucracy to act as the constituent wants, and the constituent may begin angry at the agency and end angry with both the agency and the legislator. On balance, however, casework yields considerable good will for legislators.

Administrators also benefit from casework. To be sure, an official whose agency persistently generates a huge volume of casework may develop a reputation for being a poor manager. More frequently, however, the responsive handling of casework earns credit with legislators. Furthermore, casework can help administrators identify trouble spots in agency operations. An official in the Small Business Administration explained, "We had one loan officer who was perpetually late and who didn't treat constituents properly. The congressmen got some letters, and it got to us. We had to read him out."[69]

Although casework is popular with members of Congress, nagging concerns persist. Casework could conceivably lead to the triumph of Gresham's Law of Oversight, which says that time spent on activity with limited payoffs drives out time devoted to more useful oversight. Attention is siphoned off from the analysis of the overall cost-effectiveness of programs when legislators and their staffs traffic in minutiae. Numerous requests for special investigation of particular cases may also distract officials from more significant activities. In addition, casework can undermine bureaucratic norms of universalism. It can encourage special treatment of or favoritism for individuals. In extreme cases this can lead to the triumph of good-ol'-boy practices whereby administrators violate the letter and the spirit of the law.

The precise degree to which casework spawns these negative effects remains an open question. Limited data and disagreement over appropriate criteria and standards of assessment inhibit a definitive evaluation. However, research has yielded some evidence. One sample of 48 senators and representatives as well as 232 federal administrators revealed a relatively sanguine assessment of casework. Only 26 percent of the elected officials and 20 percent of the administrators perceived that constituency service detracted from "more important things that congressmen and their staffs should be doing." Only 8 percent of the senators and representatives and 22 percent of the civil servants saw casework as detracting from the "efficient running" of executive agencies. About one-third of the administrators claimed that their offices sought to scrutinize incoming congressional requests for casework to uncover policy, program, personnel, or operating weaknesses. Only a handful of elected officials and administrators believed that casework unfairly led to preferential treatment for some citizens.[70] Given the incentives for members of Congress and administrators to perform casework, their perceptions of it may well be overoptimistic, but at a minimum the data reinforce the view that most legislators and administrators find casework to be an attractive form of oversight.

In considering the relevance of Gresham's Law to casework, critics must guard against automatic assumptions that legislators and their staffs would wisely invest any time saved from casework in more productive oversight. Even if members of Congress channel the time saved into other oversight initiatives, the trees-forest problem may persist. For instance, on taking over as chair of the Senate Armed Services Committee in January 1987, Senator Sam Nunn complained that in the past the committee had spent too much time enmeshed in budget detail, "playing congressional Trivial Pursuit, which diverts both congressional and Pentagon attention from the large challenges we face in the national security arena."[71]

Whatever the advantages or disadvantages of casework as a mechanism for oversight, its role in sustaining a sense of political efficacy among the citizenry deserves note. In a democracy filled with large, remote bureaucracies operating complex programs, government probably stands a better chance of sustaining the legitimacy of its authority if citizens believe they can turn to someone outside the bureaucracy for help in dealing with administrators.

Congressional Politicization in Perspective

Specifying the optimal degree of congressional intervention in administrative life remains very difficult. Carried to an extreme, congressional interference in administrative processes can gut the efficiency and effectiveness of government programs. Moreover, it can undermine democratic government. Rather than ensure the representation of broad segments of the public, oversight can serve the needs of certain very narrow interests. Ironically, segments of the Congress may at times become the chief opponents of vigorous administrative efforts to carry out the letter and spirit of a law. For instance, Congress has often proven much more interested in passing tough environmental protection statues than in seeing them vigorously enforced. In short, oversight in its various forms should not be viewed as an unblemished good automatically deserving of praise.

However, almost everyone agrees that the right type and dosage of oversight serve constructive ends. Occasionally oversight leads to repair of a program, enabling administrators to improve cost-effectiveness. Oversight can also foster accountability by deterring civil servants from bending the rules.

Judgments about the appropriate degree of congressional politicization cannot be detached from assessment of the appropriate extent of presidential intervention. The White House and Congress vie for control over administrative discretion. Greater congressional politicization at times undercuts presidential leadership. The issue becomes less Congress's control of the bureaucracy than Congress's control of the President. As the Watergate episode indicates, greater congressional control at times has salutary implications, but on other occasions the virtues of such control are far less obvious.

Assessments of the relative merits of congressional and presidential intervention should not obscure issues concerning the appropriate level of overall politicization. In some cases the country benefits most if administrators exercise discretion with little or no intervention by either the White House or Congress. To be sure, professionals in the bureaucracy often mask the degree to which their decisions rest on certain basic values and on limited knowledge. They understand that if their decisions appear to be technical and they can persuade others of their special expertise, their administrative discretion increases. The professionals become more powerful. This proclivity should not blind citizens to the virtues of professional judgment. For instance, the public interest would probably be ill served if grant awards from the National Institutes of Health for cancer research became highly politicized as a result of presidential or congressional intervention. In these and many other instances, administrative discretion is best left to the "experts."

Generic Politicization

Although much public administration is routine, it requires gamesmanship and strategy. The strategies used in agency life point to a kind of politicization not fully addressed by ideas of politics as discretion or as intervention by elected officials. Generic politics aims at acquiring and using resources to obtain some desired outcome when there is disagreement about appropriate action.[72] It refers to conflicts within or among organizations over budgets, authority, turf, personnel, and other matters. These conflicts vary widely in intensity and numbers of participants.

While generic politics implies administrative discretion, the exercise of such discretion need not imply generic politics. A physician may make highly discretionary judgments concerning eligibility for federal disability payments, but these need not involve disagreement or conflict with others. So, too, generic politics need not imply the active participation of elected officials and their direct appointees. Considerable infighting can occur within or among various federal agencies. At times tension and conflict erupt between professional groups. Economists and lawyers at the Federal Trade Commission bring markedly different perspectives to decisions about which antitrust cases the agency should pursue.[73] As the term *generic* implies, this form of politics can occur in many different organizational settings, including private entities.

Generic bureaucratic politics usually requires five major conditions, which are more or less present in various government agencies over time. First, those concerned with an agency's performance must disagree about ends or means or both. Given the importance of administrative decisions for who gets what from government and the uncertainty that often characterizes the best means to achieve a particular end (for instance the most effective strategies for reducing welfare dependency), disagreement tends to flourish within federal administrative agencies.

Second, the participants must be interdependent. The way in which officials in one agency exercise their discretion must affect the activities of other agencies. Otherwise, other players have little reason to care about the decisions of the agency. The interdependence of federal agencies increased during the 1960s and 1970s as the number of programs multiplied, which spawned a growing tendency for agencies' jurisdictions to overlap.[74] For instance, the Environmental Protection Agency applied pressure on another federal organization, the Tennessee Valley Authority, to reduce the pollution from its utility plants.[75] Overlapping jurisdictions often generate conflict, as administrators must build coalitions. Bargaining, compromise, and sometimes impasse result.

The third requirement is scarcity. If the pie is huge, each participant can get a piece without having to fight about it. Coalitions of agency officials, key members of Congress, and interest group representatives found it easier to escape attention and generic politics before the massive budget deficits of the 1980s. The need to watch every dollar sporadically prompts challenges to iron triangles.

Fourth, generic politics usually requires that officials see a particular issue as important. Individuals hold many views but can act on only a few of them. Relatively unimportant objectives may not seem worth fighting about. However, in considering this precondition, one should not assume that administrators define important issues as those which address the most critical government policies. For instance Califano recalls an "attempted parking putsch" by another agency.[76]

> In early 1977, the General Services Administration sought to take over allocation of precious parking spaces in HEW's headquarters building. After bickering for a year, GSA issued parking permits, claiming jurisdiction. I told Fred Bohen to ignore the action and continue to allocate parking spaces from HEW. On December 7, 1978, Administrator Jay Solomon called me to say that if we issued HEW permits, he

would send armed GSA guards to prevent holders from entering the garage the next morning. Astonished, I told Solomon he had no authority to do so and directed Bohen to go forward. The next day, GSA guards let the cars with HEW permits enter the garage to park, and the GSA aide who prompted Solomon to make his call apologized. . .

Finally, generic politics tends to flourish when power is widely dispersed. If one set of participants monopolizes resources, those who hold contrary views often refuse to fight even if the issue is important; the willingness to fight declines as the prospects for victory diminish. More than any other single condition, the substantial fragmentation of authority in the American political system contributes to the generic politicization of public administration. Not only do Congress and the president compete with each other for control of administrative discretion, the extensive reliance on third parties (other levels of government, private firms) to implement programs diffuses power.

Consider the dynamics unleashed when Congress asks state governments to implement grant-in-aid programs. State officials typically want the federal funds but seek to maximize their discretion in spending them. Federal officials adhere more readily to the view that he who pays the piper should call the tune. In attempting to resolve these and related tensions, federal administrators can seldom rely exclusively on hierarchical authority. Although they often have the right to cut off funds if state officials fail to comply with federal requirements, they have powerful incentives not to do so. Such action typically prompts bitter protest from state elected officials to the White House and Congress. Moreover, the very people federal administrators wish to help (e.g., the poor in the case of welfare programs) are hurt by fund cutoffs. Thus, federal administrators and state officials usually bargain and compromise to reconcile their differences.[77] Hierarchical authority is a limited means of control in a bureaucracy. With administration by proxy, the authority of the hierarchy weakens further.

Developments over the last quarter century have further fueled centrifugal tendencies. Two trends in particular have played an important role in this regard: the rise of court activism and the proliferation of interest groups.

Increasing Assertiveness of Courts

The courts' assertiveness is one of the major forces adding to centrifugal tendencies in the American political system. Since the New Deal federal courts have assumed administrative discretion. As a result, a broader array of interests secured representation in administrative decisions. Part of the trend toward judicial activism involved liberalization of rules concerning who has standing before the courts. In the late 1960s and early 1970s, the Supreme Court under Chief Justice Earl Warren relaxed the rules governing who could bring a suit in federal court, thereby permitting a wider range of litigation. Congress also drafted laws assuring groups access to judges, and representatives of various interests have not passed up these opportunities. Environmental groups, for instance, have frequently sued for tougher implementation of clean air laws.

An increased willingness to second-guess agencies characterizes judicial activism. Under the guise of reviewing agency decisionmaking procedures, the courts have increased pressure on administrators to justify their choices, compelling administrators to listen to all interested parties and to enter the viewpoints of these parties in official records. So, too, the courts have pushed administrators to accumulate a large volume of evidence and to indicate formally the rationale for their decisions. Even then, judges often overturn agency choices. As if these developments were not sufficient, courts have steadily expanded the liability of individual officials for their actions. Citizens who believe that administrators have violated their constitutional rights may sue individual civil servants for money on grounds of constitutional torts.

Judicial activism extends well beyond the Supreme Court; district and appellate courts also play pivotal roles. The Supreme Court itself hears approximately 150 cases per term. The twelve district courts of appeal, staffed by more than 130 judges, hear many more cases and often are the final arbiters in disputes concerning administrative agencies. Appellate courts review appeals of the decisions of federal district courts. They also review certain decisions of administrative agencies. In 1983, the various courts of appeal heard over three thousand administrative cases, about 10 percent of their total work load. The number of administrative cases handled by appellate courts nearly tripled from 1963 to 1983.[78]

Appellate, or circuit, courts are not all equal in importance to administrators. Given their proximity to federal agencies, judges in the District of Columbia hear disproportionate numbers of cases involving administrative matters. Which court hears a case is often a strategic matter. Various groups sense that a certain court will be more sympathetic to them than another. Hence, a key concern is to get a case before the "right" court. At times this literally leads to a race to the courthouse. For instance, business groups and labor unions often sue OSHA when the agency promulgates rules. Union leaders push for tough standards to promote workplace safety while business leaders decry heavy costs. Since the first party to file a legal petition can determine which court hears the case, business and labor groups have refined various strategies for quickly getting to their favorite courts, including open telephone lines, two-way radios, and runners.

As this suggests, the federal court system is decentralized. Various judges bring various perspectives to an issue. This spawns inconsistencies in rulings, heightening complexity and uncertainty for federal executives. Furthermore, the same court may over time issue inconsistent rulings. Court intervention under the Clean Air Act vividly testifies to one form of inconsistency—what Melnick calls the dualism syndrome.[79] At the prodding of environmentalists, courts have persistently pushed the Environmental Protection Agency toward tougher standards for air quality. Simultaneously they have been responsive to suits brought by business interests that complain about the draconian implications of enforcing these clean air standards, for example, that plants would close and jobs be lost. In essence, the dualism syndrome prevails where government promises much by way of formal standards and delivers relatively little by way of enforcement.

The case of the Clean Air Act also indicates two of the major ways for courts to pressure agencies. One is to limit government, as by delaying or weakening enforcement. The other is to push administrators to act boldly—to adopt broad interpretations of statutes, for instance stringent clean air standards.

The forays of federal courts into administrative arenas have given rise to new metaphors. The term *iron triangle* describes coalitions between interest groups, agencies, and congressional committees. In the wake of increased judicial activism, some observers see the rise of a *new iron triangle* consisting of the agency, the interest group, and the courts, with Congress relegated to a lesser position.[80] Others refer to an "iron rectangle" of the courts and the three traditional elements.[81] As the discussion of issue networks in a prior chapter suggests, notions of triangles and rectangles fail to allow for the permeability and unpredictability of administrative processes. Nonetheless, the new metaphors appropriately suggest that administrators may be quite pleased with court intervention. At times the courts provide officials with the authorization to do what they want to do. In the case of the Environmental Protection Agency, court challenges have prompted the creation of new bureaucratic units and contributed to growth in the size and influence of the agency's Office of General Counsel.[82]

Although the courts have become major players in administrative arenas, one should not assume a relentless march toward ever greater judicial activism. The Supreme Court under Chief Justice Warren Burger placed more restrictions on the access of groups to the courts. Moreover, the Burger court showed greater sensitivity to the costs of imposing due process requirements on agencies. Judges became somewhat more willing to defer to the expertise of civil servants in reviewing administrative decisions and in limiting the scope of remedial orders.[83] However, court intervention did not massively retreat during the 1980s. By continuing to fuel the dispersion of power, the courts contribute to the generic politicization of administrative processes.

Proliferation of Interest Groups

Chapter 3 noted the substantial increase in groups and institutions seeking representation in Washington over the past quarter of a century. This development contributes to the greater dispersal of power and in all probability to generic politicization.

Interest groups differ considerably in the degree to which they pressure the bureaucracy. Two characteristics seem pivotal in this regard.[84] First, groups with money and staff expend a greater share of their lobbying effort on administrative processes. Organizations with fewer resources disproportionately emphasize congressional strategies because the costs of mounting a comprehensive lobbying effort in Congress will probably be less than in agencies. To have much effect in the administrative arena, a group typically must influence a cluster of administrative decisions, whereas success in shaping a single decision in Congress can yield substantial benefits. Applying pressure on administrators may also require more technical expertise than exerting influence on Congress.

Second, the behavior of groups varies according to whether they primarily represent broad purposive or ideological concerns (e.g., Common Cause) as distinguished from narrower economic interests (e.g., lobbies representing oil companies). Publicity and drama are the lifeblood of purposive groups, attracting and sustaining a membership base, and with it money. Since the media usually devote much more attention to congressional decisions than to administrative ones, purposive groups gravitate toward this arena. In contrast, representatives of economic interests usually can count on support independent of the media attention they receive. In fact, the limited media coverage of administrative decisions may be to their advantage.

These broad patterns should not be construed to mean that wealthy groups representing concentrated economic interests inevitably dominate administrative politics. Civil servants may resist such pressures out of either commitment to the public interest or deference to the president, Congress, or other interest groups.

Furthermore, agencies differ in the interest group configurations they face. Contexts vary in terms of the number of groups that focus on administrators, the heterogeneity of the value preferences represented by these groups and the resources they possess. Where agencies confront heterogeneous groups with relatively equal resources, executives may play one off against the other. ("I'd like to help you, but I also have to consider the concerns of X. My hands are tied.") This heterogeneity can take its toll, as agency administrators may be damned if they do and damned if they don't. For example, OSHA faces interest groups dominated by unions and businesses. These two groups sharply disagree about the proper role of the agency. Business favors less stringent safety and health standards as well as sympathetic enforcement, and unions want the opposite. At any given time, officials at OSHA can count on either or both groups' displeasure with their performance. The constant criticism from these factions has undermined support for the agency among the public and within Congress. More homogeneous groups often get along better and allow administrators to reach a modus vivendi. However, cooperation can carry a high price. An interest group may succeed in capturing an agency to serve its own narrow purpose rather than a broader one.

Although interest groups at times dominate an agency, pressure can go the other way as well. Administrators are not the passive recipients of requests; they seek out groups that will support actions they wish to take. At times such groups primarily serve the interests of administrators rather than the reverse. Whatever the balance of influence between group and agency, the proliferation of interest groups has introduced new uncertainties and strategic challenges into the lives of administrators.

The Balance Sheet

The forces fueling the generic politicization of administrative processes could ebb. For instance, courts may retreat from behavior which has heightened the influence of a broad spectrum of groups in administrative decisions. Power would more readily become concentrated in the hands of fewer participants. Barring major constitutional reform, however, the institutions of American government will continue to guarantee a substantial dispersion of authority and influence.

Generic politicization need not be dysfunctional. Conflict in an administrative arena often yields far more sensible outcomes than would neat, frictionless processes. In fact, one study of the Federal Trade Commission concludes that conflict between lawyers and economists over which antitrust cases to pursue "has resulted in more thoughtful decisions."[85] Conflict can challenge basic assumptions; it can clarify the consequences of a course of action; it can counteract the tendency to transform questions of values into technical issues for professionals to resolve.

But if generic politicization has positive aspects, it sometimes produces undesirable outcomes. Great dispersion of power often inflates the costs of supporting a decision. Administrators and others may spend much energy jockeying for position or negotiating while making little progress in implementing a program. Moreover, the decisions reached through politics may emphasize the lowest common denominator. Attempts to please everyone rarely please anyone; they may reflect little creativity and undermine efficiency. The dispersion of power may prevent any change at all, creating a sense of being waist-deep in the Big Muddy. As Charles Lindblom has observed, "American and Western European politics suffer from serious problem-solving difficulties. One, especially pronounced in the U.S., is the dispersion of veto powers throughout the political system." The structure of veto powers can make even incremental steps difficult.[86] Failure to do anything about problems, or compromise solutions that do little to ameliorate them, can contribute to failure of programs and declining confidence in government. Various surveys indicate that Americans sustain considerable respect for the country's basic political institutions, but their confidence in government's ability to deal effectively with society's key problems has declined.[87]

Conclusion

The relationship between politics and administration is a giant part of the intellectual legacy of public administration, both as an academic field of inquiry and in practice. Well before the time of Woodrow Wilson, the framers of the Constitution considered the difficulties presented by the relationship. Since Wilson's time the debate has persisted. Despite perceptive analyses of the subject, discussions of politics and administration often prove less than gratifying. Students of the subject frequently talk past one another. One senses only modest progress in either empirical or normative theory concerning the relationship between politics and administration. In part this spinning of wheels occurs because participants bring different and often unstated definitions of politicization to these debates. In part it springs from diverging perceptions about decision processes in government agencies. For instance, one observer concludes that the Reagan administration greatly politicized the Environmental Protection Agency, while another marvels at how little influence the White House had. Beyond these factors, the debate emanates from disagreements about basic values such as efficiency as opposed to accountability or representation.

This chapter has taken a preliminary step toward sorting out some of the definitions people have in their heads when they discuss administrative politics. At times, the political character of administration refers to the fact that laws grant administrators substantial formal discretion to choose a course of action. Administrators in this broad sense cannot be neutral. They exert influence; they shape who gets what from government, when, and how. In other instances, politicization refers to the fact that elected officials and their staffs influence the way civil servants wield discretion. Finally, generic politicization is more or less present in all kinds of organizations—government, business firms, churches, athletic associations, and more. Such politicization exists to the degree that participants in an administrative arena differ about ends, means, or both, and engage in conflict.

Claims that administrative processes have become politicized demand as a first response, "In what sense?" Once this is clear, exceedingly difficult issues of measurement remain. For example, many suggest that President Reagan exerted more presidential influence and control over agency operations than his predecessors. But how much more and in what ways? What accounts for variations in the degree to which presidential politicization occurs? If analysts learn to calibrate the phenomena, understanding of the effects of politics on the effectiveness, efficiency, and accountability of government will improve and the trade-offs will become clearer.

Systematic empirical investigation of politicization will not stop debate on fundamental normative issues. How important is the enduring health of administrative agencies relative to the President's need for responsiveness from them? If certain forms of politicization yield higher levels of representation and due process but undercut efficiency, how should the trade-offs be struck? As these questions suggest, the relationship between politics and administration seems destined to remain on the front burner for students, practitioners, and other observers of public administration.

Notes

1. Richard J. Stillman, II, "Woodrow Wilson and 'The Study of Administration': A New Look at an Old Essay," *American Political Science Review* 67 (June 1973): 582–88. The essay, published in 1887, was reprinted in 1941; see Woodrow Wilson, "The Study of Administration," *Political Science Quarterly* 61 (December 1941): 481–506.
2. Wilson, "The Study of Administration," 493–95.
3. See Dwight Waldo, *The Administrative State* (New York: Ronald Press, 1948), 106–10.
4. See, for example, Frederick W. Taylor, *The Principles of Scientific Management* (New York: W. W. Norton, 1967).
5. Charles T. Goodsell, *The Case For Bureaucracy* (Chatham, NJ: Chatham House, 1983), 67.
6. Waldo, *The Administrative State;* and Paul H. Appleby, *Policy and Administration* (University, Alabama: University of Alabama Press, 1949).
7. Wilson, "The Study of Administration," 496–97.
8. Stillman, "Woodrow Wilson and the Study of Administration," 586.
9. This definition draws in part from Kenneth C. Davis, *Discretionary Justice* (Urbana: University of Illinois Press, 1976), 4.
10. In some societies administrators can rapidly modify the legal superstructure whenever they wish, or ignore it. Such discretion goes much beyond that described here.
11. Paul Sabatier and Daniel Mazmanian, "The Conditions of Effective Implementation: A Guide to Accomplishing Policy Objectives," *Policy Analysis* 5 (Fall 1979): 481–504.
12. Jeffrey M. Berry, *Feeding Hungry People: Rulemaking in the Food Stamp Program* (New Brunswick, NJ: Rutgers University Press, 1984).
13. See Phillip J. Cooper, "By Order of the President: Administration by Executive Order and Proclamation," *Administration and Society* 18 (August 1986): 233–62.
14. Ronald Randall, "Presidential Power versus Bureaucratic Intransigence: The Influence of the Nixon Administration on Welfare Policy," *American Political Science Review* 73 (September 1979): 795–810.
15. Richard P. Nathan, *The Plot That Failed: Nixon and the Administrative Presidency* (New York: John Wiley, 1975), 51.

16. Richard P. Nathan, *The Administrative Presidency* (New York: John Wiley, 1983), 93; see also Francis E. Rourke, "Grappling with the Bureaucracy," in Arnold J. Meltsner, ed., *Politics and the Oval Office: Towards Presidential Governance* (San Francisco: Institute for Contemporary Studies, 1981), 123–40.

17. The data were obtained via a phone interview with an official from the Office of Personnel Management, April 1985.

18. Huge Heclo, *A Government of Strangers* (Washington, DC: The Brookings Institution, 1977), 1.

19. Roger G. Brown, "Party and Bureaucracy: From Kennedy to Reagan," *Political Science Quarterly* 97 (Summer 1982): 279–94.

20. Joseph A. Califano, Jr., *Governing America* (New York: Simon and Schuster, 1981), 16.

21. Nathan, *The Plot That Failed,* 49.

22. Nathan, *The Administrative Presidency,* 89–90.

23. Laurence E. Lynn, Jr., *Managing the Public's Business* (New York: Basic Books, 1981), 61.

24. Heclo, *A Government of Strangers,* 171–72.

25. Laurence E. Lynn, Jr., "The Reagan Administration and the Renitent Bureaucracy," in Lester M. Salamon and Michael S. Lund, eds., *The Reagan Presidency and the Governing of America* (Washington, DC: Urban Institute, 1984), 360.

26. Ibid., 362.

27. Ibid., 339; see also Terry M. Moe, "The Politicized Presidency," in John E. Chubb and Paul E. Peterson, eds., *The New Direction in American Politics* (Washington, DC: The Brookings Institution, 1985), 258–59.

28. Nathan, *The Administrative Presidency,* 74.

29. U.S. General Accounting Office, *A 2-Year Appraisal of Merit Pay in Three Agencies* (Washington, DC: GAO/GGD-84-1, 1984), 2.

30. In fiscal 1983 OPM allocated 8,243 slots, of which about 95 percent were subsequently established by the agencies. Eleven percent of the established slots remained unfilled. See U.S. General Accounting Office, *Testimony of the Comptroller General on the Impact of the Senior Executive Service* (Washington, DC: GAO/GGD-84-32, 1983); Appendix, 3.

31. White House Personnel Office, "The Malek Manual," in Frank J. Thompson, ed., *Classics of Public Personnel Policy* (Oak Park, IL: Moore, 1979), 182–183.

32. Richard L. Cole and David A. Caputo, "Presidential Control of the Senior Civil Service: Assessing the Strategies of the Nixon Years," *American Political Science Review* 73 (June 1979): 339–413.

33. U.S. General Accounting Office, *Testimony of the Comptroller General,* 8–9; Appendix, 26.

34. Ibid.

35. Ibid., 10–11; Appendix, 31–32. See also Edie N. Goldenberg, "The Permanent Government in an Era of Retrenchment and Redirection," in *The Reagan Presidency and the Governing of America,* 394–97.

36. See, for instance, Chester A. Newland, "A Mid-Term Appraisal—The Reagan Presidency: Limited Government and Political Administration," *Public Administration Review* 43 (January-February, 1983): 1–21.

37. Patricia Ingraham and Peter W. Colby, "Political Reform and Government Management: The Case of the Senior Executive Service," *Policy Studies Journal* 11 (December 1982): 308–10.

38. Peter S. Ring and James L. Perry, "Reforming the Upper Levels of the Bureaucracy: A Longitudinal Study of the Senior Executive Service," *Administration and Society* 15 (May 1983): 133–34.

39. Ingraham and Colby, "Political Reform and Government Management," 308, 311.
40. U.S. General Accounting Office, *Testimony of the Comptroller General*, 2, 5; Appendix, 6; see also Goldenberg, "The Permanent Government," 398–402.
41. Ingraham and Colby, "Political Reform and Government Management," 315.
42. Nathan, *The Administrative Presidency*, 1, 7.
43. Moe, "The Politicized Presidency," 267–68.
44. Randall, "Presidential Power," 808.
45. Herbert Kaufman, *The Administrative Behavior of Federal Bureau Chiefs* (Washington, DC: The Brookings Institution, 1981), 47.
46. John W. Macy et al., *America's Unelected Government: Appointing the President's Team* (Cambridge: Ballinger, 1983), 6.
47. See, for instance, Lawrence C. Dodd and Richard L. Schott, *Congress and the Administrative State* (New York: John Wiley, 1979), 170; and Randall B. Ripley and Grace A. Franklin, *Congress, the Bureaucracy, and Public Policy* (Homewood, IL: Dorsey, 1984), 248.
48. Berry, *Feeding Hungry People*, 73.
49. Ibid., 116.
50. John E. Chubb, *Interest Groups and the Bureaucracy* (Stanford, CA: Stanford University Press, 1983), 47.
51. Morris P. Fiorina, *Congress: Keystone of the Washington Establishment* (New Haven: Yale University Press, 1977), 58.
52. This discussion draws heavily on William West and Joseph Cooper, "The Congressional Veto and Administrative Rulemaking," *Political Science Quarterly* 98 (Summer 1983): 285–304.
53. *Immigration and Naturalization Service* v. *Chadha*, 462 U.S. 919 (1983).
54. *Congressional Quarterly Weekly Report* 44 (6 December 1986), 3026.
55. Ripley and Franklin, *Congress, the Bureaucracy, and Public Policy*, 252.
56. Jodie Scheiber, ed., *Congressional Yellow Book: 1986 Election Special Edition* (Washington, DC: Monitor Publishing, November 1986).
57. Califano, *Governing America*, 23.
58. John E. Chubb, "The Political Economy of Federalism," *American Political Science Review* 79 (December 1985): 994–1015.
59. R. Douglas Arnold, *Congress and the Bureaucracy* (New Haven: Yale University Press, 1979), 207–08.
60. Ibid., 214–15.
61. Robert A. Katzman, *Regulatory Bureaucracy: The Federal Trade Commission and Antitrust Policy* (Cambridge, MA: MIT Press, 1981), 155.
62. Chubb, *Interest Groups and the Bureaucracy*, 262.
63. Dodd and Schott, *Congress and the Administrative State*, 173; see also 170–84.
64. Arnold, *Congress and the Bureaucracy*, 208.
65. Seven S. Smith, "New Patterns of Decisionmaking in Congress," in *The New Direction in American Politics*, 203–33.
66. Fiorina, *Congress: Keystone of the Washington Establishment*, 42–43.
67. Bruce E. Cain et al., "The Constituency Service Basis of the Personal Vote for U.S. Representatives and British Members of Parliament," *American Political Science Review* 78 (March 1984): 115.
68. See, for instance, ibid.
69. John R. Johannes, "Congress, the Bureaucracy, and Casework," *Administration and Society* 16 (May 1984): 55.
70. Ibid.
71. *Atlanta Constitution*, 13 January 1987, 1A.
72. This conceptualization and the subsequent discussion of the conditions of politics

draws heavily from Jeffrey Pfeffer, *Power in Organizations* (Marshfield, MA: Pitman, 1984). See also Douglas Yates, Jr., *The Politics of Management* (San Francisco: Jossey-Bass, 1985).

73. Katzman, *Regulatory Bureaucracy.*

74. Rourke, "Grappling with the Bureaucracy," 139.

75. See Robert Durant, *When Government Regulates Itself* (Knoxville: University of Tennessee Press, 1985).

76. Califano, *Governing America,* 45–46.

77. Helen Ingram, "Policy Implementation through Bargaining: The Case of Federal Grants-in-Aid," *Public Policy* 25 (Fall 1977): 499–526.

78. Robert A. Carp and Ronald Stidham, *The Federal Courts* (Washington: Congressional Quarterly, 1985), 42.

79. See R. Shep Melnick, *Regulation and the Courts: The Case of the Clean Air Act* (Washington, DC: The Brookings Institution, 1983).

80. Martin M. Shapiro, "The Presidency and the Federal Courts," in *Politics and the Oval Office,* 142.

81. R. Shep Melnick, "The Politics of Partnership," *Public Administration Review* 45 (November 1985): 658.

82. Melnick, *Regulation and the Courts,* 378.

83. See Phillip J. Cooper, "Conflict or Constructive Tension: The Changing Relationship of Judges and Administrators," *Public Administration Review* 45 (November 1985): 643–652.

84. Chubb, *Interest Groups and the Bureaucracy,* 256–260.

85. Katzman, *Regulatory Bureaucracy,* 54.

86. Charles E. Lindblom, "Still Muddling, Not Yet Through," *Public Administration Review* 39 (November-December 1979): 520.

87. Seymour Martin Lipset and William Schneider, "The Decline of Confidence in American Institutions," *Political Science Quarterly* 98 (Fall 1983): 401.

Chapter Six

Politics and Public Budgeting

———
———

Introduction

As various groups and individuals struggle to promote their vision of desirable ends and means through government, the budgetary process assumes enormous importance. More than a quarter of a century ago, Aaron Wildavsky observed:[1]

> The victories and defeats, the compromises and the bargains, the realms of agreement and the spheres of conflict in regard to the role of the national government in our society all appear in the budget. In the most integral sense the budget lies at the heart of the political process.

Public administrators understand the importance of budget season, when the amount of money they receive for specific functions will substantially determine their activities and priorities for the coming year and perhaps for many years to come. The budgetary process provides a mechanism for allocating available resources among many competing purposes.

Public budgeting addresses two basic and intermingled sets of questions. One set involves system-level allocation between the public and the private sectors (see Chapter 2). In principle all resources in the society are available to government, although in the United States any politician pointing that out would risk a short term in office. Critical questions nonetheless persist. How many activities or problems justify government intervention into the economy? Can the best interests of the society be better served by retaining money for consumption and investment in private hands while allowing a beneficial public program to go unfunded? Or do the equity, equality, and economic growth produced by a public project justify the use of political capital by government officials to pass and collect an additional tax or to increase an existing tax to fund that public program? Just how big should government be?[2]

In the past half century, the absolute size of the budget has become an important consideration for policymakers seeking to manage the economy. With the Keynesian "revolution" in public finance, the amount of public expenditure, especially relative to the amount of public revenue, became the principal means by which government sought to influence economic growth, inflation, and unemployment.[3] Although the stagflation of the 1970s reduced faith in the Keynesian approach, policymakers still view the budget and other dimensions of fiscal policy as important tools for influencing the health of the economy. For example, while the supply-side economists of the Reagan presidency rejected aspects of Keynesian theory, they saw tax reductions as essential to economic growth and ultimately to enhanced revenues.

The second major set of budgeting questions concerns the allocation of available resources to specific programs. Which social programs deserve how much support? Which military programs warrant substantial funding? How should defense be balanced against social needs? Because money can be divided almost infinitely, it offers a medium for the resolution of conflicts—for grounding more abstract discussions of competing social values. Public administrators, members of Congress, the president, interest groups, the courts, and others enter the fray that determines where the balance will be struck.

This chapter focuses on selected aspects of budgeting as they pertain to public administration. The first section notes some central characteristics of the budget, and the second explores the dynamics of the annual budget cycle. A third section probes some of the challenges and problems posed by contemporary budgeting practices. The chapter then discusses a phenomenon integral to budgetary processes—incrementalism. Decrementalism, a process more in evidence in the 1980s, also receives attention. Finally, this chapter assesses the perennial quest for budget reform.

Characteristics of the Federal Budget

To understand the political process that shapes the federal budget each year requires clarification of certain characteristics of the budget itself. The federal budget is an executive document that emphasizes line items and substantially follows an annual cycle.[4]

An Executive Budget

Although Congress shapes the contours of the budget, it is an executive document in key respects. The president and his staff prepare the budget, work to obtain its approval in Congress, and join with other members of the executive branch in implementing it. The president has not always played so central a role. Until 1921 the budget was prepared almost entirely in Congress and then given to the president to be executed. This practice honored the principle of congressional supremacy in taxing and spending articulated in Article I, Section 8 of the Constitution. Reformers believed that the practice undercut planned, coordinated, and coherent financial decisionmaking. In the wake of the substantial federal deficits incurred during World War I, this concern and an intensified desire for fiscal prudence helped to pass the Budget and Accounting Act of 1921. Thenceforth departments forwarded spending estimates to the Bureau of the Budget, which became the major budgetary arm of the executive. Congress could not approve an appropriation unless the president had reviewed it.

The Budget and Accounting Act of 1921 helped to galvanize conflict between the executive and legislative branches over their respective roles in the budgetary process. Since that time power has tended to shift toward the executive branch, particularly the Executive Office of the President, in large part because of the analytical dominance of the Office of Management and Budget (OMB), called the Bureau of the Budget until 1971. The excesses of the Nixon administration and to some degree those of the Johnson administration during the Vietnam War led to the passage of the Congressional Budget and Impoundment Control Act of 1974.

Among other things, this law created the Congressional Budget Office (CBO) and established a budget committee in each house of Congress. The new committees substantially bolstered the expertise of Congress on budget matters. The analytical capacity of the CBO matched that of the executive branch. Severe disagreements between the legislative and executive branches over budgetary priorities in the later years of the Reagan presidency prompted Congress to create a statement of its own budget priorities in advance, rather than merely wait for the initiation to come from the White House. Further, the necessity of passing budget resolutions each year requires Congress to pay greater attention to the aggregates of public expenditure and revenue than it had under earlier budgeting systems. Thus, Congress must now make macro as well as micro decisions. Despite all these changes, the 1974 Budget Act has not achieved all that was intended for it, and Congress largely continues to respond to presidential initiatives in the budgetary process.[5]

Line Item

Despite several attempts at reform, the federal budget remains a line-item budget. That is, the final budget document appropriating funds allocates those funds to categories (see Exhibit 6.1) such as wages and salaries, supplies, travel, equipment, and so forth. These traditional categories are extremely useful for Congress, in that they allow a substantial measure of control over expenditures. Money is appropriated for specific purposes within agencies and programs, and Congress, through the GAO, can make sure that the money is being spent under legal authority. It is more difficult to determine whether the money is being spent efficiently and effectively. In fact, a line-item budget may be an impediment to accounting for cost-effectiveness. A federal manager who determines that the goals of the organization could be better reached by using money differently may be prevented from doing so by the demands of the budgeting system. To be sure, an executive can find legal ways to transfer resources from one line to another (see below), but more flexibility in allocations in the first instance would often improve the efficiency of federal agencies.

An Annual Budget

In principle the federal budget is an annual budget. To be sure, agencies must submit five-year expenditure forecasts, but this is primarily for management purposes within OMB. The budget and appropriations constitute only an annual expenditure plan. The annual budget may present a number of problems for budgeters and managers. First, it tends to ignore the long-range implications of expenditure decisions made in any one year. A small expenditure now may result in much larger

EXHIBIT 6.1   Example of Line-Item Budget

Operation of the National Park System
Object Classification

Identification code 14-1036—0-1-303	1986 actual	1987 est.	1988 est.
NATIONAL PARK SERVICE	(in thousands of dollars)		
Direct obligations:			
Personnel compensation:			
11.1 Full-time permanent	264,649	278,793	291,594
11.3 Other than full-time permanent	59,865	69,003	71,450
11.5 Other personnel compensation	17,292	17,400	17,400
11.8 Special personnel services payment.................	351	—	—
11.9 Total personnel compensation	342,157	365,196	380,444
12.1 Personnel benefits: Civilian	53,740	61,433	79,751
13.0 Benefits for former personnel	7,383	8,850	8,850
21.0 Travel and transportation of persons	11,799	12,042	14,350
22.0 Transportation of things	8,954	9,678	10,003
23.1 Rental payments to GSA	12,865	13,500	14,000
23.2 Rental payments to others	1,148	1,157	1,180
23.3 Communications, utilities, and miscellaneous charges ...	25,736	28,357	31,010
24.0 Printing and reproduction	3,480	3,650	3,884
25.0 Other services	84,542	90,041	92,507
26.0 Supplies and materials................................	42,847	45,853	48,290
31.0 Equipment..	17,497	22,283	25,315
32.0 Lands and structures	2,536	3,028	3,230
33.0 Investments and loans	3	2	2
41.0 Grants, subsidies, and contributions	2,388	8,488	1,816
42.0 Insurance claims and indemnities	205	211	210
43.0 Interest and dividends	4	2	2
99.0 Subtotal, direct obligations, National Park Service	617,283	673,771	714,844
99.0 Reimbursable obligations, National Park Service	2,208	2,174	2,214

Source: Office of Management and Budget. *Budget of the United States Government, Fiscal Year 1988* (Washington, DC: Government Printing Office, 1987).

expenditures later, by creating clienteles that cannot be eliminated without substantial political repercussions.

For federal managers, the problem may be exactly the opposite, as they cannot necessarily depend upon continued funding to keep their programs running year after year. This is especially troublesome for capital expenditures; half a dam is of very little use. Further, difficulties in retaining spending authority from year to year mean that managers often have to spend all of their budget by the end of the fiscal year; this encourages spending decisions they would not otherwise make.

Practical problems prevent the federal budget from actually being annual. Congress often fails to complete work on all the appropriations bills in time for the beginning of the new fiscal year, or even prior to the adjournment of the congressional session, usually in December. This was particularly true in the Reagan administration, when conflicts over budgetary priorities and over funding for highly sensitive programs exacerbated tensions between the White House and Congress as well as between the two houses of Congress.

Since Congress often approves only a small proportion of all appropriations bills before the new fiscal year begins, agencies often receive their funding through continuing resolutions. Typically these measures allow the agencies to continue spending money at the previous year's level until Congress and the president act on a new appropriations bill. In 1987 no budget bills were passed before adjournment, and the government ran on a continuing resolution of some $576 billion. From the mid-1970s to the 1980s the length of continuing resolutions grew substantially—from approximately five pages to an average of a hundred. The resolutions at times were vehicles for modifying existing programs through references to authorizing legislation. In an increasingly fractious budgetary milieu, continuing resolutions became a vehicle for carrying on the struggle over spending and programs in another guise.[6]

Other factors also fueled a decline in annual budgeting. Supplemental appropriations are a significant proportion of the spending of many departments, so that the budgetary process appears to be almost continuous rather than an annual decision. OMB, which used to protect agencies from sudden reductions after approval of the budget, abandoned this role under the Reagan administration.[7] These and other forces pushed the United States toward repetitive budgeting, much like the budgetary politics of underdeveloped nations that cannot plan their expenditures or revenues adequately for an annual budget.[8] The annual budget cycle no longer provides public administrators with a sense of certainty and control over a given period. This development often undercuts the efficient and effective management of resources.

Although several factors have debased annual budgeting, the fact remains that adequate comprehension of the budget process cannot occur without understanding that cycle more fully. Exhibit 6.2 explains a few key budget terms.

The Budget Cycle

The cyclic nature of the budget has important implications for those who play the budget game. If agency executives did not have to come back year after year to get more money from the same OMB officials and the same members of Congress, they might be tempted to employ very different strategies. From an agency's perspective budgeting is a long-term game in which dependability and probity rank as important virtues and consistent gains are often more important than windfalls.

The budget cycle involves certain critical phases. First, the president and his staff set basic spending parameters. Second, agencies submit requests. Third, the president and OMB review the requests and forge them into a budget proposal submitted to

EXHIBIT 6.2   Abbreviated Glossary of Key Budget Terms

APPROPRIATION. An act of Congress that permits federal agencies to incur obligations and to make payments out of the Treasury for specified purposes.

AUTHORIZATION (AUTHORIZING LEGISLATION). Substantive legislation enacted by Congress that establishes or continues legal operation of a federal program or agency. It is usually a prerequisite for subsequent appropriations or other kinds of budget authority to be contained in appropriations acts.

BACKDOOR AUTHORITY. Budget authority provided in legislation outside the appropriations process, including borrowing authority, contract authority, and entitlements.

BUDGET AUTHORITY. Legal authority to enter into obligations that will result in immediate or future outlays of federal government funds.

CONCURRENT RESOLUTION ON THE BUDGET. Under the Congressional Budget Act of 1974, a resolution—passed by both houses of Congress but not requiring the signature of the president—that establishes expenditure and revenue targets in key substantive areas for a fiscal year. Originally two such resolutions were required. Practice and subsequent legislative change require approval of only one such resolution.

CONTINUING RESOLUTION. Legislation to provide budget authority for specific ongoing activities when the regular appropriations for such activities have not been enacted by the beginning of the fiscal year.

CURRENT SERVICES ESTIMATES. Estimated budget authority and outlays for the upcoming fiscal year, assuming that all programs and activities will be carried on at the same level as in the fiscal year in progress.

DEFERRAL OF BUDGET AUTHORITY. Action by the president or executive branch that temporarily withholds, delays, or effectively precludes the obligation or expenditure of budget authority. The president must provide a special message to Congress reporting a proposed deferral of budget authority. Deferrals may not extend beyond the end of the fiscal year in which the message reporting the deferral is transmitted. Congress can overturn the deferral by passing a law.

ENTITLEMENTS. Legislation that requires the payment of benefits to any person or unit of government that meets the eligibility requirements established by such law.

OBLIGATIONAL AUTHORITY. The sum of budget authority provided for a given fiscal year, balance of amounts brought forward from prior years that remain available for obligation, and amounts authorized to be credited to a specific account during that year (including transfers).

OUTLAYS. Disbursements by the Federal Treasury in the form of checks or cash; expenditures that derive in part from budget authority granted in prior years and in part from budget authority provided for the year in which disbursements occur.

RECONCILIATION. A process by which Congress reconciles amounts determined by taxes, spending, and debt legislation for a given fiscal year with the ceilings in the required concurrent resolution on the budget for that year.

REPROGRAMMING. Use of funds in an appropriation account for purposes other than those stipulated at the time of the appropriation.

RECISION. Action that cancels in whole or in part budget authority previously granted by Congress. Recisions proposed by the president must be submitted in a special message to Congress. Congress must approve the recision within forty-five days.

SEQUESTRATION. The withholding of budget authority, according to an established formula, up to the amount required to be cut to meet the deficit target.

TRANSFER OF FUNDS. The shifting of budget authority from one account to another.

Source: These definitions come primarily from Aaron Wildavsky, *The New Politics of the Budgetary Process* (Glenview, IL: Scott, Foresman, 1988), 440–45; see also Howard E. Shuman, *Politics and the Budget* (Englewood Cliffs, N.J.: Prentice Hall, 1988), 303–17.

EXHIBIT 6.3 Some Important Steps* in the Budget Cycle

March	Formulation of the president's budget for the fiscal year beginning nineteen months later. Development of economic assumptions.
June	OMB issues internal instructions to agencies on preparation of annual budget requests
July to September	Submission of agency requests.
September to November	OMB reviews agency requests and makes recommendations.
November	Congress receives current services budget estimates.
December	Continuing OMB review and final distillation of the president's recommendations.
January (fifteen days after Congress convenes)	The president submits the budget to Congress.
February to September	Appropriations and authorizing committees hold hearings and make recommendations.
April 15	Passage of the concurrent budget resolution for the upcoming fiscal year.
June 15	Congress completes reconciliation instructions to authorizing and appropriations committees.
August	Possibility of movement toward automatic cuts; see Exhibit 6.5.
September	Final reconciliation or a continuing resolution.
October 1	Federal fiscal year commences.
Later	Possibility of supplemental appropriations.

*The dates suggested are approximations. Slippage in schedules, especially in Congress, often occurs.
Source: *Congressional Quarterly Weekly Report* 43 (14 December 1985): 2608-09.

Congress. Fourth, Congress authorizes certain spending for specific programs. Fifth, the executive agencies spend the authorized sums and account for them. Exhibit 6.3 contains some critical dates in the budget cycle.

The President and His Allies Set Parameters

Although the president and his advisers are concerned about which agencies prosper and which do not, their first concern in the budget is with the macro question of how much to try to spend in any year. Thus they set the overall parameters for the discussion about the budget.

One of the first official acts of the budget cycle is the development each spring of the estimates of total spending for the fiscal year, which will begin some eighteen or nineteen months later. In the spring planning review the president and his advisers discuss the underlying economic and political issues in the budget. Meanwhile, the agencies begin to marshal their ammunition. A letter from the president through OMB, usually in June, contains a statement of overall budgetary strategy and specific limits within which the agencies should prepare their budgets. In addition to these formal guidelines, agency budgeting officials will use their experience to interpret the letter. For example, defense agencies may not necessarily be bound by the written limits, while domestic agencies with small clienteles and few friends in Congress may expect to do somewhat worse than the letter indicates.

The estimates used to prepare a budget must be specified some sixteen months prior to its enactment. The fiscal 1989 budget went into effect on 1 October 1988, and the planning for that budget began in June 1987. This means that the economic basis for estimates of expenditures may be far from the reality when the budget is executed. However, those economic forecasts are very important. A recession produces a reduction in revenues; people who are out of work do not pay income or Social Security taxes. At the same time, a recession means that more money will be required for unemployment compensation, welfare, and food stamps. If a balanced budget or a deficit below a certain size is an important fiscal target, these uncertainties are very troublesome.

The preparation of the economic forecasts and the estimates of expenditures evolve from the interaction of three principal institutional actors, often called the *troika*, surrounding the president: the Council of Economic Advisers (CEA), the OMB, and the Treasury (see Exhibit 6.4).[9] The CEA, as the name implies, is a group of economists who advise the President on the budget and other economic issues. Organizationally the CEA is in the Executive Office of the President. The CEA role is primarily technical, forecasting the state of the economy and advising the president accordingly. They also provide the results of mathematical models of the U.S. economy showing the economic effects of different budgets. Economic forecasting is an inexact art and can be heavily influenced by political considerations. Models based on different assumptions produce different estimates. Proponents of different models often debate sharply, and arbiters of disputes frequently have to make judgments based on very imperfect information. Consider the response of Murray Weidenbaum, chair of the CEA during the early Reagan years, to the estimates of competing models. Faced with the need to reach a consensus among different factions of economists, Weidenbaum negotiated a compromise with David Stockman, Director of OMB. When Weidenbaum presented this compromise forecast to the warring factions of economists, many expressed discontent and one sharply questioned: "What model did *this* forecast come out of, Murray?" After a moment's pause Weidenbaum asserted, "It came right out of here"—with that he slapped his belly with both hands—"my visceral computer."[10]

The Office of Management and Budget, despite its image, comes as close to being a representative of the spending agencies as any other member of the troika. It is hardly a kindly benefactor. No less a budget slasher than David Stockman found his career staff at OMB to consist of "dedicated anti-bureaucrats."[11] Nonetheless, OMB staff members are at times more favorably disposed toward certain programs than either the CEA or the Treasury. At least prior to the 1980s, budget examiners made field visits and conducted detailed reviews of agency programs. These reviews at times led them to sympathize with certain programs. Under Reagan, OMB staffers were more concerned with aggregate agency spending than with the interstices of agency operations. Meeting aggregate targets became a more salient concern than whether a given program was efficient and effective and "deserved" more funding. The posture of OMB toward agencies became more adversarial, although its staff often took a benign view of Defense Department proposals.

EXHIBIT 6.4   Some Key Staffs in the Budget Process

Council of Economic Advisers	Established by the Employment Act of 1946, the council is in the Executive Office of the President; it consists of three members appointed by the president with the advice and consent of the Senate. The President designates one of its members as chair. The council advises the president on the budget and other economic issues. In fiscal 1988 its own budget amounted to $2.4 million and it had the equivalent of thirty full-time employees.
Office of Management and Budget	Established in 1970 pursuant to Reorganization Plan No. 2, OMB is in the Executive Office of the President; it plays a key role in reviewing agency budget requests, budget preparation, and the general administration of the budget. In fiscal 1988 OMB's own budget equaled $38.8 million; it had the equivalent of 580 full-time employees.
Congressional Budget Office	Established by the Congressional Budget and Impoundment Control Act of 1974, this office is an agent of Congress. It provides Congress with basic budget data and with analyses of alternative fiscal, budgetary, and programmatic policy issues. It does economic forecasts. In fiscal 1988 CBO's own budget amounted to $18.0 million and it employed the equivalent of 238 full-time staff members.

Source: U.S. Office of Management and Budget, *Budget of the United States Government, Fiscal Year 1989, Appendix* (Washington, DC: Government Printing Office, 1988).

Finally, the Treasury to some extent represents the financial community. While this relationship was less evident during the Reagan administration, the Treasury has often been among the strongest advocates of reducing the deficit. The Treasury, by issuing government bonds or simply by printing money, must cover any deficits created by the budgetary process. Officials at the Treasury strive to preserve the domestic and international financial community's confidence in the soundness of the country's economy and the government's management of it. In addition, top Treasury officials frequently represent the United States at international organizations such as the International Monetary Fund. These organizations can greatly affect the strength of currencies on the international marketplace as well as domestic economic and social policy.

Even at this first step in the preparation of the budget, much bargaining occurs. Each member of the troika must compete for the attention of the president. Each strives to promote certain interests. The individuals involved also have ideas and careers to promote. This is true in any administration, especially in an ideologically driven administration such as that of President Reagan. Although this phase features much political discussion and infighting, it is just the first in a long series of bargaining sessions.

Agency Requests

Whether working independently or within a cabinet-level department, the agency is primarily responsible for the preparation of estimates and requests for funding. The agency makes those preparations in conjunction with OMB and at times with the department's budget committee. During the preparation of the requests OMB provides guidance and advice concerning total levels of expenditure and particular aspects of the agency's budget. Likewise, the budget committee within the executive department and the secretary's staff require the agency to coordinate its budget preparations with all the other agencies in that department. This practice helps ensure that the agency operates within the priorities of the president and the cabinet secretary.

By tradition agencies aggressively seek to expand their expenditure base, even as agency leaders recognize that they are only one part of a larger organization. The agency must be aggressive but reasonable, seeking more money but realizing that resources as a whole are finite. Likewise, the department must recognize its responsibilities to the president and his program and to the agencies under its umbrella. Cabinet secretaries tend to be major advocates for their agencies in the higher levels of government.

At the same time, agencies often have substantially greater support from interest groups and congressional committees than does the department as a whole (as do the FBI in the Department of Justice and the Weather Bureau in the Department of Commerce). Thus, a cabinet secretary may resist a president's budgetary priorities if those would damage the ongoing programs of the department's agencies. This capture of the secretary by the agencies in part reflects the general fragmentation of American government, with much of the real power and the operational connections between government and interest groups being at the agency rather than the departmental level.

To some degree the top-down budgeting of the Reagan administration tended to reduce the expansionist and exploratory nature of agency behavior in the budgetary process.[12] In most domestic agencies, officials have borne increased pressure to implement OMB policies for budget reduction. Agencies still have room for advocacy and for appeals to the director of OMB or even to the president, but there is now more restraint on budget requests.

An agency may employ any number of strategies to maintain or expand its funding, but those strategies are restrained because budgeting is an annual process and a strategic choice in any one year may preclude the use of that strategy in subsequent years.[13] Perhaps more important, the use of some strategies may destroy the confidence of OMB and Congress in the recommendations of that agency. For example, an agency may employ the "camel's nose" or thin wedge strategy to get modest funding for a program in its first year, knowing that expenditures will grow rapidly later. Once that strategy is used, the agency runs a greater risk that future requests for new programs and budget authority will be carefully scrutinized. The flip side of this strategy was especially popular in the Reagan years; an agency would promise savings in future (usually unspecified) years while asking to continue or expand appropriations in the current year.[14]

Executive Review and Recommendation

After the agency formulates its request, it sends it to OMB for review. OMB amasses all the agencies' requests and attempts to reconcile them to presidential policy priorities as well as to the desired overall level of public expenditure. This may make for a tight fit, as some programs are difficult or impossible to control, leaving little budgetary space for any new programs that the president considers important.

The requests go to OMB's budget examiners for review. These examiners, who often have considerable experience in dealing with the agency, draw on their general knowledge of its programs and the president's priorities to evaluate requested expenditures. Much depends on the examiner's relationship with the agency. Sometimes this relationship leads examiners to adopt a favorable stance. In essence, the budget examiners may over time favor the agencies they are supposed to control. On balance, however, OMB relentlessly examines ways to cut agency requests. Furthermore, priorities for spending are increasingly being determined centrally, leaving less latitude for individual examiners and the agencies.

On the basis of the agency requests and the information developed by the examiner, OMB holds hearings, usually in October or November. At these hearings the agency must defend its requests before the examiner and other members of the OMB staff. Although OMB tends to be committed to cutting expenditures, it runs some risks if it wields too sharp an ax. An agency may end-run the hearing board and appeal directly to the director of OMB, the president, or to friends in Congress. If OMB is persistently overruled, the office may develop a reputation for being incompetent and ineffective.

The results of the hearing for each agency go to the director of OMB for the director's review, which involves all of OMB's senior staff. At this stage, through additional trimming and negotiation, the staff pares the budget down to the amount desired by the president. This stage involves final appeals from agency and department personnel to OMB and on occasion to the president. It also involves last-minute estimates of revenues and expenditures to take into account the results of negotiations to that point as well as changes in economic forecasts.

These estimates often reflect political as well as technical considerations. During the early years of the Reagan administration, David Stockman, director of OMB, became increasingly alarmed by the projected deficit. However, he could not persuade the President to adopt revenue and expenditure policies to reduce the deficit. Confronted with the unpleasant political prospects of presenting the consequences of the President's program for the deficit, Stockman acknowledges that he "out-and-out cooked the books, inventing $15 billion per year of utterly phony cuts in order to get Ronald Reagan's first full budget below the $100 billion deficit level." Reflecting ruefully and somewhat facetiously on the politics of budget forecasting, Stockman concludes, "If the SEC had jurisdiction over the White House, we might have all had time for a course in remedial economics at Allenwood Penitentiary."[15] This should not be construed to mean that anything goes in producing budget estimates. Estimators realize that consistently missing the target by a large margin will undermine their credibility. However, the episode does illustrate how political forces can shape marginal estimates of the numbers.

Efforts by the Reagan administration to use the budget to pursue sweeping social and economic changes as well as serious OMB errors in estimating the deficit have pushed the CBO (see Exhibit 6.4) into a more active role in issuing and promoting its own forecasts. On average, these have been more accurate than those issued by OMB.

The law requires the president to submit his budget to Congress within fifteen days after that body convenes in January each year. Prior to that point (by November 10 of each year) the president submits the current services budget, which includes "proposed budget authority and estimated outlays that would be included in the budget for the ensuing fiscal year . . . if all programs and activities were carried on at the same level as in the fiscal year in progress." This is volume budgeting for a constant amount of public services. Changes in prices and in the eligibility of beneficiaries spur adjustments of outlays.[16] Given the rate of inflation during the 1970s and the early 1980s, the constant services budget could give Congress an early warning of the size of current commitments. Like other estimates, however, the current services budget is often inaccurate. It gives Congress only a rough estimate of expenditure requirements for planning purposes.

The budget submitted by the president in January varies somewhat in precision from year to year. For instance, President Bush tested the outer limits of ambiguity in early 1989. Having witnessed Reagan's detailed budgets routinely pronounced dead on arrival and wishing to avoid the heat for proposing unpopular cuts, Bush provided Congress with only a vague budget outline. Masterminded by OMB Director Richard G. Darman, this "nonbudget budget" let the President negotiate details in a budget summit with Congress.[17]

Congressional Action

Although the Constitution specifically grants the power of the purse to Congress, Congress had ceased to be the dominant budgetary actor by the 1960s. In 1974, however, Congress counterattacked presidential dominance with the Congressional Budget and Impoundment Control Act of 1974. Among other things, this act established a budget committee in each house of Congress to develop two concurrent resolutions. These resolutions were to contain estimates of revenues and expenditures, thereby encouraging Congress to consider the broad implications of budgetary decisions for the economy. The resolutions also set aggregate dollar figures for certain general categories of appropriations such as military spending and agriculture. The first concurrent resolution, officially due by 15 May, is to establish the basic amounts, while the second (see below) is to reaffirm or revise these figures in light of legislative and other developments. At least in theory, the budgetary decisions of the appropriations committees cannot surpass the targets embedded in the concurrent resolutions. The law also established the Congressional Budget Office to provide the budget committees capability to make informed economic forecasts.

The appropriations committees in the Senate and House of Representatives decide how to allocate total expenditures among agencies and programs. These committees are prestigious and powerful; their members tend to be veteran legislators who remain on these committees for long periods and develop both expertise and political ties with the agencies whose budgets they supervise. The two committees, especially the House Appropriations Committee, do most of their work through subcommittees, which may be responsible for a single department such as Defense or a number of agencies, such as the Department of Housing and Urban Development plus independent executive agencies. At subcommittee hearings agency personnel are summoned to testify and justify the size of their budget requests. After the hearings the subcommittee "marks up" the bill, making such changes as are deemed necessary, and then submits it to the entire committee. While according considerable deference to subcommittee recommendations, the full committee sometimes modifies the appropriation. The entire committee then recommends the appropriations bill to the membership of its house of Congress.[18] A conference committee must negotiate and reconcile any differences between the House and Senate appropriations measures. Both houses must then approve the negotiated measure. During a given session Congress may forward several appropriations bills to the president for his signature or veto.

The role of the appropriations committees has changed over the last quarter of a century. Whereas in the past these committees often sought to cut agency requests, the Reagan administration's repeated attacks on federal programs frequently prompted these committees to defend the agencies' allocations. Appropriations hearings often were forums for attacks on the Reagan administration's policies and budget proposals.

Other congressional committees get into the budget drama as well. To meet the expenditure and revenue targets promulgated by the budget committees, authorization committees may modify a program's benefits and structure, as in a change in statutory provisions for payment of physicians under the Medicare program. If the targets require new revenues, tax committees in each house may be called on to amend the tax law. These committees may balk. The many committees involved in the budget process add to its complexity. They heighten opportunities for interaction between administrators and legislators but also increase prospects for delay.

Reconciliation has played an increasingly important role in determining final appropriations. Under the 1974 budget act this is "a process used by Congress to reconcile amounts determined by tax, spending and debt legislation for a given fiscal year with the ceilings enacted in the second required concurrent resolution on the budget for that year."[19] The official timetable calls for Congress to approve the second concurrent resolution by 15 September. This second resolution set binding totals for the budget and could direct committees to determine and recommend changes in laws, bills, and resolutions to achieve conformance with the binding totals for budget authority, revenue, and public debt. The timetable calls for reconciliation in the form of a resolution or a bill approved by both houses by 25 September. If Congress adheres to this schedule and the president signs the appropriations bills, a budget is in place at the beginning of the federal fiscal year, October 1.

In fact, the timetable for the budget became at best a target and at worst a joke. Congress tended to be so far behind schedule in its action on the budget that reconciliation occurred after the first resolution.[20] A 1981 measure formally recognized this reality by providing for the first resolution to become final if Congress failed to approve the second resolution by October 1. Statutory changes in 1985 reaffirmed that Congress needed to pass only one budget resolution (see Exhibit 6.3). Even then, Congress has not always been able to stay on schedule. For instance, Congress did not approve a reconciliation bill for fiscal 1988 until December 1987, three months after the fiscal year commenced. Notwithstanding the failure to meet timetables, the reconciliation process points to the ability of the budget committees to oversee and constrain the power of appropriations committees.

This does not mean that the budget committees have absorbed all power lost by the appropriations committees. To the contrary, the budget process generally became less committee centered in the 1970s and 1980s. After 1963 the number of amendments offered to appropriations acts rose continuously. This trend indicates less deference by members of Congress to the recommendations of these committees. Leadership in the budgetary process has become more difficult as fluid, unstable coalitions arise to determine outcomes in a given year.[21]

Even with the budget act of 1974, Congress remains at a disadvantage relative to the president in the budgetary process.[22] Congress must perform a large number of tasks, only one of which is preparing the budget. Although CBO and other staffs provide considerable expertise, Congress consists of 535 different decisionmakers facing a more unitary structure in the White House. The pressures on members of Congress to satisfy a diverse array of interests make it difficult for them to act rapidly, in concert, and coherently on budgetary matters.

Supplemental Appropriations

While normally not considered part of the budget cycle, supplemental appropriations occur with sufficient frequency to justify inclusion. Agencies may require these appropriations to cover shortfalls during the fiscal year. When agencies run out of money, it can be the result of poor management. More often, however, a shortfall happens because of changes in the demand for services or because of faulty estimations of demand. For example, during a recession the demand for unemployment assistance naturally increases, and public administrators usually must seek a supplemental appropriation. Likewise, a year of poor weather may force additional funding for the Department of Agriculture for crop insurance or disaster payments. A new program such as food stamps may acquire more clients than anyone anticipated. Supplemental appropriations require significant amounts of money. For instance, the additions to agency spending authority in 1986 ranged from $235,000 for the American Battle Monuments Commission to more than $1 billion for the Department of Energy.

The request for a supplemental appropriation may be useful for an agency attempting to expand. Anticipating many clients, the agency may initiate a program with minimal appropriations and then return to Congress for a supplemental appropriation when the clients materialize and demand their benefits. Supplemental appropriations frequently receive less scrutiny than regular appropriations, allowing friendly members of Congress to hide expansion of a program. However, obvious and frequent abuse of the supplemental appropriations process often damages the relationship between the agency and Congress, threatening the agency's ability to expand its funding over the long term.

Execution of the Budget

After the executive branch receives appropriated money, the agencies use certain mechanisms for spending it. An appropriations warrant, drawn by the Treasury and countersigned by the General Accounting Office, is sent to each agency specifying the amount of its available funds. The agency plans its expenditures for the year on this warrant and submits a plan to OMB for apportionment of the funds across the fiscal year. Funds are usually made available on a quarterly basis, but some agencies differ in the amount available each quarter. For example, the Park Service spends a relatively large proportion of its appropriation during the summer because of the demand on the national parks at that time. The principal reason for allowing agencies access to only a quarter or so of their funds at a time is to provide greater control over the pace of expenditure so that an agency does not spend all its funds early in the year and then return to Congress for more. Supplemental appropriation may still be required, but apportionment helps to control profligacy.

The procedures for executing the budget are relatively simple when the president wants to spend money the way Congress does. Procedures become more complex when the president decides he does not want to spend those funds. Prior to the Congressional Budget Act of 1974, a president could impound (not spend) funds fairly easily. The numerous impoundments of the Nixon administration—for example half the money appropriated for the Federal Water Pollution Control Act Amendments—fueled congressional interest in limiting presidential discretion.

The 1974 act imposed new constraints on the president. It defined two types of impoundments—recision and deferral. Recisions are cancellations of budgetary authority to spend money. The president may decide that a program can reach its goals with less money or simply that there are good reasons not to spend. The president must request the recision from Congress. Congress must act positively on this request within forty-five days; if it does not, the money is made available to the agencies. Deferrals, on the other hand, are requests by the president merely to delay making the obligational authority available to the agency. In this case, if either house of Congress did not exercise its veto power, the deferral is granted automatically. The comptroller general, the head of the GAO, is given the power to classify the impoundment, and at times the difference between a deferral and a recision is not clear. For example, deferral of funds for programs scheduled to be phased out is in practice a recision. Reforms of the impoundment powers of the president have substantially increased the authority of Congress to determine how much federal money will be spent on what.

Recisions and deferrals are not as simple as they appear. The Supreme Court's rejection of the legislative veto by a single house of Congress in *Immigration and Naturalization Service* v. *Chadha* (1983) also made the mechanism for controlling deferrals invalid. The court ruled that the Constitution requires both houses of Congress and the president to be involved in making laws. In response Congress began to insert riders forbidding deferrals, especially in supplemental bills passed after the deferral took place.

Reprogramming and Transfers

Whereas legal provisions for deferral and recision seek to restrain presidential excesses in refusing to spend money, stipulations concerning reprogramming and transfers constrain executive branch attempts to shift money from one account or program to another. Reprogramming is the shifting of funds within a specific appropriation account. An appropriations bill contains a number of accounts, which in turn feature a number of program elements.[23] For example, the appropriations bill for the Department of Agriculture contains an account for crop supports with separate elements for cotton, corn, wheat, and other commodities. Reprogramming shifts spending authority, for example, from cotton to corn. The procedures for reprogramming have been thoroughly developed only in the Department of Defense. In general, below a certain threshold an agency is relatively free to reprogram funds, but above it, must gain approval from the appropriations committee, although not from the entire Congress.

The transfer is more substantial; it is a shift of funds from one appropriations account to another. In the case of the Department of Agriculture noted above, this might involve moving funds from crop supports to the Farmers Home Administration or to rural electrification. Fund transfers can open the door to significant abuse and circumvention of congressional authority, a problem especially evident during the Nixon administration and the Vietnam War. As with reprogramming, there are few well-established procedures for controlling transfers other than in the Defense Department.

Both reprogramming and transferring provide the executive branch with important flexibility in implementing programs and in using public funds effectively. These practices have been the subject of many abuses, however, and are probably ripe for reform and improvement. Moreover, they frequently allow an agency to circumvent the judgment of the entire Congress through an appeal to the appropriations committee, or perhaps even just its chair. If that portion or member of Congress is especially sympathetic, the agency may get what it wants with relative ease.

Budget Control

After the president and the executive branch have spent money, congressional agencies take steps to ascertain that the spending was legal and proper. The GAO and its head, the comptroller general, are responsible for auditing federal expenditures. Each year the comptroller general's report to Congress outlines deviations of executive expenditure decisions from congressional intent.

The GAO has changed from a simple financial accounting office into a policy-analytic organization within the legislative branch. It is concerned not only with the legality of expenditures but also with the efficiency with which the money is spent.[24] Although GAO reports on the efficiency of expenditures have no legal authority, any agency that wants to maintain good relations with Congress is well advised to take GAO findings into account. Further, Congress tends to consider those findings when it reviews an agency's budget the following year, and at times it expects to see changes.

The problem with GAO controls, both financial and policy-analytic, is that they are largely *ex post facto*—the money gets spent long before GAO decides whether the spending was legal, illegal, or merely unwise. Further, the agency must devote much time to congressional requests for inquiries. These requests can divert GAO from pursuing studies that would do more to foster accountability and control.

Recapitulation

The long and complex process outlined here is used to allocate federal budget money among competing agencies. The process takes almost eighteen months and involves many bargains and decisions. From bargaining and analysis emerges a plan for spending billions of dollars. Even this complex process, made more complex by reforms of budgeting procedures and the need to contend with mounting federal deficits, cannot control federal expenditures as completely as some would desire; nor can it provide the level of fiscal management that may be necessary for a smoothly functioning economic system. Among other things, it is difficult or impossible for the president or Congress to make binding decisions concerning how much money will be spent on specific programs in a given year. The absence of effective controls makes the entire process subject to error. Those elected to make policy and control spending frequently find themselves incapable of producing the types of changes they have advocated in their campaigns. This may result in disillusionment for both leaders and citizens. The budget process will never satisfy everyone, but there are identifiable problems that pose special challenges to policymakers.

Problems in the Budgetary Process

The problems that intrude on the budget process assume many guises. Five in particular deserve attention: uncontrollable entitlements, backdoor spending, the overhang, intergovernmental budget control, and gimmickry.

Uncontrollable Entitlements

The growth of major entitlement programs such as Social Security, Medicare, and unemployment insurance has dramatically altered budget processes. "Entitlements are legal obligations created through legislation that require the payment of benefits to any person or unit of government that meets the eligibility requirements established by law." These programs take nearly half of the budget.[25] Budgeting for these programs departs in fundamental ways from the dynamics described to this point. As Aaron Wildavsky notes, "A classical budget depends on classical practice—authorization and appropriation followed by expenditure, and postaudited by external auditors. But in many countries, classical budgeting does not in fact control most public spending." Rather than appropriations budgeting, these countries tend to rely on treasury budgeting, which "bypasses the appropriations process in favor of automatic disbursement of funds through the treasury."[26]

Observers often say entitlements are uncontrollable because they cannot be reduced without major policy changes that tend to be unpopular politically. For example, the president and Congress can do little to reduce spending for Social Security without either changing eligibility criteria or altering the formula for indexation (adjustments of benefits for changes in consumer prices). Either change would in all probability provoke intense political opposition leading to the defeat of these proposals. Although minor modifications such as changing the tax treatment of benefits may prove feasible, major efforts to influence program outlays seem destined to fail.

Uncontrollable entitlements also spring from difficulties in accurately estimating the costs of these programs. Entitlement outlays do not appreciably derive from some specific amount of money allocated in the annual budget process. Rather outlays are automatically triggered; eligibility, client use, and payment levels (to citizens in the case of Social Security or medical providers in the case of Medicare). These variables are intertwined with the state of the economy (e.g., unemployment, the inflation rate), population dynamics, and whether the program automatically protects beneficiaries against inflation.

Entitlement programs help accomplish many worthwhile social objectives, but they intensify pressure on the budget process. Again, Wildavsky goes to the heart of matters:[27]

> The guaranteed certainty of entitlement funding creates so much uncertainty for budgeters that it reduces the capacity of public officials to govern. Entitlements place a sizeable burden on budgetary actors: They must find a way to support large numbers of individuals while still helping manage the economy and control the deficit, all this with most of the budget 'committed' or essential.

Entitlements also siphon off funds from the discretionary portion of the budget and can make it difficult for programs with broad public support, for example conservation, to gain a "fair share" of public outlays.

Other Backdoor Spending

Uncontrollable entitlements are one form of backdoor spending, that is, spending outside of the normal appropriations process. Other back doors include borrowing authority, contract authority, and permanent appropriations. Like entitlements, these practices make fiscal management through the budget more difficult. They allow agencies to spend more than if they had to compete for annual appropriations.

Borrowing Authority.   Agencies may be allowed to borrow from the Treasury money not appropriated by Congress, as with student loan guarantees. Some argue that this is not a public expenditure, since the money presumably will be repaid. However, government frequently writes off these loans (see Chapter 3). Moreover, even if the loans are repaid, the ability of government to control expenditures for economic management is seriously impaired when the authority to pump money into the economy via loans is so widely dispersed. The Congressional Budget Act of 1974 has curtailed the use of this form of spending, but it has not eliminated it. In fiscal 1985 alone the federal government spent $50 billion to repay obligations arising from borrowing authority.[28]

Contract Authority.   Agencies at times contract to pay a certain amount for specified goods and services without going through the appropriations process. After the contract is let, the appropriations committees are placed in the awkward position of either appropriating the money or forcing the agency to renege on its debts. While this kind of spending is often uncontrollable in the short run, an agency that in this way tries to circumvent the appropriations committees may face the ire of those committees when applying for its annual budget. The 1974 budget act has sharply curtailed these types of obligations, although government corporations in particular are still able to use this form of backdoor spending.

Permanent Appropriations.   Certain programs have authorizing legislation that requires the spending of certain amounts of money each year. The largest expenditure of this sort other than entitlement programs is the interest on the federal debt; this expense constituted more than 14 percent of total federal expenditures in 1986 and is projected to increase to almost 16 percent in 1990 with the continuing large federal deficits. Likewise, federal support for land grant colleges is a permanent appropriation that began during the administration of Abraham Lincoln. The appropriations committees in Congress have little discretion over these "permanent" expenditures unless they want to renege on the standing obligations of the federal government.

The Overhang

Not all money appropriated by Congress in a fiscal year need actually be spent during that year; it must only be obligated. That is, the agency must contract to spend the money or find some other way of encumbering it so that it can be spent in some future year, as via a long-term contract. If appropriated money is not obligated in some way, it must be returned to the Treasury at the end of the fiscal year. Figure 6.1 shows how outlays in a given year, fiscal 1988, derive not only from congressional budget action for that year (new authority recommended for 1988) but from action taken previously (unspent authority enacted in prior years). The overhang in the figure refers to unspent authority for outlays in future years. This sum exceeds the amount to be spent in fiscal 1988.

The major problem with the overhang is that it impedes the president from using the budget as an instrument of economic management. One of the principal components of such management is the amount of public expenditure. If a president is trying to affect the economy through the balance of government expenditures and revenues (standard Keynesian management), it is helpful to be able to control expenditures. With the overhang, however, the president and Congress cannot always control the outlay of funds. The agencies may have sufficient budget authority, convertible into actual expenditures, to complicate forecasts of outlays, not out of malice but out of the perceived need to deliver services, especially if the president seeks to restrict new spending.

Intergovernmental Budget Control

Federalism also impedes careful estimation of public expenditures and outlays by Washington. The federal government spends roughly two-thirds of the total amount of money appropriated by all levels of government (see Chapter 2). Washington can stimulate state and local government expenditures, but it cannot tightly control them.[29] From the perspective of managing the economy, state and local policymakers at times fall out of synch with federal policymakers. For example, in 1963 the Kennedy administration pushed through a reduction in federal taxation, only to have the stimulative effect of that cut vitiated by state and local tax boosts. In the 1980s many state and local governments enjoyed budget surpluses while the federal government ran up a huge deficit. Depending on one's point of view, state and local surpluses are either a good thing (helping to reduce public borrowing) or a bad thing (counteracting the stimulative effects of the deficit). In either case, this situation represents the absence of integrated fiscal policy in the United States.

FIGURE 6.1
Flow of Federal
Funds

Source: Office of Management and Budget, *Budget of the United States Government, Fiscal Year 1988* (Washington, DC: Government Printing Office, 1987).

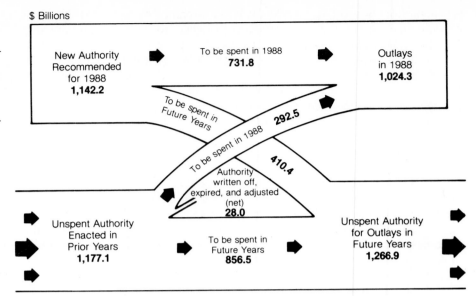

This situation has prompted some to urge that broad decisions about expenditures be decided by "diplomacy" among the several levels of government: this type of adjustment and bargaining is already practiced in other federal systems.[30] Given the fragmentation of power at the national level, patterns of partisanship, and cultural beliefs about the dangers of excessive government intervention in the economy, prospects for a coordinated approach to setting public outlays and taxes are extremely remote.

Gimmickry

Federal budgeting has become increasingly painful for top policymakers. Substantial segments of the public want the benefits of government programs; yet they do not want their taxes to go up. The deficit rises to an "unacceptable" level. Under such circumstances, gimmickry, or a smoke-and-mirrors approach, becomes highly appealing to budgeters. In essence, they give the appearance of coping with the budget deficit while they avoid cutting popular programs or raising taxes to ameliorate the problem. During the 1980s gimmickry grew "to epidemic proportions." It became more the rule and less the exception.[31]

Policymakers have proven so inventive that a complete catalog of gimmicks would require a separate volume. Let a few examples suffice. One is to redefine the budget base. The base no longer necessarily is what the agency received or spent in a given fiscal year. Different congressional committees define the base in different ways. Thus, rather than use last year's outlay, policymakers may define the base as an estimate of how much a program would cost if they failed to take some action. Congress then claims to have cut the program even though it has at best retarded its rate of growth. Another gimmick is to appear to meet spending targets by voting only eleven months of funding, knowing that the rest will have to be restored. Another is to tinker with the timing of outlays by putting an expenditure in an earlier or later accounting period. In negotiating a budget resolution for fiscal 1990, White House and congressional conferees agreed that $850 million in farm subsidies due to be paid in October 1989 (fiscal 1990) would instead be paid in September 1989 (fiscal 1989). While this worsened the deficit for the immediate year, it allowed conferees to appear to come closer to meeting deficit reduction targets for the period covered by their negotiations, fiscal 1990.[32] The 1989 negotiations also featured a willingness among policymakers to accept extremely rosy revenue estimates. This helped them avoid cutting programs or raising revenues.

Gimmickry takes its toll. When the press treats budget accords as "the usual accounting flimflam," this perception does little to bolster the legitimacy of the country's political institutions or the morale of policymakers.[33] At times policymakers cannot contain their own disrespect for such gimmickry. Thus, when President Bush invited congressional leaders to appear in a White House ceremony to mark the successful negotiation of a gimmick-riddled budget resolution in early 1989, Senator Lloyd Bentsen expressed the depth of his disgust by declining to attend. Whatever the cynicism about the practice, however, the eagerness of the President and many in Congress to avoid unpopular cuts or new taxes make it difficult to avoid the temptations of gimmickry.

Outcomes: Incrementalism and Decrementalism

Incremental, the one word used most frequently to describe changes in allocations, has any number of meanings. In budgeting incrementalism broadly means that the changes in the agency's budget from year to year tend to be predictable and relatively small.[34]

Unlike the prescriptive idea of incremental decisionmaking described in Chapter 4, budgetary incrementalism is the pattern of outcomes yielded by the budgetary process. In particular, Davis et al. found a great deal of stability in appropriations increases granted to agencies from year to year.[35] This was true not only of the executive budget but also of final appropriations by Congress. The changes in budgets were not only small for the most part but quite stable and predictable, so that the best estimate of the agency's budget in one year would be the previous year's budget (the base) plus a fixed percentage increase. Some agencies grow more rapidly than do others, but each exhibits its own stable pattern of growth.

Several factors contribute to the pattern of incremental budgeting in the United States. One is that, because a large percentage of the budget is uncontrollable, few significant changes in appropriations patterns can be made from year to year. Also, most empirical studies of incremental budgeting occurred during periods of relative economic stability and high rates of economic growth. When less favorable economic conditions apply, budget outcomes may be less stable. An agency's budget base is no longer secure from cuts.

Most important, the cyclic nature of the budgeting process tends to produce incremental outcomes.[36] A budget must be passed each year, so minor adjustments can be made annually as the need arises, thus avoiding efforts to correct all the policy problems at once. The annual cycle prevents an agency from trying to make a sudden expansion of its budget based on flimsy evidence. Agency leaders know they will have to return again next year for more money, and any attempt to deceive Congress invites punishment later. The sequential nature of the process, in which decisions are made one after the other, also tends to produce incremental outcomes. Many decisions must be made and many bargains struck. The incremental solution not only provides a "natural" choice for difficult decisions but also helps to minimize bargaining costs among institutions. Once policymakers establish a percentage increase for a particular agency, it eases their burden of calculation if they honor that rule rather than seek a "better" decision for that one year.

Criticisms of Incrementalism

Incrementalism as a description of budget outcomes has come under increasing criticism. Some analysts contend that the incremental description of the budgetary process concentrates too heavily on outcomes at the agency level. This may appear quite justifiable, given the emphasis on those organizations in American politics. However, it may be too high a level of aggregation for examining incremental budgeting. When researchers have disaggregated agency budgets to the program level, they have found a great deal of nonincremental change.[37] Thus, while agencies as a whole may have relatively stable increases in appropriations, the managers of those organizations often significantly alter priorities among programs.

In addition, when the uncontrollable elements of public expenditures are removed from the analysis, the pattern of expenditure change appears anything but incremental.[38] As inflation and citizens' resistance to taxation have squeezed budgets, increments have not been granted as usual. In some cases the base has been cut—that is, there have been real reductions in the amount of money appropriated to an agency. Incrementalism may describe only certain types of expenditures and not the budget process as a whole. Of course, given that uncontrollable expenditures account for approximately 75 percent of the total federal budget, the incrementalist approach does have some utility.[39] In a related vein, incrementalism may apply more readily to certain kinds of agencies and programs, specifically those fully accepted as part of the proper realm of government activity. Hence, veterans benefits or social security checks probably have more incremental features than more controversial organizations such as those central to the war on poverty program of the 1960s (e.g., community action agencies).

Finally, the incremental approach does little to explain how and when programs make big gains—or suffer big losses—in their appropriations.[40] Instead it focuses on general patterns.

Decrementalism

Events during the Reagan years fueled new criticisms of incrementalism as a description of the federal budget process. President Reagan worked diligently to cut public expenditures for certain programs, scoring a number of successes. This development heightened interest in a theory of decrementalism, that is, the reduction of agency and program budgets. In a certain sense decrementalism strongly resembles its incremental cousin. Typically, small cuts occur at the margins rather than a massive slashing of agency and program budgets. But decrementalism also has some distinctive features.

Decrementalism more readily applies to discretionary spending than to entitlement programs. Cuts in programs like those of the Office of Personnel Management tend to be easiest to secure and do not necessitate changes in the law. Entitlements are far more difficult to attack. Beyond this, however, decremental budgeting tends to differ from the incremental kind in three important ways. First, it often requires policymakers to make explicit decisions about taking benefits from one set of beneficiaries as opposed to another. Under incremental growth, one set of clients can get more without another set getting less. Under decremental budgeting, increases in benefits to some client group or even the preservation of the existing level of benefits necessitates a loss to some other beneficiary. The distribution of losses is a painful political process that incremental budgeting tends to avoid.

Second, decremental budgeting may be less stable and predictable. During economic declines the quest for budget savings may generate cuts that amount to a much higher percentage of the budget base. Furthermore, budget shortfalls produced by deteriorating economic conditions can produce repetitive budgeting rather than annual review. As Allen Schick notes, "The poorer the government, the more budgets it is likely to have. The affluent can ride out the storm or call upon reserves; the less fortunate must adjust to every month's or quarter's economic reports."[41]

Third, decremental budgeting leads to more conflict. Under incrementalism, policymakers can mute conflict by giving everyone a share. Participants may gripe, but they can usually live with the outcome. When policymakers attack the base of a program, fighting becomes much more intense; participants may even perceive the issue as a struggle for long-term survival. The instability associated with decremental budgeting also fuels conflict. Under incrementalism, once policymakers reach a decision, the matter tends to be settled at least for a year. The repetitive budgeting of decrementalism means that the struggle may carry on throughout much of the year—from one congressional vote to another.

Of course, much budgeting remains incremental. Many programs increase their budgets marginally each year. But to a greater degree than in the past, students of budgeting must take the dynamics of decrementalism seriously. Whichever mode of budgeting proves more pervasive, one can expect to hear that the outcomes lack rationality or are otherwise unsatisfactory. During the 1960s and 1970s this perception precipitated many attempts to reform budget processes, and the 1980s have featured their own variations on this theme.

The Quest for Budget Reform

As sure as the flowers that bloom in the spring, incrementalism nurtures efforts to make budget processes more synoptic—more comprehensively analytic of the budget base and of alternative uses of scarce resources. Program budgeting and zero-based budgeting were two of the primary initiatives in this regard. In this era of greater decrementalism, leading proposals for budget reform focus on controlling spending and deficits. Reforms of this vintage include the balanced budget amendment, the line-item veto for the president, and the Gramm-Rudman-Hollings Act.

Program Budgeting

Program budgeting was largely a product of the Johnson administration, although it had been tried previously in several federal agencies. Whereas traditional budgeting allocates personnel costs, supplies, equipment, and so forth among organizations, program budgeting allocates resources according to the activities of government and its services. It also places pronounced emphasis on the thorough analysis of expenditures and the most efficient use of all government resources.

Underlying program budgeting, or more specifically the planning programming budgeting system (PPBS), is a systems concept.[42] The PPBS approach assumes that all the elements of government are closely intertwined so that a change in one aspect of one policy may affect all others. For example, if one wants to improve the quality of health for citizens of the United States, it may be more efficient to remove funds from medical care programs and invest them in nutrition and housing programs. Program budgeters are always looking for possible interactions among policy areas and for means of producing the desired mix in the most efficient manner.

There were six major characteristics of program budgeting as it was practiced in the federal government; systems used in state and local government were in most instances similar.

1. The major goals and objectives of government must be identified. To budget effectively, one must know what government is trying to do. This decision is often made very high in the hierarchy of government, usually by the president and Congress. Whereas traditional line-item budgeting has been initiated by the agencies in most instances, program budgeting begins with the central goals and priorities of government.
2. Programs must be developed according to the specified goals. How will government attain its goals? Programs should be analytically defined and should not necessarily fall within existing organizations. For example, when Robert McNamara—who with his whiz kids was largely responsible for importing PPBS into the Department of Defense and then selling it to President Johnson for the entire government—developed the program structure for the Department of Defense, one of the programs was strategic deterrence. This program actually cut across three services within the Department of Defense. The air force had its manned bombers and some missiles, the navy had Polaris submarines, and the army had intermediate range ballistic missiles in Europe. Strategic deterrence certainly did describe one set of activities in which the Department of Defense was engaged, but no single organization was specifically responsible for that activity.
3. Resources must be allocated among the programs. Although many traditional line items were used to develop the program budget, the final budget documents within the executive branch were to state overall costs for the achievement of certain objectives. These costs would be justified as efficient and effective means of reaching goals. The idea was expressed as "more bang

for the buck." Program budgeting places its emphasis on the costs of reaching certain objectives (output), whereas line-item budgeting tends to emphasize the costs of keeping organizations or programs in operation (input).

4. Organizations are not sacrosanct in program budgeting, and there is no assumption that each program is housed within a single agency or that each agency is involved with only a single program. As with the defense example above, program budgeting attempts to expand the framework of budgeting and planning to include all the actors who contribute to the achievement of the goals. While this orientation may be realistic in one sense, it does make budgeting more difficult in an environment consisting of many organizations, each of which attempts to promote its own interest.

5. Program budgeting extends the time frame beyond the single year common in line-item budgeting. The method attempts to force those involved in making decisions to ask and then answer questions about the medium- and long-term consequences of the program. Some programs appear efficient in the short run but are less desirable when their long-term implications are considered. For example, most publicly funded health programs concentrate on acute curative medicine, whereas at times it is more efficient to emphasize preventive measures. The benefits of preventive measures are more diffuse and less likely to be identifiable to the average citizen than the "miracles" of curative medicine.

6. Budgeters systematically analyze alternative programs. Agencies scrutinize alternatives to existing program structures for more effective and efficient configurations. Agencies or groups of agencies are expected to justify their programs to show that they are superior to alternatives. Also, this aspect of program budgeting affects policy formulation (see Chapter 4), for agencies are expected to develop alternatives and to examine their relative merits using techniques such as cost-benefit analysis.

Advocates of program budgeting point with pride to the enhanced rationality and analytic rigor associated with this form of budgeting and to the way in which it breaks down organizational dominance over budgetary outcomes. Despite these apparent advantages, program budgeting has been far from successful in most of its applications, especially in the federal government. There are some technical reasons for its failures, but the most severe problems with program budgeting are political.

Technically, successful program budgeting requires a great deal of time and effort; it also demands (often unrealistically) great knowledge of the relationships of spending patterns to programs' success. The systems concept at the root of PPBS implies that if one part is modified, the entire system has been altered and should be reconsidered. This means that program budgeting may actually increase rigidity by making change appear even more threatening and difficult. Furthermore, it is difficult if not impossible to define programs, measure their results, and evaluate the contributions of individual agencies to those results.

Program budgeting has several distinct political disadvantages.

1. It tends to force decisions up the hierarchy of government. Agencies dislike this centralizing tendency, as do individual members of Congress who have

invested considerable time and effort in developing working relationships with the clientele allied with particular agencies.

2. The assumption that organizations are not the most appropriate recipients of allocations run counter to the folkways of government in the United States.
3. The quest to analyze all alternative strategies forces an agency to expose existing programs to attack.
4. The discussion of alternative policies reduces the maneuverability of the agency; it must justify its policy choices in writing, which limits its strategic use of ambiguity in dealing with diverse groups in and out of government.

In short PPBS threatened the central role of administrative agencies in the policymaking process. As such, it enjoyed minimal prospects for success.

Even if the agencies had liked PPBS, Congress would have balked at it. Some agencies used PPBS, but it failed to penetrate congressional thinking. Two factors help account for this. First, members of Congress like close connections with particular agencies—connections they can use to win benefits for their constituents. They see less strategic advantage in dealing, under PPBS, with an amorphous "program," which need not be attached to any single organization. Second, Congress likes the sense of control built into line-item budgeting. This form of budgeting can straitjacket managers, but it gives Congress a sense that they know how agencies are spending money. PPBS threatens to blur fiscal accountability—a development unlikely to please members of an institution already concerned about their diminished control over the federal purse.

Zero-Base Budgeting

Like program budgeting, zero-base budgeting (ZBB) requires superhuman analytical capability and rafts of data. Whereas traditional incremental budgeting operates from the assumption that the previous year's budget (the base) is justified and it is principally the increments that require careful examination, ZBB demands a more comprehensive examination of all expenditures. There should be no base, and the entire spending plan should be justified every year. This is supposed to terminate or at least reduce weak programs, which may have persisted largely out of inertia, and free up funds for meritorious programs. This form of budgeting came to Washington with President Carter, who tried it while he was governor of Georgia.

The *decision unit* is the building block of ZBB. A decision unit may be an agency but is frequently smaller, such as an operating program in an agency. Each budget manager is expected to prepare a number of *decision packages* to reflect priorities for funding. The manager presents these packages in rank order of importance, starting with the survival package, the lowest level of funding on which the unit can continue to exist. On top of the survival package are additional decision packages, reflecting first the existing level of the program and then expansions of service. Managers justify each decision package in terms of the services it would provide at an acceptable cost.

Decision packages prepared by lower-level budget managers go up the hierarchy to senior executives, who must prepare *consolidated decision packages* that rank priorities among the decision units. These rankings are passed along and consolidated even further, finally ending up in the OMB. All rankings from the lower levels are passed along with the consolidated packages so that higher-level decisionmakers can examine the preferences of lower-level managers and the justifications for their preferences. Like program budgeting, ZBB is oriented toward multiyear budgeting in order to convey the long-term implications of choices made in a single budget cycle.

Zero-base budgeting has several apparent advantages. It does not regard the base as beyond challenge and so fights inertia, although in practice the survival level may function as a base. It also focuses on cost-effectiveness in the rankings of decision packages, even in the survival level of funding. One principal advantage of zero-base budgeting is letting managers at lower levels consider and help set priorities and goals. The method also allocates resources in packages intended to produce a given volume of services. The standard budgeting method tends to assume that any additional amount of money can be used effectively, but ZBB realizes that after some threshold of outputs is achieved, additional allocations may well produce diminishing returns.

Nevertheless, ZBB suffers from grave drawbacks. For example, it is an obvious threat to the continued existence of some agencies. In practice a number of political factors such as client groups and uncontrollable expenditures may negate any real concern on the part of administrators. It is nevertheless clear that the intent of ZBB is to bring the existence of each organization in government into question each year.

The immensity of the task of examining each program each year is a major weakness. There is no means by which OMB, held to a reasonable size, or a Congress with a number of other tasks to perform, can carefully consider the entire budget each year. The information costs of such an enterprise would be staggering. Therefore, those asked to use ZBB resort to superficial analysis under the guise of a zero-base review or make a selective review of controversial programs. Either is an acceptable means of reducing the workload, but neither constitutes a major departure from the incremental budget or justifies the massive outlay of effort required to prepare the necessary documents.

Zero-base budgeting threatens established programs by reopening old political conflicts during each budget cycle. As noted earlier, incremental budgeting tends to reduce conflict. In contrast, ZBB (at least in theory) questions the very existence of the program each year. This makes conflict more intense and means that struggles have to be fought again and again. This is not a major problem for well-established and popular programs, but it certainly poses difficulties for new and controversial ones.

Balanced Budget Amendment

While the 1960s and 1970s spawned analytic methodologies associated with PPBS and ZBB in order to fight the inertia and narrow interests of incrementalism, the deficits of the 1980s as well as the ideological commitment of a conservative president altered the focus of budget reform. The reforms of the 1980s reflected primarily an effort to constrain either spending or deficits.

President Reagan endorsed an amendment to the Constitution requiring Congress to pass a balanced budget each year unless some extraordinary majority of Congress (possibly two-thirds of those voting) declared that an emergency existed. Such an amendment would require more explicit comparison of revenues and expenditures. It would demand that policymakers make hard decisions concerning priorities and trade-offs rather than encourage something-for-everyone politics.

However, the balanced budget amendment would face several problems. First, the planning for a budget begins more than a year ahead of execution and more than two years before the end of the budget year. During that time changes in economic conditions can eviscerate budget and revenue estimates. Forecasting is inexact. Second, rather than face the tax and spending implications of a balanced budget, policymakers may become increasingly skilled at moving expenditures off-budget and other fiscal camouflage. If all else fails, Congress may routinely declare emergencies to allow the federal government to run deficits. Whether born of imperfect forecasts or fiscal sleight of hand, failure to meet a constitutional requirement could further undermine public respect for Congress and the federal government. Finally, the pursuit of a balanced budget amendment does little to educate the public to the limits of balanced budgets in managing the economy. Keynesians, monetarists, supply-siders, and adherents of other economic schools acknowledge the value of deficits for a healthy economy in certain circumstances. Although the size of the federal deficit in the 1980s reached disturbing levels, the value of a degree of leeway in the federal budget should not be ignored.

The Line-Item Veto

In his 1984 State of the Union message President Reagan proposed that the line-item veto be made available to the president for appropriations bills. Similar to the power of governors in forty-three states, the line-item veto would allow the president to veto an "item" in a bill and permit the remainder to be put into effect. This is seen as helping the president deal with the tendency of members of Congress to add pet projects to appropriations bills, placing the president in the awkward position of having to refuse money for a large segment of the federal government in order to prevent one or two projects from being funded. Proponents of this reform see it as a means for trimming wasteful government expenditures and fighting the federal deficit. Studies of item vetoes in the states suggest that governors at times use them to shape policy priorities and possibly to practice fiscal restraint.[43]

The item veto is hardly a panacea, however.[44] It would have limited applicability to entitlement programs and other uncontrollable expenditures like interest payments on the national debt. Moreover, the line-item veto could encourage members of Congress to add more pet projects to appropriations bills and place the onus of removing them on the President. Congress would also become creative about how lines get articulated in appropriations measures. It would probably mingle things the president favors with those he disfavors. The line-item veto might also give the president powers not intended by the framers of the Constitution nor desired by the public.

Cuts by Autopilot: Gramm-Rudman-Hollings

Neither the balanced budget amendment nor the line-item veto has attracted enough political support to be approved and implemented. In contrast, the late 1980s witnessed congressional approval of a measure designed to produce automatic cuts in the event Congress failed to reduce the size of the deficit. Congress approved the

Gramm-Rudman-Hollings bill—the Balanced Budget and Emergency Deficit Control Act—in 1985. This law called for persistent reductions in the annual deficit over five years and required a balanced budget by 1991. If Congress did not meet the deficit targets, *sequestration,* or certain automatic cuts, would occur.

Processes of sequestration would commence if mid-August reports from OMB and the Congressional Budget Office to the General Accounting Office indicated that the budget for the subsequent fiscal year exceeded the deficit target. If the two estimates of the deficit differed, the GAO could average the difference or otherwise provide an estimate. If the projected deficit exceeded the target by $10 billion, then GAO had to instruct the president to begin sequestration of funds. The president and Congress then had about a month to come up with a plan to cut the deficit figure, either by raising taxes or by reducing expenditures. If GAO ruled that this plan failed to cut the deficit by the required amount, automatic cuts were to occur. Roughly half of these cuts would be from defense and half from domestic programs. Congress exempted certain programs, among them Social Security and interest payments on the national debt, and reduced the degree to which certain others could be slashed (e.g., no more than two percent in the case of Medicare).

Soon after the passage of Gramm-Rudman-Hollings, Representative Mike Synar, a Democrat from Oklahoma, challenged the law before the Supreme Court, arguing that its provisions for automatic spending cuts were unconstitutional. On 7 July 1986 the court sided with Synar. The court reasoned that GAO was an agent of Congress and could not exercise executive powers to impose expenditure cuts. The idea of automatic cuts did not die, however. In September 1987 Congress approved and the president signed a new version of the law. Among other things, the new statute assigned the president and OMB responsibility for sequestration. But it required OMB to "give due regard" to reports from the CBO on the size of the federal deficit. Exhibit 6.5 provides a brief overview of the sequestration process.

Soon after passage, sequestration received a trial run. Failure to reach deficit targets for fiscal 1988 led to mandatory cuts on 20 November 1987. Pressure from this action as well as concern over the negative effects of the deficit on Wall Street and the economy helped lay the foundation for congressional approval of a two-year deficit reduction plan in December 1987. This plan met the revised deficit targets in the new version of Gramm-Rudman-Hollings and sequestration was lifted.

As this experience suggests, the chief benefit of Gramm-Rudman-Hollings may well be to press Congress to deal with the deficit in ways other than sequestration. Such across-the-board cuts carry a number of dysfunctions. Efficient and effective programs endure the same slashes as wasteful, ineffective ones. The possibility of sequestration adds new uncertainty to the work of government executives, making it more difficult for them to make plans. Furthermore, the law stands as a vivid symbol of budgetary gridlock and raises new questions about the capacity of the nation's political institutions to govern. Policymakers in Washington are not blind to these defects. As Senator William Armstrong, Republican of Colorado, noted in a speech to the Senate before it approved the 1987 version of Gramm-Rudman-Hollings, the bill "is not worse than doing nothing. But I am not very confident of my own opinion."[45]

Will Gramm-Rudman-Hollings impose the discipline to balance the budget? Barring economic downturn, possibly. On balance, however, the barriers to a balanced budget are formidable. As the 1990s dawned, policymakers were deeply

EXHIBIT 6.5   Key Steps in Sequestration

August 15	The president provides official notice of the commencement of the deficit snapshot.
August 20	CBO estimates the size of the deficit for the coming fiscal year, the amount that federal spending must be reduced to reach the deficit target for that year, and the percentage by which program accounts must be cut to achieve the required reduction.
August 25	OMB does a separate analysis addressing the same issues as the CBO report; OMB must give due regard to the CBO report and explain any differences between its estimates and CBO's.
	The President issues an order mandating cuts on October 1.
October 1	Fiscal year commences.
October 10	CBO does new estimates and determines whether sequestration remains necessary to meet the deficit targets; if so, it recommends the automatic cuts.
October 15	OMB, after giving due regard to the CBO report, performs similar calculations. If OMB indicates that sequestration remains necessary, the president issues final orders for spending cuts.
Later	Congress may through joint resolution cancel the executive order; it may also approve expenditure or appropriations measure which would no longer make sequestration necessary.

Source: *Congressional Quarterly Weekly Report* 45 (September 26, 1987): 2309–11.

divided on what measures to pursue to reduce annual deficits. Moreover, neither the president nor Congress indicated much willingness to take the political heat for deficit reduction. In the absence of political will, it remains doubtful that Gramm-Rudman-Hollings can impose discipline on policymakers. The law may spawn more gimmickry than deficit decline. To be sure, the 1987 version attempted to prevent some accounting subterfuges, but the potential for gimmickry remains substantial. The willingness of key players to accept excessively optimistic estimates of revenue and expenditures seems particularly probable. This practice will let policymakers meet the Gramm-Rudman-Hollings deficit reduction targets on paper and avoid sequestration as well as tough political choices about program cuts and tax increases. As has commonly occurred, the actual deficit for a given year will be appreciably greater than the amount originally projected.

Conclusion

No student of public administration can safely ignore certain central characteristics of budgeting. While Congress exerts significant influence and power, the budget is an executive document featuring line items. While budgeting has become ongoing, repetitive, and late, the formal cycle driving the process remains annual. With the passage of the Congressional Budget and Impoundment Control Act of 1974, new players joined the lineup and budgeting became more complex. The process featured such staples as agency requests, OMB review of requests, and projections of the economy as well as involved efforts by newly created budget committees to set targets for expenditures and revenues.

Budgeters often point to certain phenomena as problems. These include uncontrollable entitlements, backdoor spending, the overhang, the intergovernmental challenge, and gimmickry. Analysts have also noted the special tensions created when budgeting shifts from an incremental to a decremental mode.

The quest to reform budget processes has changed directions. PPBS and ZBB represented efforts to introduce more synoptic consideration of programs—to resist the inertia of the budget base and to think more broadly and analytically about alternatives. Neither produced many significant changes in the behavior of budgetary decisionmakers. These methods threatened to impose huge information costs on government—to increase greatly the burdens of calculation for officials. Many budgeters had no incentive to support these reforms. Members of Congress saw the reforms as causing political conflict and reducing their ability to understand and control agencies. Agencies seemed more concrete to Congress than programs or decision packages. An agency has top executives to hold accountable for the expenditure of funds. A cynic could contend that the major effect of PPBS and ZBB has been the death of countless trees to make the reams of paper required by both methods. In any event, the line-item method continues to dominate budgeting.

The reforms of the 1980s focused on the budget when decrementalism and huge deficits had reared their respective heads. The balanced budget proposals, line-item vetoes, and versions of Gramm-Rudman-Hollings focused less on increasing synoptic analysis than on finding ways to discipline spending and taxing behavior. They sought to increase prospects that policymakers would agree to do politically unpalatable things. With the exception of the line-item veto, which would let Congress buck tough decisions to the president, these reforms sought to press Congress to make hard political trade-offs. The only one of the proposals to muster the support required for adoption (Gramm-Rudman-Hollings) involved a cutting mechanism that policymakers could disown. They could deplore the effects of the cuts and try to escape the political heat of voting for unpopular measures. If policymakers moved to impose reductions other than those directed by Gramm-Rudman-Hollings, they could at least claim that their actions were an improvement over the blind slashing of the law. Even then, gimmickry threatened to undermine Gramm-Rudman-Hollings.

Whatever the nature of future reforms, they will be discussed in a politically charged context far different from the one in evidence prior to the 1970s. The growth of entitlements and the budget deficit has transformed the political environment of public administrators. These developments have created a growing sense of scarcity as less money becomes available for new initiatives or to sustain the administrative infrastructure needed to deliver current programs effectively, efficiently, and accountably. Moreover, these developments have forced administrators to operate among increasingly partisan fights over the budget among members of Congress and the President. A "fiscalization of policy debate" has occurred whereby policymakers spend so much time struggling over the budget that little time exists for attention to other matters.[46] More than ever, the politics of the budgetary process sets the tone for administrative life.

Notes

1. Aaron Wildavsky, *The Politics of the Budgetary Process* (Boston: Little, Brown, 1964), 5.
2. B. Guy Peters, "The Limits of the Welfare State," in Norman J. Vig and Steven E. Schier, *Political Economy in Western Democracies* (New York: Holmes and Meier, 1985).
3. Michael Stewart, *Keynes and After* (Harmondsworth, Middlesex: Penguin, 1972); Robert Skidelsky, *The End of the Keynesian Era* (London: Macmillan, 1977).
4. Aaron Wildavsky, "A Budget for All Seasons: Why the Traditional Budget Lasts." *Public Administration Review* 38 (1978): 501–9.
5. Louis Fisher, "Ten Years of the Budget Act: Still Searching for Controls." *Public Budgeting and Finance* 5 (1985): 3–28.
6. Aaron Wildavsky, *The New Politics of the Budgetary Process* (Glenview, IL: Scott, Foresman, 1988), 222–23.
7. Ibid., 173.
8. Aaron Wildavsky, *Budgeting: A Comparative Theory of the Budgetary Process,* 2d ed. (New Brunswick, NJ: Transaction, 1986), 18–20.
9. Lawrence C. Pierce, *The Politics of Fiscal Policy Formation* (Pacific Palisades, CA: Goodyear, 1972).
10. David Stockman, *The Triumph of Politics* (New York: Avon, 1987), 105–6.
11. Jonathan Rauch, "CBO's Wishful Thinking." *National Journal* (March 3, 1987): 550–4.
12. Joseph S. Wholey, "Executive Agency Retrenchment," in Gregory B. Mills and John L. Palmer, eds., *Federal Budget Policy in the 1980s* (Washington, D.C.: Urban Institute Press, 1984), 295–336.
13. Wildavsky, *The Politics of the Budgetary Process,* 63–124.
14. Hugh Heclo, "Executive Budget Making," in Gregory B. Mills and John L. Palmer, eds., *Federal Budget Policy in the 1980s,* 287–8.
15. Stockman, *The Triumph of Politics,* 357, 383.
16. David Heald, *Public Expenditure* (Oxford: Martin Robertson, 1983), 176–9.
17. *Congressional Quarterly Weekly Report* 47 (March 18, 1989): 566.
18. Richard D. Fenno, *The Power of the Purse* (Boston: Little, Brown, 1966); John W. Ellwood and James A. Thurber, "The Politics of the Congressional Budget Process Reexamined," in Lawrence C. Dodd and Bruce Oppenheimer, eds., *Congress Reconsidered* (Washington, D.C.: Congressional Quarterly Press, 1981).
19. Allen Schick, *Congress and Money* (Washington, D.C.: Urban Institute Press, 1980), 589.
20. See Fisher, "Ten Years of the Budget Act . . .,"; Note also Dale Tate's observation that "Almost from the outset, the supposedly advisory first resolution has taken on the mandatory character of the second, the latter having become pro forma. This began as early as 1975. . . . The budget act's deadlines for the first and second resolutions long have been a dead letter." *Congressional Quarterly Weekly Report 42* (August 18, 1984): 2016–7. See also Wildavsky, *The New Politics of the Budgetary Process,* 215.
21. Wildavsky, *The New Politics of the Budgetary Process,* 192–3, 196–7, 200, 207.
22. Robert D. Reischauer, "The Congressional Budget Process," in Mills and Palmer, *Federal Budget Policy . . .,* 385–413.
23. Stanley B. Collender, *The Guide to the Federal Budget, Fiscal 1988* (Washington, D.C.: Urban Institute Press, 1987), 77–83.

24. Frederick C. Mosher, *The GAO: The Quest for Accountability* (Boulder, CO: Westview Press, 1979).

25. Wildavsky, *The New Politics of the Budgetary Process,* 259.

26. Ibid., 421.

27. Ibid., 264.

28. United States General Accounting Office, *Budget Issues: The Use of Spending Authority* (Washington, D.C.: GAO/AFMD–87–44, 17 July 1987).

29. For an analysis of the effects of grants on state and local governments, see Wallace E. Oates, *The Political Economy of Fiscal Federalism* (Lexington, MA: D.C. Heath, 1977).

30. Richard B. Simeon, *Federal Provincial Diplomacy* (Toronto: University of Toronto Press, 1973).

31. Wildavsky, *The New Politics of the Budgetary Process,* 212, 230.

32. *Newsweek,* 24 April 1989, 36.

33. Ibid.

34. M. A. H. Dempster and Aaron Wildavsky, "On Change: Or, There is No Magic Size for an Increment." *Political Studies* 28 (1980): 371–89.

35. Otto A. Davis et al., "A Theory of the Budgetary Process." *American Political Science Review* 60 (1969): 529–47.

36. Wildavsky, *The Politics of the Budgetary Process.*

37. Peter B. Natchez and Irvin C. Bupp, "Policy and Priority in the Budgetary Process." *American Political Science Review* 64 (1973): 951–63.

38. John R. Gist, " 'Increment' and 'Base' in the Congressional Appropriations Process." *American Journal of Political Science* 21 (1977): 341–52.

39. Barry Bozeman and Jeffrey D. Straussman, "Shrinking Budgets and the Shrinkage of Budgetary Theory." *Public Administration Review* 42 (1982): 509–15.

40. For an attempt at including such factors in predictive models, see Otto A. Davis et al., "Toward a Predictive Theory of Government Expenditure: US Domestic Appropriations." *British Journal of Political Science* 4 (1974): 419–52.

41. Allen Schick, "Incremental Budgeting in a Decremental Age," in Frederick S. Lane, ed., *Current Issues in Public Administration,* 3d ed. (New York: St. Martin's Press, 1986), 296. This discussion of decrementalism draws heavily on Schick's article.

42. Bertram M. Gross, "The New Systems Budgeting." *Public Administration Review* 29 (1969): 113–37.

43. See, for instance, James J. Gosling, "Wisconsin Item-Veto Lessons," *Public Administration Review* 46 (1986): 292–300; Wildavsky, *The New Politics of the Budgetary Process,* 429.

44. For a particularly piercing critique, see Wildavsky, *The New Politics of the Budgetary Process,* 429–37.

45. *Congressional Quarterly Weekly Report* 45 (September 26, 1987): 2309.

46. Wildavsky, *The New Politics of the Budgetary Process,* 186, 203.

Chapter Seven

Administrative Law and Public Administration

Introduction

Pervasive administrative discretion raises the specter of capricious action and abuse by the bureaucracy. A plethora of institutions and groups outside of an agency check such tendencies. Of particular relevance here, the courts have become more aggressive in seeking to assess and overturn decisions made by administrators (see Chapter 5). The role of the courts points to the more general importance of administrative law as a force shaping the politics of bureaucracy.

It has become a cliche to observe that Americans have a government of laws and not of persons, but to a great extent this is true. A large number of legal mechanisms protect citizens from abuse by government officials. Some of these exist in civil and constitutional law, but others reside in *administrative law*. Such law regulates how public officials exercise their duties and how they must treat citizens. In the United States administrative law is not entirely separate from the mainstream of civil law; under the proper circumstances the citizen can take a complaint from administrative tribunals into the federal court system. Although it has become a specialized branch of law, administrative law in the United States is still ultimately linked to the same constitutional and legal principles that govern other public actions.[1]

Administrative law is as broad as public administration, but it has been developed mostly to deal with the quasi-legislative and quasi-judicial functions of public administration. The bureaucracy in the United States makes many more rules than does the legislature, and it tries many more cases than does the court system. It is when the public bureaucracy plays legislator or judge that the major issues of administrative law arise. The law works to ensure that citizens are protected against arbitrary and capricious actions of the political executive, a concern that is deeply rooted in the American political consciousness. American government began in large part as a protest against excesses by the executive branch of the British government.

Administrative law involves a fundamental trade-off. The desire for due process and precise, codified, uniform rules that limit administrative discretion conflicts with the view that administrators ought to be able to respond rapidly, flexibly, and efficiently to particular situations. Consistent with the latter view, discretion becomes especially important as the tasks of government become more specialized and require the application of expertise as much as the application of the law.[2] Neither extreme is

168

fully satisfactory; hence, those involved strive to strike a balance between the two. Observers differ, however, in their interpretation of the proper balance.

While administrative law formalizes procedures for making rules and adjudicating particular cases, the role of informal processes deserves note. Interested parties may get together to see if they can hammer out an agreement on the wording of a rule. Disputant agency and client may be encouraged to reach a settlement via informal means rather than an extensive hearing. Informality can violate norms of due process as well as other values fostered by the formal procedures. However, complete dependence on formal procedures might grind public administration to a halt as the decision system overloaded.

This chapter begins its discussion of the significant issues of public law with the Administrative Procedures Act, which establishes critical parameters for administrative law. It then addresses processes the bureaucracy uses to promulgate rules. Efforts to slow the proliferation of rules and deregulate also receive attention. The chapter then considers processes of assuring that rules get applied appropriately in particular cases. Finally, the chapter develops a topic broached earlier—the judicial review of administrative decisions.

The Administrative Procedures Act

The Administrative Procedures Act of 1946 (5 USC 551 et seq.) provides the foundation for much of contemporary administrative law in the United States. This act was to promulgate principles governing the conduct of administrative agencies and thereby to formalize a body of law that had been evolving since the early days of the republic. Prior decisions on some fundamental issues, such as the right of Congress to delegate rulemaking power (*The Brig Aurora* case)[3] and a broad interpretation of the "necessary and proper" clause of the Constitution[4] allowed public agencies to expand their administrative powers. By the early twentieth century the public bureaucracy was a major rulemaker and rule adjudicator in government.

The growth in the size and powers of the federal bureaucracy during the New Deal and World War II fueled demands to formalize the huge body of rulings, precedents, and procedures that controlled what some saw as the "headless fourth branch of government."[5] These demands were reinforced by the Supreme Court's ruling that the National Industrial Recovery Act, a part of President Roosevelt's New Deal, granted too much rulemaking discretion to the agency responsible for implementing the law.[6] The American Bar Association also pushed hard for codification of administrative law and for some coherent guidance for administrative agencies that had to make rulings. These were enacted in the Administrative Procedures Act (APA).

Some details of the APA receive attention later in this chapter. The general nature of the APA is to establish standards against which the activities of administrative agencies can be judged. Actions taken by agencies outside the procedural requirements set forth in the APA are almost inherently arbitrary and capricious and susceptible to legal challenge. The procedures specified in the APA do not mean that everyone will like the substantive outcome of rulemaking or adjudication, but they are designed to ensure fairness in those processes.

The APA defines the agency in American government as an " . . . authority of the Government of the United States, whether or not it is within or subject to review by another agency."[7] Amendments in 1974 made it clear that this definition was to include off-line organizations such as government corporations as well as the Executive Office of the President. Thus, except for the operations of Congress, of the courts, and of some military organizations, the APA covers almost the entire federal government.

It also defines a great deal of federal policy concerning information. The Freedom of Information Act amends the APA, as do the Privacy Act of 1974, the Government in the Sunshine Act, and the Federal Advisory Committee Act. These acts collectively open government to citizens and foster the flow of information about government to the public while protecting citizens' privacy. Rather than standing alone, they are now considered a part of the fundamental statute governing agency activity.

The APA includes the procedures for making and adjudicating laws by federal agencies. Because it is uniform across government, organizations and citizens do not have to learn a whole new set of procedures for every agency. Differences in agencies' procedures and applications certainly exist, but the basic rules remain the same.

The APA defines the qualifications of hearing examiners or administrative law judges. Just before the passage of the APA the legal community expressed deep concern about fairness of quasi-judicial proceedings when the person hearing the case worked for one of the parties (the agency) to the case.[8] The APA attempts to ensure that administrative law judges will be qualified and as far as possible insulated from undue pressures within the agency. Further, it defines the manner in which the record of the hearing must be kept. This is important for the final section of the APA, which defines the scope and mechanisms for judicial review of decisions made in administrative hearings. As with much of administrative law, the right to judicial review of administrative hearings is a balance between the rights of citizens and the needs of the bureaucracy to keep floods of relatively minor administrative matters out of the federal court system and to act expeditiously and effectively to interpret and administer the law.

Rulemaking

Congress has long delegated some lawmaking to the executive branch. One of the early acts of Congress gave the president the right to govern the distribution of pensions to veterans of the Revolutionary War. Since that time the pace of delegation has quickened as both the number of rules and the technical content of those rules has increased. Each year the federal bureaucracy and the independent regulatory agencies make many times as many rules—frequently called regulations or "regs"—as Congress passes laws. Further, in only three major cases in American constitutional history (two involving the National Industrial Recovery Act of the New Deal) has the Supreme Court declared a delegation of authority made by Congress to be unconstitutional.[9] Thus, delegation of rulemaking authority is a well-established part of American government. (For an example of the political interplay surrounding this delegation, see Exhibit 7.1.) The magnitude of this activity can be seen by the size of the daily *Federal Register*, which publishes information concerning federal rulemaking. A week's worth of the *Federal Register* is now a compendium several inches thick of very fine type containing a vast number of rules, executive orders, proposed rules, and so on.

The administrative agencies could not make those rules if Congress had not given them the authority; otherwise they would be *ultra vires* (beyond the powers) and subject to overturn in court. Further, the agencies must make their rules within the procedures outlined in the APA. The rule cannot be "arbitrary, capricious, or otherwise not in accordance with law."

What Is a Rule?

The Administrative Procedures Act (Section 551(4)) defines a rule thus:

"Rule" means the whole or part of agency statement of general or particular applicability and future effect designed to implement, interpret or prescribe law or policy or describing the organization, procedure or practice requirements of an agency . . .

Most rules apply equally to all parties having the same characteristics. Finally, rules apply to any activities occurring in the future.

Those points are important in differentiating the quasi-legislative activities of agencies (rulemaking) from the quasi-judicial aspects (administrative adjudications). Adjudications tend to be specific, applying only to the parties in question rather than generally. In addition, adjudications tend to evaluate what has already occurred. In some instances the differences between rulemaking and adjudication will not be entirely clear, as in granting licenses for certain activities (nuclear power stations by the Nuclear Regulatory Agency or television stations by the Federal Communications Commission). Licensing is generally prospective but also involves specific decisions affecting only the parties to the application and, especially in the case of the television stations, may involve some retrospective evaluation of the performance of a current holder of the license.

Types of Rules

The APA specifies three major forms of rules, substantive, procedural, and interpretive. Each may be made in slightly different ways, and they have varying degrees of legal force. Each is important for understanding how agencies convert the broad statutes passed by Congress into specific and enforceable rules.

Substantive Rules.   In general terms, substantive rules are designed to "implement . . . or prescribe law or policy" (APA, Section 551(4)). They focus on the substance of agency activities, for example rules promulgated by the Occupational Safety and Health Administration concerning permissible levels of exposure to asbestos in the workplace. As noted above, such rules have the force of law and can be enforced in court just as if they were statutes coming from Congress.

EXHIBIT 7.1   Rulemaking Discretion: The Case of Alcohol Warning Labels

Congress makes laws for the federal government of the United States but almost never in sufficient detail to cover all eventualities. Thus, Congress explicitly and implicitly delegates a great deal of rulemaking authority to administrative agencies. When agencies exercise this discretion, they may appear to undermine or even contradict the intentions of Congress. These deviations on occasion spur members of Congress to intervene in the rulemaking process by complaining to the press, calling administrators to appear before committees, working with their colleagues to pass clarifying legislation, and so on.

The labeling provisions for alcoholic beverages described in the accompanying *Washington Post* article points to some of the political dynamics embedded in rulemaking. As is evident, a senator is displeased with the agency's proposed rule. Interest groups took different positions in their assessment of the temporary labeling policy. Thus, administrative agencies are involved in political process featuring diverse pressures when they make rules. Like the laws passed by Congress, these rules typically confer benefits on some groups and costs on others.

Alcohol Warning Labels May Be in Small Type
Congressionally Mandated Regulations for Beverages Issued

By Judith Havemann
Washington Post Staff Writer

Warning labels on alcoholic beverages, mandated by Congress last fall, may be written in type about the height of two stacked dimes on standard-sized bottles of liquor, beer or wine, according to temporary regulations issued yesterday by the Bureau of Alcohol, Tobacco and Firearms.

Smaller containers—the size of a standard eight-ounce cup or less—may be labeled using words only half that size, BATF said.

Sen. Strom Thurmond (R-S.C.), author of the requirement, said that "if the final regulations allow industry members to place minuscule labels in difficult-to-find places on the containers, the purpose of the law has been defeated."

The warnings will be required on the containers of all alcoholic beverages, including beer and wine, beginning with beverages manufactured on Nov. 18.

The labels will say: "Government warning. [1] According to the Surgeon General, women should not drink alcoholic beverages during pregnancy because of the risk of birth defects. [2] Consumption of alcoholic beverages impairs your ability to drive a car or operate machinery and may cause health problems."

The label and its wording were dictated by Congress as part of antidrug legislation passed last year.

The temporary regulations published in the Federal Register yesterday spelled out the minimum size, location and nature of the warning.

The label must be printed on a contrasting background, and may be placed on the "brand label, separate front label, or on a back or side label separate and apart from all other information."

The labels will be required only on alcoholic beverages bottled for sale in the United States, not abroad.

The public has 45 days to comment on the proposal, after which final rules will be published.

The Distilled Spirits Council of the United States, Inc., "representing the vast majority of distillers, does not believe that warning labels are necessary," said Janet Flynn, director of public affairs for the council. "However, we are prepared as a responsible industry to comply fully with the decision of Congress."

The regulations preempt states from requiring warning labels of their own. Although no states have required such labels, 10 jurisdictions, including the District of Columbia, require posters in liquor stores or sales areas warning of the dangers of alcohol to pregnant women, Flynn said.

Jeff Becker, director of the office of alcohol issues for the Beer Institute, said that his organization, too, would comply with the law although it had not changed its position that the labels are unnecessary.

Christine Lubinski, Washington representative of the National Council on Alcoholism, said, "The time for this measure is long overdue.

"This will provide urgently needed information about one of the leading causes of preventable retardation and early death in the United States."

The Washington Post, 17 February, 1989.

Most agencies have substantial powers to make rules, but congressional grants of authority do differ, with some agencies given the power to regulate activities "in the public interest"—a very broad grant of power and discretion—and other agencies having their powers and the scope of their activities more closely prescribed by Congress. The grant of authority may depend upon the nature of the agency (independent regulatory commissions tend to have broad and unspecific powers), the nature of the policy area, or simply the whim of Congress at the time.

Procedural Rules.   The APA and other statutes govern many procedures within agencies. However, these may not be sufficient to cover all needs; the agency may therefore issue its own procedural rules. Such rules make the actions of agencies in dealing with the public appear to be fairer and more just. Agencies need not follow all the requirements of the APA when they make their procedural rules. They must, however, announce them in the *Federal Register*, and once they are made, the agency must follow them.

Interpretive Rules.   Even though the rules issued by an agency are substantially more precise than the laws emerging from Congress, they may still require interpretation and explanation. Agencies therefore issue interpretive rules, or *guidelines*, which explain the agency's understanding of its own rules as well as the statutes it administers. For instance, the National Labor Relations Board at times offers interpretations of fair labor practice. Interpretive rules are specifically exempted from the procedural requirements of the APA, and they may not have the rule of law unless a court is willing to enforce them. Interpretative rules therefore come down on the side of administrative ease versus individual rights when there is such a trade-off. The agency is able to act quickly and promptly to make decisions. Interpretative rules allow agencies to render advice to clients in advance of actual decisions without the complex procedures required for making a formal rule.

How Are Rules Made?

The APA specifies how rules must be made in order to be legally binding. Rules made other ways do not have the force of law if challenged in the courts. The APA procedures provide that citizens and organizations with an interest in a particular policy area receive notice of the substance of the proposed rule. APA procedures also let interested parties comment on that new rule. In practice, they also allow them time to go to friendly members of Congress or otherwise place political pressure on the agency (for a particularly vivid example, see the case of the health planning guidelines in Chapter 4).

The APA specifies two major forms of rulemaking, informal and formal. In addition, court decisions and other legislation have produced a third category, *hybrid rulemaking,* a compromise between these two basic forms. While it will not receive detailed attention in this volume, some agencies also practice emergency, or summary, rulemaking. Officials can use such rulemaking, which is specifically exempted from APA procedural requirements, when they believe that an imminent threat to public health or safety exists.

Informal Rulemaking.   Agencies use informal procedures to deal with many issues. These procedures are relatively simple and officials frequently refer to the process as *notice and comment* rulemaking. The term *informal* in this context does *not* mean action "guided by no particular set of processes except habit, individual and group interaction, and circumstances." It refers to a more simplified, albeit standardized, process.[10]

Agencies initiate informal rulemaking with the publication of a notice of proposed rulemaking in the *Federal Register*. These notices must contain: (1) a statement of the time, place, and nature of any public rulemaking; (2) a statement of the legal authority under which the rule is to be issued; and (3) the substance of the proposed rule, or at least a mention of the topics to be covered. Those interested are given some means of commenting on the proposed rule—usually the name, address, and telephone number of someone in the agency who will receive public comments as well as the date by which comments must be made.

After the specified period, the agency is free to issue its final rule by again publishing it in the *Federal Register*. That notice must contain the substance of the rule and the legal authority under which it is made. It must be published at least thirty days prior to its effective date. Presumably, this practice gives affected parties time to come into compliance, and in practice it also allows time for additional contacts with Congress.

Informal rulemaking is a very simple procedure. It allows public input concerning the nature of the rule but does not bind the agency to follow the comments of the interested public. Again, affected interests may not always be happy with the rules, but they have some opportunity to make suggestions and complaints before the rule is issued.

Formal Rulemaking.   Formal rulemaking has some of the trappings of a judicial proceeding, although it is intended to have a legislative outcome. The enabling statutes for certain agencies specify that rules be ". . . made on the record after an agency hearing." If such language is used, formal rulemaking must be employed. Such proceedings are extremely ponderous and time-consuming compared with notice and comment proceedings. For example, it once took the Food and Drug Administration (FDA) twelve years to obtain a determination that peanut butter could contain 3 percent nonpeanut products. Formal proceedings allow full consideration of all the points of a particular rule; they also provide a complete record for future deliberations and for judicial review. They help to protect against any undisclosed biases in agency decisionmaking that could be manifested in informal rulemaking.

Formal rulemaking in many ways resembles a legal proceeding. It must be presided over by an administrative law judge or by specified members of the agency, for example one or more of the commissioners of an independent regulatory commission. Whereas informal proceedings allow the agency to disregard a good deal of the opinion of the public, a formal decision must be based on the entire record and supported by evidence. Also, unlike informal proceedings, formal proceedings lay the burden of proof on the party advocating the new rule. For example, a drug company wanting to have a new product declared safe and effective by the FDA must prove that the drug meets those qualifications under the law. In sum, these look very much like a trial rather than a legislative activity, even to the point of having cross-examination of witnesses.

These formal proceedings have the advantage of demanding full information and of promoting fairness and impartiality. However, they severely constrain administrative flexibility besides being very slow and expensive. The question also persists as to whether the adversarial nature of most Anglo-American law is the best way of making policy. It may be a very good means of protecting the rights of the accused in a criminal case but ill-suited to the compromise, negotiation, and amendment integral to successful public policy formulation in the United States.

Hybrid Rulemaking.   Given the rather extreme choice between formal and informal rulemaking, it is not surprising that a hybrid has emerged. This development occurred mostly during the 1960s and 1970s, largely as a result of judicial decisions.[11] The courts were not alone, however. Congressional legislation began to require hybrid rulemaking, and in 1978 President Carter issued Executive Order 12044, which called for greater openness, participation, and record-keeping in rulemaking. An increasing volume of rules involving complex scientific and technical questions helped spark the development of the hybrid proceedings. It became increasingly difficult for judges to review rulemaking in the face of an incomplete record that did not clarify the rationale for the agency's decisions.

The courts worked out hybrid rulemaking through a series of decisions on individual cases, especially the Vermont Yankee case.[12] The underlying logic of hybrid rulemaking is that the courts cannot determine whether an agency's decision is arbitrary or capricious without knowing whether the decision follows logically from the evidence available. Thus, judges took it upon themselves to review the evidence for particular rules and to assess the relationship between the evidence and the rule. In such proceedings the presumption is that the agency acted appropriately, but there is still an opportunity to challenge the rules. This serves as a check on arbitrary action by the agencies.

Hybrid rulemaking is the same general process as notice and comment, but it adds requirements for more stringent documentation of the agency's rationale for the rule. The record must include reference to the information used to reach a decision, evidence of adequate notice and time for comment by interested parties, evidence of any adverse comments on the proposed rule, and the agency's response to those comments (that is, reasons for accepting or for rejecting the adverse comments). In other words, the agency must be able to demonstrate to a judge that a reasonable person looking at the evidence could have arrived at the same determination as the agency.

Putting the Brakes on Rulemaking

The processes of rulemaking, especially the hybrid and formal variants, place a substantial burden of proof on the bureaucracy. They slow down the pace at which they can issue new rules. Nonetheless, the growth in the number and scope of federal regulations generated considerable alarm in the 1970s and 1980s.

Regulatory Analysis.   Political conservatives have worried that government agencies write regulations almost at will and without proper consideration of their economic effects. Thus, beginning with President Ford, the White House sought to force agencies to pay more attention to the economic and other effects of rules and to avoid promulgating unnecessary or costly rules. President Ford authorized the Office of Management and Budget to require inflation impact statements concerning proposed new rules.[13] President Carter required even more sweeping regulatory analysis.[14] He required the agency to justify its choice of a particular rule against other possible rules or simply not to issue it at all. The primary considerations were economic, but there was nothing to exclude other forms of analysis as well.

When President Reagan assumed office in 1981, he built on the work of Ford and Carter and gave more powers for review to OMB. Executive Order 12291, issued in the first month of his presidency, required agencies to submit all proposed regulations to OMB for review; the independent regulatory agencies were excluded from this provision in order to avoid confrontation with Congress. In 1985 President Reagan issued Executive Order 12498, under which OMB reviewed an annual compilation of agency regulatory policy as well as the agency's objectives and rulemaking plans for the coming year to ensure that these corresponded to the president's wishes. In the Reagan presidency the review was less technical and more political than under Ford and Carter. During this period the Supreme Court struck down the legislative veto, which allowed Congress to review and reject agency rules. This development enhanced OMB's power over rulemaking and led critics to complain that OMB had become the "regulatory KGB."[15]

Despite OMB's central powers for reviewing new rules, the agencies developed a number of ploys for escaping its control. These included using friendly members of Congress or the media to publicize the denial of regulatory power; this has been especially useful for the Environmental Protection Agency and the Occupational Safety and Health Administration, which have vocal support from interest groups. Congress's propensity to write into laws deadlines by which an agency must issue regulations can deny OMB sufficient time for review. Agencies may also circumvent OMB by interpreting existing regulations to permit new regulatory initiatives without new rules. Finally, an agency may use semantic devices such as calling a rule a guideline in order to avoid OMB scrutiny. While OMB has enhanced its power to block new regulations, it hardly looms as omnipotent in Washington's battle over policy.

Deregulation: A More Difficult Pursuit.   Through regulatory review and in other ways, a president can considerably slow the promulgation of new rules and standards. Deregulation via the elimination of rules already in the *Code of Federal Regulations* poses many more difficulties. In regulatory agencies, there often is a kind of ratchet effect, as if a toothed ratchet wheel allows regulation to turn more stringent from time to time but then locks it in place, preventing much repeal of rules. For instance, most everyone agreed that many of OSHA's first safety standards, issued in 1971, did little to protect workers and much to create a gigantic public relations problem for the agency (one was the requirement that toilet stalls have coat hangers). Yet efforts to revoke many of these rules did not reach fruition until the late 1970s.[17]

Several factors can impede the removal of regulations. Faced with limited time and resources, officials often prefer to devote their energies to new initiatives, such as a standard to regulate a newly discovered carcinogen. Furthermore, the procedures for getting rules off the books tend to be as elaborate as for putting them on. The agency must generally publish a notice of its intention to delete rules in the *Federal Register*. Frequently it must go to great lengths to document the reason for change and to let interest groups argue against the change. In the case of OSHA's efforts to delete rules, unions expressed grave reservations for fear that the action represented capitulation to business interests. Moreover, for all the speeches business leaders give about the virtue of free enterprise, they too often weigh in against various kinds of deregulation. Agencies must in some cases permit formal appeals and hearings, which make removing a rule even more costly and time-consuming.

These difficulties encourage presidents bent on deregulation to concentrate on enforcement. President Reagan had very modest success in getting administrative rules off the books. Through the budget and in other ways, however, he reduced enforcement staffs and generally made it more difficult to detect violations of rules and punish offenders. In many instances only the shell of regulation, that is, the rules themselves, remained. Future presidents may, of course, decide to commit more resources to ensuring compliance with the rules. Hence, Reagan's inability significantly to reduce rules may undermine deregulation over the long term.

As the experience of the Reagan administration suggests, the barriers to reduction of rules can thwart a president committed to cutting back government intervention in the economy. Furthermore, the procedures can thwart learning by trial and error. Agencies do err in promulgating regulatory standards. OSHA put rules on the books that did little if anything to foster safety in the workplace and aroused the ire of the business community because some were so trivial. The complexity of revocation made it very difficult for the agency to correct its mistakes.

Administrative Adjudication

Just as making rules is quasi-legislative, applying them is often quasi-judicial. The bureaucracy makes many more rules than does Congress; so too does it try many more cases than the federal courts. Administrative law judges and other officials in the Social Security Administration in 1986 heard nearly one and a half million cases. The rulemaking workload would swamp Congress without the bureaucracy, and the huge volume of cases would overwhelm the federal court system were it not for administrative law judges. (Unlike the typical civil or criminal court case, administrative adjudication frequently involves more than two parties.)[18]

Due Process As the Dominant Concern

Due process is the fundamental criterion for administrative adjudications. The Fifth Amendment to the Constitution affirms that no person shall be deprived of "life, liberty, or property, without due process of law." The Fourteenth Amendment extends the same requirements to the states (and thereby to local government). While administrative adjudications do not directly deprive anyone of life, they certainly can affect liberty and property. Due process applies to these proceedings as much as to a case tried in a federal courtroom. Assuring due process in administrative settings is often problematic. For example, critics charge that the administrative law judge, who works for the agency that is a party to the proceedings, will often be unduly sympathetic to the agency. Also, many administrative procedures are streamlined compared with those of a regular court. Again, government has sought to strike a balance between efficiency and justice. It is a point of argument whether government has tipped too far in favor of efficiency and expediency or needlessly tied the hands of administrators with elaborate due process.

Substantive versus Procedural.   Due process tends to be perceived as ensuring that the parties to a proceeding get to present their case and be heard fairly. Elements such as the right to counsel, cross-examination of witnesses, and the right to call one's own witnesses lie at the heart of due process. A formal administrative hearing has all these trappings, but less formal proceedings may exclude some or all of them.

Due process also has a substantive element. Does the law under which a person is deprived of life, liberty, or property square with acceptable notions of justice? Nearly all laws deprive some people and advantage others. Laws against murder deprive psychopaths in order to benefit their prospective victims. Laws that deprive individuals of their liberty or property on the basis of race, religion, gender, or similar attributes inherently run counter to due process. Thus, the substance of the rule may affect its acceptability.

Administrative versus Judicial Criteria.   Some of the procedural protections of judicial proceedings are absent in administrative adjudications. Under administrative law a disputant has no right to trial by jury; rules of evidence are somewhat less stringent; and the person making the final decision works for the agency. Thus, some of the features of administrative due process require special doctrines to cover contingencies. Further, administrative due process becomes all the more important as administrative tribunals determine an increasing volume of decisions important to individuals, for example on social benefits, education, and employment. In general, federal courts have been imposing constraints on the conduct of administrative adjudication, although considerable latitude does remain for administrative action.

Rights and Privileges.   An old doctrine of administrative law adheres to a fundamental distinction between the rights of individuals and the privileges government bestows upon them. Presumably, rights such as due process must be treated very differently from privileges such as public employment or social benefits. Rights receive more weight in adjudications than privileges.

The Supreme Court under Earl Warren (1954–1969) virtually eliminated the distinction between rights and privileges in administrative law.[19] In a series of decisions the court held that government may not exercise arbitrary controls over public employment or the benefits of public programs. The recipients of these privileges were entitled to many of the procedural protections of those whose rights might be denied by administrative actions. Given that such a large proportion of the population of the United States now depends upon government for some or all of their income[20] as well as for important services and amenities, effective protections against the arbitrary removal of government benefits are important for most Americans.

The Supreme Court under Burger and Rehnquist has to some degree resurrected the rights versus privileges doctrine. In a number of cases the court has held that receiving social benefits is indeed a privilege, even in the case of Social Security, which has always been justified politically as being "insurance" rather than government largesse. In *Bishop* v. *Wood* the court found that government employment, in this case at the local level, was a privilege. Hence government employees were not necessarily entitled to as much procedural protection against dismissal as they would be if a fundamental right were at stake.[21] The court has made similar decisions about rights to attend state universities and to be employed by the federal government.

Irrebuttable Presumption.   Another important doctrine in administrative law, *irrebuttable presumption,* has undergone significant change. This doctrine holds that certain characteristics of a person's situation create a presumption about other characteristics and that the individual in question cannot argue about the linkage. For instance, many state universities assumed that formerly out-of-state students could not prove they were now bona fide residents of the state. Or a state law might presume that the fathers of illegitimate children were inherently unfit parents so could not receive custody of the children after the death of the mother. Some irrebuttable presumptions exist at the federal level as well. For example, one law presumes that someone who married a Social Security recipient less than nine months prior to the recipient's death is not entitled to survivor benefits because they married the individual in anticipation of the death and the consequent benefits.

As with rights and privileges, the Warren Court tended to strike down irrebuttable presumptions denying due process. The Warren Court threw out all of the state laws mentioned above.[22] The Burger and Rehnquist courts, on the other hand, have tended to accept such provisions, including the Social Security presumption mentioned above.[23] Again, a more conservative Supreme Court has been siding with public policymakers to deny procedural protections.

The examples of rights and privileges and irrebuttable presumption demonstrate a shift in the Supreme Court's thinking during the Burger era from what one scholar called an intrinsic view of due process toward an instrumental view of procedural and substantive protections.[24] The intrinsic view of due process is that certain procedural guarantees are necessary to protect citizens against arbitrary actions by government. It considers them to be intrinsic rights of any citizen and to have a very broad applicability. This view is that due process is essential to fair and impartial administrative adjudications.

The instrumental view of due process is that the courts should protect only clearly defined, vested legal rights through procedural rules, giving administrators substantially greater latitude. To claim protection under due process, a citizen must be able to define a specific legal or property right that government has violated. For example, in the *Roth* case the court upheld without a hearing the dismissal of an untenured faculty member at a Wisconsin state university.[25] According to the court, Roth had no particular property right in the job, since it was based on an annual contract and the university simply chose not to renew that contract. The court ruled that he certainly had an interest in being rehired but that no definable property right existed. Thus the court clearly sided with administrators as opposed to procedural protections for individuals.

Hearings and Due Process

Just as the Administrative Procedures Act specifies what steps must be taken before quasi-legislative action can occur, it also regulates the issuing of orders—the outcome of administrative adjudication. Of particular importance, the APA provides the right to a hearing. In general individuals may demand a hearing when a statute, regulation, or the Constitution provides for it. If there is no specific legislative handle on which to hang the demand for a hearing, the citizen may invoke the due process clause of the Constitution in an effort to obtain procedural protections. The courts will then have to weigh that claim against the agency's clear interest in avoiding the cost and delay of a hearing.

If a hearing is required, it must occur before the individual suffers any harm from the proposed action, that is, before final action by the agency. It remains uncertain, however, exactly what is meant by final action. One view holds that the stipulation requires a hearing before anything happens to the individual, as before civil servants cut off program benefits. In a strict legal sense, however, some interpret final action as occurring when the agency has terminated its decision-making process. Although both of these criteria appear clear, in a number of instances, especially in complicated cases, the word "final" is very difficult to define.[26]

Types of Hearings.   Hearings assume many forms, ranging from extremely informal negotiation and conciliation proceedings to formal triallike hearings. Agencies use formal hearings relatively infrequently, in part because of the expense. In some instances, however, a formal hearing may be required for the full protection of the rights of the individual.

Negotiation and conciliation is the least formal type of hearing. Parties may meet informally in a prehearing conference to resolve their differences without formal proceedings. This may occur without counsel so as to keep negotiations from becoming adversarial. If the disputing parties can settle without a more formal hearing, they often save time and money.

The *paper hearing* is farther up the scale of formality. Administrative judges use this kind of hearing when they perceive a broad consensus on the facts of a case or can obtain the facts by reading written documents. The administrative law judge examines the available evidence and then renders a decision without calling for oral arguments. This saves all concerned a great deal of time but runs the risk of oversimplifying issues for the sake of convenience. It offers no opportunity for clarifying the "agreed" facts of a case, which in practice may not be nearly so straightforward as assumed. Further, such proceedings have the appearance of being bureaucratic rather than judicial, even if they are conducted by an administrative law judge.[27] Thus, they may damage the legitimacy of the administrative law process.

The next most formal type is the simple oral hearing. This avoids a trial setting but does allow the parties to present their arguments to an administrative law judge or other official. Generally counsel is not present. Unlike a paper hearing, however, this proceeding allows the affected individual to present a case to the official. Appealing parties do not always win but may perceive that they have had their day in court.

The formal hearing is the fourth category. The trappings of a regular courtroom mark these hearings, although some of the rules of regular federal court do not pertain to them. The language and legislative history of the enabling statute that created the agency substantially determine whether agency officials must use formal hearings.[28] Such hearings are more likely when administrators make decisions that can inflict great injury on an individual or group. However, officials possess some discretion in determining whether to hold a formal hearing.

A formal hearing must have:

1. Timely and adequate notice
2. Confrontation of adverse witnesses
3. Oral presentation of arguments
4. Oral presentation of evidence
5. Cross-examination of adverse witnesses
6. Disclosure to claimant of opposing evidence
7. The right to retain an attorney
8. Formal recording of the hearing
9. A statement of reasons for the final determination and an indication of the evidence that guided it
10. An impartial decisionmaker[29]

This is a rather formidable list of requirements, many of which are quite similar to those of regular courts. However, rules of evidence and rules about cross-examination may be substantially less restrictive in administrative adjudication. This is in part for administrative convenience; it is also because some issues are technically complex. While the law specifies that a formal hearing must have certain characteristics, it also leaves many questions unanswered. What is adequate and timely notice? How much information must the agency disclose? Who should be notified? Many licensing cases and other administrative adjudications have a strong element of the public interest involved, but whom to notify as representative of that broad interest?

Three issues in particular distinguished formal hearings from courtroom proceedings. First, the rules of evidence in an administrative adjudication are substantially less stringent than in regular court. In administrative adjudication hearsay or other unsubstantiated evidence is less likely to affect the decision. This is because a dispassionate administrative law judge or some other objective "expert" renders the final decision rather than an "impressionable" jury. Whether the administrative law judge in fact distinguishes the wheat from the chaff remains an open question. Nonetheless, the judge faces substantial pressure to admit all kinds of evidence, whatever its limitations, for fear of being overruled on appeal.

Second, administrative adjudication does not guarantee disputants the right to counsel. Hence, those with limited financial resources may suffer relative to plaintiffs with ample money. Industries adversely affected by government decisions can mount sophisticated efforts to overturn the decision at a formal hearing. The poor person denied Social Security benefits often has much less capacity to do so. In contrast, the poor have the right to counsel in criminal cases and even some civil proceedings before the courts.

Finally, law judges and others who preside at hearings are usually employees of agencies party to the proceedings. Can these officials be independent and impartial, or will they persistently tilt toward the agency position? The APA attempts to protect the impartiality of the presiding officer by limiting *ex parte* communications (those outside of the hearing proceedings). This practice presumably makes it more difficult for the employing agency and others to press the judge for a particular decision. Ultimately, however, the integrity of the administrative law judge and the possibility that a disputant will appeal to the regular court system are the best safeguards against undue bias toward the agency.

Judicial Review

The last quarter of a century has witnessed a more aggressive posture by the courts in reviewing administrative decisions (see Chapter 5). The courts have been less willing to give civil servants the benefit of the doubt; they have overruled administrative agencies on many occasions. Thus the courts serve as a major check on bureaucratic rulemaking and adjudication. Nonetheless, not every administrative case is open to appeal. Moreover, disputants appeal only a small fraction of administrative rules and adjudications to the federal court system. In considering what cases to hear, courts rely on certain criteria.

Criteria for Review

The courts themselves serve as crucial gatekeepers in the judicial process. Under the banner of judicial restraint and faced with heavy workloads, judges often look for reasons not to hear a case rather than the opposite. In general judges admit only cases that cannot be excluded on procedural grounds and that have some substantial federal question for review. Of course, the definition of *substantial* permits the ideology of the particular judge to come into play. Whatever the decision on whether to hear the case, however, judges usually consider issues of administrative remedies, standing, and mootness in deciding whether to hear a case.

Exhaustion of Administrative Remedies.   Judges consider whether the plaintiff has exhausted all available channels of appeal in the bureaucracy in deciding whether to hear a case. Thus, an individual dissatisfied with the ruling of a low-level employee in an independent regulatory commission must usually appeal to the commissioners before winning access to the courts. Likewise, someone dissatisfied with a ruling by an examiner in the Internal Revenue Service must usually go to the tax court before appealing to the regular federal court system.

Standing.   The courts exclude some cases because of lack of *standing to sue*. Before federal judges hear a case, they assure themselves that a real controversy exists; they avoid hypothetical cases or advisory opinions. (In contrast, agencies at times hold predetermination hearings to render such opinions.) In addition, standing requires the plaintiffs bringing the suit to have directly and substantially suffered. If citizen A does not like the way an administrative agency treated citizen B, A will usually lack the standing to have the court remedy the adverse treatment of B. Furthermore, Cooper notes:

All citizens are affected in one way or another by almost all government policies and any number of them may feel injured by government action. But the courts have held that "generalized undifferentiated injury," which a citizen may feel with regard to, say, the operation of U.S. intelligence agencies' activities, is an insufficient basis for the lawsuit challenging official action. Instead, one must point to a more specific injury, such as interference with one's freedom of religion . . . .[30]

Obviously, issues of standing require interpretation and in many instances are fuzzy. Greater judicial permissiveness in defining standing has played a key role in fueling court intervention in administrative matters over the last twenty-five years.

Mootness.   A case is moot when the injury to the plaintiff is terminated. For instance, the agency may change its ruling or the injured party may die. In one famous example the law school at the University of Washington denied Michael DeFunis admission even though nonwhite students with poorer academic credentials were admitted; he sued and the federal district court ordered him admitted.[31] The university appealed, but by the time the case reached the Supreme Court, DeFunis had almost completed law school and the school said it would grant him a degree. The Supreme Court refused to hear the case because it was moot—DeFunis had what he wanted.

Scope of Judicial Review

Once the federal courts accept a case for review, they have considerable latitude. Section 706 of the APA divides questions into those of fact and of law. While a neat and convenient distinction, issues of law and fact are often so closely intertwined as to be indistinguishable.

In reviewing administrative action, several questions often loom large for the judge. First, does the agency's evidence provide a basis for a reasonable person to reach the same decision? Administrators need not meet the stringent standards of evidence found in court proceedings, but their decisions must have a foundation in systematically gathered and assessed evidence. Otherwise the administrative decision may appear arbitrary and capricious—an open invitation to the judge to strike it down.

Second, did the agency act within its authority? While ambiguity often cloaks the law, the judge must be able to see some link between the agency's action and the statute. Otherwise the judge may rule that the agency acted *ultra vires* and set aside its decision.

Third, is the action constitutional? Behavior in accord with the APA and enabling statute may still violate the Constitution. Policymakers often learn whether the laws they pass are constitutional when agencies attempt to implement them.

Torts and Individual Civil Servants

Courts can do more than overrule an agency. They can also impose liability for direct harm to people and property (torts). Before 1946 citizens found it nearly impossible to sue the government of the United States for damages. The British legal doctrine that the Queen can do no wrong, otherwise known as sovereign immunity, had a firm grip on the courts. A citizen's main hope for obtaining damages lay in persuading Congress to pass a private bill compensating him or her. This remedy consumed much time and was quite inequitable for individuals who did not have sufficient clout to obtain such a bill.

In 1946 Congress passed the Federal Tort Claims Act (FTCA). The language of this act appeared to make the government (but not individual officials) liable for damages just as if it were an individual or corporation. The courts, however, construed the language of the act somewhat differently. In *Feres* v. *United States*,[32] one of the first cases tried under the FTCA, the Supreme Court held that government was not liable when it was performing a strictly governmental act, but only when it was performing an act similar to what private individuals or corporations do. For example, if a garbage truck runs over someone, government may be liable for the negligence of the driver, but if a tank did so, government would not be liable; few individuals have armies.

Subsequent court decisions eroded and modified this distinction between *governmental* and *proprietary* actions. In *Dalehite* v. *United States*,[33] the Supreme Court distinguished between negligence at the planning, or discretionary, levels of government and negligence at the operational level. Although there was clearly negligence in the massive explosion that killed Mr. Dalehite and more than five hundred others, and although it was clearly linked to a governmental program, the court refused to award damages because the negligence resulted from discretionary planning, specifically excluded from damages under the FTCA.

In a second case, *Indian Towing Co., Inc.* v. *United States*, the Supreme Court held the government liable for damages caused by the negligent management of a lighthouse.[34] Even though lighthouse management is overwhelmingly a public function rather than one performed by private businesses, the government could be held liable for poor performance. This decision weakened the doctrine articulated by the Supreme Court in its *Feres* opinion.

Aside from issues of government liability, questions persist as to whether individuals who work in the public sector can be held liable for their actions and the consequences of their decisions. Individual liability could serve as a mechanism for holding individual civil servants accountable but could also be abused by forcing them to spend long hours and much money defending themselves. Further, it might make them unwilling to make any decisions, so that the commonly cited bureaucratic buck-passing might become even more prevalent. Again, those considerations must be balanced against the rights of harmed citizens to receive some compensation from responsible parties.

The liability of federal officers to individual suits remains a very fuzzy area of administrative law. The Warren Court ruled in 1959 that federal officials had blanket immunity from suit on violations of common law.[35] The official who acted within the "outer perimeter of discretionary authority" could not be held liable. The court did, however, indicate that officials might be held liable for violations of the Constitution.

Later, in *Butz* v. *Economou*, the court specifically affirmed that the immunity of federal officials to tort actions did not extend to violations of the constitutional rights of citizens.[36] Hence, civil servants could claim only limited immunity from tort actions. The court did, however, hold that for an official to be personally liable, he or she must have reasonably known of the risk of violating the constitutional rights of the citizen. An official who could prove that he or she acted in good faith was unlikely to be held liable for monetary damages.

Subsequent court decisions also suggested that holding civil servants personally liable is inappropriate when statutes offer other appropriate remedies, for example under the Federal Tort Claims Act.[37] While federal officials face increased risk of legal liability for their decisions, the courts still buffer them from such suits. The implications of greater liability for the behavior of civil servants and ultimately for efficiency and effectiveness remain important, if difficult, subjects for research.[38]

Conclusion

Administrative law, whether manifested in rulemaking, adjudication, or court intervention, structures the politics of the bureaucracy; it does not eliminate politics. The fact that agencies must follow certain procedures in wielding discretion cannot eradicate the fact that their discretion affects who gets what from government. Nor does administrative law rule out intervention by top elected officials. To the contrary, the president and his top appointees understand that influence over rulemaking often allows them to accomplish many things that would be beyond their grasp if they had to obtain approval from Congress. For its part, Congress also works to influence rulemaking and at times files suit in court. Generic politics also surfaces in administrative law. Groups jockey for position at critical decision sites and in the courts. As one analysis notes, administrative rules "are not simply imposed; they are drafted with an intention of giving interests a chance to react."[39] Further, the growing willingness of the courts to intervene in administrative life has had the effect of strengthening and activating certain interest groups, for example those committed to protecting the environment (see Chapter 5).

Administrative law involves trade-offs. At times (not always) it constrains the ability of administrators to act rapidly and decisively to foster the efficiency and effectiveness of programs. For instance, rulemaking procedures and the ability of affected interest groups to appeal to the courts make it extremely costly for OSHA to promulgate new regulations. In part because of this, the agency may well find it difficult to regulate many substances widely known to be carcinogens. At a minimum, the formal rules tend to create considerable delay in dealing with health hazards. Moreover, formal hearings can make it difficult for officials to fashion acceptable political compromises in regulations. Instead, various factions dig in and fight to the last hearing, often in a federal court. William West argues that movement toward more formal rulemaking procedures at the Federal Trade Commission "impeded [the agency's] ability to fashion politically acceptable solutions to policy questions." Students of other regulatory arenas have also noted the tendency of formalized procedures to exacerbate adversarial policymaking.[40]

Whatever their limitations, these procedures provide a reasonable measure of due process to groups adversely affected by administrative discretion. They certainly stand as a barrier to arbitrary and capricious action by administrators. In this sense formal processes work to hold the bureaucracy accountable. Furthermore, courts have at times pushed administrators to be more aggressive in implementing the law. In this sense they have encouraged administrators to be more effective. Thus, the dynamics of administrative law need not invariably be at war with efficiency and effectiveness; on occasion these dynamics promote those values.

Matters of administrative law intersect with issues of government legitimacy. While there is little information on the subject, more formalized hearings may create a sense among the citizenry that processes are fair; citizens may therefore more readily obey the decisions resulting from these processes. Questions of legitimacy are complex, however. To the extent that the procedures embedded in administrative law make federal agencies appear weak and ineffectual (for example engender a perception that the Environmental Protection Agency is hamstrung), formalized processes may do little to foster a sense of government legitimacy. As these complexities suggest, the quest for the right balance in administrative law will go to the heart of important political matters.

Notes

1. Anglo-American tradition has been to link administrative law with the corpus of public law in general, while the Continental practice has been to create a separate body of law. See Z. M. Nedjati and J. E. Trice, *The English and Continental Systems of Administrative Law* (Amsterdam: North Holland, 1978).
2. Jerome R. Ravetz, "Usable Ignorance: Incomplete Science with Policy Implications," in *Knowledge: Creation, Diffusion, Utilization,* forthcoming.
3. *The Brig Aurora,* 11 U.S. 382 (1813).
4. Article 1, Section 8, Clause 18 of the Constitution. See especially *McCulloch* v. *Maryland*, 17 U.S. 1 (1819).
5. Brownlow Commission, *Report of the President's Committee on Administrative Management* (Washington, DC: Government Printing Office, 1937).
6. This was the famous "sick chicken case," *Schecter Poultry Corp.* v. *United States*, 295 U.S. 495 (1935).
7. Administrative Procedures Act, Section 551.
8. See Kenneth Culp Davis, *Discretionary Justice: A Preliminary Inquiry* (Baton Rouge: Louisiana State University Press, 1969), 28–42.
9. The third involved a rider to a piece of coal mining legislation. *Carter* v. *Carter Coal Co.,* 298 U.S. 238 (1936).
10. Phillip J. Cooper, *Public Law and Public Administration* (Palo Alto, CA: Mayfield, 1983), 115.
11. Ibid., 122–7.
12. Richard B. Stewart, *"Vermont Yankee* and the Evolution of Administrative Procedure." *Harvard Law Review* 91 (1978): 1805–1845.
13. Executive Order 11821, *Federal Register* 39 (1974), 41502.
14. Executive Order 12044, *Federal Register* 43 (1978), 12661.
15. Margaret T. Kritz, "Kibitzer with Clout." *National Journal* (30 May 1987): 1404–8.
16. Eugene Bardach and Robert A. Kagan, *Going By The Book* (Philadelphia: Temple University Press, 1982), 185–6.
17. Frank J. Thompson, "Deregulation by the Bureaucracy: OSHA and the Augean Quest for Error Correction." *Public Administration Review* 42 (May-June 1982): 202–12.
18. Amicus curiae briefs and other forms of limited third-party involvements do occur in the federal courts.

19. William Van Alstyne, "The Demise of the Right-Privilege Distinction in Constitutional Law." *Harvard Law Review* 81 (1968): 1439–1464.
20. B. Guy Peters, "The United States: Absolute Change and Relative Stability," in Richard Rose et al., *Public Employment in Western Nations* (Cambridge: Cambridge University Press, 1985), Table 7.14.
21. *Bishop* v. *Wood*, 426 U.S. 341 (1976).
22. *Vlandis* v. *Kline*, 412 U.S. 441 (1973); *Stanley* v. *Illinois*, 405 U.S. 645 (1972).
23. *Weinberger* v. *Salfi*, 422 U.S. 749 (1975).
24. Laurence Tribe, *American Constitutional Law* (Mineola, NY: Foundation Press, 1978), Section 10–7.
25. *Board of Regents* v. *Roth*, 408 U.S. 564 (1972).
26. See in particular *Eldridge* v. *Matthews*, 424 U.S. 319 (1976).
27. James Q. Freedman, *Crisis and Legitimacy: The Administrative Process and American Government* (Cambridge: Cambridge University Press, 1978).
28. It may be clear, for example, from the legislative history of an act that Congress was thinking about formal hearings even if they were not specified in the legislation.
29. Paul Verkuil, "A Study of Informal Adjudication Procedures." *University of Chicago Law Review* 43 (1976): 739, 757–71; based on *Goldberg* v. *Kelly,* 397 U.S. 154 (1970).
30. Cooper, *Public Law and Public Administration,* 182–3; see also Lief Carter, *Administrative Law and Politics* (Boston: Little, Brown, 1983), 217–21.
31. *DeFunis* v. *Odegaard,* 416 U.S. 312 (1974).
32. *Feres* v. *United States,* 340 U.S. 135 (1950).
33. *Dalehite* v. *United States,* 346 U.S. 15 (1953).
34. *Indian Towing Company* v. *United States,* 350 U.S. 61 (1955).
35. *Barr* v. *Mateo,* 360 U.S. 564 (1959).
36. *Butz* v. *Economou,* 438 U.S. 478 (1978).
37. *Bivens* v. *Six Unknown Named Agents,* 403 U.S. 388 (1971).
38. Gerald J. Miller, "Administrative Malpractice Policy before and after *Butz* v. *Economou.*" *The Bureaucrat* 9 (Winter 1980-81): 25–31.
39. Francine Rabinovitz et al., "Guidelines: A Plethora of Forms, Authors and Functions." *Policy Sciences* 7 (December 1976): 403.
40. William F. West, "Judicial Rulemaking Procedures in the FTC: A Case Study of Their Causes and Effects." *Public Policy* 29 (Spring 1981): 212.

Chapter Eight

Administration and Democracy

———
———

Introduction

The politics of public administration ultimately intersects with issues of democracy. Public bureaucracies have become a fourth branch of government, raising serious questions of accountability. Early in the twentieth century a foremost social theorist, Max Weber, saw the rise of bureaucracy as a threat to democratic government. "Under normal conditions," he wrote, "the power position of a fully developed bureaucracy is always overtowering. The 'political master' finds himself in the position of the 'dilettante' who stands opposite the 'expert' . . ."[1]

Do the power positions of public agencies in the United States fit Weber's description? In most cases, no. Nonetheless, important issues persist. The conception of democracy embedded in this nation's political culture emphasizes citizen participation, popular control, responsiveness, bureaucratic accountability, and related concepts. Empirical questions persist as to the *degree* to which public administration threatens attainment of these ends. Furthermore, it is a matter of debate how far Americans *should* go in promoting democratic values because most citizens also expect public agencies to achieve high levels of efficiency and effectiveness. These values at times collide with democratic values. To what degree does a trade-off exist? Where should the balance be struck? Students of public administration have yet to achieve consensus on these questions.[2]

While this chapter cannot answer all of the questions related to democracy and administration, it reviews some key dimensions of the problem and assesses forces that help keep public agencies accountable to elected officials, the rule of law, and the broader society. It deals first with internal psychological controls (respect for the law and the legitimate directives of superiors among civil servants) as a vehicle for democracy. It reviews the efficacy of external checks on the bureaucracy such as those employed by elected officials and the courts. Finally it addresses the special challenge for democracy of administration by proxy.

Dimensions of the Problem

In describing desirable relationships between public agencies and democratic society, three concepts—responsiveness, responsibility, and accountability—repeatedly surface. Some observers use these terms interchangeably. In fact, however, they have different meanings and at times imply contradictory courses of action. These contradictions help make the work of policymakers and public administrators complex and challenging.

Responsiveness

Citizens expect civil servants to be responsive to their requests and demands. Certainly, most conceptions of democratic theory hold that a citizen who asks something of government has the right to expect a response and to be treated as a legitimate source of demands. Difficulties arise when citizens and interest groups expect too much responsiveness. They want the bureaucracy to respond favorably even though it may lead to a dubious interpretation of the letter and spirit of the law or be harmful to other people.

"Responsive to whom?" is a central question. Does one want the Environmental Protection Agency to be responsive to the demands of an industry that wants to pollute a river? Should the local welfare office be responsive to the demand of a citizen who does not qualify for assistance but thinks he or she does? How does one decide which demands are to be met and which dismissed? Responsiveness is better understood as a *procedural* requirement for good government than as a substantive requirement. Government and public administration do not have the right in a democracy to exclude citizens from expressing their demands for public service; nor do officials have the right to exclude someone from a fair hearing concerning their claims. These institutions do, however, have the right and duty to reject claims with no basis in law. The wants and demands of citizens may be infinite, but the laws and resources of government are clearly finite.

Issues of responsiveness to the public extend beyond particular cases, such as the determination of someone's eligibility for Social Security benefits, to the formulation of policy. Administrators often show sensitivity to citizens' and interest groups' demands when they advocate changes in law to Congress. Further, the rulemaking requirements call for agencies to encourage participation by interested parties (see Chapter 7). Administrators frequently must summarize the public's comments in response to a notice of proposed rulemaking and to show how they responded to them in making a final decision.

Responsibility

Responsibility often stands in tension with responsiveness. While responsiveness requires that government officials meet the requests and demands of citizens, responsibility implies that they will adhere to the explicit and implicit values of proper administration and policy. Responsible civil servants know the law and have convictions about the proper administration of their programs. These values buffer them from the confusion, clamor, and demands of the political world in which they function. This conception of the role and behavior of civil servants approaches the old Weberian and Wilsonian notions of the public bureaucracy as acting *sine irae ac studio* (without malice or bias) in the proper administration of the law.[3] Under this conception, administrators can make decisions without constantly attending to public opinion; expertise and law rather than immediate political considerations become central.

Like responsiveness, responsibility can be carried to excess. Civil servants may become too confident of their unique ability to discern the public interest. They can assume the worst about anyone who disagrees with their interpretation of the goals of a program so that those who dissent "represent narrow, selfish interests," are "obstructionist," or are "uninformed." While the hyperresponsive bureaucrat accedes too readily to the demands of citizens, the excessively responsible administrator lacks flexibility and sensitivity.

Accountability

Accountability implies that civil servants ultimately must answer to elected public officials. It summons up the concept of overhead democracy, a method of controlling civil servants by making them subordinate to the will of elected public officials.[4] Accountability overlaps responsibility in its emphasis on bureaucratic deference to the laws passed by Congress and signed by the president. It also implies general responsiveness to the wishes of elected officials rather than great respect for the expertise and judgment of civil servants. Accountability necessitates that the public exert substantial control over elected officials through voting and in other ways.

Accountability tends to serve democracy best when administrators anticipate the legitimate preferences of elected officials and adjust their behavior accordingly. If accountability requires constant punishment for misdeeds, it leaves a legacy of inappropriate bureaucratic behavior that may have inflicted substantial harm on citizens. Such harm over time can undermine the legitimacy of government.

Efforts to ensure accountability are not an unmitigated blessing; they can heighten the sluggishness of bureaucracy. As James Fesler has observed, "an abundance of negative controls creates a pervasive climate of distrust, which can demoralize those on whom we depend for achievement of public programs." He notes that "controls external to administration may displace or undermine internal administrative controls." By increasing requirements for review of proposed decisions, they increase red tape, delay action, and may "dull administration's response to the public."[5] In a related vein, Nonet argues that emphasis on accountability leads one down the road toward formalism and legalism.[6] Thus, the desire for accountability must be weighed against responsiveness and the ability to achieve policy ends efficiently and effectively.

Students of government have often portrayed responsiveness, responsibility, and accountability as antidotes to abuse by civil servants. In contemporary Washington the phrase *fraud, waste, and abuse* has become a symbol of what people think is wrong with government. In fact, the concept of abuse demands more considered analysis. For example, at times problems arise because of excessive zeal of elected officials; on other occasions failure to act is the abuse. Paradoxically, many well-intentioned devices to prevent or control abuse create as many difficulties as they solve. If rigidity is a central problem of public bureaucracies, the introduction of more controls tends to exacerbate the problem.[7] Control must strike a delicate balance of responsiveness, responsibility, and accountability.

Democratic Control: Internal and External Forces

The tools to keep public bureaucracies safe for democracy are external and internal controls. One position, usually identified with Herman Finer, holds that the best way to enforce accountability is to develop institutions that vigorously monitor the actions of the public bureaucracy and punish those guilty of maladministration.[8] In essence, administrators behave appropriately because of the surveillance and muscle of those outside their agency.[9] Finer's assumption is that people in government are no better than people in the rest of the society. In the absence of other controls, such as the profit motive in business organizations, policymakers must monitor the performance of public administrators via formal mechanisms.

The other position, usually associated with Carl Friedrich, is that inculcation of appropriate values among administrators serves as the major check on the bureaucracy. This view holds that formal institutional checks will usually fail if officials do not have sound democratic and administrative values.[10] In essence, administrators must have an internal compass to point them in the appropriate direction.

Friedrich's and Finer's positions both have merit. Efforts to establish satisfactory control over the bureaucracy usually feature both approaches. The central issue is how to balance the two to serve the imperatives of democracy as well as those of efficiency and effectiveness.

The Internal Compass

Most people employed by government in the United States do not anticipate becoming rich and famous. That is realistic; there is little hope of either.[11] The majority feel a basic commitment to the values of public service or simply enjoy the work.[12] Many people who come into the career civil service do so because of a genuine commitment to the value of public service or to improve a particular type of policy—social services, defense, environmental protection, or whatever. Others develop such a commitment after working in government for some time. Not all government workers are saints, and many consider it just another job, but many civil servants do think of themselves as performing important public services.

Civil servants appear to be committed to democratic norms. In one survey government executives were found less likely than the general public to give antidemocratic responses to a number of questions, although they were slightly more likely to do so than delegates to political conventions.[13] In a later survey senior administrators showed a strong commitment to citizen participation and the values of participatory democracy.[14] On balance there is much to commend Charles Hyneman's view:

> The officials and employees of the federal government are typical American citizens. They are just as devoted to our ideal of government by the people and just as loyal to our form of government as the farmers of Indiana; they would be as reluctant to leave their homes in the evening to join a conspiracy against the people as the bankers of Iowa or the lumbermen of Minnesota.[15]

Aside from being committed to values of political democracy, many bureaucrats are committed to their jobs. Although their willingness to recommend public employment declined during the 1980s, surveys of federal employees still show that most would take the same type of job again if they had the opportunity.[16] Further, surveys of public employees report that they derive considerable satisfaction from the service they render in their jobs and from their relationships with the public. In short, rather than being arrogant paper-pushers, insensitive to the public and surrounded by red tape, civil servants seem truly committed to public service. Finally, the majority of citizens seem satisfied with the way public employees treat them. Interestingly, when there is comparable evidence, the federal government does rather well compared with the private sector despite the alleged remoteness of the federal government and the perception that people get the least from their tax dollars at the federal level.[17]

Values and Ethics

At the most fundamental level the control of public bureaucracy depends upon the values and ethical sense of the members of the civil service. If administrators cling to a valid sense of right and wrong and are willing to make difficult decisions accordingly, democratic control of the bureaucracy becomes easier.

Much ethics legislation at the federal, state, and local levels primarily requires public administrators and candidates for public jobs to fill out lengthy financial disclosure forms. Finance is only one small aspect of ethics in government. Ethics in more general terms deals with moral duty and obligation. It goes far beyond keeping one's personal finances legal and appropriate.

At a bare minimum ethical behavior by civil servants in a democratic society requires respect for the rule of law and the dignity of the individual. Of course, this does not mean that public administrators can achieve ethical behavior simply by following orders. For one thing, the mandates under which they operate usually allow ample room for interpretation. For another, civil servants at times find that their sense of appropriate behavior differs from the boss's. In some instances disobedience may be the ethical course. Protections for whistle-blowers can help the subordinate in such a circumstance, but it takes much moral courage to risk ethical disobedience.

Any assessment of the ethical character of civil servants must face up to the complexity of the matter. While some behavior, for example gross violation of the law, stands out as obvious abuse, a huge gray area exists. Choices frequently involve difficult trade-offs among competing values such as efficiency versus due process. The correct response often depends on the context. Moreover, civil servants frequently deal with policy issues for which crisp ethics guidelines do not exist. Issues of war, diplomacy, and inequality have long posed moral conundrums.[18] More recently, discussions of the environment and the protection of resources for future generations have presented complex ethical puzzles.[19] To compound matters, government must now wrestle with such issues as genetic engineering, the allocation of exotic lifesaving equipment, reproductive technologies, and a host of other issues about which professional ethicists—much less ordinary civil servants—can reach no consensus.

Aside from respect for the rule of law and for the dignity of the individual, some analysts suggest that it is critical for civil servants to develop a sense of personal responsibility for their actions.[20] In this view a sense of individual responsibility largely derives from interactions with others. Thus, the organizational environment and face-to-face encounters with coworkers are crucial for the formation and reinforcement of personal responsibility and presumably, ethical conduct.[21] To have moral individuals, it may first be necessary to create moral organizations—a highly complex undertaking.

The Challenge of Professionalism

In the late 1960s Frederick Mosher pointed to the rise of a professional state—one whose various professional groups increasingly dominated the employment rosters of government.[22] Any image of the civil servant as a poorly educated paper pusher became increasingly inaccurate as the growing complexity of public problems and the advancement of knowledge pushed government to hire better-educated personnel. Indeed, public service itself came to be defined as a profession. Master of Public Administration programs proliferated and the National Association of Schools of Public Affairs and Administration evolved into an accrediting agency designed to promote quality control in these programs. Aside from the new professions, government employed vast numbers of people from the established ones—medicine, law, education, engineering, and so on.

Professionalism tends to impart certain attitudes that sometimes bear on the degree to which officials are responsive and accountable. Professionals often look to their associations and publications for norms of good practice. Their desire for state-of-the-art practice may enhance the quality of government service, but it may make professionals unresponsive to policies that run against the grain of their professional norms. Professionals expect to have considerable autonomy and often find it difficult to accept hierarchical control. Their ability to move from job to job in different geographic areas may make them less motivated to obey superiors. Moreover, some posit a fundamental conflict between the professional values of expertise and technical proficiency and the political values of bargaining and compromise. Mosher argues:

> Professionalism rests on specialized knowledge, science and rationality. There are correct ways of solving problems and doing things. Politics is seen as constituting negotiation, elections, votes, compromises—all carried on by subject-matter amateurs. Politics is to the professions as ambiguity to truth, expediency to rightness, heresy to true belief.[23]

Much research on the degree to which professionals pose particular problems for accountability and responsiveness remains to be done. Conceivably the problem is less acute than some believe. One study found no correlation between professionalism and a distaste for politics and politicians among government employees.[24] Furthermore, many professionals nurture considerable respect for the law and accept the legitimacy of constraints placed on them by policymakers. Still, the rise of professionalism does raise serious questions for those who see the internal compass of officials as a vehicle for keeping public agencies under control.

Commitment to Programs

Issues of professionalism march side by side with another cluster of values that can undercut accountability and responsiveness, namely that civil servants often feel deeply committed to programs. Many within the Environmental Protection Agency, for instance, place great value on fighting hazards and eyesores in the environment. While such commitment may ebb as civil servants learn to play the game and transform zealots into conservers, substantial numbers continue to believe strongly in the goals of their agencies.

In his classic study of the U.S. Forest Service, Herbert Kaufman showed the role of selective recruitment and training in sustaining the commitment of forest rangers to the goals of the organization.[25] Such commitment can energize programs and serve the ends of accountability. If the committed become zealots, however, dogma and an excessively narrow view of the world may come to dominate the bureaucracy. The tendency of career officials to work in a single policy area during their entire stint in government can fuel this tendency. Whatever the source of zealotry, it sometimes leads to unresponsive and unaccountable behavior; officials believe that they know better than elected officials or the people.

Representative Bureaucracy

In order to ensure that administrators remain responsive to the needs of the people, some observers have pointed to the potential importance of representative bureaucracy.[26] This view holds that democracy will be served if bureaucrats mirror certain key characteristics of society. The question is, of course, which characteristics—class, sex, race, or something else? In the United States—and for that matter many other societies—race and sex figured prominently in discussions of representative bureaucracy in the 1960s, 1970s, and 1980s. For purposes of illustrating the relationship between representative bureaucracy and internal checks on administrative abuse, this discussion focuses on blacks.

Representative bureaucracy can assume two major forms. *Demographic representation* occurs when black employment in implementing agencies in general and at different levels of the hierarchy mirrors black presence in the society or work force. If, for instance, 12 percent of the work force of an agency's jurisdiction are blacks and so are 12 percent of those at various levels of the agency's hierarchy, perfect demographic representation exists. Such representation yields many dividends. It provides jobs to a disadvantaged group; it can legitimate civil service selection practices and other administrative decisions in the black community.

Demographic representation, however, need not automatically lead to *substantive representation*. For this linkage to occur, black employees must be more likely to behave as the black community wants than others in the agency. Linkage may exist because black employees have values, attitudes, and beliefs that differ from those of other employees and more closely resemble those of blacks in society. No doubt demographic representation at times finds substantive expression. For instance, black equal employment opportunity officers may be more committed to affirmative action than their white counterparts; minority police officers may be more empathetic and sympathetic in their treatment of minorities. Thus, substantively representative bureaucracy can encourage responsiveness.

Representative bureaucracy may also heighten accountability. For instance, if white employees violate the letter and spirit of antidiscrimination laws, the substantive representation of minority interests can enhance accountability in hiring practices. Of course, the responsiveness of substantively representative bureaucracy need not always serve accountability. At least in the abstract, one can imagine minority employees showing so much favoritism to the minority community as to violate the law.

Any concerns about substantively representative bureaucracy and its implications for responsiveness and accountability must acknowledge a fundamental finding—that the linkage between substantive and demographic representation is often weak or nonexistent.[27] Hiring minority employees may do little to ensure that minority interests in society gain more representation via the bureaucracy. Black and white employees often hold similar attitudes and behave in the same way. The incentive structure of agencies, the propensity of agency cultures to instill certain beliefs and values, and constraints on administrative discretion often limit the inclination and capacity of black civil servants to represent substantively their group in society. Furthermore, on many policy questions blacks and whites in society hold similar views.

The attenuated link between demographic and substantive representation need not undermine the case for affirmative action or demographically representative bureaucracy. One can make a very strong case for both in the absence of any evidence that the link exists; however, the evidence does point to the limits of representative bureaucracy as a vehicle for fueling responsiveness to some groups in society. Representative bureaucracy need not invariably serve as a desirable internal check on administrators.

External Muscle

So far this chapter has argued that most civil servants have internal compasses to keep them from grossly unresponsive, irresponsible, and unaccountable behavior. They show considerable respect for the rule of law and other norms of democracy. They often go to great lengths to be responsive. While this bodes well for democracy, most citizens would not sleep well at night if responsive, responsible, and accountable administration depended solely on the consciences of administrators.

A host of institutional, cultural, and related factors fragment political power in the United States. The general citizenry, clients of programs, interest groups, courts, the media, elected officials, and others constrain the influence of administrators. The application of external muscle to the agency can (although need not invariably) serve norms of accountability.

Information: Fishbowl or Silent Politics?

The ease with which citizens can obtain valid information about the bureaucracy profoundly affects the degree to which they can apply muscle to it. Students of public administration differ in their assessments of the availability of information.

A stock metaphor is that public managers operate in a fishbowl; that is, their activities constantly come under the scrutiny of key segments of the public.[28]

Proponents of this view generally focus on the accounts of high-level executives. Reviewing his experiences as Secretary of Health, Education, and Welfare during the Carter administration, Joseph Califano mentions the persistent presence of the media in the public executive's life. In his view, "Far more careers have been shattered in Washington because of what people say than because of what they do—and far more often through words spoken by inadvertence or ignorance than by design."[29] The image of the media as vigorously monitoring every move, eager to pounce on a mistake or inconsistency, permeates the accounts of other top executives as well. To the degree that the fishbowl metaphor applies to government, those concerned about democratic control have fewer worries of runaway bureaucracies.

Another perspective challenges the idea of the fishbowl. Douglas Yates portrays bureaucratic operations as "silent politics." Yates says that major administrative decisions "take place in a setting that is sheltered from political debate and citizen scrutiny." He sees the day-to-day operation of government as "often completely unknown to the ordinary citizen or even to organized interest groups." Professional jargon, sporadic press coverage, and the tendencies of top executives not to engage in open conflict with others presumably impede the flow of comprehensible information outside the bureaucracy.[30] If silent politics dominates public administration, defenders of democracy have much more to fear.

The different interpretations in part stem from the reference point. Proponents of the fishbowl theory usually compare public bureaucracies with those in the private sector. The vision of silent politics tends to draw on comparisons with politics in the legislative branch. Whatever the vantage point, the issue of the fishbowl versus silent politics remains important.

The clarity of the water in the fishbowl depends on several factors:

1. Hierarchical level makes a difference. High political appointees receive more attention from the media than career civil servants in the Senior Executive Service.
2. A substantial consensus that effectiveness depends on secrecy affects the flow of information to society. Most people accept that the Defense Department and the Central Intelligence Agency can legitimately refuse to disseminate certain information.
3. Executives in abstruse and remote policy spheres enjoy diminished visibility. For instance, research management at the National Institutes of Health often poses complexities beyond the grasp of most citizens. While citizens generally favor the wars against sundry diseases, they do not have immediate contact with the outputs of these institutes.
4. Executives in agencies with small budgets and few personnel usually stand a good chance of escaping the public eye. These programs rarely affect many people in major ways and so are less interesting to the media.
5. A generically politicized milieu tends to heighten visibility. Such milieus are conflictual, and conflict tends to attract the media and ultimately public attention.

Apropos of factor 5, executives in regulatory agencies often receive exposure in the media. Douglas M. Costle, administrator of the Environmental Protection Agency during the Carter years, received advice upon taking office that "If you do your job right, you'll have 60 percent of the people mad at you at least 50 percent of the time."[31] The ongoing struggles between business and proregulatory groups invite persistent news reporting of regulatory agencies' decisions.

Internal conflict within an agency heightens prospects for public attention. In January 1984 *The Atlanta Constitution* reported that forty-eight employees of the Atlanta office of the Equal Employment Opportunity Commission protested to officials in Washington because top managers in the region ordered them to dispose of employment discrimination complaints from citizens without investigations.[32]

Laws to protect whistle-blowing by bureaucrats in essence recognize the role of internal conflict in generating valuable information about agency practices. Thus, the Civil Service Reform Act of 1978 provided employees who blew the whistle with a measure of protection from reprisals by the agency. The act calls upon the Office of Special Counsel to play a particularly prominent role in this regard (see Chapter 12). The legislative effort to protect whistle-blowers in part reflected congressional reaction to the case of A. Ernest Fitzgerald, an auditor in the Department of Defense who exposed large cost overruns on the C5A airplane.[33] In retaliation, his superiors at the Department of Defense removed Fitzgerald from his job. After a long battle, Fitzgerald won reinstatement, although to a less responsible position. Aside from statutory protections for whistle-blowing, court decisions have expanded employee rights to free speech, hence greater job security to government employees who publicly criticize their agencies.[34]

On balance, neither the fishbowl nor silent politics seems to describe the visibility of executive behavior. Exposure to the media varies widely among executives. It makes little sense to view most managers as constantly under the scrutiny of a vigilant press and public. Often nobody is looking at the fishbowl. At times, major areas of the bowl's glass are so fogged or smudged that no one can see through it. (Consider the secrecy that surrounds the Central Intelligence Agency.)

By the same token, notions of silent politics often go too far, especially for domestic programs. Compared with those of other western democracies, citizens and interest groups in the United States have considerable formal access to information about the proposed decisions of public managers. Various procedural requirements reinforce this strong cultural bias. For instance, the requirements of the Administrative Procedures Act for public comment (at times via formal hearings) on proposed rules (see Chapter 7) represent a marked contrast to the more informal and closed bargaining style that often accompanies regulatory decisionmaking in European democracies.[35]

The Freedom of Information Act also works against silent politics in many agencies. Originally approved in 1966 and extensively amended in 1974, this act grants citizens substantial rights to see the vast majority of government documents. If the agency refuses to release certain records, the petitioner has the explicit authority to take the agency to court. The media and many other citizens have used this right to probe areas of government activity long immune from public scrutiny. The law subjects administrators' decisions to public scrutiny; this encourages them to be accountable to top policymakers.

To be sure, the Freedom of Information Act does not throw open all government files. The law excepts sensitive information related to national defense and foreign policy, certain trade secrets, personnel and medical files, various law enforcement records, certain inter- and intraagency memoranda, and other material specifically mentioned by statutes. In addition, the courts' interpretations of the act have not always leaned toward the release of information. In national security and other matters, judges may examine agency information in private to determine whether its release would violate individual rights or the national interest. Moreover, the courts have denied citizens access to information not specifically exempted by the Freedom of Information Act[36]; privacy laws provide additional justification for denying access to certain information.

Finally, citizens may find it difficult to use their rights. For instance, the Freedom of Information act requires that requested information be "reasonably described." Many citizens cannot name the relevant documents or even know they exist. Moreover, agencies at times have the right to charge citizens for the administrative costs of providing them with information, which inhibits citizen requests. While the Freedom of Information Act cannot abolish secrecy, it does facilitate the flow of information about administrative behavior.

The rise of a specialized press is yet another force militating against silent politics. The 1960s and 1970s witnessed the growth of publications that report specific agency developments to particular groups of readers. The *Occupational Safety and Health Reporter,* for instance, appears weekly and follows developments in its policy sphere. Specialized publications like this one disseminate information to groups particularly likely to act on it (in this case business and union leaders).

Elected Officials and the Courts Revisited

The institutions established under the separation of powers—the president, Congress, and the courts—constrain administrative discretion (see Chapter 3). However, each of these institutions deserves further consideration from the perspective of democratic theory.

For the theory of overhead democracy to be meaningful, it is not sufficient that the president and Congress acquire a measure of control over the bureaucracy. A linkage between their behavior and the preferences of the people must exist. Otherwise bureaucracy may be accountable to the president and Congress yet undemocratic because it fails to represent the general wishes of the governed. Political scientists have conducted many studies on the linkage between the populace and the officeholders they elect. One recent analysis of these studies presents a cautiously sanguine assessment. It reports that "when voter information and rationality were assessed on issues that voters felt were salient, voters were well-informed and selected candidates with political preferences similar to their own." That study finds support for the view "that voters can rationally select candidates and thus indirectly control the policy preferences of elected officials." The analysis also indicates that in general "politicians attempt to implement campaign promises after taking office."[37]

If the first link in a theory of overhead democracy garners some empirical support, can the president and Congress adequately constrain the bureaucracy and thereby forge the second critical link? To a considerable degree, yes. Earlier chapters noted the president's resources for control of the bureaucracy. Some have gone so far as to argue that a strong managerial presidency can resolve apparent conflicts between efficiency and democracy; the president is at once an elected official and the nominal head of the executive bureaucracy. In reality, even the most capable president finds it difficult to reconcile personal commitments to public accountability and efficient management. For present purposes, the degree to which the president can exert control over the bureaucracy is the central issue.

Barriers to presidential control include the sheer scale of the bureaucracy and the complexity of policy issues. The ties of the agency to Congress and interest groups also limit the president. On balance, however, the president has many levers to pull. Executive orders, the budget process, political appointments, and other devices allow the president to exert substantial control over the bureaucracy. The inroads of the administrative presidency under Nixon and Reagan provide vivid testimony in this regard (see Chapter 5). In fact, the administrative presidency has spawned concern as to whether administrators can resist unlawful pressures by the president. Deference to the chief executive and accountability to law do not always travel together. Ultimately the limits on the president's capacity to control the bureaucracy stem as much from Congress and from the courts as they do from any recalcitrance on the part of administrative agencies.

Congress has increased congressional staffs, broadened the role of the General Accounting Office, created such organizations as the Congressional Budget Office and more, in the name of more vigorous oversight (see Chapter 5). Two kinds of oversight benefit democracy—"police patrol" and "fire alarm." The former is oversight on a regular basis, for example as part of the budget cycle. The latter occurs when some event, group, or other force thrusts an issue onto the agenda of Congress and a less routine inquiry ensues (see Exhibit 8.1).

While congressional oversight has increased and one can unearth numerous examples of congressional power over the bureaucracy, nagging questions do persist. One involves the degree to which oversight (especially in the form of casework) tends to focus on the trivial rather than the important. Another involves the degree to which the oversight paradox applies. As discussed earlier, this paradox asserts that members of Congress may simultaneously be more informed of administrative activities but (given the growing dispersion of legislative power) less capable of controlling the bureaucracy. Despite these concerns, however, any notion that Congress stands impotent before the bureaucracy seems far removed from reality. Again, the failure of the bureaucracy to respond to Congress at times reflects deference to the president or to the very laws Congress has approved.

The courts have moved to constrain administrative discretion, either by forcing the bureaucracy to deal with some problem or by limiting its capacity to pursue certain options. However, the courts pose intriguing questions of democratic theory. While the judiciary clearly limits the power of the bureaucracy, it is in many respects far from democratic. Its members usually enjoy tenure for life. The public and elected officials generally stand a better chance of firing a civil servant whom they dislike than removing a judge. To be sure, a president's appointments can do much to change the ideological composition of the federal judiciary. Moreover, judicial decisions often take prevailing political views into account. Nonetheless, the judiciary is substantially buffered from popular control.

Ironically, however, the undemocratic judiciary has been a major force democratizing election processes and thereby has bolstered prospects that overhead democracy can be achieved; consider decisions to strike down barriers to black voting

EXHIBIT 8.1   Enforcing Accountability at the Environmental Protection Agency

In May 1981 the Senate confirmed Anne Gorsuch (later Burford) as administrator of the Environmental Protection Agency (EPA). Devoted to many of the ideals of the Reagan administration, such as "getting government off the backs of American business," she and her politically appointed management team began to offer "regulatory relief" to a number of industries. They did this after little or no consultation with the career employees of EPA or with environmental interest groups. This "relief," the associated pattern of close relationships with regulated industries, and cuts in the EPA budget produced an outcry by the permanent staff of the agency; in early 1983 twenty top officials resigned or were fired.

Congress began to investigate the events at EPA even before the resignations and firings and uncovered widespread improper behavior. For example, Gorsuch informed oil refinery officials that she would not enforce existing standards for lead in gasoline. She also suspended some rules governing disposal of toxic wastes in landfills (Congress almost immediately reinstated them). One aide to Gorsuch, Rita Lavelle, was accused of improperly settling a dispute with her former employer over disposal of toxic wastes. These and other EPA actions created the impression that the agency was out of control. Lavelle was convicted of perjury and Gorsuch was held in contempt of Congress for refusing to turn over subpoenaed documents to oversight committees. Eventually, Gorsuch and all of her cronies were forced out of office and she was replaced by William Ruckelshaus, who was able to build a stronger record for environmental protection.

The case of the EPA under Anne Gorsuch points to several important factors in the control of administrative agencies. First, career civil servants are not always the ones who need to be disciplined. In fact, EPA careerists took considerable risks to interpret the laws according to the intent of Congress. Career civil servants facilitated accountability to the rule of law by openly challenging top political executives at the agency.

Second, Congress has a number of controls on the bureaucracy. Congress held oversight hearings on EPA. It subpoenaed records; when they were not forthcoming, it held an official in contempt. Congress could also legislate—quickly if necessary—to counteract attempts on the part of EPA administrators to circumvent the law. Congress also enlisted the aid of the courts when it uncovered illegality, as in the case of Rita Lavelle. Moreover, Congress could have exercised its budgetary powers to eliminate certain positions or make life unpleasant for EPA malefactors. In sum, the EPA case suggests that Congress can exert substantial influence when its members believe an agency has gone astray.

Finally, the President was not very active in monitoring the actions of the agency and its leadership. The EPA administrator reports directly to the president. While he may have agreed with many of Anne Gorsuch's goals, there is no reason to believe that the president condoned the illegalities and improprieties. If he had been more aware, he could have requested changes in policies, sought resignations, or fired the administrator earlier. To some extent the president's subsequent appointment of Ruckelshaus was an attempt to restore public confidence in his supervision of the EPA.

and to support the principle of one man, one vote. The degree to which the courts serve or impede popular control of government over the long term remains a subject beyond the ken of this volume. Clearly, however, the courts have moved to check any danger of runaway bureaucracies. They have probably encouraged administrators to pay more attention to the letter and spirit of the laws they administer and so have been a force for accountability.

Interest Groups and Citizen Participation

Checks on the bureaucracy emanate from interest groups and citizen participation. To be sure, administrators at times use interest groups and citizens to promote their own preferences, but power flows in the opposite direction as well.

Among the many assets interest groups bring to bureaucratic politics, expertise ranks high. The average citizen or institution does not have the time or desire to monitor all the rulemaking and related activities of the federal bureaucracy. The burgeoning number of interest representatives in Washington has served to increase surveillance of public agencies. Many interest groups constantly monitor administrative activity to make certain that no decision adversely affecting their clientele goes unchallenged. They generally know where to go in the White House, Congress, or the bureaucracy to influence the decision.

The capacity of interest groups to disseminate information about the activities of government agencies is a significant asset. Once clients receive information, grass-roots contact with members of Congress or others may influence administrative behavior. Interest group representatives also deftly use the media to publicize (and frequently defeat) "inappropriate" actions by the bureaucracy.

From the perspective of democratic theory, interest groups' activity can be benign or malignant. Sometimes groups work in concert with citizens and elected officials to ensure responsive and accountable administration. They certainly check administrative power. At other times they serve narrow interests and seek to violate the spirit if not the letter of the law.

Aside from interest groups, public law may call for citizen participation. For instance, the law may reserve to the poor seats on the boards of community action agencies; this comprised a key element in the War on Poverty of the mid-1960s. Among other things, these agencies affected the allocation of federal funds to projects within impoverished areas. Consider the structure established by the National Health Planning and Resources Development Act of 1974. This law sought to facilitate more rational planning of health care resources, especially hospitals, by blanketing the country with roughly two hundred Health Systems Agencies. The law required a governing board for each of these planning agencies, and consumers rather than health care providers were to be a majority of these boards but no more than 60 percent.

What does citizen participation accomplish? Ideally it makes government programs more responsive and sensitive to the communities and populations they serve; it can serve the ends of program effectiveness. Moreover, it can help citizens learn about a policy and help them to participate more effectively in the political process. Some analysts see the act of participation per se as leading to "the creation of a healthy and fulfilled citizenry."[38] This citizenry may bestow greater legitimacy on government by participating in implementation of the program.

A less sanguine scenario competes with this one, however. In some instances citizen participation amounts to little more than symbolic politics aimed at providing the illusion rather than the substance of control.[39] Administrators and more organized interests in fact wield major power over program activities. Citizens may be increasingly bored and disillusioned with the processes, as when endless meetings seem to go nowhere and one would rather be coaching a Little League baseball team. Citizens may dislike decisions and become more dissatisfied with government.

There are cases to support both scenarios. On balance, positive results occur often enough that policymakers should persistently consider the desirability of citizen participation. However, in an era of large and complex federal programs, citizen participation is hardly a panacea. In most instances those who seek to foster democracy can appropriately view citizen participation as helping on the margins rather than serving as a centerpiece of control.

Sometimes citizens do not wait to be asked to participate in the control of public administration. They may use mass demonstrations, letter-writing campaigns, and even more confrontational means to get their views across to agencies. For example, popular demonstrations have helped publicize the issue of licensing nuclear power stations at Shoreham, Long Island, and Seabrook, New Hampshire, and keep them on the docket of the Nuclear Regulatory Commission. A good deal of spontaneous public participation can be associated with the NIMBY (not in my back yard) phenomenon. Public agencies, federal as well as state and local, are having an increasingly difficult time finding sites for potentially dangerous or undesirable facilities, such as nuclear waste dumps, prisons, and halfway houses. Citizens are more willing to mobilize to prevent such facilities from being put close to home. While perhaps expressing something of the spirit of democracy, these movements have made the lives of many public administrators much more difficult.

Contending Bureaucracies

Agencies also check each other. At times this serves the interest of democracy. Contending agencies come in two basic forms, regulatory and competitive. Intragovernmental regulatory agencies hold the explicit authority to promulgate rules for other agencies and to ensure compliance with rules via surveillance, persuasion, and penalties. The Merit System Protection Board and Office of Special Counsel, for example, attempt to ensure that the agencies follow certain acceptable personnel practices. In contrast, competitive agencies' jurisdictions overlap or compete. The Army and the Marine Corps, for instance, perform similar functions and constantly compete for resources. Each claims that it can do more to foster the national defense.

Intragovernmental Regulation.   Countless organizations within the federal bureaucracy are to regulate or investigate other agencies. The 1970s saw the birth of a new mechanism of control—the inspector general—within the executive branch. Reacting to popular concern about fraud, waste, and abuse within government, in 1978 Congress passed an act establishing Office of the Inspector General in a dozen federal departments and independent agencies. Six similar offices existed prior to the 1978 act or were added later. In the major executive departments, only Treasury and Justice have escaped the requirement to have such an officer.[40]

Inspectors general are housed within the executive branch, appointed by the president, and required to report directly to the secretary of their department. They have a direct connection with Congress; they make semiannual reports to that body. Moreover, when an inspector general reports on a major violation, the department secretary must pass along that report to Congress almost immediately. Inspectors general are not isolated individuals. For example, the Office of the Inspector General in the Department of Health and Human Services employs more than fourteen hundred auditors, lawyers, and policy analysts; it claims to have recovered approximately fourteen dollars for every dollar spent on staff salaries.[41]

The inspectors general have a broad mandate to uncover fraud, waste, and abuse. Some of the issues involved in coping with this vast terrain are enshrined organizationally by having two assistant inspectors general, one for investigation and the other for audit. Thus, inspectors general must decide whether they wish to focus on criminal actions such as fraud or managerial questions such as waste. Further, they must decide whether they want to punish malfeasance after the fact or develop policy-analytic techniques for preventing problems before they occur.

The two different administrations that have used the inspectors general (IG) have attempted to answer the question in different ways. The Carter administration, more concerned with legal issues, appointed a number of attorneys and prosecutors as IGs. When the Reagan Administration came into office it fired all the IGs. Although many of them were rehired, the remaining positions were filled with auditors. In addition, Reagan formed the President's Council on Integrity and Efficiency to oversee the IGs and to wage further war against waste. In general, the Reagan administration stressed strict financial management and accountability—a control orientation—rather than efficiency. In view of some managers, this use of IGs to foster strict accountability has taken a toll on efficiency.[42]

Inspectors general are only one of many agents of intragovernmental regulation. The Environmental Protection Agency regulates the Tennessee Valley Authority to control pollution.[43] The Equal Employment Opportunity Commission monitors and to some degree regulates federal employment practices to fight discrimination based on race, sex, age, and other characteristics. The Federal Labor Relations Authority sets guidelines and rules on disputes between management and unions in the federal government. The General Services Administration regulates procurement and the assignment of physical space.

Intragovernmental regulation contains the seeds of conflict; it heightens prospects that information about agency practices may leak to elected officials and the media. It thus discourages silent politics and encourages federal managers to make decisions as if someone were looking over their shoulder. Such decisionmaking may frequently fail to foster efficiency and effectiveness, but it does tend to promote accountability.

Competing Agencies.   Competition among agencies performing similar or overlapping functions can serve the interests of democracy. Such competition may lead to interagency squabbles that generate valuable information for elected officials and the public. Moreover, awareness among Agency A's administrators that their counterparts in B can seek advantage by criticizing them may keep A's managers accountable and responsive. The White House can be sensitive to the uses of internal bureaucratic conflict for purposes of control. During the 1930s President Roosevelt deliberately created overlap and ambiguity among administrative jurisdictions. This practice precipitated much infighting and kept him more fully apprised of the issues of policy implementation.

As government programs multiply, the potential for overlap and conflict increases. As one analyst notes, "many agencies have a voice in resolving a policy issue" and "none can exercise monopoly power over the decision-making process." As "bureaucratic organizations acquire the capacity to stalemate each other, issues inevitably move upward to the White House for resolution."[44] Hence, big government itself can unleash dynamics that produce information about administrative practice.

Administration by Proxy: A Special Challenge

Up to now this chapter has focused on problems of controlling federal agencies and civil servants. The tendency of the federal government to rely on other governments or private parties to implement programs makes the achievement of democratic control more complex and on occasion quite problematic.

Desire for payment and fear of losing the government contract presumably drive the private provider to be a faithful servant of the government. In fact, of course, contracting presents at least as many problems of control as the federal government's own bureaucracy. One student of the subject claims, "The ever-present political problem of accountability in public administration is only magnified with the addition of nongovernmental organizations carrying out the work of government."[45]

The case of Morton Thiokol and the *Challenger* disaster illustrates some of the complexities of assessing responsibility when private firms play a major role in program implementation.[46]

On the afternoon of 27 January 1986 it became clear to officials at the National Aeronautics and Space Administration (NASA) that temperatures for the *Challenger* launch from Florida's Kennedy Space Center the following day would scarcely reach the thirties. Upon learning of the forecast, Robert Ebeling, a manager at Morton Thiokol, one of NASA's contractors, met with the firm's engineers at their Utah plant to determine whether the cold posed any safety hazards. The meeting broke up in about an hour. Ebeling called a company liaison at the Kennedy Space Center and expressed concern about the possibility of malfunction under low temperatures of the now-famous O-rings in the solid rocket boosters that launched the *Challenger*. The liaison gave Ebeling new data about predicted temperatures and advised him to voice his concern to Bob Lund, the vice president for engineering at the Thiokol facility in Utah.

As more officials at Thiokol and NASA became aware of the problem, they scheduled an evening teleconference between NASA and Thiokol. During this teleconference several Thiokol engineers expressed concern about launching at low temperatures and urged delay. When asked directly by a NASA official, Joe Kilminster, the vice president for space booster programs at Thiokol, responded that he could not recommend a launch. Several NASA personnel questioned the conclusion; one complained that NASA would have to "wait till April to launch" given the concern over temperature. Nonetheless, the NASA managers clearly indicated that they would not recommend the launch if Thiokol executives did not believe it would be safe.

Confronted with this situation, Joe Kilminster of Thiokol requested a five-minute session among Thiokol personnel off the teleconference network. During this session, which lasted about half an hour, the Thiokol engineers continued to advise against the launch. Subsequently, however, a discussion among Lund, Kilminster, and two other top officials at Thiokol produced a reversal of their prior recommendation. In recalling the change, Lund related how a top Thiokol vice president asked him "to take off his engineering hat and put on his management hat."[47]

The teleconference with NASA administrators resumed. Kilminster of Thiokol read a rationale for recommending the launch. The rationale noted that data concerning the effects of temperature on the O-rings were unclear. But he noted that some malfunctioning of the sealing ring should not jeopardize the success of the *Challenger* flight. A top NASA administrator asked Thiokol to put the recommendation in writing. The firm complied.

The following day at 11:38 a.m., with temperatures in the thirties, the *Challenger* flight commenced with seven passengers, including S. Christa McAuliffe, a schoolteacher. A leak of hot gases soon occurred in the O-ring of the right solid rocket booster. Seventy-three seconds into the flight this leak produced an explosion that destroyed the *Challenger* and those on board. In the aftermath, one of the Thiokol engineers who strongly advised against the launch, Roger Boisjoly, filed a suit against his former employer under the False Claims Act. This law allows a private citizen to bring suit on behalf of taxpayers and receive a percentage of any award allocated. Among other things, the suit charged that Thiokol offered false safety assurances to preserve its "monopoly" as a supplier of solid-fuel rocket sections and to receive a special $75 million bonus incentive award in its contract with NASA. In February 1987 Boisjoly filed a separate defamation suit against the firm, accusing it of impugning his reputation. In the meantime, the FBI commenced an investigation of the firm.

Where does the buck stop? The *Challenger* tragedy highlights many of the complexities of accountability in government's interaction with private contractors. It illustrates the merging of public and private lines of authority. In the teleconferences federal managers indicated that they would not go ahead without a written recommendation from Thiokol. Furthermore, the firm confronted little risk of being cut off from federal contracts. NASA had too few alternatives to fire the firm immediately.

While Thiokol posed problems of control, however, it would be misreading the case to portray NASA managers as impotent servants of the private sector. Top Thiokol managers (as distinguished from the engineers) appeared to feel considerable pressure to please federal administrators who expressed exasperation over delay. (NASA executives themselves felt pressure from top policymakers to operate like a business and meet schedules.) Furthermore, while Thiokol did not suffer much risk of having its federal contract cut, it obviously faced severe problems as a result of the spectacular failure. Contractors cannot discount the prospect of a whistle-blower like Roger Boisjoly emerging from their ranks. Criminal investigations may occur. The company may face expensive suits and a tidal wave of unfavorable publicity. Thus the Thiokol case cautions against sweeping conclusions about the problems of assuring the accountability of private contractors.

Of course, the relations between the contractor and the agency in the *Challenger* disaster are a very special case. On balance the difficulties of achieving government control over private contractors do not seem to justify automatic rejection of the strategy when it promises to enhance the efficiency and effectiveness of government programs. Fewer problems of control and accountability probably exist when civil servants perform government's work, but difficulties do not vanish. In many instances the ability of the federal government to achieve democratic control of contractors depends on the willingness of Congress to provide funds to monitor the contracts.

When Washington turns to state and local governments to implement federal programs, issues of accountability take on new dimensions. Intergovernmental initiatives often invite state and local officials to put their mark on federal programs. The legislation mandating these initiatives often grants officials considerable authority to shape the program. The fact that state or local governments usually pay part of the federal program's cost out of their own revenues further reinforces the idea that they have a right to shape the program. When state and local officials refuse to implement programs as federal policymakers prefer, it may be a sign of responsiveness and accountability to citizens and elected officials within their jurisdictions. Thus, when other governments serve as proxies for Washington, a central question is: which level of government—federal, state, or local—has most control. One cannot automatically assume that state and local governments are more responsive and accountable. Undoubtedly state and local units vary enormously in this regard. Beyond this, some have suggested that the federal government may well be most subject to broadly based democratic control.[48]

In sum, administration by proxy does not make democratic control impossible, although it probably complicates it. However, this less-than-dismal assessment of the implications of third party implementation for responsiveness and accountability must acknowledge that the practice probably makes government more difficult for citizens to comprehend. Contracting may well contribute to what Ira Sharkansky has called the "incoherence" of the modern state. Incoherence means a lack of clarity— programs "are so complicated that people who should be able to know what is going on cannot do so."[49] Admittedly, programs can be plenty incomprehensible, even when administered by one agency, but proxy administration probably compounds the problem. To the degree that ordinary citizens cannot fathom what government does, they have more difficulty exerting effective control over it.[50]

Conclusion

In a political system built upon fear of centralized authority, it is not surprising that program administrators are not extremely powerful. To the contrary, they compete for influence with a host of other actors. Conceivably the balkanization of power can work to the advantage of the bureaucracy. One analyst notes, "Fragmentation does not always hold the answer to bureaucratic insularity. Given enough dispersion of power, bureaucrats can shop for the resources they need without relinquishing control."[51] Thus, they can be unresponsive and unaccountable.

However, in the federal government the internal compasses of administrators as well as the external muscle applied by overhead actors, interest groups, and internal bureaucratic contenders push federal administrators toward considerable responsiveness and accountability. To be sure, students of the subject disagree on how much control of the bureaucracy is enough. However, even those who express concern about bureaucratic power acknowledge that existing mechanisms usually can inhibit bull-in-a-china-shop behavior by agencies and prevent "unchecked, rampaging bureaucracy." In this view a form of "big loose control" clearly manifests itself.[52] When problems of accountability and responsiveness loom large, it is usually in policy areas where secrecy is vital. Hence, the implementation of foreign, military, intelligence, and law enforcement policies persistently generates difficult questions of accountability. The potential for administrative abuse looms larger. How can one keep the Central Intelligence Agency responsive and accountable without gutting its ability to accomplish its mission and protect its employees from physical harm?

Other difficult issues confront students of administration and democracy in the United States. In many policy spheres, problems of democratic control may be exacerbated by a bureaucracy too weak rather than too strong. Sometimes narrow interests triumph over law and the general public. An ever-increasing array of groups urges administrators to interpret laws favorably to them. They often use campaign contributions and other resources to encourage Congress and the White House to press the bureaucracy in behalf of narrow interests. Administrators at times capitulate to these pressures. Theories of overhead democracy often portray Congress as speaking for the general interest, but if the fragmentation of power in Congress makes its members proponents of narrow interests, congressional leverage over the bureaucracy may do little to foster administrative accountability to the law and to the public interest.

Finally, it bears repeating that the quest for democratic control at times exacts a toll on efficiency and effectiveness. This illustrates how a value good in itself is not necessarily optimized when it is maximized. The authors return to this issue in Chapter 14.

Notes

1. Max Weber, "Bureaucracy," in H. H. Gerth and C. Wright Mills, eds., *From Max Weber: Essays in Sociology* (New York: Oxford University Press, 1958), 232.
2. See, for instance, Dwight Waldo, "Bureaucracy and Democracy: Reconciling the Irreconcilable?" in Frederick S. Lane, ed., *Current Issues in Public Administration,* 3rd ed. (New York: St. Martin's, 1986), 455–68.
3. While contemporary social science finds such impartiality difficult to accept, this conception of the role of the bureaucrat is still widely accepted by many practitioners and a large portion of the public.
4. See Emmette S. Redford, *Democracy in the Administrative State* (New York: Oxford University Press, 1969); Kenneth J. Meier, *Politics and the Bureaucracy* (Monterey, CA: Brooks/Cole, 1987).
5. James Fesler, *Public Administration* (Englewood Cliffs, NJ: Prentice-Hall, 1980), 312.
6. Phillipe Nonet, "The Legitimation of Purposive Decisions." *California Law Review* 68 (1980): 163–300.
7. Aaron Wildavsky, *Speaking Truth to Power: The Art and Craft of Policy Analysis* (Boston: Little, Brown, 1979), 33.
8. Herman Finer, "Administrative Responsibility in Democratic Government." *Public Administration Review* 1 (1941): 335–50.
9. William T. Gormley, Jr., "Bureau-Bashing: A Framework for Analysis," Paper presented at 1987 annual meeting of the American Political Science Association, Chicago, IL.
10. Carl J. Friedrich, "Public Policy and the Nature of Administrative Responsibility," in C. J. Friedrich and E. S. Mason, eds., *Public Policy* (Cambridge, MA: Harvard University Press, 1940).
11. Some civil servants have received some fame among connoisseurs of the public

sector. See Jameson W. Doig and Erwin C. Hargrove, eds., *Leadership and Innovation* (Baltimore, MD: Johns Hopkins University Press, 1987).

12. See Charles Goodsell, *The Case for Bureaucracy* 2d edition, (Chatham, NJ: Chathan House, 1985), 85–109.

13. Bob L. Wynia, "Federal Bureaucrats' Attitudes toward Democratic Ideology." *Public Administration Review* 34 (1974): 158–9.

14. See Joel D. Aberbach et al., *Bureaucrats and Politicians in Developed Democracies* (Cambridge, MA: Harvard University Press, 1981), 174ff.

15. Charles Hyneman, *Bureaucracy in a Democracy* (New York: Harper, 1950), 20.

16. See Hugh Heclo, "A Government of Enemies." *The Bureaucrat* 13 (1984): 12.

17. U.S. Advisory Commission on Intergovernmental Relations, *Changing Public Attitudes on Government and Taxes, 1986* (Washington: Advisory Commission on Intergovernmental Relations, 1986).

18. Richard A. Wasserstrom, *War and Morality* (Belmont, CA: Wadsworth, 1970); Michael Walzer, *Spheres of Justice* (New York: Harper, 1984).

19. Garrett Hardin and John Baden, *Managing the Commons*. (San Francisco: Freeman, 1977).

20. Michael M. Harmon, *Action Theory for Public Administration*. (New York: Longman, 1984).

21. Ibid.

22. Frederick C. Mosher, *Democracy and the Public Service* (New York: Oxford University Press, 1968).

23. Ibid., 109.

24. Frank J. Thompson, "Professionalism, Mistrust of Politicians and the Receptivity of Civil Servants to Procedural Buffers: The Case of Personnel Officers." *Midwest Review of Public Administration* 13 (September 1979): 143–56.

25. Herbert Kaufman, *The Forest Ranger: A Study in Administrative Behavior* (Baltimore, MD: Johns Hopkins University, 1960).

26. See, for instance, J. Donald Kingsley, *Representative Bureaucracy* (Yellow Springs, OH: Antioch Press, 1944).

27. See Meier, *Politics and the Bureaucracy,* 184; Frank J. Thompson, "Minority Groups in Public Bureaucracies: Are Passive and Active Representation Linked?" *Administration and Society* 8 (August 1976): 201–16.

28. James L. Perry and Kenneth L. Kraemer, eds., *Public Management: Public and Private Perspectives* (Palo Alto, CA: Mayfield, 1983), 18–9.

29. Joseph A. Califano, Jr., *Governing America* (New York: Simon and Schuster, 1981), 57.

30. Douglas Yates, *Bureaucratic Democracy* (Cambridge, MA: Harvard University Press, 1982), 87–90.

31. *The New York Times* (24 April 1982): E23.

32. *The Atlanta Constitution* (14 January 1984): 1A.

33. Charles Peters and Taylor Branch, *Blowing the Whistle: Dissent in the Public Interest* (New York: Praeger, 1972), 195–206.

34. Samuel Estreicher, "At Will Employment and the Problem of Unjust Dismissal: The Appropriate Judicial Response." *New York State Bar Journal* 54 (1980): 146–49.

35. See Steven Kelman, *Regulating America, Regulating Sweden* (Cambridge, MA: MIT Press, 1981).

36. See Lief Carter, *Administrative Law and Politics* (Boston: Little, Brown, 1983), 107ff.

37. Meier, *Politics and the Bureaucracy,* 436–38.

38. Noted in Judith E. Gruber, *Controlling Bureaucracies* (Berkeley: University of California Press, 1987), 198–99.

39. Barry Checkoway, "The Politics of Public Hearings." *Journal of Applied Behavioral Science* 17 (1981): 566–82.

40. Mark H. Moore and Margaret Jane Gates, *Inspectors-General: Junkyard Dogs or Man's Best Friend?* (New York: Russell Sage, 1986), 9–16.

41. Richard P. Jusserow, "Fighting Fraud, Waste and Abuse." *The Bureaucrat* 12 (1983): 19–23.

42. Moore and Gates, *Inspectors-General,* 103–11.

43. See Robert Durant, *When Government Regulates Itself* (Knoxville: University of Tennessee Press, 1985).

44. Francis E. Rourke, "Grappling with the Bureaucracy," in Arnold J. Meltsner, ed., *Politics and the Oval Office* (San Francisco: Institute for Contemporary Studies, 1981), 139.

45. Ruth Hoogland Dehoog, "Theoretical Perspectives on Contracting Out for Services: Implementation Problems and Possibilities of Privatizing Public Services," in George C. Edwards, III, ed., *Public Policy Implementation* (Greenwich, CT: JAI Press, 1984), 239.

46. The following draws from *Report of the Presidential Commission on the Space Shuttle* Challenger *Accident,* Vol. I (Washington: Government Printing Office, 1986).

47. Ibid., 94, 96.

48. Grant McConnell, *Private Power and American Democracy* (New York: Alfred Knopf, 1966).

49. Ira Sharkansky, *Wither The State?* (Chatham, NJ: Chatham, 1979), 8.

50. When administration by proxy facilitates competition among different private providers of government services, the ability of citizens to choose among these providers can at times encourage administrative responsiveness and a measure of democratic control.

51. Gruber, *Controlling Bureaucracies,* 210.

52. Yates, *Bureaucratic Democracy,* 152, 167.

Part Three

Theories of Public Organization

Introduction

A philosopher once observed that nothing is so practical as a good theory. This adage certainly applies to the analysis and development of government organizations in the United States. If public administration is to be viable as a field, it must be able to speak to the question, "How should the administrative arm of government be organized?" The quest for the "right" way to organize the public sector can be traced to the nation's beginnings. With the emergence of large public and private bureaucracies in the late nineteenth and early twentieth centuries, the search for a theory of organization became more formalized and analytically rigorous.

The 1920s and 1930 featured considerable optimism about prospects for developing powerful empirical and normative theories of public organization (see Chapter 9). Leading students of public administration spoke with considerable confidence about the proper way to organize; moreover, top policymakers, especially those close to President Roosevelt, often listened. Piercing critiques by Herbert Simon and others in the wake of World War II severely undermined this confidence and spawned a search for alternative conceptual frameworks and theories. Many believed that systems theory would pick up the intellectual slack, but while systems theory gave birth to many insights about government organization, it was no panacea. The growing intellectual disunity within public administration paralleled a diminution in the agreement between top academicians and top policymakers on issues of reorganization. Whereas key figures in public administration had played pivotal roles in the reorganization initiatives of President Roosevelt, the same cannot be said of the initiatives launched by Carter and Reagan.

The quest to build consensus around new theories of public organization continues (see Chapter 10). One school of thought argues for a generic theory of organizations that makes little distinction between public and private entities. Another has its roots in human relations theory, with its emphasis on the social psychology of small groups and individuals. Public choice theory draws on economics and emphasizes the importance of client choice, competition, and redundancy. It directly challenges earlier theories that emphasized hierarchy, unity of command, and the reduction of duplication and overlap.

Each of the contending theoretical perspectives spawns insights, but none has been able to establish itself as the preeminent framework for the effective study of public organizations. Thus, academics and policymakers continue to struggle with the age-old questions: "What are the effects of organizational structures on the performance of individuals?" "What effects do these structures have on the efficiency, effectiveness, responsiveness, and accountability of government?" The student of public organizations can respond to these questions in a much more sophisticated way now than in 1900, 1935, or 1970. Even so, greater understanding has bred a certain humility; it has yielded a growing sense of the complexity of the subject. The quest for more powerful theories must persist.

———————

Chapter Nine

Organization and Reorganization in Theory and Practice

Introduction

Understanding public administration not only requires insight into the broad context of government in a mixed economy and the politics of administrative processes; it also necessitates a focus on one of the most notable features of the twentieth century—the rise of large organizations. Increasingly throughout this century, formally structured and legally chartered organizations, sometimes of immense scale and complexity, have undertaken both public and private enterprises. This complexity shows in the large number of employees and their distinct specialties, in the enormous size and wide dispersion of facilities, in the large number and wide variety of technologies and machines, in the sheer immensity of their financial transactions, and in the magnitude of problems they try to solve. As the complexity of organizations grows, it raises concerns about the right way to combine factors of production effectively, to design them to increase performance, and to institutionalize them to assure stability and reliability. It has, in short, spawned a whole field of study, organization theory.

A theory of organization is especially important to public administration because one of the field's principal beliefs is that the way government is organized makes a difference in how well it will accomplish its purposes. A better understanding of how organizations work (or don't work) can lead to more effective organizations.

Developing a useful theory for organizing public activities is hardly straightforward. Indeed, thinking up a set of abstract concepts that can be validated, tested, linked into propositions, and used to understand organizations' behavior as well as to design effective organizations has perplexed and frustrated brilliant social scientists and talented practitioners.

Because of its complexity and elusiveness, the search for effective organizational arrangements has divided researchers. What is meant by organizational effectiveness? What factors are important in determining effectiveness? What practices can be usefully transferred from private to public-sector organizations? These questions have produced discrete schools of thought. Each school has fashioned its own theories, which tend to focus on different aspects of organizational life. Consequently, theories developed by separate schools of thought provide different viewpoints on organizations. From these perspectives students address some properties or relationships considered to be important while ignoring or downplaying others.

Naturally, this practice frequently irritates people whose pet theory or approach has been devalued and has caused problems for people who would like to merge two or more approaches.

A journey into the basics of organization theory begins with this point: One important feature of contemporary public organizations is that they have been affected by theoretical movements for the past two hundred years. Therefore, today's public organizations must be understood as the product of successive waves of organizational and administrative reform, inspired by changes in the way reformers have thought about organizations. The eminent British economist John Maynard Keynes once described the process of ideas becoming institutionalized in the real world of government:

> The ideas of economists and political philosophers, both when they are right and when they are wrong, are more powerful than is commonly understood. Indeed the world is ruled by little else. Practical men, who believe themselves to be quite exempt from any intellectual influences, are usually the slaves of some defunct economist. Madmen in authority, who hear voices in the air, are distilling from some academic scribbler of a few years back.[1]

Keynes's observation, while not directed explicitly at public organization theory, applies quite well because at its base the study and practice of public administration has been the search for ideas about how best to organize public resources to produce effective government action. As new ideas are developed and gain acceptance, they become *ideas in good currency* and influence organization and reorganization.[2] Consequently the structures and processes of public organizations are the products of ideas about effective organization that gained favor, fell into disfavor, and were replaced by new ideas. Because of partial institutionalization and reorganization, most public organizations today are composed of overlays of rules, regulations, and procedures that reflect waves of ideas that came into and out of good currency.

Because no reform ever completely washes away the old rules, regulations, and procedures, vestiges of past systems carry forward to blend and conflict with new schemes. The result for the novice may be a crazy-quilt structure and doctrine seemingly conceived by a madman.[3] For the experienced observer, however, the logic of that same organization's design may unfold in a neat pattern. Thus, the challenge is to make the transition from an awed, confused, and perhaps frustrated student of public organization to a sophisticated analyst of its twists and turns.

This chapter and the next begin that transition by examining the major issues of public organization theory of the past two centuries. This chapter outlines the major schools of thought that have influenced the structures of the federal government. The next reviews some emerging approaches that may affect public organizations in the next century. Both chapters touch now and then on perhaps the two central issues in the study of organizations: Why do some organizational designs succeed and others fail? Is the formal organization the right focus for studying modern public administration?

The First Century of the American Administrative State

Organizations come into being because an individual or group wants to achieve some objective through the coordinated action of people and technologies. The Preamble to the Constitution eloquently states the purposes of the federal government:

> We the People of the United States, in Order to form a more perfect Union, establish Justice, insure domestic Tranquillity, provide for the common defence, promote the general Welfare, and secure the Blessings of Liberty to ourselves and our Posterity, do ordain and establish this Constitution for the United States of America.

The framers of the Constitution hoped to solve some of the major problems of the Articles of Confederation. The Constitution was a reorganization of government aimed at strengthening the military security of the country, assuring orderly commercial activity, and guaranteeing some rights of citizenship. The new structure centralized authority by transferring power from the states to the federal government. It also divided responsibility for policymaking among the executive, legislative, and judicial branches and established a complex system of checks and balances among them. In this new structure, decisions were to be made carefully and deliberately; stability was valued over innovation, but the structure assured that the government would be able to change policies to cope with new problems as they arose.[4]

The framers were masters of organizational design. The structure of the national government allows for the creation of subsidiary organizations, which are now the bulk of the federal government. Just as the Constitution was designed to deal with the problems facing a new nation-state, the subsidiary executive departments that came later were intended to deal with the secondary but important problems of running that nation. Thus, it was not by accident that the departments created in the first session of Congress in 1789 were Treasury, State, and War—each charged with responsibility for a function deemed necessary for a nation-state.

The Constitution makes no explicit reference to public administration. The broad framework for administrative organization is hinted at here and there, but clearly the framers considered the execution of the laws a secondary concern. James Garnett has observed:

> Article 1, Section 8 sets forth the powers of Congress, but the Constitution is conspicuously silent about how Congress and the President should exercise these powers . . . Article 2, Section 2 makes the President " . . . Commander in Chief of the Army and Navy of the United States, and of the militia of the several states . . . ," but no equally clear designation of the President as Commander in Chief of the Executive Branch exists. Article 2, Section 2 mentions "Heads" and "principal Officers" of "executive Departments." But the Constitution avoids specifying which executive departments should exist, how many are needed, and how these departments should be organized. The only mention of "organizing" appears in Article 1, Section 8, giving Congress power "to provide for organizing, arming, and disciplin-

ing, the Militia . . . " Here "organizing" more accurately means "mobilizing" than structuring . . .[5]

The framers were not negligent in their duties nor unmindful of the necessity for efficient public management. Rather, when it came to the details of executing the laws, they were more concerned about assuring that those in power would be accountable to elected officials than about how the new government would carry out its responsibilities. Furthermore, the roles of government, administration, and bureaucracy were perceived quite differently than today. For twenty years after ratification the size of the central government's work force was minute. In 1808 the total number of executive-branch employees in Washington was 126![6] Responsibility for setting up the executive branch was left to the first officials of the new government. Washington, Hamilton, and the other Federalists filled in the bare outline provided by the Constitution and created from almost nothing a competent administrative system. The following stand out among their achievements:

1. The independent chief executive with substantial administrative authority and responsibility for the conduct of official business.
2. Relations between the executive branch and Congress that give substantial freedom of action to high officials and keep Congress out of most administrative details while recognizing the responsibility of the executive to the legislative branch.
3. The delegation of authority by the president to administrators while retaining the president's controls over performance.
4. An administrative organization separate from and independent of the states, complete in itself, but with acceptance of state agencies for federal business in certain cases; and the beginning of cooperation between the two sets of officials.
5. Orderly and stable relationships among officials, based on law, instructions, and precedents.
6. A fiscal system to ensure the proper use of and accounting for funds.
7. The setting of good standards, especially canons of integrity and competence.
8. Acceptance of responsibility by the dominant party to determine the policy of the government and to conduct the administration of its affairs.
9. The right of public criticism of policy and administration, marred by the passage of the Sedition Act.
10. Recognition of the claims of local residents to fill federal offices with local and state jurisdiction.
11. Recognition of the moral authority of the government, a victory won by the character of Washington, the integrity of public services, and the decisiveness with which the challenge to federal authority in western Pennsylvania was met.[7]

These were substantial achievements for so short a period and were recognized as such at the time. According to Paul Van Riper, "The Jeffersonians inherited this system, had sense enough to leave most of it alone, and saw that it continued to function almost as well as it did under the Federalists."[8]

Despite its success, not everyone was content with Federalist government administered by the elite class. In 1828, with the election of Andrew Jackson, the organizational structure and the means to recruit civil servants underwent a gradual transformation that was to last more than fifty years. The Jackson administration changed several areas of organization and administration, especially personnel, administrative procedures, and executive responsibility.

Like his predecessors, Jackson was an administrative activist, but with a new twist. His predecessors staffed the executive branch with economically and socially prominent men who felt comfortable in the loose and personal climate of the capital. Jackson rejected government by the elite and instead recruited less privileged Democratic party loyalists. At the same time, Jacksonians recognized that "many government jobs required more ability and honesty than all commoners possessed."[9] To cope with this problem, Jackson launched an aggressive campaign of administrative reform focusing on the Post Office and the Land Office. These and other reorganizations limited administrative authority and imposed internal audits and controls to promote fiscal integrity. These reorganizations, by emphasizing rules and regulations, division of labor, job simplification, and office rather than officeholder in defining responsibilities and pay, moved the government toward a more rigidly bureaucratic structure. Through this less personal system, "the Jacksonian Democrats achieved more of a government by laws as well as a government by men—different men."[10]

The Jackson administration established the precedent that federal jobs would be filled through patronage, or the spoils system, rather than merit. In the early nineteenth century the stakes were substantial. Whereas the total federal work force in 1816 was 4,837, with just 535 employees in Washington, by 1841 the total work force was 18,038, with 1,014 in the capital. Thirty years later, in 1871, there were 51,020 federal civilian employees; the Washington work force stood at 6,222. That number doubled over the next decade.[11]

The growing number of patronage appointments fostered the growth and strength of political parties at all levels of government. It also strengthened Congress, especially the Senate (to which the Constitution gives the power to confirm presidential appointments) in its dealings with the president and the executive departments. The resulting administrative apparatus grew beyond the ability of a president to dominate through personal contacts, and a system of congressional and party involvement in administration affairs discouraged Jackson's successors from exercising authority or displaying interest in the administration.

The fragmentation of administrative authority in the years prior to the Civil War was reflected in the new organizational arrangements that were created to carry out governmental functions. For example, although the first Congress had lumped all government functions except that of prosecuting the law and postal affairs into either the War, State, or Treasury departments, in the pre-Civil War years, Congress created four "detached agencies," the Library of Congress, the Smithsonian Institution, the Botanic Garden, and the Government Printing Office. Beginning in the 1860s, "independent departments" of a status inferior to Cabinet departments, such as the short-lived Department of Education, were created as well as other "detached agencies."[12]

Movement away from departmentalism accelerated in the 1880s, with the establishment of the Civil Service Commission in 1883 and the Interstate Commerce Commission in 1887. It has ebbed and flowed ever since. In virtually every case the motive is to distance such quasi-independent entities from either congressional or presidential control, usually the latter.

It would be a mistake to conclude that the half-century after Jackson was totally devoid of concern for matters of organization and administration. Several innovations came out of the Civil War. Van Riper notes:

> There was a renewed understanding of the importance of organization, line and staff relationships, and orderly procedure . . . Precedents were set for the creation of a general staff. To Major General Montgomery C. Meigs, President Lincoln's quartermaster general, we owe the nation's first unified logistical organization in wartime. It contributed greatly to Northern success. Lincoln himself played a major role in the founding of the National Academy of Sciences. While the Radicals meddled in everything in the name of congressional government, they, Lincoln, and Grant managed to win the first great modern war and maintain the union.[13]

Nevertheless, after the Civil War administrative disarray accelerated. Congressional authority was so strong and patronage was so pervasive that their combined effects "explode[d] outward the lines of administrative responsibility, linking agencies to congressional committees and interested politicians instead of subordinating them to ordered, central lines of responsibility within the executive branch."[14] It was the administrative reformers of the last quarter of the nineteenth century who untangled the lines of administrative responsibility.

The Attack on Spoils

The casual approach to public administration that typified the middle nineteenth century gradually gave way as pressures of geographic expansion, industrial development, and population growth created new demands on the central government. Political developments that had little to do with the larger challenges facing the national government planted the seeds of reform. However, the reformers created a new system of government that rested on wholly new thinking about the organization of the national government. The foremost idea was that the operations of government could be made to work like a machine, that is, as an apolitical and rational system based on the precepts of scientific management.

The first major change in the development of what has been called the second American administrative state was in the civil service. The post-Civil War period was full of political turbulence, some of it revolving around the spoils system. Even before the Civil War Congress sought to constrain patronage. As early as 1853 it prescribed that no clerk should be appointed until three examiners selected by the head of the department found the candidate qualified. In 1871 Congress created the first, short-lived Civil Service Commission under Grant. The commission died in

1875 of the lack of an appropriation from Congress, but the recurring scandals and inefficiencies of the spoils system would not go away; eventually they sowed the seeds of countermovement.

The attack on spoils took both the high and the low road. According to Herbert Kaufman:

> A great many things were blamed on the spoils system during the fight to overthrow it. Every evidence of dishonesty. Every display of incompetence. Every suggestion of inefficiency. Everything low and mean and low and degrading that even occurred in the government service was blamed on the spoils system. [15]

Indeed, one reformer charged that the spoils system encouraged prostitution. [16]

Despite the nearly hysterical tenor of many accusations, as a matter of fact, large numbers of employees continued from one administration to another, even when party control changed. Their functions were regarded as too technical to allow for casual replacement, and they maintained at least a minimum of continuity. Furthermore, some civil servants were not only retained but moved up to key positions because their accumulated knowledge transcended the demands of parties. [17] Nevertheless, the problems of using the spoils system for staffing government agencies were sufficiently profound and obvious:

> The spoils system put a premium on the creation of extra jobs—both to provide additional political currency and also to lighten the workload so that loyal political partisans would have time for their assigned political tasks. . . .
>
> It resulted in the employment of many individuals who were not qualified to perform the duties for which they were hired. . . .
>
> It tempted government officials to use their official position for personal gain, for they had generally only four years in which to reap the harvest for which they had labored long and hard in the political vineyards. . . .
>
> It meant that a good deal of energy went into the orientation and basic training of a new work force every four years. . . .
>
> It reduced the President to the level of petty job broker, and diverted his strength and attention from important matters of state to the dispensation of hundreds of posts under the greatest pressure. The President gained bargaining leverage, but at the price of his health and vigor, his peace of mind, and the dignity and decorum of his high office. The Executive Mansion was besieged. The Chief Executive could not escape to protect either the nation's welfare or his own sanity. [18]

The defects of the spoils systems were visible and significant, and eventually they produced a broad movement to remove the powers of appointment and removal from the politicians. The disputed election of 1876, besides bringing an end to Reconstruction in the South, provided opportunity for reform.

Until the election of 1876, Republican Party control of the Congress and control of the party itself depended upon the political patronage of the big-city political machines of the Northeast. The contentious election divided Republicans into regional factions. That encouraged Republican President Rutherford B. Hayes to weaken the opposition within his own party by breaking the stranglehold of the Northeastern political machines on federal jobs, especially in the customhouses. By promoting standards of competence and open competitive exams for jobs at the customhouses and by removing Senate confirmation of appointments to customhouse jobs, Hayes began the long process of depoliticizing the civil service in order to change the balance of power in his own party.[19]

The second major impetus for reform came on the heels of the first. In July 1881 a disgruntled office seeker assassinated Hayes's successor, James A. Garfield. Garfield's death gave new impetus to a civil service reform bill introduced six months earlier by Senator George Pendleton of Ohio. A nascent reform organization, the National Civil Service Reform League (NCSRL) led by Dorman Eaton, also took on new importance. In January 1881 the NCSRL and Pendleton introduced a new bill based in part on the British personnel system, which was reformed in 1870. Finally passed in 1883, the Pendleton Act created an independent executive agency, the Civil Service Commission to screen applicants for federal jobs by administering competitive examinations, to protect federal employees against arbitrary removal, to prevent compulsory financial contributions to political parties, and generally to implement the act. The Pendleton Act gave the United States not only a new personnel system but also the beginnings of a new form of government. According to Stephen Skowronek:

> The passage of the Pendleton Act and the appointment of the commissioners brought the reformers' challenge to party into the formal apparatus of American government. With the merit system as its instrument, the Civil Service Commission set out on a task that amounted to nothing less than recasting the foundations of national institutional power. A professional, nonpartisan discipline might now take hold of governmental operations. An insulated administrative realm might now drive a wedge between party and government and force the parties themselves to adopt the responsible posture exemplified in the independent reform movement itself. Yet, . . . there was scant evidence of support for this reform agenda. . . . The merit system was born a bastard in the party state. The support it gained among the party professionals was that of another weapon in the contest for party power. The status of a merit civil service in the heyday of American party government remained uncertain at best.[20]

Once established, the Civil Service Commission's job of extending the merit system was by no means easy. For the next seventeen years the commission conducted examinations, made investigations, recommended rules to govern federal personnel, and requested disciplinary action, but its efforts were limited by the fact that enforcement powers were vested entirely with the president and the department heads. The contradictions of its creation confounded its effectiveness. Skowronek argues:

> By its very nature, it challenged the power base of the party professionals, its raison d'être was to place administrative offices outside the sphere of party politics. Yet its fate was in the hands of officials who were nothing if not good party men. To build a merit system in American government, government officers would have to move against resources and procedures vital to their power and position.[21]

But it occasionally served partisan political interests to remove a position from patronage (usually to protect a person with career status who originally was appointed through patronage). As a result, the merit system grew throughout the late nineteenth century. In January 1884 there were 131,208 positions in the executive civil service and the Pendleton Act covered 13,924, about 11 percent. In January 1900 there were 208,000 positions in the executive service; 94,839, about 46 percent, were subject to appointment by examination, but 113,161 were still left open to patronage appointment.[22] Furthermore, the positions subject to examination were largely for postal and customs clerks and some classes of professionals. "In this way, a concern for administrative efficiency was balanced with a concern for the spoils most vital to the maintenance of the party leadership and the locally based party work force."[23]

Given the partisan motives underlying most of the reforms in the federal system throughout the late nineteenth century, it is hardly surprising that until the turn of the century, American public administration existed without much theory to guide practice. True, some ideas in the Constitution, in the Federalist Papers, and in the practices of European government found their way across the Atlantic, but by and large, administration and organization in the federal government developed piecemeal, dictated by necessity and political advantage. However, some changes beginning in the mid-1880s made the subject of public administration an important concern for scholars, reformers, and managers in government.

The Classical Era of Public Organization Theory

Fortunately, the troubles with the spoils system after the Civil War did not emerge in all sectors of American society or at all levels of government. Developments in business manufacturing during and after the Civil War provided the government with one model of efficiency, and the reform of city governments in the early 1870s provided another. Reformers took two ideas from these examples: (1) Efficiency could be improved by instituting professional nonpartisan administration. (2) Better government could be achieved through the integration and coordination of authority by strong executive leadership. These ideas did not come at once but eventually complemented one another. Arnold observes:

> If the rise of the large firm exemplified new modes of large-scale management, the reform of city government exemplified that the balance between the branches of government within the separation-of-power system could be restruck. The target of municipal reform was the legislative branch of city government and its ties with political machines and private interests. The aim of the municipal reformers was to make the executive responsible for city government, with the city council serving a distant role of discussion and oversight. The reformers' success was marked by adoption of the strong mayor form of government and the spread of the idea of a politically neutral city manager. Thus the municipal reform movement suggested the utility for good administration of both a strengthened executive and a political conception of administration.[24]

The themes of neutral competence for civil servants and integrated management through executive leadership were to dominate thinking about government management for a hundred years. The beginning of what was to become the self-conscious study of public administration can be traced to 1887, when a young political scientist named Woodrow Wilson published a little-noticed article, "The Study of Administration," in the *Political Science Quarterly*. Wilson made several significant points that were to capture some of the major themes and contradictions of the next century. For example, he argued that a focus on how governments are administered is necessary because "it is getting harder to *run* a constitution than to frame one."[25] A proper study of government would not only be concerned with personnel reform and the merit system, but also with the "organization and methods of our government offices" with a view toward determining, "first, what government can properly and successfully do, and secondly how it can do these proper things with the utmost possible efficiency and at the least possible cost either in money or energy."[26]

Wilson's concern for efficiency and productivity led him to declare:

> The field of administration is a field of business. It is removed from the hurry and strife of politics; it at most points stands apart even from the debatable ground of constitutional study. It is a part of political life only as the method of the counting-house are a part of the society; only as machinery is part of the manufactured product.[27]

Thus Wilson constructed what has become known as the politics-administration dichotomy; that is, a distinction between what ought to be the proper sphere of partisan politics and what ought to be the proper sphere of nonpartisan administration (see Chapter 5). The former, Wilson argued, was broad government action of large scale, and the latter was small things and technical details. "Public administration," Wilson declared, "is the detailed and systematic execution of public law: Politics is the special province of the statesmen, administration of the technical officials."[28] Wilson acknowledged that in practice drawing a clear line between the realms of politics and administration would be no easy matter, but he believed that with enough study and careful organizational design and reform, it would be possible.

The theoretical dichotomy between politics and administration combined with several other developments around the turn of the century to give new life to the study of public administration. In 1900 Frank J. Goodnow, an influential political scientist and reformer, presented a more detailed examination of the dichotomy in his book *Politics and Administration*. About the same time, muckrakers like Lincoln Steffens, Ida Tarbell, and Upton Sinclair were exposing government corruption and incompetence in vivid detail, while progressive reformers like John Dewey and Herbert Croly in philosophy and Theodore Rosevelt and Woodrow Wilson in politics were propounding idealized possibilities of democracy. Furthermore, government continued to grow in expenditures and personnel, spurring interest in economy and efficiency. Finally, Frederick W. Taylor and other advocates of scientific management developed new approaches to factory management in the private sector, and the ideas spilled over to the public sector, as interest in the productivity of public programs was reaching new audiences.

This last development had special importance for theory in public administration in the nineteenth century because the large-scale business organization preceded large government organizations. The entrepreneur-managers of expanding manufacturing organizations had to coordinate and control large numbers of people and machines to facilitate reliably large-scale production. Organization structures and production systems were needed to take best advantage of the machines. It was thought that organizations should work like machines, using people, capital, and equipment as their parts. Just as industrial engineers sought to design the best machine to keep factories productive, scientific managers should discover the fastest, most efficient, and least fatiguing production methods—"the one best way"—and apply them to the work at hand.[29]

This mode of thinking corresponded neatly with the politics-administration dichotomy of Wilson, Goodnow, and the Progressives. If, as Wilson asserted, "the field of administration is a field of business," then the methods of business should be the methods of government administration. Politics and lawmaking could be left to the politicians, but the execution of laws should be left to managers who would control the machines of government—its departments.

For guidance about the structure of government departments, the reformers drew from the work of Taylor, who pioneered time and motion studies, and of other practitioners of scientific management. Their premise was that there was a one best way of accomplishing any given task, and by careful observation and research, scientific management could discover it. Once they found the best way, the scientific manager's job was to impose this procedure on the work force. Shafritz and Ott observe:

> Classical organization theory derives from a corollary of this proposition. If there was one best way to accomplish a task, then correspondingly, there must also be one best way to accomplish a task of social organization—including organizing firms. Such principles of social organization were assumed to exist and to be waiting to be discovered by diligent scientific observation and analysis.[30]

Europeans were also assessing the principles of scientific management of Taylor and other organization theorists in the United States. In France, Henri Fayol, a factory manager, published an influential book, *General and Industrial Management,* which propounded principles of organization based on specialization of functions and a unity of command that would later influence American theorists. In Germany, Max Weber, a sociologist, developed a theory of bureaucracy, outlining its major dimensions and presenting them as a type of formal organization ideal for controlling the routine processing of cases. Although Weber's work was not translated into English and made widely available until 1946, his theory nevertheless stands as a classic description of the public organization as a machine. In Weber's schema:

1. Official agency responsibilities would be established by laws and regulations.
2. There would be a well-defined official hierarchy and levels of graded authority; a system of impersonal supervision of lower officials by higher ones.
3. The work force would be divided into groups based on functional specialization.
4. The work force of the organization would be based on written procedures for work situations.
5. Selection for employment and promotion would be based on specialized expertise and training, that is, technical competence.

6. Management would proceed according to generally applicable rules that were stable, comprehensive, and comprehensible. Knowledge of these rules represented special technical learning or expertise.[31]

The ideal rational-legal bureaucratic structure that Weber conceived could not be found in the real world, but many countries were moving toward it. Besides promoting efficiency by division of complex tasks into smaller, manageable pieces, bureaucracy promoted reliability by making tasks routine. Most importantly, because appointment and promotion were strictly by examination, there was no room for patronage and political favoritism in either awarding jobs or providing government services. The political appeal of promoting impartiality in decisionmaking was obvious; the closed, mechanistic structure of the bureaucratic organization provided a model for both improving economy and efficiency and for sealing off administration from politics. Even though Weber's work was unknown to most Americans, the basic logic of bureaucracy crossed the Atlantic. Thus, in the first two decades of the twentieth century, several federal commissions suggested reforms for economy and efficiency in government that further sealed off the machinelike federal bureaucracies.[32] One manifestation of this trend was the extent of the merit system. By the end of World War I the federal government employed 917,760 people, of whom 642,432, or 70 percent, were under the merit civil service.[33]

The correct administrative apparatus for the federal government still lacked one important ingredient: Who would run the system? During the nineteenth century the center of government power gravitated to Congress, and into the 1930s very little had changed. During that decade the great expansion of government under Franklin D. Roosevelt encouraged public administration thinkers to consider how to endow the presidency with primary control over the executive branch. Even though there still are substantial questions as to the constitutional legality and the effectiveness of this arrangement, and although power has shifted back and forth between the branches throughout this century, there can be little doubt that at least since 1939, power and control over the executive branch have come to reside in the presidency.

The High Noon of Orthodoxy

Much of the responsibility for centralization of administrative power in the presidency can be traced to the research activities in support of Louis Brownlow and the President's Committee on Administrative Management. The Brownlow committee's report, published in 1937, reflected two developments of the 1930s: the rapid growth of government during the New Deal era and the increasing influence of the public administration research community at all levels of government. The committee focused on the concept of unity of command, first promulgated by Henri Fayol, and sought to strengthen the presidency by providing it with the tools thought necessary for control over the administrative apparatus. The committee reported:

> The Executive Branch of the Government of the United States has grown up without plan or design like barns, shacks, silos, tool sheds and garages of an old farm. To look at it now, no one would even recognize the structure which the founding fathers erected a century and a half ago to be the Government of the United States.

The structure of the Government throws an impossible task upon the Chief Executive. No president can possibly give adequate supervision to the multitude of agencies which have been set up to carry on the work of the government, nor can he coordinate their activities and policies.

The normal managerial agencies designed to assist the executive in thinking, planning and managing agencies which one would expect to find in any large-scale organization, are either undeveloped or lacking.

The constitutional principle of the separation of powers and the responsibility of the President for "the Executive Power" is impaired through the multiplicity and confusion of agencies which render effective action impossible.[34]

The committee concluded, "The President needs help." To give the president control over the executive branch, the Brownlow committee recommended reorganizing the executive branch and equipping the presidency "with the essential modern arms of management in budgeting, efficiency research, personnel and planning."[35] By strengthening the presidency, the committee sought to capture the advantages of close integration summarized several years earlier by W. F. Willoughby, an advocate of applying scientific management to public administration:

It correlates the several operating services of the government into one highly integrated and unified piece of administrative mechanism; it ensures the establishment of an effective system of overhead administration and control; it makes definite the line of administrative authority and responsibility; it lays the basis for, it if does not automatically effect, the elimination of duplication in organization, plant, equipment, personnel, and activities; it makes possible effective cooperative relations between services engaged in the same general field of activity that can be obtained in no other way; it furnishes the means by which overlapping and conflicts of jurisdiction may be avoided or readily adjusted; it facilitates greatly the standardization of all administrative processes and procedures; it permits of centralization of such general business operations as purchasing, the custody and issue of supplies, the recruitment and handling of personnel, the keeping of accounts, the maintenance of libraries, laboratories, blueprint rooms, etc., and finally, it furnishes the absolutely essential foundation for a properly organized and administered budgetary system.[36]

The advantages of a structure that centralized power in the Executive Office of the President suited the needs of Franklin D. Roosevelt. However, the idea that the president was general manager of the executive branch and that "the Presidency was established [by the Constitution] as a single strong Chief Executive Office in which was vested the entire executive power of the National Government" was hardly accepted unanimously by politicians and scholars at the time.[37] Nevertheless, in the late 1930s support for strengthening the presidency was widespread, and a succession of reorganizations of the executive branch has sought to enlarge presidential powers over the bureaucracy ever since.

Several developments in government and organization theory paved the road the Brownlow committee traveled between World Wars I and II. The conversion of America from an agricultural to a manufacturing economy changed demands on governments at all levels, enlarging scope of government activity—and budgets—to unprecedented size. The public concern for economy and efficiency in government expressed before World War I now blended with concern about corruption and accountability of public officials. Reorganization was the rule of the day. In local governments the city management movement gathered adherents nationwide. State government reorganizations strengthened governors and installed merit systems. In the federal government new agencies and procedures were created so that bureaucracies would be more efficiently managed and more tightly controlled.

Thus, to assure that federal spending would be closely monitored, the Budgeting and Accounting Act of 1921 established the Bureau of the Budget (which became the Office of Management and Budget in 1970) in the Department of the Treasury and set up the General Accounting Office as an independent agency. The Classification Act of 1923 brought classification of positions to federal employees based in Washington so that the principle of equal pay for equal work would be followed across agencies.

The 1920s also saw the beginnings of public administration as a recognized profession. The Harding administration's Teapot Dome scandals in 1923 helped prompt the establishment of public administration training programs at Syracuse University and the University of Southern California; several other universities established bureaus and institutes for municipal research. In 1926 Leonard D. White published *Introduction to the Study of Public Administration,* the field's first major textbook. White based his book on four assumptions that would give public administration a new, separate identity:

1. Public administration can be studied as a single process that covers federal, state, and local levels.
2. Its base is management, not law.
3. While administration is still art, in time it can be transformed to a science.
4. Administration "has become and will continue to be the heart of the problem of modern government."[38]

The tone and substance of White's original text[39] corresponded neatly with the works of other scholars in the field. By the late 1920s the emerging community of public administration scholars had about reached consensus on three general themes: (1) the desirability of applying principles to public organization theory; (2) the importance of integrating the executive branch; and (3) the value of the chief executive's dominance of administration and the executive branch.

During the late 1920s and the 1930s some developments, mostly outside of government, gave added importance to the new field. Academic social scientists, private philanthropists, and the federal government joined to encourage what today would be called policy science.[40] The product of one such collaboration was the Social Science Research Council (SSRC), founded in 1924 by Charles E. Merriam of the University of Chicago with financial support from the Laura Spelman Rockefeller Fund. In 1930 the Public Administration Clearing House was born in Chicago (also with funds from this foundation) under the leadership of Louis Brownlow, then the city manager of Knoxville, Tennessee. Also in 1930, Luther Gulick, then director of the Institute for Public Administration in New York, succeeded Leonard D. White as chairman of the SSRC's public administration section. The new clearinghouse and the institute had a majority of trustees in common, forming a new network for scholars and practitioners in public administration. According to Arnold:

Through this network of people and organizations, a newly influential social science-public administration network was created, offering a strongly executive-centered perspective on problem identification, policy design, and problem solving in the public sector. The motivating ambition behind the formation of this establishment was the idea of social science in the public service. Roosevelt's New Deal offered a promising opportunity for putting this idea into practice.[41]

Roosevelt's first year was a time of dramatic growth for government. New agencies were created, and established domestic departments such as Labor, Interior, and Agriculture received substantial new duties.[42] Coordinating these new programs was difficult. Overlap and redundancy pitted agencies against one another in the struggle for funds and responsibility for programs. Several attempts to fashion mechanisms for coordination failed to produce the desired results. Then, in March 1936, the President asked some old friends in public administration to study management in the federal government with an eye toward reorganization.

Roosevelt chose Brownlow to lead the study and Gulick and Merriam as the other two members of the President's Committee for Administrative Management. They assembled a staff of twenty-six political science and public administration experts from leading American universities. Their focus was to be on top-level management: What can be done for the presidency? Implicit in this question were two other issues: (1) How can the management and administrative supervision of the government be strengthened? (2) How can the president's capacity to lead be strengthened?

This last issue was particularly important to the three committee members because of developments in Europe. Brownlow and Merriam traveled through Europe in the summer of 1936 to review administrative practices there. The growing strength of fascism motivated them to find a democratic way of strengthening the presidency in order to make America ready for the impending great changes.[43]

It soon became evident that the vocabulary of public administration needed clarification because staff members' research interests ranged across public administration, American politics, and public law. To solve this problem, Gulick worked with a management expert, Lydall Urwick, to publish a group of essays, *Papers on the Science of Administration,* in 1937. In addition to providing a common vocabulary, the collection was to "provide a tool kit of administrative principles." These principles were to guide the report so that "disputes over details would [not] bury public interest in the principles."[44]

Although Gulick and Urwick's papers were not the real purpose of the Brownlow committee, they had a profound long-term effect on the theory of public organization. In addition to creating administrative management, a new focus for studies of organizations, Gulick's essay "Notes on the Theory of Organization" is generally acknowledged to be the definitive statement of the principles approach to organization and management—what Wallace Sayre later called "the high noon of orthodoxy."[45] In that essay Gulick introduced his famous acronym, POSDCORB, for planning, organizing, staffing, directing, coordinating, reporting, and budgeting, to describe the work of the chief executive.

Gulick began his essay with the assertion that the division of labor is the foundation for understanding organizations. Because of the necessity to divide work into separate units, "coordination becomes mandatory." Coordination can be achieved in two ways: (1) by subdividing work in a structure of authority "so that the work may be coordinated by orders of superiors to subordinates, reaching from the top to the bottom of the entire enterprise"; (2) by the dominance of an idea, "that is, the development of intelligent singleness of purpose in the minds and wills of those who are working together as a group. . . ."[46]

Gulick argued that the achievement of purpose required a "single directing executive authority" to coordinate the subdivision's work.[47] He also recognized "the inexorable limits of human nature," which limited "the span of control" or the number of subordinates any executive can supervise. The diversification of function, time, and space constrained executives, Gulick argued. Thus, the greater the diversity of functions of the subordinates, the narrower should be the span of control. The more rapid change in decisionmaking an organization faced, the narrower the span of control should be; in stable organizations a broader span of control was possible. Finally, "an organization located in one building can be supervised through more immediate subordinates than can the same organizations if scattered in several cities."[48]

Gulick also argued that no worker should have more than one master. There must be "unity of command" because "a workman subject to orders from several supervisors will be confused, inefficient, and irresponsible. . . ."[49] Likewise, workers should be grouped into subunits determined by the "principle of homogeneity." When nonhomogeneous activities were mixed, "the danger of friction and inefficiency" would increase.[50] Finally, Gulick proposed four methods of departmentalization to guide the grouping of workers:

1. The major *purpose* they are serving, such as furnishing water, controlling crime, or conducting education.
2. The *process* they are using, such as engineering, medicine, carpentry, stenography, statistics, accounting.
3. The *persons or things* they deal with or serve, such as immigrants, veterans, forests, mines, parks, orphans, farmers, automobiles, or the poor.
4. The *place* where they render their service, such as Hawaii, Boston, Washington, the Dust Bowl, Alabama, or Central High School.[51]

Once he identified these four bases for organizing, Gulick acknowledged that no one basis was clearly superior to the others. In fact, he believed that complex problems would require all four methods. Any one method would be more appropriate than the other three at different stages of an organization's life.

Over the next decade Gulick's principles and POSDCORB as a way to organize public administration occupied much of the academic community in fierce debates. In the meantime, despite some academic criticism and initial congressional setbacks, the work of the Brownlow committee became law with the Reorganization Act of 1939, which created the Executive Office of the President and transferred the Bureau of the Budget from the Treasury to the White House. The report greatly influenced the work of the first and second Hoover commissions (1947–49, 1953–55).

The Brownlow committee also influenced the organization of the public administration community. In 1939 the committee's leaders and its staff helped create a new organization, the American Society of Public Administration (ASPA), which gave the field a new institutional base and professional identity and a new outlet for ideas, *The Public Administration Review*.

The Attack on Orthodoxy

Almost before the ink was dry on the Brownlow committee's report and Gulick and Urwick's papers, critics began dissecting what many regard as the summary statements of the field of public administration. The first attacks were by critics who questioned the strong executive model and the administrative control that under-pinned the committee's work. After World War II, POSDCORB and the principles orientation came under even more stinging review. In the 1940s the politics-administration dichotomy was assaulted as being neither empirically correct nor possible in practice. By the mid-1950s the cumulative weight of these assaults had the field of public administration in disarray and intellectual crisis.

The change in mood and aspiration among the public administration community is noteworthy. Dwight Waldo has observed:

> In the 1930s, public administration had emerged from its childhood perhaps even from its adolescence . . . [I]n its POSDCORB and Principles days, it appeared to be self-confident and healthy . . . In the immediate postwar years . . . [a] groundswell of doubt and dissatisfaction brought about by measuring POSDCORB public administration against the war experience was topped by criticism of the most searching and damaging kind by a new generation of student. Adding to the problem in this situation of severe intellectual challenge and stress, the environment of public administration became less supportive; in fact, more demanding, indifferent, or hostile.[52]

The postwar critics of prewar public administration attacked the old orthodoxy from many angles, but there was remarkable similarity in their indictments. The charges addressed the bases for the entire field: that is "that the claim to science was, with respect to substance, premature and, with respect to method, immature or erroneous; that the 'principles' which were the issue of the science were, at best, summary statements of common sense; that economy and efficiency as goals or criteria were either too narrowly conceived or were misconceived; that the separation between politics and administration is arbitrary or false and must be abandoned" or thought through on new terms.[53] As a result of these assaults, by the late 1960s Waldo perceived "a crisis of identity for public administration." The nature and boundaries of subject matter and the methods of studying and teaching public administration were problematical.[54]

The Prewar Critiques

The first critiques of the Brownlow committee's major proposals came from scholars who believed that administrative powers should reside with the Congress, not the president. In the study *Reorganization of the National Government: What Does It Involve?* Lewis Meriam of the Brookings Institution argued that increasing the power of the presidency would not necessarily improve the economy, efficiency, or accountability of the administrative branch.[55] Furthermore, the Brookings study concluded, a strong presidency would not necessarily serve democracy, and compre-hensive reorganization would not necessarily lead to the best structure because the national government is far too large, too dynamic, and too complex for a single broad reorganization.

While Meriam's arguments were recognized as important at the time, some discounted them because he was a Republican and his work was commissioned by the Congress, and therefore thought to be biased. After the war, however, in the wake of the first Hoover Commission's recommendations for a strong administrative role for the president, other scholars echoed Meriam's themes. One critic, Charles Hyneman, charged that the concept of an administrative presidency would overburden the president by relegating him to the role of a "glorified factory superintendent."[56] Instead, Hyneman argued, "these are times when we most need to have the President free from involvement in administration so that he can devote himself most fully to political affairs of greatest current importance to the nation."[57] Others, like Edward Corwin, charged that the framers of the Constitution intended the president's role to be ministerial, not managerial.[58]

A second major stream of challenges to the Brownlow committee's view of organizations came from adherents of the human relations school. Beginning in 1933 with Elton Mayo's *The Human Problems of Industrial Civilization,* a report on studies of assembly line workers at the Western Electric Company's Hawthorne Works outside Chicago and continuing with the more detailed 1939 report of F. J. Roethlisberger and William Dickson, *Management and the Worker,* the life of the worker in organizations began to be understood in a much different way than before. The Hawthorne experiments aimed to measure changes in worker productivity and fatigue resulting from changes in working conditions. Variables like lighting, temperature, humidity, and hours of sleep were thought to play a part in determining productivity and fatigue. Later, intangibles such as workers' attitudes were related to efficiency.[59]

Although the initial series of lighting manipulations provided few clear findings about causal relations between the environment and efficiency, some anomalies eventually led researchers to shift their focus to the study of morale. Here the researchers discovered the importance of the informal organization and a new way to think about workers and their work.

To Mayo, Roethlisberger, and other early adherents of the human relations school the organization was not a machine and workers were not interchangeable cogs. Organizations were social systems composed of groups of people that gave value to their work. Employee morale was linked to productivity. Adherents of the human relations school argued that employees who were satisfied and challenged and supported by their peers produced more than those in organizations that stifle group interaction and rigidly control employees' behavior.

One of the tenets of the human relations school—that employees often consider their peers at least as important as the boss—was clearly in conflict with the hierarchical notions of orthodox theory. If informal groups and communication patterns had critical effects on morale and productivity, what was the value of the formal structures of the principles school? Furthermore, if employees form groups across formal organizational lines and across hierarchical levels, how does an organization maintain control and accountability?

Finally, the human relations school assumed that the executive now had two tasks: "the function of securing the common economic purpose of the total enterprise;

and the function of maintaining the equilibrium of the social organization so that individuals through contributing their services to this common purpose obtain personal satisfaction that makes them willing to cooperate."[60] From this perspective, an understanding of organizations based on principles of scientific management and POSDCORB was simply not enough. A more complete theory was needed.

The attack on orthodox public administration was joined by sociologists, particularly Robert K. Merton, who published an influential article in 1940.[61] Merton argued that Weber's machinelike ideal bureaucracy had inhibiting dysfunctions that prevented it from becoming optimally efficient or effective. Merton drew upon earlier critiques of bureaucracies and bureaucrats to point to the tendency of highly trained and regimented bureaucrats to develop *trained incapacity,* or blind spots. Merton observed that "[a]ctions based on training and skills which have been successfully applied in the past may result in inappropriate responses *under changed conditions.*"[62] Because the bureaucratic structure constantly presses officials to be "methodical, prudent, disciplined," they tend to adhere rigidly to rules. But "adherence to the rules, originally conceived as a means, becomes transformed into an end-in-itself; there occurs the familiar process of *displacement of goals*" whereby means become more important than the ends they are supposed to serve.[63] Bureaucracies, Merton charged, often breed overconformity to rules, ritualized discipline, and impersonal treatment of clients to the point of fostering arrogance and haughtiness, even when the agency's pruposes would be better served by more flexibility and more responsiveness.

Perhaps the most challenging development for orthodox public administration in the long run came from a source totally outside the academic and government communities. About the time the Brownlow committee submitted its report, Chester Barnard, an executive of Bell Telephone, published *The Functions of the Executive* (1935), which proposed a new, more sophisticated view of organizations. Barnard, in reading through the scholarly literature on management in the United States and Europe concluded that:

> there was lacking much recognition of formal organization as a most important characteristic of social life, and as being the principal structural aspect of society itself. Mores, folkways, political structures, institutions, attitudes, motives, propensities, instincts, were discussed *in extension* but the bridge between the generalizations of social study on the one hand and the action of masses to which they related on the other were not included, I thought.[64]

While Barnard made little impression on the field of public administration at the time, his book later gained attention because it was a bridge between the formal organization of the principles school and the more dynamic behavioral systems and decisionmaking processes that dominated organizational studies after the war. Instead of emphasizing structure, Barnard saw an organization as "a field of personal forces, just as an electromagnetic field is a field of electronic or magnetic forces."[65] The organization's field, in Barnard's conception, stretches beyond its formal boundaries to include customers and suppliers as well. Barnard argued that organizations are held together not by hierarchical authority but by the voluntary contributions of individuals with a common purpose. The mechanism for achieving purposes, an *organizational economy,* allows exchanges between individuals and the organizations and maintains dynamic equilibrium among several complex social and material processes.

To maintain this system of coordinated activities directed toward a purpose, Barnard proposed that certain executive functions must be performed: (1) organizational communication; (2) acquisition of essential services from individuals; and (3) formation of purpose and objectives. Although this is not all the work executives do, Barnard noted that it "is the specialized work of *maintaining* the organization in operation" that defines executive roles.[66] Thus, executives must attend to the framework of the organization and its personnel. The first deals with "the geographic, temporal, social and functional specializations of unit and group organization," while the latter concerns "the development of inducements, incentives, persuasion, and objective authority" that allow goals to be met.[67] Maintaining this arrangement and nurturing the belief among contributors in the purposes of the organization is a key executive function.[68] Leadership, according to Barnard, "is the aspect of individual superiority in determination, persistence, endurance, courage; that which determines the *quality* of action; which often is most inferred from what is *not* done, from abstention; which commands respect, reverence."[69]

To Barnard executive leadership not only implies complex morality and requires a high capacity for responsibility, it also requires "the faculty for creating morals for others."[70] From Barnard's perspective, leadership was an essential component of organizational life: "Cooperation, not leadership is the creative process; but leadership is the indispensable fulmination of its forces."[71]

World War II and the necessity of getting on with the business of government in the face of crisis obscured the importance of Barnard's work for most of the next decade. After the war, however, several of his main ideas were picked up by scholars who were more central to the public administration community and who were not deterred by the abstract nature of *The Functions of the Executive*.

Postwar Critiques

Lewis Meriam's attack on the Brownlow committee's report raised several issues that would not go away. Prime among them was the validity of the principles approach to designing organizations. Meriam noted at the end of his study that he and the Brookings team had "been forced to reject the theory that there is such a thing as a single controlling principle or a small group of controlling principles that dictate sound organization. . ."[72] These words were echoed and reinforced seven years later, in 1946, when the young political scientist Herbert Simon published "The Proverbs of Administration," which demolished and discredited the principles approach to organization and administration.

In 1947 Simon, who was later to win a Nobel Prize in economics for his work on decisionmaking theory, published *Administrative Behavior*, which repeated his attack on the principles school and proposed an alternative way to study administration and organizations. Simon's most telling argument was that Gulick's and others' principles of administration were contradictory.

It is a fatal defect of the current principles of administration that, like proverbs, they occur in pairs. For almost every principle one can find an equally plausible and acceptable contradictory principle. Although the two principles of the pair will lead to exactly opposite organizational recommendations, there is nothing in the theory to indicate which is the proper one to apply.[73]

Simon focused his attack on the principles that related efficiency to:

1. Specialization of task
2. Hierarchy of authority
3. Span of control
4. The grouping of workers for purposes of control according to purpose, process, clientele, or place.

In each instance he pointed to examples in government that were at odds with the principles. According to Simon, one of the major problems with these principles was ambiguity in key terms. What did words like *purpose, process, clientele,* and *place* mean? In some cases the same activity might encompass all four terms, depending on how one chose to describe it. This problem, Simon argued, made questionable the whole enterprise of the principles school:

> These contradictions and competitions have received increasing attention from students of administration during the past few years . . . All this analysis has been at a theoretical level—in the sense that data have not been employed to demonstrate the superior effectiveness claimed for the different models. But, though theoretical, the analysis has lacked a theory. Since no comprehensive framework has been constructed within which the discussion could take place, the analysis has tended either to . . . logical one-sidedness . . . or to inconclusiveness.[74]

Even though one of the Gulick-Urwick papers, "Science, Values and Public Administration," made it abundantly clear that Gulick recognized the need for measurements and testable theory about organizations,[75] Simon's attack generally was devastating. The key to a genuine administrative science, he argued, must have new beginnings. Simon subsequently set out to provide them.

Simon's skepticism about the scientific validity of orthodox public administration was joined by other voices. In 1947 Robert Dahl published an influential article that raised questions about the normative bases of American public administration, its parochial nature, and its view of workers.[76] According to Dahl, a science of public administration must (1) account for values other than efficiency, (2) find a method for comparing administrative systems across nations and social settings, and (3) develop a more elaborate and detailed understanding of the nature of man in administrative settings. In each of these areas, Dahl concluded, the American study of public administration left much to be desired.

The second branch of postwar criticism of the orthodox school focused on the role of politics in public administration, the politics-administration dichotomy, and by extension the closed machinelike model of bureaucracy implied by orthodox theory. In 1944 David E. Lilienthal, a notable public servant, wrote of his experiences in the Tennessee Valley Authority.[77] He argued that the planning and management of government was a political enterprise both healthy and beneficial for a democracy. In a follow-up study, Philip Selznick, a sociologist, outlined some of the strategies that the TVA used to build a political constituency to assure its survival.

In this book, *TVA and the Grass Roots* (1949), Selznick coined the word *cooptation* to describe an organization bringing new groups into its decisionmaking processes in order to prevent them from threatening the organization and its mission.[78] In 1945 the prominent New Deal administrator Paul Appleby published *Big Government,* which attacked the politics-administration dichotomy as a mistaken myth that could be detrimental to the workings of government.[79] Appleby also argued that political actors in administrative affairs checked the arbitrary use of bureaucratic power. Finally, Appleby shattered the notion that business and government administration are alike in all respects by asserting that "government is different because government is politics." This theme would reverberate in the literature on public administration throughout the next decade.

Several other scholars of the postwar period, most notably Norton Long, Dwight Waldo, and John Gaus, sounded the theme of openness of organizations to influences from their environment. In the 1949 article "Power and Administration" Long outlined the way public organizations and their elites play politics internally and externally to achieve their ends.[80] To Long this behavior not only challenged the idea that bureaucracies could be treated as closed passive machines responsive to their political masters but also raised serious questions of democratic accountability.

Waldo took another tack by tying the study, practice, and theory of public administration to larger issues of political philosophy and ideology. His classic 1948 work *The Administrative State* argued that "American public administration has evolved political theories unmistakably related to unique economic, social, governmental and ideological facts."[81] Waldo's work dissected the politics of ideas that underpinned the progressive movement and several streams of "the public administration as management movement." Waldo considered the notions of economy and efficiency that guided prewar public administration to be quite political. He concluded, "They have been used as weapons of attack and defense in a political struggle. They have, indeed, been key concepts in a political philosophy; that is, concepts difficult to define precisely because they are themselves regarded as ultimates, in terms of which other concepts are defined."[82]

Waldo went so far as to refer to much of public administration knowledge as orthodox ideology, promoting the belief that "true democracy and true efficiency are synonymous, or at least reconcilable."[83] Still, in the real world of government, Waldo observed, even this notion was questionable in light of the difficulties involved in defining either ideal.

By the end of the 1950s the attack on prewar orthodoxy was complete. The closed machine model that separated politics from administration had given way to a new conception of the field. John Gaus, a prominent student of public administration, declared, "a theory of public administration means in our time a theory of politics also."[84] However, with the old orthodoxy in disrepute, students of public administration became more uncertain "as to the ends, aims and methods which they should advocate."[85] With the decline of the old orthodoxy, the field of public administration entered a long era of self-doubt and theoretical disunity.

Despite the confusion in the public administration community, the actual work of government had to go on. World War II had left the federal government with a massive debt and a tangle of wartime organizations and policy. Reorganization seemed to Congress and the president a sensible way to deal with this mess.

The First Hoover Commission

In 1947 President Harry Truman asked former President Herbert Hoover to head a commission to reorganize the executive branch. Hoover sought out reorganization experts in the public administration community, most of whom were political scientists. The Commission on Government Organization, as the Hoover effort was formally named, like the Brownlow committee, was to give greater coherence to government and more central executive capacity to the president.[86] The members of the Hoover commission and certainly its staff were well aware of the scholarly criticism of the Brownlow committee, but they essentially ignored it and got on with the business of extending the Brownlow model into the postwar era.

Like the Brownlow report, the Hoover Commission report charged that the executive branch was unmanageable, its lines of communication were blurred, and the president lacked the tools to develop policy. The solution, as with the Brownlow committee, was in an integrated, hierarchical model of organization. "No single theory of administration motivated all 277 recommendations. However, many of them presumed values of coherence in governmental organization, hierarchical control, centralized authority, and organization by purpose."[87]

Because the Hoover Commission's recommendations varied greatly in their importance, it is hard to keep a box-score of success, but experts put the number of recommendations implemented somewhere between 100 and 150. Arnold notes these achievements:

> Among the recommendations implemented are a number that are among the most important ones made by the commission. The reorganization authority was renewed, albeit with a one-house veto. The recommendations for increased presidential staff support and discretion in the use and organization of the Executive Office were widely accepted and, in effect, reaffirmed changes and growth already ongoing in the development of White House organization. After the passage of the Reorganization Act, President Truman effected changes consistent with the commission's recommendations in many of the departments and independent commissions, although Congress vetoed plans that would have effected some of the departmental-level recommendations. However, following the commission's recommendations, the Post Office, and the Department of Interior, Commerce, and Labor were reformed through reorganization plans, as was the National Security Council and a number of independent agencies, such as the Civil Service Commission, the Federal Trade Commission, Federal Power Commission, the Securities and Exchange Commission, and the Civil Aeronautics Board. Some recommendations were effected through statute, the most prominent examples being the creation during 1949 of the General Service Administration, the transformation of the National Defense Establishment into the Department of Defense, and the reorganization of the State Department.[88]

The success of the first Hoover Commission represented a great breakthrough for the public administration community. Never before had a reorganization effort achieved such widespread political support. Across the country, many influential people joined the Citizens Committee for the Hoover Report, an organization intended to marshal public support for the commission's recommendations and its motto, "Better Government at a Better Price." The commission spurred taxpayers and good-government groups to form little Hoover commissions to apply the principles of good public administration to state and local governments.

In retrospect, all this support for orthodox public administration theory was ironic because it came at a time of great self-doubt in the public administration community. If the Brownlow report was "the high noon of orthodoxy" for public administration theory, then the first Hoover Commission must be considered its high noon of political legitimacy. Never again would theory and practice be in such close synchronization.

The System School

The revisionist thinking of the postwar era left public organization theory in a quandary. Simon had persuasively argued that the principles of organization promulgated by Gulick and others were merely proverbs; the human relations school had cast substantial doubt about the efficacy of hierarchical and control-oriented methods of organizing work; and political scientists had shown that public organizations and career civil servants were hardly neutral, passive implementors of directions handed down by Congress and the president. These findings argued that the politics-administration dichotomy was a fiction and neutral competence for the civil service was an unattainable ideal. In these new models the lines between politics and administration were so blurred that the world of the statesman and the administrator became a seamless web with no clear criteria for distinguishing between the two. Given this intellectual ferment, two questions naturally arose: (1) How should scholars go about understanding contemporary public administration? (2) What guidelines could they convey to policymakers for organizing government activity?

In the wake of the revisionist literature, public organization theory became fragmented and tentative, backing away from prescriptions for organizational form. Instead, research gravitated toward concern for narrow issues of economy and efficiency on the one hand and toward the description of organizational behavior on the other. Rather than asking how the government should organize its programs for old age security, students of public administration asked how they could get the most old-age pension claims processed in the least time and how social security recipients interacted with claims examiners. The first kind of question reflected the new prominence of economics and the related fields of policy and systems analysis, operations research and management science, which aimed at fine-tuning policy by improving operations. The second kind of question reflected the tradition in sociology and political science in which behavioral or descriptive analysis of organizations dominated.

Even though these studies of organizational behavior often produced rich insights into government decisionmaking, they exacerbated the identity crisis in the field. As public administration moved toward descriptive analysis, it also moved toward a normatively weak posture that eschewed predictions of the consequences of organizational change. This was, of course, the area of public administration of most interest to policymakers. Nevertheless, mindful of the stinging critiques of the revisionists, the 1950s and 1960s saw the public administration research community retreat from the world of government. Richard R. Nelson observed:

> Thus there are splendid accounts of how federal agencies, like those of the armed forces, increasingly have been contracting for work through private companies. There are good discussions of the increasingly complicated network of decision making and fund flow among the various levels of government and the various private grant-receiving groups (like scientists). But there is no persuasive analysis of how the system would in fact have worked had it otherwise evolved.
>
> Thus, while it has the form of a discipline that purports to be helpful regarding the guidance of policy, public administration has lacked two essential components of an effective intellectual structure—a useful normative apparatus, and an ability to make persuasive predictions.[89]

Though public administration lacked both a widely accepted theory for reorganizing government activity and clear criteria for choosing among alternatives, by the mid-1960s the field was gravitating toward open systems theory, a new framework useful for sorting information and structuring research.

Toward Open Systems Theory

Herbert Simon's attack on the principles school may have marked the end of an era, but it also began a new, more scientific approach to studying organizations. In *Administrative Behavior* Simon outlined an alternative way of building theory about organizations that focused on decisionmaking as the central activity of administration. One central theme of Simon's analysis revolved around the notions of *bounded rationality* and *satisficing behavior*. This spoke directly to assumptions about decisionmaking prevalent in economic theory. Simon argued that the central assumption of economics is that decisions are made rationally with complete and perfect information. In the real world, he argued, uncertainty abounds, and man does not have the luxury of complete and perfect information. Therefore, rather than choosing the best course of action from among a complete list of alternatives, administrative decisionmakers merely seek to improve their situations by making "satisficing" choices among a limited number of alternatives; thus rationality cannot be perfect, but is bounded by these constraints.

Another theme of Simon's work concerned the distinction between facts and values.[90]

> The argument runs, briefly, as follows. To determine whether a proposition is correct, it must be compared directly with experience—with the facts—or it must lead by logical reasoning to other propositions that can be compared with experience. But factual propositions cannot be derived from ethical ones by any process of reasoning, nor can ethical propositions be compared directly with the facts—since they assert "oughts" rather than facts. Hence, there is no way in which the correctness of ethical propositions can be empirically or rationally tested.
>
> The important point for the present discussion is that any statement that contains an ethical element, immediate or final, cannot be described as correct or incorrect, and

that the decision-making process must start with some ethical premise that is taken as "given."

Thus Simon proposed a dichotomy between facts and values to focus the study of administration on that which can be empirically tested in experience. Like the politics-administration dichotomy, the factual part of administration could be studied, reduced to machinelike theory, and used as tools by administrators with values of their own.

Simon, borrowing from Chester Barnard, saw the organization as a system kept in equilibrium by a balance between inducements to and contributions from organizational participants. Thus, the organization "receives contributions in the form of money or effort, and offers inducements in return for these contributions. These inducements include the organization goal itself, conservation and growth of the organization, and incentives unrelated to these two."[91]

Subordinates follow directions because the inducements of the organization are sufficient to attract their contributions,[92] but also because they fall within their "zone of indifference," an idea Simon borrowed from Barnard to describe "an area of behavior within which the subordinate is willing to accept the decisions made for him by his superior."[93] Such choices are expected to be implemented reliably and with little question. Choices outside this zone require negotiation and persuasion about inducements and contributions.

Simon's ideas about administration and organizations were to spawn a whole new approach to organizational studies. Along with colleagues, he set the stage for open systems theory, which captured the stream of thinking begun by Barnard and formalized by Simon. Thus, *Public Administration,* written with Donald W. Smithburg and Victor A. Thompson in 1950, and *Organizations,* written with James March in 1958, set the stage for Richard Cyert and James March's *A Behavioral Theory of the Firm* (1963) and March's seminal *Handbook of Organizations* (1965).[94] Embedded in these developments was the idea that a science of organization research and design could be built on a generic basis that would make distinctions between kinds of functional organizations—public versus private, hospital versus university, and so on. Toward this end Simon and other scholars of similar persuasion in 1956 founded a journal, *The Administrative Science Quarterly,* to promote generic studies. All that remained for the development of a true science of organizations was an integrative framework, and such a framework was on the near horizon.

The Systems Framework

The open systems approach to organizations had its formal beginning with the publication of two books, Robert Katz and Daniel Kahn's *The Social Psychology of Organizations* (1966) and James D. Thompson's *Organizations in Action* (1967). The two works are the intellectual basis for the mainstream of organization theory.

Katz and Kahn as well as Thompson drew their models of organization from two earlier traditions of scholarship, general systems theory and organizational sociology. General systems theory was pioneered by a biologist, Ludwig Von Bertalanfy, who sought to develop a language and methodology to formulate principles of relationships between elements of living systems and their environment.[95] In general systems theory, organizations, like other living systems, are open to environmental influences and seek to adapt to them by transforming (throughputting) energy and resources (inputs) into actions or products (outputs). The metaphor of the organization as a biological system embraces the ideal that the organization's prime imperative is survival rather than efficiency. This characteristic underscores the importance of the system finding a safe niche in its contingent environment. When such a niche is found and secured, the organization is said to be in *homeostatic equilibrium,* that is, a dynamic balance of forces and exchange of energy with the environment counteracts the forces of entropy, which break apart and wear down systems. Finding such a balance is largely a product of monitoring feedback, or information from the environment, and adapting to it.

Sociologists, most notably Talcott Parsons, one of the first to translate Weber's work into English, provided the second idea that inspired open systems theory.[96] Parsons used a *structual functional* model to explain how social systems survive over time. Parsons introduced the idea that in order to survive social systems must structure their parts to accomplish four basic functions:

1. They must *adapt* to their external environment.
2. They must use their resources to attain *goals.*
3. They must coordinate their parts through *integration* so that "control is established, deviancy is thwarted, and internal stability is maintained."
4. In order to ensure continuity of action according to some order or norm, they must exhibit *latent* pattern maintenance.[97]

The survival of a system, "from a small natural organism to a large social collectivity," depended upon the effective performance of these four functions.[98]

Parsons's analysis showed how social systems survived and changed by specializing or differentiating their parts to perform different functions. Katz and Kahn applied this idea to formal organizations and differentiated five generic subsystems that allow organizations to exist in their environment:

1. Production subsystems, concerned with the work that gets done
2. Supportive subsystems of procurement, disposal, and institutional relations
3. Maintenance subsystems to support people in their functional roles
4. Adaptive subsystems, concerned with organizational change
5. Managerial subsystems to direct, adjudicate, and control the many subsystems and activities of the structure.[99]

Katz and Kahn focused on the ways organizations regulate their subsystems.[100]

Thompson's work focused on strategies that organizations use to survive. His framework also drew heavily on Parsons's formulation of social systems. In particular, Thompson drew upon Parsons's notions that organizations are structured to meet certain environmental *contingencies,* sources of uncertainty. These contingencies present problems that the organization must cope with effectively in order to survive.

In order to meet these contingencies, organizations are motivated in two directions at once: toward openness, interacting with their environment through "boundary-spanning units"; and toward closure, by sealing off their "technical core" from uncertainty created by environmental disturbances.[101] This two-pronged strategy allows organizations to buffer their technical core from uncertainty and structure their internal workings for machinelike efficiency. This buffering requires three distinct levels of responsibility and control—technical, managerial, and institutional (the broadest).[102]

Thus, Thompson's framework helped to explain how the organization is able to accommodate open and closed systems simultaneously; that is, function as a closed machine system as well as like an open system, a living organism. Using this formulation, Thompson built a theoretical bridge between some prewar orthodoxy and the ideas and findings of later scholars.

Four other aspects of the open systems framework help to account for its success in becoming the mainstream of organizational thinking in the 1960s and 1970s:

1. It incorporated the distinction between *natural* and *artificial* systems.
2. It drew heavily upon Simon, Richard Cyert, and James March's idea of the organization as problem solver.
3. It promulgated a *contingency theory* of organizational behavior that produced testable propositions about the relationships between organizational environments, behavior, technology, and effectiveness.
4. It developed the concept of *dominant coalitions*, which allowed for politics in decisionmaking. That helped to explain why an organization picked one strategy over others in adapting to its environment.

Organizations As Artificial and Natural Systems

The distinction between natural and artificial systems is important to organization theory. Systems theory recognized that just as organizations are tools to solve problems for their owners, be they private shareholders or government entities, organizations have problems of their own and create subunits to deal with them. Thus, Victor Thompson observed, open system theory encompasses the two dominant traditions of organization studies, each reflecting separate but interrelated patterns of behavior in organizations: the closed, rational, or *artificial* system model and the open *natural* systems model.[103]

The artificial system is an organization and formal structure—that is, divisions of labor and rules and regulations that have been deliberately created to solve some specific problem or set of problems. This model addresses problems of efficiency and control and is best exemplified in the literature on bureaucratic organization, scientific management, operations research, and management science.[104] Ideally, artificial systems models are closed arrangements; there is no uncertainty in the operation of the organization, and all the factors necessary for solving problems are within the control of the system.

Natural systems models, in contrast, do not focus on the formal structure or specific goals of the organization. Rather, they view organizations as open systems, that is, as natural evolving systems whose primary purpose is self-maintenance and survival through planned and unplanned adaptions to disturbances or problems arising from the organization's external environment and internal culture.[105] The behavior of organizations and the people in them is assumed to depend to a great extent upon their interaction with external and internal environments.

In understanding organizational behavior, Victor Thompson argued, one needs to grasp two layers of intertwined activity, the artificial and the natural. The interaction between these two kinds of organizational systems is remarkably complex because no social system is static and some evolutionary changes are always taking place, either for better or for worse performance, or both at once.

These changes make up the "spontaneous, unplanned emergent quality" of organized human activity.[106] To cope with them, governments have traditionally emphasized managerial control and accountability as means to minimize negative consequences of evolutionary change. In contrast, the field of human relations has promoted the positive features of the organization's evolution through participatory approaches to management.

Taking account of the interaction between an organization's natural and artificial systems highlights some dynamics that affect performance. In addition to the ubiquitous problems of uncertainty, three kinds of problems in particular stand out: (1) *dissent* inside and outside the organization over the desirability of goals and the means to achieve them; (2) *scarcity of resources*, which limits the scope, direction, and duration of organizational activity; and (3) *entropy*, which wears down even the best-designed arrangements. To cope with these persistent problems, managers must overcome them or limit their intrusions on the routine activities of the organization.

Managers use numerous procedures and tools to limit the effects of uncertainty, dissent, scarcity of resources, and entropy on the organization's goal seeking. In all organizations this means finding ways of minimizing disturbances from the natural system, facilitating the natural system's accomplishments, and maintaining patterns of artificial goal-seeking. This leads to the conception of organizations as *purposeful* systems, that is, as social entities that make choices about what goals they will seek and how they will seek them.[107]

Organizations As Problem Solvers

Open systems theory starts from the assumption that organizational arrangements are intended responses to perceived problems. In the minds of the people who create them, something is amiss in the world, and only an organization of a particular function and form can solve it. What is amiss may be either a problem or an opportunity not seized. Simon and his followers have observed that problem solving is a powerful key for unlocking the mysteries of organizational structures and processes.

Seen from this perspective, the internal properties of organizations—that is, their rules, resources, positions, distributions of power, and technologies—can be understood as an arrangement of coordinated activity designed to change something. To illustrate, the Department of Defense (DOD) was designed to assure civilian control of the military and to coordinate military activity on land and sea and in the air. It retained the departments of the Army and Navy and created the Department of the Air Force; the Office of the Secretary of Defense, controlled by a civilian appointee; and the Joint Chiefs of Staff, controlled by the military. In similar fashion, the EPA is structured along functional lines. The agency has special divisions for water, solid waste and emergency response, air and radiation, pesticides and toxic substances, and research and development as well as several staff divisions and ten regional offices.

Because of the inherent limits on what one person can accomplish and on the number of others one person can supervise, all large organizations develop arrangements for breaking down tasks into manageable subdivisions. Into these units go resources (money, employees, machines, technology, and physical facilities) and decisionmaking authority in a complex plan its owners and managers think will produce good results. As sad experience has shown, even the most carefully planned organization can fail to produce good results. This occurs because organizations operate in a complex and changing world, and no one can claim the knowledge and insight necessary to design an organizational arrangement to cope with all its twists and turns. Organizational problems vary from simple to complex. Simple problems make it relatively easy to design organizational arrangements; complex problems make design and management more difficult. Simple problems share some common characteristics:

1. There are few goals, little conflict about goals, and few ambiguities about what the goals mean. Those with power share basic values and premises for decisionmaking.
2. Cause-and-effect relationships between the problem and the alternative solutions are clear; that is, social technologies are highly predictable and effective.
3. Measures of success are readily available; indicators of success or failure are precise; outcomes are easily measured.
4. The environment provides quick and accurate feedback on the organization's performance.
5. All resources necessary to solve the problem are readily available to the organization.

While some public-sector tasks qualify as simple problems amenable to solution via routine technologies, many do not. Fundamental features of the political system—fragmented political authority, institutionalized competition for scarce resources, ideological conflict, and multiple checks and balances at different levels of government—contribute greatly to problem complexity and can force managers of public organizations to grapple with problems in ways that are partial and disjointed. Furthermore, the forces of political as well as technological change and risk often break down even the most effective organizational arrangements. A sad example of this phenomenon may have occurred at NASA in the months before the *Challenger* tragedy.

The problem of instability combined with the complexity of most large-scale administrative arrangements forces public managers to make decisions and operate under varying degrees of uncertainty. Because of the risks of making mistakes, a premium is placed on finding managers with experience and good judgment about a problem so they can read clues to come up with a workable solution.

This suggests that when dealing with a complex problem, learning from experience is an important element of success. Formulas may readily be applied to arrive at solutions to simple problems, for example when a team of engineers designs a dam or determines the toxicity of chemical waste. In cases of this kind analysis precedes and governs action because the relationships among factors affecting success or failure are clear enough to indicate action without new experimentation. In complex situations, the action *itself* is required to generate feedback. In other words, simple problems can be dealt with by planning *before* action is taken, whereas complex problems require designs that unfold over time as each new round of action occurs and is evaluated.[108]

The strategy the national government uses on its biggest complex problems has been called *disjointed incrementalism*[109] (see Chapter 4). Charles Lindblom, a pioneer in the study of such decisionmaking, has argued that muddling through and mutual accommodation, endemic to this approach, often contributes to the intelligence of policymaking in a democratic society such as the United States.[110]

In contrast to simple calculations, disjointed incrementalism features several powerful decisionmakers pursuing several partially developed strategies simultaneously and learning about the problem as action unfolds. More specifically, disjointed incrementalism has several notable features:

1. Choices occur at the margin of the status quo.
2. A restricted number of policy alternatives contend, and these alternatives are small or incremental changes in the status quo.
3. A restricted number of consequences are considered for any given policy.
4. Adjustments in the objectives of policy produce conformity to available means of implementation, implying a reciprocal relationship between ends and means.
5. Exploration of relevant data reconstructs or transforms problems.
6. Analysis and evaluation occur sequentially, so that policy consists of a long chain of amended choices.
7. Analysis and evaluation are to remedy a problem rather than to reach a goal.
8. Analysis and evaluation permeate society; that is, the locus of these activities is fragmented or disjointed.[111]

Several features of this form of decisionmaking are important. First, disjointed incrementalism relies very heavily on the status quo as its point of departure and proceeds in small steps in several places at once. It is essentially a conservative decisionmaking strategy unlikely to produce large-scale departures from previous practices.[112] Furthermore, because it is disjointed and relies heavily on learning from experience, disjointed incrementalism defies comprehensive and integrated solutions produced by long-term planning.[113] Finally, the definition of a problem and the recognition that a problem exists are perceptual and political screening processes susceptible to error.[114] Some problems may be overlooked or assigned low priority; a program may be underfunded so as to minimize the chances that the problem will be solved.

These difficulties suggest some important points about organizations as problem solvers. First, problem solving involves the transformation of problematic states of affairs into more desired states of affairs. A problematic state arises when a person or group feels dissatisfaction or a need because of what Anthony Downs called a *performance gap*, that is, perceived disparity between a desired and a prevailing state of affairs.[115] Problem solving occurs when the dissatisfaction triggers a desire or motivation to close the performance gap.

Since an organization's recognition of a problem is a combination of perceptual and political processes, it follows that the same forces condition the kinds of proposals for solving the problem and the effectiveness of the proposals. To illustrate, if city council defines concern over a police department's response time for answering emergency calls as a problem of the misallocation of an appropriate number of police officers and cruisers on an acceptable number of well-designed patrol routes, only reconfigurations of patrol routes will be admissible as possible solutions. Executives will not consider hiring or training more police officers, buying better communications equipment, improving the morale and productivity of individual police officers, purchasing new cruisers, relocating and constructing new police stations, or training citizens to alert police to problems more quickly. Once defined, the problem determines which strategies may resolve the performance gap.[116]

To summarize, from the point of view of open systems theory, problems have a *contingent* relationship to their solution and to the processes by which solutions are achieved. As organizations search for solutions, they generally adopt form and functions that match their kinds of problems. In other words, an organization facing simple problems will likely have a simple structure and simple decisionmaking processes; an organization facing a complex environment filled with uncertainties will likely have a complex structure.[117]

Most large organizations face both simple and complex problems. In order to handle both at once, certain parts of organizations deal with the uncertain aspects of the environment and other parts operate with certainty or near certainty. How these arrangements work out and coordinate is one key to the structure and processes of organizations.

Contingency Theory

Thompson's systems framework and much of the research that followed it rested on the notion that the essence of management was to align an organization's institutionalized activity, its technology, and its structural design so that the organization occupied a viable domain with a structure appropriate to it. Jay W. Lorsch and Paul R. Lawrence capture the essence—and importance—of this idea:

> During the last few years there has been evident a new trend in the study of organizational phenomena. Underlying this new approach is the idea that the internal functioning of organizations must be consistent with the demands of the organization task, technology, or external environment, and the needs of its members if the organization is to be effective. Rather than searching for the panacea of the one best way to organize under all conditions, investigators have more and more tended to examine the functioning of organizations in relation to the needs of their particular members and the external pressures facing them. Basically, this approach seems to be leading to the development of a "contingency" theory of organization with the appropriate internal states and processes of the organization contingent upon external requirements and member needs.[118]

Contingency theory sought to refine systems theory by delineating relationships within and among subsystems as well as between the organization and its environment. It sought to understand how organizations operate under different conditions and in specific kinds of circumstances. Contingency analysis is ultimately directed toward organizational designs and strategies and managerial systems most appropriate for specific situations. Therefore, rather than the one best way of the prewar principles school, contingency theorists say it all depends.[119] Their job was to find what "it"—organizational structure and effectiveness—depends upon.

There are two central approaches for solving the problem for developing any theory of organizations: *deduction* from more general theory and *induction* from the statistical analysis of data to discover regularities among variables. Throughout the 1960s and 1970s organization researchers pursued both strategies in their search for patterns of organization structure and behavior that could be linked to characteristics of organizational environments on the one hand and effectiveness on the other. In dozens of studies, researchers identified and measured relationships among environments, internal structures, technologies, patterns of leadership, and outputs. They were looking for patterns in variables in order to explain conformity or deviance of organizations from what researchers considered optimal designs and strategies.[120]

Despite initial optimism and some promising early findings, contingency theorists have yet to explain why some successful organizations' structures resemble those of less successful ones that confront similar environments, or why two organizations with very different structures perform effectively in the same environment.[121] As a consequence, contingency theorists have been unable to predict what structure or strategy will work best on any except a very general basis.

The Dominant Coalition

Part of the explanation for the contingency theorists' difficulty in predicting organizational structure, behavior, and effectiveness appears in Thompson's idea of the *dominant coalition*.[122] According to Thompson, a coalition of the various internal and external constituencies supplying the organization's resources, support, and effort integrates and steers the organization. These constituencies control money, technology, markets, skilled workers, and so on, so they are powerful in relation to the organization and must be included in any major decisions the organization makes.

From this perspective the organization is a political system whose leader must use political tactics such as persuasion, recognition, rewards, and penalties to steer its parts into favorable alignment.[123] This dominant coalition may change as new problems arise and shift the order of priorities and the relative power of different groups. For example, if an organization's resources become scarce and can no longer be taken for granted, it will have to grant more power to those who can secure new resources and stabilize the supply. For a private firm this can mean including more bankers and financiers on its board of directors; for a public organization, it can mean consulting more closely with chairs of appropriations committees.

The notion that organizations are political systems with dominant coalitions that make choices about the future created at least three problems for systems theory in public administration.

Control of the Environment.   First, this construct implied that manipulation and control of the environment best facilitated an organization's survival. According to William Scott, this "means that organizations must ingest those necessary elements in their environment that enable them to survive even if it means that they do so at the sacrifice of other organizations, which may not be as well adapted for survival."[124] Scott saw systems theory as providing a rationale for bureaucratic empire building. While this may make some sense for a business firm, the legitimacy of a public organization depends largely upon its accountability to elected officials. Thus, the open system idea, that organizations determine their own destinies, conflicted with the doctrine of public agencies as neutrally competent servants of their political masters.

Freedom of Structure and Strategy.   Second, the idea that dominant coalitions rule organizations through strategic choices implies some freedom of selection of structure and strategy. That is at odds with the core assumptions of both the old orthodoxy and modern contingency theory that for every identifiable type of situation there is *one best way* to organize and act. Orthodox and contingency theory tended to put the leader of the dominant coalition in a passive role. This leader's job was to analyze the situation and steer the organization into an appropriate set of relationships with other organizations. A more active role in shaping both the organization and the environment was substantially precluded. The success of managers depended not on their ability to affect their environment but on their ability to read their environment and react to it.[125]

Empirically this construct has at least two flaws. The great public administrators of the 1930s through the 1980s defined *and* shaped their organization's environment through active leadership. Critics of systems theory argue that its use of an organic metaphor wrongly reified organizations by attributing to them humanlike powers of thought, motives, and actions; it is human beings who give meaning and intention to situations and change organizations and their direction.[126] To buttress their argument these critics point to bureaucratic entrepreneurs like David E. Lilienthal at the Tennessee Valley Authority, James E. Webb at NASA, and Robert S. McNamara at DOD as public administrators who made their mark by reshaping both their organization and its environment. Rather than simply reading social forces around them and reacting accordingly, they shaped them.[127]

This fact presents a difficult problem for the field of public administration because tradition assumes that public managers will interpret their role with constraint. Bureaucratic entrepreneurs, who expand their role and their agency's domain and power, often step outside the perceived formal and legitimate boundaries of their responsibilities. Proponents of traditional public administration theory considered J. Edgar Hoover of the Federal Bureau of Investigation (FBI), Robert Moses of New York State, and Admiral Hyman Rickover of the Navy to be skating on thin ice.[128]

The strategic and political behavior of public organization leaders helps to account for a major empirical and theoretical problem of systems theory. Research on large samples of organizations has often shown weak correlations among environment, structure, and performance. How to explain this finding?

Systems theory and classical public administration theory provide very different explanations. Katz and Kahn introduced von Bertalanfy's *principle of equifinality,* which states that a biological system can reach the same final state from differing initial conditions and along various paths by accommodating feedback from its environment.[129] Viewing the same phenomenon, public administration theory responds that the laws creating the organization, its goals, and its internal structure were simply different and things just worked out. In this opinion major internal adaptations and strategic change occur *only* as the result of conscious deliberation by lawmakers external to the organization. Where changes are made without changes in the law, they occur within the realm of authority delegated to the organization but *within* the constraints of the law. Clearly, in this formulation systems theory's freedom of organizations to choose structures and strategies is foreign to the constrained world of public administration.

Inherent Conservatism.   Third, and finally, the structural functional basis of systems theory has been criticized as inherently conservative. Because organizations are expected to adapt to changes in their environment, they are considered reactive, so systems theory predicts no radical change in structure or purposes for organizations. Critics charge that because systems theory concentrates on functional elements that contribute to survival and stability, they rationalize the organization's power structure and treat internal conflict as dysfunctional and even illegitimate.[130] This is unfortunate, these critics argue, because sometimes conflict helps an organization to adapt by allowing alternative courses of action to be proposed; the change in the organization's power structure allows for more effective performance. In some cases only radical change will solve a problem. Furthermore, in the world of politics, the expenditure of a large amount of resources and effort on a problem is often more important than whether or not the problem is actually solved.[131] Sometimes the public loses interest in a problem and the crisis dissolves; sometimes the problem resolves itself.[132]

By the late 1970s, the difficulties of applying systems theory to public administration cost it some attractiveness. After nearly two decades, many public administration theorists concluded that systems theory was too abstract, not directly related to the constitutional or legal foundation that underpinned public organizations. Too much was lost in the transition from theory to application. They also concluded that because the normative basis of systems theory was subtle and its prescriptions abstract, it provided a better framework for accumulating information about organizations than for prescribing how to design or administer them. In the late 1970s the historic normative impulse of the public administration profession—how to make public organizations run better—reasserted itself, and systems theory, which many had embraced so enthusiastically in the late 1960s, declined in stature.

The Decline of Organization Theory and Reorganization Practice

From the mid-1950s onward the decline of the old public administration orthodoxy combined with the rise of open systems theory and the increasing complexity of government to leave the public administration community in a quandary about what arrangements were best for the federal government. Large-scale reorganizations of the scope of the first Hoover commission were impossible because the leading actors could not agree about what was best. Thus, the government implemented far fewer of the recommendations of the second Hoover commission than of the first. President Eisenhower and the Congress rejected most of its major recommendations for changes in policy and organization.[133] Other reorganization initiatives during the Eisenhower, Kennedy, and Johnson administrations were more successful, but their scope tended to be more limited than those of the two Hoover commissions.

A decade of new program initiatives during the 1960s, most notably President Lyndon Johnson's Great Society and the Vietnam War, created a vastly more complex executive branch. Johnson appointed Ben Heineman to lead a task force on reorganization and also applied the ill-fated program, planning, and budgeting system throughout the federal government. Broad reorganization of the government, however, was never politically feasible. As Arnold has observed:

> . . . comprehensive reorganization planning never fit well within the Johnson administration; during peacetime the administration's frenetic pace and hunger for innovation were out of step with the systematic commitment necessary for planning and implementing reorganization. Later, the administration's political problems stemmed from a source that reorganization could not possibly address and were of a magnitude to overwhelm virtually any other consideration.[134]

Johnson's successor, Richard Nixon, faced no such constraints. Early in his administration he created a reorganization commission, the Ash Council, to concentrate power in the presidency. The council, led by businessman Roy Ash, recommended several major changes in the organization of the executive branch, especially the reorganization and renaming of the Bureau of the Budget into the more powerful and politically responsive Office of Management and Budget and the creation of a separate Domestic Policy Council. The combined effect of these changes was to centralize policy formation by bringing the assessment and surveillance of administrative implementation into the Executive Office of the President and to delegate more authority for managing operations to his cabinet secretaries and away from the presidential center.[135] The Ash Council proposed four new superdepartments— natural resources, economic affairs, human resources, and community development—that would subsume almost all the existing domestic programs. Increasing the president's control over these policy areas would improve policy integration and minimize overlap of programs and functions.

While this last proposal failed to achieve congressional support, the proposals to rename and reorganize OMB and to constitute a domestic policy council eventually succeeded. However, taken as a whole, the Ash Council enjoyed only modest success, and Nixon's effort to increase presidential authority eventually floundered in the Watergate scandal.

More important from the point of view of public organization theory was the fact that in several ways the Ash Council represented the last gasp of the reorganization doctrine that began more than a half century before. Arnold writes:

> This classic theme within the council's theoretic suppositions is most visible in its choices for the objects of its attentions. The council's highest priority problems were the organization of the Executive Office and the architectonics of the cabinet

departments. On the one hand, it addressed the issue of managerial capacity in the presidential office. On the other hand, it addressed the issue of manageability of the major line organization of the executive branch. The Ash Council, like its predecessors, saw these two matters as interacting, the president's managerial capacity being not only a function of his tools but a product of the manageability of the cabinet departments.[136]

The Ash Council's attention to the traditional issues of executive reorganization gave way to another conception of reorganization in 1976, when President Carter launched a quite different effort at executive reorganization. Building on his experience as governor of Georgia, where he was able to reduce the number of state agencies from three hundred to twenty-two, Carter opted to avoid grand theory and doctrine in seeking to reduce the number of federal agencies and departments. Aside from Alan Campbell, chairman of the Civil Service Commission, almost all of the leadership and staff of Carter's Reorganization Project were drawn from outside the public administration community. The lawyer Harrison Wellford, whom Carter appointed to manage the reorganization effort, explicitly rejected past reorganization plans, in part because he believed they had been developed in a "political vacuum" without adequate liaison with Congress and interested groups.[137] Furthermore, "prior reorganization efforts did not deal with problems in their real focus, at the program level where government meets the people."[138] Wellford charged that reorganization was "box shuffling" that disregarded the policy decisions "within these boxes" and that paid inadequate attention to the improvement of mangement and intergovernmental relations.[139] Instead, the Carter reorganization would emphasize consolidation and realignment of programs; it would follow a bottom-up rather than a top-down approach. It would analyze policy failures at the program level. "This is in contrast to previous reorganization efforts which have tried to impose structural reorganization from the top, guided by abstract management principles, not a study of programs."[140]

Thus Carter's Reorganization Project sought to free itself of abstract theory, whether it be the old public administration orthodoxy or some new concoction like systems theory. Even though its eleven stated goals reflected the old orthodoxy of increasing efficiency and economy, reducing fragmentation, overlap and unnecessary paperwork, and giving managers the authority necessary to do the job and then holding them accountable, the project lacked the clear theory and methodology of earlier reorganization efforts.[141] Aside from the Civil Service Reform Act of 1978, most of the Reorganization Project's efforts came to naught. Arnold notes that the Reorganization Project

> . . . lacked coherence and coordination; as its manager proudly claimed, it followed no overall conception of management. It was a collection of young professionals without significant applied or academic expertise with administration, working under a president burdened by a rigid and curiously moralistic conception of administration. These reorganizations generated a large bulk of recommendations, but little that they did enhanced the capacity of President Carter to govern effectively.[142]

By 1980, comprehensive reorganization of the executive branch had fallen into complete disfavor among political leaders. Not only was the old public administration orthodoxy regarded as obsolete, many of its strongest adherents were deceased or well along in years. Furthermore, postwar organization scholars working in universities were detached from the actual workings of government, so much so that the separation of theory and practice was nearly complete. The election of Ronald Reagan was in part based on his criticism of government and its management. Even though President Reagan appointed the Grace Commission, or Private Sector Survey on Cost Control, headed by businessman J. Peter Grace, comprehensive reorganization never gained a foothold on the Reagan agenda. The Grace Commission was intended to bring modern business structures and practices to the federal government, but the administration chose to concentrate on its cost-cutting recommendations and to ignore most of the recommendations for structural reform. The notion that propelled the study of public administration to the forefront of government during the middle third of the twentieth century—structure makes a difference—had fallen out of good currency. Instead, the Reagan administration emphasized a variety of policy, personnel, and budgetary strategies that drew from a tradition quite dissimilar from the old orthodoxy or mainstream systems theory.

Notes

1. John Maynard Keynes, *The General Theory of Employment, Interest and Money* (New York: Harcourt Brace, 1936), 383.
2. See Peter Berger and Thomas Luckmann, *The Social Construction of Reality* (New York: Anchor Books, 1967). For a more recent discussion of this phenomenon, see Richard M. Weiss and Lynn E. Miller, "The Concept of Ideology in Organizational Analysis: The Sociology of Knowledge or the Social Psychology of Beliefs?" *The Academy of Management Review* 12 (January 1987): 104–16.
3. See Dwight C. Waldo, "Organization Theory: An Elephantine Problem." *Public Administration Review* 21 (Winter 1961): 220.
4. See Charles O. Jones, *An Introduction to the Study of Public Policy,* 3d ed. (Monterey, CA: Brooks/Cole Publishing Company, 1983): 5–8.
5. James L. Garnett, "Operationalizing the Constitution via Administrative Reorganization: Oilcan, Trends, and Proverbs." *Public Administration Review* 47 (January-February 1987): 35.
6. Peri E. Arnold, *Making the Managerial Presidency: Comprehensive Reorganization Planning 1905–1980* (Princeton, N.J.: Princeton University Press, 1986), 7.
7. Quoted in Paul P. Van Riper, "The American Administrative State: Wilson and the Founders," in Ralph Clark Chandler, ed., *A Centennial History of the American Administrative State* (New York: The Free Press, 1987), 11–2.
8. Ibid., 12.
9. Garnett, "Operationalizing the Constitution via Administrative Reorganization," 36.
10. Ibid.
11. Arnold, *Making the Managerial Presidency,* 9.
12. Ronald C. Moe, *Executive Branch Reorganization: An Overview* (Washington, D.C.: U.S. Government Printing Office, 1978), 7.
13. Van Riper, "The American Administrative State," 13.
14. Arnold, *Making the Managerial Presidency*, 11.
15. Herbert Kaufman, "The Growth of the Federal Personnel System," in Wallace S. Sayre, ed., *The Federal Government Service,* 2d ed. (Englewood Cliffs, N.J.: Prentice-Hall, 1965), 30–1.

16. Ibid., 31.
17. Ibid., 29.
18. Ibid., 31–2.
19. See Stephen Skowronek, *Building a New American State: The Expansion of National Administrative Capabilities, 1877–1920* (Cambridge, England: Cambridge University Press, 1982), 59–68.
20. Ibid., 67–8.
21. Ibid., 68.
22. Ibid., 69.
23. Ibid., 69–71.
24. Arnold, *Making the Managerial Presidency,* 12–3.
25. Woodrow Wilson, "The Study of Administration." *Political Science Quarterly* 12 (June 1887). Reprinted in Jay M. Shafritz and Albert C. Hyde, eds., *Classics of Public Administration,* 2d ed. (Chicago, IL: The Dorsey Press, 1987), 10–25.
26. Ibid., 18.
27. Ibid., 19.
28. Ibid., 18. In this instance Wilson was quoting from the German writer Biuntschli to make his point.
29. Shafritz and Hyde, *Classics of Public Administration,* 3.
30. Jay M. Shafritz and J. Steven Ott, eds., *Classics of Organization Theory,* 2d ed., (Chicago, IL: The Dorsey Press, 1987), 25.
31. See H. H. Gerth and C. Wright Mills, eds., *From Max Weber: Essays in Sociology* (Oxford, England: Oxford University Press, 1946).
32. For a detailed discussion of this period, see Arnold, *Making the Managerial Presidency,* Chapter 2, "Executive Reorganization and the Beginnings of the Managerial Presidency: 1905–1913."
33. Kaufman, "The Growth of the Federal Personnel System," 42.
34. From *Report of the Committee with Studies of Administrative Management in the Federal Government,* 1937, 32–4. Represented as "The President's Impaired Responsibility" in Donald C. Rowat, ed., *Basic Issues in Public Administration* (New York: The MacMillan Company, 1961), 119–122.
35. President's Committee on Administrative Management, "Report of the Committee with Studies of Administrative Management in the Federal Government," in Rowat, *Basic Issues of Public Administration,* 121.
36. Quoted in Luther Gulick, "Politics, Administration and the New Deal." *Annals* 169 (September 1933): 55–9.
37. Stephen Hess, *Organizing the Presidency* (Washington, D.C.: The Brookings Institution, 1976), 144.
38. Leonard D. White, *Introduction to the Study of Public Administration* (New York: MacMillan, 1926).
39. White's textbook underwent three revisions over the next twenty-nine years and remained the dominant text in the field until the late 1950s. The major change from the first to the fourth edition was in the material on structure and organization. They were treated in the first edition in a four-chapter section on the mechanics of organizations, "The Administrative Machine," but were integrated into the text and deemphasized by the fourth edition. This change symbolized the loss of confidence of the public administration community after World War II in its ability to develop a general science of public administration. Arnold, *Making the Managerial Presidency,* 85.
40. Ibid., 87.
41. Ibid., 88.
42. Ibid., 89

43. Ibid., 100
44. Ibid., 97.
45. See Wallace B. Sayre, "Premises of Public Administration: Past and Emerging." *Public Administration Review* 18 (Winter 1958): 21–7.
46. Luther Gulick, "Notes on the Theory of Organization," in Luther Gulick and Lyndall Urwick, eds., *Papers on the Science of Administration* (New York: Institute of Public Administration, 1937), 6.
47. Ibid.
48. Ibid., 7
49. Ibid., 9
50. Ibid., 10
51. Ibid., 15.
52. Dwight Waldo, "Scope of the Theory of Public Administration," in James C. Charlesworth, ed., *Theory and Practice of Public Administration* (Philadelphia, PA: The American Academy of Political and Social Science, 1968), 4.
53. Ibid., 5.
54. Ibid.
55. Lewis Meriam and Lawrence F. Schmeckebier, *Reorganization of the National Government: What Does It Involve?* (Washington, D.C.: The Brookings Institution, 1939).
56. Charles S. Hyneman, *Bureaucracy in a Democracy* (New York: Harper and Brothers, 1950), 255.
57. Ibid., 256.
58. See Edward S. Corwin, *The President: Office and Powers, 1787–1957* (New York University Press, 1957).
59. See Elton Mayo, *The Human Problem of Industrial Civilization* (New York: Macmillan Co., 1933); and F. J. Roethlisberger and William J. Dickson, *Management and the Worker* (Cambridge, MA: Harvard University Press, 1939).
60. Roethlisberger and Dickson, 569.
61. Robert K. Merton, "Bureaucratic Structure and Personality." *Social Forces* 18 (1940): 560–568.
62. Ibid., 563.
63. Ibid., 564.
64. Chester Barnard, *The Functions of the Executive* (Cambridge, MA: Harvard University Press, 1938), xxix.
65. Ibid., 75.
66. Ibid., 215.
67. Ibid., 218–219.
68. Ibid., 87.
69. Ibid., 280.
70. Ibid., 272, 277. Quoted in Michael M. Harmon and Richard T. Mayer, *Organization Theory for Public Administration* (Boston, MA: Little, Brown and Company, 1986), 112.
71. Ibid., 259.
72. Meriam and Schmeckebier, *Reorganization of the National Government,* 161.
73. Herbert A. Simon, *Administrative Behavior: A Study of Decision-Making Process in Administrative Organization,* 3d rev. ed. (New York: The Free Press, 1976), 20.
74. Ibid., 259.
75. Luther Gulick, "Science, Values and Public Administration," in L. Gulick and L. Urwick, eds., *Papers on the Science of Administration* (New York: Institute of Public Administration, 1937), 191–5.
76. Robert A. Dahl, "The Science of Public Administration: Three Problems." *Public Administration Review* 7: (1947): 1–11.

77. David E. Lilienthal, *TVA: Democracy on the March* (New York: Harper and Row, 1944).

78. Philip Selznick, *TVA and the Grass Roots* (Berkeley: University of California Press, 1949).

79. Paul Appleby, *Big Democracy* (New York: Alfred A. Knopf, 1945).

80. Norton E. Long, "Power and Administration." *Public Administration Review* 9:3 (1949): 257–264.

81. Dwight Waldo, *The Administrative State: A Study of the Political Theory of American Public Administration* (New York: The Ronald Press, 1948). p. 3

82. Ibid., 192.

83. Ibid., 206.

84. John Merriman Gaus, "Trends in the Theory of Public Administration." *Public Administration Review* 10: (Summer 1950): 168. Quoted in Nicholas Henry, "The Emergence of Public Administration as a Field of Study," in Ralph Clark Chandler, ed., *A Centennial History of the American Administrative State* (New York: The Free Press, 1987), 50.

85. Richard R. Nelson, *The Moon and the Ghetto: An Essay on Public Policy Analysis* (New York: W.W. Norton, 1987), 1–47.

86. See Ronald C. Moe, *The Hoover Commissions Revisited* (Boulder, CO: Westview Press, 1982).

87. Arnold, *Making the Managerial Presidency,* 152.

88. Ibid., 153–4.

89. Nelson, *The Moon and the Ghetto,* p. 45.

90. Simon, *Administrative Behavior,* 46.

91. Ibid., 122.

92. Ibid.

93. Ibid., 133–4.

94. Herbert A. Simon et al., *Public Administration* (New York: Alfred A. Knopf, 1950); James G. March and Herbert A. Simon, *Organizations* (New York: John Wiley and Sons, 1958); Richard M. Cyert and James G. March, *A Behavioral Theory of the Firm* (Englewood Cliffs, N.J.: Prentice-Hall, 1963); and James G. March, ed., *Handbook of Organizations* (Chicago: Rand McNally, 1965).

95. See Ludwig Von Bertalanfy, *General Systems Theory* (New York: George Braziller, 1968).

96. See Talcott Parsons, *Structure and Process in Modern Societies* (New York: The Free Press, 1960); *The Social System* (New York: The Free Press, 1951); and "Suggestions for a Sociological Approach to the Theory of Organizations." *Administrative Science Quarterly* 1 (1956): 63–85.

97. See Harmon and Mayer, *Organization Theory for Public Administration,* 160.

98. Ibid., 171; Daniel Katz and Robert L. Kahn, *The Social Psychology of Organizations,* 2d ed. (New York: John Wiley and Sons, 1978), 52.

99. Ibid. Katz and Kahn

100. Ibid.

101. James D. Thompson, *Organizations in Action* (New York: McGraw-Hill, 1967), 10–1.

102. Ibid.

103. See Victor A. Thompson, *Organizations as Systems* (Morristown, N.J.: General Learning Press, 1973).

104. Ibid.

105. Ibid.

106. Ibid.

107. Russell Ackoff and Fred F. Emery, *On Purposeful Systems* (Chicago: Aldine-Atheston, 1972).

108. See Herbert A. Simon, "The Logic of Heuristic Decision Making," in Nicholas Rescher, ed., *The Logic of Decision and Action* (Pittsburgh: University of Pittsburgh Press, 1967); also Timothy J. Cartwright, "Problems, Solutions and Strategies: A Contribution to the Theory and Practice of Planning." *Journal of the American Institute of Planners* 39 (May 1973).

109. See Charles E. Lindblom, *The Intelligence of Democracy: Decision Making Through Partisan Mutual Adjustment* (New York: The Free Press, 1965); also "The Science of Muddling Through," *Public Administration Review* 19 (1959): 79–88.

110. Lindblom, *The Intelligence of Democracy*.

111. Ibid.

112. See Yehezkel Dror, "Muddling Through—Science or Inertia?" *Public Administration Review* 24 (September 1964): 154–7; Amitai Etzioni, "Mixed Scanning: A Third Approach to Decision Making." *Public Administration Review* 27 (December 1967): 385–92.

113. Ibid.

114. See Irving L. Janis, *Victims of Groupthink* (Boston: Houghton Mifflin, 1972).

115. See Anthony Downs, *Inside Bureaucracy* (Boston: Little, Brown, 1966).

116. See Charles H. Levine et al., "Organizational Design: A post Minnowbrook Perspective for the 'New' Public Administration." *Public Administration Review* 35 (July-August 1975): 425–35.

117. See Fremont E. Kast and James E. Rosenzweig, eds., *Contingency Views of Organization and Management* (Chicago: Science Research Associates, 1973).

118. Jay W. Lorsch and Paul R. Lawrence, *Studies in Organizational Design* (Homewood, IL: Irwin-Dorsey, 1970), 1.

119. See Harvey Sherman, *It all Depends: A Programatic Approach to Organization* (University, AL: University of Alabama Press, 1966); see also Harold Seidman, *Politics, Position and Power,* 2d ed. (New York: Oxford University Press, 1975).

120. For a review of this literature, see Richard H. Hall, *Organizations: Structure and Process* (Englewood Cliffs, N.J.: Prentice-Hall, 1977).

121. See John Child, "Organizational Structure, Environment, and Performance: The Role of Strategic Choice." *Sociology* (January 1972): 2–22.

122. Thompson, *Organizations in Action*.

123. Ibid.

124. William Scott, "Organicism: The Moral Anesthetic of Management." *Academy of Management Review* 4 (1979): 21–8.

125. See Donald D. Searing, "Models and Images of Man and Society in Leadership Theory." *Journal of Politics* 31 (February, 1969): 3–31.

126. See Charles Perrow, *Complex Organizations: A Critical Essay,* 2d ed. (Glenview, IL: Scott, Foresman, 1979).

127. See Robert L. Haught, ed., *Giants in Management* (Washington, DC: National Academy of Public Administration, 1985).

128. See Eugene Lewis, *Public Entrepreneurship: Toward A Theory of Bureaucratic Political Power* (Bloomington, IN: Indiana University Press, 1980).

129. See Katz and Kahn, *The Social Psychology of Organizations*.

130. See Harmon and Mayer, *Organization Theory for Public Administration,* 194–5; Frederick C. Thayer, "General System(s) Theory: The Promise That Could Not Be Kept." *Academy of Management Journal* 15 (1972): 481–94.

131. See Charles O. Jones, *An Introduction to the Study of Public Policy,* 3d ed. (Monterey, CA: Brooks/Cole, 1983); Murray Edelman, *The Symbolic Uses of Politics* (Urbana, IL: University of Illinois Press, 1964).

132. See Richard E. Neustadt and Harvey V. Fineberg, *The Swine Flu Affair: Decision-Making on a Slippery Disease* (Washington, DC: U.S. Government Printing Office, 1978).

133. Arnold, *Making the Managerial Presidency*, 200–3.

134. Ibid., p. 270–1.

135. See Don Bonafede and Johnathan Cottin, "Nixon, in Reorganization Plan, Seeks Tighter Rein on Bureaucracy." *National Journal* (21 March 1970): 621.

136. Arnold, *Making the Managerial Presidency*, 293.

137. Statement of Harrison Wellford before the House Committee on Appropriations, press release OMB, 24 February 1977. Quote in Arnold, *Making the Managerial Presidency*, 312.

138. Ibid.

139. Ibid.

140. The President's Reorganization Project, "Plan for Coordinating Federal Government Planning and Management Improvement Programs: Discussion Outline," March 1977. Quoted in Arnold, *Making the Managerial Presidency*, 313.

141. Ibid.

142. Arnold, *Making the Managerial Presidency*, 336.

Chapter Ten

The Search for a Theory of
Public Organization

Introduction

Like nature, theory abhors a vacuum. In the social sciences the decline of an old
theory sends scholars to search related disciplines for explanations and prescriptions
to fill the void. In public administration that process has been going on for nearly
thirty years. When the orthodox theory of the 1920s and 1930s fell into disfavor in the
1950s and 1960s, decision theory, systems theory, and contingency theory gained
currency as solutions for some theoretical difficulties (see Chapter 9).

Part of the problem was the limits of orthodox theory itself. The value it placed on
hierarchy, the separation of politics from administration, and the assumption that
there are clear principles for organizing government departments did not hold up
when exposed to the cold light of experience. Another part of the problem was at least
as significant: During and after World War II the American administrative state
changed in size, shape, and function. Above all, it became incomprehensibly
complex and *interdependent* with a vast array of other domestic public and private
organizations and with foreign governments and private firms.

The complexity of government organizations in the postwar era resulted from
sharing with other governments and institutions responsibility for the world's
problems. AIDS, toxic wastes, drug abuse, the depletion of the ozone layer,
terrorism, stock market regulation, and nuclear accidents are international. These
interdependencies are especially important because they magnify the consequences
of government incompetence or mismanagement; meanwhile the growing complexity of problems increases the difficulty of solving them.

The observation that the world is a smaller, more interdependent place is not new
or startling, but the objective conditions that accompany the change are indeed
startling. The government in the last two decades of the twentieth century makes
high-tech, high-finance, high-risk, and time-sensitive choices. These features of the
public policy environment have made governing more difficult. They have also made
the developing of theory for designing effective organizations more challenging than
before.

Complexity transcends the issue of big or small government to raise concerns
about the *competency* and *capacity* of governments to stabilize economic, military,
ecological, and social systems. A hundred years ago an incompetent railroad worker
could throw the wrong switch, wreck a train, and perhaps kill two hundred people.

The disaster was real; the remedies were obvious—and available. In 1986, a small number of people could collaborate in an error and launch the space shuttle *Challenger* into disaster. The deaths of seven people set back the nation's space program by some years. The disaster was just as real as the train wreck, but remedies—and the consequences—are more complex by several powers.[1]

The implications of errors combine with time pressures and complicated technology to make government decisionmaking increasingly complex and to make the design or redesign of its organizations riskier and more difficult than in the 1920s and 1930s.

The job of organization theorists now as then is twofold: (1) to make sense of the new administrative reality (that is, to explain how things are arranged and why); and (2) to prescribe organizational forms and practices to manage and coordinate these arrangements. Theorists have not been shy about either task. Indeed, several new schools of thought arose in the 1960s to fill the void left by the decline of orthodox theory. Three in particular have attracted substantial attention because they address the problems of the old orthodoxy:

- One group of scholars gravitated toward social psychology and the *human relations school,* which advocated nonhierarchical principles of management and equity-based ideals. This would deal with criticism of the machine model of bureaucracy.
- Another group moved toward sociology and systems theory, taking the *generic approach,* which concentrates on similarities rather than differences between public and private organizations. This would deal with the scientific and management weaknesses of public organization theory.
- A third group of scholars built upon the work of neoclassical economists and fostered the *public choice approach,* which promoted a focus on individual citizens' preferences and more complex policymaking and service arrangements to deal with the executive-centered and hierarchical bias in orthodox public organization theory.

Each of these groupings of scholars comprised schools of thought that adapted theories of organization from other fields to public administration in ways that they believed better captured the real world of modern government than the old orthodoxy.

The Rediscovery of Human Relations Theory

The malaise that overtook public administration theory in the late 1950s and 1960s hardly went unnoticed. It was a time of heterodoxy, not orthodoxy, a time of coming apart, not unification.[2] Ideas for new directions spilled in from all corners. Dwight Waldo proclaimed the field to be in a "crisis of identity" and suggested a professional as opposed to a scientific grounding.[3] Others, for example Fred Riggs, called for more scientific and comparative work.[4] Still others—Herbert Simon, Charles Lindblom, and Aaron Wildavsky—sought to refocus the field by concentrating its attention on decisionmaking.[5]

For a short time in the late 1960s the most important influence on public administration theory came not from academia, but from government. The 1960s were turbulent. Civil rights, urban rioting, affirmative action, student protests, the War on Poverty, the Vietnam War, and a host of other crises pressed themselves upon public administration as a practice and as a theory. In the view of several mostly younger academics in the field, the crises facing government revealed inadequate basic thought about what government should do and how it should do it: "Needed were new approaches, philosophies, and arrangements—a 'new public administration.'"[6]

While the views of those calling for a new public administration were diverse, they did share a critical pessimism about the organizing values, conceptual frameworks, and accepted practices of the field. Particularly deficient, in their view, were (1) the emphasis on efficiency and economy to the exclusion of other values, particularly equity; (2) the advocacy of centralized and hierarchical forms of organization rather than decentralized structures that stressed participation by workers and citizens; and (3) preference for machineline passivity instead of active advocacy from public administrators.[7] To the more radical proponents of the new public administration, not only did the old orthodoxy limit solutions to problems, it was part of the problem itself:

> . . . there is growing evidence that the institutions of public administration have failed to finish what they set out to do and, worse, are now suspected of aggravating or intensifying the very problems they were designed to solve.[8]

The new public administration would need new theories, philosophies, and ethics to change society. Public organizations would have to be less instruments of control for the establishment and the privileged and more instruments of advocacy to improve the lot of the politically powerless and poor. Policy and action would be based upon knowledge gained from an exchange of views between administrators and their clients. Decisionmaking would be shared and new institutions of *structured nonhierarchy* would have to be designed.[9]

For new ideas these critics turned to human relations theory, which itself was reviving. The human relationists said there was an informal as well as formal organization structure and that it could be managed to increase effectiveness. This blended neatly with the criticisms of orthodox theory. These proponents of new PA argued that formal organizations and machinelike hierarchies depersonalized workers, promoted overnarrow specialization, and supported repressive supervision and control. They argued that this alienated and frustrated employees and produced less than optimum performance.[10]

A better way to organize, they contended, would be to liberate the potential of employees by making their work intrinsically more satisfying and their relationships with fellow workers and supervisors more open, authentic, and supportive. Such a system of management would improve morale, job satisfaction, and work groups' performance by changing supervisory styles, decisionmaking procedures, job content, and relationships among work groups. According to Felix Nigro and Lloyd Nigro, human relations theorists believe:

• The average employee wants some control over the work environment and likes interesting work that allows some discretion.

- In many cases jobs can be redesigned so as to satisfy basic psychological needs.
- Close supervision and administrative control do not automatically produce efficiency.
- Tightly centralized decisionmaking in a rigid hierarchy makes workers powerless and subject to constant manipulation.
- Authoritarian management prevents the healthy psychological development of the person; over the long run it fails to produce the desired contributions to organizational efforts.[11]

The remedy for these maladies was forms and leadership styles that were not centralized, hierarchical, control-oriented supervision but decentralized, nonhierarchical, participative, and democratic. If this were done, human relations theory argued, positive outcomes would occur: better employee morale and self-development and higher productivity. Employees would take more responsibility for the quality and quantity of their work and contribute to the betterment of the whole organization.

The attraction of human relations theory to the new generation of public administration scholars in the 1960s is easily apparent. The leading figures of the human relations school—among them Abraham Maslow, Chris Argyris, Douglas McGregor, Rensis Likert, Warren Bennis, and Frederick Herzberg—were eminent researchers and theoreticians trained in psychology and social psychology, not political science or old-fashioned administrative management. Furthermore, their work was clearly normative; it extended beyond purely descriptive studies and so-called sterile exercises in behavioral analysis. For those interested in a new way to organize public agencies, the human relations school provided a fresh vehicle for theory *and* action.

Postwar Foundations of Human Relations Theory

To understand the attraction of human relations theory for public administration theorists one must examine basic assumptions and main ideas. For a decade, beginning in the early 1950s with the work of Abraham Maslow and extending to the mid-1960s, human relations theorists produced several seminal works that have influenced the study of management and organizations ever since.

Abraham Maslow

The second wave of activity for the human relations school began in 1954 with the publication of Abraham Maslow's *Motivation and Personality*. Maslow's ideas about human motivation inspired others to build theories for fitting organizations to their workers in contrast to the scientific management school's bias of fitting workers to their organizations.

Most of Maslow's writings were in psychology; only in later years did he apply his theories to organizations and management. His most important contribution to organization theory is his notion that human motivation can be understood as responses to a hierarchy of needs. Maslow's hierarchy rests on the assumption that there are several levels of needs. The bottom level is *physiological needs* like food, water, and shelter. At the next level is *safety*. Maslow described this level as encompassing not only safety from physical harm but also stability, "seen in the very common preference for familiar rather than unfamiliar things."[12] At the third level, Maslow observed, are *psychological* needs. The first of these is the need for love and belonging, often called the *social needs*. Next comes the need for *esteem*, which encompasses the desire for both self-respect and for respect from others. The final and highest need, *self-actualization*, Maslow defined as "the desire. . . to become everything that one is capable of becoming."[13]

Maslow went on to point out two important aspects of his hierarchy. First, he warned that it is not a fixed order. While it fit most people with whom he had worked, he noted that for some people there may be a different order. Maslow stressed the importance of seeing needs on a hierarchical basis. Once a need has been satisfied, he argued, it can no longer serve as a motivator. Needs ". . . when chronically gratified cease to exist as active determinants or organizers of behavior."[14] Once one need is satisfied, the next higher one on the hierarchy becomes the main motivator.

Maslow's theory was very important because it suggested that material incentives like pay and job security were not the only or most effective motivators for employees. Indeed, Maslow's work reinforced the idea that reshaping organizations and their incentives was an important avenue for improving individual and group performance.

Maslow's theory was not universally accepted. The peak of his hierarchy, the concept of self-actualization, was called ". . . a fuzzy term, drenched in value connotation. . . "[15] A more serious problem has been the lack of empirical evidence to support Maslow's theory. In later years, Maslow himself called for more experimentation. He wrote of the ways others had used his theory: "But I of all people should know just how shaky this foundation is as a final foundation."[16]

Chris Argyris

Despite the conceptual and empirical problems associated with Maslow's work, the intuitive appeal of his hierarchy attracted many other scholars. Chris Argyris was the first to apply Maslow's work on motivation to organizational theory. Argyris saw a fundamental conflict between the organization and the individual: "We conclude that the needs of healthy individuals (in our culture) tend to be incongruent with the maximum expression of the demands of the formal organization."[17]

Earlier theorists suggested that a given structure produced certain responses. Argyris, using Maslow's motivation theories, extended this idea and theorized that an intermediate variable—human personality and its needs—mediated between the organization and its employees' behavior. He went on to describe three basic propositions:

1. There is a lack of congruency between the needs of healthy individuals and the demands of the formal organization.
2. The results of this disturbance are frustration, failure, short-time perspective, and conflict.
3. The nature of the formal principles of organization subject subordinates at all levels to competition, rivalry, hostility, and a focus on the parts rather than the whole.[18]

Argyris argued that formal organizations require the individuals within it to behave rationally and to specialize in certain tasks. These requirements conflict with the healthy individual's needs for growth—for self-actualization. To assuage this conflict, Argyris argued, the informal organization would:

1. Decrease feelings of dependence, submissiveness, subordination, and passivity toward management.
2. Reduce arbitrary unilateral action by the people in power, increasing the possibility of individual responsibility.
3. Allow expression of pent-up feelings ranging from outright aggression and hostility to passive internalization of tensions arising from the formal organization, directive leadership, management controls, and manipulative human relations programs.
4. Create an informal world with its own culture and values, offering psychological shelter and a firm anchor to maintain stability while constantly adjusting and adapting to the formal organization and directive leadership. The informal world also lets the employee actively influence the formal organization.[19]

Argyris did not suggest a means to counteract the incongruence between the formal and informal organizations. Instead he suggested three ways to decrease the dependency, subordination, and submissiveness of employees and increase their potential; job enlargement; participative leadership; and *reality leadership*, in which the leader varies "his leadership style according to the situation in which he exists."[20]

Argyris's job enlargement strategy would let individuals use their intellectual and interpersonal skills. He warned against simply increasing the number or nature of tasks, as some advocates of job enlargement suggested. True job enlargement, Argyris contended, means allowing the workers to use more of their own judgment and in varying their tasks. Herzberg would later call Argyris's idea of job enlargement *job enrichment* to distinguish it from a mere increase in demands on employees.

Argyris's notion of employee-centered leadership changes the focus of decision-making and group definition from the leader to the employees. In this model the group as a whole defines the rules that will guide the leader's decisions. Once these rules are defined, the leader takes command of the group's daily work. Situations outside formulated guidelines call for a reconvening of the group. Argyris argued that this allows employees more participation in the formal organization and so better use of their abilities. It also encourages the employee to identify with the organization and its goals.[21]

Argyris argued that over time these techniques and others would integrate individual and organizational needs. Although he did not explicitly state what form of organization would promote this goal, he did summarize its properties.

First, management would give more thought to basic values and their manifestations. In Argyris's ideal organization, feelings and social skills would be as important as rationality and intellectual competence. Authority would expand through methods that minimize dependence. This would be no easy change, he cautioned, because it required ". . . people who are not threatened by, but actually value, psychological success, self-esteem, self-responsibility, and internal commitment."[22]

Second, Argyris's ideal organization would have some structural enlargement. The hierarchies of formal organizations would not be totally replaced but would exist along with several other structural forms. A set of rules would explicitly determine when to use each structure and how to make the transition from one structure to another.

Finally, Arygris's framework would need changes in the control systems of the organization. Instead of restrictions, controls would be instruments to help employees increase their sense of responsibility and psychological success. To aid this process, employees would collect their own information about their work performance and evaluate it themselves to determine how well they were doing and how to improve.[23]

Douglas McGregor

Douglas McGregor, like Argyris, thought managers should take a new approach to leadership and supervision. He wanted managers to examine their assumptions in light of new theories of motivation in the social sciences. The manager, McGregor argued, rather than acting strictly on personal experiences, should study these theories and integrate them into his or her own management philosophy. This, he believed, would eventually produce new, more efficient and effective management practices.[24]

In examining the management practices of the time, McGregor formulated *Theory X*. He argued that this set of incorrect assumptions guided most organizations and management actions:

1. Management is responsible for organizing the elements of productive enterprise—money, materials, equipment, people—in the interest of economic ends.
2. With respect to people, this is a process of directing their efforts, motivating them, controlling their actions, modifying their behavior to fit the needs of the organization.
3. Without this active intervention by management, people would be passive—even resistant—to organizational needs. They must therefore be persuaded, rewarded, punished, controlled—their activities must be directed. This is management's task.[25]

McGregor observed that behind this conventional view are several additional beliefs—less explicit, but widespread:

4. The average man is by nature indolent—he works as little as possible.
5. He lacks ambition, dislikes responsibility, prefers to be led.
6. He is inherently self-centered, indifferent to organizational needs.
7. He is by nature resistant to change.
8. He is gullible, not very bright, the ready dupe of the charlatan and the demagogue.[26]

McGregor went on to argue that the assumptions underlying Theory X are false. He observed they were likelier to be self-fulfilling prophecies: Managers build organizations based on these assumptions, and that structure forces individuals to conform to the assumptions. Instead, McGregor argued, these behaviors are symptoms of deprivation of the individual's higher-level psychological needs. Management generally seeks only to satisfy physiological and safety needs through pay and benefits—the carrot and the stick—and ignores all else. While this may work to a certain level, eventually in modern society it fails, so management must meet higher needs in order to motivate modern workers.[27]

McGregor then presented Theory Y, based on newer assumptions of human nature and motivation:

1. Management is responsible for organizing the elements of productive enterprise—money, materials, equipment, people—in the interest of economic ends.
2. People are *not* by nature passive or resistant to organizational needs. They have become so as a result of experience in organizations.
3. The motivation, the potential for development, the capacity for assuming responsibility, the readiness to direct behavior toward organizational goals are all present in people. It is a responsibility of management to make it possible for people to recognize and develop these human characteristics for themselves.
4. The essential task of management is to arrange organizational conditions and methods of operation so that people can achieve their own goals *best* by directing *their own* efforts toward organizational objectives. [emphasis McGregor's][28]

The assumptions behind Theory Y were quite different from those behind Theory X:

1. The expenditure of physical and mental effort in work is as natural as play or rest.
2. External control and the threat of punishment are not the only means of bringing about effort toward organizational objectives. A person will exercise self-direction and self-control in the service of objectives to which he or she is committed.
3. Commitment to objectives is a function of the rewards associated with their achievement.
4. The average human being learns, under proper conditions, not only to accept but to seek responsibility.
5. The capacity to exercise a relatively high degree of imagination, ingenuity, and creativity in the solution of organizational problems is widely, not narrowly, distributed in the population.
6. In modern industrial life the intellectual potentialities of the average human being are only partially used.[29]

McGregor recognized several difficulties in implementing Theory Y. For example, he observed that the social scientists' knowledge of human personality and motivation is incomplete, making specific application a problem. Further, past practices have accustomed people to Theory X, and changing attitudes will take time and effort.

Unlike Argyris, McGregor did not see perfect integration of organizational objectives and individual goals as possible. Instead, Theory Y seeks a degree of integration that lets the individual best achieve personal goals by working for the organization's success. This is not necessarily the point at which the organization's goals are reached with optimal effort, McGregor observed, but to settle for less by ignoring the assumptions of Theory Y will cause organizational performance to suffer.[30]

McGregor's Theory Y[31] won immediate attention and support from management scholars, but as with most previous human relations theories, when it came to implementing his central notions, all McGregor had to recommend was a patchwork of old techniques and good intentions, not a complete structure of organizational design.

Rensis Likert

It was left to Rensis Likert to develop a model organizational structure that took into account the new theories of motivation. In 1961 he published *New Patterns of Management,* in which he expounded the use of working groups as the basis for a new organizational design. Likert began with the principle of *supportive relations*:

> The leadership and other processes of the organization must be such as to ensure a maximum probability that in all interactions and all relationships with the organization each member will, in the light of his background, values, and expectations, view the experience as supportive and one which builds and maintains his sense of personal worth and importance.[32]

This principle was derived from Likert's studies of supervisory relationships. Likert found leadership to be relative, requiring the leader to adapt his behavior to the expectations, values and interpersonal skills of those around him in order to lead effectively and communicate clearly.[33]

Likert believed effective organizations to be built upon effective work groups.[34] He observed that several common properties combine to make the group function smoothly. Loyalty to the group, confidence and trust among workers, and a satisfactory integration of relevant values and goals are key properties. These properties combine to create a supportive atmosphere within the group, facilitating integration of individual and organizational goals. The members of the group have strong influence over each other, which produces constant evaluation of the values and goals of the group. This increases the flexibility and adaptability of the group, enabling it to adjust to changing needs and objectives, but this flexibility occurs within a context of stability derived from the group's commonality of goals and values.[35]

According to Likert, the work group is the optimal unit for harmonizing the objectives of the organization with the needs and desires of the majority of the organization's members. Likert observed that the leader of the effective work group carries out two key functions, one internal and one external. The internal function is to maintain effective supportive relationships among the members while being careful to minimize the influence of the leadership position. This requires, Likert noted, low-key leadership of the effective group.[36]

Externally, the group leader is what Likert called the key *linking pin*. The linking pin connects working groups within the organization. A linking pin is a member of two working groups at once. This dual membership promotes organization-wide integration of goals and facilitates cooperation between groups. Likert argued that although any member of a group may be the linking pin, it is the formally designated leader who must make the vital linkage upward in the organization. Through this hierarchical link the tasks and objectives of the group are communicated throughout the organization, after the leader—as a member of a higher working group—has helped to define them.[37]

The main criticism of Likert's theory addressed the requirement that all members of the organization attain a high level of interpersonal skill. Skeptics have argued that a failure to develop this skill may lead to poorly functioning work groups, lack of goal and value integration, and inability to attain objectives. They also question whether the cost of reaching that level of skill is worth the improved productivity that might result.[38]

Warren Bennis

The ideas of Likert and the other human relations theorists prompted Warren Bennis to predict the eventual decline of the bureaucratic form. In its place, Bennis predicted, would arise a more democratic organization. Bureaucracies, Bennis argued, would soon find themselves obsolete in the face of rapid social changes. Bennis catalogued the faults of bureaucracy and the problems they caused and concluded that only radical change in the nature of organizations could keep them effective. Besides criticizing the bureaucratic organization, Bennis outlined what he saw as the organization of the future. He began by observing that in order to survive, organizations have to accomplish two tasks:

1. Maintain their internal system and coordinate the "human side of enterprise"—a process of mutual compliance called *reciprocity*
2. Adapt to and shape the external environment—a process he called *adaptability*.[39]

Bennis's reciprocity mainly covers the methods by which an organization handles the conflict between organizational and individual goals. While Bennis agreed with the arguments of Argyris and the other human relations theorists, he said that they did not go far enough in recommending changes to mediate this basic conflict. Bennis considered Argyris's suggestions to be "fuzzy" and utopian, essentially unfeasible. He argued that McGregor's "tragic view" of organizations was more realistic, as it came to grips with the value of conflict and the steps necessary to integrate individuals and organizations. Overall, Bennis thought the work of the earlier theorists could go far toward resolving the inherent conflict between individuals and organizations but that more work was needed to solve the problem.

Bennis saw the acceleration of change as the driving factor in the decline of bureaucracy. He observed that the ". . . major shock to bureaucracy has been caused by the scientific and technological revolution. It is the requirement of adaptability to the environment which leads to the predicted demise of bureaucracy and to the collapse of management as we know it."[40] The main fault of bureaucracy, Bennis concluded, was that it was rigid. While rigidity was acceptable for simple tasks in static conditions, during rapid change it would break down as events overtook the organization's responses.

Bennis turned to science to deal with rapid change. He saw science as "the only institution based on, and geared for, change. It is built not only to adapt to change but to overthrow and create change."[41] In examining scientific institutions, Bennis concluded that they encouraged—indeed required—a democratic environment. Therefore, in order for organizations to adapt to change, they too needed a democratic form.

According to Bennis, the democratic organization embodies a system of values governing behavior. The main values are:

1. Full and free communication, regardless of rank and power.
2. A reliance on consensus, rather than on the more customary forms of coercion or compromise, to manage conflict.
3. The idea that influence is based on technical competence and knowledge rather than on the vagaries of personal whims or prerogatives of power.
4. An atmosphere that permits and even encourages emotional expression as well as task-oriented acts.
5. A basically human bias, one which accepts the inevitability of conflict between the organization and the individual but which is willing to cope with and mediate this conflict on rational grounds.[42]

Finally, as a basis of judging organizations, Bennis developed the idea of *organizational health*. He defined the concept as "the degree to which the organization maintains harmony—and knowledge—about and among the manifest, assumed, extant, and requisite situations."[43] According to Bennis, the *manifest* situation is the formal organization; the *assumed* situation is the organization as it is perceived by its workers; the *extant* situation is the organization as it is derived from investigation; and the *requisite* situation is the organization as it should be. Bennis observed that organizational health does not require that the four be the same, but that the organization and its managers recognize each type and take their differences into account in management decisions.[44]

Frederick Herzberg

Frederick Herzberg took Maslow's motivation theories one step further: he applied them to the individual and studied specific motivations and discouragements of employees. From his research Herzberg developed his *motivation hygiene theory*. Herzberg found that some factors associated with job satisfaction were not normally associated with job dissatisfaction. Similarly, certain factors closely associated with job dissatisfaction had virtually no correlation with job satisfaction. This apparent paradox led him to conclude that:

> The opposite of job satisfaction would not be job dissatisfaction, but rather *no* job satisfaction; and similarly the opposite of job dissatisfaction is *no* job dissatisfaction—not job satisfaction.[45]

Herzberg observed that the factors that led to job dissatisfaction (dissatisfiers) all related to the work environment. Herzberg called these *hygiene factors*. He found that hygiene factors could be related to Maslow's lower needs, those of physiology and safety. Herzberg argued that because these needs are easily satisfied in modern society, they fail to act as motivators but could act as nonmotivators if the employee found them unsatisfactory. To increase happiness and thereby motivate the modern worker, Herzberg observed, some psychological growth seemed to be required. Because factors of hygiene did not promote this growth, he concluded that they could not motivate workers.

Herzberg also concluded that the factors of job satisfaction all described the worker's relationship to the work. Herzberg called these *motivation factors,* and he observed that they can be related to the higher needs in Maslow's hierarchy: because these factors do promote psychological growth, they can motivate employees.[46] Herzberg stressed that the two sets of factors worked in opposite directions: poor hygiene causing job dissatisfaction and good motivators causing job satisfaction. He felt that industry had been treating only half of human nature, the hygiene factors, and ignoring the actual motivating half. He recommended that in order to treat both, organizations separate industrial relations into two parts.

One part would ensure that hygiene did not lead to job dissatisfaction. The other part would use motivators to ensure that the employees put forth optimal effort. This division would be involved with: (1) education; (2) job enrichment; and (3) remedial action. The education he advocated would deal with workers' and managers' attitudes. It would seek to increase employees' pride in their work and to teach managers to respect the employees' perceptions of themselves. Herzberg stressed the need to enrich the content of the job and not simply to enlarge the tasks involved. He argued that the recognition of achievement, increased responsibilities, and opportunities for growth were prerequisites for true job enrichment. Remedial action would respond to technical obsolescence, poor performance, and administrative failures.

Extending Human Relations Theory

The work of Maslow, Argyris, McGregor, Likert, Bennis, and Herzberg in the 1950s and 1960s produced several significant developments for the field of public administration. Three in particular stand out: (1) The normative implications of human relations theory fed the thinking of an emerging group of younger scholars who became advocates of the "New Public Administration;" (2) The theoretical work of the human relations scholars provided a starting point for the empirical work of a rapidly growing community of scholars who developed a subfield of organization theory called *organizational behavior* (or OB); and (3) Its normative structure and orientation toward planned organization change for more satisfying and productive work settings encouraged the growth of a new field, *organizational development* (or OD). Each of these streams of activity set off a new ferment that challenged the field's core assumptions—its orthodoxy—and brought forth new concerns about what exactly constituted the proper scope and methods of analysis for the field.

The New Public Administration

H. George Frederickson articulated perhaps the most complete statement of the new PA. He said it rested on changing the value emphases and normative foundations of the field.[47] The orthodox values that traditionally underpinned public administration—economy, efficiency, effectiveness, accountability to elected officials, and political nonpartisanship—were not wrong; they were incomplete. Other important values included "citizen responsiveness, worker and citizen participation in decision making, the equitable distribution of public services, the provision of a range of citizen choices, and administrative responsibility for program effectiveness."[48] With greater sensitivity to these values the field of public administration would be able to satisfy its ". . . primary normative premise: the reduction of economic, social, and psychic suffering and the enhancement of life opportunities for those inside and outside the organization."[49]

Perhaps the most controversial aspect of the new PA concerned its advocacy role. Peter Savage found the source of "old" public administration's deficiencies in the bias of pluralist politics:

> Pluralism has become a kind of self-fulfilling prophecy, in which public administration increasingly acts as an arbitrator between unequal competing interests, frequently deciding in favor of those in power rather than acting as an advocate of some larger public need.[50]

To Savage and others the only solution to this bias was a new generation of public administrators who would act as "change agents who would instead pursue the objectives of social equity *within* the bureaucracy."[51] These new bureaucrats would deliberately violate the politically useful myth of the separation between politics and administration. In such an arrangement "new Public Administration might well foster a political system in which elected officials speak basically for the majority and for the privileged while courts and administrators are spokesmen for the disadvantaged minorities."[52]

The ideas of the academics who advocated new PA were hardly accepted in all quarters. Critics attacked the movement's central ideas for lack of originality, feasibility, and constitutionality.[53] Some criticism was based on experience. In the real world of practicing public administrators, policymakers "experimented with initiatives which could have been drawn from New Public Administration essays—citizen participation requirements, decentralized service delivery arrangements, and expansive interpretations of rights and entitlements."[54] Although these experiments may have had positive implications, they did not always make for successful public management. For several critics of the new PA, these experiences proved that the movement's theoretical work failed utterly to provide the means to enable practitioners to handle their daily challenges.[55]

The new PA movement faded out almost as quickly as it emerged. By the mid-1970s its principal proponents had moved on to other interests or back to the disciplines from which they had come. Perhaps John Gangin advanced the best postmortem on the movement:

At base, the New Public Administration proposed a reordering of political power and political roles. In the existing order, local, state, and national administrators were undoubtedly aware that they influenced policy and political processes, their influence was contextually determined, and their interests and the interests of political systems were served by the rhetoric and symbolism of a separation of politics and administration. Administrators' power was derived from extant praxis. To ask that public administrators set aside their derived power and become advocates *for* and, therefore, newly derive their political power *from* the politically powerless was to ask much. . . [56]

As things turned out, not only was the new PA asking much, it was asking *too much*. However, not all of the ideas that made up the new PA were consigned to the trash heap of history by the public administration community. One stream of ideas—organizational behavior theory—attracted the attention of scholars before, during, and after the new PA movement.

Organizational Behavior

Almost from the beginning of the twentieth century, theories of industrial and organizational psychology were applied to business and public administration. Frederick W. Taylor's work on scientific management is generally recognized as defining its early scope and direction. Through systematic empirical research Taylor investigated the influence of financial incentives, tool design, and work layout on job performance. The idea behind scientific management was to find the most efficient, least fatiguing, and least expensive way to do a job. An appropriately selected, supervised, trained, and rewarded worker would do an acceptable job. Despite the limitations of scientific management, as dramatized by the Hawthorne experiments, much of the work in industrial psychology continued to focus on perfecting scientific systems of testing, selection, supervision, training, incentives, and job design. It was not until the publication of the work of Maslow, Argyris, and other organizational humanists in the 1950s and 1960s that the field widened its scope to include the social and interpersonal aspects of the work environment.

The work of Taylor and the human relations theorists shared a focus on work motivation, job satisfaction, and job design. Despite their obvious differences, "there was one characteristic they had in common, the implicit underlying assumption that a satisfied worker was a more highly motivated worker than one who was not."[57] Several research studies in the 1950s and 1960s severely shook this widely held belief. The studies concluded that despite many years of research, a strong, pervasive, and direct influence of job satisfaction on performance could not be found.[58]

That finding produced the *work itself,* or *growth,* school, a third view on the nature, sources, and processes of work motivation and job satisfaction. This view was that job satisfaction through growth in skill, efficacy, and responsibility was made possible by mentally challenging work.[59] Herzberg's hygiene theory of motivation was a very significant addition, creating a strong interest in job enrichment as a way to motivate workers.

Over the next two decades a large number of studies and theories explored various dimensions of the relationship between job satisfaction and performance. These studies produced controversies that divided the sizable community of concerned scholars into different camps. However, over time it came to be well accepted that organizational performance is determined by:

1. The needs, values, expectations, and abilities of the individuals who constitute the organization's work force
2. Interpersonal, group, and intergroup processes which make up the organization's behavioral dynamics
3. Organizational structure, job structure, controls, and administrative systems, which constitute the organization's internal environment
4. Political, economic, and social properties in organizational environments which create forces or contingencies that influence an organization's strategies and success.[60]

More than thirty years of scientific research have shown that the combinations and subcategories of these factors are almost endless. Indeed, from the late 1950s through the 1980s, hundreds of researchers did studies on two or more variables that were thought to affect performance. However, studies on different kinds of organizations and different measures of performance have shown only small relationships between structure and behavior, and even these relationships vary in statistical significance. Nevertheless, in such journals as the *Administrative Science Quarterly, The Academy of Management Journal, Organizational Behavior and Human Performance,* and *Personnel Psychology,* scholars continue to report research aimed at analysis of these complex relationships.

One subject especially intriguing to students of organizational behavior is leadership. From early interest in supervision scholars have progressed through a series of questions about leadership. Early theorists used the *trait approach;* they attempted to determine personal attributes that yield effective leadership in all kinds of situations.[61] From the end of World War I to the end of World War II, researchers analyzed successful and unsuccessful leaders, looking for physical, psychological, and social traits of success. The object was to select leaders who already had them.

Unfortunately, most research on traits failed to produce clear results. One review of 124 studies indicated "that leaders tend to be more fluent, more original, more adaptable, more responsible, more popular, and know how to get the job done. For other characteristics, however, the results were less clear and certainly not conclusive."[62] Scholars concluded that it was more useful to consider leadership as a relationship between people in particular situations than as a set of characteristics held by the leader.

As trait theory was falling into disfavor in the late 1940s, social scientists at Ohio State University and the University of Michigan began to take more behavioral approaches. Although one of the principal objectives of the Ohio State team was to reveal how the situation determines a leader's behavior, much of the research was to identify the types of behavior leaders display and to determine the effects of leadership style on the work group's performance and satisfaction.[63]

The University of Michigan studies focused on subordinates' performance and job satisfaction and tried to identify leadership behavior that would maximize both. Although they and the Ohio State team found several factors that were often but not always related to performance, neither effort at finding a "best" leadership style under all conditions proved successful.[64]

In the 1960s and early 1970s, other researchers, most notably Fred E. Fiedler, Robert House, and Victor H. Vroom, developed empirical *situational theories* of leadership. These theories drew upon the systems theorists' contingency approach. The research found evidence that effectiveness depended on: (1) the personality traits and behavioral style of the leader, (2) the characteristics of the subordinates, and (3) environmental pressures and demands. The implications of contingency theories of leadership are very significant for both management theory and education. For example, Behling and Schresheim have observed:

> The fact that leadership effectiveness is not dependent upon a single set of personal characteristics with which an individual is born or acquires at an early age should provide a sense of relief to many managers and potential managers. This conclusion indicates that success in leadership is not limited to a small elite, but rather can be attained by almost any individual, assuming that the situation is proper or that the manager can adjust to it. The process leading to effective leadership, in other words, is not so much one of changing the characteristics of the individual as it is one of either assuring that he is placed in a situation appropriate to his particular pattern of behavior or teaching him to modify his behavior to fit the situation.[65]

The importance of contingency theories of leadership cannot be underestimated: If leaders must "fit their style to the situation" to be effective, an understanding of both leadership styles and of various situations in which they find themselves must be at the core of the study of management. This finding has directed a great deal of attention in management education to the assessment of leadership styles and in training managers to diagnose political and interpersonal dynamics.

Organizational behavior theory, including leadership theory, has had mixed consequences for the field of public administration. On the one hand, very few public administration scholars have contributed actively to the research base of organization behavior theory, which comes largely from people trained in psychology and management. Furthermore, most public administration scholars research only the formal institutions of government. On the other hand, most university-based public administration programs and many management training programs in government draw heavily from the insights of the organizational behaviorists. Therefore, among scholars in public administration one finds a pronounced bifurcation between research production and the consumption of organization behavior studies. However, one variant of human relations theory, *organization development* (OD) has attracted a sizable number of public administration scholars as both producers and consumers.[66]

Organization Development

Since the late 1950s a number of public administration scholars have gravitated to OD. This occurred for three reasons: (1) Its *prescriptive* ideas advocated more participatory decisionmaking. (2) It was an *applied* approach consistent with the field's hands on tradition. (3) It promised researchers an *active* role in organizational change.

French and Bell have provided a well-accepted definition of OD:

> . . . organization development is a long-range effort to improve an organization's problem solving and renewal processes, particularly through a more effective and collaborative management or organization culture—with special emphasis on the culture of formal work teams—with the assistance of a change agent, or catalyst, and the use of the theory or technology of applied behavioral science, including action research.[67]

OD tends to concentrate on the internal environment of an organization with a concern for more effectively integrating the organization's human resources with its goals. "A manager committing his organization to an O.D. process makes two important assumptions: (1) an important aspect of the job is the challenge it presents to expand personally in ways which are enriching to all aspects of one's life; and (2) work associates have an important part to play in providing learnings that facilitate personal and professional development."[68] In addition, OD seeks to build strategy and design capabilities in the organization with an eye toward the future. "The future time reference of O.D. is concerned with (1) preparing the manager to learn from the present so that future applications are available; (2) inculcating an assessment of long-term consequences both in managerial planning and programming; and (3) valuing a proactive-adaptive philosophy as a means of maintaining a managerial stance that moves on both a future as well as concurrent basis."[69]

In the most thorough OD interventions, outside consultants work with an inside team first to diagnose the organization's internal environment and then to design and implement a program of team development, intergroup relations, and structural changes. Tactics range from sensitivity training, T-groups, and other forms of laboratory training for individuals and groups to leadership training and team building.[70]

It is important to stress that these tactics serve a distinctly normative purpose. While not every advocate would agree, according to Bennis OD has these common goals:

1. Improvement in interpersonal competence.
2. A shift in values so that the human factors and feelings come to be considered legitimate.
3. Development of increased understanding between and within working groups in order to reduce tensions.
4. Development of more effective "team management," i.e., the capacity . . . for functional groups to work more competently.
5. Development of better methods of "conflict resolution." Rather than the usual bureaucratic methods, which rely mainly on suppression, compromise, and unprincipled power, more rational and open methods of conflict resolution are sought.
6. Development of "organic" or open and fluid systems rather than "mechanical" or machine-like systems.[71]

This list shows that OD has been very controversial in public administration. Its advocates say OD promises to make public agencies more adaptive and responsive to their increasingly complex environments. Leadership and work force management would be more open, authentic, and satisfying to the average worker. Morale would improve, and along with it productivity and responsiveness to clients.

Critics of OD have been skeptical of its promises and hostile to its implications. They say OD breeds a permissive work environment where it is more important to "feel good" than to produce. At the extreme the philosophy of OD has been called psychobabble.[72] In real public administration, where the formal organization is encased in law, OD has been seen as a threat to the chain of command and the legal accountability of public employees. Efforts to diffuse responsibility to work groups rather than individuals and to decentralize decisionmaking have been seen as threats to processes of democratic accountability. In orthodox theory there were clear lines of accountability between civil servants and elected officeholders. In OD theory, critics charged, these lines would become hopelessly blurred.

Despite these criticisms and reservations, OD has sustained considerable popularity as both a theory and a practice in public administration. Moreover, some studies suggest that it is often effective. An analysis by Robert Golembiewski claims that OD's rate of producing positive intended effects on target organizations is around 85 percent, and its success does not diminish as one moves from the private to the public sector.[73] As is often the case with social science, definitive proof of OD's effectiveness or ineffectiveness cannot be produced, in part because of methodological difficulties of evaluating it. Nonetheless, studies like Golembiewski's suggest that OD—and the human relations philosophy upon which it is based—will continue to be a major part of public administration theory in the years ahead.

Generic Theories: Do Differences Make a Difference?

One surprising outcome of the "diversity, heterogeneity, competition and changing fashions"[74] in organization theory over the past thirty years has been a growing commonality among scholars in the terms and concepts for describing and studying organizations. Indeed, as decision theory and open systems theory spread into the study of public administration, some of the field's distinctiveness seems to be fading away.[75] In its place some scholars advocate the widespread adoption of generic theories of organizations based on organizational sociology, open systems theory, decision theory, and organizational behavior.

The general vocabulary for studying organizations also has had practical consequences for management in public agencies: If there are no significant differences between public and private organizations, why shouldn't government be run more like a business? This question implies that government agencies should search the business world for efficiency-enhancing techniques that their work processes can use. It also suggests that many functions performed by government can be privatized, without appreciable loss of government authority or democratic accountability.

There are old issues for public administration. Richard Stillman has observed that business management methods dominated much of the early development of the field: "Frederick W. Taylor and his business-oriented scientific management concepts served as the core of much of the field of public administration prior to World

War II. The Brownlow Committee Report (1937). . . largely mirrored the business organization practices of the day."[76] Today, many practices that began in business—performance budgets, cost-benefit analysis, cost-accounting procedures, performance appraisals, management by objectives and more—are in use in the public sector. Other techniques developed in the public sector, for example operations research, are widely used in the private sector. Despite these transfers, two questions remain: Is government like business? If there are differences, which ones are important?

One of the major ideas underpinning the study and practice of public administration is that public organizations and their management are different from the private sector. Indeed, one of the oft-quoted statements about public administration is Wallace Sayre's "law" that public and private management are fundamentally alike in all *un*important respects.[77] If this is the case, the argument goes, the tools and techniques of designing and managing public organization must be at least somewhat different from those used for private-sector organizations.

Ideally, a clear distinction between public- and private-sector organizations should be possible, but none of the several efforts to draw clear lines of distinction between the two types of organizations has been fully successful.[78] The wide, varied, and continually evolving role of government in the economy has in fact produced a blurring, or convergence, in the organizational structure and practices of the public and private sectors.[79] In addition to the conceptual convergence in organization theory and analysis, this blurring seems to arise from two aspects of contemporary government: First, there is an intermingling of government and nongovernmental activities, which is observable in (1) government regulation of various industries; (2) various mixed undertakings such as public corporations (like the Postal Service and the Tennessee Valley Authority), and (3) the contracting of government services to private firms. Second, there is some overlap and similarity in the functions, contexts, roles, and structures of organizations in the two sectors. Thus, for example, Louis Gawthorp has argued that coping with increasingly rapid and unpredictable changes in their environments is such a major concern to both public and private organizations that differences between them on other counts will be overshadowed.[80] Murray Weidenbaum has observed that some corporations—especially some defense manufacturing firms—are so dependent on government contracts that they take on certain attributes of government agencies.[81] In contrast, John Kenneth Galbraith has argued that many business firms have so much market power and influence that it is no longer appropriate to regard them as private. If so, he continues, society needs mechanisms to ensure that these firms are made "accountable to elected officials in a manner similar to government agencies."[82]

Therefore, the blurring between organizations in the two sectors complicates the problem of distinguishing between them, but the real question is how much to make of it. A distinction can be blurred and still be meaningful. In this case there is no consensus; there are two camps—those who emphasize the similarities and those who emphasize the difference between business and government organizations.

All organizations share at least some similarities. They all have environments, they all interact with other organizations, they all have internal structures of rules, procedures, and authority relationships, and they all have human relations of one kind

EXHIBIT 10.1 Functions of General Management

Strategy

1. Establishing objectives and priorities for the organization (on the basis of forecasts of the external environment and the organization's capacities).

2. Devising operational plans to achieve these objectives.

Managing internal components

3. Organizing and staffing: In organizing the manager establishes structure (units and positions with assigned authority and responsibilities) and procedures (for coordinating activity and taking action); in staffing he tries to fit the right persons in the key jobs.

4. Directing personnel and the personnel management system: The capacity of the organization is embodied primarily in its members and their skills and knowledge; the personnel management system recruits, selects, socializes, trains, rewards, punishes, and exits the organization's human capital, which constitutes the organization's capacity to act to achieve its goals and to respond to specific directions from management.

5. Controlling performance: Various management information systems—including operating and capital budgets, accounts, reports and statistical systems, performance appraisals, and product evaluation—assist management in making decisions and in measuring progress towards objectives.

Managing external constituencies

6. Dealing with "external" units of the organization subject to some common authority: Most general managers must deal with general managers of other units within the larger organization—above, laterally and below—to achieve their unit's objectives.

7. Dealing with independent organizations: Agencies from other branches or levels of government, interest groups, and private enterprises that can importantly affect the organization's ability to achieve its objectives.

8. Dealing with the press and public whose action or approval or acquiescence is required.

Source: Graham Allison, "Public and Private Management: Are They Fundamentally Alike in All Unimportant Respects?" in Richard J. Stillman, ed., *Public Administration,* 3d ed. (Boston: Houghton Mifflin, 1984), 455–6.

or another. The management of all organizations features commonalities. As Gulick pointed out in the *Papers on the Science of Administration* (1937), all chief executives engage in POSDCORB activities; that is, planning, organizing, staffing, directing, coordinating, reporting, and budgeting.[83] Other writers, like Barnard, have extended and modified this list, but the point is that at least at one level of abstraction public and private organizations and their management *are* similar—and theoretically these similarities ought to be identifiable in a simple list. Graham Allison has developed one such list (see Exhibit 10.1).

Allison's list of management functions is both general and abstract. He is careful to point out that "the character and relative significance of the various functions differ from one time to another in the history of any organization, and between one organization and another. But whether in a public or private setting, the challenge for the . . . manager is to integrate all these elements . . . to achieve results." Nevertheless, Allison cautions that even though public and private management functions may "bear identical labels," they "take rather different meanings in public and private settings."[84] Therefore, finding these meanings and their significance, he concludes, is a necessary endeavor.

Distinguishing Features of Public Organizations

Those who agree with Allison have found distinctive features of public organizations at each of the three principal levels of organizational analysis: (1) organizational environments, (2) transactions between the organization and the environment, and (3) internal structures and processes. Proponents of a separate theory of public organizations have argued that these sets of distinctive features flow from the special purposes of public and private organizations. Wamsley and Zald have observed that public organizations' most notable features stem from the fact that a "government is a system of rule. . . that: (1) . . . ultimately rests upon coercion and a monopoly of force, and (2), if legitimate, it symbolically speaks for the society as a whole, or purports to do so."[85] This makes citizens and ruling elites feel that their rights and expectations regarding government agencies are different from those of private firms. In addition to the symbolic significance of public organizations and the importance of legitimacy in shaping and delivering public policy, Wamsley and Zald note that public organizations rely largely on allocated budgets. That is, they receive their resources through political processes rather then through the sale of goods and services in the marketplace. From these three essential characteristics—*symbolism;* perceptions of *ownership,* or rights and privileges; and differences in *funding*—come a number of characteristics that distinguish government organizations from business organizations.

Environmental Factors

Contingency theorists assume that much about organizations can be understood from their environment. Environmental factors are external forces that affect the way organizations behave and how they organize their structures and processes. Environmental factors are largely beyond the control of the organization. Three of these factors are particularly important to the distinction between public and private organizations: (1) market exposure; (2) legal and formal constraints; and (3) political influences.

Market Exposure.   One of the most fundamental and frequently mentioned distinctions between public and private organizations is the latter's involvement with economic markets as a source of resources, information, and constraints. As a source of revenues and resources, it is argued, the market enforces relatively automatic penalties and rewards on business firms, providing them with incentives to pursue cost reduction, operating efficiency, and effective performance.[86] In contrast, public organizations tend to obtain resources through an appropriations process embedded in a political context. Public organizations are therefore less subject to such operating pressures. Also, the budget of a public organization often is based on direct political influences or on a number of vague criteria of "public interest."[87]

Furthermore, it is sometimes argued that managers of organizations financed by appropriations seek organizational growth and personal aggrandizement by maximizing appropriations and thus tend to *de*-emphasize operating efficiency.[88] Using this reasoning, a number of critics of public organizations, particularly public choice theorists, stress the inefficiencies inherent in allocating resources through political decisionmaking rather than through market forces.[89]

Intermingled with these criticisms about operating and allocational inefficiencies of government organizations are frequent references to the importance of the market as a source of relatively clear, quantitative indicators of demand, goals, and performance measures (that is, prices, sales, and profits). They argue that such relatively clear information is conducive to operating efficiency and effectiveness because it provides indicators of users' preferences, economies of scale, and demand for particular services.[90]

Legal and Formal Constraints.   A second source of environmental influence on organizations is the legal structure surrounding them. It gives them more or less autonomy and flexibility depending upon how clearly and tightly laws are written and enforced. Generally, private organizations need only obey the law and the regulations enforced by governmental regulatory agencies, but the law tends to define the purposes and methods of operation of public organizations to a much greater degree. One effect is that public managers have less choice about when to enter and to withdraw from various undertakings, whether they are effective or not.[91]

The importance of legal constraints has led more than one writer to note a tendency toward legalism in the public sector—that is, a proliferation of formal, legal specifications and controls by statute, regulations, court rulings, and executive orders.[92] This propensity to use detailed, formal procedures to run organizations is called red tape. It reflects the fact that public agencies are subject to hierarchic controls from elected officials.[93] Indeed, the electoral process itself can strongly affect government organizations. Leadership changes following regular popular elections and new political appointments often disrupt internal operations of public organizations. They can also create intense short-term time pressures on managers. For example, new presidents and their staffs often perceive that they have only a short time to make changes in policies and programs at the start of a new administration. This perception can put enormous pressure on an agency to act quickly. In contrast, "private managers appear to take a longer time perspective oriented toward market developments, technological innovation and investment, and organization building."[94]

Political Influences.   Reference to popular elections and political appointments brings up another set of observations about the importance of political influences on government organizations. These influences encompass not only those that come from Congress, the White House, and city hall and that typify all government decisionmaking, but also the less formal processes of influence, such as interest group demands and lobbying. Some argue that the presence of these multiple, diverse, and often competing interests in government spawns bargaining, and therefore, make the process of setting objectives and implementing policy in government much more complex than in the private sector.[95] Because public decisionmakers always need to be on the alert for the reactions of various interests to their choices, they must consult a wider variety of constituencies, interest groups, and authorities than is usually demanded in the private sector.

Transactions between Organizations and the Environment

A number of differences between public and private organizations have been found in their relationship to other entities in their environment. These differences:

1. Coerciveness
2. Policy impacts
3. Public scrutiny
4. The nature of goods produced.

Coerciveness.   Sometimes, the coercive, monopolistic, or unavoidable nature of government activities is cited as a distinction between public and private organizations.[96] Thus, citizens are stuck with government entities for many functions ranging from national defense to tax collection and law enforcement. For some of these functions a simple market mechanism will not ensure sufficient and guaranteed levels of service. Individual voluntary choice cannot be trusted to produce the necessary goods and services in functions like national security, law and order, or basic scientific research. Such collective goods require coercion in the form of taxation or regulation to assure that appropriate levels of these goods are produced. To assure that this exercise of the power of government is not abused, it is checked and balanced by extensive formal constitutional guarantees and political processes that assure fairness and due process. In contrast, in private business greater stress is placed upon efficiency and competitive performance.[97]

Policy Impacts.   A number of commentators have noted the relative importance of government decisions compared with private sector choices. Governmental decisions frequently have wide-ranging implications for society as a whole, while business decisions rarely have such wide scope. Paul Appleby cited this as a distinctive aspect of public administration. Government's unique breadth, impact, and importance for so many people, he argued, put it in a special category for making comparisons.[98] Wamsley and Zald note that government's unique importance gives it a special symbolic significance to citizens.[99] Edward Banfield has added that participation in government decisionmaking gives one the chance to achieve both great power and great glory.[100] To add experience to these academic observations, several high-ranking administrators with experience in both the sectors have reported that they found themselves making more important and influential decisions when they served in government than in the private sector.[101]

Public Scrutiny.   Another important distinction is that public administrators are subject to greater public scrutiny than their private-sector counterparts (see the discussion of fishbowl management in Chapter 8). Banfield argues that this makes government organizations more subject to outside monitoring and less able to keep secrets than businesses.[102] Government managers must contend regularly with the media.[103] Indeed, much of the heavy overlay of formal rules in government can be interpreted as a method of ensuring public scrutiny to enhance oversight and accountability to elected officials. Furthermore, the normally large numbers of interest group representatives involved in the consideration of an agency's actions also assures an extensive amount of public awareness. Even though there are indications of increasing public scrutiny of large private corporations and increasing concerns about their impact on the general public, rarely does the spotlight on private firms come close to the extensive oversight of public agencies exercised by elected officials, lobbyists, and the media.[104]

Nature of Goods Produced.   Economists have noted that government organizations are usually involved in the production of *public* and *quasi-public goods*. Public goods are special because they are not *divisible*; that is, they cannot be sold to individual consumers in pieces. Thus, a strong national defense, clean air, and a safe and secure society are *natural monopolies*—goods that everyone in a society has an interest in and from which they cannot be excluded by setting some price for the goods.[105] Thus, much of what government produces is not appropriate for the market. In contrast, quasi-public goods are a government product sufficiently "packageable" to allow for the application of prices (for example, tolls and other user fees). These goods involve significant *externalities* or *spillover effects* so they are often provided below the cost of production. Thus, government subsidies for doctors' educations have been justified on the grounds that society benefits later through the physician's contribution to better public health. Without the subsidy the market would produce fewer and less qualified doctors and public health would suffer. Business firms, in contrast, are expected to market goods that cover the full costs of production and produce a profit.

A third form of public goods are *merit* or *meritorious* goods. These goods include government services that distribute benefits to individuals under nonmarket conditions because either society as a whole benefits or because it is considered the right thing to do. Thus, localities in the United States provide free education to age sixteen for all children, states provide welfare benefits to the impoverished, and the federal government provides food stamps and other forms of aid to the needy because it is considered the correct thing to do, irrespective of its market consequences.

Internal Structures and Processes

One major assumption of organization theory is that environments and transactions shape the internal operations and structures of organizations. This means that if there are significant differences between the environments and transactions of public and private organizations, their internal properties must also differ. Indeed, several systematic studies have found considerable differences between the two kinds on at least five dimensions:

1. Their objectives and criteria for evaluation
2. Hierarchical authority and administrative roles
3. Performance characteristics
4. Incentives
5. The motivations and attitudes of individual employees.[106]

Objectives and Evaluation Criteria.   Probably the most frequently mentioned distinction between business and government organizations concerns their goals and performance measures. The objectives and performance criteria of public sector organizations tend to differ from those of business organizations in at least three important ways:

1. *Multiplicity and diversity.* The mix of objectives and criteria in the public sector is said to be more complex than in business. Multiple formal program objectives and a number of important political considerations such as accountability, openness, and equity are built into the operations of public sector agencies.
2. *Vagueness and intangibility.* Public organizations often face unique difficulties in specifying and quantifying effective performance. Lacking a clear goal like profit, public organizations are forced to fall back on less specific measures of output and impact.
3. *Goal conflict.* Conflicts and trade-offs among objectives and performance criteria in the public sector are not surprising in view of the many complex constraints and expectations focused on government. For example, in government operating efficiency is often deemphasized in relation to other criteria like fairness and accountability.[107] This is not to suggest that businesses seek only sales and profits. Clearly, they too are faced with a complex mix of objectives, and frequently with inadequate quantitative measures of performance; nevertheless, when comparing their managerial experience, many executives who have worked in both sectors have noted the greater multiplicity, vagueness, and conflict of objectives in the public sector.[108]

Hierarchical Authority and Administrative Roles.   The political and legal influences on public organizations are related to attributes of government authority with significant implications for the behavior of managers. In general, observers regard hierarchical authority as weaker in the executive branch than in business.[109] Sometimes this weakness is traced to the fragmentation and complexity of governments at all levels. More often the "lack of control" that plagues government executives is attributed to the ability of subordinates to bypass their superiors by appealing to legislators and other political actors. Furthermore, public managers usually have less flexibility and autonomy in making decisions than their private-sector counterparts. This stems from the heavy overlays of legal, statutory, and procedural controls that constrain public managers. For example, decisions regarding the hiring, firing, promoting, and rewarding of employees are often outside the formal discretion of managers, and even when subject to some managerial authority, are often encased in elaborate frameworks of appeals to assure fairness and due process.[110]

This pattern of constricted managerial authority suggests some unique difficulties in supervision and delegation in the public sector. The relative inability to specify clear objectives and performance measures makes it harder to supervise and control subordinates. This leads to reluctance to delegate authority, multiple levels of review and approval for decisions, and a proliferation of regulations. The lack of specific and quantitative criteria is also said to promote overcautious management and to limit innovations because it is difficult to evaluate their outcomes.[111]

The necessity to maintain the support of constituencies for programs, to deal with multiple external influences, and to seek appropriations from elected officials strongly influence the behavior of managers in government. Political skills and contacts often play a pivotal role in determining a manager's effectiveness. Stockfish argues that the need to combine political adroitness with managerial expertise sets the public manager apart.[112] Mintzberg concludes from a study of managerial work that the requirement to deal with external coalitions and to make politically sensitive decisions make the "liaison, spokesman, and negotiator roles" more important for top executives of public organizations than for business executives.[113]

Performance Characteristics.   A number of observers comparing the performance of government and business organizations have focused on the special dysfunctions that plague government agencies. Robert Dahl and Charles Lindblom have asserted that agencies suffer more than enterprises from red tape, buck-passing, timidity, and rigidity.[114] Anthony Downs has noted tendencies in bureaus to inertia, routinization, and inflexibility.[115] Golembiewski has asserted that government organizations have a greater tendency to procedural regularity and caution than business firms.[116] Finally, Weidenbaum has noted the tendency of some corporations to become so dependent on government contracts that they lose their *essential privateness;* that is, their capacity to innovate and their willingness to take risks.[117] The issue of risk taking by government managers is important to many observers. Former OMB director Charles Schultze argued that the inadequate performance measures in government produce risk avoidance because success cannot be easily recognized, but mistakes can be singled out and punished.[118]

Incentives.   There are significant differences between the incentives available to employees in the public and private sectors. Banfield argued that the most important incentives to private-sector employees are material—primarily money. In government, he says, nonpecuniary incentives such as job security, involvement in important affairs, and power and glory figure more prominently.[119] Lawler adds that those who work in business attach more importance to pay than do persons in government. These observations suggest greater constraints on the ability of public managers to manipulate incentives to motivate employees and differences between public and private employees in the value they attach to various incentives.

Individual Differences.   The differences of incentives available to public and private organizations suggest that there may be several significant differences in the kinds of people who work in them. One study compared students planning employment in the private sector with students planning for jobs in the nonprofit and public sectors. The latter were more likely to have been agents of change in their school; their responses on personality scales were higher on attributes of dominance, flexibility, and capacity for status; and they placed a lower value on economic wealth.[120] Other studies have found that government managers show lower work and need satisfaction, lower commitment to the organization, higher need for achievement, and lower need for affiliation.[121] These findings suggest important differences in the motivations of public- and private-sector employees, but one must be cautious in taking them as definitive; they may merely reflect the relatively weak financial incentives available to managers and workers in public organizations.

Implications for Organizational Design and Management

The differences between public and private organizations have important implications for public administration. They suggest that the distinctive features of public organizations must be considered in designing public organizations and in improving management. Rainey and his associates have identified three broad implications of the differences between public and private organizations:

1. *Purposes, objectives, and planning*. Because public administrators generally have little flexibility and autonomy in defining the purposes of their organizations and programs, and because their objectives are more diverse and harder to specify, planning is usually subject to a more complex set of influences and is more difficult than is common in the private sector.
2. *Selection, management, and motivation*. Since there are likely to be constraints on public managers' ability to select and control subordinates, they may need to consider a different set of employee needs and motivational problems in hiring and in rewarding outstanding performance.
3. *Controlling and measuring results*. A public manager may find it not only harder to measure results, but also—partially because of that difficulty— harder to attain results and effective performance.[122]

These differences are important, but the questions persist: Are they fundamental to the context and purposes of the public sector? Do they justify a separate set of theories, tools, and techniques for public organizations? If so, is it reasonable to conclude that tools for managing business firms are not likely to work in the public sector with equivalent success?

Generic theorists say no to all these questions. They consider the differences to be a matter of degree, not of kind. They argue that at a minimum, organization theories and management techniques that address extreme complexity should transfer from business to public administration. Furthermore, they observe that many problems in public organizations, particularly those involving the routine production of goods and services, are similar to those in business firms. Techniques that work in business organizations ought to work equally well in similar public-sector systems. This reasoning has led researchers in organization theory and management in at least four directions:

1. *Publicness*, or government penetration through regulation or contracting, that affects all organizations, public and private. Barry Bozeman has argued that "all organizations are public" to the extent that laws and regulations constrain their decisions.[123]
2. *Complexity* and its demands on theories of decisionmaking and organizational effectiveness. James March and his colleagues have described a garbage can model to explain decisionmaking under conditions of ambiguity

and uncertainty.[124] John Kingdon and Nelson Polsby have extended these ideas to government decisionmaking.[125]

3. *Classifications,* or *taxonomies* of organizational structure, tools, and techniques appropriate for different classes of problems. Decision theorists have sorted organization problems into three categories, those that involve *certainty,* those that involve *risk,* and those that involve *uncertainty.* They then classify familiar decisionmaking techniques into each of these categories to show where they are most appropriate.[126]

4. *Tailoring* of management techniques to the particular context. These scholars study such management techniques as performance appraisal, pay-for-performance bonus systems,[127] strategic management,[128] and integrated financial management and budgeting systems in the public sector.[129]

The transfer of theories and tools from business to public organizations has been a major concern for public administration from its beginnings. Such transfers have at least implicitly accepted the key assumption of generic theory, that the differences between public and private organizations are of degree, not kind.

Not all scholars agree. Allison concludes "that public and private management are at least as different as they are similar, and that the differences are more important than the similarities."[130] He goes on to draw several lessons for research on public management:

> . . . the demand for performance from government and efficiency in government is both real and right. The perception that government's performance lags private business performance is also correct. But the notion that there is any significant body of private management practices and skills that can be transferred directly to public management tasks in a way that produces significant improvements is wrong.
>
> . . . performance in many public management positions can be improved substantially, perhaps by an order of magnitude. That improvement will come not, however, from massive borrowing of specific private management skills and understandings. Instead, it will come, as it did in the history of private management, from an articulation of the general management function and a self-consciousness about the general management point of view. The single lesson of private management most instructive to public management is the prospect of substantial improvement through recognition of and consciousness about the public management function. . .
>
> . . . the effort to develop public management as a field of knowledge should start from problems faced by practicing public managers.[131]

The debate over the validity and usefulness of generic theory in public administration seems to flare up every decade.[132] Its implications speak to the essence of the field. If it is indeed valid and useful, much of public administration as a separate theoretical endeavor, educational curriculum, and professional practice may fade away without harm. But if it is not valid, critics contend, enthusiasm for generic organization and management can produce more harm than good in government.[133] However, one thing is certain: Because of the prestige of business in the United States, research on generic theory and the transfer of business techniques to the public sector is bound to persist, and the debate over their applicability will continue.

Economics and Public Organization Theory

The third major school of thought about public organizations to arise in the 1960s derived from economics. Just as human relations theory came from social psychology and generic theory came from sociology and systems theory, so the economic approach, often called *public choice theory,* adopted the underlying assumptions of neoclassical economics. According to Keith Baker, the public choice school is made up of:

> . . . a rather loose community of economists and political scientists who, increasingly have adopted theoretical variants of classic political economy as a means of studying how scarce public goods and services might best be allocated in society.[134]

Building on the work of such political economists as James Buchanan, Gordon Tullock, and William Niskanen, public choice scholars have addressed three central questions:

1. Why a society chooses to provide goods and services through its government.
2. Why there are public agencies as opposed to alternative arrangements for delivery of service.
3. How elected officials can control their bureaucratic subordinates.

Thus, public choice theory begins with a model of a human being as a decisionmaker and proceeds to describe how that person will make choices about the consumption and production of public goods and services under different decision-making rules and structures.[135] Ostrom and Ostrom summarize this *methodological individualism* as follows: "The decision maker will confront certain opportunities and possibilities in the world of events and will pursue his relative advantage within the strategic opportunities afforded by different types of decision rules or decision-making arrangements."[136] They assume that individuals will act purposefully, not randomly, and so will choose from a set of alternatives based on their preferences in order to achieve preferred outcomes. This key assumption of public choice theory is an abstraction; it does not postulate that individuals will make pen-and-paper calculations of the costs and benefits of each alternative. Instead, public choice models assume that individuals act "as if" they make such calculations and "as if" they use them in choosing courses of action.[137]

This assumption leads in turn to three others: (1) People in and out of bureaucracies will be self-interested, that is, to fulfill their ambitions and to advance themselves. Thus clients and interest groups will seek more benefits if others bear the cost. (2) The government work force is populated by "intelligent, ambitious, and somewhat unscrupulous" men and women who behave "predictably in the quest of self-interested outcomes."[138] (3) The processes of self-interested choicemaking can be described, explained, and predicted by formal deductive, logical, and mathematical models that produce new insights about effective design of government activities. Despite some promising findings, these assumptions and their implications have come under severe criticism from all quarters. There are several sound reasons for this criticism, but it is important to note at the outset that public choice theory is a direct challenge to both orthodox public organization theory and its more recent competitors, human relations theory and generic organization theory. Public choice theory does this in at least six ways:

1. It directly addresses the issue of what goods and services governments ought to produce. Orthodox theory essentially begged this question by labeling it outside the proper scope of administrative decisionmaking.
2. It questions the belief of orthodox theorists that "good administration . . . will be hierarchically ordered in a 'one best way' system of graded ranks subject to political direction by heads of departments at the center of government."[139] Instead, public choice theory equates good administration with varying degrees of centralization in decisionmaking, depending upon the good or service in question.
3. It challenges the orthodox idea that bureaucrats are dedicated to the precepts of "neutral competence" by viewing bureaucrats as self-interested political actors who are in constant struggle with their superiors to expand their budgets and avoid hierarchical control.
4. It rejects the assumption of the human relations theorists that complex social forces that take place in groups motivate "organization men." Instead, public choice theory begins with the assumption that organization man pursues his self-interest.
5. It challenges generic theorists' belief that all organizations are alike, separating private and public organizations into categories it calls *market* and *nonmarket* decisionmaking groups.
6. It replaces the detached, descriptive methods of generic organization theory with a pronounced normative orientation. It promises theory that will lead to new ways of conducting the real business of government. Because of this orientation, public choice approaches aim for greater impact on government than either human relations or generic theory. Rather than simply making minor modifications in the old orthodoxy and the structures and processes it left behind in government, public choice theory seeks to replace them with an entirely new approach to organizing governmental activities.

Public choice theory has been built upon three foundations: (1) criticism of the old orthodoxy of Woodrow Wilson and the Brownlow committee, (2) new departures of Herbert Simon and his colleagues in decision and systems theory, and (3) the economic theory of public goods. The public choice critique of orthodox public organization theory centered on the older theory's notion of efficiency as an essential criterion of good administration. According to Vincent Ostrom, orthodox public administration theory has tended to judge efficiency indirectly by administrative structure: The greater the degree of specialization, professionalization, and linear organization in a unitary chain of command, the greater the efficiency."[140] In contrast, Ostrom argues that efficiency is most appropriately measured by a cost calculus, "accomplishment of a specifiable objective at least cost; or, a higher level of performance at a given cost. . ."[141]

This second criterion argues that organization structures are composed of a set of variables and that their efficiency will vary over time, place, and the nature of the good produced. Ostrom criticized the orthodox theorists for depicting a centralized hierarchical structure as "the" proper form for producing public goods and services. According to Ostrom, this model amounted to a revealed truth, or myth, that produced inefficiencies as well as damaging results. He argued that if efficiency is to be raised, alternative arrangements for the production of public goods and services must be considered.

Ostrom and other public choice theorists argue that production of public services by civil servants in bureaucracies is not the only way to meet citizen preferences. The provision and production of public services can be separated into two decisions: first, whether a government should provide a service; second, *how* to provide that service—a government bureaucracy being only one of several options. Alternatives include intergovernmental agreements, contracts with private firms, franchises, grants, and vouchers. Public choice theory even questions taxation as the best way to fund public goods and services. Its theorists frequently propose quasi-market mechanisms like user fees and tolls to raise funds and deliver services to those who really want them.[142]

Public choice theory also suggests—even advocates—that under certain conditions, diverse, fragmented, and overlapping delivery systems are an effective way to organize. In orthodox theory, diversity, fragmentation, and overlap were considered inefficient and should be eliminated by reorganization. In contrast, public choice theory regards these arrangements as potentially quite efficient—and adds that by increasing citizens' choices, overlapping services can best satisfy citizen preferences. Public choice theorists also argue that in a market for public services, competition will check the proclivity of centralized bureaucracies to grow and become less efficient.[143] While recognizing that small decentralized service arrangements are not always preferable to large centralized ones, public choice theorists contend that other things being equal, as size increases, bureaucrats' ambitions combine with bureaucratic politics to allow fewer resources for the primary mission and more for management and control.[144]

Public choice theorists also diverge from orthodox theory in the way they deal with public employees. Instead of regarding them as "neutrally competent" implementors of decisions made by elected officials, much of the literature assumes public employees adopt strategies that (1) lead to promotion to higher rank; (2) increase their discretion (freedom from close supervision by superiors, elected officials, citizens, or clients); and (3) increase the budget and the organization's size. All this activity is assumed to lead to increases in *in*efficiency and to excess production. As a consequence, public choice theorists frequently argue that a strong bureaucracy yields an oversized government.[145] Other have found that these assumptions should be modified because: (1) many bureaucrats have other motives besides promotion, discretion, and larger budgets; (2) even those with expansionary ambitions are checked by superiors and legislators; and (3) marketlike competition might in fact increase government growth and inefficiency rather than decrease it.[146]

These concerns have made public choice theory a lively arena for research and debate among scholars in the field of public administration. By promoting privatization through contracting out and marketlike arrangements for delivering public services, public choice theory has elevated the importance of public preferences in service delivery. This has threatened the professional standing of the civil service.

According to Vincent Ostrom, successful delivery of services often depends upon *coproduction,* or cooperative exchanges between producers and consumers of services. In law enforcement, education, and even garbage collection, joint cooperative action by civil servants and citizens produces higher levels of effectiveness. According to Ostrom, excessive civil service professionalism may negate these advantages of coproduction.

> Professionalization of public services can be accompanied by a serious erosion in the quality of those services. This is especially true when professionals presume to know what is good for people rather than provide people with opportunities to express their own preferences, and when they fail to regard citizens as essential coproducers of many public goods and services. Higher expenditures for public services supplied exclusively by highly trained cadres of professional personnel may contribute to a 'service paradox,' where the better that services are, as defined by professional criteria, the less satisfied that citizens are with those services. An efficient system of public administration will depend upon professionals working under conditions where they have incentives to assist citizens as essential coproducers rather than assume that citizens are incompetent to realize their own interests.[147]

Thus, from this observation and others about decisionmaking and organization structure, Ostrom and other public choice theorists have developed what amounts to a full-blown new theory of public administration that constitutes a direct challenge to the old orthodox theory. To public choice theorists, the success of the orthodox prescriptions for hierarchical arrangements, clear lines of authority, technical proficiency, and political neutrality has meant "large, distant, and unresponsive bureaucracies; inefficient and ineffective public programs; and unrealistic expectations about the abilities of elected chief executives."[148] To remedy these ills, public choice advocates have proposed major and sometimes radical changes in the structure and processes of public administration. During the past two decades, using new criteria, public choice theorists and conservative think tanks like the Heritage Foundation and the Cato Institute in Washington have promoted new financing and arrangements to deliver services in local, state, and federal government. As a result, marketlike arrangements such as contracting out, user fees, and coproduction schemes have been considered and in some cases adopted for public services throughout the United States and abroad. Despite these successes, some fundamental questions about the assumptions underlying public choice theory and its implications for public administration have prevented its adoption for more services and in more jurisdictions.

Criticisms of Public Choice Theory

The criticisms of public choice theory have generally focused on four problems:

1. Its lack of accessibility to government officials and law makers
2. Its inattention to problems of equity
3. Its implicit bureaucrat bashing
4. Its complex third party service arrangements, which tend to make management difficult.

The Accessibility Problem.   The great strength of orthodox public organization theory was that it spoke directly to the laws and institutions of government. By using the language of public law and focusing on the laws and regulations that needed to be changed, orthodox theorists were able to communicate their ideas to lawmakers. In contrast, public choice theory is abstract. Even when addressing specific government programs and agencies, public choice theorists tend to speak a language that public administrators and lawmakers have a hard time understanding. Louis Weschler has observed that although the rigor of public choice reasoning is a virtue, its formal and deductive methodology makes the "costs of participation in public choice theory" very high. [149] Indeed, this problem seems to be escalating as public choice theorists use ever more elaborate mathematical models. Terry Moe, while praising the "great deductive power" of economic methods, notes that:

> A corresponding disadvantage, however, is that such a framework encourages highly complex mathematical treatment of trivial problems: form tends to triumph over substance, and analytical concerns tend to take on lines of their own that have little to do with the explanation of empirical phenomena. [150]

In general, public choice theorists dismiss the accessibility problem as a temporary inconvenience and an inappropriate measure of theoretical progress. Thus they are able to brush aside criticism that human beings—both bureaucrats and clients—are not narrowly rational; a variety of motives, group orientations, values, and preferences affect their behavior. The defense is that this is pretheory: "intermediate, transitional structures that cannot explain empirical phenomena, but may point the way toward theories that do." [151] In the meantime, most public administration scholars either await events or ask for demonstrations.

The Equity Problem.   The key assumption of public choice theory for public administration is that markets deliver public services more efficiently and responsively than do monopolies. Therefore, public services ought to be organized into markets, either through price mechanisms or geographically, differentiated and bundled so that citizen consumers can vote with their feet. In other words, if citizens do not like the services offered by one jurisdiction, they can move to another one where the services and their costs better fit their preferences. An implication of this assumption is that several, single-purpose special districts with different sizes and funding bases will be more efficient than consolidated multiple-purpose local governments that predominate in the United States.

For critics of public choice theory these ideas create a potentially serious equity problem because they assume that every citizen has the financial resources necessary to pay user fees or can move from one jurisdiction to another freely. [152] By advocating special districts, user fees, and tolls, critics argue, public choice theory would unfairly exclude the poor from consuming services. In recreation services, for example, user fees would exclude poor people from enjoying the good life that ought to be available to everyone in a community. Furthermore, because services and facilities are often subsidized by public funds, poor people who pay taxes but cannot afford the admission fee would be subsidizing the middle class and rich who can afford to pay.

The issue of requiring citizens to vote with their feet by moving to jurisdictions with a better service mix has also attracted critics. It is no accident, they observe, that the suburbs of the middle class and rich have the best services, often the lowest taxes, and the fewest poor and minority people. If people could indeed freely vote with their feet, why don't the poor and minorities move to these jurisdictions? The answer, critics contend, is exclusionary zoning and discrimination that deny to poor people and minorities access to the rich suburbs and their services. Until this problem is solved, critics charge, the public choice prescription of a free market for public services is a pipe dream.

In response to the problem of income inequities, public choice theorists have suggested vouchers for services. Their best-known proposal deals with elementary and secondary education. In this plan people of all income groups receive vouchers, so they could "shop around" for the school that would most meet their needs. A school system would therefore be converted from a monopoly producer of standardized educational services to a competitive marketplace where schools can differentiate their products in order to attract students. Advocates of vouchers argue that competition will improve the performance of schools.

This scheme has serious problems. Besides threatening a major upheaval of school systems and forcing schools into intense and perhaps counterproductive competition, critics contend that it will not solve the equity problem. Indeed, if students who are enrolled at private schools are included, the plan can result in the middle class and rich benefitting disproportionately. Furthermore, the most successful schools will probably have their choice of students and may be able to exclude poor and minority students. Finally, voucher plans rarely allow students to cross school system boundaries. This means that familiar disparities between city and suburban service would likely persist. (For additional discussion of vouchers, see Chapter 14.)

The Problem of Bureaucrat Bashing.

Public choice theory challenges the role of civil servants in the policy process. According to public choice theory, ambitious bureaucrats use expertise to expand their budgets and secure higher salaries and promotions. Public choice theorists contend that bureaucrats are not passive instruments of political officials or motivated by the public interest; they have expansionary motives that stimulate the growth of government and its expenditures. The oft-recommended solution is to place more levels of political appointees between elected officials and career civil servants, decreasing civil servants' participation in the policy process.[153]

A second implication of public choice theory is that the best and the brightest workers should be channeled away from government service into the private sector, where wealth is created. Some argue that because the civil service creates no wealth, it should be composed of adequately skilled, trained, and motivated employees, not the best and the brightest.[154] One way to assure this outcome—and to save money—is to suppress the salaries and benefits of the civil service relative to those of the private sector.

A way to achieve both these ends has been to engage in what critics call bureaucrat bashing. This is criticizing the bureaucracy for alleged abuses of power, incompetence, fraud, waste, and abuse. Such accusations rationalize several practices that downgrade the career civil service and decrease the attractiveness of civil service careers: (1) increasing the number of political appointees to control career employees; (2) eroding civil service salaries and benefits; and (3) channeling as much public-sector work as possible to private firms.

Undoubtedly the most provocative part of this strategy lies in the argument that the best and brightest should be steered away from government and toward the private sector, where wealth is created. This reasoning overlooks the contribution of public employees to creation of wealth through the stable infrastructure of national defense, scientific and technical knowledge, and government housekeeping functions within which the private sector can operate.[155] The proposal to separate government work from activities that contribute to GNP would diminish the significance of government functions. Even in the constricted concept of government held by economic conservatives like Milton Friedman, the environment for creation of wealth requires certain minimum governmental functions such as national defense, an efficient revenue-raising system, skillful diplomacy, and sound currency.[156] Liberals extend this list substantially, but the important point is that a model of government based first on a rigid division between public and private sectors and second on the presumption of a marginally competent government work force simple misreads the current and likely future role of government—and its work force—in increasingly complex and interdependent economic systems.

The Third Party Problem.   The major policy contribution of public choice theory to government in the 1980s was the broad concept of *privatization*. Public choice theory argues that forms of privatization would:

1. Lessen the perverse outcomes of individual bureaucrats acting in their self-interest
2. Create businesslike practices within public agencies
3. Promote competition for contracts
4. Turn government programs over to private companies to increase their operating efficiency

In the two most commonly used forms of privatization, contracting out and grants, government decides whether to provide services, and the private sector (or a nonprofit entity) actually produces and delivers them.

Critics contend that this is hardly novel because it describes a fundamental change occurring in government action since the early 1950s—without the help of public choice or orthodox public administration theory. Indeed, Lester Salamon has argued that the field of public administration has become increasingly out of touch with the operation of the public sector.[157] The concepts and mind-sets of the field have lagged behind the changes. He goes on to argue that the old concepts do not even examine the right units of analysis. Salamon's major point is that federal programs and activities, and increasingly state and local ones, come in a wide variety of forms. The real issue is the number of types and forms of government action and the different mechanisms they use. Many of these mechanisms are quite different from each other, but these differences have not been explored. Shifting the focus of public administration away from agencies and programs onto the tools of government action, Salamon argues, produces a new view of government operations (see Chapter 3).

According to Salamon, each instrument has its own political economy—its own characteristics, procedures, network of organizational relationships, and skill requirements. For example, a loan guarantee program requires credit judgment, estimates of payback potentials, foreclosures, and linkages with banks and financiers. In contrast, a regulation is a set of rules prescribing proper behavior, enforcement agents, and penalties. Each has its own actors and actions. Many of these tools (for example loans and loan guarantees), though quite large, do not appear in the federal budget and so escape attention.[158]

Each substantive federal area has not just many programs but different forms of assistance. At the state and local level, special authorities borrow more than governments do for capital construction, and city governments contract out a variety of services. Over the past forty years there has been a proliferation of ways to take public action, a widespread and often ingenious surge of innovation.

The forms of government action are not just more numerous. Many of the new tools of government action share a common characteristic: They are *indirect;* nonfederal third parties—states, cities, banks, corporations, hospitals, nonprofit organizations—operate them. While federal expenditures increased fourfold in real dollars, federal employment increased just 50 percent from 1950 to 1978.[159] Salamon notes that the federal government increasingly operates by proxy. It turns to other institutions to deliver the services it funds. Grants-in-aid are a classic example. They have increased thirtyfold from 1955 to 1980, while total federal spending increased only eightfold.[160] The key point is that grants-in-aid make pursuit of federal purposes dependent on the good offices of state and local officials.

Salamon has observed that use of third party instruments has become so widespread it is sometimes difficult to figure out who is doing what. Tracing the flow of funds and delivery of human services in local areas reveals that most services government pays for are delivered not by government agencies but by private nonprofit and commercial organizations.[161]

Third party government is not merely the contracting of specific activities or purchases from outside suppliers; it shares a more basic government function: *exercise of discretion over the use of public authority and the spending of public funds.* For example, the availability of loan guarantees depends on the decisions of local bankers to participate and how they interpret qualifications of applicants for loans. The Small Business Administration found it difficult to get bankers to make guarantees available. The concept of third party government makes it clear that while power is flowing in from the sides, it is also going out the bottom, as agencies surrender controls to third parties.[162]

Several problems with third party government cause management headaches. Because it blurs the distinction between the public and private sectors and creates shared authority, public managers must create and coordinate complex networks of actors and institutions over which they have limited control. Accountability becomes a problem, and coordination is made difficult by the proliferation of tools. The responsibility to manage cannot be contracted away. Third party government has contributed to the steady decline in the federal blue-collar work force, since fewer employees are needed for direct provision of services. The percentage of civil servants rated GS9 or higher increased from 40.8 in 1967 to 50.4 in 1983. Increasingly federal civil servants manage third parties instead of producing services themselves.[163]

Donald Kettl has observed that traditional public administration theory is disturbed by the lack of a hierarchy or unity of command when service providers belong primarily to organizations outside government. He argues that management of public policy depends more on coordination among organizations both public and private than on control of employees within government. This presents three fundamental problems for public managers: (1) bearing responsibility without control, (2) obtaining leverage on third parties, and (3) ensuring that third parties remain responsive to elected officials.[164]

Kettl adds that some of the government's responses to these problems are more harmful than helpful. One is the "regulatory/recentralization reflex." As third party government is a decentralizing process, recentralization can be an automatic response, although centralization, has its own set of problems.

Third party strategies require different approaches, particularly movement beyond traditional notions of authority and hierarchy. Kettl notes four issues that dominate the challenge to modern public administration:

1. The growth of third party instruments has dealt a blow to the concept of neutral competence. As federal administrators broker services between elected officials and third-party producers, their role is to reconcile differences in values.
2. How can government ensure the old goals under new conditions?
3. Government by third parties has tied federal, state, and local governments more tightly; the private sector becomes less private as government's activities increase.
4. Third party government produces a more complex policy system, promoting the power of those who can understand and operate in a complex environment.

It also may produce partnerships of distant administrators and outside contractors. In contrast to public choice expectations, Kettl notes that these two factors may in fact discourage citizen participation.[165]

The Future of Public Choice Theory

Despite its conceptual and operational problems, the future of public choice theory seems very bright from both an academic and political point of view. Public choice theory is gaining more academic adherents, and their research articles are no longer consigned exclusively to journals specializing in public choice. They also can be found in such general journals as the *American Political Science Review* and the *Public Administration Review*. In addition, concepts from other branches of organizational economics are mixing and merging with public choice ideas to produce new legitimacy.[166] One sign of the new status of public choice theory occurred in 1986, when James Buchanan, one of the field's pioneers, received the Nobel Prize in economics.

Public choice theory has also arrived politically. Almost from its inception, its critiques of government spending and bureaucratic practices won the support of conservatives. The nation's fiscal problems created a policy environment in which many proposals for less costly service arrangements won attention from all bands of the political spectrum. Thus, the Reagan administration promoted public choice ideas, and many states and localities with democratic leadership have embraced, adopted, and considered service delivery systems that came out of the theoretical framework of public choice.[167] The nation's fiscal problems are unlikely to disappear in the near future, so one can expect even more pure privatization, contracting out, and user fees. This will not occur without complications for practitioners and theorists in public administration.

Public Organization Theory: Retrospect and Prospect

If the oldest question to intrigue students of politics is how to organize a government, the second oldest must be how to organize government's work. The first question has been the province of political theorists from ancient times. Political theory is a field whose relevance remains obvious and contemporary. The second question has generally been addressed by administrative practitioners, who mostly prefer to act rather than write. Thus one can unearth little historical record of their theories. This intellectual division of labor has continued to the present, although around the turn of this century a few practitioners began to write down their theories of the best ways to do the work of government.

The immediate impetus for the growth of interest in organization to accomplish government's tasks was the growth of the administrative state in the early twentieth century and particularly the requirements of a complex war. From about 1900 through the mid-1950s, some of the finest minds in American and European social science turned their attention to government organization and management. Their theories became guiding doctrine for the creation and reorganization of a burgeoning bureaucracy. The purpose of administrative theory was to assist lawmakers and practitioners in running the modern state.

In the United States the field of public administration flourished between roughly the close of World War I and the publication of the reports of the second Hoover commission in 1955. In that era there was a consensus that the public and private sectors had distinctive characteristics and roles and that these distinctions had both a legal and a political basis. There was also general agreement on how a government ought to be organized, and this agreement was reflected in both the Brownlow and first Hoover commission reports. Scholars and practitioners worked together for mutual support. Some nostalgically recall these decades as the golden years.[168]

That culture of consensus and shared purposes began to unravel in the mid-1950s. The prevailing tenets of American public administration became targets of the emerging school of behavioral scientists. The field tried to accommodate this wave of criticism and in so doing entered a period of self-doubt and theoretical atrophy that continues to the present day. For some years, however, lawmakers continued to rely on concepts that the scholars in the field itself had generally abandoned. This intellectual capital, accumulated during the golden years, was fully expended by the mid-1970s, when lawmakers began to turn elsewhere for advice. This situation has prompted more than one political scientist to pronounce that public administration has become a scholarly wasteland, bereft of sophisticated research and meaningful theory.

In the late 1980s the traditional subject of concern to public administration—the organization of government's work—underwent substantial change. Some responsibility for this change rests with the Reagan administration. By setting new conservative policy for the way government and the private sector produce goods and services, the Reagan administration established the legitimacy of dialogue about the essential features of the American administrative state. Thus, by promoting supply-side economics, deregulation, the contracting out of government operations, and privatization, the Reagan administration both explicitly and implicitly questioned what government should do, how it should do it, and who should do it. So far the debate surrounding these issues has been remarkably one-sided, with conservatives flaying what they perceive to be an outdated and misguided administrative orthodoxy and the public administration community standing mostly silent on all but the narrowest technical aspects of the conservative proposals for change.[169]

The asymmetry of the debate is not a function of politeness or political cunning on the part of the public administration community. Rather, it reflects that those most directly involved in the operations of government have no well-formulated and well-integrated doctrine about the proper scope and functions of the state in the contemporary world. In the 1980s free market economists and public choice theorists, who are not shy about proposing solutions to public policy problems, have willingly filled this theoretical vacuum. These latter groups consider that their theories have universal applicability and sometimes present impressive empirical evidence. Public administrators generally find themselves unable to cite any general theory to defend the traditional ways of doing the work of government and thus have found to their dismay that persons unfamiliar with and unsympathetic to their concerns control the agenda for public administration. Despite this gloomy and confused situation, there is opportunity for scholars to rebuild the field's theoretical base. Indeed, there is reason to believe that in the next decade the so-called wasteland is likely to be fertile ground for exciting new research and theories. A theoretical departure is likely to combine several ideas to address both old and new problems of the administrative state.

The first step toward reconstructing a theory of public administration is to recognize that the world has changed, probably irreversibly. In the 1980s alone the verities that sustained the old public administration orthodoxy came undone. Today we live in a complex market-oriented world in which the ability of nations to insulate themselves from outside competition is severely limited. This competition is not just between the private sectors of the respective countries, but between governments as well.

In addition to recognizing both the universal and particular elements of American public administration, some scholars have argued that to reconstruct American public administration theory it is necessary to return to certain basics of the field.[170] The proper foundation for public administration, they contend, lies in its public law tradition and not in the traditions of social psychology, sociology, or economics.

Such an orientation, they argue, would provide the basis for normative judgments by political leaders. To do so it would have to answer several questions central to the field:

- What are the distinctive features and character of public and private organizations? Are they really alike in all unimportant respects? To which sector and what kinds of organizations should public functions be assigned?
- What are the differences between politics and administration? Which jobs in government should political appointees perform and which jobs should career civil servants handle?
- Does the structure of organizations make a difference in their performance? Do the degrees of centralization, hierarchy, formalization, and task specialization affect the performance of government and its agencies? Do reorganizations solve more problems than they create?
- Is the organization the right focus of analysis? Can we understand the modern administrative state as a single unit, or must we view it as a highly complex network of loosely coupled and tightly joined relationships among federal agencies; state, local, and special district entities; and domestic and foreign private-sector and nonprofit organizations? If so, how do we control and coordinate this system?

Answering these questions with surety and authority is by no means easy, but it is necessary. Without such answers the executive branch will continue to change its structure and function without any overarching logic or theory to guide its development, and this process will have its costs. Lines of responsibility and accountability blur. The line between public authority and private rights will continue to tangle as delegations of authority become more confused. And private parties will be the dispensers of more public funds.

While the drive for policy and organizational autonomy has been a trait of government since the inception of the republic, this drive has generally been countered by the tendency of presidents and agencies to strive for centralized supervision and a hierarchical executive branch. For going on two decades, however, the centrifugal tendencies of the bureaucracy and political process have not been effectively balanced by the centripetal tendencies of the institutional presidency.[171]

Trenchant centrifugal forces, along with the inability of public administration theorists to provide a firm intellectual basis for countering them, have issued a severe challenge to management. While the administrative presidency often looms large (see Chapter 5), much organizational and management authority has shifted to Congress, the courts, and private parties. Throughout this dispersal of power, students and practitioners of public administration have often been passive bystanders; they lack an institutional advocate for a coherent theory of management. Consider the Office of Management and Budget, once the preeminent managerial arm of the president. Lamenting this state of affairs, the National Academy of Public Administration concluded in 1983 that "while OMB continues to be capable of occasional excellent performance, it has irretrievably lost its overall effectiveness as government-wide leader in management matters."[172]

Conclusion

For nearly three decades, the field of public administration has generally been silent on the subject of executive branch organization and management. Insofar as it has an accepted position on the subject it is that the government ought to look to the private sector for guidance. That posture is not sufficient and may in fact be wrongheaded to the point of danger.

Still, these developments suggest that the next decade will be an especially exciting time for public administration theorists. They have the opportunity to redesign their discipline and possibly their government. As the rise of public choice theory indicates, if they cannot do it, there are plenty of others ready to do it for them. Thus the task at hand is urgent.

There is another reason for optimism about public organization theory. Nearly thirty years ago Dwight Waldo observed that the disarray in organization theory resembled "three blind men trying to describe an elephant."[173] While that may suggest that developing a theory of public organizations is a hopelessly confusing problem, one can give another, more optimistic interpretation of the situation. As Herbert Simon aptly notes: "Science, like all creative activity, is exploration, gambling, and adventure. It does not lend itself very well to neat blueprints, detailed road maps, and central planning. Perhaps that's why it's fun."[174]

Notes

1. Barbara S. Romzek and Melvin J. Dubnick, "Accountability in the Public Sector: Lessons from the *Challenger* Tragedy." *Public Administration Review* 47 (May-June 1987): 227–38; *Report of the Presidential Commission on the Space Shuttle* Challenger *Accident*, (Washington, DC: 6 June 1986).
2. See Allen Schick, "Coming Apart in Public Administration." *Maxwell Review* 10 (Winter 1973–74): 13–24.
3. Dwight Waldo, "Scope of the Theory of Public Administration," in James C. Charlesworth, ed., *Theory and Practice of Public Administration: Scope, Objectives, and Methods* (Philadelphia: American Academy of Political and Social Science, 1968), 1–26.
4. Fred W. Riggs, *Administration in Developing Areas* (Boston: Houghton Mifflin, 1964).
5. See, for example, Herbert A. Simon, *Administrative Behavior: A Study of Decision-Making Processes in Administrative Organization,* 2d ed. (New York: Free Press, 1957); Charles E. Lindblom, "The Science of Muddling Through." *Public Administration Review* 19 (January-February 1959): 79–88; Aaron Wildavsky, *The Politics of the Budgetary Process* (Boston: Little, Brown, 1964); Martin Landau, "The Concept of Decisionmaking in the Field of Public Administration," in Sidney Mailick and Edward H. Van Ness, eds., *Concepts and Issues in Administrative Behavior* (Englewood Cliffs, NJ: Prentice-Hall, 1962).
6. John J. Gargan, "The Public Administration Community and the Search for Professionalism" (unpublished manuscript), 24 November 1987, 62.
7. Ibid.
8. Peter Savage, "Contemporary Public Administration: The Changing Environment

and Agenda," in Dwight Waldo, ed., *Public Administration in a Time of Turbulence* (Scranton, PA: Chandler Publishing, 1971), 46.

9. See, for example, Frederick C. Thayer, *An End to Hierarchy and Competition: Administration in the Post-Affluent World,* 2d ed. (New York: Franklin Watts, 1981); Orion J. White, Jr., "Organization and Administration for New Technological and Social Imperatives," in Waldo, *Public Administration in a Time of Turbulence,* 151–68.
10. See Gargan, "The Public Administration Community and the Search for Professionalism."
11. Felix A. Nigro and Lloyd G. Nigro, *Modern Public Administration,* 6th ed. (New York: Harper & Row, 1984), 160–1.
12. A. H. Maslow, *Motivation and Personality* (New York: Harper & Brothers, 1954), 88.
13. Ibid., 92.
14. Ibid., 83–4.
15. Warren G. Bennis, *Changing Organizations* (New York: McGraw-Hill, 1966), 74.
16. A. H. Maslow, *Eupsychian Management* (Homewood, IL: Richard D. Irwin, 1965), 55.
17. Chris Argyris, *Personality and Organization* (New York: Harper & Brothers, 1957), 229.
18. Chris Argyris, "The Individual and Organization: Some Problems of Mutual Adjustment." *Administrative Science Quarterly* 2 (1957): 20–2.
19. Argyris, *Personality and Organization,* 230.
20. Chris Argyris, *Integrating the Individual and the Organization* (New York: John Wiley & Sons, 1964), 216.
21. Ibid., 216–20.
22. Ibid., 274.
23. Ibid., 273–7.
24. Douglas McGregor, *The Human Side of Enterprise* (New York: McGraw-Hill, 1960), 6–8.
25. Douglas McGregor, "The Human Side of Enterprise." *The Management Review* (November 1957), 23.
26. Ibid., 23.
27. Ibid., 27–8, 88.
28. Ibid., 89.
29. McGregor, *The Human Side of Enterprise,* 47–8.
30. Ibid., 50–6.
31. Ibid., 246.
32. Rensis Likert, *New Patterns of Management* (New York: McGraw-Hill, 1961), 103.
33. Ibid., 90–5.
34. Ibid., 98–9.
35. Ibid., 166–9.
36. Ibid., 170–2.
37. Ibid., 113–6.
38. David Silverman, *The Theory of Organization* (New York: Basic Books, Inc., 1971), 83–4.
39. Warren G. Bennis, *American Bureaucracy* (Chicago: Aldine Publishing, 1970), 7.
40. Warren G. Bennis, *Changing Organizations* (New York: McGraw-Hill, 1966), 10.
41. Ibid., 21.
42. Ibid., 19.

43. Ibid., 54.

44. Ibid., 50–5.

45. Frederick Herzberg, "The Motivation-Hygiene Concept and Problems of Manpower." *Personnel Administration* 2 (1964): 3.

46. Frederick Herzberg, *Work and the Nature of Man* (New York: Thomas Y. Crowell, 1966), 74–80.

47. See H. George Frederickson, "Toward a New Public Administration," in Frank Marini, ed., *Toward a New Public Administration* (Scranton, PA: Chandler Publishing, 1971), 304–31; "The Lineage of New Public Administration," in Carl J. Bellone, ed., *Organization Theory and the New Public Administration* (Boston: Allyn and Bacon, 1980), 33–51; *New Public Administration* (University, AL: University of Alabama Press, 1980).

48. Frederickson, "The Lineage of New Public Administration," 49.

49. Todd R. LaPorte, "The Recovery of Relevance in the Study of Public Organizations," in Marini, ed., *Toward a New Public Administration,* 17–48.

50. Peter Savage, "Contemporary Public Administration: The Changing Environment and Agenda," in Waldo, ed., *Public Administration in a Time of Turbulence,* 48.

51. Frederickson, "Toward a New Public Administration," 331.

52. Ibid., 329.

53. See, for example, Alan K. Campbell, "Old and New Public Administration in the 1970's," *Public Administration Review* 32 (May-June 1972): 343–7; York Wilbern, "Is the New Public Administration Still with Us?" *Public Administration Review* 33 (May-June 1973): 373–8; and Victor A. Thompson, *Without Sympathy or Enthusiasm: The Problem of Administrative Compassion* (University, AL: The University of Alabama Press, 1975).

54. See John Gargan, "The Public Administration Community and the Search for Professionalism," 64.

55. See, for example, Robert Golembiewski, *Public Administration As a Developing Discipline: Perspectives on Past and Present* (New York: Marcel Dekker, 1977), especially Chapter 4.

56. Gargan, "The Public Administration Community and the Search for Professionalism," 65.

57. Don Mankin et al., eds., *Classics of Industrial and Organizational Psychology* (Oak Park, IL: Moore Publishing Company, 1980), "Introduction to Section V," 227.

58. Ibid., 228.

59. Ibid.

60. For reviews of this literature see Marvin D. Dunnette, ed., *Handbook of Industrial and Organizational Psychology* (Chicago: Rand McNally, 1976).

61. Orlando Behling and Chester Schriesheim, *Organizational Behavior: Theory, Research and Application* (Boston: Allyn and Bacon, 1976), 315.

62. Ibid., 196; see also Ralph M. Stogdill, "Personal Factors Associated with Leadership: A Survey of the Literature," *The Journal of Psychology* 25 (1948): 35–72.

63. Behling and Schriesheim, *Organizational Behavior,* 298; see also C.L. Shurttle, "Introduction," in Ralph M. Stogdill and A. E. Coons, eds., *Leader Behavior: Its Description and Measurement* (Columbus, OH: The Ohio State University, Bureau of Business Research, 1957).

64. Behling and Schriesheim, *Organizational Behavior;* see also Robert L. Kahn and Daniel Katz, "Leadership Practices in Relation to Productivity and Morale," in Dowrin Cartwright and Alvin F. Zander, eds., *Group Dynamics,* 2d ed. (Evanston, IL: Row, Peterson, 1960).

65. Behling and Schriesheim, *Organizational Behavior,* 313; for an outstanding overview of leadership research see Ralph M. Stogdill, *Handbook of Leadership* (New York: The Free Press, 1974).

66. Robert T. Golembiewski, "The Basic Approaches to Organizational Phenomena: Insularities and Interfaces," in Golembiewski, ed., *Approaches to Organizing* (Washington, DC: American Society for Public Administration, 1981), 1–23.

67. Wendell L. French and Cecil H. Bell, Jr., *Organization Development* (Englewood Cliffs, NJ: Prentice-Hall, 1973), 15.

68. See Samuel Culbert and Jerome Reisel, "Organization Development: An Applied Philosophy for Managers of Public Enterprise." *Public Administration Review* 31 (March-April 1971): 161.

69. Ibid.

70. Ibid.

71. Warren G. Bennis, *Organization Development: Its Nature, Origins, and Prospects* (Reading, MA: Addison-Wesley, 1969), 15.

72. Golembiewski, "Three Basic Approaches to Organizational Phenomena," 14.

73. Ibid., 15–6; see also Robert T. Golembiewski, "Organization Development in Public Agencies: Perspectives on Theory and Practice." *Public Administration Review* 29 (July-August 1969): 367–8.

74. Waldo, "Scope of the Theory of Public Administration," 4.

75. See, for example, Barry Bozeman, *All Organizations Are Public: Bridging Public and Private Organizational Theories,* (San Francisco, CA: Jossey-Bass Publishers, 1987).

76. Richard J. Stillman, *Public Administration,* 3d ed. (Boston: Houghton Mifflin, 1984), 452.

77. Graham T. Allison, "Public and Private Management: Are They Fundamentally Alike in All Unimportant Respects?" in Stillman, ed., *Public Administration,* 453.

78. See Gerald E. Caiden, *The Dynamics of Public Administration* (Hinsdale, IL: Dryden Press, 1971).

79. The remainder of this section draws extensively from Hal G. Rainey et al., "Comparing Public and Private Organizations." *Public Administration Review* 36 (March-April 1976): 234.

80. Louis C. Gawthorp, *Administrative Politics and Social Change* (New York: St. Martin's Press, 1971).

81. Murray L. Weidenbaum, *The Modern Public Sector: New Ways of Doing the Government's Business* (New York: Basic Books, 1969).

82. John Kenneth Galbraith, *Economics and the Public Purpose* (Boston: Houghton Mifflin, 1973).

83. Luther Gulick and Al Urwick, eds., *Papers on the Science of Administration* (New York: Institute of Public Administration, 1937).

84. Allison, "Public and Private Management: Are They Fundamentally Alike in All Unimportant Respects?", 455–6.

85. Gary L. Wamsley and Mayer N. Zald, *The Political Economy of Public Organizations* (Lexington, MA: D. C. Heath, 1973), 63.

86. Armen A. Alchian, "Cost Effectiveness of Cost Effectiveness," in Stephen Enke, ed., *Defense Management* (Englewood Cliffs, NJ: Prentice-Hall, 1967), 74–86; Jesse Burkhead and Jerry Miner, *Public Expenditure* (Chicago: Aldine, 1971); Robert A. Dahl and Charles E. Lindblom, *Politics, Economics, and Welfare* (New York: Harper & Row, 1953); Robert A. Levine, "Redesigning Social Systems," in Erich Jantsch, ed., *Perspectives on Planning* (Paris: Organization for Economic Cooperation and Development, 1969), 449–69; William A. Niskanen, Jr., *Bureaucracy and Representative Government* (Chicago: Aldine, 1971); and Charles L.

Schultze, "The Role of Incentives, Penalties, and Rewards in Attaining Effective Policy," in R. Haveman and J. Margolis, eds., *Public Expenditures and Policy Analysis* (Chicago: Markham Publishing Co., 1970), 145–72.

87. Rainey et al., "Comparing Public and Private Organizations," 235.

88. Dahl and Lindblom, *Politics, Economics, and Welfare;* Peter Drucker, "Managing the Public Service Institution." *The Public Interest* 33 (Fall 1973): 43–60; Niskanen, *Bureaucracy and Representative Government;* and J.A. Stockfish, *The Political Economy of Bureaucracy* (New York: General Learning Press, 1972).

89. Robert L. Bish and Vincent Ostrom, *Understanding Urban Government* (Washington, DC: American Enterprise Institute for Public Policy Research, 1973); Harley H. Hinrichs and Graeme M. Taylor, *Systematic Analysis* (Pacific Palisades, CA: Goodyear Publishing Co., 1972); Vincent Ostrom, *The Intellectual Crisis in American Public Administration* (University, AL: University of Alabama Press, 1973).

90. Burkhead and Miner, *Public Expenditure;* Dahl and Lindblom, *Politics, Economics, and Welfare;* Anthony Downs, *Inside Bureaucracy* (Boston: Little, Brown, 1967); John D. Millet, *Organization for the Public Service* (Princeton, NJ: D. Van Nostrand, 1966), 10ff; O. Glenn Stahl, *Public Personnel Administration* (New York: Harper & Row, 1971).

91. Edward C. Banfield, "Corruption as a Feature of Governmental Organization," *Journal of Law and Economics* 20(July, 1977): 587–605.

92. Robert T. Golembiewski, "Organization Development in Public Agencies: Perspective on Theory and Practice," 367–8; Lewis C. Mainzer, *Political Bureaucracy* (Glenview, IL: Scott, Foresman, 1973), 14ff.

93. Dahl and Lindblom, *Politics, Economics, and Welfare*.

94. Allison, "Public and Private Management: Are They Fundamentally Alike in All Unimportant Respects?", 457.

95. Charlesworth, ed., *Theory and Practice of Public Administration: Scope, Objectives, and Methods;* Dahl and Lindblom, *Politics, Economics, and Welfare*.

96. Banfield, "Corruption as a Feature of Governmental Organization"; Caiden, *Dynamics of Public Administration;* Theodore Lowi, *The End of Liberalism* (New York: Norton, 1969); Mainzer, *Political Bureaucracy;* O. Glenn Stahl, *Public Personnel Administration;* Weidenbaum, *The Modern Public Sector: New Ways of Doing the Government's Business*.

97. Rainey et al., "Comparing Public and Private Organizations," 239.

98. Paul H. Appleby, *Big Democracy* (New York: Alfred A. Knopf, 1945).

99. Wamsley and Zald, *The Political Economy of Public Organizations*.

100. Banfield, "Corruption as a Feature of Governmental Organization."

101. Herman L. Weiss, "Why Business and Government Exchange Executives." *Harvard Business Review* (July-August 1974): 129–40.

102. Banfield, "Corruption as a Feature of Governmental Organization."

103. Rainey et al., "Comparing Public and Private Organizations," 239.

104. Ibid.

105. Ibid.

106. Ibid., 239–41.

107. Appleby, *Big Democracy;* Mainzer, *Political Bureaucracy;* E. S. Savas, "Municipal Monopolies Versus Competition in Delivering Services," in Willis D. Hawley and David Rogers, eds., *Improving the Quality of Urban Management* (Beverly Hills, CA: Sage, 1974), 473–500; Harold Seidman, *Politics, Position, and Power* (New York: Oxford University Press, 1970).

108. Rainey et al., "Comparing Public and Private Organizations," 240.

109. Ibid.
110. Banfield, "Corruption as a Feature of Governmental Organization"; Bruce Buchanan II, "Government Managers, Business Executives, and Organizational Commitment," *Public Administration Review* 35 (July-August 1975): 339–47; and Gawthorp, *Administrative Politics and Social Change.*
111. Bish and Ostrom, *Understanding Urban Government.*
112. Stockfish, *The Political Economy of Bureaucracy.*
113. Henry Mintzberg, *The Nature of Managerial Work* (New York: Harper and Row, 1973).
114. Dahl and Lindblom, *Politics, Economics, and Welfare.*
115. Downs, *Inside Bureaucracy.*
116. Golembiewski, "Organization Development in Public Agencies: Perspectives on Theory and Practice."
117. Weidenbaum, *The Modern Public Sector: New Ways of Doing the Government's Business.*
118. Schultze, "The Role of Incentives, Penalties and Rewards in Attaining Effective Policy," 145–72.
119. Banfield, "Corruption as a Feature of Governmental Organization."
120. James R. Rawls et al., "A Comparison of Managers Entering or Reentering the Profit and Non-Profit Sectors." *Academy of Management Journal* 18 (September 1975): 616–22.
121. See, for example, Hal G. Rainey, "Public Agencies and Private Firms: Incentive Structures, Goals, and Individual Roles." *Administration and Society* 15 (August 1983): 207–42; and James L. Perry and Hal G. Rainey, "The Public-Private Distinction in Organization Theory: A Critique and Research Strategy," paper presented at the annual meeting of the American Political Science Association, the New Orleans Hilton, 30 August 1986.
122. Rainey et al., "Comparing Public and Private Organizations," 242.
123. Bozeman, *All Organizations are Public.*
124. See James G. March and Johan P. Olsen, *Ambiguity and Choice in Organizations* (Bergen, Norway: Universitetsforlaget, 1976).
125. John W. Kingdon, *Agendas, Alternatives and Public Policies* (Boston: Little, Brown, 1984); Nelson W. Polsby, *Political Innovation in America: The Politics of Policy Initiation* (New Haven: Yale University Press, 1984).
126. See, for example, Kenneth R. MacCrimmon and Donald N. Taylor, "Decision Making and Problem Solving," in Dunnette, *Handbook of Industrial and Organizational Psychology,* 1397–454; and R. Duncan Luce and Howard Raiffa, *Games and Decisions: Introduction and Critical Survey* (New York: John Wiley and Sons, 1957).
127. See Patricia W. Ingraham and Carolyn Ban, eds., *Legislating Bureaucratic Change: The Civil Service Reform Act of 1978* (Albany: State University of New York Press, 1984).
128. See, for example, Barton Wechsler and Robert W. Backoff, "Policy Making and Administration in State Agencies: Strategic Management Approaches." *Public Administration Review* 46 (September-October 1986): 321–7; Peter Ring and James L. Perry, "Strategic Management in Public and Private Organizations: Implications of Distinctive Contexts and Constraints." *Academy of Management Review* 10 (1985): 176–286.
129. See Aaron Wildavsky, *The Politics of the Budgetary Process* (Boston: Little, Brown, 1979).
130. Allison, "Public and Private Management," 465.

131. Ibid.

132. George W. Downs and Patrick D. Larkey, *The Search for Government Efficiency: From Hubris to Helplessness* (New York: Random House, 1986).

133. See Ronald D. Moe, "Exploring the Limits of Privatization." *Public Administration Review* 47 (November-December 1987): 456.

134. Keith G. Baker, "Public Choice Theory: Some Important Assumptions and Public Policy Implications," in Robert T. Golembiewski, et al., eds., *Public Administration: Readings in Institutions, Processes, Behavior, Policy* (New York: Rand McNally, 1976), 41–60.

135. Vincent Ostrom and Elinor Ostrom, "Public Choice: A Different Approach to the Study of Public Administration." *Public Administration Review* 31 (March-April 1971): 203.

136. Ibid., 205.

137. Peter C, Ordeshook, *Game Theory and Political Theory* (New York: Cambridge University Press, 1986).

138. Gordon Tullock, *The Politics of Bureaucracy* (Washington, DC: Public Affairs Press, 1965), 26.

139. Ostrom and Ostrom, "Public Choice," 204.

140. Vincent Ostrom, *The Intellectual Crisis in American Public Administration* (University, AL: University of Alabama Press, 1974), 48.

141. Ibid.

142. See E. S. Savas, *Privatizing the Public Sector* (Chatham, NJ: Chatham House, 1982).

143. William A. Niskanen, *Bureaucracy and Representative Government* (Chicago: Aldine-Atherton, 1971).

144. See, for example, Tullock, *The Politics of Bureaucracy;* Anthony Downs, *Inside Bureaucracy* (Boston: Little, Brown, 1967).

145. Gordon Tullock, *Private Wants, Public Means: An Economic Analysis of the Desirable Scope of Government* (New York: Basic Books, 1970).

146. A review of this literature is found in Patricia M. Patterson, "Foundations for a Social Choice Theory of Bureaucratic Decision-Making," unpublished paper, The American University, 20 November 1987; see also Albert Breton and Ronald Wintrobe, "The Equilibrium Size of a Budget Maximizing Bureau: A Note on Niskanen's Theory of Bureaucracy." *Journal of Political Economy* 83 (1975): 195–207.

147. Vincent Ostrom, "Structure and Performance," in Vincent Ostrom and Francis P. Bish, eds., *Comparing Urban Service Delivery Systems: Structure and Performance* (Beverly Hills, CA: Sage Publications, 1977), 35–6.

148. Gargan, "The Public Administration Community and the Search for Professionalism," 69–70.

149. Louis F. Weschler, "Public Choice: Methodological Individualism in Politics." *Public Administration Review* 42 (May-June 1982): 288–94.

150. Terry M. Moe, "On the Scientific Status of Rational Models." *American Journal of Political Science* 23 (February 1979): 237.

151. Ibid.

152. See Thomas DeGregori, "Caveat Emptor: A Critique of the Emerging Paradigm of Public Choice." *Administration and Society* 6 (1974), 205–28.

153. See Patricia W. Ingraham, "Building Bridges or Burning Them? The President, the Appointees, and the Bureaucracy." *Public Administration Review* 47 (September-October 1987): 425–435.

154. See Terry W. Culler, "Most Federal Workers Need Only Be Competent," *The Wall Street Journal,* 21 May 1986, 33.

155. See Elliot L. Richardson, "Civil Servants: Why Not the Best," *The Wall Street Journal,* 20 November 1987, 32.

156. Milton Friedman, *Capitalism and Freedom* (Chicago: University of Chicago Press, 1962).

157. Lester M. Salamon, "The Rise of Third-Party Government: Implications for Public Management," in Donald F. Kettl, ed, *Third-Party Government and the Public Manager: The Changing Forms of Government Action* (Washington, D.C.: National Academy of Public Administration, 1987).

158. Ibid, 7–9.

159. Ibid, 12.

160. Ibid, 14.

161. Ibid, 15–6.

162. Ibid, 18.

163. Donald F. Kettl, "Performance and Accountability: The Challenge to Public Administration," in Kettl, ed., *Third-Party Government and the Public Manager,* 34.

164. Ibid, 40.

165. Ibid, 50.

166. See, for example, Jay B. Barney and William G. Ouchi, eds., *Organizational Economics* (San Francisco, CA: Jossey-Bass, 1986); more specifically Terry M. Moe, "The New Economics of Organization." *American Journal of Political Science* 28 (1984): 739–77.

167. See Savas, *Privatizing the Public Sector.*

168. For a discussion of the so-called golden age of public administration, see Frederick C. Mosher, *A Tale of Two Agencies: A Comparative Analysis of the General Accounting Office and the Office of Management and Budget* (Baton Rouge, LA: Louisiana State University Press, 1984).

169. For one notable exception to this general pattern see Charles T. Goodsell, "The Grace Commission: Seeking Efficiency for the Whole People?" *Public Administration Review* 44 (May-June 1984): 196–204.

170. Moe, "Exploring the Limits of Privatization."

171. Ibid.

172. National Academy of Public Administration, *Revitalizing Federal Management: Managers and Their Overburdened Systems* (Washington, DC: National Academy of Public Administration, 1983).

173. See Dwight Waldo, "Organization Theory: An Elephantine Problem." *Public Administration Review* 21 (Autumn 1961): 210–25; "Organization Theory: Revisiting the Elephant." *Public Administration Review* 38 (November-December 1978): 589–97.

174. Herbert A. Simon, "Approaching the Theory of Management," in Harold Kootz, ed., *Toward a Unified Theory of Management* (New York: McGraw-Hill, 1964), 85.

Part Four

Government Operations and Management

Introduction

This volume has marched along the continuum from macro to micro concerns. It has broached empirical and normative issues concerning the role of government in a mixed economy. It has reviewed the diverse organizational forms and tools endemic to federal programs and the dynamics of the policy process. It has probed the interstices of the relationship between politics and administration—the ways in which politics permeates administrative processes as well as the balance of administration, the rule of law, and ultimately democracy. The volume has reviewed the status of efforts to explain how large, complex organizations behave and why; it has assessed the capacity of public administration to advise government officials concerned with the efficiency, effectiveness, responsiveness, and accountability of organizations.

With this backdrop in place, the spotlight shifts to those who manage the daily operations of public programs. Although sometimes denigrated as "nuts and bolts" issues, these are crucial for the success of any agency. Congress may hand an agency the most innovative and exciting program ever devised, but if managers cannot hire capable personnel, find appropriate office space, or develop suitable information systems, failure probably awaits. Thus, managerial questions are important extensions of this volume's general concern with the effects of administration on policies and on society at large. In a nutshell, management makes a difference for who gets what from government. Just as the field of public administration must be able to speak to broad questions of design of organizations and programs as well as to the relationship of administration to politics, it must be able to address micro issues of management. How do public managers behave, and why? How can one improve management in government?

While, given available evidence, this section cannot provide definitive, finely honed answers to these questions, it can at least cast some light on them. Thus, this section describes the nature of managerial work and the four basic imperatives that do much to shape it—legal, consensual, programmatic, and personal. It also addresses certain challenges public executives face. The first challenge is a political culture that casts public managers in a negative light and thereby heightens risks of defensiveness, dependence, and defeatism. The second is technology—the particular problems that certain types of tasks tend to generate. The final challenge stems from the need to manage certain pivotal resources—authority, personnel, information, physical resources, and money.

Chapter Eleven

Federal Management in Perspective

Introduction

Ultimately, fundamental questions of policy, politics, and organization theory impinge on those who manage the day-to-day operations of government. Definitions of management vary. Seen in a general way, management can be characterized as whatever those formally in charge of organizations actually do. Defined somewhat more specifically, management is "the organization and direction of resources to achieve a desired result." This presumably involves responsibilities inside the organization to integrate the diverse contributions of specialized subunits; it also involves work outside to relate the organization to its suppliers, clientele, and environment.[1]

Useful as these definitions can be, they conjure up images of management as orderly, rational, even wooden. This view misleads. For instance, it hardly seems consistent with the frequency of generic politics (see Chapter 5). Indeed, the strategic aspects of administrative life have prompted some observers to portray government operations as a set of loosely interrelated games and successful public management as effective gamesmanship.[2] *Game* evokes notions of sundry players marshaling diverse resources and consciously plotting strategies in hopes of winning. Most games include an element of chance. A player may confront an unlucky roll of the dice and be dealt a bad hand.

Certain caveats are in order in thinking of the day-to-day operations of federal agencies as games, however. Unlike athletic contests or most board games, various players in federal games keep score in different ways. A manager at the Social Security Administration may define winning as getting to choose the computer system; another may gauge victory in terms of promotion.[3]

Participants in government games seldom can complete one game before moving on to another. Instead, the typical pattern is more like playing a large number of games all over the floor of a huge convention center. New games constantly get added; some games get removed.

Many contestants, especially high-level managers, rush from one game to the next every five or ten minutes. Phones at each table ring; allies urge the manager to join another game to overcome opponents who are taking advantage of his or her absence. The players at least implicitly sense the wisdom of Woody Allen's dictum, "Eighty percent of success is showing up."[4] Their problem is that they lack the time to participate in all the games. Unless the manager can adroitly assemble a team of like-minded supporters and coordinate their participation in the potpourri of games, contests in which the manager cannot steadily participate often get forfeited to those who invest more time in them. For an executive, Gresham's Law of Managerial Gamesmanship threatens: that is, less important games crowd out more significant ones. Given the many games taking place and the stream of new ones, the manager faces minimal prospects of winning them all.

As this imagery of disorderly gamesmanship suggests, managers can seldom concentrate on highly deliberate and rational problem solving. They usually confront diverse issues ranging from the trivial to the momentous and can devote only minutes to each. Furthermore, fragmentation tends to prevail; they cannot move smoothly from issue to issue but face constant interruptions and abrupt shifts of attention. Faced with unrelenting demands to deal with many matters, successful managers must become "proficient at superficiality."[5]

Consistent with this view, studies of successful managers indicate that they do not slavishly follow the rational model of decisionmaking—that is, they do not always clarify goals, formulate options, assess the likelihood that each will produce certain costs and benefits, make a decision, and then implement it. Instead, managers respond to considerable ambiguity by groping along with different combinations of approaches while attempting to gauge the results. Hunches, intuition, and gut feelings play a role in much managerial behavior. These factors are not arbitrary, metaphysical, or irrational but rather learned behavior sequences based on extensive practice and experience. Given the intuitive nature of much of their action, managers often know what is right before they can analyze and explain it. They act before they think; at times their preferences follow rather than precede behavior.[6]

Routines, or standard operating procedures, also greatly reduce the burdens of calculations for executives. Laws, administrative regulations, and organizational culture embed formal and informal decision rules that do much to guide behavior. Each month, for instance, the Social Security Administration routinely distributes billions of dollars according to a formula. The pervasiveness of routines means that major activities go on without senior executives paying much attention to them. Moreover, rules dictate the executive's behavior in many instances. Letters of inquiry from the public may, depending on their substance, evoke a programmed response. The executive may routinely refer them to a staff member or have a clerk type the appropriate form letter. The enormous importance of standard operating procedure in organizations points to the limits of the game metaphor in describing government operations and management. Much of a manager's day does not involve the conscious plotting of strategy and the artful assembly of winning coalitions.

Keeping these general qualities of management in mind, this chapter examines the context and character of federal management. Humility seems appropriate to this task. One seasoned observer of the academic literature on public management asserts that it consists mostly of "speculation tied to bits and pieces of evidence about the tail or the trunk or other manifestation of the proverbial elephant."[7] Clearly, social scientists have many miles to travel to describe and explain variations in the behavior of federal executives. Nonetheless, an observer can discern the broad contours of federal management along with certain factors that shape it.

This chapter first examines the major imperatives of senior career executives in the federal government—legal, consensual, programmatic, and career. It then considers three important challenges to senior executives who manage federal programs. The first challenge is a political culture that casts civil servants in a bad light. The second challenge springs from the diverse technologies federal executives confront. These technologies include regulatory, allocative, and inducement versions. A third challenge is the need to manage key resources effectively and efficiently. This chapter will discuss the uses and limits of one resource—formal authority.

While the chapter examines these imperatives and challenges from the perspective of senior federal managers, many of the observations also apply to state and local executives.

The Imperatives of Public Executives

Who are the career managers employed by the federal government? Approximately six thousand career executives populate the Senior Executive Service, the primary focus of this chapter. Another hundred ten thousand middle managers (GS13 to GS15) occupy the ranks just below the SES.[8] Many other civil servants handle lower management tasks, for instance, supervising employees at the bottom of the hierarchy. Career SES members spend more time on the specifics of managing government than do the political executives above them. They face fewer demands to testify before congressional committees, make public speeches, or otherwise provide liaison outside the agency. Unlike middle managers, they tend to be in on major agency decisions as to how to interpret laws; they usually possess considerable administrative discretion. Members of the SES are overwhelmingly white men, although the proportion of women appears to be increasing slightly (see Table 11.1).

What general orientations characterize the behavior of senior career executives? Perceptions vary. One view holds that federal executives are aggressive and entrepreneurial in building agency resources. A comparative analysis of administrative styles in Australia, Israel, and the United States suggests that public managers in the latter two countries are more entrepreneurial.[9] Another study holds that the fragmentation of authority endemic to American political life brings out the entrepreneurial proclivities of administrators. Consistent with this view, the percentage of senior administrators reporting regular contacts with members of the legislative branch, political parties, and representatives of clientele groups tends to be greater in the United States than in Great Britain, the Netherlands, and Sweden. The study asserts that "Institutions and history have pushed American bureaucrats toward more traditionally political roles as advocates, policy entrepreneurs and even partisans. . ."[10]

In the absence of specific prohibitions against action, entrepreneurial managers aggressively pursue their objectives. In essence, these executives take the forgiveness factor seriously. This maxim holds that it is easier to obtain forgiveness for an action taken than it is to obtain permission to act; sensing this, officials test the limits of tolerance in their efforts to shape programs.[11]

TABLE 11.1   Selected Characteristics of SES Members 1979, 1983, and 1988

	1979	1983	1988
SES Members on Board	6,836	6,933	7,076
Percent Career	92	89	90
Percent Noncareer and Limited[a]	8	11	10
Percent Minority[b]	6	7	6
Percent Female[b]	5	7	9

Source: U.S. General Accounting Office, *Testimony of the Comptroller General on the Impact of the Senior Executive Service* (Washington, DC: GAO/GGD-84-32, 1983), Appendix, 3–4. U.S. Office of Personnel Management, EPMD Report No. 41, May 1988.
[a]Includes a few limited term and limited emergency appointments. By law these positions may not exceed 5 percent of total SES positions. This is in addition to a 10 percent cap on noncareer employees.
[b]While data on the attributes of a small number of individuals were not available, these are reasonably precise estimates.

Others undercut the idea of federal managers as highly entrepreneurial. Some see federal executives as above all seeking to avoid uncertainty and risk. One analyst portrays federal managers as motivated by a hierarchy of goals. Budget security, a rather conservative goal, sits at the top, and budget growth ranks second. The desire to promote a particular version of the public interest comes in third. Presumably, officials place a very high premium on reducing prospects that the financial base of their operations will erode. They strive for budget growth and certain innovations only if they can do so without jeopardizing their budget base.[12]

Another perspective that emphasizes the avoidance of uncertainty and risk paints the senior executive as a "constrained maximizer."[13] This vision holds that managers worry primarily about maintaining current programs and avoiding controversies. They attempt to carve out a particular agency niche and stick within it. To be sure, expansion continues to appeal, but managers generally prefer inching ahead to moving rapidly into new territory. The executive seeks to advance as much as possible while avoiding issues that generate intense conflict. In essence, executives sense that it may well be "useful to charge down the corridors of indifference."[14] They seek to leave their mark in areas that others in their milieu view as uncontroversial.

Notions of managers' motivations that focus on the desire to avoid uncertainty and risk seem much closer to reality than those that view executives as aggressively power-hungry. Executives tend to be entrepreneurial within the bounds of prudence. While understanding this tendency is important, further information about the imperatives that drive federal managers is desirable. At least four major imperatives deserve attention—legal, consensual, programmatic and career or personal.[15] Each imperative is a psychological force that managers feel. The force springs from factors in the agency and its environment as well as from the particular personality of the executive. The force of the different imperatives varies among career executives and over time within a single individual. The mix of imperatives substantially affects whether an executive is an aggressive entrepreneur, a constrained maximizer, or some other type.

The *legal imperative* is to obey the law and the formal interpretations of it. These interpretations include court opinions, official regulations, guidelines in the *Federal Register,* executive orders, and so on. This documentary superstructure places more or less precise demands on senior executives. At times it creates a thicket of constraints that the executive can ignore only at considerable risk. Managers in the Internal Revenue Service, for instance, implement a remarkably detailed statute that goes to great lengths to define such pivotal terms as *gross income* and *capital gains*.

Other laws amount to little more than carte blanche invitations to managers to do something to accomplish something. The Emergency Health Personnel Act of 1970 sought to ameliorate shortages of physicians in certain parts of the country. The drafters expected that doctors who volunteered for a tour of duty with the U.S. Public Health Service would go to these needy areas. However, the four-page statute left fundamental objectives and terms undefined. What was a health manpower shortage area? Should the physicians be assigned to the most impoverished and deprived areas where there was little prospect that they would subsequently enter private practice? Or should these doctors be dispatched to more affluent areas of shortage, where they might be attracted to private practice after the stint with the Public Health Service? The law remained silent with respect to these and other important questions. In subsequent years this vague mandate led to major shifts in program emphases as different administrators became involved with the program.[16]

Precision can be a boon or barrier to performance. Precise statutes allow the executive to resist pressures from inside and outside the organization to interpret the law in ways they view as undesirable. "I'd like to help, but the law won't let me" can be a handy response. (At times, the desire to use this excuse may prompt a manager to impute greater precision to the statute than it actually has.) On the other side of the ledger, precision in law may thwart the administrator's efforts to get something accomplished. Congressional processes often impede the marriage of workability and precision in statutes. For instance, amendments to the Clean Air Act in 1977 set up conflicting dates within the same bill for accomplishing certain objectives.[17] A precise law that authorized the government to provide grants, loans, and loan guarantees to encourage the spread of health maintenance organizations proved so constraining that substantial amounts of the allocations went unspent during the early years of the program. (Health maintenance organizations are groups of medical providers which, for a prospectively determined premium, agree to deliver a comprehensive set of primary and acute care services to enrollees whenever these clients seek care.)

The documentary superstructure may be overwhelming. How could anyone be expected to keep up with it all? Most managers do not. Some rely on experts to know different rules and keep them out of trouble. Some managers remain oblivious to certain rules. Others bend or even ignore formal requirements. If the documentary superstructure cannot determine all aspects of their behavior, career managers generally take the legal imperative seriously, in part because they believe in the rule of law and in part because they are constrained maximizers.

The *consensual imperative* encourages executives to rally supporters and avoid major controversy. At one level this consensus is simply the absence of negative sentiment and criticism. Others may not so much endorse the executive's action as accede to it; such action falls within their zone of indifference.

At another level various groups go beyond tolerance of the executive's decisions; they provide active support. In general, an executive faces more difficulties in pursuing the consensual imperative to the degree that he or she confronts a generically politicized milieu—a milieu where basic disagreements exist about ends, means, or both, and various groups stand ready to fight about their differences. This milieu may drive an executive toward one of several strategies. One is to forge a compromise whereby each of the contestants wins some concession. A much more difficult course is to remove the foundation for conflict by persuading interested parties to change their minds. For example, an executive bent on removing certain occupational safety standards from the books may attempt to persuade protesting union leaders that the change is not a sellout to business. He or she may portray the initiative as an effort to exorcise picayune rules with no real bearing on workers' well-being. Those who see federal executives as constrained maximizers eager to avoid risk and uncertainty at least implicitly assign the consensual imperative considerable importance.

The *programmatic imperative* is the values and beliefs of officials concerning the ends and means of the programs they administer. It is a vision of what the agency ought to do to promote the public interest. It entails preferences about the best means to achieve these goals. The intensity with which career executives adhere to certain programmatic convictions has often been a source of concern for those who fear that the bureaucracy will be unresponsive to top policymakers. Henry Kissinger captures the flavor of this concern in his discussion of the "particular problem of the Secretary of State." While acknowledging that career officials in the department are "intelligent, competent, loyal and hardworking . . . the reverse side of their dedication is the conviction that a lifetime of service and study has given them insights that transcend the untrained and shallow-rooted views of the political appointee." Desk officers become advocates for the countries with which they deal. "They will carry out clear-cut instructions with great loyalty, but the typical . . . officer is not easily persuaded that an instruction with which he disagrees is really clear-cut."[18]

Countless examples of the programmatic imperative are at work in domestic agencies. During the 1970s senior executives at the Occupational Safety and Health Administration strongly favored engineering over personal solutions to occupational hazards. Revamping a plant's ventilation system in order to make the air safe to breathe illustrates the engineering approach; requiring the plant's workers to wear face masks that filter out impurities exemplifies a personal solution.

The *career, or personal, imperative* is the interest of the manager in his or her own prospects for sustaining and obtaining desirable employment. Notions of desirability vary considerably. In some cases the career imperative overlaps with programmatic and consensual imperatives. For instance, a manager may place a premium on working in a relatively unpoliticized agency with low potential for conflict or in one that provides moral satisfaction from being associated with the agency's program, for example providing medical care to veterans. In other instances the desire for status, perquisites, and a certain life-style dominate the career imperative. One can easily imagine an ambitious executive making certain choices in pursuit of promotion, a higher salary, and a more powerful position. The career imperative may also push in another direction. An elderly executive may strive for employment that does not demand fifty- or sixty-hour work weeks and is generally less taxing. Another manager may prefer a job involving little travel and a low prospect of reassignment so that he or she can spend more time with the family and can live in the Washington area.

The more the four imperatives indicate a certain course of action, the more likely is an executive to pursue it. Often, however, trade-offs exist. An executive must slight one imperative in order to obey another. Thus, following the letter and spirit of the law may force the manager into strong conflict that makes consensus impossible. The desire to obtain broad support for agency actions may incline the manager to make concessions that violate his programmatic sense of the public interest.

Programmatic and career imperatives may trade off. In an era of retrenchment federal executives have frequently felt painful tension—career rewards may accrue to those most willing to slash the programs they have strongly supported in the past. Career concerns may also clash with the legal imperative. For instance, one source of tension between political and career executives stems from the desire of the latter not to be too closely identified with the former. When a different political party comes to power, a career official prefers not to be seen as energetically committed to the agenda of the opposing party. While keeping one's distance from political executives may be quite rational in this sense, it may also lead the career official to be less responsive to legitimate White House initiatives than strict deference to the legal imperative would dictate. In a similar vein, the career imperative can raise issues of *conflicts of interest*. Critics of regulatory administration often charge that top regulatory officials aspire to obtain more lucrative positions in the very industries they regulate. These critics view any propensity of regulated industries to hire these officials as a kind of "delayed bribe."[19]

Again, the relative force of the imperatives depends upon context and the personality of the manager. The important point is that the four motivational factors frequently influence government executives as they deal with the day-to-day operations of government and cope with the challenges of society, technology, and resource management.

The Societal Challenge

The societal task environment constrains, energizes, and challenges the federal executive. This environment consists of elements outside of the federal government that have a relatively immediate bearing on the manager of government operations.[20] These include forces of nature both physical (e.g., hurricanes in the case of agencies involved in disaster relief) and biological (e.g., the reactions of bears to policies designed to regulate their interaction with visitors to the national parks.) Human behavior, as manifested in myriad social institutions and groups, is central to the societal task environment. The executive typically works with suppliers of resources to the agency; clients; competing agencies with similar missions; groups that bear the direct costs of agency activities; and media, which observe the agency's performance in order to report to society.

The elements in an executive's task environment vary considerably in complexity and fluidity. Complexity increases as the number, heterogeneity, and interdependence of these elements grow. Heterogeneity refers to the degree to which diversity prevails among the elements. For instance, some executives must deal with groups that hold conflicting perspectives on what the agency ought to do; other agency managers deal with groups that hold more or less uniform views about the mission. Interdependence occurs when changes in the behavior of one element precipitate prompt alterations in others. When considerable interdependence exists, the modification of one variable affects almost everything else in the executive's task environment. Task environments also vary in the rapidity with which they change. Some executives work with universities and other research institutions that constantly produce new discoveries of direct relevance to the agency's mission. In other agencies the advancement of pertinent knowledge in society proceeds at a snail's pace.

This volume has already discussed several key groups and forces in the societal task environment. For present purposes three implications of a political culture that denigrates public bureaucracy deserve attention. While this culture can check any proclivity toward heavy-handed, arrogant behavior by civil servants, it can also contribute to managerial weakness and failure by engendering defensiveness, dependence, and defeatism.

First, the relatively low status of federal managers may exacerbate the tendency for public administration to become a defensive and nonexperimental exercise whose officials spend much time maneuvering to avoid scrutiny, blame, and responsibility.[21] In the face of a negative political culture, the slightest misstep by a bold and innovative public executive can easily be blown out of proportion to cast doubt on his or her fundamental competence as a manager. When they visibly err, federal executives tend to bear the brunt of moralistic blame rather than receive the benefit of the doubt and a helping hand. Trial-and-error learning is much more difficult. In circumstances like these, the avoidance of scandal, fraud, and embarrassment can easily become a stronger concern than actual program performance. Self-protection and maintaining proper appearances can crowd out results-oriented management.

The fishbowl environment that many public managers face encourages the defensive approach that the political culture encourages. Obviously, greater visibility can foster accountability. Some managers may be more inclined to stay on their toes, attempt to carry out the letter of the law, and guard against any hint of impropriety. Visibility also entails costs, however. The tendency of the media to emphasize man-bites-dog stories is a critical intervening variable in this regard. Television, radio, and the press gravitate toward isolated cases of egregious abuse rather than to systemic issues that are often far more relevant to program performance. For instance, the media frequently pay much more attention to fraud by medical providers or clients than to the dry, technical but more important issues concerning Medicare payment formulas and the day-to-day incentives they establish for hospitals and physicians. The media also frequently portray administrative episodes as morality plays involving flawed character or incompetence; in fact these episodes often reflect errors and malfunctions rooted in more basic factors that drive program implementation. Given media propensities, visibility can encourage executives to manage appearance rather than substance. Face-saving and posturing may become more important as executives strive to be consistent and look like winners. The programmatic imperative may thereby become less salient to officials, and results-oriented management may suffer.

Second, the political culture heightens the dependence of federal managers on oversight actors or groups in their environment; it makes the consensual imperative much more important than it might otherwise be; it means that executives often bargain from a position of weakness in implementation games. The limited status or prestige of the federal executive fuels the desire to avoid open conflict with others. If such conflict erupts, there is a high risk that the public will blame the bureaucrat rather than another entity such as a community hospital that condones dubious admissions to maximize Medicare receipts. In essence, the quest for consensus may draw officials' attention away from the letter and spirit of the law or from their own programmatic sense of how to accomplish a task, damaging accountability and cost-effectiveness.

Third, the negative strain in the political culture can induce defeatism among federal managers. Defeatism is a kind of inferiority complex that leads an executive to take too limited a view of what can be accomplished. Defensiveness and defeatism are closely related. However, while a defensive manager may be entrepreneurial and strive to accomplish ambitious goals, defeatism brings about resignation to subpar performance. The executive tends to give up too easily out of a conviction that forces out there will prevent him or her from doing what needs to be done.[22] In a certain sense, the executive comes to accept the cultural stereotypes.

Defensiveness, dependence, and defeatism heighten the risk of a self-fulfilling prophecy for federal management. At worst they ratify and reinforce the theme pervasive in the broader political culture. Portrayed as ineffectual, federal managers risk becoming so. Most career executives resist such tendencies; many of them set high standards of creativity and effectiveness in managing public programs. Several factors help buffer them from the self-fulfilling impact of a negative political culture. The subcultures surrounding particular agencies or civil servants are one such buffer. While citizens may rail against government bureaucracy in general, they often respect the importance and competence of certain agencies in particular, for example the National Institutes of Health. Nonetheless, bureaucrat bashing is a formidable obstacle to effective management.

The Challenge of Diverse Technologies

While society conditions executive behavior, the technology of an agency usually does more to determine its particular problems and the roles of the manager. *Technology* here does not mean hardware but the practices and means a public agency uses to accomplish certain ends.[23] Each month, for instance, the Social Security Administration assembles resources and applies techniques to deliver checks to millions of citizens. Myriad qualities characterize the technologies of the federal government.

Some technologies are better established than others. A well established technology rests on a widespread consensus among knowledgeable individuals on how to accomplish some end. While one may debate the relative merits of a nine-digit zip code and complain about delays, there is a substantial consensus about how to get a letter from Atlanta to Akron. Other technologies do not enjoy such credibility.

Evidence of their efficacy remains inconclusive; experts disagree about their suitability. The Veterans Administration cannot rely on proven technologies for treating veterans with certain mental problems. Mental health specialists often differ on the diagnosis and best treatment for various kinds of mental disorders.

The programmatic imperative tends to increase in importance relative to legal and consensual forces when an executive manages a well-established technology. Confident that he or she knows what works, the manager resists demands from outside groups or overhead actors if they seek deviations from proven ways of doing things. Weak technology requires managers to work harder at building a consensus about the wisdom of agency actions. Praise, or at least the absence of criticism from outside the agency, usually is an important means of validating the executive's success.

Alternatively, an executive may become more inclined to play it by the book in the face of uncertain technology. In essense, he or she attempts to follow the letter of the law or the *Code of Federal Regulations*. This defensive strategy shields the manager from criticism with arguments that the law and other documents require certain practices, whatever their ultimate efficacy.

Technologies vary in other respects. Boundaries between different types of technologies are fuzzy, and most programs feature unique combinations of them. Three types of technology—regulatory, allocative, and induced (or proxy)—are particularly common. Each of these technologies poses distinct issues for those who manage the day-to-day operations of the federal government.[24]

Regulatory Technology

Regulatory technology calls on the public agency to prescribe and control behavior for a designated group in its task environment. It typically features the promulgation of rules or standards (e.g., specifying acceptable levels of exposure to toxic substances), the monitoring of groups to determine compliance with standards, and the imposition of penalties for failure to comply. Each component of technology raises problems for federal executives.

In the case of rule promulgation, questions involving priorities are often central. For instance, OSHA standards cover only a small number of the many known carcinogens. If agency officials wish to issue new standards, which carcinogens should receive attention first? Should it be those that affect the most workers? Those that have the severest effects on the exposed workers? Those found in industries with less political power to make trouble for the agency? Those whose affected firms can comply with the new standard at low economic cost? Those that have caught the attention of the media? Uncertainty often shrouds the answers to questions like these. To be sure, executives involved with regulatory technologies need not invariably grapple with these questions explicitly. During the early 1980s the White House strongly pressured these agencies to refrain from issuing new standards. Over the long term, however, regulatory executives must set priorities for addressing hazards.

Deregulation also poses problems for executives (see Chapter 7). The quest to sustain due process as well as other factors can prevent managers and their agencies from getting rid of obsolete rules. In order to delete regulations executives must often muster considerable evidence, motivate employees to devote themselves to a task far less exciting than rulemaking, and overcome suspicions of outside groups that repeal represents going soft on the regulated rather than error correction.

The deployment of investigatory resources for efficient and effective enforcement of existing standards also presents executives with significant challenges. Which kinds of violations of standards should receive attention? Which groups or sectors in society should be marked for surveillance? Managers consider many factors as they decide these questions.

Consider how OSHA executives have resolved the question of the relative priority that ought to be assigned to enforcing safety as opposed to health standards. Safety hazards tend to produce immediate injuries such as a broken leg or electrocution; health threats cause occupational illness (e.g., cancer)—often after many years of exposure to a toxic substance. Although most knowledgeable observers believe that health rather than safety should receive priority, the agency has done just the opposite.[25] Targeting uncertainty and the labor market are among the variables that have produced this safety bias. OSHA's executives have much greater confidence in their ability to address safety risks than health risks. Occupational injury statistics are far superior to occupational illness data. This means that managers can readily develop models to focus safety inspections on the most hazardous industries; in contrast, they must rely much more heavily on guesswork to target the firms most likely to foster occupational illness. The labor market also encourages the tilt toward safety. During much of the 1970s, skilled health inspectors were much more difficult to recruit than safety experts.

There are other examples of recruitment, motivation, and turnover of personnel shaping enforcement priorities. For instance, the Federal Trade Commission administers both antitrust and trade regulation laws. The law grants it broad discretion to foster competition in the economy and to attack business monopolies. Although some argue that the agency should invest its limited resources only in important cases with the potential for great impact, executives routinely instigate suits with few ramifications for the functioning of economic markets. This in part reflects a desire to sustain the morale of the lawyers within the agency. These attorneys crave trial experience. Moreover, many of them view their stint at the Federal Trade Commission as a stepping-stone to a lucrative career in the private sector. By pursuing smaller cases that take only a year or two to bring to court, executives boost the morale of these lawyers. They also reduce the problem of trying to litigate major cases in the face of high turnover among the agency's legal staff.[26]

The distribution of scarce enforcement resources affects responsiveness. A manager faces a strong incentive to investigate citizen complaints about violations of agency rules. The culture of the United States places a great value on responsiveness for its own sake. Ignoring or even deferring complaints offends that value.[27] However, too much responsiveness to complaints can distort an agency's enforcement priorities so that compliance officers spend more time on trivial than on major infractions of the rules. After criticism of its slow handling of complaints from severely ill workers at a Kepone plant in Hopewell, Virginia, in the mid-1970s, executives at OSHA placed a higher priority on following up complaints. Eventually, however, in some regions responses to complaints consumed nearly all of the inspection staff's time. Programmed inspections based on evidence as to which worksites posed the most hazards dropped precipitously. Soon the agency came under criticism from GAO for allowing complaints to impede inspection of workplaces with the most serious hazards.[28]

Managing a regulatory technology also involves important choices concerning the appropriate response to infractions. In general terms, executives may pursue a legalistic or consultative approach. Under the former, top management urges inspectors to cite all infractions, however minor, and seek stiff penalties. Under the latter, executives encourage inspectors to use their judgment. Compliance officers have discretion to size up the situation and to refrain from issuing citations and proposing penalties if they believe that hazards can be abated more effectively in other ways. Each approach features advantages and disadvantages. The legalistic version allows managers to defend themselves against charges of playing favorites or caving in to industry. However, this strategy tends to engender considerable hostility as the agency comes to be perceived as picayune and unreasonable. When OSHA encouraged this approach in the 1970s, it meant that nearly all inspected employers received citations, often for what they perceived as trivial infractions. These nuisance citations, some of which sprang from questionable rules (for example that toilets have a hinged open-front seat and that toilet stalls have coat hangers), subjected the agency to public ridicule.

A consultative approach, wherein the inspector judges the context and uses discretion, can avoid this antagonism; it can militate against unreasonableness. The risk is that enforcement officers will go beyond proper bounds in wielding discretion. Inspectors may do favors for employers when they should not; corruption may rear its head. More probably, a consultative approach can easily breed suspicion of corruption or excessive leniency.[29] During the Reagan years OSHA pursued a consultative approach; agency managers negotiated citations, penalties, and abatements with employers. Whatever goodwill the approach engendered in the business community, it prompted Ralph Nader to say that the agency had become little more than a "hollow percussion chamber" intent on gutting enforcement and getting "the federal cop off the corporate beat."[30]

Nader's blast testifies to an important factor confronting many executives who manage regulatory technologies. They operate in conflict. No matter what path the executive follows, a major group becomes unhappy and unleashes a barrage of criticism. Pursuit of the consensual imperative often becomes quite difficult.[31]

Direct Allocative Technology

Direct allocative technology uses government's own personnel to deliver income, services, or goods to groups or individuals who apply for them. While those who manage regulatory technologies often meet resistance from their target group, those who oversee allocative programs often are so popular as to be swamped with demand. Executives who manage allocative technologies encounter several issues, among them eligibility, access, and quality.

Federal laws generally deem certain categories of individuals eligible to apply for benefits. Determination of eligibility need not be perplexing. Anyone who has a stamp can mail a letter. However, most social programs cannot rely on such simple market tests of eligibility. They leave ample room for errors of liberality or stringency. The former is allowing someone who is not eligible to receive a benefit; the latter is the opposite. Errors of eligibility, especially those of liberality, are a particular concern for allocative technology. The manager of a local supermarket can usually make a hard economic decision to accept a certain amount of shoplifting as the cost of doing business. He or she can determine that at some level the cost of setting up mechanisms to control theft exceeds the value of the stolen goods. A federal manager encounters difficulties in adopting this economically rational perspective because of the heavy symbolic overtones attached to eligibility errors. The media often treat these errors as a kind of morality play. The script has it that welfare cheats conspire to rip off government while lethargic and incompetent bureaucrats stand by. Errors of stringency, especially in the case of the deserving poor, such as the elderly and veterans, may also become a public relations nightmare. Outsiders may interpret such errors as "yet another" indicator of callous bureaucratic behavior.

Eligibility errors frequently spring from much more systemic sources. Extremely complex regulations often play a role. These rules confuse those who apply for benefits as well as intake workers, who must determine eligibility. To compound problems, low pay for intake workers often heightens turnover and reduces expertise. In dealing with the two kinds of eligibility errors, the executive often confronts the trade-off that reducing one will increase the other. If managers place a greater burden of proof on those seeking federal benefits, errors of liberality may well decline while those of stringency rise.

Other things being equal, intake errors tend to decline if eligibility criteria are crisp and workers have ready and timely access to pertinent information about applicants. For instance, civil servants who decide eligibility for Social Security enjoy relatively crisp criteria—generally, age specifications. In contrast, the Supplemental Security Income program, which among other things provides income to the disabled, suffers far fuzzier eligibility standards. The meaning of disability is nebulous; eligibility determinations often require very subjective judgments by physicians and others.[32]

The manager of an allocative program must see to it that valid information about the applicant for aid flows rapidly to the intake worker. Often this proves difficult. An applicant's income and wealth may be important criteria. The intake worker may not be able to obtain accurate information about these factors. How can one be sure that an applicant who claims he has no bank account is telling the truth? Sometimes eligibility workers have it much easier. The federal government keeps extensive, readily retrievable records on veterans and contributors to Social Security. These records dramatically reduce the threat of eligibility errors.

Allocative technologies also call for the management of access. Access increases to the degree that those eligible under the law for program benefits can obtain them at minimal cost and inconvenience to themselves. Barriers to access assume many guises. Information about eligibility for benefits and procedures to obtain them may be scarce. Burdensome application forms, long queues, busy phone lines, limited business hours, hostile intake workers, and remote locations that clients must visit also impede access. Where market tests of eligibility apply (as with supplemental Medicare insurance for physicians' services), those who desire the benefit may lack the money to pay for it.

Executives faced with decisions affecting access typically confront many trade-offs. Steps to enhance access usually boost costs and may precipitate a backlash as Congress looks for ways to cut the program. Increased demand may damage the quality of the agency's work. (For instance, hospital personnel may rush from one patient to the next without completing medical histories.) Eligibility errors may increase as intake workers struggle to cope with a soaring volume of applications. Even if lawmakers allocate more resources to the agency, problems may persist. If Veterans Administration hospitals have large numbers of beds, many veterans may remain in the hospital well beyond a medically justifiable point. Excessive hospital stays not only waste resources; they expose patients to certain diseases that they might otherwise avoid.

Sustaining the quality of output concerns managers of allocative technologies. In the case of income, do clients receive the appropriate amounts in timely fashion? Does a service agency provide the right amount and blend of service? Where products are allocated, does the good meet societally defined standards of acceptability? (For instance, does the surplus food delivered to the poor meet sanitation codes, have nutritional value, and taste and look right?) Judging the quality of agency outputs is often difficult, especially for service programs. For example, directors of Veterans Administration hospitals must take into account that medical experts do not agree on how to measure the quality of hospital services. Some observers, including accrediting agencies, define it primarily in terms of the resources available to a hospital—equipment, the staff's credentials, and so on. Others stress the outcomes of hospital care. Here the hospital's success in reducing the presence of the five D's (death, disease, disability, discomfort, dissatisfaction) in its patients is pivotal. While it may seem obvious that for hospitals outcome definitions of quality are superior, successful implementation of this approach requires expensive, methodologically complex studies. In contrast, Veterans Administration executives can much more readily acquire data on the resources in their hospital system.

Induced Technology

Induced technology is administration by proxy. The federal agency authorizes third parties such as private firms, private nonprofit grantees, and other governments to carry out programs. Effective use of this technology usually requires three conditions:[33] (1) Federal executives must find suitable proxy organizations that have the basic ability to perform some task or role. (2) Federal executives have inducements to motivate the third parties to perform as desired. (3) Executives must structure and manage those inducements so as to encourage the third party to avoid waste and achieve desired performance. These conditions may be elusive, as the case of the Social Security Administration and the Paradyne Corporation suggests.[34]

In 1981, the Social Security Administration entered into a $115 million contract with the Paradyne Corporation of Largo, Florida. Under the contract, which the agency awarded through competitive bidding, the corporation pledged to install more than 1,800 communications terminals in some 1,350 Social Security offices nationwide. These offices depend on the terminals for timely access to data that support such services as issuing Social Security numbers, maintaining records of earnings, and taking claims for benefits. The contract called for the Social Security Administration to lease this equipment with an option to buy. By September 1982, Paradyne had installed nearly 1,400 terminals.

Late in that year executives in the Social Security Administration awarded a follow-on sole-source contract (without bidding) to Paradyne to modify terminal software and to enhance the data transmission capabilities of the leased terminals. Officials also decided to take their option and purchase 841 of these terminals.

Federal administrators took these steps in the face of mounting evidence that the equipment was defective. Complaints about the new system began as soon as it was installed. A district office in Roanoke, Virginia, reported 238 terminal malfunctions in one month. The New York regional office of the Social Security Administration estimated that the terminal system malfunctioned an average of eight to ten times per day. While Paradyne slowly worked some of the bugs out of the system, a 1984 analysis indicated that the equipment still failed three to four times as often as similar terminals.

Complaints about the contract ultimately sparked concern in Congress and the General Accounting Office. Subsequent investigations produced charges that the Social Security Administration had mismanaged its contract procedures. Social Security executives permitted each competing bidder to structure the demonstration of its product. When a bidder did not have a component of the system, federal executives allowed the company to substitute written analysis for actual tests of the product. The first equipment Paradyne installed did not meet the contract's standards, so officials at the Social Security Administration modified the contract to allow the company to pass muster. Officials also bought many of the leased terminals without an adequate analysis of their options.

By 1983, concern about the contracts had reached new proportions. The Securities and Exchange Commission sued Paradyne, charging it with bidding fraud, among other things. Other bidders on the contract filed civil suits against Paradyne for misrepresentation. In February 1984 a key official at the Social Security Administration's Office of Data Communications was charged with attempting to extort money in order to assure a software subcontractor favored treatment.

Not all cases are so dramatic. Procurement often works smoothly. However, the Paradyne episode illustrates the pitfalls that can trap executives as they attempt to satisfy the three conditions for effective management of inducements.

Consider the first condition, finding a third party with the capacity to perform the task. Sometimes it is a serious question whether any organization in the environment of the public agency can do the job (for instance develop a new military technology). The agency may want the impossible. However, the Paradyne case points to a different problem of capacity. It seems likely that various companies had the capacity to provide the terminals, but serious questions exist as to whether Paradyne did. Selection of a contractor often depends on educated guesses. Organizations, such as Paradyne, that seem capable of delivering benefit X at cost Y at time Z may subsequently encounter difficulties that make it impossible.

Having found a third party capable of delivering the service, officials must be able to induce performance. Money is a primary incentive, as the Paradyne episode shows. Skilled executives may also employ nonmonetary inducements to achieve objectives.

Executives at the Equal Employment Opportunity Commission have used information in this way. The law requires the commission to investigate complaints of employment discrimination and to seek penalties and corrective action where appropriate. The commission receives such a large volume of charges that it cannot investigate all of them thoroughly, let alone sue all employers that seem to be guilty of discrimination. The law provides a safety valve for this congestion. If after a specified time the commission fails to file suit or otherwise satisfy the complainant, he or she can hire a lawyer and sue the employer directly.

Sensitive to the vital role of the private bar in enforcing equal employment laws, commission executives have provided inducements for these lawyers to take discrimination cases. In particular, they reduced the information costs of private attorneys who pursued such suits. Despite statutory provisions against distributing information obtained in its investigations to the public, commission executives decided to furnish these files to complainants and their lawyers. This practice often helped complainants with well-grounded charges to hire private attorneys on a contingent fee basis. (Under this arrangement, the client pays the lawyer only if he or she wins the case.) While business groups strongly opposed the commission's release of information, the Supreme Court subsequently upheld the practice.[35] The commission also attempted to use information as an inducement in other ways. Under the Area Bar Center Program, the agency established litigation support centers to update the private bar on significant developments in employment discrimination law and to provide more specific technical assistance to lawyers who requested it.

The case of the Equal Employment Opportunity Commission more fundamentally illustrates the use of inducements to facilitate *coproduction,* in which the beneficiaries of the program and their nongovernmental allies participate in implementation without payment from the agency.[36]

Those who manage inducement technologies often have trouble with the third condition for effectiveness, the linking of rewards to performance. The Social Security administrators' handling of their contract with Paradyne illustrates this point. These executives chose to purchase leased equipment from the company and enter into another contract with it for software despite abundant evidence that Paradyne's performance was mediocre at best. Problems in linking rewards to performance happen not only with major decisions, such as taking options or entering into another contract; problems can also surface in day-to-day payment decisions. Errors occur when an agency pays a third party an amount other than that prescribed by guidelines or procedures. Defense contractors have constantly been in the headlines for receiving inappropriate payments; such errors afflict social programs as well. Medicare and Medicaid have made various payment errors. Government may pay a doctor twice for the same service; authorize payment for a service not delivered; pay a physician X amount when the guidelines call for Y; or reimburse for services that the client's private insurance company should have covered.

Linking inducements to performance requires both carrots and sticks. Federal executives can threaten to terminate a relationship with an agent unless it changes its ways. Usually, however, firing the party is much easier said than done. In certain situations federal officials may be unable to replace an agent. Many statutes give state governments exclusive authority to implement a federal program. In that case the federal government's primary formal sanction is its authority to withhold funds if states prove unable or unwilling to carry out the programs as effectively as federal officials would like. However, suspensions of funds often carry heavy costs for federal executives. They arouse the wrath of state officials and their political allies; they often hurt the clients federal officials wish to help, such as the poor in the case of welfare programs.

Authority to shop for another provider can free officials from such Hobson's choices, but as the Paradyne affair suggests, federal managers have incentives to retain a provider even in these circumstances. Government executives may see termination of a contract or a grant as an embarrassment, an admission that the selection process erred. In a political system that encourages people to play blame-the-bureaucrat, admissions of mistakes commonly elicit condemnation rather than a pat on the back for honesty. Besides, executives may simply have a hard time admitting that the third party whose bid looked so good could be so incompetent, conniving, or uncommitted as to deserve termination. Fear of legal action by the contractor may also bring pause. Furthermore, executives may calculate that working with the contractor to improve its performance stands a better chance of fostering cost-effectiveness than facing the delays, uncertainties, and expense of termination and of seeking a new implementing agent.

In contemplating an induced technology, one tends to think in terms of an executive dealing with *an* external implementing agent. In fact, the manager must often coordinate multiple providers to accomplish a single activity. These arrangements complicate the management of inducements. For instance, Medicare executives contract with private insurance companies, such as Blue Cross, which in turn pay community hospitals to serve elderly beneficiaries. Throughout much of Medicare's history, administrators worried that the insurance companies under contract had failed to review critically the charges submitted by hospitals. Part of this problem was the difficulty of drafting precise standards for reviewing claims. Other parts were a strong tradition of deference to medical providers and the difficulties of judging whether a hospital had provided unnecessary care. Moreover, federal executives wanted the insurance companies to process claims quickly and to hold down the administrative cost per claim processed. This hardly encouraged insurance companies to spend time scrutinizing particular hospital charges. To compound the problem, the law for many years allowed hospitals to select the reimbursing insurance company from a substantial list of eligible intermediaries. An insurance company that objected to excessive hospital charges might find itself out in the cold as the hospital turned to another company. This graphically illustrates the complexities of managing inducements on top of inducements. Such cases reaffirm that the line between master and servant often blurs when the federal government turns to external agents for implementation.

A political culture that dislikes "big government" in Washington has helped spread indirect implementation and elevated the importance of induced technology. The appeal of this technology reached particular intensity during the 1980s with much talk of the need to contract out many government functions. However, induced technology probably poses at least as many management problems as regulatory and allocative technologies. These problems will receive additional attention in Chapter 14.

The Challenge of Resource Management

The challenges from society and technology intermingle with complexities of managing certain basic resources, or factors of production. Five factors—authority, personnel, information, physical resources (building, land, equipment), and money—loom particularly large. The ways executives husband and use these resources profoundly affects their ability to achieve objectives.

Among these resources, authority may seem to students of public administration to be the most obvious. Bureaucracies are, after all, authority structures that feature a chain of command. Executives usually have the formal right to guide a wide range of employee behavior. In many respects, however, authority is a less useful resource for managers than this view suggests.

In considering this claim, one must keep in mind that a definition of authority may be broad or narrow. The broad view is that authority is a type of power. Authority exists when a superior gives an order to a subordinate *and* the subordinate obeys. The subordinate acts not because he or she chooses to but because of the command or signal. Alternatively, the subordinate may anticipate what the superior wishes and behave accordingly. In this broad sense authority does not exist if a subordinate ignores or disobeys an order from a manager.[37] The narrow definition distinguishes between authority as a resource and the actual exertion of power.[38] In this view, authority is a formal legal right (e.g., as declared by statutes or administrative regulations) to make certain decisions and order certain actions. For instance, laws may grant certain managers the authority to order inspectors to investigate particular firms for violations of safety or health standards. This formal legal authority exists whether or not the subordinate obeys. In essence, authority is a resource that may or may not assist managers in exerting power over subordinates. For purposes of this analysis, the formal definition of authority will apply.

Executives are often reluctant to issue overt, direct, authoritative commands to subordinates. One study of federal bureau chiefs concludes that these executives seldom found it necessary to issue orders or crack the whip. They did not behave in a highly "authoritarian fashion."[39]

Several factors help account for this. First, persuasion and suggestion may well stimulate subordinates to greater commitment and motivation to the manager's objectives. In essence, persuasion and suggestion heighten prospects that subordinates will "buy into" management decisions as ones they have freely agreed to carry out. They may also be more appealing to managers, many of whom dislike thinking of themselves as heavy-handed bosses forcing subordinates to do things against their will.

Second, the acute fragmentation of authority in American bureaucratic life limits the potency of authority as a vehicle for controlling subordinates' behavior. Frequently executives find their authority checked by other civil servants, as when the Office of Personnel Management considers reductions in force. Without a clear monopoly of authority, persuasion and suggestion become all the more critical.

Third, authoritative executives run the risk of disobedience, which will undercut their power position. Subordinates who ignore, deflect, or disobey orders are not uncommon. Executives at least implicitly understand the wisdom of Chester Barnard, who observed in the late 1930s: "There is no principle of executive conduct better established than that orders will not be issued that cannot or will not be obeyed."[40] To invite subordinates to ignore or disobey an order may devalue executive authority in other contexts. Unless the executive severely punishes the disobedient, as by firing, subordinates may conclude that they have little to fear from resisting authoritative commands.

This is not to suggest that authority is irrelevant. A manager's success with persuasion and suggestion may in part depend on the subordinates' recognition that the manager can ultimately order an action. A single encounter between manager and employee frequently involves a mix of persuasion, suggestion, and command.[41] Moreover, the executive routinely manifests authority by signing off on a host of documents such as financial statements. Finally, when persuasion and suggestion completely fail, the manager can often draw on formal authority to prevail. When managers find it necessary to issue commands, prospects for obtaining obedience improve when the following conditions hold:

1. It is clear to the subordinate that the executive has personally and with forethought issued an order expressing a definite decision.
2. The order is clear.
3. The subordinate has the means to carry out the command.
4. The subordinate believes that the executive has the legitimate right to order the particular behavior.[42]

Conclusion

While authority ranks as an important management resource, its limits prompt more extensive treatment of other factors of production in Chapters 12 and 13. Those factors—personnel, information, money, physical facilities and equipment—are not all of the relevant ones. One could consider other factors such as professional reputation and time.[43] But if Chapters 12 and 13 cannot claim comprehensiveness, the resources they examine are critical and pervasive. As will become evident, their management often requires executives to juggle legal, consensual, programmatic, and career imperatives. Their management also highlights how government processes exhibit a mix of strategy, luck, change, disorderliness, and firmly entrenched ways of doing things.

Notes

1. Graham T. Allison, Jr., "Public and Private Management: Are They Fundamentally Alike in All Unimportant Respects?" in Frederick S. Lane, ed., *Current Issues in Public Administration* (New York: St. Martin's Press, 1982), 15; see also Henry Mintzberg, *The Nature of Managerial Work* (New York: Harper & Row, 1973); Stephen R. Rosenthal, *Managing Government Operations* (Glenview, IL: Scott, Foresman, 1982).
2. See, for instance, Eugene Bardach, *The Implementation Game* (Cambridge, MA: MIT Press, 1977); Laurence E. Lynn, Jr., *Managing The Public's Business* (New York: Basic Books, 1981).

3. Games in government assume various forms. Zero-sum games resemble athletic contests in that one player's gain is another's loss. In well-played positive-sum games, all participants win. In negative-sum games potential winnings shrink with the onset of the game and the risk that all players will lose runs high.

4. Cited in Thomas J. Peters and Robert H. Waterman, Jr., *In Search of Excellence* (New York: Warner, 1982), 119.

5. Mintzberg, *The Nature of Managerial Work,* 31–2.

6. Robert D. Behn, "Management by Groping Along." *Journal of Policy Analysis and Management* 7 (Fall 1988): 643–63; Daniel J. Isenberg, "How Senior Managers Think." *Harvard Business Review* 62 (November-December 1984): 81–90.

7. Allison, "Public and Private Management," 15.

8. U.S. General Accounting Office, *A 2-Year Appraisal of Merit Pay in Three Agencies* (Washington: GAO/GGD–84–1, 1984), 2; other data obtained from the Office of Personnel Management via phone interview, April 1985.

9. Ira Sharkansky, *Wither the State?* (Chatham, NJ: Chatham House, 1979).

10. Joel D. Aberbach et al., *Bureaucrats and Politicians in Western Democracies* (Cambridge, MA: Harvard University Press, 1981), 243.

11. Beaumont R. Hageback, "The Forgiveness Factor: Taking the Risk Out of Efforts to Integrate Human Services." *Public Administration Review* 42 (January-February 1982): 72–76.

12. R. Douglas Arnold, *Congress and The Bureaucracy* (New Haven: Yale University Press, 1979), 21–2.

13. Douglas Yates, *Bureaucratic Democracy* (Cambridge, MA: Harvard University Press, 1982), 90, 103–4.

14. Hugh Heclo, *A Government of Strangers* (Washington, DC: The Brookings Institution, 1977), 200.

15. This typology builds on Martin Rein and Francine F. Rabinovitz, "Implementation: A Theoretical Perspective," in Walter D. Burnham and Martha W. Weinberg, eds., *American Politics and Public Policy* (Cambridge, MA: MIT Press, 1978), pp. 307–35.

16. See Frank J. Thompson, *Health Policy and the Bureaucracy* (Cambridge, MA: MIT Press, 1981), 81–108.

17. R. Shep Melnick, *Regulation and the Courts* (Washington, DC: The Brookings Institution, 1983), p. 104.

18. Henry Kissinger, *White House Years* (Boston: Little, Brown, 1979), 27.

19. Paul J. Quirk, *Industry Influence in Federal Regulatory Agencies* (Princeton, NJ: Princeton University Press, 1981), 143.

20. For a more extensive discussion of this concept, see James D. Thompson, *Organizations in Action* (New York: McGraw Hill, 1967), 27–9.

21. Bardach, *The Implementation Game,* 37.

22. See Joseph W. Whorton and John A. Worthley, "A Perspective on the Challenge of Public Management: Environmental Paradox and Organizational Culture," in James L. Perry and Kenneth L. Kraemer, eds., *Public Management: Public and Private Perspectives* (Palo Alto: Mayfield, 1983), 126–32.

23. Yates, *Bureaucratic Democracy,* 130.

24. This typology in part derives from Eugene Bardach, "Implementation Studies and the Study of Implements," unpublished paper delivered at the annual meeting of the American Political Science Association, Washington, DC, 1980.

25. See, for instance, John Mendeloff, *Regulating Safety* (Cambridge, MA: MIT Press, 1979).

26. Robert A. Katzman, *Regulatory Bureaucracy* (Cambridge, MA: MIT Press, 1980).

27. Colin S. Diver, "A Theory of Regulatory Enforcement." *Public Policy* 28 (Summer 1980): 275.

28. Thompson, *Health Policy and the Bureaucracy,* 244.

29. Eugene Bardach and Robert A. Kagan, *Going by the Book* (Philadelphia: Temple University Press, 1982).

30. Ralph Nader, "Foreword," in Phillip J. Simon, *Reagan in the Workplace: Unraveling the Health and Safety Net* (Washington, DC: Center for the Study of Responsive Law, 1983), i.

31. This pattern particularly applies to the "new social regulation" that became common in the 1960s and 1970s.

32. See, for instance, Deborah A. Stone, *The Disabled State* (Philadelphia: Temple University Press, 1984).

33. Bardach, "Implementation Studies and the Study of Implements."

34. U.S. General Accounting Office, *Social Security Administration's Data Communications Contracts with Paradyne Corporation Demonstrate the Need for Improved Management Controls* (Washington, DC: GAO/IMTEC–84–15, 1984).

35. Thomas Yamachika, "Beyond *Equal Employment Opportunity Commission* v. *Associated Dry Goods Corporation:* A New Defense of the EEOC's Role in the Title VII Enforcement Process." *California Law Review* 70 (May 1982): 816–49.

36. This definition in part derives from Gordon P. Whitaker, "Coproduction: Citizen Participation in Service Delivery." *Public Administration Review* 40 (May-June, 1980): 240–46.

37. Herbert A. Simon, *Administrative Behavior* (New York: Free Press, 1965), 123–7.

38. Warren F. Ilchman and Norman Thomas Uphoff, *The Political Economy of Change* (Berkeley: University of California Press, 1969), 81.

39. Herbert Kaufman, *The Administrative Behavior of Federal Bureau Chiefs* (Washington, DC: The Brookings Institution, 1981), 86.

40. Chester I. Barnard, *The Functions Of The Executive* (Cambridge, MA: Harvard University Press, 1966), 167; see also 162.

41. Simon, *Administrative Behavior,* 127.

42. See Richard E. Neustadt, *Presidential Power* (New York: John Wiley and Sons, 1964), 29–37.

43. Drawing on Neustadt (ibid., 64), one can define professional reputation as the capacity of a manager to persuade others that he or she has the skill and the will to use the advantages at his or her disposal. Occasional demonstrations of tenacity and skill along with careful management of appearances may permit the executive to prevail even without personally intervening in a particular decision. Usually a manager's professional reputation is linked to actual behavior, but at times executives may manage appearances so as to build an inflated reputation for some quality that is absent or minimal. In essence, the emperor has no clothes (or only underwear and socks), but others do not recognize it.

    As the introductory section of this chapter implied, time also can be seen as a resource. The ability of an executive to carve out the hours needed to focus on a matter heightens prospects that he or she will effectively use other resources to influence a particular decision.

Chapter Twelve

The Management of Personnel

Introduction

In April 1978 Harry Cain, Director of the Bureau of Health Planning and Resources Development in the U.S. Public Health Service, started to deliver a resignation speech to his fellow civil servants. Soon, however, Cain became so overcome with emotion that he could not continue. His immediate superior, Henry Foley, stepped to the lectern and finished reading Cain's statement, which included the following: "I have totally lost my tolerance for the bureaucratic swamp through which a bureau like this must wade. The widest and deepest channel in the swamp, of course, is affectionately known as the personnel system." Complaining that he was unable to hire the people he wanted or fire those he did not, Cain declared that the time had come to quit—"to swim over to the side, climb up and dry out."[1] Cain's resignation followed considerable turbulence over his approach to personnel management. Deeply committed to hiring the best and the brightest to plan and regulate health facilities, Cain attempted to avoid dependence on mid-level employees inherited from other programs. Bitter internal conflict, court suits, and ultimately critical reports from the Civil Service Commission and General Accounting Office ensued.

Not all cases lead to such a dramatic denouement, nor should this example prompt automatic conclusions that those who manage personnel in the government invariably meet defeat. To the contrary, unsung cases of the adroit use of human resources abound. The example does, however, convey the critical importance of personnel management to top officials, the emotional strain it can induce, and the pitfalls it can present. In many respects, personnel remains the most challenging factor of production for top executives to manage.

The issues of personnel management are many. *Position determination* is allocation of formal slots or roles within the agency. How many of what types of positions does the executive need to accomplish some task? How, precisely, should jobs be designed and classified? The management of *human resource flows* focuses on recruitment from outside the agency, promotion, transfer, demotion, and removal. How can executives assure that the movement of people into and out of positions contributes to the achievement of their objectives? *Appraisal of performance* also occupies a central role in personnel management. How do executives find out how their employees perform? What normative standards do they apply to this information; that is, what distinguishes good from bad performance? Executives also control many processes having to do with the *motivation and enablement* of subordinates. How can executives evoke desired behavior from subordinates? How can they ensure that motivated employees have the training and implements to perform their tasks?

As in other arenas, executives face programmatic, legal, consensual, and career imperatives as they manage human resources. Harry Cain's strong commitment to accomplishing certain health planning objectives led him to attempt several innovative personnel strategies. More than in many other management spheres, however, the president, Congress, the courts, and federal agencies have constructed an elaborate edifice of rules for personnel management. With the growth of court activism over the past quarter of a century and the new legal rights conveyed to various classes of individuals during this time, personnel management has become more legalistic. Cain's inattention to legal technicalities ultimately did much to increase his management problems. In varying degrees executives are also sensitive to the consensual imperative, that is, the desirability of avoiding conflicts with subordinates. Harry Cain's intense commitment to program objectives led him to elevate conflict within his bureau. The career imperative also looms large. An executive's opportunity to rise in the hierarchy, or as Cain illustrates, to avoid great personal frustration, may hinge on the processes and outcomes of the personnel game.

This chapter assesses some of the issues of managing human resources. It begins by reviewing five core values that compete for attention in personnel management. It then presents a few players that constrain and occasionally assist executives in the human resource sphere—the Office of Personnel Management, the Merit System Protection Board, the Office of the Special Counsel, the Federal Labor Relations Authority, the Equal Employment Opportunity Commission, unions, and others. With central values and the lineup established, the chapter reviews some critical dynamics in position management, personnel flows, performance appraisal, motivation, and enablement.

Competing Values

Certain core values in human resource management give more specific content to the general imperatives that drive executives.[2] These values are instrumental achievement, political responsiveness, merit, social equity, and employee rights and well-being. These core values compete for the executive's attention; they coexist in some tension with each other.

Instrumental achievement (or agency competence) is managing human resources to foster economy (cost containment), efficiency (as expressed by the ratio of output to cost), and effectiveness (achievement of program goals), as specified, or at least suggested, by law. Commitment to these instrumental goals can lead executives to shortcuts. Administrators may, for instance, decide that it makes little sense to invest time and money searching extensively for the most competent applicant available if a lesser expenditure of resources can attract employees who are "good enough."

Political responsiveness requires that the immediate preferences of elected officials and their appointees weigh heavily in personnel management. Political officials may use personnel processes to carry out their interpretations of laws. Or they may use personnel processes to distribute patronage to their allies. At times deference to the personnel preferences of elected officials and their appointees helps ensure respect for the rule of law and reduces any prospect for the abuse of administrative discretion. On occasion, however, efforts by public executives to honor the preferences of elected officials push them to violate the letter and spirit of the law. Furthermore, responsiveness to one set of elected officials (say the White House) often entails unresponsiveness to another set (say a congressional subcommittee).

Meritocratic norms have deep roots in the classic liberal tradition of the United States. In the case of personnel management, they direct that rewards go to the most competent—those with the best record of or potential for achievement. In this view society is a market where individuals compete and the prize goes to the fittest. Meritocratic norms apply to many aspects of personnel management but probably bear most heavily on recruitment. Viewed from one perspective, government hiring can be seen as an exercise in allocating a scarce resource, namely, a job with reasonably attractive perquisites attached to it. Strong sentiment and legal requirements often insist that jobs go to the most competent applicants available.

Social equity concerns the uses of federal employment to help "worthy" societal groups deemed disadvantaged or potentially disadvantaged. One manifestation of this is that certain group characteristics are off-limits in decisions. This helps protect these groups from adverse discrimination. Individuals, for instance, generally enjoy the right not to be discriminated against on the basis of being a Catholic or 55 years of age. Another version of commitment to social equity goes beyond protection to obtaining representation of certain groups in the bureaucracy's ranks. Representative Patricia Schroeder (Democrat of Colorado) captured some of the flavor of this concern when she remarked during a house hearing: "I think one of the very important things is to make sure that the Federal government represents the population that pays the taxes to make the Federal Government work. Affirmative action is the key to all of that."[3] Executives have in varying degrees faced pressures to hire women, minorities, veterans, the handicapped, and so on.

Employee rights and well-being also shape federal personnel management. A pervasive norm, buttressed in many instances by law, asserts that individuals enjoy certain substantive and procedural rights by virtue of their employment. Employee rights increase to the degree that four conditions, among others, hold. First, they increase to the extent that rules limit the reasons for which executives can take adverse action (e.g., firing) against employees. For instance, federal executives are constrained from taking action against subordinates for engaging in certain activities off the job, such as contributing money to a political campaign. Second, employee rights increase as the procedures for taking adverse action become more elaborate and place a greater burden of proof on executives. Third, employee rights loom larger when those who have more seniority within the agency enjoy greater protection from adverse action than those with less. Fourth, employee rights grow as formal procedures require executives to consult or bargain with official representatives of subordinates over a broader scope of issues.

Beyond these characteristics, the concept of employee well-being implies a concern that government ought to pay attention to the quality of work life. Work that provides civil servants with psychological gratification and promotes their physical well-being goes to the core of this concern. Some observers suggest that the federal government possesses particular obligations vis-à-vis employee rights and well-being. In the words of Representative Mary Rose Oakar (Democrat of Ohio), "The Federal Government ought to serve as a role model for how we treat workers and retirees across the country."[4]

While instrumental achievement, political responsiveness, merit, social equity, and employee rights compete for the executive's attention they do not inevitably clash. For instance, orders to protect racial minorities from discrimination allowed many employers to cast aside blinders that had historically led them to prefer less capable white applicants. In a similar vein, the federal government's willingness to grant employees procedural and substantive rights may facilitate efficiency and effectiveness; at least some subordinates may be more loyal and better motivated as a result. But if values need not invariably conflict, at times they do. Supporters of the Civil Service Reform Act of 1978 charged that employees possessed so many rights that efficiency had been undermined. The Committee on Ability Testing of the National Academy of Science concluded that employment selection "is caught up in a destructive tension between the employer's interest in promoting work force efficiency and the governmental effort to ensure equal employment opportunity."[5]

Considerable uncertainty generally marks any assessment of trade-offs among core values. The precise degree to which value A works at the expense of value B remains fuzzy. This fact frequently allows advocates of a particular value to play the free lunch game. Proponents of some view will persuade executives that concessions to a particular value will entail no costs to others. Those making this argument may be quite sincere and in some situations undoubtedly correct. However, executives can seldom employ a precise calculus to judge their claims.

Other Bureaucratic Players

As executives attempt to balance the claims of competing values in various personnel arenas, they face a cast of other executive branch players who constrain their authority to act. Sometimes these participants serve as allies of the executive, but they also stand ready, like Monday morning quarterbacks, to question the executive's judgment or actions. Unlike such quarterbacks, they often have the authority or power to compel officials to modify decisions and to make restitution for damage.

Overseers

The Office of Management and Budget and the General Accounting Office influence personnel management. Other overseers have specific assignments to monitor and shape developments in the personnal arena in particular. These agencies include the Office of Personnel Management (OPM), the Merit System Protection Board, the Office of Special Counsel, the Federal Labor Relations Authority, and the Equal Employment Opportunity Commission. Exhibit 12.1 is a brief description of

EXHIBIT 12.1   Overseer Agencies in Personnel

Agency	Primary Functions	Formal Leadership	Full-Time Equivalent Employment Fiscal 1987[a]
Office of Personnel Management	Conducts or delegates recruitment, examination, personnel investigations, employee development and training, position classification, and compensation. Operates information systems and manages federal employee benefit programs. Promulgates rules governing personnel operations and monitors practices to determine compliance with standards. Conducts research and provides advice on management issues.	Director appointed by the president to a four-year term with the advice and consent of the Senate.	5,108
Merit System Protection Board	Provides for hearings and adjudication of grievances concerning alleged violations of personnel laws and rules that apply to federal employees. Issues compliance orders to federal agencies found to be in violation of these rules. Conducts special studies as to whether the personnel system adequately protects employees from prohibited personnel practices. May order corrective actions recommended by the Office of the Special Counsel.	Three members appointed by the president for seven-year terms with the advice and consent of the Senate. Members serving a seven-year term cannot be reappointed. No more than two may be adherents of the same political party. President designates chairman of board, who serves as chief executive officer.	302
Office of the Special Counsel	Investigates allegations of prohibited personnel practices. Conducts independent investigations. Can request disciplinary or corrective action from the Merit System Protection Board or others. Has special obligation to probe violations of the Hatch Act, which restrains the partisan political activities of civil servants. Provides channel for whistle-blowers to bring charges of waste, fraud, illegality, or major mismanagement; protects whistle-blowers against retaliation. Relationship to the Merit System Protection Board resembles that of prosecutor to court.	Director is an attorney appointed by the president to a five-year term with the advice and consent of the Senate.	77
Federal Labor Relations Authority	Issues policy interpretations of pertinent laws. Rules on negotiability disputes, exceptions to arbitration awards, union representation, and complaints about unfair labor practices. Supervises the Federal Services Impasse Panel, which provides assistance when unions and management are at loggerheads.	Three members appointed by the president for five-year terms with the advice and consent of the Senate.	263

EXHIBIT 12.1 *Continued*

Agency	Primary Functions	Formal Leadership	Full-Time Equivalent Employment Fiscal 1987[a]
Equal Employment Opportunity Commission	Enforces prohibitions against work-place discrimination based on race, color, religion, sex, national origin, age, or handicap. Requires federal agencies to develop affirmative action programs for minorities, women, and the handicapped. Issues rules and guidelines concerning employment discrimination. Enforces equal employment opportunity laws outside the federal bureaucracy. (Outside groups subject to its jurisdiction include state and local governments and private firms with fifteen or more employees.)	Five members appointed by the president for five-year terms with the advice and consent of the Senate. The president appoints one member to chair the commission.	2,941

[a]U.S. Office of Management and Budget, *Budget of the United States Government, Fiscal Year 1989, Appendix* (Washington: Government Printing Office, 1988).

the primary functions, formal leadership structure, and personnel resources of these agencies.

OPM performs or delegates a wide variety of personnel functions, such as recruitment and performance appraisal. In the wake of the Civil Service Reform Act, OPM increasingly yielded authority to the line agencies of government. By the early 1980s career executives could look to personnel staffs in their own departments to provide a range of personnel services. This probably made it easier for agency executives to influence personnel decisions, although it hardly gave them fine control. However, the delegation in some instances carried a price tag. It forced executives to strip resources from other activities to perform personnel functions OPM once handled. A top official from the Veterans Administration complained in 1983 that his agency had to establish some fifty special examining units in hospitals to select licensed practical nurses, medical technicians, food service workers, and housekeeping aides. This expedited recruitment "but at a cost of reduced VA employee hours available for health-care facilities."[6]

OPM provides more support services than other overseers. It is also likelier to buttress executive authority relative to employees. Reporting directly to the White House, it may be a conduit for presidential preferences about personnel processes. Other major bureaucratic overseers operate more as intragovernmental regulators. The Merit System Protection Board, Office of Special Counsel, and Federal Labor Relations Authority function as major arbiters of employee rights. The Equal Employment Opportunity Commission (EEOC) interprets and enforces laws concerned with social equity.

Certain basic characteristics of the relationship between overseers and federal executives deserve attention. First, overseers' jurisdictions overlap. This makes it

Certain basic characteristics of the relationship between overseers and federal executives deserve attention. First, overseers' jurisdictions overlap. This makes it harder for the executive to guess which agency will take up a given episode. It can also foster delay. In 1984 the Office of Special Counsel charged a Customs official with sexually harrassing and assaulting female employees. When the Office of Special Counsel brought the case before an administrative law judge of the Merit System Protection Board, the judge dismissed some of the counts on grounds that the case fell under the jurisdiction of the EEOC. The three members of the Merit System Protection Board subsequently endorsed the decision of the administrative law judge but reinstated certain related charges filed by the Office of the Special Counsel.[7]

Second, the attitudes and behavior of overseers tend to change over time. They may become more or less supportive of career executives as the years go by. During the Carter administration OPM's director, Alan Campbell, devoted considerable attention to research and advice to line agencies on personnel management. The Reagan administration and a new director, Donald Devine, returned to "bedrock personnel management." Faced with cutbacks, OPM de-emphasized research and consulting. Instead, the agency stressed staffing services and the administration of health, life, and retirement benefit systems.

Third, overseers set constraints for career executives, but they are far from juggernauts in their capacity to enforce their preferences. Ample information about management practices is one prerequisite for enforcement. Overseers do not necessarily have the substantial monitoring capacity to gather intelligence about agency practices. Overseers tend to be reactive; they respond to complaints, usually from employees or unions, that some personnel decision violates the rules. They seldom have the resources to launch any major investigations other than those triggered by complaints to detect violations of standards. Cuts and retrenchment at OPM in the early 1980s diminished its compliance reviews so far that the agency came under criticism from the General Accounting Office.[8]

Vigorous enforcement also requires resources to persuade or compel agencies to correct undesirable behavior. Overseers often lack such potency. In the early 1980s the EEOC required agencies to submit affirmative action plans that included targets and timetables for hiring minorities and women. Expressing their ideological opposition to such targets, officials in the Justice and Education Departments, among others, refused to comply. In the face of this open resistance, top officials at the EEOC perceived that they lacked the clout to prevail. In the words of the commission chairman, the EEOC has "no ability to achieve compliance" and must basically rely on "friendly persuasion . . . and tattle-tale powers."[9]

The capacity of overseers to enforce their preferences generally rests on a firmer foundation when they rule on specific employee appeals. If the Merit System Protection Board orders a fired employee reinstated, compliance usually follows. However, the enforcement capacities of overseers suffer from limits even in processing complaints.[10] The volume of complaints frequently exceeds the capacity of overseers to process them quickly. Delay and backlog often result, especially in cases of social equity. One analysis in the early 1980s indicated that sixty-two federal agencies averaged more than a year and a half to reach a verdict on discrimination appeals. Some, such as the Department of Justice and the Environmental Protection

Agency, averaged close to three years to arrive at a decision. These figures exclude the additional time involved if the complainant appeals the department's decision to the EEOC.[11]

The limited enforcement muscle of agencies like the EEOC has prompted some observers to question whether the sundry overseers are paper tigers. Wilson and Rachal argue that "in general, it is easier for a public agency to change the behavior of a private organization than of another public agency."[12] While sound in some instances, the view probably overstates the point. Federal employees are not shy about filing appeals, often receive prompt consideration of them, and stand a reasonable chance of winning.

Employees file substantial numbers of complaints and appeals. It is not uncommon, for instance, for the Merit System Protection Board and its regional offices to face nearly ten thousand cases in a single year.[13] The prosecutorial arm of this overseer, the Office of Special Counsel, received nearly fourteen hundred complaints of prohibited personnel practices in fiscal 1984. (At one point, the number of complaints prompted its director to state publicly that the agency is not "a federal Ann Landers.")[14]

For its part, the EEOC received some forty-five hundred requests for hearings on charges of employment discrimination in fiscal 1982. This figure underestimates the number filed, since EEOC enters the picture only after the executive's own personnel staff has investigated the charge. After this inquiry, the employee or agency executive can request that the EEOC hold a hearing on the charge. Top executives at the EEOC then reach a verdict on the employee complaint, which the subordinate can formally appeal to the EEOC. In fiscal 1982 these appeals numbered approximately three thousand.[15] Finally, the Federal Labor Relations Authority received nearly fifty-eight hundred charges of unfair labor practices in fiscal 1984.[16]

While delay and backlog characterize the appellate process, the fact remains that the overseers process large numbers of appeals. From fiscal 1982 through fiscal 1986, the regional offices of the Merit System Protection Board (primarily administrative judges) decided 46,349 appeals. The board itself issued rulings on 16,476 cases during this time. (The MSPB handles appeals of regional office decisions as well as requests from OPM, the Office of Special Counsel, and others.) Moreover, the MSPB has striven to improve its processing time. In fiscal 1983, deluged with appeals from air traffic controllers whom President Reagan had fired, the regional offices of the board decided only 17 percent of appeals within 120 days. In fiscal 1985 and 1986, after introducing a voluntary expedited appeals procedure and with the return of the caseload to normal levels, the regional offices decided within 120 days 95 percent and 99 percent respectively.[17]

Nor do overseers shrink from siding with employees in struggles with executives. While systematic data on appellate decisions are elusive, the available evidence points to considerable employee success. In the period from fiscal 1982 through 1985, the regional offices of the MSPB modified the decisions of federal executives about 25 percent of the time. (This excludes the appeals of the fired air traffic controllers—a highly atypical set of cases). Modification is reversal of the agency's decision or a reduction in the penalty to the employee.[18] If overseers reject an appeal, the subordinate can carry the fight to the federal court system.

The capacity of overseers to inhibit certain behavior of executives is not limited to overturning adverse actions. Anticipation of the time and energy involved in dealing with overseers can, itself, have a chilling effect on executive willingness to take adverse action. Furthermore, legal or other imperatives may drive executives to comply with rules in the absence of any major threat from the overseer. Hence, overseers cannot be readily dismissed as paper tigers even if it is also incorrect to portray them as ferocious.

Aside from enforcement, overseers have important symbolic status. The public rhetoric and behavior of those who lead oversight agencies (especially agencies widely visible to Congress and federal employees) hint at the way the personnel system will balance the five core values—instrumental achievement, merit, political responsiveness, social equity, and employee rights. The cues may have a ripple effect influencing the way that executives and subordinates perceive human resource decisions. These perceptions at times matter as much as the priorities overseers actually set for their agencies.

The experience of Donald Devine as director of OPM during the first term of the Reagan administration illustrates this point. As director, Devine openly and fervently endorsed the "Reagan revolution," at times taking to the hustings on behalf of Republican candidates for office. Moreover, Devine often expressed his views on personnel matters in pungent, colorful terms that the media rushed to cover. Unhappy about delays in reforming the government pension system, he is said to have put out a press release entitled "House Committee Fiddles While the Government Pension System Burns." Whether accurate or not, the image of Devine was that he stood ready to place political responsiveness to the White House above other core values in the personnel arena. Some feared that he was excessively partisan on personnel issues. In part as a result, his dealings with certain committees in Congress quickly deteriorated. One member of Congress likened him to Spiro Agnew, going "for the tougher or cruder word" at some "sacrifice" to "more direct and honest analysis."[19] President Reagan nominated Devine for a second four-year term in 1985. However, Devine's contentious relations with Congress, intense opposition from employee groups, and other events ultimately prompted the President to withdraw Devine's name from consideration. Of greater significance, Devine's behavior probably exacerbated the distrust and anxiety in many quarters of the bureaucracy during the retrenchment of the 1980s.

Unions

Aside from bureaucratic overseers, federal executives must in varying degrees contend with employee unions. (For a general perspective, see Exhibit 12.2.) Unions have gained a foothold in some although by no means all agencies of the federal bureaucracy. Labor relations in the federal sector inhabit at least three different worlds. In one, unions of federal employees are unable to bargain collectively over the "gut stuff" of labor relations—wages and fringe benefits. They generally lack such major power resources as a massive dues-paying membership base. In another, unions representing civil servants enjoy both these advantages. In the third, which consists of private contractors and other agents of indirect implementation, patterns of

EXHIBIT 12.2   Perspective on Public Sector Union Membership

Considering membership at all levels of government in the twentieth century, public-sector unionism has evolved through three major periods. A period of slow, steady growth marked the period from 1900 to 1961; 1962 through 1976 featured explosive increases in membership; finally, the post-1976 phase emphasized stabilization and minor erosion. The figures below reveal this pattern.

	Membership (in thousands)	Density (percent of all public employees unionized)
1897	11	—
1930	268	9
1962	2162	24
1976	5922	40
1987	6055	36

The percentage of all public sector union members who work for the federal government has declined steadily from 91 percent in 1930 to 30 percent in 1962 to 19 percent in 1982. This in part reflects the fact that employment at the state and local levels has increased more rapidly than at the federal level.

Source: Leo Troy and Neil Sheflin, "The Flow and Ebb of U.S. Public Sector Unionism." *Government Union Review* 5 (Spring 1984): 1–149; Leo Troy, "Public Sector Unionism: The Rising Power Center of Organized Labor." *Government Union Review* 9 (Summer 1988): 1–35. Reprinted by permission of the Government Union Review.

labor relations vary enormously. Since federal executives seldom deal directly with labor relations issues in this third world, this chapter will not examine it.

The First World.   Weak unions tend to represent the general schedule work force. As of the early 1980s, 98 different unions represented more than 1.2 million nonpostal employees in some 63 agencies and 2,432 bargaining units. Unions represented about 60 percent of the nonpostal civilian work force.[20] Figures on the percentage of employees legally represented by unions are misleading. For a union to become the representative of employees in a given organizational unit, 30 percent of the employees in that unit must file a petition requesting that bargaining be handled by one union. The union must then receive a majority of the votes cast by eligible employees in a secret ballot. Unlike its counterparts in much of the private sector, the victorious union cannot under the law establish a union shop. That is, it cannot require that all employees in the bargaining unit who do not join the exclusively recognized union pay a fixed amount, usually equivalent to members' dues. Hence, union leaders in the nonpostal service carry a substantial number of free riders, who do not join the union but nonetheless obtain the advantages of collective bargaining.

While data on union membership in the federal government leave much to be desired, it appears that fewer than 40 percent of those legally represented by unions actually belong to them. The largest nonpostal unions are the American Federation of Government Employees (about 250,000 members), the National Treasury Employees' Union (about 50,000), the National Association of Government Employees (roughly 50,000), and the National Federation of Federal Employees (approximately

40,000).[21] Membership in these and other unions rose sharply from 1963 through 1975. As austerity struck the federal bureaucracy in 1980, union memberships and revenues declined. In 1983 the American Federation of Government Employees witnessed a $600,000 decline in dues revenue; the union cut its own staff, which helped to precipitate a nine-week strike by the remaining staff.[22]

The prohibition against bargaining collectively over salaries and fringe benefits in this federal sphere means that union leaders focus on other matters in labor negotiations and use traditional political channels to lobby Congress on pay and fringe benefits. Contracts with these unions often call for more extensive grievance procedures than executives would otherwise face. Union contracts can also constrain executives in assigning employees to organizational subdivisions, work projects, or terms of duty.

Unions persistently seek to expand the scope of issues subject to negotiation by appealing to the Federal Labor Relations Authority. Often these appeals focus on significant issues such as the circumstances under which executives can reassign personnel or contract out certain agency functions. For their part, executives frequently complain that unions strive to make the most trivial decisions subject to negotiation by filing "frivolous" appeals with the Federal Labor Relations Authority. Top executives at the Veterans Administration cited unfair labor practice charges over such matters as the agency's refusal to bargain over a union proposal to provide PacMan machines for use during work breaks and over greens fees charged employees at Veterans Hospital golf courses.[23]

The Second World.   This is primarily the postal service, which employs nearly 25 percent of federal civilian workers. The Postal Reorganization Act of 1970 is the legal foundation for labor relations in this agency. Whereas unions of nonpostal employees began to gain impetus in the 1960s, the Postal Service has a tradition of union activity dating to the nineteenth century. Postal unions represent the vast majority of the department's employees. Moreover, the law permits union shops. It is not surprising, therefore, that an estimated 85 percent to 90 percent of postal employees belong to a union.[24] Ten unions represent the great bulk of this membership; two-thirds of the union members belong to the two largest groups, the National Association of Letter Carriers or the Postal Workers Union; both are AFL-CIO affiliates.[25]

Postal workers are the largest group of federal employees who can use collective bargaining to set pay and fringe benefits. Some sixty-two thousand employees in nineteen other federal agencies, among them the Government Printing Office and the Tennessee Valley Authority, also have this prerogative. Postal and other unions have successfully used their right to bargain over pay. A study in the early 1980s indicated that employees whose salaries were set through collective bargaining generally earned more than those doing comparable work in agencies where unions lacked this right. In fiscal 1981 letter carriers received $5,490 more in annual salary than their general schedule counterparts.[26]

On balance, unions and overseers contribute to centrifugal tendencies in the personnel system. Under the banner of various core values, they accelerate the dispersal of power and influence over human resource management. Whether these players foster a system where the competing values receive appropriate weight in personnel decisions remains an open question. Examining position management, the administration of personnel flows, performance appraisal, and motivation can provide additional insight into this issue.

Position Management

Career executives know that agency tasks require a division of labor. If they could start from scratch, officials could consider a plethora of options for bundling tasks into positions (job design). They could determine the number of different types of positions needed; they would have free rein to place these positions in the hierarchy and into particular subunits of the agency. They would face perennial uncertainty. Officials can seldom calibrate the precise relationship between position management and the cost-effectiveness of the agency. Will the marginal return in outputs from adding ten more of position type X justify the additional salary expense? Will placement of positions in subunit A rather than B yield greater efficiency and effectiveness? Such questions seldom submit to proven and unequivocal answers. Nevertheless, executives starting from scratch could test their pet theories of effective position management.

Executives seldom if ever start with so clean a slate; instead they must work at the margins. They inherit some number and structure of positions. Through various processes they may succeed in adding slots, getting some positions changed to different types, or reorganizing them. Even if they succeed, change tends to come at a snail's pace. Many factors constrain their ability to act.

The formal classification systems of the federal government set critical parameters for the design and labeling of positions. The Office of Personnel Management defines and sorts jobs into positions—cartographic technician, mail clerk, file clerk. The different positions require certain qualifications, entail certain duties, and are associated with certain levels of pay. OPM and its delegated representatives in the departments are responsible for assuring that the classification structure remains accurate—that the employee classified as being in position X actually performs the duties associated with this job rather than those of position Y.

The largest classification structure for civilian employees is the general schedule (GS) system, which covers about 1.4 million predominantly white-collar employees. It contains 442 occupations and some 18 pay grades; hence the common reference to a job as being a GS 7 or some other level. The federal wage system (FWS) covers some 520,000 blue-collar trade, craft, or laboring employees in 372 occupations.[27] Both GS and FWS emphasize position analysis; scrutiny of duties determines classification. Other smaller systems, such as those associated with the Foreign Service and the Department of Medicine and Surgery in the Veterans Administration, use the *rank-in-person* approach. That is, the qualifications and accomplishments of an employee (e.g., a physician in the Department of Medicine and Surgery) rather than a highly detailed analysis of the particular job to be performed determine his or her title and pay.

Aside from having to structure work life according to formal classification systems, executives face many other pressures that limit their discretion. Among these pressures, two in particular stand out, namely, pressures that seek to limit the total number of positions within the agency and pressures to hold down the hierarchical level of jobs. The degree to which these forces contribute to efficient position management is debatable.

Ceilings: Control versus Management?

In determining how many positions they will have to accomplish agency tasks, executives face the limits of budget allocation. Obviously, positions cannot be filled unless executives have the money to pay the personnel who fill them; nor do the controls end here. Aside from the constraints of budget outlays, executives typically confront personnel ceilings—formal limits on the number of civil servants the agency can employ. These ceilings are often only loosely related to appropriations. Lacking specific statutory specifications of total positions, the Office of Management and Budget sets numerical limits on personnel. Annual budget requests from agency officials to OMB contain estimates of the positions they need to fill. Around the time the president submits his budget to Congress, OMB notifies departments of their employment ceilings. Ceilings often reflect the preferences of the White House, and appropriations reflect those of Congress. Many an executive has the money to hire personnel but not the authority to do so because of ceilings.[28]

For many years, personnel ceilings were calculated on the final day of the fiscal year. Beginning in fiscal 1982, however, all agencies except the Department of Defense commenced with the full-time equivalent system of calculation. Instead of meeting an end-of-the-year count, the executive had to keep a running tab on the actual work years being expended, making sure that they did not exceed the ceiling.

Like most constraints, ceilings encourage certain management practices. For instance, under the end-of-the-year system for ceilings, executives at the Internal Revenue Service often furloughed large numbers of seasonal employees just before the end of the fiscal year and brought them back after the new year. Executives in the agency viewed the practice as expensive and disruptive. With the shift away from counting only on the last day of the year, the ceilings heightened the importance of certain other incentives. Ceilings elevate the appeal of overtime work; they also heighten the allure of contracting out for services, since ceilings do not apply to third parties. *Hence, the strong cultural bias toward administration by proxy finds reinforcement in the nitty-gritty of personnel management.*

Two OMB circulars govern executives when they seek to contract with those outside of government. Circular A–76, issued in 1966, requires agencies to compare costs of certain "commercial and industrial activities" (protective services, janitorial work, keypunching, and so on) to determine the most economical source of performance. Technically, an in-house activity cannot be converted to contract unless it saves 10 percent in personnel costs. The circular also vaguely asserts that some functions "are inherently governmental, being so intimately related to the public interest as to mandate performance by Federal employees." Uncertainty and disagreement characterize efforts to define exactly what services can be contracted out and the techniques to be used in conducting cost comparisons. Union leaders have often complained that existing interpretations of A–76 manifest undue bias in favor of contracting. More objective observers have also called attention to this bias.[29] In the view of the General Accounting Office, "personnel ceilings, among other things, caused agencies to use contractor personnel to perform work that Federal employees should have performed."[30]

OMB circular A–120 governs the hiring of consultants. These consultants are supposed to provide advice; in some instances, however, they come close to making decisions reserved for government officials. As with A–76, ambiguity in the regulation provides career executives with considerable discretion in using consultants when ceilings prevent them from hiring civil servants.

Do personnel ceilings ultimately prompt career executives to pursue undesirable management strategies? Some say yes. The GAO ranks among the most persistent critics of ceilings as a barrier to effective work force planning. In the GAO view, "arbitrary personnel ceiling constraints are a major reason why Federal agencies have not extensively used sound work force planning procedures."[31] This view holds that budgetary limitations coupled with human resource planning can provide the necessary control over the size and cost of federal personnel. "Additional controls imposed by personnel ceilings deprive agency management of options for accomplishing essential work through the most effective, efficient, and economical use of the most appropriate manpower in specific circumstances."[32]

Others within government, particularly OMB, have rejected these views. In 1976 James T. Lynn, then director of OMB, praised ceilings as a significant check on the "natural" inclination of federal managers to add personnel and "to disregard the indirect costs" of such additions. He also expressed the view that the ceilings are important in and of themselves "regardless of any other considerations."[33]

This latter remark in particular shows how personnel ceilings represent a fundamental tension between cost-effectiveness and political responsiveness. Consistent with GAO arguments, a plausible case can be presented—although certainly not proven—that abolishing ceilings and relying on budgetary constraints alone would let executives manage their programs more effectively. However, top political officials often see virtues in redundant control mechanisms; they will often trade a measure of effectiveness for greater accountability.

Ceilings seem valuable to political officials for several reasons. For one thing, elected officials appreciate their symbolic utility. In a culture fearful of centralized bureaucracy and under the misconception that the federal bureaucracy (as distinct from the federal budget) is huge, actions to hold down the number of bureaucrats in Washington have considerable public appeal. If elected officials have a difficult time controlling spending, they can at least control the number of civil servants. Beyond this, ceilings further an ideological commitment to the privatization of government. Big appropriations and low ceilings feed the pervasive tendency to contract services to the private sector. Proponents of privatization believe that it has many virtues. One is that it may reduce pressures to expand government programs and make concessions to civil servants. This view holds that government employees (as opposed to private firms under contract) are more likely to generate pressures for "big government." In addition, ceilings help the White House control the bureaucracy. In the early 1980s President Reagan attempted to use ceilings to cut some programs beyond the levels Congress had mandated.[34]

Given the various functions of ceilings for numbers of political officials, they seem likely to persist as a major constraint on position management. The prospect that these ceilings will derive from sophisticated analysis of human resource needs in various federal agencies remains slight. In light of this circumstance, the already formidable barriers to human resource planning, in large part limits to knowledge, seem even more substantial.

The Struggle against Grade Creep

Executives not only encounter substantial pressure to hold down the number of federal civil servants; they also face pressure to reduce the grade level of positions in the bureaucracy. Overseers have sought to generate this pressure in order to check grade creep, or the propensity for positions to be reclassified to a higher pay scale. Grade creep is persistent. The average grade of full-time general schedule employees rose from 5.4 in 1950 to 6.7 in 1960 to 7.8 in 1970 to 8.3 in 1983.[35]

Some observers view grade creep as the result of Machiavellian executives attempting to bolster their status by surrounding themselves with high-level personnel. In fact, however, other factors probably do more to account for this executive propensity. Advances in technology and the quest to buffer the agency against uncertainty can fuel the quest for upward classification. Executives inhabit an environment that persistently produces new equipment and techniques. These developments often create a demand for more "professionals." Furthermore, higher classifications enable some executives to build in skills slack. Even if the day-to-day operations of the agency do not require certain skills, executives may desire the surplus skills as a hedge against uncertainty. An executive who encounters an atypical problem, more complex than those ordinarily confronted, will have the human resources to adapt and cope with it.

The differential in the flow of information concerning classification errors and the desire to win support from subordinates also fuel grade creep. Errors of undergrading much more readily come to the attention of executives than errors of overgrading. An employee who feels undergraded (that is, doing more demanding work than is conveyed by the class specifications) is likely to report the problem. Subordinates have every incentive to draw these circumstances to the attention of the executive because upward classification will lead to more pay. In contrast, subordinates who are doing less than the duties specified in their job classification are much more likely to shield information from the executive. Reporting this information could lead to their downgrading and an attendant loss of pay and status. Aside from the differential in the flow of information concerning the two types of classification errors, executives have more incentive to act on upgradings. Such actions can win them considerable goodwill and support from subordinates. Efforts on their part to downgrade employees tend to have the opposite effect.

Finally, the more constraints on executives in terms of the number of personnel they can hire, the more they tend to be left with high-grade positions. In this respect, the implications of personnel ceilings come home to roost. These ceilings heighten the appeal of contracting out government functions. Such contracting tends to be easiest for low-grade positions such as cafeteria and custodial work. As these jobs disappear, the average grade tends to increase. Moreover, executives may push for higher-grade personnel to manage contracts or grants.

While the upward pressures on classification are considerable, other incentives militate against executives being excessively zealous in seeking to upgrade subordinates. To some degree the legalistic imperative inclines managers not to pursue upgradings of individual positions that would grossly violate classification standards. Furthermore, a classification structure ridden with inaccuracies is not particularly useful to the executive in monitoring and projecting the personnel needs of the agency. These inaccuracies may create hard feelings among employees who see themselves as doing the same work as better-paid coworkers in higher classes. On balance, however, the pressure for upward classification tends to be more potent than countervailing forces.

In the abstract one might expect OPM to do more to inhibit upward movement in the classification structure. This overseer is ultimately responsible for monitoring compliance with classification standards. However, OPM and its designated representatives in the line agencies lack the resources to engage in constant monitoring. Moreover, these personnel specialists have some incentive to give executives the benefit of a doubt on classification issues. Much contemporary personnel administration emphasizes the personnel staff's role as a facilitator for executives rather than as an enforcer of the letter of classification policy.

Sporadically, those looking for ways to cut government budgets have attempted to stem or reverse grade creep. During the Reagan administration OPM and OMB initiated the "battle of the bulge." Spurred in part by the Grace Commission's charges of overgrading, the two agencies sought to reduce the number of federal positions in the GS 11 to GS 15 categories (those just below the Senior Executive Service) by two percent per year from 1985 through 1988.[36] As could be expected, executives resisted. Hospital directors in the Veterans Administration asserted that the policy would damage morale, hurt recruiting, thwart retention of employees, and threaten the quality of care delivered to veterans.[37] This and other resistance appeared to have an effect. With criticism in Congress growing, officials at OMB acknowledged that the bulge project "doesn't seem to be catching fire" in the agencies and that "a lot of these management things are a lot more difficult to get at than we thought."[38] In the face of these difficulties, officials at OPM and OMB put the project on the back burner in mid-1985.

Uncertainty about the origins of grade creep make it difficult to legitimate projects like the bulge initiative. In launching this project, OPM estimated that 32 percent of the grade increases over time stemmed from poor position management and classification. However, this estimate soon came under fire from other analytic staffs such as the GAO.[39] Several factors other than misclassification or poor position management can account for grade creep. These include technological advances as well as the propensity of the federal government to contract out lower-level jobs. To be sure, in some instances agencies accomplish just as much with a lower grade structure, but determining how much grade creep stems from illegitimate sources remains difficult. This uncertainty helps assure that efforts to reduce grade levels will unleash considerable bureaucratic infighting.

Critics of personnel ceilings, such as the GAO, see similar problems with grade controls. They believe that budgetary appropriations mingled with careful attention to work force planning will serve efficiency and effectiveness more satisfactorily than arbitrary caps on grade levels.[40] Sporadic attempts at grade controls seem likely to continue, however. These controls and personnel ceilings will not only add to the challenge of position management, they will set basic parameters for executives as they manage the flow of personnel.

Managing the Flow of Personnel

Managers have a clear stake in the position management processes that create a skeletal structure of formal organizational roles. Their fortunes also depend heavily on who occupies these roles. The ability of executives to move people into and out of jobs can markedly affect their capacity to accomplish critical objectives.

Finding the Right People

In attempting to find and appoint the appropriate people to vacant positions, executives face a number of constraints. (1) They face the inevitable limits on their time. They can usually recruit subordinates to positions one or two steps down the hierarchy from them, but they must rely on subordinates for most other appointments. (2) They face limits on their information. Does the applicant pool include adequate numbers of the best qualified job hunters? Among applicants, who would prove to be the most competent? Neither question can be answered definitively. (3) They have limited authority to appoint people. Statutes and other rules delegate considerable authority to OPM and personnel staffs in winnowing down the list of those certified for employment.

These barriers are less formidable when executives seek to fill positions via promotions or transfers. In these circumstances they can learn about applicants from the grapevine as well as from formal performance appraisals. Furthermore, OPM tends to permit the executive more discretion when appointing from within. These factors, along with the desire of executives to build support and organizational involvement among subordinates, make promotions the more popular vehicle for filling many positions. Nonetheless, hiring from the outside remains important. Low-level workers hired from the outside perform significant tasks; over time, they become the pool for future promotions.

OPM as well as personnel specialists in line agencies do much to structure the selection of applicants for the federal work force. Officials may appoint applicants from a register kept either by OPM or the agency. A standing register is an ongoing list of applicants judged acceptable for appointment. A deferred register is created when a position opens. A register ultimately lists successful applicants in rank order. Executives can usually pick from the top three on the register who continue to express interest in the job. Only a small number of those listed on the register ultimately win federal positions.

Job hunters obtain a place on the register via an examination. The Civil Service Reform Act generally gave federal departments more authority to construct their own competitive examinations. It did, however, require OPM to conduct competitive examinations for positions common to several federal agencies. The first Director of OPM, Alan Campbell, interpreted this provision very liberally, attempting to delegate broad authority for competitive examinations to line departments. Under

Campbell's successor, Donald Devine, OPM moved to reclaim some of its testing authority. Devine believed that excessive delegation had spawned a duplication of examination efforts, placed undue burdens on job hunters to file multiple applications, and led to inadequate public notice of exams.[41]

The 1970s and 1980s not only witnessed debate over the proper locus of examination authority, they also produced ferment concerning the kind of tests to use. For many years, the assembled, or written, test dominated the federal government's examinations and stood as the major symbol of the merit system. As of the late 1970s, just under 60 percent of all outside applicants for general schedule jobs took written or performance tests.[42] The Professional and Administrative Career Examination (PACE) played a particularly prominent role. This test was the primary screening device for college graduates seeking entry in GS 5 through GS 7 positions for 120 different federal occupations from food assistance program specialist to veterans claims examiner to customs inspector. The PACE sought to tap certain generic abilities presumed to be critical for successful performance in these occupations. For example, it purported to measure the ability to understand complex reading material and to use language effectively in written communications.

The degree to which the PACE and other written examinations presented career executives with the most competent applicants available remains an open question. The examinations made it more difficult to influence the ranking of applicants, a primary goal of early civil service reformers. However, only complex validation studies can demonstrate the precise degree to which examinations lead to the hiring of the most able. Since meritocratic norms had long emphasized that government should hire the best applicants available, federal personnel specialists were sensitive to issues of validation. Prior to the 1970s, however, the pressures on these personnel administrators to present ample proof of examination validity was modest. The Supreme Court's decision in *Griggs* v. *Duke Power Company* (1971) dramatically altered matters. Among other things, this decision affirmed that the absence of discriminatory intent did not redeem hiring procedures that had not been validated and disproportionately screened out minority job hunters. Armed with this court opinion, minority advocates put new legal pressure on employers to meet stringent standards of proof in demonstrating the validity of their selection processes, a very expensive and difficult exercise. Short of exacting validation, they wanted employers to hire minority applicants in at least the same proportion as white applicants.[43]

Under the pressure of a 1975 appellate court ruling, federal officials agreed to abandon their prior examination, the Federal Service Entrance Examination; subsequently, the Civil Service Commission (OPM after 1978) poured substantial resources into the PACE. By 1979, their efforts at validation had consumed more than two million dollars.[44]

Whatever validity the PACE achieved, white applicants tended to score better on it than blacks. A study released in 1979 indicated that 58 percent of the white applicants passed, while only 12 percent of black applicants did.[45] Nor surprisingly, results like these prompted further litigation by black advocates challenging the validity of the PACE. After several rounds of legal sparring between federal administrators and minority plaintiffs, federal officials threw in the towel in 1982. As a result of a consent decree negotiated in the case of *Luevano* v. *Devine,* federal officials agreed to abolish the PACE and develop alternative examining procedures.

At least over the short term, federal officials would employ outsiders for the PACE positions through a special hiring authority under Schedule B. Schedule B appointments take place when OPM determines it is impractical to hold a competitive examination and when the appointee does not serve in a confidential or policymaking position. In the past some executives used Schedule B to meet unusual hiring requirements. For instance, ACTION, a federal poverty agency, recruited certain employees under this schedule on grounds that they needed particular empathy with clients; agency officials believed that standard civil service tests could not measure this quality. For many years Schedule B appointees could not win career jobs in the civil service unless they took the appropriate examination. Of course job experience would help Schedule B appointees get better scores on competitive examinations. In 1987 even this modicum of competition vanished. Responding to court action, Executive Order 12596 provided for noncompetitive conversion of Schedule B appointees to career posts. From 1983 through 1986, Schedule B placements were roughly 15 percent of all appointments to professional and administrative positions in the federal service. More than 70 percent of these appointments went to federal civil servants seeking promotions or transfers.[46]

In general the great difficulties of constructing and validating written tests that withstand minority challenges in courts encouraged reliance on unassembled examinations. These examinations evaluate education, training, and experience in ranking applicants for jobs. Aside from pressures applied by minority advocates, the growing professionalism in government galvanized the use of unassembled tests. Over the years the federal government increasingly came to be made up of different clusters of professional groups (e.g., doctors, nurses, social workers, accountants) each with their university degrees. The federal government demonstrated increased willingness to accept these degrees as proof of competence for a wide range of positions.

Technically, unassembled examinations pose as many problems of validation as written tests. Personnel analysts must develop reliable and valid techniques for interpreting and scoring the education, experience, and training of applicants. The opportunity for error is ample. Despite the fact that unassembled examinations are no cure-all, they draw less criticism than written tests, possibly in part because minority applicants often perform better on them.[47]

Greater Discretion: A Double-Edged Sword?

The demise of the PACE and the rise of unassembled examinations has in some respects increased the discretion of career executives over appointments. Sometimes executives know beforehand whom they wish to hire, and unassembled examinations open the door to job tailoring. In essence, an executive drafts a job description that fits the desired applicant. The official then coaches the preferred applicant to use the right words and emphases on the application form. Working from these written documents and looking for certain key phrases, personnel specialists tend to give higher ranking to these preselected applicants and certify them for hiring.[48]

However, executive discretion can invite outside pressure for appointments. Elected officials interested in political responsiveness may be one source of such pressure. While political officials usually pay more attention to top-level jobs, the possibility of interest in lower positions cannot be dismissed. In recent years, interest among elected officials in middle- and lower-level jobs has been less a matter of patronage than of gaining control over the bureaucracy. Sensitive to the discretion civil servants wield at nearly all levels of the bureaucracy, various groups have pressed elected officials for ideological representation. For instance, in 1984 the American Coalition for Traditional Values, a national network of churches, initiated a program to rectify what its leaders saw as underrepresentation of born-again Christians in federal agencies. Schedule C positions have long symbolized the quest for political responsiveness below the top ranks. Schedule C employees win appointments outside regular competitive civil service channels. Ranked at the GS 15 or below, they serve in policy determining positions requiring a close, confidential relationship with top political officials.

With the PACE gone, some observers expected schedule B appointments to ease intervention by elected officials. Two observers foresaw a "return to the spoils system."[49] In a similar vein, the Merit System Protection Board termed schedule B appointments "the weakest link in. . . the merit system chain." As of the mid-1980s, however, concern among career executives over abuse of schedule B appointments was not widespread.[50] In fact, officials in many agencies preferred the schedule B flexibility. Furthermore, one study of federal recruitment uncovered no evidence that the Reagan administration systematically used Schedule B to extend political control to the lower echelons of the bureaucracy.[51]

In the meantime, OPM worked throughout the 1980s to develop alternatives to both PACE and Schedule B. As of mid-1988, OPM had created six new exams that covered about 52 percent of the positions formerly filled through PACE (e.g., computer specialists and tax technicians). The new examinations differ from PACE because they test for the ability to do a specific job rather than a more general aptitude to do professional and administrative work.

Hiring Discretion and Social Equity

More hiring discretion could also intensify pressures for social equity. The Civil Service Reform Act of 1978 raised this prospect by requiring all executive agencies to conduct a continuing recruitment program to eliminate underrepresentation of racial minorities. The implementors, primarily EEOC and OPM, expanded the program's coverage to women as well. By 1980 the initiative had come to be known as the Federal Equal Opportunity Recruitment Program (FEORP).

Those implementing the program initially sought to apply considerable pressure on agencies to bolster affirmative action. To that end they adopted a definition of underrepresentation that amounted to a kind of double jeopardy for agencies. Underrepresentation occurred when the percentage of protected group A (e.g., blacks, women) in certain agency jobs lagged behind the percentage of A in that occupation in the civilian labor force. Federal guidelines required executives to examine the percentage of group A in that occupation in *both* the local and the national labor force. The *higher* of the two labor force figures was the benchmark for underrepresentation in certain agency jobs. This meant that an agency that recruited locally for clerical positions (for example in Boise, Idaho, where few members of racial minorities live) might have to seek applicants nationally to achieve adequate "representation." This method of calculating underrepresentation also meant that in full compliance with the guidelines, the federal work force would contain higher proportions of minorities and women in various occupations than would the entire civilian labor force.

Many executives perceived that this standard set their agencies up for failure, a view at least implicitly endorsed by the General Accounting Office.[52] Sluggish implementation became the rule, in part because of the limited enforcement muscle of the EEOC. Moreover, the opposition of many top Reagan appointees to anything resembling "racial quotas" in hiring signaled that FEORP ranked low in priority. One agency director of personnel put it this way in the early 1980s:

> When I talk to people out in the field, I see that their sense is that OPM has back-burnered or shelved EEO programs. They don't feel they have to pay attention anymore. Their attitude is that FEORP and these other programs will get changed, and eventually they won't be held accountable for them anymore.[53]

Or in the words of another agency executive:

> The Carter Administration went (overboard) in the EEO area and made life terrible for us . . . Our hiring, frankly, became very race and sex conscious . . . Since that time, there has been a Department level change and we are now hiring purely on the basis of ability again.[54]

While many federal executives no doubt disagree at least in part with these views, few dispute that pressure to use hiring discretion on behalf of social equity declined during the 1980s. The sense that FEORP was neglected angered minority advocates. In the view of one black leader, FEORP "has become a nonprogram of paper-mâché substance."[55]

Various groups with special claims to employment based on social equity to some degree place conflicting pressures on career executives. Observers have criticized veterans preference as a barrier to affirmative action. Veterans receive preference points on entry-level examinations that often permit them to move to the top of the register. A study based on a 1 percent sample of all general schedule employees suggests that over the short term the preference points help veterans obtain federal jobs, largely at the expense of women rather than racial minorities because higher proportions of minorities serve in the military than whites. However, the analysis goes on to conclude that veterans who win jobs but who lack education and experience lose out over time to other employees in obtaining promotions. Over the long haul, veteran status predicts little about the grade level achieved by an employee relative to other factors traditionally associated with merit, such as education.[56] In essence, executives use their discretion to offset the initial bias in favor of veterans.

Whatever the precise dynamics, certain data indicate that women and racial minorities are obtaining more and better-paying federal jobs. As Table 12.1 indicates, the overall proportion of women in general schedule jobs rose from 42 percent in 1974 to 47 percent in 1985. Of greater importance, the percentage of females in GS 9 through GS 12 positions nearly doubled, and the percentage rated GS 13 through GS 15 more than doubled. Increases among blacks were slightly less

TABLE 12.1 Percentage of Women and Blacks in General Schedule Positions, 1974–1985

	1974		1980		1985	
	Black	Female	Black	Female	Black	Female
All GS Levels	13%	42%	14%	45%	15%	47%
GS 1–4	22	76	24	77	27	78
GS 5–8	17	58	20	65	21	69
GS 9–12	7	19	9	27	11	34
GS 13–15	3	5	5	8	5	12

Source: U.S. General Accounting Office, *Distribution of Male and Female Employees In Four Federal Classification Systems* (Washington, DC: GAO/GGD-85-20, 1984), Appendix 33; Office of Personnel Management, November 1985. Data on female representation in 1974 and 1980 come from the GAO report; OPM furnished the remaining data.

dramatic. Their overall representation rose from 13 percent to 15 percent from 1974 to 1985. Their representation in the grades GS 9 through GS 12 rose from 7 percent to 11 percent and in the GS 13 through GS 15 from 3 percent to 5 percent.

Other analyses reaffirm that the Reagan administration did not end gains in the hiring of minorities and women. One study of employment at GS 13 and above concludes that "despite Reagan rhetoric and actions against affirmative action, progress seems to have continued at the same rate since his election as during the previous few years."[57] Another study documents that minorities received a higher percentage of Schedule B appointments than via PACE or other examinations.[58] The results may stem from declining public-sector pay, which makes federal employment less attractive to white men. The results may also indicate that many career officials continued to pursue affirmative action despite the antipathy of the White House to anything resembling gender- or race-conscious hiring.[59] Whatever the reason, the findings provide some hope for those committed to social equity in federal employment.

Time-out: The Hiring Freeze

In playing the hiring game, the career executive perennially faces the prospect that the White House will impose a hiring freeze. President Carter imposed three such freezes—one that ran from 3 March to 17 June 1977, one from 24 October 1978 through February 1979, and one from 14 March 1980 until President Reagan took office. In January 1981 President Reagan initiated his own freeze, which lasted until mid-March 1981. Freezes vary in severity. Carter's 1980 freeze allowed officials to fill 50 percent of the vacancies in full-time positions and did not apply to part-time and temporary employment.

Like personnel ceilings and grade quotas, sporadic freezes make it more difficult for executives to manage agencies. There is evidence that the freezes have exacerbated problems of managing grant programs. Freezes may also inhibit the government's ability to collect funds. One analysis asserts that the Carter freezes hampered the collection of taxes by the Internal Revenue Service and slowed loan collections at such federal agencies as the Farmers Home Administration, the Small Business Administration, and the Veterans Administration.[60] While difficult to assess with precision, hiring freezes may also lead to ineffective staffing configurations (e.g., imbalances between professional and clerical support staff because attrition rates among the latter tend to be higher). Whatever inefficiency and ineffectiveness they cause, however, freezes have considerable appeal to elected officials. Freezes may ease cash flow problems over the short run. Of vastly greater importance, they symbolize the federal government's capacity to keep the bureaucracy in line. A presidential announcement of a hiring freeze can convey that the White House plans to get tough with the bureaucracy. Freezes are much easier to achieve than significant victories over the substance of federal programs and their costs.

Sporadic hiring freezes create certain incentives for managers. They are yet another reason to use other governments and private entities to implement government programs. Freezes also create incentives to have subordinates work overtime; they spur a quest for loopholes. If a freeze applies to full-time or permanent employees, executives look more favorably on hiring part-time or temporary workers. At times, officials hire more employees than the freeze order permits. (Lest this be blown out of proportion, some White House freezes have violated statutory provisions for staffing.)

Removal for Unsatisfactory Performance

The management of personnel requires more than finding and hiring the right people; it also entails efforts to dislodge certain incumbents through demotion, transfer, or termination. In attempting to remove employees for unsatisfactory performance, executives must generally be careful to follow procedures and build a carefully documented case against the employee. (This assumes that the executive anticipates formal action such as firing. Informal means such as encouraging an employee to resign by means of a transfer to an undesirable posting may be easier.)

Conventional wisdom holds that it is far too hard to fire the inept government worker. Partly because of this charge, proponents of the Civil Service Reform Act of 1978 attempted to reduce use of procedural technicalities to overturn firing decisions. They cited the case of an employee who, dismissed for beating his supervisor with a baseball bat, won reinstatement with back pay because of a minor procedural irregularity.[61] The new law contained provisions designed to streamline the appeals process. Among other things, it removed some levels of appeal and set a time limit to the appeals process. It permitted executives to remove an employee for failure to achieve an acceptable rating on only one critical element of the performance appraisal.

Whether the Civil Service Reform Act has made it appreciably easier to fire employees remains unclear. An earlier section of this chapter described the substantial number of overseers with whom executives must still contend. Moreover, an evaluation conducted soon after the act's passage suggests that change will not be dramatic. This study found that while the number of adverse actions overruled on procedural grounds had declined, the overall reversal rate remained about the same. This was because the number of reversals based on substantive grounds (disagreement with the executive's action based on the facts of the case) had increased sharply.[62]

Findings such as these ostensibly reinforce the view that cumbersome removal procedures result in the triumph of employees' rights over efficiency and effectiveness. Matters are not so simple. For one thing, federal executives have often succeeded in documenting poor performance and obtaining removals. More fundamentally, an unrelenting effort to purge the inept from the agency's employment roster does not necessarily serve cost-effectiveness. Leaving aside the time and energy an executive must take from other pressing matters to do so, such an initiative could ultimately create a kind of dog-eat-dog work culture, which would erode the employees' motivation and productivity. Respect for employee rights, even to the point of carrying older subordinates who have "lost their stuff," may ultimately spawn greater organizational involvement and productivity within the work force. Ultimately, the executive needs to strike a delicate balance between excess in ferreting out the inept and excess in tolerating their presence.[63]

In dealing with issues of removal, career executives confront an ambivalent political culture. On the one hand, many believe that it is too hard to fire people from government. On the other, the culture emphasizes the importance of subordinates who blow the whistle on executives. The image of the lone public employee—a sort of John Wayne of the civil service—taking on lethargic, inefficient, or corrupt executives has a special place in the minds of the citizenry. The Civil Service Reform Act assigned responsibility for protecting whistle-blowers to the Office of Special Counsel.

The Office of Special Counsel has tended to give executives the benefit of a doubt. It refrains from prosecuting whistle-blower cases unless it perceives at least a 75 percent chance of success.[64] The Merit System Protection Board has established exacting standards of proof for those who wish to pursue such cases. Among other things, the special counsel must be able to demonstrate a clear causal link between the employee's allegation of mismanagement or corruption and the agency's adverse treatment of him or her. Given these standards, the Office of the Special Counsel prosecutes only a small percentage of whistle-blower complaints. The relatively low rate of prosecution attracted considerable criticism from some members of Congress.[65]

Yet, a study of seventy-six randomly selected whistle-blower charges concluded that closures of these cases "appear reasonable." Nor did the study uncover evidence that whistle-blowers had fallen victim to a lack of investigatory effort.[66] Some whistle-blower complaints are the last refuge of employees who have appropriately been removed for incompetence.

All this is not to suggest that whistle-blowing invariably lacks validity and is harmless to executives if documented. In mid-1985, for instance, the Merit System Protection Board ordered an executive in the Defense Department fired for retaliating against George Spanton, an employee who had sharply criticized defense contracting practices. At this writing it appears likely that Congress and the president will take additional steps to protect whistle-blowers.

While concerns about whether executives could fire the incompetent dominated much of the political struggle for the Civil Service Reform Act, this issue became much less important under the Reagan administration, when cutback management took center stage. Procedures for laying off employees who had solid records of performance got the attention.

The Intricacies of Reduction in Force

The reduction in force (RIF) is for most executives personally unpleasant, complicated, and unpredictable. As of the early 1980s, the regulations governing RIFs called for notification of the employee at least thirty days in advance. Such employees face reassignment to another position at a similar grade, demotion to a lower position without loss of pay over the short term, or separation.

In order to lay the groundwork for demotions or transfers, executives undertaking RIFs were to establish *competitive areas*. These are geographic and organizational areas within which employees compete for retention during RIFs. Within each competitive area are *competitive levels,* or jobs with similar qualifications, duties, and pay schedules. The executive must establish a retention register for each competitive level. The higher on this register employees are, the less likely are they to be laid off. Tenure (nonprobationary career status), military service, seniority, and good performance appraisals all help employees earn a higher place on the list. An employee whose position is eliminated may be able to move into another job at the same competitive level. When no one is lower on the retention roster in his or her competitive level, an employee can *bump* other employees in a lower level out of a position so long as he or she possesses the skills to do the job. An employee may also *retreat* to a position that is identical to, or substantially the same as, a position from or through which he or she was promoted.

Hence, the elimination of a high position can set off bumping and retreating clear down the hierarchy. Sometimes these chain reactions create public relations problems. OPM Director Donald Devine complained in 1983 that "newspapers have kind of had a heyday of showing a mailroom sorter earning $50,000 a year, or one case in HHS [Health and Human Services], the chief of one of the computer divisions was bumped down to be an animal cage cleaner."[67]

While the rules governing RIFs pay substantial homage to employee rights, they leave executives with some discretion to consider merit. Occasionally federal courts have reaffirmed the right of executives to consider the relative abilities of employees in determining which slots to eliminate.[68] Moreover, executives can reduce the unpredictability of bumping and retreating. Top officials can narrowly define competitive areas and levels. If they do so, employees whose positions are eliminated will have less latitude to remain with the agency. Thus, executives can more easily target not only specific positions but particular subordinates as well. Conceivably, executives could also use avenues of discretion to foster social equity. RIF's emphasis on seniority means that minorities and women, often more recently hired, may bear the brunt of RIFs. Executives can manage RIFs to soften the blow to these groups.

Exercising discretion in the name of merit, social equity, or some other value is not without risk. Executives cannot afford to ignore the threat of appeal to the Merit System Protection Board and ultimately to the courts. Unions use particular care to scrutinize executives' behavior for violations of the rules.

More fundamentally, executives may compound formidable problems of sustaining employees' motivation and productivity during cutbacks if subordinates believe executives have abused their authority in conducting RIFs. RIFs affect more than those who lose their jobs or get bumped. As one federal manager expressed it: "In an organization undergoing a RIF, 100 percent of the people are affected . . . Employee attitudes will generally be negative regardless of whether they are *personally* affected by the RIF."[69] Many within the agency (often the most capable, who have more options) will devote considerable energy to searching for alternative employment. To avoid exacerbating these problems, some executives may decide that ample respect for the letter and spirit of RIF procedures governing employee rights will best enhance agency cost-effectiveness. Many executives are adept at creating a sense that they have been equitable. In the early 1980s a survey found that more than half of the employees who had received RIF notices did not plan to file a complaint because they felt they had been "treated fairly."[70]

Concern with an appropriate balance of employees' rights and other core values does not surface only when executives make discretionary decisions during RIFs but also when overseers attempt to modify the rules of the RIF game. In late October 1983, OPM announced in the *Federal Register* that it had among other things increased the weighting of performance appraisals relative to seniority in retention decisions.[71] These rules also limited bumping and retreating.

Such changes can evoke considerable conflict. In this case employee groups protested to Congress, which banned use of the new rules. This ban expired in July 1985 after considerable efforts at compromise by OPM, employee groups, and members of Congress. To facilitate this compromise, the new Director of OPM, Constance Horner, agreed to a smaller increase in weight for performance appraisals in retention decisions. Union leaders continued to complain that "the OPM regulations would largely substitute notoriously uneven, unfair, and unreliable performance evaluations for seniority in RIF situations."[72] They saw the rules as opening the door to political reprisals and favoritism and appealed unsuccessfully to the Supreme Court to stay the OPM edict. Union leaders were not alone in questioning the value of performance appraisals in RIF decisions. A survey in various departments of the federal government found that more than 71 percent of senior personnel officials did not believe performance appraisals were accurate enough to be a major factor in layoff decisions.[73]

Given the strategic difficulties and possible detrimental effects of RIFs, executives often prefer to consider attrition, early retirements, and furloughs. These strategies are often more cost-effective than RIFs but can entail substantial costs. Attrition is reducing the work force by not replacing those who leave. Rather than systematically configuring the staff to foster effectiveness, executives rely on the luck of the draw. For unlucky officials turnover may yield unbalanced staffing, which hampers the agency's ability to accomplish its mission. Encouraging certain elderly employees to take early retirement can yield a measure of control over attrition. However, this option proved to be of limited help in reducing the federal work force in the early 1980s. Many candidates concluded that they could not afford to retire.[74]

A furlough is a limited cutback in work and pay. In 1985 the Interstate Commerce Commission furloughed about a thousand employees one day a week from 15 April through 15 June in order to avoid RIFs.[75] Furloughs impose significant administrative costs. They disrupt the flow of work and burden personnel record keepers. Where budget shrinkage is likely to be severe and protracted, they tend to be less efficient than layoffs.

As with other facets of managing personnel flows, reductions in force entail uncertainty and trade-offs among core values. Executives must attend to these issues amidst countless other demands on their time.

In managing personnel flows the importance of performance appraisals is persistent. Reliable and valid appraisals facilitate selection practices and inform promotion and removal. Like other aspects of human resource management, however, effective appraisal poses many difficult challenges.

The Appraisal of Performance

Executives committed to accurate performance appraisal need minimally be able to accomplish two tasks. First, they must know good performance when they see it. This requires valid criteria and standards for judging performance. Where their subordinates work at highly discretionary jobs (e.g., as middle managers or physicians), the development of sharply honed indicators of performance often proves particularly difficult. Furthermore, the indirect contributions of an employee to agency productivity almost always prove difficult to evaluate. For instance, some employees foster productivity primarily by sustaining the cohesion and sociability of primary groups in the agency.

Second, executives need properly interpreted and accurate information about employees' behavior. This too can present problems. Subordinates possess considerable incentive to see that information casting them in a disproportionately favorable light reaches the executive. Executives often need to correct for this distortion.

Performance appraisal proceeds informally and formally. Executives develop impressions of the quality of subordinates through firsthand encounters and the grapevine. They store most of these impressions in their minds without putting anything in writing. These informal evaluations often involve rather simple rules of thumb. Consider the remarks of former Postmaster General Paul Carlin on how he could tell whether a local post office was well run. According to Carlin, "I can tell whether their [speed of delivery] is good, their sick leave performance is good, and so on. I can tell it by the quality of their housekeeping. If that floor is neat and clean, I invariably find that everything else in that operation works well."[76]

While informal assessments play a critical role in organizational life, the late 1970s witnessed increased emphasis on formal judgments in written appraisals. The Civil Service Reform Act of 1978 required agencies to develop one or more appraisal systems under OPM regulations. The law and subsequent regulations raised the stakes in appraisal by more tightly linking these appraisals to a host of personnel decisions, particularly those related to merit pay and removal.

"Objective" appraisal seldom proves simple. Not surprisingly, considerable delay occurred as agencies attempted to revise performance appraisals according to the Civil Service Reform Act. Many agencies did not fully succeed in developing persuasive measures of work quality, quantity, and timeliness.

Once established, indicators of performance may motivate desirable behavior;

but they can also fuel gamesmanship and other unproductive practices. Executives in the Social Security Administration, for example, appraise managers partly on the basis of such indicators as processing time per claim. Their counterparts in the Internal Revenue Service rely heavily on numerical quotas, such as the processing of some number of tax returns per week by workers under a given manager's supervision. In response, managers and supervisors in the Social Security Administration have devised various strategies for "gaming" the statistics; they manipulate activities to help them look better on the indicators even though these activities do little to improve the performance of field offices.[77] In the case of the Internal Revenue Service, processing quotas and staff limitations put so much pressure on employees that some of them shredded tax returns to increase the appearance of productivity.

Executives who seek to encourage accurate assessments on official appraisal forms usually depend on lower-level managers and supervisors to accomplish this task. This dependence can contribute to inconsistency. Some supervisors, like some professors, grade harder than others. Furthermore, some supervisors more accurately observe pertinent behavior by their employees. This means that equally competent employees may receive quite different appraisals. Executives can have supervisors trained to appraise performance, but some inconsistency usually remains.

The tendency of supervisors to be generous in their appraisals may also concern executives. In March 1983 a top official at the Veterans Administration expressed concern over the agency's "highly skewed" performance ratings, which persisted despite continuing efforts to discourage such "over-rating."[78] Nalbandian captures some of the interpersonal dynamics of this proclivity. He notes that the "great majority of employees tend to see the manager's evaluation as being less favorable than self-estimates . . . the tendency to overrate themselves produces employee apprehension and disappointment with a formal review process." Thus, a supervisor who gives candid appraisals knows that they may well produce subordinates who "argue, sulk, look bewildered or disappointed, threaten to file grievances, or in some other way react negatively to their appraisal."[79] Evaluation inflation, or overstating the merits of subordinates, may mute hostility and avoid an emotionally uncomfortable experience.

The tendency toward inflated appraisals has evoked consideration of corrective measures. Some executives have at least tacitly endorsed forced rating distributions. Like grading curves in undergraduate classes, forced ratings require supervisors to keep high ratings below certain percentages.[80] However, executives must be circumspect with forced rating distributions. OPM regulations prohibit them and unions make it their business to fight them. In negotiating a pact with the Internal Revenue Service, the National Treasury Employees Union won a promise from agency administrators to eliminate any tendency toward rating employees by a quota or bell curve system.[81] Forced rating systems may compel supervisors to make performance distinctions among employees where no valid differences exist.

Whether inflated appraisals constitute a major problem remains open to debate. The practice violates meritocratic norms that demand the "true" quality of employee performance be stated. It can fuel complacency, impede removal of the inept, and inhibit the effective operation of a performance-based reward system. However, inflated appraisals may at times have positive effects. They may build employee confidence, heighten loyalty, and reduce job dissatisfaction.

Whatever the technical features of the performance appraisal system and the ratings it produces, whether employees view them as equitable largely determines its motivational effects; thus, it is important for executives to sell the appraisal system to subordinates. Surveys of federal employees' attitudes toward appraisal suggest that this is not easy. About half of the respondents in one survey of federal managers expressed skepticism that their productivity could be accurately measured. More than 40 percent doubted that their most recent performance rating accurately reflected the quality of their performance.[82] While such data point out the challenges of appraisals, many executives have successfully used appraisals to motivate employees, improve their performance, and when all else fails, to remove or redeploy them.

Motivation and Enablement

Motivation is the management of incentives to induce desired effort and contributions from employees. One cannot neatly compartmentalize this aspect of human resource management. It interacts with position allocation, management of personnel flows, performance appraisals, and countless other executive actions. Drawing on expectancy theory, one can view employee motivation as a function of: (1) the degree to which subordinates believe they can achieve the desired level of performance; (2) the outcomes that they perceive are associated with accomplishing that level of performance; and (3) the value that they place on those outcomes. Executives concerned about increasing motivation may choose to intervene at any of the three points.

Condition 1 intersects with enablement. Enablement refers to the transmission of information and other resources that give subordinates the means and self-confidence to accomplish some task. Training and employee development programs deserve particular attention as instruments of enablement. Among other things, these programs provide employees with important knowledge and skills. Executives tend to have ambivalent attitudes toward training initiatives. One the one hand, they frequently see them as a major palliative for organizational problems. On the other, they often criticize the relevance of training and slash training budgets at the least sign of fiscal austerity.[83] Even without formal training, employees learn things that contribute to condition 1. Their immediate supervisor and peers serve as teachers day in and day out; they build skills by performing tasks over and over again. However, problems arise if these informal mechanisms fail to impart the desired knowledge and skills or if they foster perceptions that certain performance levels cannot be achieved.

Apropos of condition 2, executives may bolster motivation by altering their employees' perceptions of the result of achieving objectives. They may, for instance, link bonus awards to the achievement of some task or announce that failure to perform will greatly heighten the employee's risk of being fired or demoted.

Condition 3 may also be an avenue for enhancing motivation. Training programs and other management initiatives may induce employees to care about some goal critical to the organization (e.g., improved service by the Veterans Administration for soldiers disabled in the Vietnam War).

Certain psychological phenomena may well prove important to motivation. Job satisfaction is one. While no clear link exists between job satisfaction, motivation, and productivity, discontent tends to fuel absenteeism and turnover. The degree of organizational involvement among employees also looms large in potential importance. Organizational involvement refers to "attitudinal components which indicate the level and direction of psychological attachment employees develop toward their employing organization, ranging from intensely committed to alienated." It includes, among other things, a sense of loyalty to, identification with, and pride in working for a particular agency.[84] High organizational involvement probably prevents absenteeism and turnover; greater involvement may well facilitate executive efforts to motivate employees.

The capacity to monitor job satisfaction, organizational involvement and motivation would be useful to executives. Seldom, however, do they have access to finely honed indicators of these phenomena. Instead, they must usually rely on certain symptoms, such as absenteeism, turnover, and complaints from the public, to alert them to possible problems. A more highly calibrated diagnosis of agency problems would require social science research. The costs of this research as well as other factors frequently make it infeasible to pursue.

The Portfolio of Incentives

Executives can draw on four basic kinds of incentives—material, solidary, purposive, and task—to influence the behavior of their subordinates.[85] Material, or extrinsic, incentives are direct tangible rewards such as money and fringe benefits. Although national policies set by Congress and the President establish fundamental boundaries for these incentives, career executives can use them indirectly through promotion, removal, merit pay, and so on.

Solidary incentives are intangible satisfactions that stem from associating with an agency and particular primary groups within it. Friendship and a sense of loyalty to one's coworkers may do much to motivate employees and build their organizational involvement. Executives face considerable uncertainty in managing solidary incentives. How does one create a work atmosphere in which employees will become attached to cohesive primary groups committed to cost-effectiveness? The answer is far from clear. Executives run some risk that any cohesive group will develop norms emphasizing employee rights or running counter to productivity. The sheer complexity of managing solidary incentives frequently discourages executives from thinking about them in any systematic fashion. Nonetheless, certain executive behaviors reflect respect for these incentives. For example, executives frequently tolerate a degree of socializing during work hours and support the annual holiday party each December.

Purposive incentives tap employees' idealism; they draw on the promise of accomplishing organizational goals to motivate employees. An executive at the Environmental Protection Agency might use rhetoric and other actions to make employees feel that their efforts determine whether the citizenry will have clean water. Sustaining and tapping such idealism day in and day out is difficult. Nor does substantial commitment to the agency's purposes invariably yield higher organizational involvement and motivation. Consider the case of the U.S. Commission on Civil Rights, an agency charged with investigating and reporting discrimination based on race or sex. Although nonwhite employees of this agency evince stronger commitment to the fight against discrimination than their white coworkers, they reveal significantly lower levels of organizational involvement. This tendency probably reflects a perception among minority employees that the agency lacks the capacity to accomplish its goals.[86] In such circumstances emphasis on purposive incentives may damage motivation.

Task incentives enhance the enjoyment or fulfillment that an employee obtains from the work itself. A statistician at the National Center for Health Statistics may find stimulating and absorbing the task of developing more sophisticated procedures to measure the incidence of various diseases. Some students of management have emphasized the importance of designing jobs that provide more demanding and interesting work.[87]

In considering incentives, uncertainty again must be underscored. No one knows how much the different types of incentives contribute to motivation at any given time. Efforts to alter these incentives can unleash unanticipated outcomes. Change in society contributes to this complexity. During economic recessions material incentives may be more important to employees; grateful to have employment, they may be satisfied and loyal even if their work bores them.

Material Incentives to Center Stage

However useful the different kinds of incentives, concern about pay and fringe benefits increased during the 1970s and 1980s, partly because of fundamental policy questions. For instance early in the Reagan administration policymakers debated how closely federal employees' pay matched that of the private sector. High salaries could cost government more money than necessary to accomplish its task; low salaries would make it difficult to attract and retain able employees. Issues of social equity also impinged on payment policy. Many persons debated whether the federal government had done enough to promote equal pay for work of equal worth and should move to establish a policy of comparable worth.

For career executives in the SES, however, the more pressing material issues involved the allocation of merit pay to managerial subordinates. In addition to subjecting SES members to merit pay provisions, the Civil Service Reform Act of 1978 initiated a similar system for the roughly 110,000 supervisors and managers rated GS 13 through GS 15. The law specified that these employees would not automatically receive the full annual salary adjustments granted to general schedule employees in the past. (These adjustments were usually salary boosts approved by Congress and the president as well as within-grade increases.) Instead the managers would receive at least half of the annual salary increment and compete against each other for the remaining amount. Many proponents of this approach believed that it would introduce a valuable motivational tool adapted from the private sector. In the words of Donald Devine, Director of OPM during the early 1980s, "automatic increases," rather than those based on merit pay, are "something we can't justify to the private sector. It's the kind of thing that's given Federal employees a bad name."[88]

As of the mid-1980s, however, there was little evidence that merit pay for the federal government's middle managers had succeeded. One survey of three federal agencies found that the great majority of managers did not believe that merit pay had increased their productivity.[89] A study of the Social Security Administration examined over time four performance indicators (such as the average number of days for a supplemental income claim to be paid or denied an elderly person). The analysis concluded that performance-contingent pay for program managers had no statistically significant effects on productivity in eleven out of twelve tests.[90]

These results are not surprising. Perry correctly notes that "pay-for-individual-performance is based on the assumption that organizational performance is the simple additive combination of individual's separate performances."[91] In fact, even if the merit pay plan motivates individual managers, a wide array of other factors such as limited resources and uncertainty can weaken the link between a manager's behavior and the agency's performance. Moreover, merit pay plans based on individual performance may unleash too much competition among those exposed to it. This can inhibit the willingness of managers to share information and otherwise cooperate to accomplish a goal. In an extreme case merit pay might actually damage the agency's performance.

Even at the level of the individual manager's behavior, merit pay plans pose many implementation problems. Such pay systems work best when they feature valid, widely accepted measures of performance that do not call for highly subjective judgments from evaluators and when rewards are great. Without these conditions, members of the merit pay pool may have little respect for the system. Envy, bickering, lower job satisfaction and diminished organizational involvement can result.

There is a strong case that none of the conditions necessary for strong motivation applied to the merit pay system for GS 13 through GS 15 managers. The appraisal of managers is a highly subjective process in which the development of broadly accepted and valid indicators of performance remains extremely difficult. Aside from the general problem of appraisal, other factors undercut confidence in the system. For instance, variations in the composition of merit pay pools (groups of employees who compete directly for fixed merit pay funds) assured that equally meritorious managers at the same grade level could receive widely divergent pay boosts because the distribution of performance ratings varied substantially from one pay pool to the next. In some pools more than 90 percent of the performance ratings were in the top two levels (i.e., outstanding and highly satisfactory) compared with 20 percent in others. The more managers receiving top ratings, the smaller the merit pay increase for any one manager. Having Schedule C (political) employees in merit pay pools also fanned distrust. In the words of one middle manager at the Department of Housing and Urban Development, "The system seems to have been politicized, with top political appointees changing the ratings of career people in order to reward themselves and their appointed subordinates."[92]

As if these problems were not sufficient, the financial squeeze that afflicted the federal government in the 1980s greatly limited the amount of money available for merit pay allocations. During the early stages of the program, this problem worsened when disagreement broke out between OPM and GAO over the size of the merit pay fund. When the dust had cleared, the merit fund for fiscal 1982 was roughly 80 percent of the original amount. The forces limiting the amount available for merit pay allocations are potent. In 1985 President Reagan proposed a reduction in pay for civil servants. Congress ultimately modified the president's proposal by voting for no increase.

Hence, greater discretion over pay may create as many problems as it solves. A survey of managers in three federal agencies found that 37 percent to 46 percent supported the general principle of merit pay, but fewer than ten percent favored retention of the 1978 merit pay system for GS 13 through GS 15 managers.[93] In a similar vein, Perry concludes that "requiring a public organization's compensation system to harness pay for motivating short-term managerial performance is not realistic."[94] The formidable barriers to successful merit pay policy have prompted some observers to caution against extension of the policy to GS 1 through GS 12 workers.[95]

Whatever the wisdom of this view, government policies seem likely to continue to pay homage to merit pay as a motivator. In the mid-1980s a demonstration project at two Navy research laboratories in China Lake, California, sought to explore the feasibility of extending merit pay below GS 13. In part, the continued interest in merit pay reflects the view that for some jobs, especially routine nonmanagerial ones, the approach has desirable motivational effects. The appeal of merit pay is partly symbolic. A skeptical political culture biased toward the techniques of business means that some personnel practices take life as much because they cater to these biases as because they stand a chance of enhancing core personnel values.[96]

As federal policymakers gain more experience with merit pay, they may correct some of the defects of the Civil Service Reform Act. In November 1984 policymakers replaced the old system with the Performance Management and Recognition System. The new law established a five-tier performance rating for GS 13 through GS 15 managers and supervisors. The third level denotes fully satisfactory performance. The two levels above it reflect increasingly better performance and the two below, increasingly worse. The law links the rating of a middle manager to four vehicles for increasing their pay—general pay increases granted by Congress and the president, annual within-grade merit increases, special performance awards, and cash awards. The four mechanisms assure that those in the highest categories receive the most remuneration. In the case of general pay increases, for instance, the law requires that those who rank in the third tier or higher receive the full pay increase mandated by law. Those in the fourth tier receive one-half the pay boost, and those in the bottom tier, no increases. With the exception of those at the maximum rate for their grades, those in the top three tiers receive annual merit increases. Subject to certain restrictions, the higher the performance ranking, the greater the merit increase.

On balance, the new pay system is probably an improvement over the old one, at least in the sense that employees are likelier to view it as fair. The new policy assures that fully satisfactory employees will receive about as much as they would have under the compensation system in effect prior to 1978 (and possibly more). The Civil Service Reform Act produced lower pay increases for many of these employees than for GS 13 through GS 15 civil servants who were not managers. This fueled the sense that the 1978 merit pay provisions contributed to dog-eat-dog competition, in which fully satisfactory employees could lose appreciable sums of money. The Performance Management and Recognition System reduced this negative prospect while leaving the door open to the possibility that employees in the first or second tiers would earn extra compensation.

The financial crunch afflicting federal agencies in the 1980s tended to eradicate any positive effects of merit pay as a motivator. The amounts available to federal executives for merit pay allocations may often be too small to have much motivational impact on subordinates.[97] Executives interested in motivating employees must also focus on intrinsic (solidary, purposive, and task) incentives.

In attempting to manage intrinsic incentives, federal executives face the fundamental challenge of the bash-the-bureaucrat political culture. This cultural strain troubles the merit pay system by breeding suspicion among employees that it is more for punishment than for reward. The evidence also suggests that this antibureaucratic theme may thwart executives who try to manage intrinsic incentives. One study found that employees' perceptions of public recognition of service, or the degree to which public and elected officials respect them for their work, correlated more strongly with organizational involvement than did their own job security and cuts in agency staffing levels. Hence, public respect, which is largely beyond the control of executives, may be important in shaping the organizational involvement and motivation of their subordinates.[98] The external political culture of the federal government further complicates the already uncertain process of managing incentives.

Conclusion

In the abstract one can compartmentalize personnel management into such categories as position management, personnel flows, appraisal, motivation, and enablement. In fact, these activities frequently overlap and are interdependent, which heightens the complexity of human resource administration.

Management of personnel has become more challenging over the last twenty-five years, largely because the arena is more generically politicized. Not only do social equity, merit, instrumental achievement, employee rights, political responsiveness, and so on compete, they do so vigorously; each has advocates. Legislation and court decisions have put racial minorities, women, the unions, and others in the middle of the personnel game. Various advocacy agencies such as the Federal Labor Relations Authority promote or safeguard certain values within the federal establishment. The competing values that undergird personnel management require the executive to manage conflicting expectations.

Moreover, as one observer notes, "the difficulty of pursuing important values simultaneously stimulates the cyclical nature of much of personnel reform."[99] The quest by policymakers to modify laws and regulations to reassert some value slighted by the last adjustment in rules often impinges on career executives. The Reagan administration attempted to weaken rules that buttressed the position of minorities and unions. But even with these initiatives, the dispersal of power over human resources remains considerable and elevates the need for executives to be adroit tacticians.

This review of efforts to manage personnel should not veil the fact that the federal government frequently gives the problem away through administration by proxy.

Constraints on management discretion such as position ceilings and hiring freezes reinforce the strong cultural bias in this direction. Executives have fewer employees to manage than if the government assumed more direct responsibility for implementing public programs. Ultimately, much personnel management pertinent to the success or failure of Washington's programs occurs outside of the federal bureaucracy. Federal executives shape it only indirectly.[100]

Notes

1. Frank J. Thompson, *Health Policy and the Bureaucracy* (Cambridge, MA: MIT Press, 1981), 54.
2. This typology derives in part from Donald E. Klingner and John Nalbandian, *Public Personnel Management* (Englewood Cliffs, NJ: Prentice-Hall, 1985).
3. U.S. House Committee on Post Office and Civil Service, *Civil Service Oversight* (Washington, DC: U.S. Government Printing Office, 1983), 512.
4. *Federal Times,* 25 February 1985, 24.
5. U.S. House Committee on Post Office and Civil Service, *Civil Service Oversight,* 449.
6. Ibid, 570.
7. *Federal Times,* 15 July 1985, 6.
8. U.S. General Accounting Office, *Delegated Personnel Management Authorities: Better Monitoring and Oversight Needed* (Washington, DC: GAO/FPCD–82–43, 1982).
9. U.S. House Committee on Post Office and Civil Service, *Civil Service Oversight,* 509–10.
10. See U.S. General Accounting Office, *Problems Persist in the EEO Complaint Processing System for Federal Employees* (Washington, DC: GAO/FPCD–83–21, 1983). This analysis concludes that existing laws did not provide the EEOC with authority to enforce its decisions on discrimination complaints filed by federal employees.
11. Ibid.
12. James Q. Wilson and Patricia Rachal, "Can The Government Regulate Itself?" *Public Interest* 46 (Winter 1977): 4.
13. U.S. General Accounting Office, *Merit Systems Protection Board: Case Processing Timeliness and Participants' Views on Board Activities* (Washington:GAO/GGD–87–97, 1987).
14. *Federal Times,* 8 July 1985, 6.
15. Equal Employment Opportunity Commission, *17th Annual Report, FY 1982* (Washington DC: 1983).
16. U.S. House Committee on Appropriations, *Treasury, Postal Service, and General Government Appropriations for Fiscal Year 1985, Part 4* (Washington: U.S. Government Printing Office, 1984), 536.
17. U.S. General Accounting Office, *Merit Systems Protection Board: Case Processing Timeliness and Participants' Views on Board Activities,* 12, 20.
18. Ibid., 12–3.
19. U.S. House Committee on Post Office and Civil Service, *Civil Service Oversight,* 5, 10.

20. U.S. General Accounting Office, *Labor Contract Negotiations under the Civil Service Reform Act of 1978* (Washington: GAO/GGD–84–68, 1984), 5.

21. Sar A. Levitan and Alexandra B. Noden, *Working for the Sovereign* (Baltimore: Johns Hopkins University Press, 1983), 17.

22. *Federal Times,* 8 April 1985, 24.

23. U.S. House Committee on Post Office and Civil Service, *Civil Service Oversight,* 566.

24. Alan L. Sorkin, *The Economics of the Postal System* (Lexington, MA: Lexington, 1980), 68.

25. U.S. Department of Commerce, *Statistical Abstract of the United States, 1985* (Washington: U.S. Government Printing Office, 1984), 423.

26. U.S. General Accounting Office, *Comparison of Collectively Bargained and Administratively Set Pay Rates for Federal Employees* (Washington: GAO/FPCD–82–49, 1982).

27. U.S. General Accounting Office, *Description of Selected Systems for Classifying Federal Civilian Positions And Personnel* (Washington, DC: GAO/GCD–84–90, 1984), 3–5.

28. The entire discussion of personnel ceilings draws heavily upon U.S. General Accounting Office, *Personnel Ceilings—A Barrier to Effective Manpower Management* (Washington: FPCD–76–88, 1977); and *Savings from 1981 and 1982 Personnel Ceiling Reductions* (Washington, DC: GAO/FPCD–82–23, 1982).

29. U.S. General Accounting Office, *Civil Servants and Contract Employees: Who Should Do What for the Federal Government?* (Washington, DC: GAO/FPCD–81–43, 1981).

30. U.S. General Accounting Office, *Savings From 1981 and 1982 Personnel Ceiling Reductions,* Appendix I, 10.

31. U.S. General Accounting Office, *Civil Servants and Contract Employees: Who Should Do What for the Federal Government?* 14.

32. U.S. General Accounting Office, *Personnel Ceilings—a Barrier to Effective Manpower Management,* 21.

33. Ibid., 73–4.

34. Irene S. Rubin, *Shrinking the Federal Government* (New York: Longman, 1985), 9, 36, 50.

35. U.S. General Accounting Office, *Information on the Administration's Program to Reduce Grade 11–15 Positions* (Washington, DC: GAO/GGD–85–48, 1985), 2.

36. *Federal Times,* 14 April 1985, 3.

37. *Federal Times,* 13 May 1985, 16.

38. *Federal Times,* 22 April 1985, 3.

39. U.S. General Accounting Office, *Information on the Administration's Program to Reduce Grade 11–15 Positions.*

40. U.S. General Accounting Office, *Employment Trends and Grade Controls in the DOD General Schedule Work Force* (Washington, DC: GAO/FPCD–81–52, 1981).

41. See Carolyn Ban and Toni Marzotto, "Delegations of Federal Examining." *Review of Public Personnel Administration* 5 (Fall 1984): 1–11.

42. U.S. General Accounting Office, *Federal Employment Examinations: Do They Achieve Equal Opportunity and Merit Principle Goals?* (Washington, DC: GAO/FPCD–79–46, 1979), 3.

43. For an overview of some of the issues involved in selection validation, see Dennis L. Dresang, *Public Personnel Management and Public Policy* (Boston: Little,

Brown, 1984), 208–14; "Uniform Guidelines on Employee Selection Procedures." *Federal Register* 43 (1978): 38290–38315.

44. U.S. General Accounting Office, *Federal Employment Examinations: Do They Achieve Equal Opportunity and Merit Principle Goals?* 28.

45. Ibid., 11.

46. Carolyn Ban and Patricia W. Ingraham, "Retaining Quality Federal Employees: Life after PACE." *Public Administration Review* 48 (May-June, 1988): 710.

47. U.S. General Accounting Office, *Federal Employment Examinations: Do They Achieve Equal Opportunity and Merit Principle Goals?* 51.

48. Hugh Heclo, *A Government of Strangers* (Washington, DC: The Brookings Institution, 1977), 125–6.

49. Levitan and Noden, *Working for the Sovereign,* 107.

50. U.S. General Accounting Office, *Appointments to Professional and Administrative Career Positions* (Washington, DC: GAO/GGD–85–18, 1984), 6.

51. Ban and Ingraham, "Retaining Quality Federal Employees: Life After PACE," 710.

52. U.S. General Accounting Office, *Achieving Representation of Minorities and Women in the Federal Work Force* (Washington, DC: GAO/FPCD–81–5, 1980).

53. U.S. House Committee on Post Office and Civil Service, *Civil Service Oversight,* 442.

54. Ibid.

55. Ibid., 613. Statement of Mildred Goodman, President, Blacks in Government.

56. Gregory B. Lewis and Mark A. Emmert, "Who Pays For Veterans Preference?" *Administration and Society* 16 (November 1984): 328–45.

57. Gregory B. Lewis, "Progress toward Racial and Sexual Equality in the Federal Civil Service?" *Public Administration Review* 48 (May-June, 1988): 705.

58. Ban and Ingraham, "Retaining Quality Federal Employees: Life after PACE," 714.

59. Lewis, "Progress Toward Racial and Sexual Equality in the Federal Civil Service?" 705.

60. U.S. General Accounting Office, *Recent Government-Wide Hiring Freezes Prove Ineffective in Managing Federal Employment* (Washington, DC: GAO/FPCD– 82–21, 1982).

61. Carolyn Ban, Edie N. Goldenberg, and Toni Marzotto, "Firing the Unproductive Employee: Will Civil Service Reform Make a Difference?" *Review of Public Personnel Administration* 2 (Spring 1982): 90.

62. Ibid.

63. See U.S. General Accounting Office, *Poor Performers: How They Are Identified and Dealt with in the Social Security Administration* (Washington: GAO/GGD– 89–28, 1989); William J. Goode, "The Protection of the Inept." *American Sociological Review* 32 (February 1967): 5–19.

64. U.S. General Accounting Office, *Whistleblower Complaints Rarely Qualify for Office of the Special Counsel Protection* (Washington: GAO/GGD–85–53, 1985).

65. *Federal Times,* 24 June 1985, 15.

66. U.S. General Accounting Office, *Whistleblower Complaints Rarely Qualify For Office of the Special Counsel Protection,* 19–26.

67. U.S. House Committee on Appropriations, *Treasury, Postal Service, and General Government Appropriations for Fiscal Year 1984, Part 4,* 570.

68. *Federal Times,* 7 October 1985: 6.

69. U.S. Merit Systems Protection Board, *Reduction-In-Force in the Federal Government, 1981* (Washington, DC, 1983), 75.

70. Ibid., 56–7.

71. *Federal Register* 48 (1983): 49462.

72. *Federal Times,* 30 September 1985, 7. The compromise also affected bumping and retreating rights; see U.S. General Accounting Office, *Information on the Office of Personnel Management's Reduction-in-Force Rules* (Washington, DC: GAO/GGD 86–39 FS, 1986).

73. U.S. Merit System Protection Board, *Reduction-in-Force in the Federal Government,* 71.

74. Ibid., 94; see also U.S. General Accounting Office, *Reduction in Force Can Sometimes Be More Costly to Agencies Than Attrition and Furlough* (Washington, DC: GAO/PEMD–85–6, 1985).

75. *Federal Times,* 7 October 1985, 6.

76. *Federal Times,* 18 March 1985, 16.

77. Jone L. Pearce and James L. Perry, "Federal Merit Pay: A Longitudinal Analysis." *Public Administration Review* 43 (July-August, 1983): 321.

78. U.S. House Committee on Post Office and Civil Service, *Civil Service Oversight,* 563.

79. John Nalbandian, "Performance Appraisal: If Only People Were Not Involved." *Public Administration Review* 4 (May-June, 1981): 394.

80. U.S. General Accounting Office, *A 2-Year Appraisal of Merit Pay in Three Agencies* (Washington: GAO/GGD–84–1, 1984), 12–3.

81. *Federal Times,* 4 March 1985, 6.

82. U.S. General Accounting Office, *A 2-Year Appraisal of Merit Pay in Three Agencies,* 67–9.

83. See Dresang, *Public Personnel Management and Public Policy,* 230–1.

84. Barbara S. Romzek and Stephen J. Hendricks, "Organizational Involvement and Representative Bureaucracy: Can We Have It Both Ways?" *American Political Science Review* 76 (March 1982): 77, 81–2. Organizational involvement is closely related to two other concepts—organizational identification and organizational commitment.

85. This typology draws heavily on James Q. Wilson, *Political Organizations* (New York: Basic Books, 1973), 30–55; see also James L. Perry and Lyman W. Porter, "Factors Affecting the Context for Motivation in Public Organizations." *Academy of Management Review* 7(1982): 89–98.

86. Romzek and Hendricks, "Organizational Involvement and Representative Bureaucracy: Can We Have It Both Ways?"

87. See Robert T. Golembiewski, "Civil Service and Managing Work: Some Unintended Consequences." *American Political Science Review* 66 (September 1962): 961–73.

88. U.S. House Committee on Post Office and Civil Service, *Civil Service Oversight,* 8.

89. U.S. General Accounting Office, *A 2-Year Appraisal of Merit Pay in Three Agencies,* 67.

90. Jone L. Pearce, William B. Stevenson, James L. Perry, "Managerial Compensation Based On Organizational Performance: A Time Series Analysis of the Effects of Merit Pay." *Academy of Management Journal* 28 (June, 1985): 261–278.

91. James L. Perry, "Merit Pay In The Public Sector: The Case For a Failure of Theory." *Review of Public Personnel Administration* 7 (Fall, 1986): 58.

92. U.S. General Accounting Office, *A 2-Year Appraisal of Merit Pay in Three Agencies,* 19.

93. Ibid., 48.

94. Perry, "Merit Pay In The Public Sector: The Case For a Failure of Theory," 67.
95. Pearce and Perry, "Federal Merit Pay: A Longitudinal Analysis."
96. David K. Cohen and Richard J. Murnan, "The Merits of Merit Pay." *The Public Interest,* 80 (Summer, 1985): 23.
97. It deserves note that under the new system performance awards to employees with the same grade and rating still vary. This could fuel discontent with the system among civil servants. For a general assessment, see James L. Perry, Beth Ann Petrakis, and Theodore K. Miller, "Federal Merit Pay, Round II: An Analysis of the Performance Management and Recognition System." *Public Administration Review* 49 (January/February, 1989): 29–37.
98. Barbara S. Romzek, "The Effects of Public Service Recognition, Job Security and Staff Reductions on Organizational Involvement." *Public Administration Review* 45 (March/April, 1985): 282–291.
99. Edie N. Goldenberg, "The Grace Commission and Civil Service Reform: Seeking a Common Understanding," in Charles H. Levine, ed., *The Unfinished Agenda For Civil Service Reform* (Washington, DC: The Brookings Institution, 1985), 91.
100. The federal government has attempted to shape the personnel management practices of grantees and contractors through laws and regulations concerning merit systems and equal employment opportunity.

Chapter Thirteen

Other Challenges: Information, Physical Resources, and Money

In 1981, Senator Charles Percy (Republican of Illinois) introduced legislation designed to aid collection of more than $25 billion in overdue federal loans to college students, small businesses, and others. The legislation also sought to discourage loans to poor credit risks. The bill authorized use of addresses from Internal Revenue Service (IRS) files by private collection agencies whom federal officials hired to track down delinquent borrowers. The proposed legislation also authorized IRS to disclose to another federal agency whether a loan applicant had outstanding tax liabilities and was therefore a poor credit risk. Opponents of the bill portrayed it as a threat to the privacy rights of citizens.[1]

In 1983 President Reagan issued Executive Order 12411, which established an objective of not more than 135 square feet per person as an average for office space in the federal government. The General Services Administration (GSA) assumed responsibility for implementing the order. Executives in many agencies resisted the initiative. Negotiations between line agencies and GSA ensued.

In fiscal 1984 a payment center for GSA made thirty-two duplicate payments amounting to $1.3 million. In essence, vendors got paid twice for the service or product they provided. Part of the problem arose when the agency processed bills manually rather than on automated computer systems with internal control mechanisms designed to prevent duplicate payments.[2]

As these examples attest, the management of information, physical resources, and money poses challenges for federal executives. These activities involve value tensions such as those between an agency's need for information and citizens' rights to privacy. They can affect conflict and bargaining among different actors within the bureaucracy, as with the struggle over office space. Moreover, the management of these resources interconnect and overlap. Thus, Senator Percy's desire to improve financial management required better coordination of information systems. Problems of financial management at GSA in part stemmed from failure to use a computerized system. Of course, some management of information, physical resources, and money works smoothly and attracts limited executive attention. Routine or strategic, however, the successful handling of these resources goes to the heart of an executive's ability to respond to programmatic, consensual, legal, and career imperatives.

This chapter begins with a discussion of information—issues involved in acquiring and transmitting it. The different media of communication, the information preferences of managers, the conflicting legal imperatives that affect information policy, the efforts to rationalize decisions through the use of formal analysis, and the computer revolution all receive attention. The chapter then turns to the management of facilities, equipment, and furnishings. Among other things, the ways in which the management of physical resources influences personnel issues is a central concern. Finally, the chapter briefly analyzes issues of financial management, primarily for budget execution. As will become apparent, executives at times have trouble paying, collecting, and accounting for money.

Information: Talk, Analysis, Computers

Few topics in management have precipitated such a torrent of vivid prose as information. For instance, Harlan Cleveland describes the "informatization of society," in which "information becomes the dominant resource" in an organization's life. In his view, this process has "mind-blowing implications . . . for four of the old hierarchies" with which executives must contend—those "based on control, secrecy, ownership, and structural unfairness." Cleveland believes that the "information era features a sudden increase in humanity's power to think and therefore to organize."[3] Other students of public administration express doubt that the increase in ability to use and process information can keep pace with the growing complexity of society's problems.[4] Observers agree that the advent of the computer, along with other technologies, has greatly elevated the importance of managing information.

Discussions of the "informatization" of society provide a useful perspective on the general milieu in which public executives operate. However, it is also important to grasp certain basics about communication.

The Media

Executives confront at least three primary media of communication—written or printed, oral, and nonverbal. *Written or printed communication* conjures up basic images of bureaucracy and what seem like endless amounts of official paperwork. In some agencies executives send and receive printed messages on video display terminals. Moreover, executives often receive important printed information from such unofficial sources as *The Washington Post*.

Oral communication is talk and other vocalizations, face-to-face or over the phone. It includes the formal content of a language ("Guy, I need your work plan by Friday"); it also includes *paralanguage,* or speech other than formal words and meanings. For instance, some communication is through vocal tone—loudness, pitch, pause, and tempo. Paralanguage also includes sighing, laughing, crying, and so on.[5]

Nonverbal communication is the physical presentation of self. It includes clothes as well as body language such as gaze, facial expression, distance, touch, and arm movements. While frequently subject to several interpretations, nonverbal communication can do much to influence a person's reaction to an executive. Hence, in part as an effort to convey credibility, male executives wear suits and ties (as opposed to open shirts, beads, and earrings); in similar fashion, female managers usually come to work in conservative "professional" dress rather than miniskirts. Nonverbal communication also involves the management of physical resources. One need only recall the postal official who saw clean floors as a key indicator of managerial effectiveness to understand the relevance of this form of nonverbal communication.

Criteria for Media Assessment.   Modes of communication differ in their appeal depending on at least four factors.

1. The cost in effort and money of acquiring or disseminating information varies widely. Darting into a colleague's office down the corridor to relay information usually takes less effort than drafting a formal memorandum.
2. Speed of transmission varies. An executive, for example, can frequently obtain information more quickly via a telephone call than through written requests.
3. Information may be more or less precise and clear. Failures of communication are legion even under the best of circumstances. Part of the problem arises from language itself. One study claims that each word in the English language has on the average twenty-eight different meanings.[6] Yet another analysis contends that American English has become increasingly intolerant of sharp linguistic distinctions.[7] Whatever the problems created by language in general, some forms tend to be more conducive to precision than others. Printed communications often convey information more clearly than oral and nonverbal means.
4. The mode of communication may be more or less congenial to building an organization's memory. A file of documents (in a metal cabinet or on computer disk or tape) establishes a record that can extend beyond the recollections of current agency members. Among other things, the records can cement commitments via formal agreements. Information received orally or nonverbally often (but not inevitably) fades from the organization's memory.

In selecting media of communication, executives more or less consciously realize the costs and benefits of various forms, but they also have a bias—toward oral communication. In part, this bias reflects a very rational response to the environment. At times, however, it may inhibit them from effectively managing information.

The Triumph of Talk.   As a rule, information does not flow smoothly to managers during a work day. Brevity, variety, and fragmentation tend to prevail. In other words, executives deal with a broad range of subjects for brief periods with little prospect of a smooth transition or continuity from one issue to the next. Interruptions occur constantly. Hence managers often lack the time to draw appropriate lessons from written documents. Of even greater importance, executives tend to prefer live action and the spoken word. This preference manifests itself in the desire for "instant" or "hot" information. In the words of one study, "Gossip, speculation, and heresay form a most important part of the manager's information diet." Talk was the primary medium of communication close to 80 percent of the time in one sample of managers.[8]

No doubt federal executives vary greatly in their preference for talk over other modes of communication. On balance, however, it seems plausible that many of them would only grudgingly increase the amount of time they spend on written communications. Many might resemble the bank executive interviewed by a journalist about his attitudes toward a new paperless information system installed by his employer. When the journalist entered the executive's office, he noticed that the computer terminal was unplugged and facing the wall. In response to questioning, the bank executive acknowledged that he hated to type in the instruction necessary to retrieve information from the computer and went on to observe: "I think most managers, including me, are talkers . . . I would much rather talk than write."[9] To this one can add that many managers prefer listening to reading.

The preference for hot information acquired through conversation is usually quite sensible. Oral communication tends to be suited for conveying strategic information. Much of the information that flows to the manager through informal channels provides insight into the prevailing configuration of support, indifference, and opposition within the agency and its environment. Who are the relevant actors with respect to some issue? What values and opinions do they hold? To what degree do they possess the skill and related resources necessary to exert leverage on an issue? A trustworthy network of contacts can do much to reduce the manager's uncertainty with respect to these questions. Informal channels can also alert managers to fast-breaking developments, allowing them to use finely honed timing.

Written communication is often poorly suited to providing strategic information such as how to outflank an opposing official. Such communication generally takes more time; delay often presents problems because the strategic value of information can plummet virtually overnight. Beyond this, written strategic information threatens considerable embarrassment if it falls into the wrong hands. Such embarrassment can disrupt the very coalitions the manager has succeeded in building. Thus, in most public organizations putting certain strategic information in writing is taboo.

All of this is not to say there is any inevitable superiority of the spoken over the written word. Talk is often less precise and frequently serves poorly when organizational memory is critical. Moreover, it may become an escape from the more systematic thinking and analysis that the written word demands. The preference for talk also interferes with movements to rationalize and inform government decisions through the systematic collection, storage, reporting, and analysis of information.

Whatever the information preferences of executives, their environment constantly poses new challenges to their management of this resource. As in other areas, policymakers establish a legal framework within which managers operate—one that attempts to reconcile competing values of privacy, openness, and efficiency. Executives are subject to persistent pressures to become more analytic and rational in their decisions. In this and other respects they must grapple with the implications of the computer revolution.

Policy: Privacy, Openness, and Efficiency

Many laws and rules constrain the acquisition and transmission of information by federal executives (see Chapters 7 and 8). Two of the major statutes governing executives, the Freedom of Information Act of 1966 and the Privacy Act of 1974, reveal particular sensitivity to the power implications of information distribution.

Knowledge is *not* power, but it is a major resource that can be used to exert power.[10] The Freedom of Information Act sought to bolster the public's right to know by permitting access to a vast range of executive branch records. In contrast, the Privacy Act requires agencies to maintain the confidentiality of certain personal files. It reflects a popular concern that in the words of one editorial ("Big Brother Alive in Fed's Computers"), the federal bureaucracy has the "capacity to intrude as never before on personal privacy" and great dangers exist if "federal bureaucrats wind up with wholesale snooping rights."[11] Aside from this concern, policymakers believe that their ability to persuade firms and citizens to report accurate information to a government agency tends to increase if they promise not to release the information to other agencies or to the public.

Executive Discretion.   While setting general guidelines for executives, the information and privacy laws are sufficiently ambiguous to require difficult judgment calls.[12] Managers often cannot be sure which personal information they must release under the Freedom of Information Act or safeguard under the Privacy Act. If executives refuse to disclose information, they risk criticism and possibly a lawsuit by the party denied access. If they disclose the content of records, they run a similar risk and must also pay the costs of gathering and transmitting the information to the requesting party. In deciding whether to release information, executives deal with an increasingly sophisticated set of requesters. The number of law firms and businesses that specialize in this area has increased substantially. For example, FOI Services Incorporated specializes in invoking the Freedom of Information Act to the Food and Drug Administration, among other agencies. It sells the information it gets to subscribers. Many executives also face an internal bureaucratic constituency of *access professionals,* who nurture firm views on the subject and who in 1980 formed the American Society of Access Professionals.[13]

The cost of responding to requests for information has influenced executive discretion under the Freedom of Information Act. The cost can include hours of searching for records, scrutiny of their contents to determine what can be divulged, and reproduction. Originally, some executives expressed their resentment of these costs by dragging their feet, often taking weeks to respond to an initial request for access to public records. Repeated delays prompted Congress to amend the law, imposing certain deadlines for processing information requests—for example, the agency must respond to initial requests within ten days.[14]

Executives also reacted to the costs of providing information by charging fees for information. Since many requests come from corporations and individuals who seek economic profit from the information, the eagerness of some executives to impose fees is understandable. However, fees can prevent citizens from readily obtaining information they need for legitimate personal reasons. Because of concern that agencies had gone too far in charging for information, Congress amended the Freedom of Information Act to constrain executive discretion. Among other things, the amendments permitted agencies to charge only the actual cost of searching out and copying public records; they forbade agencies from charging for requests when the cost of collecting and processing the fee was equal to or greater than the fee itself.[15]

Like the Freedom of Information Act, the Privacy Act can interfere with efficiency. Consider computer matching, which is a comparison of two or more files containing information on persons or organizations of interest to administrators.[16]

Typically the administrator uses a computer match to generate a list of persons or organizations who have violated a program's rules and regulations; the list is usually called "computer match hits." Presumably, discovery of these hits can aid administrators in fighting fraud and abuse. For instance, managers of entitlement programs have been interested in using information on federal tax returns to detect ineligible beneficiaries. The lack of data to verify income and assets reported by applicants and recipients in entitlement programs has contributed to significant overpayments—an estimated one billion dollars by five programs in fiscal 1980.[17] A computer match with IRS could uncover "hits" who had inaccurately reported their income. Driven by a programmatic imperative, executives in many agencies have promoted the use of computer matching.

Concern for citizens' privacy has led some individuals and groups such as the American Civil Liberties Union to question the constitutional and statutory legitimacy of such matching. Some privacy advocates attack matching as fishing expeditions that violate the Fourth Amendment right to be free from unreasonable search and seizures. They also assert that the practice violates the letter and spirit of the Privacy Act, which restricts disclosure of personally identifiable information without consent of the subject.[18]

Efforts to strike the proper balance between secrecy and information dissemination continue. The balance varies over time, depending to some degree on the presidential administration. The 1980s witnessed increasing restriction of the Freedom of Information Act. It took more time for requesters to receive documents and they had to provide more detailed justifications and specifications in their requests. Moreover, the Reagan administration revised the rules governing the classification of government documents, making it easier to keep certain files secret.[19]

Other things being equal, the greater the cultural tilt toward openness over privacy, the more incentive executives have to communicate orally rather than in writing. Candid memoranda often carry high risks if they become available to anyone requesting a certain file.

Efficiency to the Fore.   The Freedom of Information and Privacy Acts deal with important values, but they do not address efficiency. The Paperwork Reduction Act of 1980 was the first major and self-conscious effort by Washington to forge general guidelines with efficiency in mind. The Paperwork Reduction Act proclaimed six formal goals, only one of which, the last, considered privacy. The first goals concern managing information as a resource. Among other things, they call for reducing information costs, maximizing the usefulness of collecting information, and coordinating federal information gathering. The objective puts Congress on record as endorsing the computer revolution. It requires executives "to ensure that automatic data processing and telecommunications technologies are acquired and used by the Federal Government in a manner which . . . increases productivity, reduces waste and fraud, and . . . reduces the information processing burden."

Part of the law had little to do with cutting government's costs of obtaining information. Instead, costs that Washington had shifted to individuals, small businesses, and state and local governments were the target. In hearings on the law, complaints about the huge costs and inconvenience of filling out federal forms flew thick and fast. Classroom teachers complained that they had to spend at least twenty-six working days each year completing required federal paperwork. Local government officials, university presidents, and community leaders estimated that 10 percent to 30 percent of federal grant money was wasted on paperwork. One attorney taped end to end the federal forms required to start a small business and stretched them the length of the meeting hall.[20] The accuracy of these estimates remains an open question, but whatever their validity, the new law called for a 25 percent reduction in the paperwork burden.

The Paperwork Reduction Act envisioned that a new Office of Information and Regulatory Affairs in the Office of Management and Budget would play a major role in implementation. The law required the director of the new office to develop a federal information locator system to coordinate information gathering by agencies. Presumably, more sharing among agencies would reduce redundancy and therefore the economic costs of information gathering. More fundamentally, the director of the Office of Information and Regulatory Affairs had to review and clear agency requests to collect information (for example, survey questionnaires going to ten or more persons). Armed with this organizational device, the Reagan administration generally sought to reduce federal efforts to gather statistics. The law also called upon OMB to advise the General Services Administration on records management and automatic data processing.

Information Systems, Analysis, and Rationality

Laws governing privacy, freedom of information, and paperwork lay out general rules of the game for career executives' use of the information they get through formal monitoring systems and analyses. Whatever the appeal of talk to executives, the computer revolution, the complexity of policy problems they confront, and other factors have elevated the importance of formal reports. Computer-based information systems that routinely present data on certain aspects of agency operations abound. Analytic staffs within the bureaucracy and countless contractors stand ready to provide systematic studies of some subject (e.g., for plans, designs, evaluations, cost-benefit analyses). These studies may come from the social, physical, and biological sciences. They cover issues ranging from effective teaching in ghetto schools to the efficacy of rocket boosters for space shuttles to the relationship between tobacco chewing and cancer of the mouth.

Of course, any attempts to rationalize decisions through better information confront the limits on human ability to acquire, absorb, and process information. No one can possibly gather all the facts about a problem, consider all alternatives, and precisely anticipate the costs and benefits of each alternative. As Herbert Simon has observed, "human beings satisfice because they have not the wits to maximize." They tend to rely on "a drastically simplified model of the buzzing, blooming confusion that constitutes the real world."[21] Although monitoring systems and formal analysis can enlighten the simplified models of executives, information costs and the perils of overload caution against assumptions that more is inevitably better.

Executives interested in improving their understanding of programs and their organizations must realize that information comes with a price tag. Computerized management information systems are often expensive; so are formal studies produced by analytic staffs. Ideally, executives would know the precise value of certain information (for example a report on improved organizational performance). They would know the exact costs of obtaining the information. They would then compare the marginal benefits produced by the information with the costs to see whether or not to invest. In fact, executives seldom have access to such exact information, so decisions on purchasing information systems and formal studies remain judgment calls.[22]

The perils of overload also loom large. Paradoxically, managers with too much printed communication at times use *less* information in decisionmaking than those who receive fewer reports. In essence, executives may "experience an information glut as a shortage" as overload breaks down their psychological ability to process information.[23] To avoid drowning in formal reports, executives must become masters of superficiality.[24] They must have a firm sense of when to stop their quest for information.

Ultimately, federal executives must strike a delicate balance. If too many reports can hinder them, so can too few. Have federal executives struck this balance? Students of public administration lack the evidence to answer this question with confidence. However, a dominant theme in much of the literature is the difficulty management scientists and analysts have in getting executives to use the information that monitoring systems and formal studies generate.

Barriers to Instrumental Use of Information.   Many students of information management have argued that formal reports seldom directly influence the decisions executives make. After studying policy analysis in the federal bureaucracy, one author concludes: "The notion that knowledge will carry the day is absurd." Organizations seem to generate many more reports than executives bother to read or to act upon.[25]

What inhibits the instrumental use of information systems and formal analyses? Several factors account for this pattern. The psychological disposition of an executive often undercuts instrumental use of information. Poring over lengthy reports runs against the grain of the manager's preference for talk and the cultivation of informal networks of information. A sense of psychological threat may make it difficult for the manager to accept the findings of a report. Executives are particularly likely to resist evaluation results critical of them. Such findings call into question the long hours they may have committed to program goals and can seriously threaten their career aspirations (e.g., for promotion). Confronted with such dissonance, executives often reject the conclusions of the analysis. In fact, their commitment to practices criticized in the formal report may increase.[26]

The selection or focus of a project can also retard the instrumental use of reports. Analyses or information systems may focus on factors over which the executive has very little control, which is to say that the research may not address variables executives can manipulate at reasonable cost. In essence, executives may lack the resources and opportunity to act on evidence from the analyses or monitoring systems. Problems with project selection may also arise via a misinterpretation of the executive's priorities. A report may address factors that the official can influence (e.g., new procedures for allocating grants by the agency) but the official may not assign much importance to the recommendation. Other issues may demand more attention.

Lack of timeliness also contributes to the executive's lack of interest in a report. Officials may be intensely interested in a study's focus at its beginning but have moved on to other priorities by the time it is done, particularly with major studies. Paradoxically, the larger and longer a study, the greater the prospect for definitive findings—but the greater the likelihood that the results will fail to reach executives in time to be used.

Inappropriate communications strategies by policy analysts also inhibit the use of formal analysis. Researchers and executives tend to belong to separate communities with different values, ideologies, and language.[27] The prose in a report may seem loaded with abstruse jargon and incomprehensible statistics. Shrewd analysts know that they must translate their findings if they are to persuade executives to use them. Carefully prepared oral briefings may serve this purpose. So do artfully constructed executive summaries at the beginning of formal reports.

Executives may ignore a formal analysis because they do not find it authoritative.[28] Poor-quality research may generate this concern. Sometimes, however, lack of authoritativeness arises from more basic sources. Scientists seek to develop empirically supported theories that describe and explain what is. With good theories, or models, they can predict the results of certain courses of action (for instance the implications of lower interest rates for housing construction). Developing these theories and testing them with valid data often present great difficulties, however. Problems of empirical verification in the social sciences loom particularly large. Even high-quality, state-of-the-art analyses leave readers with a substantial measure of uncertainty. Furthermore, valid findings may become obsolete with the passage of time. For instance, a merit pay plan may successfully motivate employees for a while but with the arrival of an economic downturn no longer do so. Moreover, contradictory findings abound in the social sciences. Rather than yielding a growing convergence of viewpoints, successive studies of social phenomena often yield inconsistent findings.

Ironically, the desire to study variables that executives can manipulate sometimes undercuts the authoritativeness of studies. The systematic exclusion of political phenomenon in many applied reports serves as an example. It may be, for instance, that opposition from the local medical society, hostility of various political leaders, and outbreaks of racial prejudice in a community help explain why some neighborhood health centers are less effective than others. (These centers, among other things, seek to increase poor people's access to medical care.) However, examination of these factors might incite political forces to attack not only the study but also the evaluation team. Hence, evaluators may exclude political variables that are too hot to handle.

Finally, applied research cannot speak in very conclusive fashion about values. Scientists may be able to advise the Occupational Safety and Health Administration on the risk to the health of workers exposed to some substance. They cannot, as scientists, proclaim with any special authority that the risk is acceptable given some level of economic and social benefit associated with the continued use of the substance. Such issues fall into the bailiwick of moral philosophy and of course politics.

Thus the barriers to the instrumental use of formal analysis—the psychological predispositions of managers, faulty project selection, a lack of timeliness, poor translation skills among analysts, limited authoritativeness—encourage executives to neglect reports.

Excessive Pessimism about Instrumental Use.   While formal reports of information systems and analytic staffs often go unused, executives rely on them more than this vision portrays. The magnitude and complexity of agency activities often make information systems valuable to the manager.[29] They provide a means of keeping score. These systems do not automatically define problems for executives and indicate appropriate remedies. Rather, the systems provide clues. In the words of one high-level manager in the federal bureaucracy, the "statistics and reports do . . . throw up some signals that things aren't happening at the point of impact." Executives then turn to personal contacts to understand the source of the problem.[30]

Beyond routine statistical reports, formal studies influence executive decisions directly. Officials at the National Aeronautics and Space Administration rely heavily on certain engineering reports. Executives at the Occupational Safety and Health Administration must come to grips with studies of the toxicity of substances that may adversely affect workers' health before regulating them. Certain executives at the Office of Personnel Management pay attention to validation studies of federal examinations. Executives may not read these studies in detail, but their findings often directly influence these officials' actions.

The law sometimes requires the instrumental use of formal studies. At times Congress has sought to institutionalize analysis to assure that executives consider certain values so as to encourage the more accurate assessment of trade-offs by federal executives. Consider the National Environmental Policy Act of 1969, which requires that agencies planning major construction projects prepare an environmental impact statement.[31] These impact analyses differ somewhat according to the type of project and the agency, but nearly all of them discuss the physical setting of a project (e.g., the construction of a dam or harbor), adverse effects on the environment, alternatives to the proposed project, and their comparative costs and benefits. The analyses vary in length from fifty pages to several thick volumes. Among the distinguishing features of these reports two stand out: (1) They must be made available to the public; (2) courts have the authority to review and use them if citizens bring suit.

Executives tend to heed these reports, especially when certain conditions apply. One is pressure from environmentalists. In the San Francisco Bay Area, the Army Corps of Engineers faces vigorous environmental advocates. The corps plans and builds water resource projects; it is a civilian agency in personnel and major mission but housed in the Department of Defense and headed by a military engineering elite. Given the activities of environmentalists in the Bay Area, corps executives cannot safely ignore or downplay the concerns in environmental impact statements. To do so heightens prospects that environmental groups will use the analysis to block the project in the courts.

The benefit-cost ratio of a project also influences the effect of the environmental impact statement. Through data gathering and analysis, staffs in the federal government develop estimates of the benefits of a project (e.g., construction of a dam) relative to its costs. The higher the ratio of benefits to costs, the more likely is a project to win approval by executives and policymakers. When a project has a "fat," or substantial, benefit-cost ratio, executives tend to pay more attention to concerns expressed in environmental impact statements. In essence, they can afford to be responsive. Officials can make the project more expensive by building pollution controls and environmental safeguards into the design and still have a satisfactory benefit-cost ratio.

The authoritativeness of the knowledge base also influences the degree to which executives pay attention to environmental impact statements. For instance, certain geological studies designed to predict hazards rest on research techniques widely accepted as scientifically valid. Executives can ignore these studies only at considerable risk that a project will be delayed in the courts or ultimately generate visible, undesirable side effects. In contrast, landscape architects tend to emphasize the visual impact of the projects and wrestle with highly subjective issues such as the nature of beauty. Lacking an aura of scientific authoritativeness, landscape architects run greater risk that executives will ignore their concerns.

Depending on legal requirements and other circumstances, information systems and formal analyses often directly influence executive choices. Furthermore, reports have uses that extend beyond the instrumental.

Enlightenment and Symbolism.   Analyses may influence executives by providing them with general enlightenment on a subject. This influence of analysis on the actions of public managers is less specific and direct than that implied by the instrumental use of studies. The period between the appearance of the study and its impact on the values, beliefs, and behavior of executives may be quite lengthy. This general enlightenment may occur as studies become absorbed into the conventional wisdom, or ordinary knowledge, in the agency or society.[32] Whether executives open themselves to such enlightenment in some degree depends on their proclivities to read and their tolerance for ostensibly "irrelevant information."[33]

Information systems and reports also have symbolic value for federal executives. The undertaking of such analysis, especially when highly visible, often sends powerful signals to groups within the bureaucracy, members of Congress, lobbyists, the news media, and others. In essence, formal study states one's interest in a problem and the worthiness of one's approach to it. This symbolic approach has roots in a dominant value of Western culture—that information ought to be systematically applied to decisions. At the extremes this cultural perspective degenerates into a naive faith that officials can ameliorate almost all problems through analysis and subsequent action. Formal information gathering and analysis provide a ritualistic assurance to interested observers (and often executives themselves) that proper attitudes about decisionmaking exist.[34] This symbolic dimension has prompted various students of organization to liken the pursuit of much formal analysis to religion, ritual, and magic.[35,36,37]

The symbolic uses of information can make life easier for federal executives in several ways. The conspicuous consumption of information can legitimize a decision to employees, segments of the public, oversight actors, and others. Studies can also help public managers avoid criticism if things go wrong. Given the costs of acquiring information, executives can err by spending too much on it, but they are much less likely to face criticism for excess study than for failing to conduct an analysis that would have alerted them to some problem. Analysis becomes a means of self-protection. Research can also take the heat off executives to do something about a particular problem. When officials oppose certain options being thrust upon them, they may hope that by the time the study is done, pressure for the decision they do not wish to make will have dissipated. Or the delay produced by the study may buffer interference and buy time to assemble a coalition in favor of a solution. The threat of analysis may also serve as a device for hierarchical control. Knowledge that an evaluation staff will be undertaking a study may lead its subjects to pay more attention to complying with the law. Even though program executives may never read the report, they have influenced the behavior of other administrators.

Examples of the symbolic uses of analysis abound. Top executives at the Office of Personnel Management used evaluation studies to deflect pressures on them during the early phases of the Civil Service Reform Act of 1978. This law's controversial provisions regarding merit pay and the establishment of the Senior Executive Service produced considerable suspicion among union leaders, members of Congress, and senior career executives. As one observer notes, "The political environment of civil service reform was hypersensitive, anecdote-hungry, and suspicious. The potential existed for isolated instances of personnel abuse to be generalized as evidence of the failure of the whole reform program."[38] To reduce this possibility, top officials at the Office of Personnel Management early evinced a clear commitment to long-term evaluation of the program. The evaluation staff aggressively sought out other studies of the reform and publicized its own research. The commitment of executives to evaluating the various initiatives launched by the Civil Service Reform Act helped buy time for managers to get the program off the ground. The promise of subsequent evaluation made it more difficult for potential critics to rush to judgment and attack the program.

Consider also the uses of PERT—a formal analytic exercise designed to describe graphically the interrelationship of steps, or events, involved in developing a specific product. PERT received much favorable publicity for contributing to the success of a Navy project office in developing the *Polaris* missile (a nuclear warhead fired from a submerged submarine). A careful analysis of the uses of PERT in the development of this project, however, notes that the technique, per se, was as "effective technically as rain dancing."[39] It did little to shape employee behavior or prevent delays. The highly visible use of the technique did protect project managers from interference by comptrollers, auditors, and others. In essence, the technique worked not because it guided the behavior of executives but because it persuaded outsiders not to interfere with the team working on missile development.

The symbolic uses of formal analysis do not rule out subsequent use instrumentally or as a source of general enlightenment. Once produced, a report may unexpectedly modify the attitudes, beliefs, and behavior of public managers.

The Coming of the Computer

The management of information merges with the management of equipment. The computer is the analytic engine that powers efforts to make more analysis-intensive decisions and to make bureaucracy more efficient in handling routines. The Paperwork Reduction Act formally makes computers the centerpiece of information management.

Within the federal government and more generally, the 1950s and 1960s were the era of large, powerful mainframe computers. Centralization prevailed. Access to the computer entailed use of a terminal connected to the mainframe. Highly skilled computer experts tended to these systems and provided assistance to those who wished to use them. During this period computers allowed officials to handle the routine functions of government faster. Computer technology came to dominate the processing of Social Security checks and tax returns.

During the 1970s and the 1980s, major new developments occurred with respect to computer technology—developments some describe as "quantum leaps" and as ushering in a "management revolution."[40] The proliferation of microcomputers helped this revolution. Their relatively low cost permitted federal agencies to purchase large numbers of them. These microcomputers have separate memory modules and great capacity to link directly to remote locations through telecommunications networks. Many are as powerful as the mainframe of a generation ago. At the same time, the growing availability of user-friendly software (word processing programs, statistical packages, and so on) meant that civil servants with little formal training in computers could easily operate them. These technological developments militated against centralization and bolstered access to computers. Officials throughout the bureaucracy could develop their own procedures for data base management and for applying computers to an agency's particular needs.

For instance, the Department of Medicine and Surgery in the Veterans Administration (VA) adopted a system called MUMPS (Massachusetts General Hospital Utility Multi-Programming System) for medical record keeping.[41] This system has about thirty thousand users in some 172 VA hospitals. It permits personnel to create, consult, and update the medical records of patients through a few simple commands. Not only can the VA staff obtain data about specific patients, but they can use the system to conduct management analyses, for example on the cost of performing certain medical procedures.

Problems on the Way to the Revolution.   Whether in business or government, the march of the computer revolution has been uneven. Although computers have become more accessible, many federal executives have not understood the broader uses of computer technology in managing information. Nor has computerization invariably moved ahead at great speed. In May 1983 Congressman Jack Brooks (Democrat of Texas) charged that the Office of Management and Budget had concentrated far too little attention on implementing the provisions of the Paperwork Reduction Act aimed at computerizing federal offices.[42] By one rough estimate, the federal bureaucracy had about 13,700 major computer systems and 82,000 word processors as of the mid-1980s.[43]

In some respects the purchase and operation of computer technology is like mining for gold. The potential benefits are great, but pitfalls are plentiful. Difficulties arise early, when officials attempt to estimate benefits and costs of purchasing a computer system. Vendors almost inevitably claim that the latest equipment will work wonders. Some vendors have gone so far as to argue that executives will not only have paperless offices but will not need desks other than those required to hold up their computer consoles. Prudent executives take this hype with a grain of salt and are sensitive to the threat of the "Trojan computer."[44] In sum, computers may have unforeseen and undesirable effects. Often the machinery and software do not perform as well as promised. Moreover, the rapid rate of advance in computer technology means that the timing of decisions can come back to haunt executives. A delay of a month or two may let the executive buy a more powerful system for less money, but no one can be certain of this.

Once the system is operating, maintenance can be a problem. Issues of data quality loom large. The initial feeding of valid information into the system is the least of the problems. Typically, new data must be fed into the system to keep its outputs accurate and timely. In the long run updating often ranks as the single largest cost associated with these systems, a fact executives frequently underestimate when they purchase them. The fact that growing numbers of micro- and minicomputers are linked to each other, or networked, can elevate the importance of preserving data quality. Data inaccurately entered into a widely accessible information system increase the possibility that decisions will be based on erroneous data.[45]

A federal executive bent on improving information management through computers also confronts the possibility of a spillover into issues of personnel management—sometimes in dramatic ways. It is unclear whether video display terminals pose health hazards to those who constantly use them. Furthermore, concern that computer installations will cost federal jobs has entered into labor-management negotiations. In 1985 the Social Security Administration and the American Federation of Government Employees signed an agreement to ease the agency's efforts to install computer equipment in more than thirteen hundred field offices around the country. The agency and union agreed to short-circuit traditional bargaining to resolve more directly issues of automation, work space, assignment of work, and equipment design.[46]

These and related questions pose substantial uncertainties for executives in purchasing computer systems and mean that guesstimates often predominate in these decisions. Of course, the executive can reduce uncertainty. At least in theory, executives can force the vendor to develop a prototype and do a performance test to demonstrate how it will serve the agency. Simulating agency conditions in a performance test often proves quite difficult, however. In addition, opinions on the standards that can reasonably be applied in designing and judging these performance tests differ. Thus, these tests are hardly foolproof devices for anticipating problems and avoiding criticism. In 1985 the Federal Aviation Authority decided to spend approximately $725 million to develop, acquire, and operate new computers for twenty air traffic control centers.[47] Executives at the agency hoped that the new computers would provide the capacity to handle without delay air traffic anticipated in the late 1980s and in the 1990s. Critics accused the agency of rushing to imprudent judgment in the purchase decisions. Among other things, they charged that executives had conducted inadequate performance testing of the proposed system in the design phase.

The pitfalls of acquiring and maintaining computer systems would be less dangerous if staffs could easily correct deficiencies in the systems, but error correction often proves difficult without considerable sums of money or staff time or both.

Problems with computers are not confined to the public sector. An article in the *Harvard Business Review* observes, "As any executive involved with the purchase of computer service knows, users are frequently disappointed in the performance of their computer installations, sometimes to the point of desperation."[48] The article provides advice on negotiating with and even suing unsatisfactory computer vendors.

Computers and Power.   As union interest in issues of computerization suggests, the acquisition and management of computers goes beyond technology to power. One question is who should control basic decisions about the purchase and use of computers and software. Since microcomputers and user-friendly software have encouraged agencies to tailor systems to their particular needs, some officials worry about the excesses of decentralization. In extreme form decentralization inhibits communication among agencies, as each uses different software and related equipment. It can lead agencies to create their own information systems when they could just as easily obtain the pertinent reports from elsewhere in the bureaucracy. Decentralization can draw those with little expertise about computers and little capacity to obtain volume discounts into purchasing.[49]

To counter the excesses of decentralization, agencies such as the General Services Administration have long played an important role in the purchase of computers. The Paperwork Reduction Act of 1980 tried to create a measure of centralized control over computer technology. The law required officials at the Office of Management and Budget to consult with GSA and line managers to prepare a five-year plan for automatic data processing in the federal government. It charged OMB with enforcing information processing standards, particularly software language standards, at all federal installations. It also required OMB and GSA to ensure that "information systems do not overlap each other or duplicate the systems of other agencies." How strongly these provisions will counteract centrifugal forces in the management of computer systems remains an open question. Some observers see considerable virtue in granting agency executives more authority over such purchases.[50]

Once systems are purchased and operating, who gains power as a result of computerization? One view is that the advance of computer technology has shifted power up the hierarchy. Presumably top executives can use management information systems to monitor activities or outputs at the bottom levels. They thereby enhance their control over subordinates.[51] Is this view correct? One study used survey research techniques to determine its veracity. While focused on local governments rather than the federal establishment, the study is suggestive.[52]

The study divided the types of officials affected by computing innovations into four major categories:

1. Managers or top-level administrators who mainly use summarized information from automated files on an occasional basis
2. Staff professionals who provide formal analysis and advice to managers
3. Desktop bureaucrats—the administrative and clerical employees extensively involved in recording, processing, searching, and producing the information contained in files
4. Street-level bureaucrats, the line personnel who directly provide goods or services to clients

The study provides some support for the centralization hypothesis. While a majority of employees in each category felt that computerization had not modified their influence, more than 40 percent of the managers and staff professionals believed that their influence over others had increased as a result of computerization. The study goes on to suggest that an "information elite," that is, the staff professionals with expertise in computer-assisted analysis, may be the primary beneficiaries. Of course, perceptions of power shifts may not accurately gauge transformations of power.

Moreover, the centralization hypothesis coexists with another that sees power dispersion resulting from the spread of computer literacy and user-friendly micro-computers. This thesis portrays executives as losing control over access to computer systems. Presumably, employees may enter or obtain data when they should not. Fraud is one aspect of this problem. A few readily portable plastic discs can contain information that once filled several file cabinets. Hence, theft becomes simpler.[53] The ability of outsiders to break into government computers also presents problems. For instance, at a 1983 congressional hearing, teenage hacker Neal Patrick described how he had broken into the computer system at the Los Alamos National Laboratory in New Mexico.[54] In essence, executives may not be able to control information. In the case of criminal justice and national security, information leakage has particularly ominous implications. It can also violate the privacy rights of citizens.

Federal officials have responded with a variety of measures to prevent leakage. Constant changing of passwords (codes that allow access to the data base) is one approach. It is far from foolproof, however, as employees afraid of forgetting their password often write it down on the terminal or give it to coworkers, defeating the purpose of the system. At more advanced and expensive levels, systems can check the retinal patterns or handprints of users, but these checks lack practicality in the great majority of cases.[55] In order to heighten computer security, the OMB issued a directive in the 1980s requiring agencies to do a risk analysis for their computer systems. Officials surveyed their systems and attempted to estimate losses to the agency in the event of unauthorized entry.

Information in Perspective

Developments in communication technology and science have made the federal executive's world more information- and analysis-intensive, but it is important not to exaggerate the implications of these trends. Talk and informal information networks remain central to an executive's life. Nonverbal communication also ranks high in importance, although its precise role is difficult to determine. Moreover, in spite of efforts to rationalize decisions, uncertainty remains a staple of managerial life. One observer goes so far as to assert that management is in large part "the art of making decisions with insufficient information."[56] Another says that the essence of manage-ment is decisionmaking under ambiguity. "Very little information is given to the manager faced with a strategic issue, and almost none of that is structured."[57] Federal executives often operate amid considerable disagreement about desirable goals or priorities and the means to achieve various ends.

This is not to suggest that efforts to rationalize the decisions of federal executives through better information will fail. Executives may become more computer- and analysis-literate and so heighten their use of systematic formal information. Profes-sional analysts may follow in the path of software specialists and make their reports user-friendly. The ability of analysts to convert formal studies into informal oral presentation with minimal distortion is probably a central requirement of advancing the instrumental use of their products.

Certain tensions are evident in the advice of those who seek to improve information use by managers. Some specialists see considerable virtue in sustaining redundant sources of information, which runs counter to the Paperwork Reduction Act of 1980. In this view managers should encourage the use of multiple and competitive sources of information. The manager needs different points of view and contrary opinions.[58] Duplication and overlap in agencies may encourage this redundancy. By the same token, however, virtually everyone acknowledges the problems of information overload. One student of management information systems emphasizes the importance of controlling "the rate of information bombarding the manager" and the "intelligent filtering of information."[59] Both redundancy and filtering make sense, but striking the proper balance between the two is a major challenge for information specialists.

Whatever the degree to which computer-based information systems and formal analysis affect executive decisions, they should not mask the political character of information. Because the flow of information affects who gets what from government, there are temptations to deceive and lie, and executives must constantly assess the information they receive for its veracity. They must wrestle with the ethics of telling the truth as they know it. Deception occurs when through action or inaction (even silence), officials intentionally communicate misleading messages. Evasions, euphemisms, and exaggeration may be part of deception. Lies—intentionally false messages that people explicitly state—are a subcategory of deception.[60]

Lying springs from many sources. Officials may tell white lies to reduce unpleasantness and tension. Or an executive may falsely praise a colleague to get cooperation on a project. Or in the name of compassion, a doctor in the VA medical system may choose not to tell a patient that he has terminal cancer. State department executives may deliberately spread misleading information to confuse a government hostile to the United States. As these examples suggest, lying and deception may be born of good intentions—a desire by managers to respond to programmatic and consensual imperatives. Some lying may be ethically justified. But however good the intentions, an official's lie may ultimately have undesirable effects on the person who hears it (it would have been better to be honest with the dying patient), corrode the moral sensibility of the person telling it, undermine credibility and trust within the federal bureaucracy, and engender suspicion of and hostility toward government among the citizenry.

The Management of Physical Resources

The management of information overlaps the management of physical resources. A manager may use office decor as nonverbal communication. Good paintings may testify to a State Department official's worldly, sophisticated, cultured outlook; books and journals may serve a manager of an evaluation unit as a badge of academic and technical sophistication. Moreover, computers, telephones, and other apparatus of communication are simultaneously sources of information and physical resources. The overlap is not complete; the management of physical resources deserves consideration in its own right. While relatively neglected in standard efforts to understand public management, the forces affecting the nature and distribution of buildings, equipment, and supplies markedly affect the ability of executives to meet their programmatic, consensual, legal, and personal imperatives.

The neglect of the study of physical resources may in part reflect the belief that the typical career executive exerts very little influence over their allocation. Major decisions in this realm (the construction of VA hospitals, the development of weapons systems) often seem to be the preserve of top political officials. However, as will become evident, executives frequently have more control over physical resources than conventional views suggest. To some degree it depends on the type of physical resource involved. The jargon of the federal establishment distinguishes between real and personal property. *Real property* is land and buildings; *personal property* is everything else—furniture, equipment, supplies, and materials.[61]

Turf: Buildings and Space

The federal government ranks as one of the largest owners and users of buildings in the world. Congress plays a major role in shaping the expansion and allocation of buildings. As of the early 1980s, space acquisition requiring net rental or alteration costs of half a million dollars or more required a prospectus, which had to be approved by Congress under the Public Buildings Act of 1959. Members of Congress often view decisions related to real property as the stuff of pork barrel politics—of providing jobs and other benefits to their district or state. Major decisions concerning the location of VA hospitals often produce intense political infighting. While officials at the VA go to some lengths to conduct analyses and present technical criteria for their capital investments, pressures from affiliated medical schools, which use VA hospitals for training purposes, and the interest of members of Congress in scoring a victory for the folks back home substantially affect such decisions.

Aside from Congress and political appointees, career executives contend with other bureaucracies to get physical property. Established in 1949, the General Services Administration supervises the leasing and construction of real property as well as the assignment of office space to particular agencies. Sensitive to the importance of such decisions, various federal agencies have been sufficiently powerful to remain outside the ambit of GSA authority. These agencies include the Postal Service, the VA, and the Defense Department.

In the acquisition of buildings, leasing from the private sector rather than construction often prevails. In 1985 an official from GSA reported that the agency leased about forty-seven hundred buildings; it owned another twenty-three hundred.[62] By the mid-1980s some observers thought the balance between leasing and building failed to foster cost-effectiveness. Officials at the GSA began to emphasize the importance of owning buildings to avoid, as one congressional aide put it, "ending up with a pile of rent receipts after 20 years."[63]

Frustrations of Delay.   Federal executives frequently have trouble obtaining space. This derives from the obvious fact that space is a scarce resource. Beyond this, however, managers of federal facilities have often lacked sensitivity to the preferences of executives and employees. In 1985 William Sullivan, Commissioner of the Public Buildings Service in the GSA, acknowledged that "the tenants in a new Federal Building . . . are often overlooked in planning and decision-making. Not surprisingly, this can result in dissatisfaction with both the process and the product."[64] Delay is one source of executive unhappiness. A study of how long it took GSA to process requests for space found that the average delay had gone from 125 days in 1977 to 240 days in 1980.[65] Delay in part stems from the large number of evaluations required for approval of a building. For instance, the building must meet standards prescribed by the Occupational Safety and Health Administration.

While the delay these standards impose may irritate executives, the hours spent in reviewing buildings ahead of time may well save trouble later. As sensitivity to workplace hazards has grown, facilities planners have paid more attention to hazards ranging from asbestos to rug fungus. In the 1980s the GSA invested heavily in reducing the presence of the carcinogen asbestos in federal buildings. At times executives get caught in the middle on safety and health issues. When an employee of the Library of Congress contracted a serious respiratory illness, he attributed it to the inadequate ventilation system in the James Madison Building in Washington. This episode plus general complaints from employees about ventilation and air conditioning led to a meeting of Library of Congress officials with union representatives and health inspectors in January 1986.[66]

Neglect As a Legacy of Hawthorne.   The task of executives does not end with the struggle to obtain enough space that meets appropriate standards of aesthetics, safety, and physical comfort. The interior design of offices also affects the ability to pursue objectives. Interior design can, for instance, affect the organizational commitment, motivation, and productivity of subordinates.[67]

The Hawthorne studies and the resulting human relations movement have done much to relegate the behavioral implications of physical facilities to the back burner in the study of management. Conducted at the Hawthorne plant of Western Electric (then a subsidiary of AT&T) in the 1920s and 1930s, this series of studies explored the influence of certain physical conditions such as lighting on the productivity of workers. The studies failed to produce much support for the hypotheses of experimenters concerning the effects of physical factors on productivity. Unexpectedly, however, two groups of workers—one experimental and one control—isolated for one phase of the study both demonstrated increases in productivity. Researchers theorized that workers understood the study to be an expression of management interest and concern and concluded that morale and productivity increased as a result.

While the human relations lessons of Hawthorne subsequently came under considerable criticism, the study heightened interest in the social context of work. Physical setting and its implications for behavior received much less attention from students of management. In fact, however, facilities can do much to shape employee attitudes, beliefs, and behavior. Obviously, executives seldom start from scratch in interior design. The building itself sets basic structural constraints. Moreover, employees set the character of their own work space by hanging pictures and rearranging the furniture. While these and other factors constrain executive discretion, however, they do not eliminate it.

How does interior design affect organizational involvement, motivation, and productivity? While federal executives cannot turn to social science literature for precise answers, certain tendencies are evident. For example, interior space provides employees with greater or fewer opportunities to interact—to share thoughts, feelings, and values. This can markedly affect the degree to which employees become attached to primary groups within the agency and the extent to which executives can use solidary incentives to accomplish organizational ends. So, too, office character-istics affect noise levels and opportunities for privacy, thereby influencing the ability of workers to think without distraction and to have a sense of autonomy.

One study focused on four factors—openness, density, architectural accessibil-ity, and darkness.[68] Openness is the ratio of the square footage of an office to the total length of its interior walls and partitions. A related quality, architectural accessibility, is the degree to which walls and doors surround each employee's individual work space. Density is the total square footage of the office divided by the number of employees working in it. Darkness derives from the color of office walls and the level of office illumination. Among other things, the study indicated that dense, accessi-ble, dark offices damp job satisfaction. While the effect of interior design on employees' values, perceptions and behavior cannot be stated precisely, prudent executives cannot afford to ignore the implications of such design for personnel management.

The Great Space Initiative.   At times a concern with interior design and space prompts executives to mobilize and resist oversight actors. In the early 1980s President Reagan issued an executive order designed to increase density in federal office space. The order called for an average of 135 square feet per person in the federal government, down from an estimated 165 square feet in the early 1980s.[69] GSA assumed responsibility for implementing the executive order and set the goal of a ten percent annual reduction in office space per person until agencies achieved the desired level. In the debate between GSA and line executives, proponents of different views mustered private-sector comparisons designed to strengthen their position. The GSA asserted that private-sector space ranged from 110 to 150 square feet per person. Those sympathetic to federal managers countered with a report of the Building Owners and Managers Association International that found an average of 230 square feet per employee in the private sector.[70]

The conflict led to bargaining over definitions. Program managers complained that GSA failed to take into account that some spaces, such as hearing rooms and recreation areas, did not constitute individual work areas. They argued that this space should not count toward the quota for square footage. Executives scored a minor victory when GSA issued regulations creating a new category, "supplemental space," which agencies could deduct when calculating square footage per employee. The degree to which the GSA will fully implement the executive order remains an open question. As of the mid-1980s, GSA officials estimated that square footage per employee had dropped by only five over two years. Moreover, top administrators in the executive branch remained skeptical of GSA's prospects for success. Officials in the Office of Management and Budget indicated that they planned to place little emphasis on space reduction on grounds that it would produce only minor savings, at least in the short run. Moreover, a GSA report raised doubts as to whether the agency had the clout to prevail over executives in line agencies.[71]

On balance, this case testifies to the occasional ability of executives to deflect regulations they view as undesirable. Changes in space standards are particularly likely to attract the attention of managers. Such standards not only have concrete implications for the comfort and productivity of agency personnel; they also have a heavy symbolic overlay. Many managers read President Reagan's order reducing space as yet one more assault on the bureaucracy he campaigned against. Moreover, office space conveys social rank. Internal agency standards that call for differences in office space depending on an official's position in the hierarchy in effect allocate status.

Executives and "Personal Property"

As one of the largest buyers and users of equipment, supplies, and furnishings, the federal government purchases everything from paper clips to major weapons systems. The issues of dealing with this type of property fall into several major categories, including procurement, storage, security, use, maintenance, repair, and disposition. More than a hundred thousand federal employees administer these processes.[72]

Ideally, procurement agents obtain appropriate equipment and supplies in a timely fashion at a reasonable cost. This process often proves frustrating for executives. As with office space, they frequently complain about excess paperwork and slow response time by such purchasing agencies as the GSA.[73] Beyond this, the unpredictability of the procurement process can be considerable especially when the government seeks to purchase expensive new technology. The problems often encountered in buying computers and weapons systems serve as vivid examples. Equipment that fails to meet performance expectations is only part of the problem. Cost can be a thorny issue. Vendors who understate costs in order to obtain federal contracts may subsequently appeal for more funds to complete their contractual obligation. Federal officials may, depending on the nature of the contract, deny this request, but to do so introduces the risk that the contractor will not furnish the product at all, on time, or at the level or quality originally promised.

Neglect of the Human Factor.   As with the design of office space, procurement processes have often slighted the human factor. The relationship between equipment design and employee performance is particularly important.[74] When employees use equipment inappropriately, there is a strong tendency to cite human error; the machine did its job, but the operator goofed. Most design engineers have had little incentive or basic inclination to take human factors into account in their work on equipment. In fact, machine design can be a powerful variable shaping whether human errors occur. Since World War II, a small discipline known as human factors engineering, or ergonomics, has addressed these issues. Human factors engineers seek to broaden the perspective of ordinary design engineers by advising them on the physical and psychological characteristics of operators and maintenance personnel. Still, in the federal government as well as more generally, the power of human factors engineers over purchasing and design decisions often remains quite limited.

Moreover, critics question whether human factors engineers have fully grasped how organizational context can affect the operators' relationships to their machines. Human factors engineers focus on such variables as anthropometric limits (reach, strength, and so on), response time, visual sensitivity, cognitive capacity, and memory limits. Critics suggest that while useful, the perspective is "that of the isolated human, subject only to biological limitations."[75] Critics contend that human factors engineers inadequately consider primary work group, supervisorial patterns, organizational culture, and so on. These contextual variables do much to shape the mental models of machine operators.

Whatever the limits of human factors engineering, the degree to which top executives pay attention to it in procuring equipment depends on several factors. Where the consequences of poor design are highly visible to the public, hence threaten the status of officials, and where law requires investigation of accidents by independent agencies, executives have more incentive to pay attention. Airplane accidents fit this description, so human factors engineering has received considerable attention in designing equipment for air traffic controllers in the Federal Aviation Administration.

Aside from procurement, keeping track of personal property and sustaining its security are a managerial concern. While usually a routine matter handled through periodic inventories, this aspect of property management can be troublesome. The possibility of theft sparks particular concern in agencies involved with criminal justice and national defense. The increase in terrorism has escalated the importance of security at federal installations overseas and to some degree at home.

Executives face a host of issues related to the use of equipment and other property by employees. This concern interacts with personnel management. To assure the effective use of certain equipment, executives may have to influence recruitment processes so that personnel with adequate skills win jobs. Or they may have to use training programs to this end.

"Abuse" and the Telephone Offensive.   Concern with control and the prevention of abuse also guides executives' attempts to control use of equipment. Sometimes federal executives have this issue thrust at them whether they like it or not. In 1985, for instance, GSA launched a campaign against alleged phone abuse by federal civil servants. The President's Council on Integrity and Efficiency (a group of inspectors general charged with ferreting out fraud and abuse) sponsored the project. Benjamin Friedman, GSA's acting deputy inspector general, explained the project in the following terms: "If people know that someone is checking on calls they make, we hope they will be more shy about abusing the system." Hence GSA announced plans to sample calls made from government phones in Washington, using computers to pick out the calls that appeared most suspicious. Among other things, GSA planned to target the phone numbers of well-known resort areas and the dial-a-porn industry (companies offering sexually explicit conversations for a fee). Friedman noted that while the system did not intend to track down and prosecute individual employees, those who "have run hog wild" in making illicit phone calls could face legal prosecution. GSA officials estimated that the project might save the government as much as $150 million per year.[76]

A 1986 GSA report asserted that 30 percent of the long distance calls sampled at the Department of Housing and Urban Development were for personal rather than business reasons. GSA pointed to highly questionable calls such as one to a New Jersey gambling casino. Other "personal calls," however, seemed far less extraordinary. Large numbers of them were calls to employees' homes in suburban Washington. In mid-August 1986, GSA installed a device in the main switchboard of the HUD building in Washington so that any employee who dialed a number for the time, the weather, dial-a-porn, or certain other "non-business" connections would get a busy signal.[77]

External attempts such as these can provide information and control to executives, but they also contribute to a climate of mistrust that undermines organizational involvement and motivation among employees. These initiatives may appear to be, as one official expressed it, "another little deal to punish federal employees."[78] Moreover, efforts at control often collide with values concerning employee rights. Unions and members of Congress complained that phone audits were an unwarranted intrusion into the privacy of civil servants. Union leaders vowed that attempts at disciplinary action based on the audit would meet opposition as an unfair labor practice.

Maintenance and Disposal. Executives also face decisions about the maintenance and disposal of certain properties. Using sophisticated techniques, executives may perform various financial and technical analyses to determine the appropriate time to dispose of rather than repair property. Such techniques also assess whether the latest technological advances justify replacement of well-functioning but less modern equipment. Aside from these obvious concerns, problems with the incentives created by the mere presence of equipment and furnishings may motivate executives to dispose of them. For instance, students of health policy have long noted the tendency of hospital staffs to fill the beds. Excess bed capacity tempts administrators and doctors to hospitalize individuals who could best be treated as outpatients. This creates financial waste. Moreover, since hospital patients are exposed to diseases during their stays and at times acquire new illnesses because of this exposure, needless hospitalization threatens health. Suspicions that this was occurring in VA hospitals prompted the Office of Management and Budget to press the agency to reduce beds, and they declined from roughly 121,000 in 1964 to fewer than 90,000 at the end of the 1970s.[79]

Along with the management of buildings and space, the management of personal property is largely neglected among students of public management. This may also reflect the legacy of Hawthorne with its emphasis on human relations. Whatever the reason, these issues deserve more attention than they ordinarily receive.

Federal Managers and Money

Chapter 6 presented the high drama of budgetary politics, in which the White House, Congress, interest groups, the courts, and political executives play leading roles. Although less visible, career executives also have parts to play. They help draft the budget requests that ultimately filter up to the highest levels of the executive branch. The performance of these executives has often provided the litmus test as to whether various budget formats such as PPBS and ZBB live up to their much-vaunted objectives of rationalizing the budget process.

Career executives are eager spectators of budget processes. How much money these processes funnel to their programs dramatically affects their ability to respond to the various imperatives that drive them. Over the last two decades, circumstances have forced considerable change in the rules of the budget game. The notion that an executive receives an annual budget that clearly specifies how much to spend frequently bears little resemblance to reality. Executives who administer funds for entitlement programs (such as Medicare, a health care program for the elderly) have open-ended spending authority. In essence, the federal government agrees to entitle specific citizens to certain benefits. Outlays in a given year depend in large measure on the number of eligible program beneficiaries who show up to claim that benefit.

Uncertainty stemming from the growth in entitlements need not be particularly troubling to career managers. In fact, it may please them to know that Congress has given their program a blank check. More problematic is the uncertainty stemming from the fact that Congress often fails to approve agency budgets prior to the beginning of the federal fiscal year on October 1. By the 1980s it was common for all twelve months of a fiscal year to go by with Congress unable to pass the regular appropriations bills for an agency. Executives in many agencies faced a succession of two- to four-month continuing resolutions, which usually preserve existing levels of funding in the absence of specific congressional commitments. In many respects, budgeting by Congress in the 1980s became continuous, so executives "have to devote considerable time to simply 'crunching' the changing numbers and ensuring compliance with legal spending limitations."[80] This short-term preoccupation undercuts executive attention to a whole range of strategic management issues.

Concern with the high drama of the federal budget and its changing rules should not divert executives' attention from other aspects of financial management. Once budget figures come down from Congress, executives may well be able to influence the timing and nature of expenditures. As in other aspects of policy implementation, the issue of how much discretion executives ought to possess in financial management remains the subject of considerable debate. In the early 1980s the National Academy of Public Administration criticized congressional budget appropriations for becoming too detailed. It noted that the president's budget accounts listing had 1,250 separate accounts covering some 180 pages.[81] Elected officials, of course, frequently see considerable virtue in detailed accounts as a means of obtaining specific information about programs and exerting more control over the bureaucracy.

Federal executives' discretion in financial management intersects with three sets of issues, among others. One concerns the disbursement of funds—the timing of payments, the recipient, and the amount. Another set, less universally applicable, concerns the collection of money, usually fees or loans. Yet another set of issues concerns the recording and verification of financial transactions—accounting and auditing.

Disbursement: Variable Discretion and Error

Depending in part on the statute governing a program, federal executives have varying degrees of discretion in influencing the targets, amounts, and timing of a program's disbursement of funds. Some executives exert considerable leverage over which group obtains a contract or grant to undertake certain activities such as to heighten awareness and preparation for health careers among minority youths.

In other circumstances managers have much less discretion. Even then, however, executives frequently have some room to maneuver. Sometimes they shift funds among object classifications in the budget. Common categories are personnel, travel, supplies, and equipment. The amounts ultimately assigned to the various object classifications usually appear in the Appendix to the Budget approved by Congress. Unless specifically prohibited, executives in agencies can usually realign funds within the same general program area among the various objects of expense. For instance, if a lag in hiring creates salary savings, often executives can use this money to purchase supplies and equipment.[82] While executives can influence shifts in funds among object classifications within a program area, major reallocations among programs typically require congressional approval. Moreover, Congress has occasionally plunged into micromanagement by constraining fund transfers among object classifications within programs. Travel, consulting services, furniture, and furnishings have borne the brunt of these interventions.

Aside from making explicit decisions about the allocation of funds, federal executives know that breakdowns in the routines of payment can bring adverse publicity and undermine program efficiency. Students of financial management emphasize the importance of *payables monitoring*. This activity assures that payments get made in a timely fashion—a requirement of the Prompt Payment Act of 1982. Many agencies have not had an easy time meeting the requirements of this act. For example, the VA operates a payment system called CALM (Centralized Accounting for Local Management). In fiscal 1983 CALM processed about 6.1 million invoices and paid approximately $2.5 billion to vendors. Because of late payments to some of these vendors, the agency lost roughly $413,000 in discounts in fiscal 1983; during the same year, it paid penalties for tardiness amounting to roughly $88,500.[83] Another analysis of thirty-nine payment centers in thirteen different agencies found that they made 24 percent of their payments after due dates.[84]

With late payments, executives cannot escape criticism by adopting an earlier-the-better orientation. Early payment (operationalized as five days or more before the due date) can cost the government money due to additional borrowing costs and eat into interest income. (Banks hold cash not needed for current disbursement by the Treasury and pay interest on the deposits.) Moreover, paying too early may vitiate vendor incentives to offer discounts for rapid payment. Hence, executives face pressure to time payments precisely. Given the inevitable ebb and flow of workload, such precise timing can be very difficult.

Breakdown also occurs when agencies err in the recipient or amount of payment. Occasionally the Social Security Administration sends checks to people who are not eligible for benefits. Payment of the incorrect amount to the designated party can also come home to haunt the executive, as when one GSA payment center made substantial numbers of duplicate payments to vendors in the early 1980s (see the introduction to this chapter). GSA problems in part stemmed from such practices as assigning the same vendor more than one identification number. The episode also illustrates the occasional tension between accuracy and timeliness. In order to assure that certain companies received prompt payment, personnel at the agency occasionally processed bills manually rather than rely on the automated system with its internal control mechanisms designed to avoid duplicate payment.[85] Once payment errors surface, an agency generally succeeds in recovering the lost sums, but the embarrassment and administrative costs of doing so can be significant.

At times, the complexity of the formula involved in paying vendors drives payment error. For instance, the Department of Medicine and Surgery in the VA provides some care to veterans by paying private doctors to treat them. In fiscal 1984 the Department of Medicine and Surgery paid $93 million on about one million invoices for these physician services. The payment formula for these providers depends on several variables and requires a constant infusion of new data. For instance, VA payment in part hinges on the median fee charged to members of the public for a certain service by private doctors in a given area. The VA staff did not routinely update prevailing physician charges to the general public; this spawned errors. Nearly a quarter of the payments to private physicians fell outside the range specified by the payment formula of the Department of Medicine and Surgery.[86]

Collection of Funds

Executive fortunes generally depend on the money budgetary processes yield, but for some managers, collections also constitute an aspect of financial management. Some federal agencies, such as the Postal Service, charge fees for services. The work of other executives is more like that of bankers seeking to collect loans. The collection and management of loans has often troubled and embarrassed federal managers. In yet another manifestation of congressional preference for indirect administration, laws often require federal executives to guarantee loans made by private financial institutions.

For instance, the Small Business Administration guarantees loans to certain individuals who wish to invest in small businesses but are presumably unable to obtain private financing. If the borrower defaults on the guaranteed loan, the federal government reimburses the private lender and attempts to collect the money. At times, the staff of the Small Business Administration has devoted inadequate financial analysis to loan applications prior to approval. This lapse has led to substantial default rates. Consider the problems of the agency's Pollution Control Financing Guarantee Program. This program sought to help qualified small businesses finance the costs of pollution abatement equipment. The staff of the Small Business Administration did not systematically apply credit analysis criteria to loan applicants to determine whether these firms could repay the cost of the equipment. In part as a consequence, the Small Business Administration had paid $17 million out of a $46 million fund established for loan defaults by August 1984.[87] Executives at the Small Business Administration are not alone in these problems. The Department of Education has similar difficulties in managing student loan programs. Established by the Higher Education Act of 1965, this program guarantees loans made by private lenders to college students. Many recipients of these loans defaulted and the Department of Education has often been unable to collect the overdue sums.[88]

These examples point to the pitfalls of managing agency collections, especially loans. The cases do not purport to show that loan programs inevitably fail. Many who have borrowed federally guaranteed funds have not defaulted and have become better equipped to serve themselves and society as a result of these programs. Moreover, some loans that result in defaults represent reasonable gambles by an agency to help some disadvantaged groups, such as students from the most impoverished families.

Keeping Score: Accounting and Auditing

Aside from the sensible allocation and collection of funds, the recording and verification of monetary transactions is a key concern of financial management, largely to keep civil servants subservient to law. Accounting and auditing systems put executives on notice that they should be able to justify their spending in terms of statutory or budgetary policies handed down by Congress and the White House. Beyond this, however, accounting and auditing information can advance the quest for efficiency and effectiveness. Through analysis of comparable financial data from different agencies, top officials may diagnose obstacles to achievements. Current modes of accounting and auditing in the federal bureaucracy make this difficult, however.

Methods: Cash, Obligation, Accrual.   While practices vary from one agency to the next, federal accounting procedures tend to emphasize fund control—the monitoring of cash flow and obligations. Recording economic events on a cash basis consists of keeping track of the money received and disbursed in a given time. Establishing records on an obligation basis means that cost is recorded at the time funds become committed to some party (possibly well in the future). An obligation is the placing of an order or the awarding of a contract. In and of themselves, cash and obligation accounting can present a misleading picture of agency expenditures. Too much emphasis on cash flow can allow financial reports to understate an agency's financial obligations in subsequent years. It leads to a very short time perspective on an agency's financial health. Accounting for obligations can also produce distorted impressions. It can make agency expenditures seem huge in a given year, such as the year executives sign a contract for a new and expensive computer system, when in fact the agency incurs the benefits and costs of the system over several years. Together, cash and obligation accounting to some degree offset each other's weaknesses.

The limits to the financial picture provided by these systems have prompted officials at GAO to endorse accounting on an accrual basis.[89] Under this system agency executives report revenues when received; they recognize an expenditure when the agency consumes the resources. For instance, the purchase of a car is recognized not when an official orders (obligation basis) or pays for it (cash basis), but when an employee actually begins to drive it. Proponents of the accrual method believe that it leads to a more accurate presentation of total resource usage in a given period of time.

Supplementing cash and obligation accounting with accrual could give executives a better grasp of agency financial life; it could facilitate oversight by the White House, Congress, and the General Accounting Office. Even if accrual accounting becomes more common, however, another barrier to financial insight persists—the diversity in accounting practices within and among federal agencies. Those who wish to obtain a clear overview of the expenditures made by agencies generally favor uniformity in financial terminology and the rules of the accounting game. Among other things, this uniformity heightens their ability to compare the costs of similar operations across government. As of the late 1980s, this uniformity remained far from realization in the federal government. Instead, federal executives in different agencies went their own ways to develop financial systems; this led to a situation GAO described as "fragmented."[90] The diverse accounting languages and procedures in federal agencies summoned up images of a financial Tower of Babel.

The Quest for a Common Language.   Top executives at GAO have emphasized the need to combat this diversity—to develop a common language of accounting and auditing. They have suggested that federal agencies imitate the private sector by preparing consolidated financial statements each year based on uniform accounting procedures. (Requirements that corporations prepare these statements followed the stock market crash in 1929, after which many observers complained about the unreliability and noncomparability of the books and financial statements of corporations.) For executives at GAO acquiring enough power to impose this and other manifestations of uniformity has been a strategic concern. Charles Bowsher, the Comptroller General, observed that "the Federal Manager's Financial Integrity Act of 1982 represents important progress."[91] This act requires each executive agency to report annually on its compliance with GAO's internal control standards.

In the wake of this legislation, the GAO issued a plethora of reports critical of agency practices. These reports chronicled considerable agency difficulty in meeting accounting standards. For instance, staff members in the Department of Education responsible for the Student Loan Insurance Fund reported certain cash receipts incorrectly. This produced errors in records concerning the loan principal and interest owed to the fund.[92] GAO also found that VA reports to the Treasury Department did not square with the figures in the agency's own annual report. The study concludes that the agency's "accounting system may not produce and report to Treasury reliable financial information on a consistent basis."[93]

GAO initiatives such as those under the Federal Manager's Financial Integrity Act may give some impetus to uniformity, but forces resisting such initiatives are potent. Resistance from line agencies springs from several sources. So long as executives can obtain accurate and pertinent cost information about their own programs, they have little incentive to bring their accounting practices into line with those of other agencies. In fact, furnishing information to GAO, the White House, and Congress in a format that permits different programs to be compared may threaten executives. The ambiguity of inconsistent accounting procedures may protect them from substantial criticism and from interagency comparisons. Most executives understand that accounting and auditing cannot be treated as purely technical matters; the information they produce has power implications and can alter resource allocation so as to hurt their programs. Aside from sensitivity to the power considerations of uniformity, executives often view modifications in their financial management systems as costly and inconvenient. Now that budget cuts have heightened the sense of scarcity in many agencies, many federal managers see accounting improvements as a luxury. The value of improved accounting must be compared not only with the costs of acquiring it but also with competing items on which an agency could spend limited funds.

The problems of federal accounting and auditing practices should not be construed to mean that executives cannot keep track of funds. By and large, federal expenditures are accounted for in an honest and coherent way. Cases of fraud, abuse, and ineptitude in financial management remain few and far between. GAO's initiatives to improve financial management reflect efforts to make a reasonably good system better.

Conclusion

The management of critical resources—authority, personnel, information, physical resources, money—presents senior executives with a complex challenge. One cannot neatly divide this challenge into compartments. The management of different resources overlaps. One resource cannot sensibly be discussed without considering the implications for the others. The complicated, interactive relationships among these management spheres introduce considerable uncertainty for executives. They must often contend with competing values such as the need to know versus respect for privacy. They cannot predict precisely the implications of management strategy X for phenomenon Y (say, the ramifications of certain equipment or internal office arrangements for the organizational involvement of employees). Their problem does not stem from failure to read the literature of administrative science and public administration, although this may contribute. Such literature provides general guidelines but does not treat specific situations; moreover, it has tended to neglect the behavioral implications of office and machine design. If managers are uncertain, however, this is not to suggest that they fall prey to analysis paralysis. Used to making decisions in the face of ambiguity, executives often reconcile conflicts between values and uncertainty about the best means to the end with great aplomb and acumen.

As in dealing with other factors of production, executives concerned with managing information, physical resources, and money face changing circumstances. To be sure, certain constants hold. One cannot escape the fact that the distribution of information affects the distribution of power and therefore that innovations in information technology are much more than purely technical matters. However, time-honored notions about the management of these resources are in flux. Developments in computer technology loom largest of all in this regard. Will increases in computer literacy modify executives' preference for talk and elevate their receptivity to formal reports? Will the spread of such literacy make secrecy more difficult, threatening the executive's ability to control the flow of information in sensitive areas? Will those who develop computers pay adequate attention to their implications for the organizational involvement, motivation, and performance of personnel? Will growing computer sophistication ultimately reduce payment errors and facilitate the efforts of those who wish to assure greater uniformity in the language and rules of accounting? Attempts to answer these and a host of related questions will make the subsequent study and practice of federal management important and intriguing.

The management of resources in the face of many factors that constrain discretion is only part of the challenge. The political culture necessitates that executives remain vigilant in their resistance to dependence, defensiveness, and defeatism (see Chapter 11). Besides, they need to grapple with the specific problems of the particular technologies they manage. These challenges, plus other factors assessed in the next chapter, have substantial bearing on the pursuit of excellence in public administration.

Notes

1. *Congressional Quarterly Weekly Report* 39 (26 December 1981): 2596.
2. U.S. General Accounting Office, *General Services Administration Needs to Improve Its Internal Controls to Prevent Duplicate Payments* (Washington: GAO/AFMD–85–70, 1985).
3. Harlan Cleveland, "The Twilight of Hierarchy: Speculations on the Global Information Society." *Public Administration Review* 45 (January-February 1985): 185, 194.
4. Barry Bozeman, *Public Management and Policy Analysis* (New York: St. Martin's Press, 1979), 241.
5. See Marianne LaFrance and Clara Mayo, *Moving Bodies: Nonverbal Communication in Social Relationships* (Monterey, CA: Brooks/Cole, 1978).
6. Cited in Arnold J. Meltsner and Christopher Bellavita, *The Policy Organization* (Beverly Hills, CA: Sage, 1983), 28.
7. Richard M. Merelman, *Making Something of Ourselves* (Berkeley: University of California Press, 1984), 60–2.
8. Henry Mintzberg, *The Nature of Managerial Work* (New York: McGraw Hill, 1973), 36, 39–41; see also Herbert Kaufman, *The Administrative Behavior of Federal Bureau Chiefs* (Washington, DC: The Brookings Institution, 1981).
9. *The Wall Street Journal,* 24 June 1980, 1.
10. Power exists when A causes B to do something B would not otherwise do in the manner intended by A. Knowledge may help A exert power over B but per se cannot guarantee it.
11. *The Atlanta Constitution,* 5 June 1986, 10A.
12. David O'Brien, "Freedom of Information, Privacy, and Information Control: A Contemporary Administrative Dilemma." *Public Administration Review* 39 (July-August 1979): 323–8.
13. Lottie E. Feinberg, "Managing the Freedom of Information Act and Federal Information Policy." *Public Administration Review* 46 (November-December 1986):615–21.
14. Samuel J. Archibald, "The Freedom of Information Act Revisited." *Public Administration Review* 39 (July-August 1979): 311–8.
15. U.S. General Accounting Office, *Freedom of Information: Cost of Collecting and Processing Fees* (Washington, DC: GAO/GGD–87–58FS, 1987).
16. U.S. General Accounting Office, *Computer Matching: Assessing Its Cost and Benefits* (Washington, DC: GAO/PEMD–87–2, 1986).
17. U.S. General Accounting Office, *GAO Observations on the Use of Tax Return Information for Verification in Entitlement Programs* (Washington, DC: GAO/HRD–84–72, 1984).
18. U.S. General Accounting Office, *Privacy Act: Federal Agencies' Implementation Can Be Improved* (Washington, DC: GAO/GGD–86–107, 1986).
19. James D. Carroll et al., "Supply-Side Management in the Reagan Administration." *Public Administration Review* 45 (November-December 1985): 810.
20. *Congressional Quarterly Weekly Report* 38 (29 November 1980): 3456.

21. Herbert A. Simon, *Administrative Behavior* (New York: Free Press, 1957), xxiv, xxv; see also Charles Lindblom, "The Science Of Muddling Through." *Public Administration Review* 19 (Spring 1959): 79–88.

22. Some suggest that officials tend to underestimate information costs. See Martha S. Feldman and James G. March, "Information in Organizations as Signal and Symbol." *Administrative Science Quarterly* 26 (June 1981): 171–86.

23. Ibid., 175; see also Henry Mintzberg, *Impediments to the Use of Management Information* (New York and Hamilton, Ontario, Canada: National Association of Accountants and the Society of Management Accountants of Canada, 1975), 13.

24. Mintzerg, *The Nature of Managerial Work,* 35.

25. Quotation is from Arnold J. Meltsner, *Policy Analysts in the Bureaucracy* (Berkeley: University of California Press, 1976), 270. See also Feldman and March, "Information in Organizations As Signal and Symbol."

26. Janice M. Beyer and Harrison M. Trice, "The Utilization Process: A Conceptual Framework and Synthesis of Empirical Findings." *Administrative Science Quarterly* 27 (December 1982): 591–622.

27. Ibid., 608.

28. This part of the discussion draws heavily from Charles E. Lindblom and David K. Cohen, *Usable Knowledge* (New Haven: Yale University Press, 1979), 41–53.

29. U.S. General Accounting Office, *EPA Could Benefit from Comprehensive Management Information on Superfund Enforcement Actions* (Washington, DC: GAO/RCED–85–3, 1984).

30. Hugh Heclo, *A Government of Strangers* (Washington, DC: The Brookings Institution, 1977), 207.

31. This discussion draws extensively from J. Serge Taylor, *Making Bureaucracies Think* (Stanford, CA: Stanford University Press, 1984).

32. Lindblom and Cohen, *Usable Knowledge,* 2.

33. Bozeman, *Public Management and Policy Analysis,* 256.

34. Feldman and March, "Information in Organizations As Signal And Symbol."

35. On religion, see Jeffrey Pfeffer, *Power in Organizations* (Marshfield, MA: Pitman, 1981), 194.

36. On ritual, see Lindblom and Cohen, *Usable Knowledge,* 84.

37. On magic, see Russell Stout, Jr., *Management Or Control?* (Bloomington: Indiana University Press, 1980), 75–6.

38. Edie N. Goldenberg, "The Three Faces of Evaluation." *Journal of Policy Analysis and Management* 2 (Summer 1983): 520–1.

39. Harvey Sapolsky, *The Polaris System Development* (Cambridge, MA: Harvard University Press, 1972), 246.

40. National Academy of Public Administration, *Revitalizing Federal Management: Managers and Their Overburdened Systems* (Washington, DC: 1983), 49–50.

41. *Federal Times* (24 March 1986): 11.

42. *Congressional Quarterly Weekly Report* 41 (7 May 1983): 895.

43. *Federal Times* (14 April 1986): 17.

44. Lynn M. Salerno, "What Happened to the Computer Revolution?" *Harvard Business Review* 63 (November-December 1985): 129–38.

45. Ibid., 136

46. *Federal Times* (12 August 1985): 5.

47. U.S. General Accounting Office, *Federal Aviation Administration's Host Computer: More Realistic Performance Tests Needed before Production Begins* (Washington, DC: GAO/IMTEC–85–10, 1985).

48. Richard Raysman and Peter Brown, "Don't Rush to Court When Your Computer Fails." *Harvard Business Review* 62 (January-February 1984): 119.
49. Warran F. McFarlan and James L. McKenney, "The Information Archipelago—Governing the New World." *Harvard Business Review* 61 (July-August 1983): 91–9.
50. National Academy of Public Administration, *Revitalizing Federal Management*.
51. See, for instance, Stout, *Management Or Control?* 87–8.
52. Kenneth L. Kraemer and James N. Danziger, "Computers and Control in the Work Environment." *Public Administration Review* 44 (January-February 1984): 32–42.
53. Martin D. J. Bass and Lynn M. Salerno, "Common Sense and Computer Security." *Harvard Business Review* 62 (March-April 1984): 112–21.
54. *Congressional Quarterly Weekly Report* 43 (2 November 1985): 2235.
55. *Federal Times* (4 November 1985): 18.
56. Martin Landau and Russell Stout, Jr., "To Manage Is Not to Control: Or the Folly of Type II Errors." *Public Administration Review* 39 (March-April 1979): 149.
57. Mintzberg, *The Nature of Managerial Work,* 191.
58. Mintzberg, *Impediments to the Use of Management Information,* 21; see also Russell Stout, *Management or Control?,* 121–4.
59. Mintzberg, *Impediments to the Use of Management Information,* 19–20.
60. See Sissela Bok, *Lying* (New York: Vintage, 1979), 14.
61. While land management ranks high in importance, this chapter discusses only buildings, which in one form or another most executives must consider.
62. U.S. House Committee on Appropriations, *Treasury, Postal Service, and General Government Appropriations for Fiscal Year 1986* (Washington, DC: Government Printing Office, 1985), 304.
63. *Federal Times* (10 March 1986): 3.
64. U.S. House Committee on Appropriations, *Treasury, Postal Service, and General Government Appropriations,* 281.
65. National Academy of Public Administration, *Revitalizing Federal Management,* 56.
66. *Federal Times* (3 February 1986): 5.
67. See Franklin D. Becker, *Workspace: Creating Environments in Organizations* (New York: Praeger, 1981).
68. Greg R. Oldham and Nancy L. Rotchford, "Relationships between Office Characteristics and Employee Reactions: A Study of the Physical Environment." *Administrative Science Quarterly* 28 (December 1983): 542–56.
69. *Federal Times* (15 July 1985): 7.
70. National Academy of Public Administration, *Revitalizing Federal Management,* 60.
71. *Federal Times* (15 July 1985): 7.
72. National Academy of Public Administration, *Revitalizing Federal Management,* 60.
73. Ibid., 61.
74. Charles Perrow, "The Organizational Context of Human Factors Engineering." *Administrative Science Quarterly* 28 (December 1983): 521–41.
75. Ibid., 523.
76. *Federal Times* (25 March 1985): 3.
77. *Federal Times* (14 April 1986): 1, 16; *Federal Times* (15 September 1986): 4.
78. *Federal Times* (25 March 1985): 4, 11.
79. Frank J. Thompson, *Health Policy And The Bureaucracy* (Cambridge, MA: MIT Press, 1981), 201.
80. Charles A. Bowsher, "Governmental Financial Management at the Crossroads: The Choice Is between Reactive and Proactive Financial Management." *Public Budgeting and Finance* 5 (Summer 1985): 15; see also Naomi Caiden, "The New Rules of

the Federal Budget." *Public Administration Review* 44 (March-April 1984): 109–18; "The Myth of the Annual Budget." *Public Administration Review* 42 (November-December 1982): 516–23.

81. National Academy of Public Administration, *Revitalizing Federal Management*, 23.
82. Bernard T. Pitsvada, "Flexibility in Federal Budget Execution." *Public Budgeting and Finance* 3 (Summer 1983): 83–101.
83. U.S. General Accounting Office, *Veterans Administration Financial Management Profile* (Washington, DC: GAO/AFMD–85–34, 1985), 46.
84. U.S. General Accounting Office, *Prompt Payment Act: Agencies Have Not Achieved Available Benefits* (Washington, DC: GAO/AFMD–86–69, 1986).
85. U.S. General Accounting Office, *General Services Administration Needs To Improve Its Internal Controls.*
86. U.S. General Accounting Office, *VA Needs Better Control over Its Payments to Private Health Care Providers* (Washington, DC: GAO/HRD–85–49, 1985).
87. U.S. General Accounting Office, *The Small Business Administration's Second-Year Implementation of the Federal Managers' Financial Integrity Act* (Washington, DC: GAO/RCED–86–24, 1985).
88. For a useful analysis of student loan programs, see Donald Kettl, *Government by Proxy: (Mis?)Managing Federal Programs* (Washington, DC: Congressional Quarterly, 1988).
89. See Bowsher, "Governmental Financial Management at the Crossroads"; U.S. General Accounting Office, *Managing the Cost of Government, Vol. II* (Washington, DC: GAO/AFMD–85–35–A, 1985), 27–9.
90. U.S. General Accounting Office, *Managing The Cost of Government, Vol. II.*
91. Charles A. Bowsher, "Sound Financial Management: A Federal Manager's Perspective." *Public Administration Review* 45 (January-February 1985): 183.
92. U.S. General Accounting Office, *Adverse Opinion on the Financial Statements of the Student Loan Insurance Fund for the Fiscal Year Ended September 30, 1980* (Washington, DC: GAO/AFMD–82–52, 1982).
93. U.S. General Accounting Office, *Veterans Administration Financial Management Profits* (Washington, DC: GAO/AFMD–85–34, 1985), 7.

Part Five

The Future

Public administration must confront its future—a future replete with challenges. A growing federal deficit, political gridlock over how to cope with it, the siren call of budget gimmickry, bureaucrat bashing, increased competition from abroad, and so on—all contribute to the conundrum. Little wonder that one observer has noted: "Bureaucracy used to be for the timid, now it is only for the brave . . . Public service is the highest service, because it is also the hardest service."[1]

The news is not all bad, however. Some people in and out of government are concerned about the erosion of the federal civil service. The wave of preference for the private sector appears to have given way to opportunities for more reasoned discussion of the proper role of government in society. Most hopeful of all is the fact that many people in government, especially in the career civil service, have come to regard problems as challenges to be overcome rather than as death sentences for their careers and values. They have responded by enhancing efforts to improve their own performance and the performance of their organizations. Just as the need to search for excellence in the private sector was a major theme in the 1980s, a similar search in the public sector may gain momentum in the 1990s.

Chapter 14 explores the challenges in the search for excellence in public administration. True to the conceptual framework of this book, the examination runs from the macro to micro level—from the broad problems of political culture and structure to the specific issues of encouraging certain attitudes, values, and behavior among public managers. The final chapter looks to the future of public administration by examining the potent legacy of the Reagan administration. Do the Reagan years presage a major transformation in the role people assign to government in society, the way government goes about its work, and the quality of the federal work force? In a nutshell, what will public administration be like in the year 2000?

Notes

1. Aaron Wildavsky, " 'Ubiquitous Anomie' or, Public Service in an Era of Ideological Dissensus" in *The Campus and the Public Service* (Washington, DC: National Academy of Public Administration, 1988), 10.

Chapter Fourteen

Enduring Problems in the Search for Excellence

―――――――
―――――――

In Search of Excellence catapulted into the limelight in 1982. It sold one million copies in ten months, making it one of the fastest-selling books of all time.[1] Subsequently released in paperback, it continued to enjoy brisk sales in 1984 and 1985. What attracted such a wide audience? Its authors, Thomas Peters and Robert Waterman, described management practices in what they judged to be the most successful private corporations and concluded that these companies had certain basic attributes. These included a bias toward action, a tendency to stay close to the customer, willingness to foster autonomy and entrepreneurship among employees, and the capacity to motivate personnel toward productivity. Successful businesses also had executives who kept in touch with the firm's essential business (hands-on, value driven) and who stuck to matters the firm knew best. Successful corporations featured lean staffing with few administrative layers; they also fostered simultaneous loose-tight properties by blending a culture of dedication to central company values with great tolerance for differences among employees who accepted these values.

Read as social science, *In Search of Excellence* suffered from many afflictions. The authors often praised practices in corporations that did not meet their criteria of excellence. They did not systematically compare management in successful and unsuccessful companies. These and other defects prompted one reviewer to dismiss the book as a "missed opportunity" that may have "needlessly delayed" movement toward excellence in management.[2] Although the book was flawed as social science, many of its propositions seemed plausible. Moreover, its sales figures attest that it captivated great segments of the public. Just when Americans were down in the mouth about the international competitiveness of American business, *In Search of Excellence* held out hope. It offered an alternative vision to defeatism and the decline of America as an economic power. The appeal also extended to many in the public administration community, often castigated for alleged inefficiency and ineffectiveness during the Carter and Reagan years.

Clearly, students and practitioners of public administration need to remain vigilant in the search for excellence. But what is excellence? In analyzing private firms, Peters and Waterman relied on six measures of financial performance to help them define the companies that had achieved excellence. These indicators included compound asset growth from 1961 through 1980, the average ratio of market to book value of stock, and the average return on capital from 1961 through 1980.[3] Developing credible numerical indicators of excellence in the public sector is much

402

more difficult. As has been evident in this volume, public administrators confront multiple criteria for judging the caliber of their agencies and often lack reliable performance measures.

If judging excellence in the public sector is complex, however, one need not be daunted by the task. In general, two principles inform most notions of excellence in public agencies. One is the traditional political value of accountability. Are civil servants law-abiding and answerable to elected officials and the courts? The other is economy, efficiency, and effectiveness. Do programs deliver goods or services at the lowest feasible financial cost? Do the outputs and outcomes of these programs succeed in ameliorating some problem? Given these two dominant principles, the search for excellence in the public sector primarily involves steps to increase the efficiency and effectiveness of government programs while remaining within bounds prescribed by law, court opinions, and the legitimate preferences of elected officials. This definition does not offer a precise numerical calibration of excellence but at least provides a conceptual underpinning.

Obviously, the quest for excellence cannot be isolated from context. This volume has wrestled with issues of public policy and administration from macro to micro levels. In this vein, it has probed broad questions related to the private and public shares of the economy, the political culture and institutions that set parameters for public administration, and the politics of policy processes and bureaucracy. It has assayed theories of how one can organize complex work in fruitful ways; it has examined some of the challenges that high-level career managers face as they confront specific aspects of their work. The point of this chapter is that all of these variables, from macro to micro, affect the quality of public administration in the United States. While the chapter can lay no claim to comprehensive coverage of all pertinent factors, it does highlight certain critical problems in the search for excellence. The problems spring from the political culture, governmental institutions that fragment power, the substantial reliance on administration by proxy, the bias toward rule-oriented control and streamlined hierarchy, and the complex qualities public executives need.

Culture and Excellence: Waste and Eating Cake

For all its virtues, the political culture of the United States poses an ongoing problem in the search for excellence in public administration. The antigovernment, antibureaucracy ethos heightens risks of dependence, defensiveness, and defeatism in the administration of public programs. Most executives occupy a relatively weak position vis-à-vis interest groups, which often spurs responsiveness to these groups at the expense of efficient, effective, and accountable implementation. The negative culture also drives executives toward (although does not automatically trigger) a self-protective syndrome leading to nonexperimental, unimaginative management. Finally, a negative culture can create defeatism—a conviction among public executives that they have no real chance of success and are inferior to their private-sector counterparts. This last element of political culture gives public managers an excuse to *avoid* the search for excellence. One may imagine a culture that posed the opposite problems—a culture that cast civil servants in such favorable light that it led them to hubris, unaccountable behavior, and insensitivity to personal liberties. But, in this society the antipathy toward government bureaucracy is a critical inhibitor of excellence.

While popular culture has long held public bureaucracies to be perpetrators of many unfortunate things, the view that government programs are wasteful became particularly pervasive in the 1980s. The veneration of private enterprise—a disposition encouraged by many economists in the absence of much hard evidence—has fueled the assumption that governmental administration lacks the efficiency found in business.[4] President Reagan's Private Sector Survey on Cost Control (otherwise known as the Grace Commission) reinforced this view. In the mid-1980s, the Grace Commission issued forty-eight reports containing close to twenty-five hundred recommendations. The commission concluded that eradication of waste could save the federal government a staggering $424 billion over three years. Moreover, the citizenry could have its cake and eat it too; according to Grace, these savings could be realized without weakening defense or harming necessary social welfare programs.[5] Read superficially, the report reinforced the idea that gains in efficiency could yield a relatively painless solution for the massive federal deficit.

Beliefs about so-called government waste become a handy way for citizens to reconcile two conflicting impulses. Opinion polls persistently show strong public support for many expensive government programs. For instance, surveys indicate that more than half of the public believes government spends too little on the environment, the educational system, and health. Fewer than 10 percent believe that government spends too much in each of these policy spheres. These same surveys show that citizens do not want their taxes to increase and believe that the federal budget should be cut. In one survey conducted in 1985, more than 80 percent of respondents were strongly in favor of cuts in government spending in order to help the economy. Survey trends from 1961 to 1982 suggest that the percent who believe taxes are too high increased from 46 percent to 69 percent.[6]

To some degree, these findings reinforce the view that the public can hold highly inconsistent attitudes, but beliefs about "waste" provide a more orderly way to reduce dissonance. One can have both lower taxes and vast public programs if getting rid of waste can abolish the trade-offs. The data clearly indicate a growing conviction that the government wastes a lot of money (see Table 14.1). In the late 1950s and early 1960s, less than half the populace adhered to this view. By the late 1970s and early 1980s, roughly three-quarters of the population nurtured this sentiment.

Perceptions of great waste need not automatically cause citizens to blame public administrators. One should distinguish between waste as bureaucratic inefficiency and waste as inappropriate goals. The former occurs when administrators do not maximize desirable outputs per unit of cost. The latter develops when lawmakers pursue a program that observers oppose. Some liberals, for instance, see the Defense Department budget as too large regardless of whether civil servants implement its programs efficiently. Presumably, elected officials are a more natural target of blame for waste stemming from inappropriate goals and administrators for that rising from bureaucratic inefficiency. Unfortunately, those most eager to cry "waste" seldom distinguish between these two forms. Many of the recommendations of the Grace Commission required Congress to change laws. When Peter Grace publicized the results of his commission's findings, however, the accompanying press packet

TABLE 14.1   Beliefs about Waste in Government, 1958–1985

"Do you think that people in government waste a lot of money we pay in taxes, waste some of it, or don't waste very much of it?"

Year	A lot	Some	Not Very Much
1958	45%	44%	10%
1964	48	45	7
1968	61	35	4
1972	67	31	2
1976	76	21	3
1980	80	18	2
1984	69	28	3
1985 (Dec.)	76	21	3

Source: Surveys from the Center for Political Studies, University of Michigan; CBS/*New York Times* Poll; *New York Times* poll as reported in "The Role of Government an Issue For 1988?" *Public Opinion* 9 (March–April 1987): 27.

included a chart entitled "Ten Random Examples of Bureaucratic Absurdity."[7] Administrators frequently provide a more vulnerable and convenient target than the elected officials who make the policies.

In sum, perceptions of waste contribute to the negative culture, which can breed administrative defeatism, dependence, and defensiveness. This is not to suggest that public administrators never waste money, but the amount arising from bureaucratic inefficiency is not "a lot," or forty-eight cents of every federal dollar spent. (These amounts are mentioned in public opinion surveys.) In order to save that much money, the government will have to pursue fundamental changes in policy rather than administrative reform.[8]

Can the public develop more sensitive understanding of "waste" and less stereotypically negative attitudes toward public administration? Change will not come easily. Antibureaucratic strains have very deep roots in the country's culture. The tendency of the mass media to sieze upon bureaucratic foibles perpetuates the problem. Running against the bureaucracy remains an attractive option for those seeking election to public office.

Public understanding and opinion need not be viewed as immutable. For one thing, some elected officials have increasingly come to realize that attacks on the bureaucracy can be counterproductive. Few, except for the most extreme radicals on the right and left, would see enormous diminution of bureaucratic capacity as a blessing. Elected officials may also choose to help by debunking the mythology of waste—that the country can attack the deficit painlessly. More serious measures to deal with the deficit (eliminating programs or raising taxes to fund them or both) would counter some of the mythology that public administrators, if they were good enough, could come up with the savings to allow the public to have many expensive programs and low taxes.

Other initiatives can help, at least on the margins.[9] Groups such as the American Society for Public Administration can go to greater lengths to inform the public and counter unfair media coverage. Academics also have a role to play. While their influence is indirect, their research and writings filter into the classroom and to the nation's leaders of opinion. Over the past twenty years, academic views of public administration rooted in intellectually impressive economic theories (public choice models) have gained stature. Much work, such as that by Nobel Prize winner James Buchanan, has been unrelenting in its assumption that waste and inefficiency permeate public enterprise.[10]

While most of this literature is long on theory and short on data, students of public administration cannot afford to ignore it. Where they find models based in economics deficient, they must propound competing theories of comparable or superior potency.

Excellence and the Fragmentation of Power

In forging a government based on the separation of powers, the Constitution laid the foundation for a political system that fragmented power. With the proliferation of interest groups, the rise of large, interconnected administrative agencies, the move toward subcommittee government in Congress, the growing assertiveness of the judiciary, and so on, fragmentation has become more pronounced. Some analysts contend that the substantial dispersal of power within the federal government produces incoherent policy and ineffective administration.

Consider the views of the Committee on the Constitutional System, a group that surfaced in the mid-1980s with support from such private foundations as Ford, Rockefeller, and Hewlett. The board of directors of this committee consisted of nearly fifty prominent Americans, including C. Douglas Dillon, former secretary of the Treasury; Lloyd Cutler, former counsel to President Carter; Senator Daniel Moynihan of New York; and Senator Nancy Kassebaum of Kansas. In a 1987 report the committee noted that the separation of powers had served well in preventing tyranny and the abuse of the high office but had the negative side effects of "encouraging confrontation, indecision and deadlock" along with the diffusion of accountability. "Because the separation of powers encourages conflict between the branches and because the (political) parties are weak, the capacity of the federal government to fashion, enact and administer coherent public policy has diminished and the ability of elected officials to avoid accountability for governmental failures has grown."[11]

One can argue that the pursuit of excellence in public administration will stall unless fundamental reform occurs—reform aimed at reducing the vast dispersal of power in the American political system. In essence, improvement of public administration becomes a matter of broader, often constitutional, change in political institutions. The prospect of such change may strike some as too remote to demand serious consideration. By the same token, however, a balanced perspective on the quest for excellence in a volume that stresses relationships between macro and micro issues demands that such reform be considered. Moreover, some alterations in political institutions may prove feasible.

Reforms designed to counteract the dispersal of power and improve administration come in many forms. Given its recency and the prestigious set of policymakers associated with the Committee on the Constitutional System, the modifications this

EXHIBIT 14.1   Selected Reforms to Cope with Political Fragmentation

Reform	Alleged Power Implication	Constitutional Amendment Required?
1. Require political parties to entitle all winners of party nominations for the House and Senate plus holdover senators to sit as uncommitted delegates at presidential nominating conventions.	Improve cooperation between the president and members of Congress.	No
2. Require all states to include a line or lever on federal election ballots enabling voters to cast a straight-line party ballot.	Reduce ticket splitting; lessen the likelihood of divided government.	No
3. Create a Congressional broadcast fund available to each party on the condition that the party expend no other funds on campaign broadcasts. Half of each party's share would go to the nominees themselves.	Create party loyalty and cohesion by requiring candidates to depend on party leaders for needed funds.	No
4. Require that the president and members of the House of Representatives serve four-year terms and that one senator from each state be elected for an eight-year term at each presidential election.	Due to coattail effects in elections, improve incentive of members of Congress to cooperate with the president and be less dependent on interest groups for campaign support.	Yes
5. Permit members of Congress to serve as heads of administrative departments or agencies.	Closer collaboration between Congress and the president.	Yes
6. Make the approval of foreign treaties possible by majority vote of both Houses of Congress.	Strengthen the president in international relations.	Yes
7. Have Congress set reasonable limits on campaign expenditures in a legislative race.	Remove some influence of wealthy interest groups.	Yes
8. In Congress, vest in the speaker of the House or the majority leader the authority to select and remove committee chairs; to choose which committees have jurisdiction over bills and which bills will come to the floor for a vote. Allow House and Senate campaign committees to raise and spend large sums for individual candidates and place control of these committees in the hands of the speaker or majority leader. Reduce the ability of members of Congress to create political action committees (PACs) and receive funds from them.	Centralize power within Congress; reduce the number of legislators with whom the president must negotiate over legislation.	No

Sources: The first seven recommendations come from the Committee on the Constitutional System, *A Bicentennial Analysis of the American Political Structure* (Washington, DC: 1987). The final recommendation derives from James Q. Wilson, "Does the Separation of Powers Work?" *Public Interest* 86 (Winter 1987): 51–2. Reprinted with permission.

group proposed are pertinent. A majority of the committee's governing board endorsed the first seven reforms presented in Exhibit 14.1, which also shows how (hypothetically) the reform would counteract political fragmentation and whether a change would require a constitutional amendment. As is evident, the Committee on the Constitutional System sought to strengthen political parties as agents of cohesion, to improve collaboration between the executive and legislative branches, and to reduce "the divisive influence of interest group contributions."[12] Aside from the seven reforms backed by the Committee on the Constitutional System, Exhibit 14.1

contains an eighth aimed at counteracting the vast dispersal of power within Congress.

Whether these reforms would attain the hypothesized effects remains open to question. Unanticipated outcomes remain the rule rather than the exception when political reform occurs. Moreover, those who stress the problems associated with fragmented power do not lack for critics.[13] For present purposes, however, it is useful to assume that the reforms specified in the chart would have the projected results and to explore whether they would ease the pursuit of excellence in public administration. *Other things being equal, the proposed reforms would probably assist the quest for excellence, but they also carry risks.*

The reforms could produce more coherent and sensible policy. Concentration of power could help lawmaking processes surmount "free-for-all pluralism and something-for-everyone politics."[14] This would be a major contribution. When programs fail because Congress passes inconsistent, unworkable, theoretically flawed laws, civil servants take much of the blame for subsequent program failures. More sensible policies enhance possibilities that public managers will look like winners.

The reforms might also increase responsiveness to law and enhance efficiency during implementation. Making members of Congress financially less dependent on interest groups and more on political parties may well diminish congressional responsiveness to narrow group pressures. Elected officials would see less need to obtain special consideration for these groups in the administrative process. Furthermore, the reduced power of subcommittees would curtail the number of access points for these groups. These circumstances could translate into more support for administrators when they implement measures that are opposed by some group (e.g., imposing cost cutting measures on hospitals or physicians under Medicare or penalizing employers guilty of occupational safety and health violations). The ability of interest groups to undermine the efficiency and effectiveness of policies during implementation would diminish.

While possibly beneficial, the reforms entail risks. Consider their propensity to enhance presidential power. Presidents have become increasingly aware of the possibilities of an administrative presidency; they understand that through implementation they can obtain fundamental changes in programs without persuading Congress to alter the law (see Chapter 5). To be sure, a president could use the enhanced powers from reform to bargain more effectively with top leaders in Congress and so might feel less compelled to rely on administrative means to modify programs. The greater concentration of power in Congress could make it easier to change laws. However, if the president did use administrative processes to modify policy, administrators would have fewer levers to pull in an effort to resist. They could not so readily turn to interest groups or committee chairs to protect themselves and their programs. Sometimes the weaker position of administrators would serve excellence in public administration, but it would also make presidential abuse of authority more difficult (although certainly not impossible) to resist.

The reforms sketched in Exhibit 14.1 would probably be even tougher to achieve than those aimed at modifying the political culture. Constitutional change does not come easily. Other forms of institutional change can also meet strong opposition. For instance, individual members of Congress hardly have an incentive to shift significant power to the speaker of the House and the majority leader. Instead they prefer to carve out small spheres of influence for themselves, contributing to fragmentation and incoherent policy as well as the oversight paradox. Moreover, some reforms may fail to generate the expected power shift or do little to advance the quest for excellence in public administration. The implications of allowing members of Congress to serve as heads of administrative agencies remain very cloudy. The questionable theoretical underpinnings of some of the reforms further damage their prospects.

Students of public administration must remain alert to the potential benefits of reforming political institutions, but they must also recognize that the quest for excellence in public administration will in all probability proceed in a policy context of potent centrifugal forces.

Excellence and Administration by Proxy

Whether administration by proxy is a boon or barrier to the pursuit of excellence in government is still a matter of debate. One analyst views the proxy as the best hope for restoring the "social contract" between government and its citizens—for helping to overcome the lost confidence in government by improving the delivery of services.[15] Another claims that government bureaucracies are "set up for 'failure' . . . by heavy reliance on indirect means of administration through grants, loans, and contracts."[16]

Who is right? Since social scientists have produced few systematic studies comparing the efficiency and accountability of direct and indirect administration, choosing the winning argument amounts to educated guesswork. Ultimately researchers need to specify the conditions under which various forms of administration by proxy foster excellence. In pursuing such inquiry, it is pertinent to distinguish between reliance on other governmental units to deliver federal programs and reliance on private firms and individuals. To be sure, commonalities exist between these two types of administration by proxy (see the discussion of induced technologies in Chapter 11). As will become evident, however, the two types pose distinct issues in the search for excellence.

Private Contracting and Excellence

While evident in myriad forms for many years, the concept of privatization became a dominant intellectual focus of public administration during the 1980s. Definitions of the concept vary greatly. For instance, a task force of the Grace Commission broadly defined privatization as the turning over of an activity or part of an activity currently performed by the federal government to a nonfederal entity.[17] This includes load shedding, wherein government withdraws completely from a program; grants to local governments to deliver a service; seeking volunteers to provide the program. While this broad definition may be useful for certain purposes, this section focuses on arrangements in which government pays a private party to provide goods or services. In this regard, three types of contractual relationships deserve note: direct, consumer-driven, and franchise.

Direct arrangements more explicitly and exclusively involve government officials in the role of provider. In the purest case of this type, the government contracts with a provider to deliver a certain service or product (for instance, with corporation X, to deliver components of a weapons system under particular terms and conditions of payment).

Consumer-driven models rely on the beneficiaries of government programs to pick the provider. For instance, clients of Medicare have substantial latitude to choose their physicians and hospitals. The federal government pays the provider or reimburses the client for the service. To be sure, the federal government may attempt to exert quality and cost control by certifying only some providers for reimbursement (e.g., hospitals X and Y but not Z for Medicare beneficiaries). But program beneficiaries must have some choice of providers for the model to apply.

While this section will not deal with the franchise model in detail, its broad characteristics deserve note. This model of government assures citizens access to a service or product but does not pay the provider for them. Typically the government designates some firm as the supplier, usually with some price regulation. Consumers purchase the item with their own funds from the franchised dealer. For instance, some state governments franchise certain firms to provide automobile service and restaurants on toll roads.

Advocates of direct and consumer-driven contracting point out several virtues of these modes of administration by proxy. Some perceived benefits are explicitly political. One analyst suggests that such arrangements serve as a check against "big government." He argues (without presenting hard evidence) that public employees have a higher voter turnout and will naturally tend to vote for more government programs. He even goes so far as to imply that election endorsements and campaign contributions by public-sector unions (generally a legal activity) are similar to bribes by officials from firms seeking to obtain a government contract (an illegal activity).[18] Whatever the intellectual gymnastics required to accept this analogy, note the central thesis: that keeping down the number of federal employees via contracting and other means will depress the expansion of the public sector.

The more important case for direct and consumer-driven contracting rests on their efficiency and effectiveness. A market model lies at the heart of this justification. The scenario runs as follows. Private agents compete vigorously with one another to become the supplier of some governmental good or service. This competition stimulates a drive for efficiency. Providers seek to impress purchasers with the amount and quality of the output they deliver relative to its cost. Government officials or clients (in the consumer-driven model) have access to this information and readily understand it. They choose the most efficient alternative (not necessarily the lowest bid). If providers fail to deliver the promised service or product at the agreed cost, purchasers move on to another provider. Government programs presumably come to enjoy the efficiency and effectiveness that competition can produce.

The case for private contracting based on economic theory deserves to be taken seriously. However, the quest for excellence will be better served if advocates of such contracting do not enjoy the benefit of the doubt in government decision processes. Instead, they should have to demonstrate the benefits of private contracting in particular circumstances. The rationale for this prescription becomes evident if one considers the problems that can arise in attempting to reap the efficiency gains of administration by private proxy.

Limits to the Economic Rationale.   Several factors can undermine the capacity of contracting to foster excellence in public administration (see Chapter 11). The limits of competition are a major one.[19] In many policy spheres, relatively few firms have the capacity to deliver the product or service. There are only a handful of firms that can provide major weapons systems. In fact, the federal government frequently enters into contracting on a sole-source basis. Public officials justify a continuing relationship with a supplier on grounds that the firm is uniquely qualified to deliver.

Follow-on contracting also occurs frequently. Under this practice firm A, which has a sole-source or competitive government contract, gets a new contract or very substantial modification in its current one without having to compete with other firms. One analysis found that in fiscal 1985, bidding competition preceded only 44 percent of all federal contracting.[20] Another disclosed that in fiscal 1984, more than $42 billion in Defense Department contracts (32 percent of the department's prime contract awards over $25,000) were for follow-on contracts.[21] Furthermore, firms may tacitly or even explicitly collude to avoid vigorous competition. Each may be content to have a share of government's business at a relatively generous price.

Some firms compete on grounds having little to do with the cost and quality of their outputs. They may offer bribes or other blandishments to government officials in order to influence the contracting decision. Moe aptly observes, "A high percentage of instances of corruption that have occurred over the two centuries of American administrative history has involved contracts with private providers to perform a public service. . . The stakes for private parties are often high"; they not infrequently prove "willing to go to the edge of the law."[22]

Alternatively, competition may center on which contractor is most adroit at lobbying Congress. Just as elected officials view the placement and preservation of post offices and Veterans Administration hospitals as political plums, they may steer major federal contracts to firms that play a key role in the economy at home.

One analysis notes that over the past twenty years Congress has played a larger role in managing weapons procurement. Individual legislators often elevate the interests of their district or state over broader concerns with military effectiveness and efficiency. "Because weapons are expensive and their industries employ large numbers, receiving and then sustaining a steady stream of contracts is very important to legislators and their constituency."[23]

Competition on grounds other than efficiency may also mark consumer-driven models. In the early 1970s health maintenance organizations (HMOs) in California vigorously competed to enroll beneficiaries of Medicaid, a federal and state health program for poor people. To persuade beneficiaries to sign with his HMO, one salesman promised them access to narcotics.[24]

Effective contracting also depends on the ability of the purchaser to acquire and assess valid and reliable information concerning the cost and quality of a product or service. Sometimes the producer has genuine problems in furnishing these estimates. Contracts that extend well into the future are especially hard to predict. Major weapons systems frequently require ten to fifteen years to plan, design, produce, and deploy. It stands to reason that estimating the cost of a ten-year project will be more difficult than for a one-year enterprise. Inflation and changes in market conditions can make once-reasonable cost estimates completely inaccurate. New and uncertain technology also increases the burdens of calculation. Research and development firms building new weapons systems frequently face this problem.

Besides, producers often have an interest in distorting information. Some firms offer loss leaders to get a contract. They deliberately underrepresent their costs to win the contract in the hope that the purchaser will subsequently permit payment increases rather than endure the cost and inconvenience of seeking a new provider. In the case of weapons procurement, bidders who make unrealistically low cost proposals often win major contracts. In essence, these firms buy into a defense contract and then try to "get well" financially via contract changes or follow-on contracts. Often they succeed.[25] In consumer-driven contracting, producers may do little to help consumers rationalize choices. Physicians and hospitals, for example, are notoriously reluctant to publicize the costs and quality of their service.

The ability of the purchaser to process pertinent information in the most rational way also varies greatly. Government officials frequently have the expertise and experience to make realistic estimates of costs and benefits, but many consumers do not. Much research suggests that consumers have trouble processing and understanding information about the products they buy, even in relatively simple comparisons of quality and prices in grocery stores. Moreover, the less educated and poor tend to have particular problems acting as the rational purchasers of classical economic theory. Because many citizens are illiterate or semiliterate, there are perils in assuming that a consumer choice model will lead to the selection of more efficient providers.[26]

Payment practices also undercut the ability of private contracting to induce efficiency. Ideally, the provider promises the purchaser a fixed price for the service or product to be delivered prior to the commencement of work. If the provider fails to estimate the cost accurately, it absorbs the loss. This practice protects the purchaser from surprises. It also creates incentives for the provider to estimate costs accurately. However, providers frequently enjoy a cost-plus arrangement, wherein the government agrees to pay a firm its cost for producing some good or service plus some predetermined profit. These contracts provide little incentive for efficiency; subject to restrictions concerning what constitutes "reasonable" cost, government agrees to pay whatever bill the provider presents.

The frequent use of cost-plus payment in part reflects the political potency of providers in persuading policymakers to offer them generous terms. It also springs from other sources. Uncertainty about the time, steps, and expenditures needed to produce some service or product increases the allure of cost-base contracting. Firms may be unwilling to take the risks involved in attempting to perform uncertain tasks for a fixed price.

Concerns for quality may also heighten the appeal of cost-based contracting. In the early 1980s Medicare converted to a system based on a relatively fixed payment to hospitals per admission of an elderly person. Before then the program paid hospitals on the basis of their "reasonable" costs for providing service. This gave hospitals considerable incentive to provide very intensive and expensive care to older people. Under the new system hospitals got paid a fixed amount depending on the diagnosis of the patient. This created an incentive for hospitals to hold down the costs of treatment and to discharge elderly patients "quicker and sicker." Some observers believe that movement from a cost-based to a fixed-price system has eroded the quality of care.

Limited numbers of capable providers may promote cost-based contracting. In the case of defense policy, for instance, only a handful of firms can provide certain weapons. Given their importance to national security, many policymakers and administrators believe that they cannot allow these firms go out of business. In such circumstances fixed-price contracting loses its bite. Managers of these firms expect rescue if they fail to estimate costs accurately.[27]

The respective problems of fixed-price and cost-based contracts have unleashed the quest for a hybrid. One version, occasionally used in the Defense Department, is the fixed-price incentive contract. For this type of contract the government and the firm negotiate a *target cost,* the sum they believe it will cost to complete the contract. They also set a *target profit,* the payment the contractor receives if the actual costs of the contract exactly match the target cost. The *sharing ratio* apportions cost overruns or (less likely) underruns between the government and contractor. For instance, a fifty-fifty sharing ratio would evenly split between government and contractor the responsibility for any cost overruns. In contrast, under a strict fixed-price arrangement, the contractor would assume responsibility for all costs of overruns (at least in theory). Finally, most fixed-price incentive contracts feature a *ceiling price,* the maximum amount that the government will pay for the contract.[28] Proponents of fixed-price incentive contracts hope that they will foster a greater commitment to efficiency without imposing unrealistic requirements on contractors to estimate the exact cost of long-term projects featuring technological uncertainty.

Aside from the problems of limited competition, information deficits, and cost-based pricing, government contracting only in part aims at efficiency and effectiveness. The federal government attempts to accomplish many goals through contracting requirements. For instance, the Small Business Administration provides noncompetitive government contracts to socially and economically disadvantaged businesses under Section 8(a) of the Small Business Act. The law assumes that these firms will ultimately develop and graduate from this status to compete for contracts in the open market. The program benefits many firms operated by minorities. However, studies have found that it often results in high contract prices and necessitates greater administrative efforts by government to secure delivery.[29] The number of contracts let under special provisions is substantial. In 1987 officials at the Health Care Financing Administration announced their commitment to award 25 percent of their contracts to small businesses each year.[30] Fears that special contracting requirements undercut efficiency have prompted a call by the National Academy of Public Administration and others to reconsider the advisability of using contracting for so many social purposes.[31]

Contracting, Accountability and the Cultural Problem.   Aside from efficiency and effectiveness, private contracting affects another dimension of excellence—accountability to law and elected officials (see Chapter 8). Contracting can exacerbate problems of accountability. When chains of contractors and subcontractors are involved in delivering a government program, public executives often, though not inevitably, find it more difficult to exert control than if they could turn to civil servants in their own bureaucracies for implementation. Moreover, extensive reliance on contracting probably makes government incoherent to average citizens; it makes it all the more difficult to be an informed citizen.

The potential for contracting to make government more complicated for citizens gives rise to a serious question. Does contracting feed the strain in the nation's political culture that holds federal government in low repute and creates barriers to excellence? Whether complexity per se contributes to the problem must await research. Clearly, however, the occasional horror stories in the press about contracting spawn doubt that the practice bolsters government credibility.

Stories abound of government paying ludicrous prices for spare parts—$110 for a four-cent diode and $9,609 for a 12-cent Allen wrench. Faced with news stories like these, what citizen would doubt that huge waste and inefficiency characterize government contracting?

In fact, these stories often present a misleading picture. Distorted impressions often spring from per-unit allocations of overhead. When government buys a product, it pays not only for the direct costs of the materials and technology needed to produce it but also for a portion of the company's overhead expenses. Thus, a $10 million contract to produce a weapon may include an additional 20 percent for overhead. When the Department of Defense orders spare parts, it has often allowed overhead to be charged on an item rather than a value basis. Imagine that the Pentagon orders a thousand parts, some of which cost thirty thousand dollars and some, five cents. A value-based accounting system allocates the overhead charge on this shipment according to the price of the part. Parts that cost a lot carry large overhead sums; small parts carry small sums. Item-based accounting simplifies by allocating the same amount of overhead to each part in the shipment regardless of its value. The thirty-thousand-dollar part carries the same overhead charge, say of $100, as the part that costs five cents. Whatever the technical virtues of this approach, it reinforces negative views about the inefficiency of government administration.[32]

This is not to exonerate Defense Department contractors from all charges of waste. However, media coverage of contracting relationships poses many of the same difficulties as that of programs the government itself administers. Disappointment probably awaits those who view contracting as a vehicle for countering negative stereotypes about public program administration.

Private Provision in Perspective.   The use of private companies or individuals to implement the programs of the federal government can foster excellence in public administration, but it is no panacea. Many factors can prevent the gains in efficiency and effectiveness envisioned by its advocates. Policymakers are well advised to have some public bureaucracies directly implement programs. Given this circumstance, excellence seems most likely to advance if officials approach private providers with four caveats in mind:

1. The virtues of private contracting are not so overwhelming that the burden of proof should automatically be on the shoulders of those who wish to have public agencies deliver a service or good. Politicians constantly struggle over the rules relating to the contracting out of government functions. Circular

A–76 (see Chapter 12) prescribes that those seeking to contract out services now provided by government must justify the move. During the Reagan years, proponents of privatization strove to weaken A–76. The Grace Commission recommended that many activities be exempted from cost comparisons so that contracting would not have to be justified on this basis. In 1987 the staff of the Office of Management and Budget prepared revisions to A–76 which would expedite achievement of this objective. Moreover, two lawmakers, Senator Gordon Humphrey (Republican of New Hampshire) and Representative David Dreier (Republican of California), introduced legislation to give A–76 the force of law and delete the requirement that public-private comparisons add 10 percent to the cost of private firms. (The 10 percent is to pay for transferring the program to the private sector.) Given the problems of contracting and the massive degree to which the federal government already relies on private parties to deliver goods and services, stacking the rules of the administrative game to favor more contracting is a dubious initiative.

2. Better targeting of policy areas where reliance on private firms seems more likely to yield efficiency and effectiveness would enhance prospects for excellence. Other things being equal, private contracting makes sense when government does not have the necessary experience, equipment, or expertise to provide the service, and the private sector does. It makes sense when there is bona fide competition over quality and cost among private providers, and government administrators can choose from among them on that basis. This requires that purchasers have valid and comprehensible information about the performance and cost of products. Contracting also becomes more attractive when government can reasonably expect to reward or punish a firm for its performance.

3. The conditions facilitating the efficient and effective use of private contracting seldom exist naturally; government must work to create them. For instance, Congress approved the Competition in Contracting Act of 1984 in an effort to stimulate market forces likely to benefit government procurement. For its part, the Grace Commission recommended that the Defense Department consult with industry to give contractors a better understanding of projects. The commission hoped that this would lead to better estimates of cost in bids and therefore more rational selection of contractors. The commission also recommended that the Defense Department encourage dual sourcing, or preserving at least two firms capable of supplying desired equipment.[33] In essence, the successful exploitation of competitive forces in private contracting often depends on appropriate law and administrative rules as well as their implementation by talented contract officers. These officers must be skilled negotiators and managers. If private contracting is to provide efficiency and effectiveness, policymakers and administrators must continually upgrade and sustain the skills of contract personnel.

4. Policymakers should be open to the advantages of allowing public agencies to compete with private firms. A leading student of privatization argues that one of the best defenses against uncompetitive practices in the private sector is to

have "part of the work done by a government agency and part by contractors. . . The performance of the public agency serves as a yardstick to measure the performance of the private agency, and vice versa."[34] If the private contractors show signs of sluggish performance, the proportion of the work done by public agencies can increase; the same threat hangs over the head of government agencies. This recommendation stands in considerable tension with the privatization-must-be-better mentality of the Grace Commission. Indeed, in many spheres it could prompt policymakers to beef up the federal government's share of the direct delivery of service or goods. For instance, the federal government might decide to operate some of its own nursing homes for Medicare beneficiaries in the hope that this would put pressure on private providers to pursue more efficient and effective practices.

Federalism and Excellence

Administration by proxy also takes the form of reliance on state and local governments to implement some of Washington's programs. This form of indirect implementation poses somewhat different issues than private contracting. Much of the case for private contracting rests on market models which extoll the virtues of competition as the midwife of efficiency. Competition and efficiency are much less significant in justifying the use of other levels of government. State and local governments frequently monopolize implementation rights in their respective jurisdictions. If the federal agency wants a program in a given territory, it often must rely on the government of that jurisdiction. The case for employing other levels of government as implementing agents often rests on political ideas about the appropriate division of labor among Washington, the states, and localities—on the desire to limit the centralization of power within the public sector. Debate focuses more on the meaning of the Constitution and responsiveness than on efficiency.

The formal theory of accountability is more complex in federalism than in private contracting. When government issues a contract to a private firm, the master-servant relationship is normatively lucid: the firm works for the federal government. While government officials often have a hard time controlling private firms and holding them accountable, few dispute their right to exert such control. In contrast, theoretical doctrines pertaining to the administrative relationships among the federal government, states, and localities are much less crisp. Usually Washington must approach state and local governments under the banner of partnership rather than hierarchy. Recalcitrance by state and local officials seldom evokes rhetoric that these officials ought to be fired or even penalized and disciplined. Often their resistance proceeds under the banner of responsiveness to the citizenry of their jurisdictions and calls into question federal policy or the bureaucracy's interpretation of it. Federal administrators frequently feel compelled to retreat and negotiate.

Whether intergovernmental administration facilitates or impedes the quest for excellence in public administration depends largely on the capacity and commitment of state and local governments. Capacity here refers to agencies' resources (such as skilled personnel and adequate information systems) to implement policy effectively, efficiently, and lawfully. Commitment connotes the degree to which state and local governments exert themselves to carry out the letter and spirit of federal policy.

Advances and Variations in Capacity.   In the past skepticism has dominated assessments of state and local capacity. Their legislatures lacked professional staffs; their top elected executives, especially governors, had minimal formal authority over departments; low pay and patronage characterized personnel administration; election processes in many parts of the country inhibited minority voting. These and other deficiencies prompted many to view state and local governments as inferior to the federal government. Where these conditions persist, intergovernmental administration vitiates the search for excellence in public administration.

There is good reason to believe that state and local governments have bolstered their capacity. A 406-page report of the U.S. Advisory Commission on Intergovernmental Relations points to a "profound restructuring of the state governmental landscape" in the 1960s and the 1970s. The report finds state governments to be "more representative, more responsive, more activist, and more professional in their operations than they ever have been."[35] While the available evidence does not permit definitive conclusions, state and local governments have in all probability enlarged their administrative capacity. The professionalism of state administrators has increased. Procurement practices have improved, and the merit system covers greater numbers of personnel. Federal civil servants have sensed improvements in capacity. A survey of federal grant administrators conducted in 1964 and again in 1975 found a great decline in the percentage citing personnel deficiencies in state and local governments. In 1964, 79 percent of these federal grant administrators believed that salaries were too low in state and local bureaucracies; 69 percent perceived that these levels of government had inadequate training programs. By 1975 the percentages of federal grant administrators feeling this way had dropped to 25 percent and 16 percent respectively.[36]

The federal government has contributed to capacity at the state and local levels. The 1939 Amendments to the Social Security Act required state governments to place most employees who implemented the act under merit systems. While the federal government has probably influenced personnel practices the most, it has affected other areas as well. Budget circular A–102 prescribes procurement practices for state and local governments receiving federal assistance. The regulations imposed on state and local implementing agents as a condition of receiving federal aid do not invariably enhance their capacity. Some regulations complicate management, albeit usually in the name of honorable objectives. For instance, most state and local agencies that administer federal programs must comply with rules for fair labor practices, safety and health, and equal employment opportunity. On balance, however, the federal government has increased the administrative capacity of other governments.

The capacity of state and local governments should be put in perspective. As the capacity of the federal government declines relative to that of state and local agencies, intergovernmental administration becomes more attractive. Any superiority of the federal government over state and local bureaucracies probably diminished in the late 1970s and 1980s. Negligible pay increases, antibureaucracy rhetoric, attacks on fringe benefits, reductions in force, and other factors have posed severe threats to the capacity of the federal bureaucracy (see Chapter 15).

Any discussion of state and local capacity must acknowledge their wide variation. Local governments in particular differ enormously in their size and professionalism. Given these variations, an intergovernmental strategy confronts uneven prospects. Some state and local agencies have less capacity than the federal government to implement a program effectively, efficiently, and lawfully. Others have more, and still others, about the same capacity. While a multitude of forces impels state and local governments toward greater and more homogeneous capacity, discrepancies seem destined to persist. Consider in this regard the capacity of states to tax—the amount of money a jurisdiction would raise if it applied a nationally uniform set of tax rates to specified revenue sources. Tax capacity is a measure of wealth. It affects the ability of government to pay competitive salaries and generally invest in administrative infrastructure. Some evidence points to growing disparity rather than homogeneity of the tax capacity of states since the mid-1970s.[37]

Common Professionalism Promotes Commitment.   Capacity will do little to foster excellence in intergovernmental administration if policymakers and executives lack commitment to the spirit and letter of federal law. A distinction between the policy commitments of elected officials and those of administrators looms large here. Many initiatives, such as welfare programs for mothers with dependent children (AFDC) and health programs for the poor (Medicaid), give states ample discretion to determine how generous these programs will be. The commitments of state administrators may influence this policy decision, but the authority to choose a penurious or generous program remains in the hands of state elected officials. If some states such as Alabama and Georgia adopt minimal programs to assist the poor and if this is undesirable, the problem is not so much one of intergovernmental administration as it is the design of federal policy, which explicitly grants state elected officials great latitude.

The connection to public administration becomes more explicit when state administrators lack commitment to federal goals and use their discretion to undermine these programs. However, the growth of professionalism in state agencies tends to weaken any such proclivity. For instance, the professionals who staff federal welfare bureaucracies tend to share values and beliefs with their counterparts at the state and local levels. Many of them have earned degrees in social work or related fields. The common perspectives of professionals at different levels of government reduce friction that might impede intergovernmental implementation.

Common professionalism may well be critical for socially redistributive programs. Redistributive programs provide benefits to populations who pay relatively small amounts of taxes and have special needs for public services—the poor and other disadvantaged. As a rule, states and localities have less incentive to pursue these programs vigorously than those which benefit the middle class or promise to spur economic development. Migration theory holds that competition among states and localities for economic resources produces a bid-down effect on redistributive programs. Decisions by these jurisdictions to provide generous benefits to the poor and disadvantaged may drive up taxes, since federal programs frequently require some kind of matching allocation by the state or local government. At some threshold higher taxes for redistributive ends discourage firms and affluent individuals from remaining in or moving to the jurisdiction, which erodes its tax base. Simultaneously, generous redistributive programs entice needy people to move to the area, draining public resources.

Although state and local elected officials make the most fundamental decisions about programs' generosity, administrators have some discretion over eligibility and other administrative matters bearing on program costs. The importance of administrative discretion at times prompts state and local elected officials to influence it. These interventions can severely undermine redistributive programs. Many of the poverty programs of Johnson's Great Society floundered because local elected officials feared power shifts to the poor and energetically intervened to block such shifts. Thus, migration theory suggests that the barriers to excellence in intergovernmental administration are greater for redistributive programs.

However, as the research of Peterson and his associates suggests, substantial professional autonomy at the state and local level can counteract this tendency. These authors studied the implementation of several federal programs by four local governments, Baltimore, Dade County, Milwaukee, and San Diego. The programs studied included those aimed at economic or physical development (e.g., the Hill-Burton program for hospital construction) and redistribution (e.g., the compensatory education provisions of the Elementary and Secondary Education Act of 1965). Among other things, the researchers conclude that in cities where local administrators achieved greater autonomy vis-à-vis elected officials, redistributive programs were implemented in a manner consistent with federal policy. They assert: "Professionals helped secure the long-term success of most new redistributive programs. The value of their efforts became even more evident where we examined those few instances when a politicized context kept them from significant participation."[38]

Such studies caution against assumptions that intergovernmental administration will erode the pursuit of excellence in public administration. State and local agencies often have considerable commitment and capacity. Insofar as the public holds administrators at state and local levels in higher esteem than their federal counterparts, the value of intergovernmental administration increases. This may reduce the destruction that a negative political culture visits on program management. However, available data do not consistently support this possibility. To be sure, in a 1986 survey 23 percent of the respondents indicated that the federal government did the best job of dealing with the problems it faced; 35 percent chose the state; and 41 percent, local government.[39] When asked in 1983 which level of government gives the most for your money, however, 31 percent of a national sample named the federal government, 20 percent the state, and 31 percent, the local level; 19 percent responded "Don't know."[40]

Excellence, Control, and Redundancy

The search for excellence concerns not only issues of administration by proxy but also leading and managing the federal bureaucracy itself. This volume has explored some of the dynamics of managing authority, personnel, information, physical resources, and money. Each of these resources presents particular challenges; each could generate a specific set of proposals for reform. For purposes of this volume, however, it is more pertinent to address two broad themes related to excellence. Specifically, excellence stands a greater chance of flourishing if two related developments occur: (1) Officials place less emphasis on control and more on entrepreneurship. (2) Officials remain sensitive to the benefits of messy and ambiguous administrative arrangements, especially those involving competitive redundancy.

Less Emphasis on Control

No one can plausibly argue against the need for bureaucratic accountability in a democratic society, but control and accountability can be achieved in different ways and in different degrees. There is a strong case that the federal government's emphasis on control now inhibits the quest for economy, efficiency, and effectiveness.

Many management theorists have pointed to the problems of emphasizing rule-driven control. Peters and Waterman stress that autonomous and entrepreneurial managers foster innovation. These managers try a lot of things; they experiment and learn; they recognize that some experiments will fail. Autonomy and entrepreneurship help create a "bias toward action" that Peters and Waterman see as a distinguishing characteristic of the best-run companies.[41] Their popular volume recalls Woodrow Wilson's endorsement of "large powers and unhampered discretion" for administrators (see Chapter 5). It casts light on the growing interest in entrepreneurship among students of public policy and management.[42]

Public organizations have often stressed control rather than autonomy and entrepreneurship. Stout notes, "Public organizations are particularly susceptible to generalizing control to inappropriate realms, partly because of demands for bureaucrats to be 'in control' of their organizations and accountable to superior authority."[43] Kelman contends that public administration is more rule-bound than that of the private sector, which magnifies the risk of turning government managers into "clerks" and slows government's ability to respond to new situations. In his view, "Public managers need to be freer to make decisions, to take initiatives, and to innovate; then they must be held responsible for the results."[44] A report of the National Academy of Public Administration on the federal government draws a similar conclusion. It charges that federal management systems are too centralized, too negative, too constraining, too rigid, and too expensive. The "systems have become so burdensome and constraining that they reduce rather than enhance management effectiveness."[45]

Precise calibration of the degree to which federal management features rule-oriented control remains impossible. In general, however, these assertions appear to be on target. Thus the search for excellence requires effort to deregulate managers—to grant them more autonomy to pursue various strategies. This need not be inconsistent with accountability. The degree to which top executives and Congress have access to information about a program's direction, activities, and performance is a critical intervening factor. Ample flow of such information allows managers to be held accountable for their use of discretion. If top policymakers dislike the results, with such information they can intervene to alter a program. This can apply to goals as well as means. Students of democracy frequently worry that vague legislation allows public managers to pursue objectives no member of Congress envisioned when he or she voted for a law. If Congress has access to information about program direction, this need not be undesirable. In fact, the evolution of goals may let members of Congress discover new preferences. While they did not originally expect an agency to pursue a certain objective, they may applaud the pursuit of this value.

There are barriers to the flow of information about program activities. Earlier chapters discussed the limits of oversight. On balance, however, top officials can acquire considerable general information about domestic programs. Thus, some rule reduction need not gut accountability.

The quest to unfetter executives must recognize that internal deregulation has implications for power and values. For instance, eliminating rules that govern reductions in force could help managers keep the employees they want and possibly enhance effectiveness. Simultaneously, it could undermine the power of employee groups. It could diminish the weighting of employee rights as a value in personnel processes. Moreover, abolition of rules might open up managers to greater pressures from interest groups. When approached by lobbyists, managers could no longer so readily say, "I'd like to help, but the rules won't let me." Sometimes these pressures could undercut the efficiency and effectiveness of programs.

As this suggests, any initiative to deregulate federal managers must distinguish among rules. Many rules compel managers to consider important values. Regulations designed to ensure equal opportunity employment are an example. Moreover, sometimes there is a case for imposing precise requirements on managers. For instance, standardization of certain accounting and general reporting requirements would let policymakers compare performance and cost information across agencies. While reducing rule-oriented control makes sense, decisions to deregulate require careful examination of specific cases.

In general, the case for deregulation is strongest when three conditions apply. First, a strong organizational culture of shared values, beliefs, and rules conducive to efficiency and effectiveness facilitates deregulation. Culture constitutes the other side of the argument Peters and Waterman make for discretion. They contend that winning companies have "simultaneous loose-tight properties." These companies "allow (indeed, insist on) autonomy, entrepreneurship, and innovation" yet obtain a great measure of control through cultures featuring "rigidly shared values."[46] Strong culture may inhibit control and undermine efficiency. It may emphasize values running counter to those espoused by top executives and impeding the trial of new techniques. Furthermore, many public agencies lack a strong culture or have many subcultures. In such instances executives often see a greater value in rules to guide behavior.

Second, ample information about an agency's activities and performance weakens the need for rules to govern behavior. If top officials receive sufficient information about agencies, they can turn more to error-correction rather than to error-prevention strategies. In some fields, for instance defense, foreign intelligence, and law enforcement, secrecy is a vital component of technology. This strengthens the case for elaborate rules to govern agency practices.

Third, uncertain technology and considerable environmental change or instability make rule reduction more attractive. Elaborately prescribed systems of rules presume considerable consensus on values and great cause-effect understanding of the best ways to produce desired outcomes. Some cases, such as procedures for issuing Social Security checks, are clear and simple. In other instances, such as treating the chemically dependent at Veterans Administration hospitals, professional judgment is essential. Instability in the environment heightens the risk that rule-oriented control will yield dysfunctional results. It takes time and energy for bureaucracies to ferret out and modify outdated rules. When change occurs rapidly and assumes unexpected forms, the prospect that rules will undermine efficiency and effectiveness increases.

Internal Competitive Redundancy: A Neglected Alternative

If substantial emphasis on rule-oriented control has dominated public administration, so too has the imagery of neat hierarchical lines of authority, crisply defined agency jurisdictions, and minimal duplication and overlap. These accoutrements are supposed to produce lean, efficient administration. Such thinking ignores, however, the considerable importance of redundancy—of building components into an organizational system that perform the same or similar functions. A moment's reflection yields insight into why this practice may well foster effectiveness. In abstract terms, redundancy within agencies can lead to the construction of a reliable complete organization from a set of less reliable parts. A system's probability of failure or ineffectiveness may be considerably less than the probability of failure of each of its parts. In essence, redundancy can allow organizations to absorb error and malfunction without breaking down.[47]

Types of Redundancy.   The meaning of these abstractions becomes clearer in the light of three general types of redundancy: backup, clearance and competitive.

Backup redundancy strives to assure that the system continues on course. The rockets designed to boost space shuttles feature considerable backup redundancy. If one mechanical component fails, another takes its place to save the mission from disaster. The calamity that sent the seven *Challenger* astronauts to their deaths in January 1986 stemmed in part from a failure to build in sufficient redundancy for the O-ring seals on the rocket boosters. Manufacturers had designed the system so that a secondary O-ring would activate if the primary O-ring did not seal the rocket joint (thereby preventing the escape of hot gases that would cause an explosion). However, experiments with the rocket boosters made it clear to certain experts that a completely redundant system did not exist. Hence, those responsible for classifying parts changed the certification of the O-ring from Criticality 1R to Criticality 1. Criticality 1R designates systems with redundancy where complete failure of both systems would doom a mission. Criticality 1 connotes the importance of the subsystem to mission success and acknowledges that a reliable backup component does not exist. In the *Challenger* disaster, it appears that top management at NASA and Morton Thiokol were unaware that the classification of the O-ring seal had changed from Criticality 1R to Criticality 1.[48]

Backup redundancy is not limited to the design, operation, and management of machines. The National Guard and Army Reserve serve as backup units for the president during a national emergency when the regular army cannot cope with the situation. The Occupational Safety and Health Act allows states to serve as implementing agents of the federal government. However, if a state program fails, OSHA can claim jurisdiction and enforce standards in that state.

Clearance redundancy aims at preventing action unless reviews at several decision sites give a go-ahead. When the National Science Foundation submits grant proposals to reviewers for comment, for instance, project officers often require that several reviewers report favorably on the proposal before it is funded. Decisions to launch missiles against the Soviet Union require multiple clearances and the pressing of many switches. Clearance redundancy contains a bias against action unless substantial evidence supports it.

Competitive redundancy exists when different units within an organization have identical or overlapping functions that each can simultaneously perform. Competitive redundancy differs from backup redundancy in that activity by unit A does not depend on malfunction by unit B. Competitive redundancy differs from clearance redundancy in that units A cannot authoritatively prevent B from acting. In the analysis of management excellence, Peters and Waterman show considerable sympathy for competitive redundancy. They see successful firms as "driven by internal markets and internal competition."[49] Competitive redundancies can contribute to excellence in two major ways. First, as a "hidden stimulus" resembling the market, they serve to create "a form of organizational Darwinism" that presumably boosts prospects of efficiency and effectiveness.[50] Administrators try harder and are more innovative. Competitive redundancy often permits comparative evaluation of alternative approaches to some problem. Second, such redundancies can heighten the accountability of civil servants to top officials. Overlap and competition increase prospects that information will flow to policymakers. President Franklin Roosevelt deliberately created conflict between overlapping jurisdictions in order to ensure that major issues would reach his desk.[51]

Limits to Redundancy.   While more redundancy might well fuel the achievement of excellence, it is no elixir. The primary need is to consider ways in which backup and competitive redundancy can help. There is a strong case that decision-making in the United States already features so much clearance redundancy that delay, inaction, and lowest-common-denominator solutions pervade. For instance, concerns about the debilitating effects of excessively fragmented power within Congress are basically concerns about a surfeit of clearance redundancy.

Aside from this issue, policymakers and managers must remain alert to the importance of gauging the costs of redundancy. Virtually all forms of redundancy involve extra money and staff. Officials must pour resources into at least two distinct organizational or mechanical components. Whether long-term benefits to efficiency and effectiveness offset the short-term costs of such action is problematic. Redundancy can foster inefficiency by preventing economies of scale. Up to some point increases in organizational size increase efficiency and effectiveness. After that optimal point, a decline may occur.

Information issues can damp the allure of redundancy. Too many channels of information can overload executives and others who must deal with the agency. In this regard, redundancy increases the incoherence of government for ordinary citizens. It can make it ever more difficult for citizens to fathom who makes what decisions. Their information costs of dealing with government increase; their sense of political efficacy may diminish. These dynamics, in part, make a strong case for preserving a monopoly in some spheres. For instance, much evidence indicates that the Social Security Administration performs its mission efficiently and effectively. A redundant unit to perform certain of its functions would probably only confuse the beneficiaries. Given their difficulties in gathering, absorbing, and processing information, the poor and poorly educated would probably suffer a disproportionate decline in service.

Competitive redundancy presents the additional threat that interaction will occur on nontask rather than task grounds. Units A and B may compete not only by task-oriented methods such as trying to do a job more efficiently and effectively but also via nontask methods such as public relations campaigns, deception, cultivating certain members of Congress, catering to certain interest groups, and "dirty tricks." Interaction among the branches of the armed services generally features a mix of task and nontask competition.

Given the limits of redundancy, scholars should specify the circumstances under which a particular form of redundancy is appropriate. In general redundancy tends to be attractive when the probability of error or failure is high or when the consequences of failure are severe or both. (Consider toxic contamination of a residential area and the accidental launching of a warhead.) The appeal of redundancy also increases when parallel units cost less to establish and maintain. Clearance redundancy becomes more attractive when one wishes to prevent errors or ascertain that broad agreement exists on the need for action. In contrast, backup and competitive redundancy are biased toward doing something. They elevate the system's tolerance for error or malfunction once action commences.

The Quest for Constructive Overlap, Duplication, and Blurring.   Of the three forms of redundancy, the potential benefits of the competitive version deserve more acknowledgement among students and practitioners of public management. To be sure, aside from competition public agencies have a number of reasons to stay on their toes. These include the threat of budget cuts, bad publicity, citizen complaints, congressional oversight, and so on. However, the right kind of competitive redundancy can yield dividends in efficiency, effectiveness, and accountability; it can enlarge the capacity of government to learn and to absorb error.

An open-minded perspective on competitive redundancy can facilitate informed responses to the forces that affect internal competition. The growth of interdependent governmental programs has heightened prospects of jurisdictional duplication and overlap. The appearance of such redundancy should not immediately precipitate efforts by policymakers to stamp it out.

Top officials should be sensitive to forces that threaten to erode competitive redundancy. High-level civil servants tend to be constrained maximizers (see Chapter 11); they want to stabilize their environments by forging consensus on their respective domains. This reduces overt competition. Instead, gradual and subtle encroachment tends to prevail. Other forces also undermine competitive redundancy. The information generated by competition among agencies may at times reach the news media. The media delight in reports of bureaucratic infighting and tend to interpret such conflict as a sure sign of organizational pathology. This goads politicians and others to clean up the mess—in essence, to eliminate the competition. Too much success for one competitor can also gut redundancy. If one agency visibly outperforms the other, policymakers may eliminate or drastically cut the budget of the loser. Once established as the sole supplier of some service or good, the dominant agency may become lazy and lose its competitive edge.

Fiscal austerity also militates against competitive redundancy. Policymakers may well become tempted to save costs over the short run by eliminating or combining redundant units. (However, the competition that remains in an environment of cutback may be more intense.)

As these barriers to competition suggest, redundancy needs nourishment, management, and evaluation. Given prevailing cultural biases, redundancy featuring jurisdictional overlap rather than pure duplication is more feasible. Redundancy in which competing agencies employ distinctive technologies such as different weapons systems to accomplish the same task will also prove more viable.

The Bottom Line

Valid and reliable performance measures would expedite the search for excellence via internal deregulation and greater receptivity to competitive redundancy. Top officials will more readily accept discretion and competition if they can find a bottom line for agency performance. The federal government has demonstrated initiative in this regard. Throughout the 1970s and 1980s, a division of the Department of Labor's Bureau of Labor Statistics developed, collected, and reported data on agency productivity. As of the mid-1980s, it had gathered data on some thirty-four hundred different indicators of output.[52] Expansion of this system could assist performance measurement.

Measurement entails risks. Performance indicators can motivate officials to be very active while paying little attention to quality, as when they conduct large numbers of safety inspections that are not intelligently targeted to boost overall levels of compliance. Also, performance indicators can skew an agency's effort to emphasize measurable outputs relative to equally important intangible ones. Even proponents of measurement systems allow that some agencies' outputs "are difficult or impossible to specify."[53] Moreover, officials must guard against equating agency and managerial performance. Managers, whether in baseball or the federal government, can affect only some of the factors that determine success.

If performance measurement presents risks, refusal to pursue it seems even less promising. In the absence of performance data, evaluation of alternative strategies is all the harder. Learning is harder. The siren call of rule-oriented control is louder. The effort to develop better performance measures will cost money. The quest for efficiency and effectiveness often costs more rather than less, at least over the short term. Hence, a milieu featuring austerity and cutbacks may well be barren ground for gains in measurements of performance.

Excellence and Qualities of Public Executives

The pursuit of excellence rests on more than political, cultural, and organizational factors; it also depends on the individual qualities of public executives. In general theorists have abandoned the quest to isolate *the* traits of good managers.

Students instead espouse a contingent approach that holds that good management is a function of the critical interaction between personality and circumstances. Personality here refers to "distinctive qualities of mind, emotion, and character as manifested in behavior or temperament."[54] Personalities successful in one administrative context may be disastrous in another. Allowing for the contingencies of managerial excellence, certain general observations seem possible, at least with respect to senior executives in the federal government. In particular and other things being equal, the quest for excellence will be abetted if managers possess democratic sensitivity, political skills, a finely honed capacity for strategic opportunism, and a proclivity to treat action as complex hypothesis.

Democratic sensitivity exists when public administrators respect institutions and processes that serve the ideals of individual rights and the consent of the governed. Civil servants need to be safe for democracy (see Chapter 8). In part, they are safe if the legal imperative drives their choices. Democratically sensitive executives nurture an acute sense that in the final analysis they must be civil *servants* of the Constitution, statutes, and court interpretations of them. Within the constraints set by this legal framework, they must remain deferential to the preferences of elected officials and the populace. Beyond this, democratic sensitivity implies a respect for the sanctity of the individual and human life. Executives imbued with democratic sensitivity understand due process and know that ends do not automatically justify the means—that lying and deceit can seldom be justified. The role of democratic sensitivity points to the importance of offering moral philosophy and ethics in programs to educate and train executives for the public service.

Public executives need *political skills* for the pursuit of excellence. These skills are especially important in contexts featuring generic politicization (see Chapter 5). That is, with power and authority dispersed and heterogeneous preferences present, actors must mobilize resources and engage in strategic behavior in order to prevail. Politicization may increase to the extent that competitive redundancies become more common in organizations.

Politically sophisticated executives understand that conflict over ends and means lies at the heart of much managerial work. They accept the positive side of conflict and do not personalize it. They see managing and shaping conflict along constructive lines as one of their major tasks. They sense the importance of civility and mutual respect in debate; they work against the development of an "enemy psychology" during conflict.[55] Administrative politicians are adroit at mapping their strategic environment. They understand the relevant actors and processes affecting decisions, the values held by these actors, their power resources, and the likelihood that they will pursue certain strategies to influence a decision. Administrative politicians must be "dirty-minded" to anticipate how various groups or interests can impede program implementation.[56] They rank high in negotiating skills, which often help them in the critical art of forming and sustaining coalitions. They possess skills of advocacy. They tend to be articulate and at least implicitly sense the importance of paralanguage, body language, and symbols.

Although these qualities are neglected in theories of management, astute administrative politicians often have a sense of humor and the ability to use it for strategic purposes. Humor helps an executive cope with the stress of the job. The ability to laugh at one's own foibles as well as those of others can lend perspective and release tension. The use of such humor in dealing with others can help keep conflict focused on mountains rather than molehills. It can reduce the tendency for conflict over issues to degenerate into personal antagonism. Humor may help an executive acknowledge certain realities and escape the negative consequences of errors. Columnist Lou Cannon noted how President Reagan's self-deprecating sense of humor became a "shield and saving grace in moments of political and personal crisis."[57]

While it seems obvious that executives interested in pursuing excellence must be adroit administrative politicians, many of them cringe at the label. To them, the terms *politics* and *politician* often carry negative connotations. In part this problem derives from the vulgar self-help literature found on airport book racks and similar outlets. This literature frequently features an amoral and exploitive tone. Consider an exhortation from a volume of 225 pages of advice to managers on the art of "power lunching."[58]

> Remember, at a restaurant your guest can't be the same tough, mean son-of-a-bitch he is in his office. When he's savoring tender veal or delicious trout, or when he's ducking his calorie count and indulging in a Napoleon, he's more vulnerable to your pitch. At a power lunch, *you have control*.

While the amoral, exploitive perspective on administrative politics often provides dubious advice, focusing on the relatively trivial (lunches) at the expense of a broader understanding of political context and strategy, it underscores a critical point. Political skills detached from democratic sensitivity and an enlightened vision can yield undesirable consequences. Winning at administrative politics cannot be a suitable end in itself. In the United States above all it must be evaluated in terms of the degree to which it fosters efficiency, effectiveness, and accountability. However, if political skills are not a sufficient condition for achieving excellence, they are almost always a necessary one.

Strategic opportunism tends to facilitate the pursuit of excellence.[59] Many constraints restrict an executive's options at a given time. Managers confront rules and procedures limiting their use of critical factors of production; they inherit personnel; they become involved with a specific technology and face a particular constellation of forces in the agency's environment. Many variables lie well beyond their control. They also live with change, serendipity, and the random confluence of events. This combination of stability and change has prompted various students of management to emphasize the importance of seizing the time. As one analyst notes, "the strategic manager uses the small openings presented by the agency's routine to induce change toward an identified goal, step by step, as the deep sea fisherman lands the fish in the occasional moments when the line is slack."[60] As another observer puts it, "The effective manager of public policy is a skilled opportunist . . . skilled in taking advantage of random policy making opportunities," who uses "events, whether or not they are of the executive's own doing, as opportunities to achieve strategic gains."[61]

At its core, strategic opportunism lets the manager remain focused on long-term program objectives while dealing with day-to-day tasks—striking a balance between flexibility and direction. Strategic thinking requires a programmatic vision. Managers need an overriding image of where they wish to take a program. Events may alter that vision, but it should not be purely a function of the opportunities in the environment.

The cognitive orientation of executives also influences the pursuit of excellence. Cognitive orientation is the ways individuals store, evaluate, and use information. It takes "the form of beliefs, images, models, and ideas about reality"—how one interprets the world.[62] *An orientation that treats action as complex hypothesis heightens prospects for excellence in public management.* Hypotheses state expectations about relationships among variables. A scientific manager may reason if one does A and B at time 1, consequences X and Y will follow at time 2. Moreover, having thought of action as hypothesis, the manager is alert to information that can shed light on the validity of the hypothesis.

Why is this cognitive orientation so attractive? Primarily because it increases the probability that dogma and overcommitment will not swamp the judgments of executives—that they will be genuinely evaluative in outlook. Although political scientists and others have often expressed concern that top executives will be insufficiently committed to some program preferred by policymakers, the problem of overcommitment can be just as great. Driven to making programs work, to staying the course, and to avoiding the blame and insecurity of being charged with failure, executives tend to resist evaluation. They often continue to pursue programs and strategies long beyond their point of effectiveness (if they ever were effective). This problem is not confined to public managers. An issue of the *Harvard Business Review* published in the late 1980s dealt with the difficulties of businesses in "knowing when to pull the plug" on programs.[63] To treat action as hypothesis implies that managers constantly look for opportunities to experiment, reflect, debug, and retest. They remain open to information and explanations that run counter to expectations. They constantly question themselves without permitting this to degenerate into self-doubt or hostility.[64]

In treating action as hypothesis, however, the manager should not automatically transform uncertainty into skepticism. Given the fluid, overlapping, and ambiguous properties of much of organizational life, executives seldom have the luxury of definitively testing a hypothesis. They seldom if ever conduct formal, rigorous experiments.[65] In the face of uncertainty, the manager should not always prefer the null hypothesis, that program A does not produce outcome B. Instead, a more optimistic stance ("while we can't be sure, program A may well be yielding outcome B") may serve better. Otherwise, a scientific perspective can cause excessive skepticism, which may be contagious as executives transmit it to subordinates. In turn, this doubt may undermine the commitment and motivation of employees. Thus, skepticism itself can cause a program to fail.

Finally, executives must not let a view of action as hypothesis undermine their sense of complexity. Managers feel a strong emotional pull toward certainty, simplicity, and consistency. This predisposition has positive functions; it encourages them to remain action-oriented. However, thinking of strategy as hypothesis can become a pitfall if it imputes excessive order to organizational life. Karl Weick has argued that "most managers get into trouble because they fail to think in circles." They adhere rigidly to "such things as unilateral causation, independent and dependent variables, origins, and terminations." He urges managers to complicate themselves as a strategy for achieving greater effectiveness.[66] Among other things, they must understand that causation tends to be reciprocal. When A affects B, B's response alters A. These dynamics require managers to remain alert to the complexity of the systems in which they operate. They should be alert to the probability of unanticipated outcomes and to the likelihood that each solution will unleash a new (hopefully better) set of problems for them to work on.

Conclusion

The quest for excellence must meet challenges raised by governmental institutions, political culture, administration by proxy, the bias for control and against competitive redundancy, and the need to find talented executives. None of these will be easy to conquer. Some will be more intractable than others. These enduring problems should not, however, be construed as a counsel for defeat. Even the more stubborn problems may submit to amelioration. For instance, it may be possible over time to educate the public that waste reduction in the bureaucracy cannot abolish the need for unhappy choices—that policymakers cannot eviscerate financial support for public programs and sustain or increase services. Furthermore, there is enough evidence of outstanding achievement by federal programs to suggest that excellence can take root.

Aside from these hurdles, the quest for excellence features internal tension. As defined here, it implies a search for effectiveness and efficiency as well as a quest for accountability. Trade-offs among these dimensions need not invariably exist. In some forms and contexts, for example, redundancy serves the interests of both efficiency and accountability. Where a trade-off does exist, however, one can often make a strong case for tilting toward efficiency and effectiveness.[67] When much of the public believes that government cannot make things work, efforts to foster efficiency and effectiveness may well do more to buttress the credibility of public administration than the quest for greater accountability. The chief exception to this argument is policy spheres where big, loose control seems most threatened, as with the Central Intelligence Agency.

Finally, this book suggests that the pursuit of excellence must extend beyond public administration narrowly defined. Students of public administration have tended to concentrate on the management of organizations at the core of government—governmental agencies with civil service systems and other familiar accoutrements. The policy and management issues posed by those core units deserve primary attention, but the pervasiveness of administration by proxy demands a broader focus, one emphasizing public *program* administration. The implementation of a program typically involves several government agencies and private organizations. The management of interorganizational seams becomes critical. The concept of bureaucratic hierarchy becomes less relevant. Thus, students of public administration must not only grasp how agencies like NASA operate and why; they must also fathom the dynamics of their relationships with firms like Morton Thiokol. They must come to grips with the forces that drive firms when they do government's work. In summary, the ability to generate ideas for pursuing excellence substantially hinges on the capacity of public administration specialists to expand their intellectual horizons.

Notes

1. *Publisher's Weekly* 225 (16 March 1984): 30. Thomas J. Peters and Robert H. Waterman, Jr., *In Search of Excellence* (New York: Warner, 1984).
2. Daniel T. Carroll, "A Disappointing Search for Excellence." *Harvard Business Review* 61 (November-December 1983): 88; see also Robert T. Golembiewski, "Toward Excellence in Public Management: Constraints on Emulating America's Best-Run Companies." Unpublished paper, University of Georgia, 1987.
3. Peters and Waterman, *In Search of Excellence,* 22–3.
4. For an overview, see George W. Downs and Patrick D. Larkey, *The Search for Government Efficiency* (New York: Random House, 1986), 20–1.
5. Steven Kelman, "The Grace Commission: How Much Waste in Government?" *Public Interest* 78 (Winter 1985): 62–82.
6. These data are the results of various surveys reported in "The Role of Government: An Issue for 1988?" *Public Opinion* 9 (March-April 1987): 21–33; and Paul E. Peterson, "The New Politics of Deficits," in John E. Chubb and Paul E. Peterson, eds., *The New Direction in American Politics* (Washington, DC: The Brookings Institution, 1985), 388.
7. Cited in Kelman, "The Grace Commission," 63.
8. Ibid., 62.
9. See Charles T. Goodsell, *The Case for Bureaucracy* (Chatham, NJ: Chatham House, 1985), 179–80.
10. James M. Buchanan and Gordon Tullock, *The Calculus of Consent* (Ann Arbor: University of Michigan Press, 1974); William A. Niskanen, *Bureaucracy and Representative Government* (Chicago: Aldine/Atherton, 1971).
11. Committee on the Constitutional System, *A Bicentennial Analysis of the American Political Structure.* (Washington, DC: Committee on the Constitutional System, 1987), 3, 5.
12. Ibid., 13.
13. See, for instance, James W. Ceaser, "In Defense of Separation of Powers," in Robert A. Goldwin and Art Kaufman, eds., *Separation of Powers—Does It Still Work?* (Washington, DC: American Enterprise Institute, 1986), 168–93.
14. Douglas Yates, Jr., *The Politics of Management* (San Francisco: Jossey-Bass, 1985), 247.
15. E. S. Savas, *Privatizing the Public Sector* (Chatham, NJ: Chatham House, 1982).
16. Goodsell, *The Case for Bureaucracy,* 67.
17. General Accounting Office, *Compendium of GAO's Views on the Cost Savings Proposals of the Grace Commission,* vol. 2 (Washington, DC: GAO/OCG–85–1, 1985), 15.
18. Savas, *Privatizing the Public Sector,* 22, 84.
19. This section draws heavily on Ruth Hoogland DeHoog, "Theoretical Perspectives on Contracting Out for Services: Implementation Problems and Possibilities of Privatizing Public Services," in George C. Edwards, III, ed., *Public Policy Implementation* (Greenwich, CT: JAI Press, 1984), 227–59.
20. Donald F. Kettl, *Government by Proxy: (Mis?)Managing Federal Programs* (Washington: Congressional Quarterly Inc., 1988), 37.
21. U.S. General Accounting Office, *Federal Regulations Need to Be Revised to Fully Realize the Purposes of the Competition in Contracting Act of 1984* (Washington, DC: GAO/OGC–85–14, 1985), 13.

22. Ronald C. Moe, "Exploring the Limits of Privatization." *Public Administration Review* 47 (November-December 1987): 458.

23. William B. Burnett, "Competition in the Weapons Acquisition Process: The Case of U.S. Warplanes." *Journal of Policy Analysis and Management* 7 (Fall 1987): 22.

24. Frank J. Thompson, *Health Policy and the Bureaucracy* (Cambridge, MA: MIT Press, 1981), 127.

25. William B. Burnett, "Competition in the Weapons Acquisition Process: The Case of U.S. Warplanes," 28.

26. Susan Haddon, *Read The Label* (Boulder, CO: Westview, 1986), 215–25.

27. See Raymond G. Hunt, "Cross-Purposes in the Federal Contract Procurement System: Military R&D and Beyond." *Public Administration Review* 44 (May-June, 1984): 247–56.

28. U.S. General Accounting Office, *Incentive Contracts: Examination of Fixed-Price Incentive Contracts* (Washington, DC: GAO/NSIAD–88–36BR, 1987).

29. General Accounting Office, *Compendium of GAO's Views on the Cost Savings Proposals of the Grace Commission,* vol. 2 (Washington, DC: GAO/OCG–85–1, 1985), 193–4.

30. *Federal Times* (27 April 1987): 17.

31. National Academy of Public Administration, *Revitalizing Federal Management: Managers and Their Overburdened Systems* (Washington, DC: National Academy of Public Administration, 1983), 27–35.

32. Kelman, "The Grace Commission," 62–65.

33. General Accounting Office, *Compendium of GAO's Views on the Cost Savings Proposals of the Grace Commission,* 154–8.

34. Savas, *Privatizing the Public Sector,* 154.

35. U.S. Advisory Commission on Intergovernmental Relations, *The Question of State Government Capability* (Washington, DC: Government Printing Office, 1985), 364.

36. Ibid., 168–9.

37. Frank J. Thompson, "New Federalism and Health Care Policy: States and the Old Questions." *Journal of Health Politics, Policy and Law* 11 (1986): 664–5.

38. Paul E. Peterson et al., *When Federalism Works* (Washington, DC: The Brookings Institution, 1986), 26. This analysis of professionalism draws heavily upon this volume.

39. "The Role of Government: An Issue For 1988?" 27.

40. U.S. Advisory Commission on Intergovernmental Relations, *Changing Public Attitudes on Governments and Taxes* (Washington, DC: Government Printing Office, 1983), 7.

41. Peters and Waterman, *In Search of Excellence.*

42. In 1985, for instance, the Brookings Institution invited prominent scholars to a conference entitled Entrepreneurial Leadership in Public Administration.

43. Russell Stout, Jr. *Management or Control? The Organization Challenge* (Bloomington: Indiana University Press, 1980), 13.

44. Kelman, "The Grace Commission," 81.

45. National Academy of Public Administration, *Revitalizing Federal Management: Managers and Their Overburdened Systems,* 1–4.

46. Peters and Waterman, *In Search of Excellence,* 318, 320.

47. This discussion of redundancy draws heavily from Martin Landau, "Redundancy, Rationality, and the Problem of Duplication and Overlap." *Public Administration Review* 29 (July-August, 1969): 346–58; Dan S. Felsenthal, "Applying the Redundancy Concept to Administrative Organizations." *Public Administration Review* 4

(May-June, 1980): 247–52; and especially Jonathon B. Bendor, *Parallel Systems* (Berkeley: University of California Press, 1985).

48. *Report of the Presidential Commission on the Space Shuttle* Challenger *Accident,* vol. 1 (Washington, DC: Government Printing Office, 1986), 125–7.

49. Peters and Waterman, *In Search of Excellence,* 51, 118, 215.

50. Louis K. Bragaw, *Managing a Federal Agency: The Hidden Stimulus* (Baltimore: Johns Hopkins, 1980), 229, 246.

51. Arthur M. Schlesinger Jr., *The Coming of the New Deal* (Boston: Houghton Mifflin, 1959).

52. U.S. Senate Committee on Governmental Affairs, *Management Theories in the Private and Public Sectors* (Washington, DC: Government Printing Office, 1985), 48–83.

53. Ibid., 60.

54. Laurence E. Lynn, Jr., *Managing Public Policy* (Boston: Little, Brown, 1987), 110.

55. For an extremely perceptive treatment of strategies for dealing with conflict, see Yates, *The Politics of Management,* 130–65.

56. Martin A. Levin and Barbara Ferman, *The Political Hand* (New York: Pergamon, 1985), 19.

57. Lou Cannon, "Reagan Uses Humor to Disarm His Critics." *The Atlanta Constitution,* 27 April 1987, 11A.

58. E. Melvin Pinsel and Ligita Dienhart, *Power Lunching* (Chicago: Turnbull & Willoughby, 1984), 17.

59. Daniel J. Isenberg, "The Tactics of Strategic Opportunism." *Harvard Business Review* 65 (March-April 1987): 92–7.

60. Donald E. Stokes, "Political and Organizational Analysis in the Policy Curriculum." *Journal of Policy Analysis and Management* 6 (Fall 1986): 55.

61. Lynn, *Managing Public Policy,* 269–71.

62. Ibid., 112.

63. Barry M. Straw and Jerry Ross, "Knowing When to Pull the Plug." *Harvard Business Review* 65 (March-April 1987): 68–74.

64. Chris Argyris, "Some Characteristics of Successful Executives." *Personnel Journal* 32 (May 1953): 50–5.

65. See Robert D. Behn, "Management by Groping Along." *Journal of Policy Analysis and Management* 7 (Fall 1988): 645.

66. Karl Weick, *The Social Psychology of Organizing* (Reading, MA: Addison-Wesley, 1979), 86, 261.

67. For discussion of the potential for this trade-off, see Judith E. Gruber, *Controlling Bureaucracies: Dilemmas in Democratic Governance* (Berkeley: University of California Press, 1987); Dwight Waldo, "Bureaucracy and Democracy: Reconciling the Irreconcilable?" in Frederick S. Lane, ed., *Current Issues in Public Administration,* 3d ed. (New York: St. Martin's Press, 1986), 455–68.

Chapter Fifteen

The Federal Government in the Year 2000: Legacies of the Reagan Years

——————
——————

For most of their history Americans have been relentlessly optimistic about the future and their ability to shape it. Immigrants have seen rich natural resources, an open economic system, and political liberties as opportunities to fulfill their dreams. For their part, native-born Americans have expressed their optimism via geographic and occupational mobility as they sought economic and social opportunity. Both groups of Americans, old and new, have viewed the future as malleable by their hopes and designs for a better life.

C.P. Snow, an Englishman, captures the value of such optimism:

> The world's greatest need is an appetite for the future . . . all healthy societies are ready to sacrifice the existential moment for their children's future and for their children after these. The sense of the future is behind all good policies. Unless we have it, we can give nothing wise or decent to the world.[1]

The American appetite for the future, so pronounced in our personal lives, has characterized the governmental system as well, particularly over the past fifty years. Since the New Deal of the 1930s, the desirability of government intervention in social and economic affairs has been a well accepted doctrine, no matter how unpopular a single policy, program, or government agency. This support for government rests on the general belief that Americans share some control over their destiny and that government can make their social and natural environment more secure and benign.

Society's deeply held optimism about the future and about government's ability to predict and shape it has been tested in the 1970s and 1980s. Even the most casual observer can see that the United States is in the midst of a long-term technological and economic transformation that is rapidly creating problems and opportunities for people and government. The nation is passing out of the industrial era, during which the United States dominated the world economy through finance and the manufacture of durable goods toward what some call a *postindustrial* or *technoservice* society.[2] In this new era the world economic system is quickly becoming more complex than before, as the movement of money and the production of goods and services are increasingly internationalized. Furthermore, in this new arrangement the economic dominance of the United States is less certain than at any time since World War II. In 1945 the U.S. economy accounted for 50 percent of the GNP of the capitalist world; in 1978 for 33 percent; and in the year 2000, it is estimated, only 20 percent.[3] This is a sizable figure, but it does reflect a change in U.S. control of international markets and underscores the importance of international flows of material, knowledge, money, and finished products for the economic health of the nation.

If international competition has eroded confidence that the nation can control its destiny, movement toward a more "knowledge-intensive" society has also created dislocations. The shift from an economy dominated by manufacturing to one of information and communication means that some industries, regions, and occupations will decline while others grow.

Stagflation has contributed to a sense of vulnerability among the citizenry. From the end of World War II through 1973, adjusted for inflation, the wages of families grew markedly. During the Eisenhower years real family income grew by 30 percent; a similar growth rate marked the Kennedy and Johnson years. However, after the Arab oil embargo of 1973, workers' real incomes grew at a much lower rate, about 10 percent from 1976 to 1986. This quiet depression, along with the rapidly rising costs of housing and higher education in many parts of the country, began to erode the assumption that the next generation would enjoy a more bountiful life than this one.[4]

As economic and related factors gave rise to insecurities about prospects for achieving the American dream, the belief that government could solve society's problems also came under attack. Government policies are usually predicated on the assumption that a more desirable state of affairs will occur as a result of its actions, but what if the prediction is wrong? All predictions are subject to error; the further out the time horizon of the prediction, the greater the chance that errors will occur. In attempting to forecast outcomes, policymakers may rely on poor models, for example of the factors contributing to low reading scores among the poor. These models may exclude relevant variables. They may fail to depict the relationships among the model's components accurately. (That is, X turns out not to cause Y.) Some observers question whether the world is simply too complex to be modeled, predicted, controlled, or reshaped with any confidence.[5]

Many major and minor errors of public policy have produced unanticipated and undesirable side effects. Some were correctable or reversible; some were not. Some cropped up immediately, some long after the policy was initiated. Some arose from complicated technological change, some from economics, some from demographic shifts, and some from the policies and their accompanying politics. The important point is that in their zeal to produce a better world, governments have used instruments with confidence in their efficacy that frequently underestimated the complexity and the risks of the situation.[6]

Policy failures like the Vietnam War and certain (by no means all) poverty programs raised doubts about the feasibility of predicting the future and shaping it through government action in the United States. Skeptics of government efficacy often attach the pejorative label of *social engineering* to attempts to use government power and policy to do such things as regulate financial markets, reduce poverty, fight crime, and educate children. In their view the future is so unpredictable, complex, and uncontrollable, and government decisionmaking is so slow, cumbersome, and politically motivated, that public programs almost inevitably spawn more problems than they solve. They argue that a decentralized free market system with very limited government will more adroitly make swift and efficient adjustments to the rapidly unfolding changes that lie ahead.[7]

Doubts about the nation's economic future and government efficacy certainly began to penetrate public thinking before the Reagan administration. The dominance of that administration during the 1980s interacted with these two themes in important ways. Reagan sought to bolster optimism about the accomplishments and future of the United States while reinforcing skepticism about government's ability to accomplish constructive ends other than the national defense. As the first two-term president since Eisenhower, and one deeply committed to conservative ideology, Reagan left a legacy of government and public administration that demands attention. A primary outcome of the Reagan administration is the reopening of debate on three major issues:

- What government should do
- How government should do it
- Who should work for government

The Reagan administration, through its own words and actions as well as its links to conservative thinkers, has stimulated public debate about the role and reach of government in a mixed economy, the organizational apparatus that should be used to carry out government's role, and the role of government employees—career civil servants and political appointees—in the policy process. With due deference to the complexities of predicting the future, this chapter speculates about the content of that debate in the 1990s.

What Will Government Do?

Chapter 2 traced the rise of the federal government as a driving force politically and economically. Trends in terms of the percentage of the GNP accounted for by federal expenditures testify to the rise of a more centralized administrative state. Governments in general, and the federal government in particular, penetrate nearly all aspects of society.

Upon taking office, President Reagan vowed to reverse this pattern. Reagan's first inaugural address contained much of this ideological flavor. After citing a litany of economic problems, the President asserted:

> In this present crisis, government is not the solution to our problem; government is the problem. From time to time we've been tempted to believe that society has become too complex to be managed by self-rule, that government by an elite group is superior to government for, by, and of the people. Well, if no one among us is capable of governing himself, then who among us has the capacity to govern someone else? . . .
>
> So, as we begin, let us take inventory. We are a nation that has a government—not the other way around. And this makes us special among the other nations of the Earth. Our government has no power except that granted it by the people. It is time to check and reverse the growth of government which shows signs of having grown beyond the consent of the governed.
>
> It is my intention to curb the size and influence of the Federal establishment and to demand recognition of the distinction between the powers granted to the Federal

government and those reserved to the States or the people. All of us need to be reminded that the Federal government did not create the States; the States created the Federal government.

Now, so there will be no misunderstanding, it's not my intention to do away with government. It is rather to make it work—work with us, not over us; to stand by our side, not ride our back. Government can and must provide opportunity, not smother it, foster productivity, not stifle it. . . .

In the days ahead I will propose removing the roadblocks that have slowed our economy and reduced productivity. Steps will be taken aimed at restoring the balance between the various levels of government. Progress may be slow, measured in inches and feet, not miles, but we will progress. It is time to reawaken this industrial giant, to get government back within its means, and to lighten our punitive tax burden. And these will be our first priorities, and on these principles there will be no compromise.[8]

Reagan's words are important for the future—perhaps more so than his accomplishments—because they have forced a reexamination of some of the basic premises of American government. This is particularly noteworthy because since the New Deal, significant public debate between opposing philosophies about the role and scope of government in the United States has steadily diminished. In its place arose a public philosophy Theodore J. Lowi has called "interest group liberalism." This philosophy provided the underpinning for a system in which interest group support was the primary basis for legitimizing government intervention.[9] In this century, especially since the 1930s, the growing reach and activities of the federal government have been fueled by an almost endless assortment of such groups representing virtually every imaginable breakdown of the population by social, economic, occupational, and geographical designation.

During his presidency, Reagan attempted to live up to his first inaugural address by reversing the trend of government growth.[10] However, the Reagan administration's efforts to redirect the role of American government encountered the problems that all political reformers face. Because it is cumbersome and complicated, barring crisis, the policymaking system generally does not take or reverse direction quickly. This helps to explain why Reagan's successes in redirecting the role of government, while significant in a few policy areas, must be considered marginal in the aggregate. A look at government programs and legislation passed since January 1981 shows that the great preponderance of programs the Reagan administration inherited are still in place and that their funding levels, while smaller in places, have not appreciably diminished. There are several notable exceptions, of course, but generally speaking there have been no significant program terminations since the fall of 1981.

An editorial by conservative columnist William Buckley in mid-1988 testifies to developments. Responding to a campaign proposal by Vice President Bush to increase federal involvement in providing day care, Buckley ruefully noted:

The Reagan Administration, of which Mr. Bush is a part and the principal political beneficiary, began by huffing and puffing about the New Federalism and ends by inaugurating a new Cabinet department of veteran affairs, maintaining in the Cabinet a department of education and another for energy; and now are going to look after babies as a federal responsibility.[11]

Hence, the Reagan administration did not leave a greatly reduced role for the federal government in the 1990s. Certain basic features of American government and political culture—features likely to persist into the next century—push in the opposite direction. Interest group liberalism and the dependence of well-organized groups on the federal government make up one such feature.[12] Behind nearly every federal program stands a network of groups ready to defend their pet projects by lobbying Congress and the executive to spare them budget cuts. These groups often represent middle-class or affluent constituencies. No matter how strongly an administration professes its desire to cut back programs, the combined weight of these interest groups—often expressed by their political action committees and voting power—discourages anything more than incremental reductions at the margins of programs. Furthermore, many of the older programs, like Social Security, agricultural subsidies, and real estate tax incentives, are deeply woven into the fabric of American social and economic life. Families have made investment decisions based on the expectation that these programs will continue into the distant future. Changing their direction is bound to be considered a betrayal of a promise, and very few members of Congress are likely to vote for legislation that promises to incur the wrath of masses of voters.

Furthermore, there is considerable demand for expansion of these programs from powerful constituencies. A majority of Americans prefer more government spending in several major policy spheres. Demographic trends could also increase pressure for the federal government to do more. For instance, the growing proportion of the population over age 65 and especially over 75 (the "old old") will generate new demands on the federal treasury for Social Security, medical treatment, and custodial care in nursing homes. In addition, the rise of immigration, legal and illegal, from Asia and Latin America will cause new problems and expenses for social service organizations, school systems, and other government institutions. As if these developments were not sufficient, the continued shift of population from the frostbelt of the Northeast and Midwest to the sunbelt of the Southwest and Southeast will press government to fund a deteriorating infrastructure in the North and a developing one in the South. Moreover, new economic circumstances—international competition and high technology—will galvanize demands on government to work more closely with the private sector to compete abroad and facilitate economic development.

While the pressures to expand the federal government augur against a diminished federal presence in the 1990s, a greatly enhanced role seems unlikely. The huge federal deficit, the costs of servicing the interest payments on it, and public distaste for tax increases will militate against major new programs or the rapid expansion of old ones. This points to a major legacy of the Reagan presidency. The enormous growth in the deficit during the Reagan years (largely a product of substantial tax cuts, increases in defense spending, and the political difficulty of cutting entitlements) has significantly altered political debate. Rather than a struggle between those espousing bold, new, and expensive programs and those seeking to hold the line or retrench, debate revolves around marginal adjustments to existing programs. Debate does not center on whether government ought to be involved in some sphere; it boils down to disagreements about the degree and nature of appropriate government involvement and how to get more bang for the buck.

Given substantial public distaste for both tax hikes and cuts in major programs, the 1990s seem likely to be characterized by fiscal stringency and policy deadlock in government. No doubt the competing pressures will also encourage inventiveness in raising money and hiding the costs of programs. The affluent who receive entitlements such as Social Security may find a larger portion taxed. Policymakers may look for accounting innovations to mask the amount of the deficit or shift the costs of programs to the private sector or both. For example, rather than directly subsidize health insurance for significant segments of the public, Congress could require all businesses with more than 10 employees to provide insurance.

Of course, certain factors may throw this projection off course. A marked increase or decline in the threat of war could either heighten or reduce defense spending. The pressure to cut social programs might increase, or the public might be willing to accept a greater role for the federal government in the economy. If the threat of war, hence defense spending, declined, the prospect for bolder initiatives in undertaking social programs (the "peace dividend") might grow. A range of economic factors may also change the scenario. If interest rates stay low and the economy healthy, some of the pressures to raise taxes and cut programs will be less. If the economy takes a downturn or inflation flourishes, policymakers would face intense pressure in the form of greater demands for social support (e.g., unemployment compensation) and diminished revenues. Major new initiatives to increase taxes and to bolster government's presence in the economy would be more likely.

Politics also matters. The Republican party has generally stood for less involvement by the federal government in social programs. When Republicans inhabit the White House and increase their share of seats in Congress, the prospects for major new social programs decline. The shift of more House seats to conservative sunbelt states after the 1990 census will reinforce the resistance of the system to new social outlays and higher taxes.

On balance, the 1990s seem likely to be full of risks and agonizing challenges, but not to change much in the basic concept of the role of government. The Reagan administration made it harder to contemplate bold new forays by government but did not succeed in whetting appetites for major retrenchment.

How Will Government Carry Out Its Role?

A major legacy of the Reagan administration—perhaps the one with the most lasting effect—has been to legitimize debate over the tools and techniques of policy implementation. The Reagan administration brought into the open the full implications of the subtle shift over the past fifty years from direct delivery of services, income and goods to administration by proxy.[13] While its version of a "new federalism" hardly proved pathbreaking or long-lived, its emphasis on the virtues of privatization substantially reoriented debate within the field of public administration. The Reagan administration also vividly illustrated the potential for a president to achieve substantial success in pursuing an administrative presidency.

Early in his term President Reagan emphasized the theme of *devolution*—of charting a new course in intergovernmental affairs. This thrust aimed less at improving the management of existing intergovernmental programs than at fundamentally redistributing responsibilities among federal, state, and local governments.

One initiative was the swap: a state would assume complete responsibility for one policy (e.g., occupational safety and health), and the federal government would take another from the states (e.g., Medicaid). Another initiative gave states more discretion to administer federal grant programs. In general the Reagan proposals assumed that the federal government ought to do less and that if government intervention was needed at all, states and localities ought to take the lead. While Reagan did cut funding for intergovernmental programs and shift some authority to states and localities, no large-scale devolution occurred. The centerpiece of his initiative, that the federal and state governments swap functions, made little headway.

The 1990s will no doubt feature debate over intergovernmental relations and their implications for public administration as well as a more general theory of government. As sure as the flowers that bloom in the spring, another proposal for a "new federalism" will surface. This is a long-standing issue that marks many presidential administrations rather than a distinctive legacy of the Reagan years.

In contrast, the Reagan administration did much to spark consideration of privatization as a program strategy. Assuming that more privatization was better, Reagan officials did little to develop a practical theory of the precise circumstances under which privatization in one form or another ought to be pursued, but they did push the topic to center stage. Debate over the subject and new initiatives to foster privatization seem likely to flourish during the 1990s regardless of which political party dominates Washington.

The staying power of privatization comes from several sources:

1. Major federal programs (e.g., Medicare, Defense Department weapons procurement) already are privatized. It would require massive and costly restructuring of these programs to turn them over to the civil service.
2. The political culture of the United States makes privatization appealing. It lets Americans have their ideological cake and eat it too. They can get government programs without big public bureaucracies. This harmonizes with American individualism and antisocialist values and comports with the customary American preference for reliance on the private sector.
3. The eroded capacity of the federal work force—another legacy of the Reagan administration—reinforces privatization. If the federal government cannot attract and retain enough highly competent employees, the attractiveness of contracting out the work of government will grow.
4. Privatization will draw strength from the reluctance of politicians to allow career executives to manage in a manner consistent with the pursuit of excellence (see Chapter 14). In particular, the federal management system's rule-bound, control-oriented nature seems unlikely to change. Hence, the allure of the more flexible, "creative" management of private firms will remain potent.

The persistence of a control-oriented approach to public administration is not exclusively the result of inertia and recalcitrance. Top policymakers understandably place a heavy premium on accountability; they can point with pride to the fact that the federal government has been relatively free of corruption. The prevailing approach has, after all, provided the United States with a very substantial measure of bureaucratic integrity, reliability, and responsiveness. Moreover, an emphasis on control gives a president many levers to pull in an effort to redirect policy. The chief constituency for an improved management system is federal career managers and their professional associations. Federal management is too complex and the stake in improving it too uncertain for most Americans to mobilize on behalf of change.

In considering possible developments in privatization, it is wise to look beyond conventional contracting arrangements. These will undoubtedly be important, but new combinations of public-private arrangements also seem likely to evolve. In order to facilitate international competitiveness of American business and domestic economic development, the federal government may well create a variety of public-private special-purpose hybrid organizations to carry out new programs or reshape old ones. These new organizations, which will range from government corporations to federally insured private ventures, will widen the range of management systems the government uses by capitalizing on the flexibility afforded private firms while retaining at least some of the control of government agencies. As this occurs, the distinction between public and private organizations will blur.

While privatization has staying power both as an intellectual challenge and in terms of administrative practice, it cannot be expected to usher in a radical replacement of traditional public agencies. Indeed, in drawing attention to privatization, President Reagan helped bring its assumptions under critical scrutiny. Chapter 14 shows how private contracting can produce undesirable results. Initially on the defensive, critics of privatization have become more sophisticated in their attacks on it.[14] Moreover, corruption and mismanagement in government contracting such as the Pentagon and HUD scandals of the late 1980s tend to erode confidence that privatization via contracting serves goals of efficiency and effectiveness. Representatives of public employees will also be sure to point out the foibles of privatization. Hence, both as an intellectual force and as a movement to transform government, privatization faces obstacles that will keep it from radically reshaping government administration in the 1990s.

Aside from privatization, the Reagan years leave a potent legacy of the administrative presidency. Future presidents will study these lessons. The Reagan administration demonstrated considerable skill in imposing its will on the bureaucracy. Reagan established a political personnel apparatus to ensure that top appointments in the bureaucracy went to people who supported him ideologically (see Chapter 5). In the view of one observer, the consequences of the high priority placed on White House control of personnel was that Reagan "achieved a degree of loyalty and coherence in the bureaucracy that other presidents have longed for." In this regard Reagan's practices "differ from those of his predecessors in their effectiveness, not their intent."[15]

The Reagan White House used other mechanisms for control. Of particular note was the marked acceleration in the use of the Office of Management and Budget as an instrument of presidential control. This surfaced not only in the budget process as David Stockman used his formidable intellect and political skill to heighten the leverage of the office but also in the behavior of the Office of Information and Regulatory Affairs, a unit of OMB. This office assumed responsibility for approving rules proposed by regulatory agencies and others and did much to slow the promulgation of new rules.

Presidents in the 1990s may well pursue similar centralizing strategies, but with variation. The enormous dispersal of power in Congress and the resulting difficulty in getting legislation through the House and Senate almost guarantee that a president will look for levers like the ones Reagan used. Reagan's successors will appreciate that substantial policy redirection can occur via administration, without changes in law. The appointment process and OMB will continue to be important tools of leadership, but not necessarily used the same way. For that matter, Reagan's successors may not have comparable skill using them. A Democrat would, for instance, face more difficulty in pursuing a personnel strategy aimed at ideological purity because of the greater heterogeneity of that party. Moreover, the risks of elevating the importance of ideological compatibility became evident during the Reagan years. Many of Reagan's major policy setbacks and political embarrassments (e.g., Iran-Contra) resulted from the actions of political zealots, both in the White House and the executive branch. Reagan demonstrated the risks of delegating too much to fervent supporters and avoiding the details of executive leadership.

While privatization and successful centralization are primary administrative legacies of the Reagan years, his administration also encouraged certain forms of "management improvement." Operating through its several councils on administration and via OMB, Reagan's Reform '88 program was to improve the way the federal government handled cash management, debt collection, real property, procurement, computer planning, travel, and the administration of overhead expenses. Some of these initiatives commenced in the Carter administration; the General Accounting Office instigated others; still other reforms were stimulated (or publicized) by the Grace Commission. The Reagan administration played a pivotal role in getting several of these initiatives implemented. The Reagan administration's achievements in securing these low-visibility but often costly management reforms are likely to encourage future presidents to carry on the modernization effort as new ideas and opportunities develop.

In sum, although the "what" of government in the United States is unlikely to change much during the 1990s, the "how" probably will. In particular one can expect increased use of many conventional privatization strategies as well as the birth of new ones.

Who Will Work for Government?

The Reagan years also brought to a head some long-standing problems in the civil service system. During the 1980s concern over the quality, morale, and effectiveness of the federal service grew rapidly. Anecdotal and impressionistic evidence suggest a serious problem that may well be getting worse. Although no one seems sure of the precise nature and origin of the problem, informed observers tend to agree that the federal government cannot attract, educate, and retain the high-caliber career service it will need for the year 2000.

Erosion: Some Signs and Sources

What signs point to erosion in the human resource base of the federal civil service? Resignations by members of the Senior Executive Service are a central target of concern. From 1979 through 1983 approximately 40 percent of the SES retired; the rate of resignation (as a percentage of SES positions allocated) leveled off during the mid-1980s at between 8 percent and 9 percent but rose above 10 percent in 1985 and 1986. This sparked concern that the federal government was suffering a serious brain drain.[16] The full meaning of any brain drain becomes more apparent when one remembers that as of the late 1980s, about one-third of the SES members were scientists and engineers; one-fifth were other professionals such as attorneys, economists, accountants, and medical officers.[17]

Assertions of declining morale among SES members abound. A recent study by the Federal Executive Institute Alumni Association rated morale at 3.6—down from 3.8 in 1983—on a scale of 1 to 7.[30]

On the whole, the evidence suggests that the human resource base of the federal work force is in decline. However, convincing explanations for the decline are harder to come by. One thing is clear: The problem didn't begin with the Reagan administration or with Carter's Civil Service Reform Act of 1978; nor is it likely to end with the Bush administration in the 1990s.

Few highly qualified and ambitious people want to work in a system perceived to be failing and not satisfying. Such disparate groups as the Grace Commission and the National Academy of Public Administration have noted this unhappy state of affairs.[18] While they and other informed observers acknowledge that the federal civil service continues to attract and hold many well-qualified and hard-working employees, some of whom achieve impressive results, by and large they view the system in pessimistic terms. In support of this prognosis they point out an array of factors such as restrictive ethics requirements, red tape, congressional intervention in program management, and a management system with no room for discretion, flexibility, and rewards.

Above all, federal pay for executives has garnered attention as a major source of the capacity problem. One survey of SES members who left federal employment in 1985 found that approximately 40 percent mentioned the unfair distribution of pay bonuses and frustration with proposed and actual compensation plans as being of great or very great importance in their decision to leave. Among those who resigned (as distinct from those who retired or retreated to a position in the General Schedule not covered by SES), 44 percent cited salary inadequacy as being of great or very great importance.[19] Another survey found that 61 percent of the SES members employed by the federal government in 1985 were either dissatisfied or very dissatisfied with their salary. It reported that about half of those who left the SES in 1985 to assume a new position moved to a job with a larger salary.[20]

In April 1987, concerns about salaries for top executives prompted President Reagan to appoint the Commission on the Compensation of Career Federal Executives, which consisted of three high-level government employees and two representatives from the private sector. It reported in 1988 that "the Federal Government is at a substantial disadvantage in competing for the best of our nation's executive talent." More specifically, it concluded that from 1979 to 1987 real (that is, inflation-adjusted) SES pay had slightly declined. It found that both the averge salary and total compensation (salary plus fringe benefits) of private sector executives were "substantially above" those of their federal counterparts. The commission also noted that the range of pay among different levels of the SES was so small as to be "meaningless in terms of a compensation incentive." It found that poor pay appears to create recruitment and retention problems in some occupations, for example among attorneys and medical researchers, but suggested that "ongoing analysis" must "begin measuring the health of the SES recruitment/retention effort with any real adequacy."[21] Major barriers are lack of public understanding and the unwillingness of members of Congress to see top executives receive salaries higher than their own.

While President Reagan endorsed better pay for high-level executives, he espoused a different line with respect to the civil service more generally. Through the Grace Commission and other avenues, Reagan pushed to hold down and even cut salaries and fringe benefits for rank-and-file civil servants. The Federal Pay Comparability Act of 1970 asserted that federal and private-sector salaries for similar work ought to be comparable. From 1977 into the late 1980s, however, presidents proposed and Congress accepted salary adjustments that were not enough to achieve comparability between the private sector and federal white-collar employees. As a result, the federal government's pay agent, an advisory group consisting of the director of the Office of Personnel Management, the director of OMB, and the secretary of Labor, estimates that federal employees' pay on the average lagged behind that of their private-sector counterparts by close to 24 percent. Debate persists as to whether the pay survey used to make comparisons overestimates the private sector's advantage.[22] Even if officials revise the methodology to remove this bias, the gap appears considerable. Nor do the retirement and health benefits of federal employees appear to compensate for this difference.[23] Whatever the adequacy of federal benefits compared to private firms, Reagan's efforts to reduce the perquisites associated with civil service employment symbolize his opposition to the federal bureaucracy.

Another factor serving to discourage the highly qualified and ambitious from joining the federal government in the near future is the change in the mission of several domestic agencies. Budgetary cutbacks, a few program terminations, and a general decline in program activism have combined to reduce the sense of achievement that often prevailed in these agencies during the 1960s. Few people who have contributed to the creation, development, and growth of a program can be expected to approach retrenchment with equal enthusiasm. Nor will the process of adapting organizations and programs to austerity strike many federal employees as a rewarding challenge.

Increased politicization of the higher civil service in the form of intervention by elected officials and their appointees also eroded human resources during the Reagan years. The more extensive use of central controls through the budget and regulatory review were one element of this development. The increased numbers and importance of political appointees contributed to this trend. One study found that from fiscal 1980 to 1986 the number of career SES members declined by about 5 percent while the number of noncareer SES members rose by just over 13 percent. Schedule C employees (political appointees in lower positions) increased by nearly 13 percent over the same period.[24] An often-cited example of this trend occurred at the Office of

Personnel Management under the leadership of Donald J. Devine. During his four-year term at OPM, the number of career professionals fell 18 percent, while the number of political appointees increased 169 percent.[25]

Critics of this personnel policy argue that it amounts to a significant reduction in the policy roles of the top levels of the career civil service and with it an assault on the concept of "neutral competence," which guided civil service doctrine for much of the past fifty years. Without some involvement in policy planning, these critics argue, career employees are kept ignorant of policy directions by short-term political appointees who often do not value their advice or institutional memory. This arrangement not only frustrates and confuses career employees but also increases the risk of errors and policy failures.[26]

Politicization appeared to contribute to the resignations of significant numbers of career SES members during the 1980s. One survey of individuals who left the SES during fiscal 1985 found that 43 percent pointed to "dissatisfaction with political appointees" as a factor of great or very great importance in their decision to leave. Over 33 percent mentioned "too much political interference."[27] Hence, the quest for an administrative presidency may give rise to dissatisfaction among career civil servants and lessen the availability of competent people that a president needs to implement initiatives efficiently and effectively.

Many federal employees and longtime supporters of the civil service blame the politicization on the Civil Service Reform Act of 1978. In the words of one critic, the reform bill was "Carter's gift to Reagan," making it easier for the latter to gain control over the bureaucracy.[28]

However, for many government employees the disappointments of the Civil Service Reform Act, politicization, and compensation may be less important to job satisfaction and commitment to the federal service than the negative image of the civil servant in American society. The 1985 survey of individuals who left the SES found that 40 percent cited "frustration with criticism of federal workers by press, politicians, or public" as being of great or very great importance in their decision.[29] While bureaucrat bashing is deeply embedded in the political culture, the fact remains that the rhetoric of both Carter and Reagan reflected and reinforced this sentiment.

In such a political culture it is remarkable that the federal government gets as many highly qualified employees as it does. Of course, the law of averages dictates that some employees will be excellent, but that hardly explains why some whole agencies seem to attract and retain superior work forces. A better explanation is that the federal government has a monopoly or near-monopoly on some interesting occupations. For example, professionals who want to work in advanced archival techniques, space exploration, diplomacy, and intelligence have been unable to find many opportunities to practice their profession that compare with those available at the Library of Congress, NASA, the State Department, and the CIA. Another explanation is rooted in social history. Many women, members of minorities, and first-generation college graduates see the corporate world as alien. In contrast, the civil service, with its social and ethnic diversity, affirmative action programs, and merit-based entrance and promotion systems, has been regarded as comfortable and secure.

Yet another explanation lies in the expansion of government into new areas to contend with a variety of social problems, first during the New Deal and later with the Great Society. Many government employees say the prospect of contributing to the solution of social problems attracted them to federal service. Many of these people were imbued with an ethic of public service when they first entered government. Many who took up employment at the Department of Housing and Urban Development or the Agency for International Development, for example, were attracted to government service by their agency's mission.

Finally, there is a more utilitarian explanation: the chance to combine retirement credits gained through military service with the civilian retirement system has induced many well-qualified people to join and stay in the federal civil service. No matter what their initial motivation to join the civil service, once there, many federal employees have advanced to general management roles. As a consequence, over the years the federal government has enjoyed a cadre of capable employees, many of whom have transferred to other agencies, enriching the capacity of the civil service as a whole.

If the assessments offered in several recent studies of the federal civil service are correct, the system of recruitment and retention that worked reasonably well in the past may no longer work. According to agency recruiters, fewer highly qualified, technically trained college graduates are interested in federal employment. They report that graduates see more challenging work, greater flexibility, and higher rewards in the private sector. Furthermore, of the factors accounting for the high quality of recruits attracted into federal employment in the past, almost all have lost some of their pull. For example, the barriers to corporate employment of women, minorities, and first-generation college graduates are lower. Moreover, the redirecting of federal policy away from social programs has channeled the interest of many public-spirited workers toward state, local, nonprofit, and private-sector social service agencies. Furthermore, in a society that tends to regard working for the federal government in negative terms, there is little prestige in such a career. Given these factors and the issue of compensation, it is hardly surprising that in a recent survey of the career members of the SES, 72 percent responded no when asked if they would recommend a career in the federal government for their children.[30] This response is all the more disturbing because experts project that the labor force will grow more slowly in the 1990s than at any point since the 1930s and that federal jobs will require higher skills than ever before.[31] The federal government's capacity to compete with other employers for able recruits may well diminish just as the competition intensifies.

The United States runs great risk of moving toward a new political economy with a rigid, poorly trained, unimaginative, and unmotivated civil service. This condition could produce many episodes of policy failure. Programs whose employees use high science and technology could be especially hard hit. These programs often have major consequences that are the product of seemingly minor decisions by mid-level government employees. These programs vividly testify that a government populated by the error-prone, be they ill-informed, misinformed, lazy, or incompetent, can produce small administrative nightmares that add up to a general breakdown of government effectiveness.

By the year 2000 the risks involved in the small decisions of mid- and upper-level federal employees will be even greater. Not only is the economy of the United States becoming more complex and its technology more sophisticated, the political pressures on government agencies require more sensitive responses than in the past. There will be a premium on knowledgeable and savvy officials at the mid- and upper-levels of the bureaucracy, which in turn means that the federal work force will need more skillful and committed employees than before. Yet current trends augur the opposite. If they continue much longer, only a major overhaul of the system may be adequate to forestall serious problems.

Prospects for Reform

In the view of many observers, the most desirable overhaul of the system would allow the federal government to be truly competitive with the private sector in compensation, management systems, and opportunities to innovate. Such a reform would be possible only if critical actors in the White House, Congress, the media, business, unions, and public interest groups reached some consensus about the magnitude and significance of the problem. In the 1980s the alignment of these political forces militated against compromise and change.

Since the mid-1960s a fundamental transition has occurred in the political arena surrounding the federal civil service system. Before that, civil service reforms were often motivated and guided by "good government" groups and associations of career civil servants espousing progressive notions of "neutral competence." In recent years this coalition has given way to a new, more politicized and polarized alignment of friends and foes of the civil service. To be sure, the "good government" period enjoyed a revival under Alan K. Campbell, Chairman of the Civil Service Commission under Carter and later the first Director of the Office of Personnel Management. Campbell played a critical role in designing and promoting the Civil Service Reform Act of 1978.

Despite this brief throwback to an earlier era of relative consensus about the goals of civil service reform, the politics surrounding the civil service for much of the past two decades—and particularly during the 1980s—have featured a high degree of polarization. The White House is on one side, hoping to cut the size, cost, and autonomy of the federal work force. Civil service unions and employee associations are on the other, resisting any erosion of pay, benefits, and perquisites by capturing the support of sympathetic congressional committees and members.[32] In this contentious atmosphere, a consensus for civil service reform to promote a more productive work environent—hence "the public interest—has largely disappeared. Interested third parties—the business community, public interest groups, professional associations, and so on—have either been drawn into one side or the other or have fled the field to avoid being "burned" by well-intentioned advocacy. This has changed the dialogue about civil service policy from management improvement (i.e., to attract, retain, and better deploy an appropriately skilled and motivated workforce) to confrontation and political stalemate.

Polarization of civil service policy made a broad-scale reform of the system infeasible during the 1980s. Without some reforms, the capacity and performance of the executive branch may well decline. This suggests that the civil service may become a drag on the economy, so it is perhaps in the interests of the business community, which so far has been mostly silent on the issue, to bring the problem of civil service decline to the public's attention. In doing so, it could become a "third force" between the polarized factions to build a consensus for reforms to strengthen the system.

The president has a major responsibility to assure that the system does not erode. A weak civil service impedes the president's constitutional responsibility to "take care that the laws be faithfully executed." It is not enough to control the system. In order to carry out responsibilities, the president must have a competent administrative apparatus. Therefore the president has the greatest stake in this issue, and a president committed to change could provide the leadership necessary to reform the system. Ignoring the issue or encouraging the processes of erosion is to force the government to live on borrowed time and ignore the long-term consequences of a weakened civil service. Presidential leadership can persuade the public that a highly competent and motivated civil service is a public good that hostility, indifference, and neglect will erode unless it gets new ideas, talent, and public support. With the exception of President Reagan's support for higher salaries for top executives and a few management reform initiatives, processes of neglect and decline dominated the federal civil service during the 1980s. Reversing that trend and setting off a countervailing process of revitalization could occur by the year 2000, although this development is far from assured.

In sum, if present patterns of erosion continue, the civil service will become an impediment to rather than a facilitator of desirable social, economic, and technical transformation. In the 1990s the civil service will have to be more technologically sophisticated, better schooled in the ways of the business community, and more savvy about emerging international economic trends and their implications.

As the deficiencies of the system become more and more apparent, an environment more amenable to broad reform may materialize. As the 1980s closed, promising signs were showing. In 1988, for example, neither presidential candidate ran against the federal bureaucracy in the way of Carter and Reagan. President Reagan's appointment of the Commission on the Compensation of Career Federal Executives reflected recognition of the need to increase the remuneration of top career officials. While in early 1989 public outcry galvanized congressional rejection of a pay package that would have increased the salaries of executives, judges, and members of Congress, President Bush promised to press for pay hikes in the future. In late 1989, Congress finally approved a pay boost. Moreover, with funding from such private organizations as the Ford Foundation and the Rockefeller Foundation, Paul Volcker, the former and widely respected chairman of the Federal Reserve Board, agreed to head the National Commission on the Public Service. The Commission was "dedicated to placing high on the Nation's agenda the need to strengthen the effectiveness of the career service of government." It released its report in early 1989.[33]

Will American Public Administration Be Ready for the Year 2000?

Now to the bottom line: Will the federal administrative structure, systems, and work force be able to meet the challenges of the year 2000? There is evidence to support both optimistic and pessimistic answers. On the whole, however, historic American optimism is likely to prove warranted. This conclusion is largely based on one important aspect of American government: When confronting crises and contingencies, the system in the United States has proved remarkably adaptive. When wars, domestic problems, and economic difficulties posed a serious and pressing challenge, leaders emerged to pass laws and create administrative arrangements to grapple with the problem. There is no reason to expect such a scenario not to play out again, although there will no doubt be some tempering of optimism and a keener recognition of the nation's fiscal and social limits.

Barring unforeseen events and politically improbable coalitions, the fiscal stringency that dominates public policy in the 1980s is likely to continue into the 1990s; public attitudes and the national debt will continue to dictate a large but constrained role for the federal government in domestic affairs. At the same time one can expect a more diverse and dynamic government, especially hybrid organizational forms and policy implementation strategies. The good news is that government is likely to continue as a large and positive force in American society; the better news is that it may carry out its role in ways that minimize the negative aspects of bureaucracy, take advantage of joint public-private administrative arrangements, and borrow appropriate private sector management techniques.

The bad news is the erosion in quality of the civil service. The problems of the civil service are not inherently insolvable. Erosion can be stabilized and even reversed with new compensation policies and structural changes in the rules and procedures used to attract and retain federal employees. Furthermore, contracting out, government corporations, and other alternative service delivery arrangements can strengthen the talent pool available to government managers for carrying out their responsibilities.

Even if erosion can be arrested, a significant intellectual and practical challenge remains. Since the late 1930s, the administrative apparatus of the federal government has been shaped by a widely shared administrative philosophy about the proper way to organize and administer operations and the role of public employees in that arrangement. In the 1980s considerable theoretical confusion about these issues prevails. Without a clear doctrine based on guiding principles of organization and management, the executive establishment has evolved into a much more varied and complicated structure of governance that increasingly uses third parties, public-private hybrids, and indirect means to carry out national policy. Lacking the firm theoretical ground of an earlier era provided by such efforts as the Brownlow and first Hoover Commissions, policymakers and government executives have tended to narrow the scope of their thinking to tackle more tractable second-order problems. While this incrementalism may solve problems in the short run—and in the aggregate move government to a better fit with its problems and opportunities—it also creates difficulties and makes many observers suspect that these efforts lack clear direction. Unless there is a clearer resolution of the central issues of what government should be doing, how it should be doing it, and who should be doing it, the debate over the focus and activities of the federal government will be increasingly dominated by grand ideologies that are inappropriate for the problems at hand. The result may be that large-scale initiatives grounded in inapplicable theories of governance and public management will eviscerate the good work done to manage narrow problems.

This plagued all the developed democracies in the 1980s. The governments of Britain, France, Sweden, and Canada struggled with austerity by redefining their roles and reshaping their administrative systems. Lacking a well-accepted public philosophy on the role of administrators, the political leaders of these nations tried to reduce the scope of the public sector and the discretion traditionally provided to their civil servants. In part, the fiscal problems of these countries and their retrenchment at the margins of the welfare state explain this development. It also reflects some confusion about the operational practices of these governments.

In this context is another major legacy of the Reagan years. Besides opening up a discussion of alternative ends and means of government action, the difficulty the Reagan administration had in fashioning administrative tactics within the framework of a conservative ideology suggests that neither the liberal nor the conservative—nor for that matter the neoconservative—approach to public management provides complete guidance for arranging and managing the public sector in a mixed economy. This intellectual deficit, which seems likely to be even more apparent in the 1990s, promises to spur activity to fill it. Therefore, while in the 1980s the intellectual study of public administration was in the doldrums, the next decade promises to be a period of lively debate and theory building.

Governments worldwide, including the United States, have changed both their ends and their means since the Brownlow and Hoover commissions—and will surely change more before the next century. To do so with minimal problems and errors, they will need a new doctrine to guide governance and management. Setting forth such a doctrine may well be the central challenge confronting scholars and public officials in the next decade; it may be their most valuable contribution to the public interest of the future.

Notes

1. Quoted in Walter A. Hahn and Dennis L. Little, "Public Administration in the Third Century: Overview." *Public Administration Review* 36 (September/October 1976): 577.
2. Many different terms have been used to describe the era the United States is entering, but there is a remarkably high consensus about what its main technical and economic shape is likely to be and how it will depart from the past. See, for example, Daniel Bell, *The Coming of Post-Industrial Society* (New York: Basic Books, 1973); Michael Maccoby, "A New Way of Managing," *IEEE Spectrum* (June, 1984): 69–72; and John Naisbitt, *Megatrends* (New York: Warner Books, 1982).
3. Richard Rose and B. Guy Peters, *Can Government Go Bankrupt?* (New York: Basic Books, 1978).
4. Frank Levy, *Dollars and Dreams* (New York: Russell Sage, 1987), 3–4; Frank Levy, "Incomes, Families, and Living Standards," in Robert E. Litan et al., eds., *American Living Standards: Threats and Challenges* (Washington, DC: The Brookings Institution, 1988), 112–7.
5. See Joseph F. Coates, "Why Think About the Future: Some Administrative and Political Perspectives," *Public Administration Review* 36 (September/October, 1976): 580–585.
6. Todd R. LaPorte, ed., *Organized Social Complexity: Challenge to Politics and Policy* (Princeton, NJ: Princeton University Press, 1975).
7. For one of the clearest expositions of this position, see Milton Friedman, *Capitalism and Freedom* (Chicago: University of Chicago Press, 1962).
8. Inaugural address of President Ronald Reagan, January 20, 1981.

9. See Theodore J. Lowi, "Ronald Reagan—Revolutionary?" In Lester M. Salamon and Michael S. Lund, eds., *The Reagan Presidency and the Governing of America* (Washington, DC: Urban Institute, 1985), 29–56.

10. In at least one respect President Reagan's approach to restricting the role of government has been contradictory. According to Lowi, rather than restricting government's role, "what Reagan was ultimately trying to accomplish was considerably more important to him than merely relieving corporations of some of their regulatory burdens. Reagan's goal as a conservative was to try to shift and extend government's authority toward realms where government concerned itself with the morality of conduct." This has extended to Reagan's support for the so-far unsuccessful right-to-life amendment to the Constitution, other antiabortion measures, his firm support of the proposed school prayer amendment, and his endorsement of firm discipline in the nation's schools. See Lowi, "Ronald Reagan—Revolutionary?", 38–9.

11. William F. Buckley, "Day Care Becomes Federal," *Albany Times Union,* 27 July 1988, A–14.

12. See Harold Wolman and Fred Teitelbaum, "Interest Groups and the Reagan Presidency," in Salamon and Lund, eds., *The Reagan Presidency and the Governing of America,* 297–329.

13. See Frederick C. Mosher, "The Changing Responsibilities and Tactics of the Federal Government." *Public Administration Review* 40 (November-December 1980): 541–7.

14. See, for instance, Ruth Hoogland DeHoog, "Theoretical Perspectives on Contracting Out for Services: Implementation Problems and Possibilities of Privatizing Public Services," in George C. Edwards, III, ed., *Public Policy Implementation* (Greenwich, CT: JAI Press, 1984), 227–59.

15. Elizabeth Sanders, "The President and the Bureaucratic State," in Michael Nelson, ed., *The Presidency and the Political System* (Washington, DC: Congressional Quarterly, 1988), 392.

16. Reported in Peter M. Benda and Charles H. Levine, "Reagan and the Bureaucracy: The Bequest, the Promise, and the Legacy," in Charles O. Jones, ed., *The Reagan Legacy* (Chatham, NJ: Chatham House, 1988, 134).

17. *The Report of the President's Commission on Compensation of Career Federal Executives* (Washington, DC: PCCFE 1988), 9.

18. See *President's Private Sector Survey on Cost Control* (Washington, DC, PPSSCC 1983) and the National Academy of Public Administration, *Revitalizing Federal Management: Managers and Their Overburdened Systems* (Washington, DC: National Academy of Public Administration, 1983).

19. U.S. General Accounting Office, *Reasons Why Career Members Left in Fiscal Year 1985* (Washington, DC: GAO/GGD–87–106FS, 1987), 8, 19.

20. U.S. General Accounting Office, *Senior Executive Service: Answers to Selected Salary-Related Questions* (Washington, D.C.: GAO/GGD–87–36FS, 1987).

21. *The Report of the President's Commission on Compensation,* 4, 30.

22. U.S. General Accounting Office, *Federal Pay: Changes to the Methods of Comparing Federal and Private Sector Salaries* (Washington, DC: GAO/GGD–87–8, 1987), 9.

23. See, for instance, U.S. General Accounting Office, *Analysis of Grace Commission Proposals to Change the Civil Service Retirement System* (Washington, DC: GAO/GGD–85–31, 1985); U.S. General Accounting Office, *Health Insurance: Comparison of Coverage for Federal and Private Sector Employees.* (Washington, DC: GAO/HRD–87–32BR, 1986).

24. U.S. General Accounting Office, *Federal Employees: Trends in Career and Noncareer Employee Appointments in the Executive Branch* (Washington, DC: GAO/GGD–87–96FS, 1987).

25. See Edie N. Goldenberg, "The Grace Commission and Civil Service Reform: Seeking a Common Understanding," in Charles H. Levine, ed., *The Unfinished Agenda for Civil Service Reform* (Washington, DC: The Brookings Institution, 1985), 69–94.

26. Edie N. Goldenberg, "The Permanent Government in an Era of Retrenchment and Redirection," in Salamon and Lund, eds., *The Reagan Presidency and the Governing of America,* 396.

27. U.S. General Accounting Office, *Senior Executive Service: Reasons Why Career Members Left,* 8.

28. B. Guy Peters, "Administrative Change and the Grace Commission," in Charles H. Levine, ed., *The Unfinished Agenda for Civil Service Reform,* 19–35.

29. U.S. General Accounting Office, *Senior Executive Service: Reasons Why Career Members Left,* 8.

30. Results of a survey conducted by the Federal Executive Institute Alumni Association, draft report, November 1984.

31. Demographic projections come from Hudson Institute, *Civil Service 2000* (Washington, DC: U.S. Office of Personnel Management, 1988); U.S. Department of Labor, *Opportunity 2000* (Washington, DC: U.S. Government Printing Office, 1988).

32. See Bernard Rosen, "Effective Continuity of U.S. Government Operations in Jeopardy." *Public Administration Review* 43 (September-October, 1983): 383–91.

33. Extracted from a brochure of the National Commission on the Public Service.

Index

A

Accessibility problem, 288
Access professionals, 371
Accountability, 5-6
  administrative, 104
  Challenger disaster and, 204-205
  of civil servants, 190
  contracting and, 413-414
  enforcement of, 191
    at EPA, *200*
  formal theory of, 416
  lines of, 295
  problem of, 76
  in public versus private sector, 278-279
  in representative bureaucracy, 195
Accounting, 393-395
  innovations in, 438
  methods of, 393-394
Accrual accounting, 393-394
Action
  bias toward, 420
  as hypothesis, 428-429
Activism, support for, 6
Adaptability, 265-266
Adaptation, 239
Adjudication. *See* Administrative
  adjudication
Administration, by proxy, 204-206,
  320-323, 429
  excellence and, 409-419
Administrative adjudication, 177
  due process as dominant concern in,
    177-180
  hearings in, 180-182
Administrative agencies. *See also* Agencies
  agenda setting by, 90-91

discretion of, 108
  evaluation of, 96-98
  legitimation by, 92-93
  policy evaluation by, 96-98
  policy formulation by, 91-92
  policy implementation by, 95-96
  as policymaking participants, 88-99
  in policy process, 10-11
  resource attachment by, 93-95
  response of to policies, 98-99
Administrative authority, fragmentation of,
  217-218
Administrative Behavior, 232, 237
Administrative law
  definition of, 168
  trade-off in, 168
Administrative politics, 105, 130-131
  dichotomy in, 105-107
  as discretion, 107-108
  elected officials and, 109-124
  generic, 124-130
Administrative Procedures Act, 169-170
  amendments of, 170
  procedural requirements of, 173
  Section 553(4) of, 171
  Section 706 of, 183
Administrative remedies, 182
Administrative roles, 280-281
Administrative Science Quarterly, The,
  founding of, 238
Administrative State, The, 234
Advocacy, 268
Affirmative action, 330
  pressure for, 347-348
AFL-CIO
  affiliates of, 338
  lobbying of, 91-92

About the Authors

CHARLES H. LEVINE (deceased) was a Senior Staff Member at the Brookings Institution in Washington, D.C., and Edwin O. Stene Distinguished Professor of Public Administration in the Department of Political Science and School of Business at the University of Kansas. Dr. Levine received his B.S. degree from the University of Connecticut and his M.B.A., M.P.A., and Ph.D. degrees from Indiana University. A well-known and respected expert on public administration, Dr. Levine served as a consultant for many cities, states, and organizations such as IBM, the Department of Energy, and the Centers for Disease Control. He was widely published in professional journals and served on the editorial boards of the *Journal of Urban Affairs, Policy Studies Review, Administration and Society,* and other journals. His books include *The Politics of Retrenchment: How Local Governments Manage Fiscal Stress* (with Irene S. Rubin and George G. Wolohojian), *Urban Politics: Past, Present, and Future* (edited with Harlan Hahn), and *Racial Conflict and the American Mayor: Power, Polarization, and Performance.* Dr. Levine received the William E. Mosher Award for distinguished writing from the American Society for Public Administration.

B. GUY PETERS is Maurice Falk Professor of American Politics at the University of Pittsburg and Honorary Research Fellow at the Centre for the Study of Public Policy at the University of Strathclyde. Dr. Peters holds a B.A. degree from the University of Richmond and M.A. and Ph.D. degrees from Michigan State University. His professional experience includes a Senior Fulbright Lectureship at the University of Strathclyde, and research grants from the National Science Foundation, Exxon Foundation, Sloan Foundation, Swedish Kennedy Foundation, and Ford Foundation. He also directed the Metropolitan Leadership Forum for the City of New Orleans and served on the State of Louisiana Governor's Cost Control Commission. Dr. Peters has published in many professional journals on comparative politics, public policy, and public administration, and is currently co-editor of *Governance.* He is author of *The Pathology of Public Policy, American Public Policy: Problems and Prospects, 2/e, Comparative Politics: An Introduction* (with Dan Jacobs, David Conradt, and William Safran), and other books.

FRANK J. THOMPSON is a Professor and Dean of the School of Public Affairs and Associate Provost of Rockfeller College at the State University of New York, Albany. He received his B.A. degree from the University of Chicago, and his M.A. and Ph.D. degrees from the University of California, Berkeley. Dr. Thompson worked as an analyst for the Department of Health, Education, and Welfare and for the City of Oakland's Civil Service Department and Office of the City Manager. He also served as a consultant with many universities and public agencies such as the U.S. Public Health Services and Office of Personnel. Dr. Thompson has been active on several committees for the National Association of Schools of Public Affairs and Administration, including service as chair of its commission on peer review and accreditation. His articles have appeared in many professional journals and he has been on the editorial boards of *Public Administration Review, Administration and*

Society, and other journals. Dr. Thompson is author of *Personnel Policy in the City* and of *Classics of Public Personnel Policy.* He has received several awards including the William E. Mosher Award for distinguished publication from the American Society for Public Administration.